WEBSTER'S

ENGLISH
DICTIONARY

CONCISE EDITION
For school, home and office

This edition published 2005 by
STRATHEARN BOOKS LIMITED
Toronto, Canada

© 1997 Geddes & Grosset,
David Dale House, New Lanark ML11 9DJ, Scotland

First published 2000, reprinted 2000, 2001, 2002, 2003,
2004, 2005

This book is not published by the original publishers of
Webster's Dictionary or by their successors

ISBN 1 85534 956 6

Printed and bound in Canada

Abbreviations used in this book

abbr	abbreviation		*myth*	mythology
adj	adjective		*n*	noun
adv	adverb		*naut*	nautical
anat	anatomy		*neut*	neuter
approx	approximately		*news*	news media
arch	archaic		*nf*	noun feminine
archit	architecture		*npl*	noun plural
astrol	astrology		*n sing*	noun singular
astron	astronomy		*orig*	original, originally, origin
Austral	Australia, Australasia		*p*	participle
aux	auxiliary		*pers*	person, personal
biol	biology		*philos*	philosophy
bot	botany		*photog*	photography
Brit	Britain, British		*pl*	plural
c	*circa*, about		*poet*	poetical
cap	capital		*poss*	possessive
Cdn	*Canadian*		*pp*	past participle
cent	century		*prep*	preposition
chem	chemical, chemistry		*pres t*	present tense
compar	comparative		*print*	printing
comput	computing		*pron*	pronoun
conj	conjunction		*pr p*	present participle
demons	demonstrative		*psychol*	psychology
derog	derogatory, derogatorily		*pt*	past tense
econ	economics		*RC*	Roman Catholic
eg	*exempli gratia*, for example		*reflex*	reflexive
elect	electricity		*Scot*	Scotland
esp	especially		*sing*	singular
fig	figuratively		*sl*	slang
geog	geography		*superl*	superlative
geol	geology		*theat*	theatre
geom	geometry		*TV*	television
gram	grammar		*UK*	United Kingdom
her	heraldry		*US*	United States
hist	history		*USA*	United States of America
ie	*id est*, that is		*usu*	usually
imper	imperative		*vb*	verb
incl	including		*vb aux*	auxiliary verb
inf	informal		*vi*	intransitive verb
interj	interjection		*vt*	transitive verb
math	mathematics		*vti*	transitive or instransitive verb
mech	mechanics		*vulg*	vulgar, vulgarly
med	medicine		*zool*	zoology
mil	military			

A

A *abbr* = ampere(s).

a *adj* the indefinite article; one; any; per.

AA *abbr* = Alcoholics Anonymous; anti-air-craft; Automobile Association.

AB *abbr* = Alberta.

aback *adv* **taken aback** startled.

abandon *vt* to leave behind; to desert; to yield completely to an emotion or urge. * *n* freedom from inhibitions.—**abandonment** *n*.

abate *vti* to make or become less; (*law*) to end.—**abatement** *n*.

abattoir *n* a slaughterhouse.

abbey *n* a building occupied by monks or nuns; a church attached to an abbey; the community of monks or nuns.

abbot *n* the head of an abbey of monks.

abbreviate *vt* to make shorter, esp to shorten (words) by omitting letters.

abbreviation *n* the process of abbreviating; a shortened form of a word.

abdicate *vti* to renounce an official position or responsibility, etc.—**abdication** *n*.

abdomen *n* the region of the body below the chest containing the digestive organs; the belly; (*insects, etc*) the section of the body behind the thorax.—**abdominal** *adj*.

abduct *vt* to carry off (a person) by force.—**abduction** *n*.—**abductor** *n*.

abet *vt* (*pt* **abetted**) to encourage or assist.—**abetter**.

abhor *vt* (*pt* **abhorred**) to detest, despise.

abide *vt* (*pt* **abode** *or* **abided**) to endure; to put up with.

ability *n* being able; power to do; talent; skill.

ablaze *adj* burning, on fire.

able *adj* having the competence or means (to do); talented; skilled.—**ably** *adv*.

abnormal *adj* unusual, not average or typical; irregular.—**abnormality** *n*.

aboard *adv* on or in an aircraft, ship, train, etc.—*also prep*.

abolish *vt* to bring to an end, do away with.

abolition *n* the act of abolishing; (*with cap*) in UK, the ending of the slave trade (1807) or slavery (1833), in US, the emancipation of the slaves (1863).—**abolitionist** *n*.

abominable *adj* despicable, detestable; (*inf*) very unpleasant.—**abominably** *adv*.

aborigine *n* any of the first known inhabitants of a region; (*with cap*) one of the original inhabitants of Australia.

abort *vti* to undergo or cause an abortion; to terminate or cause to terminate prematurely. * *n* the premature termination of a rocket flight, etc.

abortion *n* the premature expulsion of a foetus, esp if induced.

abortive *adj* failing in intended purpose; fruitless; causing abortion.

abound *vi* to be in abundance; to have in great quantities.

about *prep* on all sides of; near to; with; on the point of; concerning. * *adv* all around; near; to face the opposite direction.

above *prep* over, on top of; better or more than; beyond the reach of; too complex to understand. * *adv* in or to a higher place; in addition; (*text*) mentioned earlier.

abrasive *adj* causing abrasion; harsh, irritating. * *n* a substance or tool used for grinding or polishing, etc.

abreast *adv* side by side and facing the same way; informed (of); aware.

abridge *vt* to shorten by using fewer words but keeping the substance.—**abridgement, abridgment** *n*.

abroad *adv* in or to a foreign country; over a wide area; out in the open; in circulation, current.

abrupt *adj* sudden; unexpected; curt.—**abruptly** *adv*.

abscess *n* an inflamed area of the body containing pus.

abscond *vi* to hide, run away, esp to avoid punishment.

absence *n* the state of not being present; the time of this; a lack; inattention.

absent[1] *adj* not present; not existing; inattentive.

absent[2] *vt* to keep (oneself) away.

absentee *n* a person who is absent, as from work or school.

absenteeism *n* persistent absence from work, school, etc.

absent-minded *adj* inattentive; forgetful.

absolute *adj* unrestricted, unconditional; complete; positive; perfect, pure; not relative; (*inf*) utter, out-and-out.

absolutely *adv* completely; unconditionally; (*inf*) I completely agree, certainly.

absolve *vt* to clear from guilt or blame; to give religious absolution to; to free from a duty, obligation, etc.

absorb *vt* to take in; to soak up; to incorporate; to pay for (costs, etc); to take in (a shock) without recoil; to occupy one's interest completely.—**absorber** *n*.—**absorption** *n*.

absorbent *adj* capable of absorbing moisture, etc.—**absorbency** *n*.

abstain *vi* to keep oneself from some indulgence, esp alcohol; to refrain from using one's vote.—**abstainer** *n*.—**abstention** *n*.

abstemious *adj* sparing in consuming food or alcohol.

abstinence *n* an abstaining or refraining, esp from food or alcohol.—**abstinent** *adj*.

abstract *adj* having no material existence; theoretical; (*art*) non-representational. * *n* (*writing, speech*) a summary or condensed version. * *vt* to remove or extract; to separate; to summarize.

absurd *adj* against reason or common sense; ridiculous.—**absurdity** *n*.

abundance *n* a plentiful supply; a considerable amount.

abundant *adj* plentiful; rich (in).—**abundantly** *adv*.

abuse *vt* to make wrong use of; to mistreat; to insult, attack verbally. * *n* misuse; mistreatment; insulting language.

abusive *adj* insulting.

abysmal *adj* extremely bad, deplorable.

abyss *n* a bottomless depth; anything too deep to measure.

academic *adj* pertaining to a school, college or university; scholarly; purely theoretical in nature. * *n* a member of a college or university; a scholarly person.

academy *n* a school for specialized training; (*Scot*) a secondary school; (*with cap*) a society of scholars, etc.

Acadian *n* one of the settlers in the former French colony of Acadia, or a descendant in the Maritime Provinces of Canada, southeast Quebec, or eastern Maine. * *n* of or pertaining to Acadia or Acadians.

ACCC *abbr* = Association of Canadian Community Colleges.

accede *vi* to take office; to agree or assent to (a suggestion).

accelerate *vti* to move faster; to happen or cause to happen more quickly; to increase the speed of (a vehicle).

acceleration *n* the act of accelerating or condition of being accelerated; the rate of increase in speed or change in velocity; the power of accelerating.

accelerator *n* a device for increasing speed; a throttle; (*physics*) an apparatus that imparts high velocities to elementary particles.

accent *n* emphasis on a syllable or word; a mark used to indicate this; any way of speaking characteristic of a region, class, or an individual; the emphasis placed on something; rhythmic stress in music or verse.

accept *vt* to receive, esp willingly; to approve; to agree to; to believe in; to agree to pay.—**acceptance** *n*.

acceptable *adj* satisfactory; welcome; tolerable.

access *n* approach, or means of approach; the right to enter, use, etc. * *vt* (*comput*) to retrieve (information) from a storage device; to gain access to.

accessory *adj* additional; extra. * *n* a supplementary part or item, esp of clothing; a person who aids another in a crime.

accident *n* an unexpected event; a mishap or misfortune, esp one resulting in death or injury; chance.

accidental *adj* occurring or done by accident; non-essential; (*mus*) a sign prefixed to a note indicating a departure from the key signature.—**accidentally** *adv*.

acclaim *vt* to praise publicly; to welcome enthusiastically; (*Cdn*) elect without opposition. * *vi* to shout approval. * *n* a shout of welcome or approval.—**acclamation** *n*.

acclamation *n* a demonstration of approval or assent; an outburst of joy or praise; the adoption of a resolution *viva voce*; a mode o f papal election; (*Cdn*) the act or fact of being elected without opposition.

acclimatize *vt* to adapt to a new climate or environment * *vi* to become acclimatized.—**acclimatization** *n*.

accommodate *vt* to provide lodging for; to oblige; supply; to adapt, harmonize.

accommodating *adj* obliging, willing to help.

accommodation *n* lodgings; the process of adapting; willingness to help.

accompaniment *n* an instrumental part supporting a solo instrument, a voice, or a choir; something that accompanies.—**accompanist** *n*.

accompany *vt* (*person*) to go with; (*something*) to supplement.

accomplice *n* a partner, esp in committing a crime.

accomplish *vt* to succeed in carrying out; to fulfil.

accomplished *adj* done; completed; skilled, expert; polished.

accomplishment *n* a skill or talent; the act of accomplishing; something accomplished.

accord *vi* to agree; to harmonize (with). * *vt* to grant. * *n* consent; harmony.

accordance *n* agreement; conformity.

accordingly *adv* consequently; therefore.

accordion *n* a portable keyboard instrument with manually operated folding bellows that force air through metal reeds.—**accordionist** *n*.

accost *vt* to approach and speak to.

account *n* a description; explanatory statement; business record or statement; a credit arrangement with a bank, department store, etc; importance, consequence. * *vt* to think of as; to consider. * *vi* to give a financial reckoning (to); (*with* **for**) to give reasons (for); (*with* **for**) to kill, dispose of.

accountable *adj* liable; responsible.—**accountability** *n*.

accountancy *n* the profession or practice of an accountant.

accountant *n* one whose profession is auditing business accounts.

accumulate *vti* to collect together in increasing quantities, to amass.—**accumulation** *n*.—**accumulative** *adj*.

accurate *adj* conforming with the truth or an accepted standard; done with care, exact.—**accuracy** *n*.—**accurately** *adv*.

accusation *n* the act of accusing or being accused; an allegation.

accuse *vt* to charge with a crime, fault, etc; to blame.—**accuser** *n*.—**accusingly** *adv*.

accustom *vt* to make used (to) by habit, use, or custom.

accustomed *adj* usual, customary.

ace *n* the one spot in dice, cards, etc; a point won by a single stroke; an expert. * *adj* (*inf*) excellent.

ache *n* a dull, continuous pain. * *vi* to suffer a dull, continuous mental or physical pain; (*inf*) to yearn.

achieve *vt* to perform successfully, accomplish; to gain, win. —**achievable** *adj*.—**achiever** *n*.

acid *adj* sharp, tart, sour; bitter. * *n* a sour substance; (*chem*) a corrosive substance that turns litmus red; (*sl*) LSD.

acknowledge *vt* to admit that something is true and valid; to show that one has noticed or recognized.—**acknowledgement** *n*.

acne *n* inflammation of the skin glands producing pimples.

acorn *n* the nut of the oak tree.

acoustic *adj* of the sense of hearing or sound; of acoustics.

acoustics *npl* (*room, concert hall, etc*) properties governing how clearly sounds can be heard in it; (*in sing*) the physics of sound.—**acoustical** *adj*.—**acoustically** *adv*.

acquaint *vt* to make (oneself) familiar (with); to inform.

acquaintance *n* a person whom one knows only slightly.

acquire *vt* to gain by one's own efforts; to obtain.

acquisition *n* gaining, acquiring; something that is acquired.

acquisitive *adj* eager or greedy for possessions.—**acquisitively** *adv*.—**acquisitiveness** *n*.

acquit *vt* (*pt* **acquitted**) to free from an obligation; to behave or conduct (oneself); to declare innocent.—**acquittal** *n*.

acre *n* land measuring 4840 sq yards.

acrimony *n* bitterness of manner or language.—**acrimonious** *adj*.—**acrimoniously** *adv*.

acrobat *n* a skilful performer of spectacular gymnastic feats.—**acrobatic** *adj*.—**acrobatically** *adv*.

acrobatics *npl* acrobatic feats.

across *prep* from one side to the other of; on or at an angle; on the other side of. * *adv* crosswise; from one side to the other.

act *vi* to perform or behave in a certain manner; to perform a specific function; to have an effect; to perform on the stage. * *vt* to portray by actions, esp on the stage; to pretend, simulate; to take the part of, as a character in a play. * *n* something done, a deed; an exploit; a law; a main division of a play or opera; the short repertoire of a comic, etc; something done merely for effect or show.

acting *n* the art of an actor. * *adj* holding an office or position temporarily.

action *n* process of doing something; an operation; a movement of the body, gesture; a land or sea battle; a lawsuit; the unfolding of events in a play, etc.

activate *vt* to make active; to set in motion.—**activation** *n*.—**activator** *n*.

active *adj* lively, physically mobile; engaged in practical activities; energetic, busy; (*volcano*) liable to erupt; capable of producing an effect; radioactive; (*armed forces*) in full-time service. * *n* (*gram*) the verb form having as its subject the doer of the action.—**actively** *adv*.

activity *n* being active; energetic, lively action; specific occupations (*indoor activities*).

actor *n* a person who acts in a play, film, etc.—**actress** *nf*.

ACTRA *abbr* = Alliance of Canadian Cinema, Television and Radio Artists.

actual *adj* real; existing in fact or reality.—**actually** *adv*.

acumen *n* sharpness of mind, perception.

acupuncture *n* the insertion of the tips of fine needles into the skin at certain points to treat various common ailments.—**acupuncturist** *n*.

acute *adj* (*hearing*) sensitive; (*pain*) severe; very serious; (*angles*) less than 90 degrees; (*disease*) severe but not long lasting.—**acutely** *adv*.—**acuteness** *n*.

ad *abbr* = *anno Domini* (in the year of Our Lord) in dates of the Christian era, indicating the number of years since the birth of Christ.

Adam's apple *n* the hard projection of cartilage in the front of the neck.

adapt *vti* to make or become fit; to adjust to new circumstances.—**adaptability** *n* —**adaptable** *adj*.

adaptation *n* the process or condition of being adapted; something produced by modification; a version of a literary composition rewritten for a different medium.

adapter, adaptor *n* a device that allows an item of equipment to be put to new use; a device for connecting parts of differing size and shape.

add *vt* to combine (two or more things together); to combine numbers or amounts in a total; to remark or write further. * *vi* to perform or come together by addition.

adder *n* the venomous viper.

addict *n* a person who is dependent upon a drug.—**addiction** *n*.

addition *n* the act or result of adding; something to be added; an extra part.—**additional** *adj*.

additive *adj* produced by addition. * *n* a substance added (to food, etc) to improve texture, flavor, etc.

address *vt* to write directions for delivery on (a letter, etc); to speak or write directly to; to direct one's skills or attention (to); (*golf*) to adjust one's stance and aim before hitting the ball; * *n* a place where a person or business resides, the details of this on a letter for delivery; a speech, esp a formal one; (*comput*) a specific memory location where information is stored.

adenoids *npl* enlarged masses of tissue in the throat behind the nose.

adept *adj* highly proficient. * *n* a highly skilled person.

adequate *adj* sufficient for requirements; barely acceptable. —**adequacy** *n* —**adequately** *adv*.

adhere *vi* to stick, as by gluing or suction; to give allegiance or support (to); to follow.—**adherence** *n*.—**adherent** *n*.

adhesion *n* the action or condition of adhering; the attachment of normally separate tissues in the body.

adhesive *adj* sticky; causing adherence. * *n* a substance used to stick, such as glue, paste, etc.—**adhesiveness** *n*.

adjacent *adj* nearby; adjoining.

adjective *n* a word used to add a characteristic to a noun or pronoun.—**adjectival** *adj*.

adjoining *adj* beside, in contact with.

adjourn *vt* to suspend (a meeting) temporarily. * *vi* (*inf*) to retire (to another room, etc).—**adjournment** *n*.

adjust *vt* to arrange in a more proper or satisfactory manner; to regulate or modify by minor changes; to decide the amount to be paid in settling (an insurance claim). * *vi* to adapt oneself.—**adjustable** *adj*.—**adjuster** *n*.—**adjustment** *n*.

adjutant *n* a military staff officer who assists the commanding officer.—**adjutancy** *n*.

ad-lib *vti* (*pt* **ad-libbed**) (*speech, etc*) to improvise. * *n* an ad-libbed remark. * *adv* spontaneous, freely.

administer *vt* to manage, direct; to give out as a punishment; to dispense (medicine, punishment, etc); to tender (an oath, etc).

administration *n* management; the people who administer an organization; the government; (*with cap*) the executive officials of a government, their policies, and term of office.—**administrative** *adj*.

administrator *n* a person who manages or supervises; (*law*) one appointed to settle an estate.

admiral *n* the commanding officer of a fleet; a naval officer of the highest rank.

admiration *n* a feeling of pleasurable and often surprised respect; an admired person or thing.

admire *vt* to regard with honor and approval; to express admiration for.—**admirer** *n*.—**admiring** *adj*.—**admiringly** *adv*.

admission *n* an entrance fee; a conceding, confessing, etc; a thing conceded, confessed, etc.

admit *vb* (*pt* **admitted**)*vt* to allow to enter or join; to concede or acknowledge as true. * *vi* to give access; (*with* **of**) to allow or permit.

admittance *n* the act of admitting; the right to enter.

admittedly *adv* acknowledged as fact, willingly conceded.

admonish *vt* to remind or advise earnestly; to reprove gently.—**admonition** *n*.—**admonitory** *adj*.

ado *n* fuss, excitement, esp over trivia.

adolescent *adj* between childhood and maturity; (*inf*) immature. * *n* an adolescent person.—**adolescence** *n*.

adopt *vt* to take legally into one's family and raise as one's child; to take as one's own.—**adoption** *n*.

adore *vt* to worship; to love deeply.—**adoringly** *adv*.

adorn *vt* to decorate; to make more pleasant or attractive.—**adornment** *n*.

adrenaline *n* a hormone that stimulates the heart rate, blood pressure, etc in response to stress and that is secreted by the adrenal glands or manufactured synthetically.

adrift *adj, adv* afloat without mooring, drifting; loose.

adroit *adj* skilful and clever.—**adroitly** *adv*.—**adroitness** *n*.

ADT *abbr* = Atlantic Daylight Time.

adult *adj* fully grown; mature; suitable only for adults, as in pornography, etc. * *n* a mature person, etc.

adulterate *vt* to make impure or inferior, etc by adding an improper substance.—**adulteration** *n*.

adultery *n* sexual intercourse between a married person and someone other than their legal partner.—**adulterous** *adj*.

advance *vt* to bring or move forward; to promote; to raise the rate of; (*money*) to lend. * *vi* to go forward; to make progress; to rise in rank, price, etc. * *n* progress; improvement; a rise in value; payment beforehand; (*pl*) friendly approaches. * *adj* in front; beforehand.

advanced *adj* in front; old; superior in development.

advanced green *n* (*Cdn*) a flashing green traffic light that comes on before a steady green light, showing that oncoming traffic is halted.

advancement *n* promotion to higher rank; progress in development.

advance poll *n* (*Cdn*) a poll for voters prior to the official election day.

advantage *n* superiority of position or condition; a gain or benefit; (*tennis*) the first point won after deuce. * *vt* to produce a benefit or favor to.

advantageous *adj* producing advantage, beneficial.—**advantageously** *adv*.

advent *n* an arrival or coming.

adventure *n* a strange or exciting undertaking; an unusual, stirring, often romantic, experience.—**adventurous** *adj*.—**adventurously** *adv*.

adventurer *n* a person who seeks adventure; someone who seeks money or power by unscrupulous means.—**adventuress** *nf*.

adverb *n* a word that modifies a verb, adjective, another adverb, phrase, clause or sentence and indicates how, why, where, etc.—**adverbial** *adj*.

adversary *n* an enemy or opponent.

adverse *adj* hostile; contrary or opposite; unfavorable.—**adversely** *adv*.

adversity *n* trouble, misery, misfortune.

advert *n* (*inf*) an advertisement.

advertise *vt* to call public attention to by buying space or time in the media, etc. * *vi* to call public attention to things for sale; to ask (for) by public notice.—**advertiser** *n*.

advertisement *n* advertising; a public notice, usu paid for by the provider of a good or service.

advertising *n* the promotion of goods or services by public notices; advertisements; the business of producing adverts.

advice *n* recommendation with regard to a course of action; formal notice or communication.

advisable *adj* prudent, expedient.—**advisability** *n*.

advise *vt* to give advice to; to caution; to recommend; to inform. * *vi* to give advice.—**adviser, advisor** *n*.

advisory *adj* having or exercising the power to advise; containing or giving advice.

advocate *n* a person who argues or defends the cause of another, esp in a court of law; a supporter. * *vt* to plead in favor of.

aegis *n* protection, sponsorship.

aerial *adj* belonging to or existing in the air; of aircraft or flying. * *n* a metal device for transmitting and receiving radio waves, an antenna.

aerie, aery *n* variant spellings of **eyrie**.

aeroplane, airplane (*US*) *n* a power-driven aircraft.

aerosol *n* a suspension of fine solid or liquid particles in gas, esp as held in a container under pressure, with a device for releasing it in a fine spray.

aesthetics, esthetics (*US*) *n* the philosophy of art and beauty.—**aesthetic** *adj.*—**aesthetically** *adv.*

AF *abbr* = Air Force.

affable *adj* friendly; approachable.—**affability** *n* —**affably** *adv.*

affair *n* a thing done or to be done; (*pl*) public or private business; (*inf*) an event; a temporary romantic or sexual relationship.

affect[1] *vt* to have an effect on; to produce a change in; to act in a way that alters or affects the feelings of.

affect[2] *vt* to pretend or feign (an emotion); to incline to or show a preference for.

affect[3] *n* an emotion, feeling or desire associated with a certain stimulus.

affectation *n* a striving after or an attempt to assume what is not natural or real; pretence.

affected *adj* (*manner, etc*) assumed artificially.

affection *n* tender feeling; liking.

affectionate *adj* showing affection, loving.—**affectionately** *adv.*

affiliate *vt* to connect as a subordinate member or branch; to associate (oneself with). * *vi* to join. * *n* an affiliated person, club, etc.—**affiliation** *n.*

affinity *n* attraction, liking; a close relationship, esp by marriage; similarity, likeness; (*chem*) a tendency in certain substances to combine.

affirmation *n* affirming; an assertion; a solemn declaration made by those declining to swear an oath, eg on religious grounds.

affix *vt* to fasten; to add, esp in writing; to attach.

afflict *vt* to cause persistent pain or suffering to; to trouble greatly.

affliction *n* persistent pain, suffering; a cause of this.

affluent *adj* rich, well provided for.—**affluence** *n* —**affluently** *adv.*

afford *vt* to be in a position to do or bear without much inconvenience; to have enough time, money, or resources for; to supply, produce.

affront *vi* to insult or offend openly or deliberately. * *n* a deliberate insult.

afield *adv* far away from home; to or at a distance; astray.

afloat *adj* floating; at sea, on board a ship; debt-free; flooded.—*also adv.*

AFN *abbr* (*Cdn*) = Assembly of First Nations.

afraid *adj* full of fear or apprehension; regretful.

afresh *adv* anew, starting again.

African-Canadian *n* a Black Canadian. * *adj* pertaining to Black Canadians, or their culture, history, etc.

aft *adv* at, near, or toward the stern of a ship or rear of an aircraft.

after *prep* behind in place or order; following in time, later than; in pursuit of; in imitation of; in view of, in spite of; according to; about, concerning; subsequently. * *adv* later; behind. * *conj* at a time later than. * *adj* later, subsequent; nearer the stern of a ship or aircraft.

aftereffect *n* an effect that occurs some time after its cause.

afterlife *n* life after death.

aftermath *n* the result, esp an unpleasant one.

afternoon *n* the time between noon and sunset or evening.—*also adj.*

aftershave *n* lotion for use after shaving.

afterthought *n* a thought or reflection occurring later.

afterwards *adv* at a later time.

again *adv* once more; besides; on the other hand.

against *prep* in opposition to; unfavorable to; in contrast to; in preparation for; in contact with; as a charge on.

age *n* the period of time during which someone or something has lived or existed; a stage of life; later years of life; a historical period; a division of geological time; (*inf: often pl*) a long time. * *vti* (*pr p* ageing *or* aging, *pt* aged) to grow or make old, ripe, mature, etc.

aged *adj* very old; of a specified age.

agency *n* action; power; means; a firm, etc, empowered to act for another; an administrative government division.

agenda *n* a list of items or matters of business that need attention.

agent *n* a person or thing that acts or has an influence; a substance or organism that is active; one empowered to act for another; a government representative; a spy.

agent general *n* the official representative of a Canadian province or Australian state in a foreign country or region.

aggravate *vt* to make worse; (*inf*) to annoy, irritate.—**aggravation** *n.*

aggregate *adj* formed of parts combined into a mass or whole; taking all units as a whole. * *n* a collection or sum of parts; sand, stones, etc, mixed with cement to form concrete. * *vt* to collect or form into a mass or whole; to amount to (a total).

aggression *n* an unprovoked attack; a hostile action or behaviour.

aggressive *adj* boldly hostile; quarrelsome; self-assertive, enterprising.—**aggressively** *adv.*—**aggressiveness** *n.*

aghast *adj* utterly horrified.

agile *adj* quick and nimble in movement; mentally acute.—**agility** *n.*

agitate *vt* to shake, move; to disturb or excite the emotions of. * *vi* to stir up public interest for a cause, etc.—**agitation** *n.*—**agitator** *n.*

AGM *abbr* = Annual General Meeting.

ago *adv* in the past. * *adj* gone by; past.

agony *n* extreme mental or physical suffering.

agree *vb* (*pt* **agreed**)*vi* to be of similar opinion; to consent or assent (to); to come to an understanding about; to be consistent; to suit a person's digestion; (*gram*) to be consistent in gender, number, case, or person. * *vt* to concede, grant; to bring into harmony; to reach terms on.

agreeable *adj* likeable, pleasing; willing to agree.—**agreeably** *adv*.

agreement *n* harmony in thought or opinion, correspondence; an agreed settlement between two people, etc.

ag rep *n* (*Cdn*) (*inf*) agricultural representative, an employee of a government agriculture department who advises farmers.

agriculture *n* the science or practice of producing crops and raising livestock; farming.—**agricultural** *adj*.—**agriculturally** *adv*.

aground *adj* on or onto the shore.—*also adv*.

ahead *adj* in or to the front; forward; onward; in advance; winning or profiting.—*also adv*.

aid *vti* to help, give assistance to. * *n* anything that helps; a specific means of assistance, eg money; a helper.

aide *n* an aide-de-camp; assistant.

AIDS, Aids *n* (*acronym for* acquired immune deficiency syndrome) a condition caused by a virus, in which the body loses immunity to infection.

ailment *n* a slight illness.

aim *vti* to point or direct towards a target so as to hit; to direct (one's efforts); to intend. * *n* the act of aiming; purpose, intention.

air *n* the mixture of invisible gases surrounding the earth; the earth's atmosphere; empty, open space; a light breeze; aircraft, aviation; outward appearance, demeanour; a pervading influence; (*mus*) a melody; (*pl*) an affected manner. * *vt* to expose to the air for drying; to expose to public notice; (*clothes*) to place in a warm place to finish drying.

airborne *adj* carried by or through the air; aloft or flying.

Air Command *n* the Canadian air force.

air conditioning *n* regulation of air humidity and temperature in buildings, etc.

air-cooled *adj* cooled by having air passed over, into, or through.

aircraft *n* (*pl* **aircraft**) any machine for travelling through air.

aircraft carrier *n* a warship with a large flat deck, for carrying aircraft.

airgun *n* a gun that fires pellets by compressed air.

air hostess *n* a stewardess on a passenger aircraft.

air letter *n* a sheet of light writing paper that is folded and sealed for sending by airmail.

airline *n* a system or company for transportation by aircraft.

airlock *n* a blockage in a pipe caused by an air bubble; an airtight compartment giving access to a pressurized chamber.

airmail *n* mail transported by aircraft.

airplane *n* the US spelling of **aeroplane**.

airport *n* a place where aircraft can land and take off, with facilities for repair, etc.

air raid *n* an attack by military aircraft on a surface target.

airship *n* a self-propelled steerable aircraft that is lighter than air.

airstrip *n* an area of land cleared for aircraft to land on; a runway.

airtight *adj* too tight for air or gas to enter or escape; (*alibi, etc*) invulnerable.

airy *adj* (**airier, airiest**) open to the air; breezy; light as air; graceful; light-hearted; flippant.—**airily** *adv*.

aisle *n* a passageway, as between rows of seats; a side part of a church.

ajar *adv* partly open, as a door.

alarm *n* a signal warning of danger; an automatic device to arouse from sleep or to attract attention; fear arising from apprehension of danger. * *vt* to give warning of danger; to fill with apprehension or fear.

Albertan *n* a person who lives in, or is from, Alberta. • *adj* of or pertaining to Alberta.

album *n* a book with blank pages for the insertion of photographs, autographs, etc; a long-playing record, cassette, or CD.

alchemy *n* chemistry as practised during medieval times, with the aim of transmuting base metals into gold.—**alchemist** *n*.

alcohol *n* a liquid, generated by distillation and fermentation, that forms the intoxicating agent in wine, beer and spirits; a liquid containing alcohol; a chemical compound of this nature.

alcoholic *adj* of or containing alcohol; caused by alcohol. * *n* a person suffering from alcoholism.

alcoholism *n* a disease caused by excessive consumption of alcohol.

alcool *n* (*Cdn*) in Quebec, unflavoured alcohol sold as a beverage.

alcove *n* a recess off a larger room.

ale *n* beer.

alert *adj* watchful; active, brisk. * *n* a danger signal. * *vt* to warn of impending danger, put in a state of readiness.—**alertly** *adv*.—**alertness** *n*.

algebra *n* the branch of mathematics dealing with the properties and relations of numbers; the generalization and extension of arithmetic.—**algebraic** *adj*.

Algonquian *n* a group of eastern North American Indian languages; a member of a North American Indian people who speaks one of these languages. * *adj* of or pertaining to these peoples or their languages.

Algonquin *n* a member of a First Nations people living in eastern Ontario; the Algonquian language spoken by this people. * *adj* of or pertaining to this people or their language.

alias *adv* otherwise called. * *n* (*pl* **aliases**) an assumed name.

alibi *n* (*pl* **alibis**) (*law*) the plea that a person charged with a crime was elsewhere when it was committed; (*inf*) any excuse.

alien *adj* foreign; strange. * *n* a person from another country, place, etc; a person of foreign birth who has not been naturalized;

a being from outer space.

alienate *vt* to render hostile or unfriendly; to make less affectionate or interested.—**alienation** *n*.

alight¹ *vi* to come down, as from a bus; to descend after a flight.

alight² *adj* on fire; lively.

align *vt* to place in a straight line, to bring into agreement, etc. * *vi* to line up.—**alignment** *n*.

alike *adj* like one another. * *adv* equally; similarly.

alimony *n* an allowance for support made by one spouse to the other; maintenance.

alive *adj* having life; active, alert; in existence, operation, etc.

alkali *n* (*pl* **alkalis**) (*chem*) any salt or mixture that neutralizes acids.—**alkaline** *adj*.

all *adj* the whole amount or number of; every one of. * *adv* wholly; supremely, completely; entirely. * *n* the whole number, quantity; everyone; everything.

allay *vt* to lighten, alleviate; to pacify or make calm.

all-candidates meeting *n* (*Cdn*) a public meeting held during an election campaign in which all candidates present their views and answer questions.

all-dressed *adj* (*Cdn*) pertaining to an item of food, such as a pizza or a hot dog, that is topped with all available garnishes.

allege *vt* to assert or declare, esp without proof; to offer as an excuse.—**allegation** *n*.

allegedly *adv* asserted without proof.

allegiance *n* the obligation of being loyal to one's country, etc; devotion, as to a cause.

allegory *n* a fable, story, poem, etc, in which events depicted are used to convey a deeper, usu moral or spiritual, meaning.—**allegorical** *adj*.

allergy *n* an abnormal reaction of the body to substances (certain foods, pollen, etc) normally harmless; antipathy.—**allergic** *adj*.

alleviate *vt* to lessen or relieve (pain, worry, etc).—**alleviation** *n*.

alley *n* a narrow street between or behind buildings; a bowling lane.

alliance *n* a union by marriage or treaty for a common purpose; an agreement for this; the countries, groups, etc in such an association.

alligator *n* a large reptile similar to the crocodile but having a short, blunt snout.

all-in *adj* (*inf*) exhausted.

allocate *vt* to distribute or apportion in shares; to set apart for a specific purpose.—**allocation** *n*.

allophone *n* a phonetic term describing any of various possible contextual or environmental variants of the same phoneme; (*Cdn*) in Quebec, an immigrant to Canada whose first language is neither English nor French. • *adj* having a first language as an immigrant other than English or French.—**allophonic** *adj*. **allot** *vt* (*pt* **allotted**) to distribute, allocate.

allotment *n* allotting; a share allotted; a small

area of land rented for cultivation.

all-out *adj* using maximum effort.

allow *vt* to permit; to acknowledge, admit as true; (*money*) to give, grant as an allowance at regular intervals; to estimate as an addition or deduction. * *vi* to admit the possibility (of).

allowance *n* an amount or sum allowed; a discount; a portion of income not subject to income tax; permission; admission, concession.

alloy *n* a solid substance comprising a mixture of two or more metals; something that degrades the substance to which it is added. * *vt* to make into an alloy; to degrade or spoil by mixing with an inferior substance.

all-round *adj* efficient in all respects, esp sport.

all-time *adj* unsurpassed until now.

allude *vi* to refer indirectly to.

allure *vt* to entice, charm. * *n* fascination; charm.

alluring *adj* attractive.

allusion *n* alluding; an implied or indirect reference.—**allusive** *adj*.

ally *vti* to join or unite for a specific purpose; to relate by similarity of structure, etc. * *n* a country or person joined with another for a common purpose.

almighty *adj* all-powerful. * *n* (*with cap*) God, the all-powerful.

almond *n* the edible kernel of the fruit of a tree of the rose family; the tree bearing this fruit. * *adj* (*eyes, etc*) oval and pointed.

almost *adv* all but, very nearly but not quite all.

alms *npl* money, food, etc, given to the poor.

alone *adj* isolated; without anyone or anything else; unassisted; unique. * *adv* exclusively.

along *adv* onward, forward; over the length of; in company and together with; in addition. * *prep* in the direction of the length of; in accordance with.

alongside *prep* close beside. * *adv* at the side.

aloof *adv* at a distance; apart. * *adj* cool and reserved.—**aloofness** *n*.

aloud *adv* with a normal voice; loudly.

alphabet *n* the characters used in a language arranged in conventional order.—**alphabetical** *adj*.—**alphabetically** *adv*.

alpine *adj* of the Alps; of high mountains. * *n* a mountain plant, esp a small herb.

already *adv* by or before the time specified; before the time expected.

also *adv* in addition, besides.

Alta. *abbr* = Alberta.

altar *n* a table, etc for sacred purposes in a place of worship.

alter *vti* to make or become different in a small way; to change.—**alteration** *n*.

alternate¹ *vt* to do or use by turns. * *vi* to act, happen, etc, by turns; to take turns regularly.

alternate² *adj* occurring or following in turns.—**alternately** *adv*.

alternating current *n* an electric current that reverses its direction at regular intervals.

alternative *adj* presenting a choice between two

things. * *n* either of two possibilities.—**alternatively** *adv.*

alternator *n* an electric generator that produces alternating current.

although *conj* though; in spite of that.

altitude *n* height, esp above sea level.

alto *n* (*pl* **altos**) the range of the highest male voice; a singer with this range.

altogether *adv* in all; on the whole; completely.

aluminium, aluminum (*US*) *n* a silvery-white malleable metallic element notable for its lightness.

always *adv* at all times; in all cases; repeatedly; forever.

am *see* be.

a.m. *abbr* = *ante meridiem*, before noon.

A/M *abbr* = Air Marshall.

amalgamate *vt* to combine, unite.—**amalgamation** *n.*

amass *vt* to bring together in a large quantity; to accumulate.

amateur *n* one who engages in a particular activity as a hobby, and not as a profession. * *adj* of or done by amateurs.

amateurish *adj* lacking expertise.—**amateurishly** *adv.*

amaut *n* among the Inuit, a fur-lined pouch in back of a woman's parka, used to carry an infant.

amaze *vt* to fill with wonder, astonish.—**amazement** *n.*—**amazing** *adj.*

ambassador *n* the highest-ranking diplomatic representative from one country to another; an authorized messenger.—**ambassadorial** *adj.*

amber *n* a hard yellowish fossil resin, used for jewellery and ornaments, etc; the color of amber; a yellow traffic light used to signal "caution."

ambiguous *adj* capable of two or more interpretations; indistinct, vague.—**ambiguity** *n.*—**ambiguously** *adv.*

ambition *n* desire for power, wealth and success; an object of ambition.

ambitious *adj* having or governed by ambition; resulting from or showing ambition; requiring considerable effort or ability.—**ambitiously** *adv.*

amble *vi* to walk in a leisurely way.

ambulance *n* a special vehicle for transporting the sick or injured.

ambush *n* the concealment of soldiers, etc to make a surprise attack; the bushes or other cover in which they are hidden. * *vti* to lie in wait; to attack from an ambush.

amenable *adj* easily influenced or led, tractable; answerable to legal authority.—**amenably** *adv.*

amend *vt* to remove errors, esp in a text; to modify, improve; to alter in minor details.—**amendment.**

amends *npl* (*used as sing*) compensation or recompense for some loss, harm, etc.

amenity *n* pleasantness, as regards situation or convenience.

amethyst *n* a gemstone consisting of bluish-violet quartz.

amiable *adj* friendly in manner, congenial.—**amiably** *adv.*

amicable *adj* friendly; peaceable.—**amicably** *adv.*

amid, amidst *prep* in or to the middle of; during.

amiss *adj* wrong, improper. * *adv* in an incorrect manner.

ammunition *n* bullets, shells, rockets, etc; any means of attack or defence; facts and reasoning used to prove a point in an argument.

amnesia *n* a partial or total loss of memory.—**amnesiac** *n.*

amnesty *n* a general pardon, esp of political prisoners.

among, amongst *prep* in the number of, surrounded by; in the group or class of; within a group, between; by the joint efforts of.

amoral *adj* neither moral nor immoral; without moral sense.

amorous *adj* displaying or feeling love or desire.—**amorously** *adv.*—**amorousness** *n.*

amorphous *adj* lacking a specific shape, shapeless; unrecognizable, indefinable.

amount *vi* to be equivalent (to) in total, quantity or significance. * *n* the total sum; the whole value or effect; a quantity.

ampere *n* the standard SI unit by which electric current is measured.

amphibious *adj* living on both land and water; (*mil*) involving both sea and land forces.

amphitheatre *n* an oval or circular building with rising rows of seats around an open arena.

ample *adj* large in size, scope, etc; plentiful.—**amply** *adv.*

amplifier *n* a device that increases electric voltage, current, or power, or the loudness of sound.

amplify *vt* to expand more fully, add details to; (*electrical signals, etc*) to strengthen.—**amplification** *n.*

amputate *vt* to cut off, esp by surgery.—**amputation** *n.*

amuse *vt* to entertain or divert in a pleasant manner; to cause to laugh or smile.—**amusement** *n.*

an *adj* the indefinite article ("a"), used before words beginning with the sound of a vowel except "u" as pronounced "y".

anaemia, anemia (*US*) *n* a condition in which the blood is low in red cells or in haemoglobin, resulting in paleness, weakness, etc.

anaemic, anemic (*US*) *adj* suffering from anaemia; weak; pale; listless.

anaesthetic, anesthetic (*US*) *n* a drug, gas, etc used to produce anaesthesia, as before surgery. * *adj* of or producing anaesthesia.

anaesthetist, anesthetist (*US*) *n* a person trained to give anaesthetics.

analogy *n* a similarity or correspondence in certain respects between two things.

analyse, analyze (*US*) *vt* to separate (something) into its constituent parts to investigate its structure and function, etc; to examine in detail; to psychoanalyse.

analysis *n* (*pl* **analyses**) the process of analysing; a statement of the results of this; psychoanalysis.

analyst *n* a person who analyses; a psycho-analyst.

analytic, analytical *adj* pertaining to analysis.—**analytically** *adv*.

anarchist *n* a person who believes that all government is unnecessary and should be abolished.—**anarchism** *n*.

anarchy *n* the absence of government; political confusion; disorder, lawlessness.—**anarchic** *adj*.

anathema *n* anything greatly detested; an ecclesiastical denunciation with excommunication.

anatomy *n* the science of the physical structure of plants and animals; the structure of an organism.—**anatomical** *adj*.—**anatomically** *adv*.

ancestor *n* one from whom a person is descended, a forefather; an early animal or plant from which existing types are descended; something regarded as a forerunner.—**ancestral** *adj*.—**ancestress** *nf*.

ancestry *n* ancestors collectively; lineage.

anchor *n* a heavy metal implement that lodges at the bottom of the sea or a river to hold a ship in position; something that gives support or stability. * *vt* to fix by an anchor; to secure firmly.

anchorage *n* a safe anchoring place for ships; the charge for anchoring.

anchor ice *n* (*Cdn*) ice formed at the bottom of a body of water.

anchovy *n* a small Mediterranean fish resembling a herring with a very salty taste.

ancient *adj* very old; dating from the distant past; of the period and civilizations predating the fall of the Roman Empire; old-fashioned. * *n* a person who lived in the ancient period; (*pl*) the members of the classical civilizations of antiquity.

and *conj* in addition to; together with; plus; increasingly; as a consequence, afterwards; expressing contrast.

anecdote *n* a short entertaining account about an amusing or interesting event or person.

anew *adv* afresh; again, once more; in a new way or form.

angakok *n* an Inuit shaman or healer.

angel *n* a messenger of God; an image of a human figure with wings and a halo; a very beautiful or kind person.—**angelic** *adj*.

anger *n* strong displeasure, often because of opposition, a hurt, etc. * *vti* to make or become angry.

angina *n* sharp stabbing pains in the chest, usu caused by angina pectoris.

angle[1] *n* a corner; the point from which two lines or planes extend or diverge; a specific viewpoint; an individual method or approach (eg to a problem). * *vt* to bend at an angle; to move or place at an angle; to present, news, etc from a particular point of view.

angle[2] *vi* to fish with a hook and line; to use hints or artifice to get something.—**angler** *n*.

Anglican *adj* belonging to or of the Church of England or churches in communion with it.

* *n* a member of the Anglican Church.—**Anglicanism** *n*.

Anglo *n* (*Cdn*) (*inf*) a person who speaks English as a first language, especially in Quebec.

Anglo-Canadian *adj* pertaining to England and Canada, as to commerce or population. * *n* a Canadian citizen whose first language is English.

anglophone *adj* (*Cdn*) English-speaking. * *n* a person whose first language is English.

angry *adj* (**angrier, angriest**) full of anger; inflamed.—**angrily** *adv*.

anguish *n* agonizing physical or mental distress.

angular *adj* having one or more angles; forming an angle; measured by an angle; stiff and clumsy in manner, thin and bony.—**angularity** *n*.

animal *n* any living organism except a plant or bacterium, typically able to move about; a lower animal as distinguished from man, esp mammals; a brutish person. * *adj* of or like an animal; bestial; sensual.

animate *vt* to give life to; to liven up; to inspire, encourage. * *adj* alive; lively.

animosity *n* strong dislike; hostility.

aniseed *n* the seed of the anise plant, used as a flavoring.

ankle *n* the joint between the foot and leg, the part of the leg between the foot and calf.

annex *vt* to attach, esp to something larger; to incorporate into a state the territory of (another state).—**annexation** *n*.

annihilate *vt* to destroy completely; (*inf*) to defeat convincingly, as in an argument.—**annihilation** *n*.

anniversary *n* the yearly return of the date of some event; a celebration of this.—*also adj*.

annotate *vti* to provide with explanatory notes.—**annotation** *n*.

announce *vt* to bring to public attention; to give news of the arrival of; to be an announcer for. * *vi* to serve as an announcer.—**announcement** *n*.

annoy *vt* to vex, tease, irritate, as by a repeated action.—**annoyance** *n*.

annual *adj* of or measured by a year; yearly; coming every year; living only one year or season. * *n* a plant that lives only one year; a periodical published once a year.—**annually** *adv*.

annuity *n* an investment yielding fixed payments, esp yearly; such a payment.

annul *vt* (*pt* **annulled**) to do away with; to deprive of legal force, nullify.—**annulment** *n*.

anoint *vt* to rub with oil; to apply oil in a sacred ritual as a sign of consecration.—**anointment** *n*.

anomaly *n* abnormality; anything inconsistent or odd.—**anomalous** *adj*.

anonymous *adj* having or providing no name; written or provided by an unnamed person; lacking individuality.—**anonymity** *n*.—**anonymously** *adv*.

anorak *n* a waterproof jacket with a hood.

another *adj* a different or distinct (thing or person); an additional one of the same kind;

some other.—*also pron.*

answer *n* a spoken or written reply or response; the solution to a problem; a reaction, response. * *vt* to speak or write in reply; to satisfy or correspond to (eg a specific need); to justify, offer a refutation of. * *vi* to reply; to act in response (to); to be responsible (for); to conform (to).

answerable *adj* capable of being refuted; (*with* **for** *or* **to**) responsible, accountable.

ant *n* any of a family of small, generally wingless insects of many species, all of which form and live in highly organized groups.

antagonism *n* antipathy, hostility; an opposing force, principle, etc.

antagonist *n* an adversary; an opponent.—**antagonistic** *adj.*—**antagonistically** *adv.*

antagonize *vt* to arouse opposition.

Antarctic *adj* of the South Pole or its surroundings. * *n* the Antarctic regions; the Antarctic Ocean.

antelope *n* any of the family of fast-running and graceful deer-like animals of Africa and Asia.

antenatal *adj* occurring or present before birth.

antenna *n* (*pl* **antennae**) either of a pair of feelers on the head of an insect, etc; (*pl* **antennas**) an aerial.

anthem *n* a religious choral song; a song of praise or devotion, as to a nation.

anthill *n* a mound thrown up by ants or termites in digging their nests.

anthology *n* a collection of poetry or prose.—**anthologist** *n.*

anthropology *n* the scientific study of human beings, their origins, distribution, physical attributes and culture.—**anthropological** *adj.*—**anthropologist** *n.*

anti- *prefix* opposed to; against.

antibiotic *n* any of various chemical, fungal or synthetic substances used against bacterial or fungal infections.

anticipate *vt* to give prior thought and attention to; to use, spend, act on in advance; to foresee and take action to thwart another; to expect. * *vi* to speak, act, before the appropriate time.—**anticipation** *n.*

anticlimax *n* a sudden drop from the important to the trivial; an ending to a story or series of events that disappoints one's expectations.

anticlockwise *adj* moving in a direction contrary to the hands of a clock as viewed from the front.—*also adv.*

anticyclone *n* a body of air rotating about an area of high atmospheric pressure.

antidote *n* a remedy that counteracts a poison; something that counteracts harmful effects.

antifreeze *n* a substance used, as in car radiator, to prevent freezing up.

antipathy *n* a fixed dislike; aversion; an object of this.

antiquated *adj* old-fashioned; obsolete.

antique *adj* from the distant past; old-fashioned. * *n* a relic of the distant past; a piece of furniture, pottery, etc dating from an earlier historical period and sought after by collectors.

antiquity *n* the far distant past, esp before the Middle Ages; (*pl*) relics dating from the far distant past.

antiseptic *n* a substance that destroys or prevents the growth of disease-producing microorganisms. * *adj* destroying harmful organisms; very clean.

antisocial *adj* avoiding the company of other people, unsocial; contrary to the interests of society in general.

antler *n* the branched horn of a deer or related animal.—**antlered** *adj.*

anus *n* the excretory orifice of the alimentary canal.

anvil *n* the heavy iron block on which metal objects are shaped with a hammer.

anxiety *n* the condition of being anxious; eagerness, concern; a cause of worry.

anxious *adj* worried; uneasy; eagerly wishing; causing anxiety.—**anxiously** *adv.*

any *adj* one out of many, some; every.

anybody *pron* any person; an important person.

anyhow *adv* in any way whatever; in any case.

anymore *adv* now; nowadays.

anyone *pron* any person; anybody.

anything *pron* any object, event, fact, etc. * *n* a thing, no matter what kind.

anyway *adv* in any manner; at any rate; haphazardly.

anywhere *adv* in, at, or to any place.

apart *adv* at a distance, separately, aside; into two or more pieces.

apartheid *n* a policy of racial segregation implemented in South Africa.

apartment *n* a room or rooms in a building; a flat.

apathy *n* lack of feeling; lack of concern, indifference.—**apathetic** *adj.*—**apathetically** *adv.*

ape *n* a chimpanzee, gorilla, orang-utan, or gibbon; any monkey; a mimic. * *vt* to imitate.

apéritif *n* an alcoholic drink taken before a meal.

aperture *n* an opening; a hole.

apex *n* the highest point, the tip; the culminating point; the vertex of a triangle.

aphrodisiac *adj* arousing sexually. * *n* a food, drug, etc that excites sexual desire.

apiece *adv* to, by, or for each one.

aplomb *n* poise; self-possession.

apologetic *adj* expressing an apology; contrite; presented in defence.—**apologetically** *adv.*

apologize *vi* to make an apology.

apology *n* an expression of regret for wrongdoing; a defence or justification of one's beliefs, etc; (*with* **for**) a poor substitute.

apoplexy *n* a sudden loss of consciousness and subsequent partial paralysis, usu caused by a broken or blocked artery in the brain.

apostle *n* the first or principal supporter of a new belief or cause.

apostrophe *n* a mark (') showing the omission of letters or figures, also a sign of the possessive case or the plural of letters and figures.

appal, appall (*US*) *vt* (*pt* **appalled**) to fill with terror or dismay.

appalling *adj* shocking, horrifying.—**appallingly** *adv.*

apparatus *n* the equipment used for a specific

task; any complex machine, device, or system.

apparent *adj* easily seen, evident; seeming, but not real.—**apparently** *adv*.

apparition *n* an appearance or manifestation, esp something unexpected or unusual; a ghost.

appeal *vi* to take a case to a higher court; to make an earnest request; to refer to a witness or superior authority for vindication, confirmation, etc; to arouse pleasure or sympathy. * *n* the referral of a lawsuit to a higher court for rehearing; an earnest call for help; attraction, the power of arousing sympathy; a request for public donations to a charitable cause.

appear *vi* to become or be visible; to arrive, come in person; to be published; to present oneself formally (before a court, etc); to seem, give an impression of being.

appearance *n* the act or occasion of appearing; that which appears; external aspect of a thing or person; outward show, semblance.

appease *vt* to pacify; to allay; to conciliate by making concessions.—**appeasement** *n*.

appendage *n* something appended; an external organ or part, as a tail.

appendicitis *n* inflammation of the appendix of the intestine.

appendix *n* (*pl* **appendixes, appendices**) a section of supplementary information at the back of a book, etc; a small tube of tissue that forms an outgrowth of the intestine.

appetite *n* sensation of bodily desire, esp for food; (*with* **for**) a strong desire or liking, a craving.

appetizing *adj* stimulating the appetite.—**appetizingly** *adv*.

applaud *vt* to show approval, esp by clapping the hands.

applause *n* approval expressed by clapping; acclamation.

apple *n* a round, firm, fleshy, edible fruit.

appliance *n* a device or machine, esp for household use.

applicable *adj* that may be applied; appropriate, relevant (to).—**applicability** *n*.

applicant *n* a person who applies, esp for a job.

application *n* the act of applying; the use to which something is put; a petition, request; concentration, diligent effort; relevance or practical value.

apply *vt* to bring to bear; to put to practical use; to spread, lay on; to devote (oneself) with close attention. * *vi* to make a formal, esp written, request; to be relevant.

appoint *vt* to fix or decide officially; to select for a job; to prescribe.

appraise *vt* to estimate the value or quality of.—**appraisal** *n*.

appreciable *adj* capable of being perceived or measured; fairly large.—**appreciably** *adv*.

appreciate *vt* to value highly; to recognize gratefully; to understand, be aware of; to increase the value of. * *vi* to rise in value.

appreciation *n* gratitude, approval; sensitivity to aesthetic values; an assessment or critical evaluation; a favorable review; an increase in value.—**appreciative** *adj*.

apprehend *vt* to arrest, capture; to understand, to perceive.

apprehension *n* anxiety; the act of arresting; understanding; an idea.

apprehensive *adj* uneasy; anxious.—**apprehensively** *adv*.

apprentice *n* one being taught a trade or craft; a novice.—**apprenticeship** *n*.

approach *vi* to draw nearer. * *vt* to make a proposal to; to set about dealing with; to come near to. * *n* the act of approaching; a means of entering or leaving; a move to establish relations; the final descent of an aircraft.—**approachable** *adj*.

appropriate *adj* fitting, suitable. * *vt* to take for one's own use, esp illegally; (*money, etc*) to set aside for a specific purpose.—**appropriately** *adv*.—**appropriateness** *n*.

approval *n* approving; favorable opinion; official permission.

approve *vt* to express a good opinion of; to authorize. * *vi* (*with* **of**) to consider to be favorable or satisfactory.

approximate *adj* almost exact or correct. * *vt* to come near to; to be almost the same as. * *vi* to come close.—**approximately** *adv*.

approximation *n* a close estimate; a near likeness.

apricot *n* a small, oval orange-pink fruit resembling the plum and peach.

apron *n* a garment worn to protect clothing; anything resembling the shape of an apron used for protection; the paved surface on an airfield where aircraft are parked, etc.

apt *adj* ready or likely (to); suitable, relevant; able to learn easily.—**aptness** *n*.

aptitude *n* suitability; natural talent, esp for learning.

aqualung *n* portable diving gear comprising air cylinders connected to a face mask.

aquarium *n* (*pl* **aquariums**) a tank, pond, etc for keeping aquatic animals or plants; a building where collections of aquatic animals are exhibited.

Aquarius *n* (*astrol*) the eleventh sign of the zodiac, the Water-carrier, operative 20 January-18 February.

aquatic *adj* of or taking place in water; living or growing in water.

aqueduct *n* a large pipe or conduit for carrying water; an elevated structure supporting this.

arbiter *n* an arbitrator.

arable *adj* (*land*) suitable for ploughing or planting crops.—*also n*.

arbitrary *adj* not bound by rules; despotic, absolute; capricious, unreasonable.—**arbitrarily** *adv*.—**arbitrariness** *n*.

arbitrate *vi* to act as an arbitrator. * *vt* to submit to or act as an arbitrator.

arbitration *n* the settlement of disputes by arbitrating.

arbitrator *n* a person chosen to settle a dispute between contending parties.

arc *n* a portion of the circumference of a circle or other curve; a luminous discharge of electricity across a gap between two electrodes or terminals. * *vi* (*pt* arced *or* arcked) to form an electric arc.

arcade *n* an arched passageway; a covered walk or area lined with shops.

arch[1] *n* a curved structure spanning an opening; the curved underside of the foot. * *vti* to span or cover with an arch; to curve, bend into an arch.

arch[2] *adj* (*criminal, etc*) principal, expert; clever, sly; mischievous.

archaeology, archeology *n* the study of past human societies through their extant remains.—**archaeological, archeological** *adj*.—**archaeologist, archeologist** *n*.

archaic *adj* belonging to ancient times; (*language*) no longer in use.

archbishop *n* a bishop of the highest rank.

archer *n* a person who shoots with a bow and arrow.

archery *n* the art or sport of shooting arrows from a bow.

archetype *n* the original pattern or model; a prototype.—**archetypal** *adj*.

archipelago *n* (*pl* **archipelagos**) a sea filled with small islands; a group of small islands.

architect *n* a person who designs buildings and supervises their erection; someone who plans something.

architecture *n* the art, profession, or science of designing and constructing buildings; the style of a building or buildings.—**architectural** *adj*.—**architecturally** *adv*.

archives *npl* the location in which public records are kept; the public records themselves.

archway *n* an arched or vaulted passage, esp leading into a castle.

arctic *adj* (*often with cap*) of, near, or relating to the North Pole or its surroundings; (*inf*) very cold, icy.

arctic boot *n* (*Cdn*) a heavy, felt-lined, rubber-soled boot worn in cold weather.

arctic char *n* a freshwater fish of northern North America, similar to salmon.

arctic cotton *n* a northern sedge whose flower heads have long white cottony hairs.

arctic hare *n* a large hare of northern Canada and Greenland, whose coat is brown in summer and white in winter.

arctic poppy *n* a northern plant with four-petalled golden flowers.

ardent *adj* passionate; zealous.—**ardently** *adv*.

arduous *adj* difficult, laborious; steep, difficult to climb.—**arduously** *adv*.

are *see* **be**.

area *n* an expanse of land; a total outside surface, measured in square units; a part of a house, district, etc; scope or extent.

arena *n* an area within a sports stadium, etc where events take place; a place or sphere of contest or activity.

aren't = are not.

arguable *adj* able to be asserted; plausible.—**arguably** *adv*.

argue *vt* to try to prove by reasoning; to debate,

dispute; to persuade (into, out of). * *vi* to offer reasons for or against something; to disagree, exchange angry words.

argument *n* a disagreement; a debate, discussion; a reason offered in debate; an abstract, summary.

arid *adj* very dry, parched; uninteresting; dull.—**aridity** *n*.—**aridly** *adv*.—**aridness** *n*.

Aries *n* (*astrol*) the first sign of the zodiac, the Ram, operative 21 March-21 April.

aright *adv* correctly.

arise *vi* (*pt* arose, *pp* arisen) to get up, as from bed; to rise, ascend; to come into being, to result (from).

aristocracy *n* (a country with) a government dominated by a privileged minority class; the privileged class in a society, the nobility; those people considered the best in their sphere.

aristocrat *n* a member of the aristocracy; a supporter of aristocratic government; a person with the manners or taste of a privileged class.

aristocratic *adj* relating to or characteristic of the aristocracy; elegant, stylish in dress and manners.—**aristocratically** *adv*.

arithmetic *n* (*math*) computation (addition, subtraction, etc) using real numbers; calculation.—**arithmetic, arithmetical** *adj*.—**arithmetically** *adv*.

ark *n* (*Bible*) the boat in which Noah and his family and two of every kind of creature survived the flood; an enclosure in a synagogue for the scrolls of the Torah.

arm[1] *n* the upper limb from the shoulder to the wrist; something shaped like an arm, as a support on a chair; a sleeve; power, authority; an administrative division of a large organization.

arm[2] *n* (*usu pl*) a weapon; a branch of the military service; (*pl*) heraldic bearings. * *vt* to provide with weapons, etc; to provide with something that protects or strengthens, etc; to set a fuse ready to explode. * *vi* to prepare for war or any struggle.

armchair *n* a chair with side rests for the arms. * *adj* lacking practical experience.

armful *n* as much as the arms can hold.

armistice *n* a truce, preliminary to a peace treaty.

armour, armor (*US*) *n* any defensive or protective covering.

armpit *n* the hollow underneath the arm at the shoulder

arms *see* **arm**[2].

army *n* a large body of soldiers for waging war, esp on land; any large number of persons, animals, etc.

aroma *n* a pleasant smell; a fragrance.—**aromatic** *adj*.

arose *see* **arise**.

around *prep* on all sides of; on the border of; in various places in or on; approximately, about. * *adv* in a circle; in every direction; in circumference; to the opposite direction.

arouse *vt* to wake from sleep; to stir, as to action; to evoke.

arpent n (Cdn) (hist) a unit of land area of about one acre, esp in French Canada.

arrange vt to put in a sequence or row; to settle, make preparations for; (mus) to prepare a composition for different instruments other than those intended.* vi to come to an agreement; to make plans.—**arrangement** n.—**arranger** n.

array n an orderly grouping, esp of troops; an impressive display; fine clothes; (comput) an ordered data structure that allows information to be easily indexed. * vt to set in order, to arrange; to dress, decorate.

arrears npl overdue debts; work, etc still to be completed.

arrest vt to stop; to capture, apprehend esp by legal authority; to catch and hold the attention of. * n a stoppage; seizure by legal authority.

arrival n arriving; a person or thing that has arrived.

arrive vi to reach any destination; to come; to achieve success, celebrity.

arrogance n an exaggerated assumption of importance.

arrogant adj overbearing; aggressively self-important.—**arrogantly** adv.

arrow n a straight, pointed weapon, made to be shot from a bow; a sign used to indicate direction.

arsenal n a workshop or store for weapons and ammunition.

arsenic n a soft grey metallic element, highly poisonous.

arson n the crime of using fire to destroy property deliberately.—**arsonist** n.

art n human creativity; skill acquired by study and experience; any craft and its principles; the making of things that have form and beauty; any branch of this, as painting, sculpture, etc; drawings, paintings, statues, etc; (pl) the creative and nonscientific branches of knowledge, esp as studied academically.

artefact, artifact n a product of human craftsmanship, esp a simple tool or ornament.

artery n a tubular vessel that conveys blood from the heart; any main channel of transport or communication.—**arterial** adj.

artful adj skilful at attaining one's ends; clever, crafty.—**artfully** adv.—**artfulness** n.

arthritis n painful inflammation of a joint.—**arthritic** adj.

artichoke n a thistle-like plant with a scaly flower head, parts of which are eaten as a vegetable.

article n a separate item or clause in a written document; an individual item on a particular subject in a newspaper, magazine, etc; a particular or separate item; (gram) a word placed before a noun to identify it as definite or indefinite. * vi (Cdn) serve a period of apprenticeship as a law student.

articulate adj capable of distinct, intelligible speech, or expressing one's thoughts clearly; jointed. * vti to speak or express clearly; to unite or become united (as) by a joint.

artificial adj lacking natural qualities; man-made.—**artificiality** n.—**artificially** adv.

artillery n large, heavy guns; the branch of the army that uses these.

artisan n a skilled workman.

artist n one who practises fine art, esp painting; one who does anything very well.—**artistic** adj.

artistry n artistic quality, ability, work, etc.

artless adj simple, natural; without art or skill.—**artlessly** adv.—**artlessness** n.

as adv equally; for instance; when related in a certain way. * conj in the same way that; while; because. * prep in the role or function of.

ASA abbr = (Cdn) Acetylsalicylic acid; (Brit) Amateur Swimming Association; (US) American Standards Association.

asbestos n a fine fibrous mineral used for making incombustible and chemical-resistant materials.

ascend vti to go up; to succeed to (a throne).

ascendancy, ascendency n dominating influence.

ascent n ascending; an upward slope, means of ascending.

ascertain vt to acquire definite knowledge of.—**ascertainable** adj.

ascetic adj self-denying, austere. * n a person who practises rigorous self-denial as a religious discipline; any severely abstemious person.—**ascetically** adv.—**asceticism** n.

ascribe vt to attribute.—**ascribable** adj.

ash[1] n a tree with silver-grey bark; the wood of this tree.

ash[2] n powdery residue of anything burnt; fine, volcanic lava.

ashamed adj feeling shame or guilt.

ashen adj like ashes, esp in color; pale.

ashore adv to or on the shore; to or on land.—also adj.

ashtray n a small receptacle for tobacco ash and cigarette stubs.

aside adv on or to the side; in reserve; notwithstanding. * n words uttered and intended as inaudible, esp as spoken by an actor to the audience and supposedly unheard by the others on the stage.

ask vt to put a question to, inquire of; to make a request of or for; to invite; to demand, expect. * vi to inquire about.

askance, askant adv with a sideways glance; with distrust.

askew adv, adj to one side; awry.

asleep adj sleeping; inactive; numb. * adv into a sleeping condition.

asparagus n a plant cultivated for its edible young shoots.

aspect n the look of a person or thing to the eye; a particular feature of a problem, situation, etc; the direction something faces; (astrol) the position of the planets with respect to one another, regarded as having an influence on human affairs.

aspersions npl slander; an attack on a person's reputation.

asphalt n a hard, black bituminous substance,

used for paving roads, etc. * *vt* to surface with asphalt.

asphyxiate *vt* to suffocate.—**asphyxiation** *n*.

aspiration *n* strong desire; ambition; aspirating; the act of breathing; the withdawal of air or fluid from a body cavity.

aspire *vi* to desire eagerly; to aim at high things.

aspirin *n* a pain-relieving drug.

ass *n* a donkey; a silly, stupid person; (*sl*) the arse, the buttocks.

assail *vt* to attack violently either physically or verbally.

assailant *n* an attacker.

assassin *n* a murderer, esp one hired to kill a leading political figure, etc.

assassinate *vt* to kill a political figure, etc; to harm (a person's reputation, etc).—**assassination** *n*.

assault *n* a violent attack; (*law*) an unlawful threat or attempt to harm another physically. * *vti* to make an assault (on).

assemble *vti* to bring together; to collect; to fit together the parts of; (*comput*) to translate.

assembly *n* assembling or being assembled; a gathering of persons, esp for a purpose; the fitting together of parts to make a whole machine, etc.

assembly line *n* a series of machines, equipment and workers through which a product passes in successive stages to be assembled.

assent *vi* to express agreement to something. * *n* consent or agreement.

assert *vt* to declare, affirm as true; to maintain or enforce (eg rights).

assertion *n* asserting; a statement that something is a fact, usu without evidence.

assertive *adj* self-assured, positive, confident.—**assertively** *adv*.—**assertiveness** *n*.

assess *vt* to establish the amount of, as a tax; to impose a tax or fine; to value, for the purpose of taxation; to estimate the worth, importance, etc of.—**assessment** *n*.

asset *n* anything owned that has value; a desirable thing; (*pl*) all the property, accounts receivable, etc of a person or business; (*pl*: *law*) property usable to pay debts.

assign *vt* to allot; to appoint to a post or duty; to ascribe; (*law*) to transfer (a right, property, etc).—**assignable** *adj*.

assignment *n* the act of assigning; something assigned to a person, such as a share, task, etc.

assimilate *vt* to absorb; to digest; to be ascribed; to be like.—**assimilation** *n*.

assist *vti* to support or aid.—**assistance** *n*.—**assistant** *n*.

associate *vt* to join as a friend, business partner or supporter; to bring together; to unite; to connect in the mind. * *vi* to combine or unite with others; to come together as friends, business partners or supporters. * *adj* allied or connected; having secondary status or privileges. * *n* a companion, business partner, supporter, etc; something

closely connected with another; a person admitted to an association as a subordinate member.

association *n* an organization of people with a common aim; the act of associating or being associated; a connection in the mind, etc.

assorted *adj* distributed according to sorts; miscellaneous.

assortment *n* a collection of people or things of different sorts.

assume *vt* to take on, to undertake; to usurp; to take as certain or true; to pretend to possess.

assumption *n* something taken for granted.

assurance *n* a promise, guarantee; a form of life insurance; a feeling of certainty, self-confidence.

assure *vt* to make safe or certain; to give confidence to; to state positively; to guarantee, ensure.

asterisk *n* a sign (*) used in writing or printing to mark omission of words, etc. * *vt* to mark with an asterisk.

astern *adv* behind a ship or aircraft; at or toward the rear of a ship, etc; backward.

asthma *n* a chronic respiratory condition causing difficulty with breathing.—**asthmatic** *adj*.—**asthmatically** *adv*.

astir *adv* moving or bustling about; out of bed.

astonish *vt* to fill with sudden or great surprise.—**astonishing** *adj*.—**astonishment** *n*.

astound *vt* to astonish greatly.—**astounding** *adj*.

astray *adv* off the right path; into error.

astride *adv* with a leg on either side. * *prep* extending across.

astrology *n* the study of planetary positions and motions to determine their supposed influence on human affairs.—**astrologer** *n*.—**astrological** *adj*.—**astrologically** *adv*.

astronaut *n* one trained to make flights in outer space.

astronomy *n* the scientific investigation of the stars and other planets. —**astronomer** *n*.

astute *adj* crafty, shrewd.—**astutely** *adv*.—**astuteness** *n*.

asylum *n* a place of safety, a refuge; (*formerly*) an institution for the blind, the mentally ill, etc.

at *prep* on; in; near; by; used to indicate location or position.

ate *see* eat.

Athapaskan *n* a large group of First Nations languages in northwest Canada; a member of a First Nations people who speaks one of these languages. * *adj* of or pertaining to these peoples or their languages.—*also* **Athabaskan**.

atheism *n* belief in the nonexistence of God.—**atheist** *n*.

athlete *n* a person trained in games or exercises requiring skill, speed, strength, stamina, etc.

athletic *adj* of athletes or athletics; active, vigorous.—**athletically** *adv*. —**athleticism** *n*.

athletics *n* (*used as sing or pl*) running, jumping, throwing sports, games, etc.

atigi *n* a type of Inuit parka.

Atlantic Canadian *n* a person who lives in or is from New Brunswick, Nova Scotia, Prince Edward Island, or Newfoundland. • *adj* of or pertaining to such a person.

Atlantic salmon *n* a salmon of the coastal North Atlantic Ocean and its tributaries.

atlas *n* a book containing maps, charts and tables.

atmosphere *n* the gaseous mixture that surrounds the earth or the other stars and planets; a unit of pressure equal to the pressure of the atmosphere at sea level; any dominant or surrounding influence.—**atmospheric** *adj*.

atom *n* the smallest particle of a chemical element; a tiny particle, bit.

atomic bomb *n* a bomb whose explosive power derives from the atomic energy released during nuclear fission or fusion.

atomizer *n* a device for atomizing liquids, usu perfumes or cleaning agents.

atone *vi* to give satisfaction or make amends (for).

atrocious *adj* extremely brutal or wicked; (*inf*) very bad, of poor quality.—**atrociously** *adv*.

atrocity *n* a cruel act; something wicked or repellent.

attach *vt* to fix or fasten to something; to appoint to a specific group; to ascribe, attribute. * *vi* to become attached; to adhere.—**attachable** *adj*.

attack *vt* to set upon violently; to assault in speech or writing; to invade, as of a disease. * *vi* to make an assault. * *n* an assault; a fit of illness; severe criticism; a beginning of a performance, undertaking, etc.

attain *vt* to succeed in getting or arriving at; to achieve. * *vi* to come to or arrive at by growth or effort.—**attainable** *adj*.

attainment *n* something attained; an accomplishment.

attempt *vt* to try to accomplish, get, etc. * *n* an endeavour or effort to accomplish; an attack, assault.

attend *vt* to take care of; to go with, accompany; to be present at. * *vi* to apply oneself (to); to deal with, give attention to.

attendance *n* attending; the number of people present; the number of times a person attends.

attendant *n* a person who serves or accompanies another; someone employed to assist or guide. * *adj* accompanying, following as a result; being in attendance.

attention *n* the application of the mind to a particular purpose, aim, etc; awareness, notice; care, consideration; (*usu pl*) an act of civility or courtesy; (*mil*) a soldier's formal erect posture.

attentive *adj* observant, diligent; courteous.—**attentively** *adv*.—**attentiveness** *n*.

attest *vt* to state as true; to certify, as by oath; to give proof of. * *vi* to testify, bear witness (to).—**attestation** *n*.

attic *n* the room or space just under the roof; a garret.

attire *vt* to clothe; to dress up. * *n* dress, clothing.

attitude *n* posture, position of the body; a manner of thought or feeling; the position of an aircraft or spacecraft in relation to certain reference points.

attorney *n* (*pl* **attorneys**) one legally authorized to act for another; a lawyer.

attract *vt* to pull towards oneself; to get the admiration, attention, etc of. * *vi* to be attractive.

attraction *n* the act of attraction; the power of attracting, esp charm; (*physics*) the mutual action by which bodies tend to be drawn together.

attractive *adj* pleasing in appearance, etc; arousing interest; able to draw or pull.—**attractively** *adv*.—**attractiveness** *n*.

attribute *vt* to regard as belonging to; to ascribe, impute (to). * *n* a quality, a characteristic of.—**attributable** *adj*.—**attribution** *n*.

attrition *n* a grinding down by or as by friction; a relentless wearing down and weakening.

aubergine, eggplant (*US*) *n* the dark purple fruit of the egg plant used as a vegetable; its color.

auburn *adj* reddish brown.

auction *n* a public sale of items to the highest bidder. * *vt* to sell by or at an auction.

auctioneer *n* one who conducts an auction.

audacious *adj* daring, adventurous; bold; rash; insolent.—**audaciously** *adv*.—**audacity** *n*.

audible *adj* heard or able to be heard. —**audibly** *adv*.—**audibility** *n*.

audience *n* a gathering of listeners or spectators; the people addressed by a book, play, film, etc; a formal interview or meeting.

audiovisual *adj* using both sound and vision, as in teaching aids.

audit *n* the inspection and verification of business accounts by a qualified accountant. * *vt* to make such an inspection.

audition *n* a trial to test a performer.* *vti* to test or be tested by audition.

auditor *n* a person qualified to audit business accounts.

auditorium *n* the part of a building allotted to the audience; a building or hall for speeches, concerts, etc.

augment *vti* to increase.—**augmentation** *n*.

augur *vti* to prophesy; to be an omen (of).

August *n* the eighth month of the year, having 31 days.

august *adj* imposing; majestic.

aunt *n* a father's or mother's sister; an uncle's wife.

au pair *n* a person, esp a young woman, from abroad who performs domestic chores, child-minding, etc, in return for board and lodging.

aura *n* a particular quality or atmosphere surrounding a person or thing.

aurora trout *n* a brightly spotted brook trout of northern Ontario.

auspice *n* an omen; (*pl*) sponsorship; patronage.

auspicious *adj* showing promise, favorable.—**auspiciously** *adv*.

austere *adj* stern, forbidding in attitude or appearance; abstemious; severely simple, plain.—**austerely** *adv.*—**austerity** *n.*

authentic *adj* genuine, conforming to truth or reality; trustworthy, reliable. —**authentically** *adv.*—**authenticity** *n.*

author *n* a person who brings something into existence; the writer of a book, article, etc. * *vt* to be the author of.—**authoress** *nf.*

authoritarian *adj* favoring strict obedience; dictatorial. * *n* a person advocating or practising authoritarian principles.

authoritative *adj* commanding or possessing authority; accepted as true; official.—**authoritatively** *adv.*

authority *n* the power or right to command; (*pl*) officials with this power; influence resulting from knowledge, prestige, etc; a person, writing, etc cited to support an opinion; an expert.

authorize *vt* to give authority to, to empower; to give official approval to, sanction.—**authorization** *n.*

auto *n* (*pl* **autos**) (*US inf*) a motor car.

autobiography *n* the biography of a person written by himself or herself.—**autobiographer** *n.*—**autobiographical** *adj.*

autocrat *n* an absolute ruler; any domineering person.—**autocratic** *adj.*—**autocratically** *adv.*

autograph *n* a person's signature. * *vt* to write one's signature in or on.

automate *vt* to control by automation; to convert to automatic operation.

automatic *adj* involuntary or reflexive; self-regulating; acting by itself. * *n* an automatic pistol or rifle.—**automatically** *adv.*

automation *n* the use of automatic methods, machinery, etc, in industry.

automaton *n* (*pl* **automatons, automata**) any automatic device, esp a robot; a human being who acts like a robot.

automobile *n* a motor car.

autonomy *n* freedom of self-determination; independence, self-government.—**autonomous** *adj.*

Auto Pact *n* (*Cdn*) (*inf*) an agreement between Canada and the US that removed tariffs from the sale of motor vehicles and parts between the two countries.

autopsy *n* a post-mortem examination to determine the cause of death.

autumn *n* the season between summer and winter; in US, fall.—**autumnal** *adj.*

auxiliary *adj* providing help, subsidiary; supplementary. * *n* a helper; (*gram*) a verb that helps form tenses, moods, voices, etc of other verbs, as *have, be, may, shall*, etc.

avail *vti* to be of use or advantage to. * *n* benefit, use or help.

available *adj* ready for use; obtainable, accessible.—**availability** *n.*

avalanche *n* a mass of snow, ice, and rock tumbling down a mountainside; a sudden overwhelming accumulation or influx.

avalanche lily *n* a plant of the lily family with a large yellow flower found near the snow line on mountains.

avant-garde *n* (*arts*) those ideas and practices regarded as in advance of those generally accepted. * *adj* pertaining to these and their creators.

avarice *n* greed for wealth.—**avaricious** *adj.*—**avariciously** *adv.*

Ave, ave *abbr* = avenue.

avenge *vt* to get revenge for.—**avenger** *n.*

avenue *n* a street, drive, etc, esp when broad; means of access.

average *n* the result of dividing the sum of two or more quantities by the number of quantities; the usual kind, amount, etc. * *vt* to calculate the average of; to achieve an average number of.

averse *adj* unwilling; opposed (to).

aversion *n* antipathy; hatred; something arousing hatred or repugnance.

avert *vt* to turn away or aside from; to prevent, avoid.

aviation *n* the art or science of flying aircraft.

avid *adj* eager, greedy.—**avidly** *adv.*

avocado (pear) *n* a thick-skinned, pear-shaped fruit with yellow buttery flesh.

avoid *vt* to keep clear of, shun; to refrain from.

avoidable *adj* able to be avoided.

await *vti* to wait for; to be in store for.

awake *vb* (*pt* **awoke** *or* **awaked**, *pp* **awoken** *or* **awaked**) *vi* to wake; to become aware. * *vt* to rouse from sleep; to rouse from inaction. * *adj* roused from sleep, not asleep; active; aware.

award *vt* to give, as by a legal decision; to give (a prize, etc); to grant. * *n* a decision, as by a judge; a prize.

aware *adj* realizing, having knowledge; conscious.—**awareness** *n.*

awash *adj* filled or overflowing with water.

away *adv* from a place; in another place or direction; off, aside; far. * *adj* absent; at a distance.

awe *n* a mixed feeling of fear, wonder and dread. * *vt* to fill with awe.

awesome *adj* inspiring awe.

awful *adj* very bad; unpleasant. * *adv* (*inf*) very.—**awfulness** *n.*

awhile *adv* for a short time.

awkward *adj* lacking dexterity, clumsy; graceless; embarrassing; embarrassed; inconvenient; deliberately obstructive or difficult to deal with.—**awkwardly** *adv.*—**awkwardness** *n.*

awning *n* a structure, as of canvas, extended above or in front of a window, door, etc to provide shelter against the sun or rain.

awoke, awoken *see* **awake.**

awry *adv* twisted to one side. * *adj* contrary to expectations, wrong.

axe, ax (*US*) *n* a tool with a long handle and bladed head for chopping wood, etc. * *vt* to trim, split, etc with an axe.

axiom *n* a widely held or accepted truth or principle.—**axiomatic** *adj.*

axis *n* (*pl* **axes**) a real or imaginary straight line about which a body rotates; the centre line of a symmetrical figure; a reference line of a coordinate system; a partnership, alliance.—**axial** *adj*.

axle *n* a rod on or with which a wheel turns; a bar connecting two opposite wheels, as of a car.

B

babble *vi* to make sounds like a baby; to talk incoherently; to murmur, as a brook. * *n* incoherent talk; chatter; a murmuring sound.—**babbler** *n*.

baby *n* a newborn child or infant; a very young animal; (*sl*) a girl or young woman; a personal project. * *vt* to pamper.—*also adj*.—**babyish** *adj*.

baby beef *n* (*Cdn*) meat from young beef cattle, older than those producing veal.

baby bonus *n* (*Cdn*) a government allowance paid to families.

baby-sit *vti* to look after a baby or child while the parents are out.—**baby-sitter** *n*.

bachelor *n* an unmarried man; a person who holds a degree from a college or university.—**bachelorhood** *n*.

bachelor apartment *n* (*Cdn*) an apartment that has one large room serving as a bedroom and living room, together with a kitchenette and bathroom.

back *n* the rear surface of the human body from neck to hip; the corresponding part in animals; a part that supports or fits the back; the part farthest from the front; (*sport*) a player or position behind the front line. * *adj* at the rear; (*streets, etc*) remote or inferior; (*pay, etc*) of or for the past; backward. * *adv* at or toward the rear; to or toward a former condition, time, etc; in return or requital; in reserve or concealment. * *vti* to move or go backward; to support; to bet on; to provide or be back for; (*with* **down**) to withdraw from a position or claim; (*with* **off**) to move back (or away, etc); (*with* **out**) to withdraw from an enterprise; to evade keeping a promise, etc; (*with* **up**) to support; to move backward; to accumulate because of restricted movement; (*comput*) to make a copy (of a data file, etc) for safekeeping.

backache *n* an ache or pain in the back.

back bacon *n* round, lean bacon cut from a pork loin.

back bay *n* (*Cdn*) a shallow bay of a lake.

backbencher *n* a Member of Parliament who does not hold an important office.

backbiting *n* spiteful talk behind a person's back.—**backbite** *vt*.

backbone *n* the spinal column; main support; strength, courage.

back channel *n* a person who acts as a secret intermediary, esp in diplomacy; (*Cdn*) a backwater or side channel of a river.

back concession *n* (*Cdn*) a land concession distant from heavily populated areas.

backdate *vt* to declare valid from some previous date.

backfire *vi* (*automobiles*) to ignite prematurely causing a loud bang from the exhaust; to have the opposite effect from that intended, usu with unfortunate consequences.—*also n*.

back forty *n* (*Cdn*) (*inf*) the area at the rear of a rural property.

backgammon *n* a board game played by two people with pieces moved according to throws of the dice.

background *n* the distant part of a scene or picture; an inconspicuous position; social class, education, experience; circumstances leading up to an event.

backhand *n* (*tennis, etc*) a stroke played with the hand turned outwards.

backhanded *adj* backhand; (*compliment*) indirect, ambiguous.—*also adv*.

backhander *n* a backhanded stroke; (*inf*) a backhanded remark; (*sl*) a bribe.

backing *n* support; supporters; a lining to support or strengthen the back of something; musical accompaniment to a (esp pop) singer.

backlash *n* a violent and adverse reaction; a recoil in machinery.

backlog *n* an accumulation of work, etc still to be done.

backside *n* (*inf*) buttocks.

backsplit *n* (*Cdn*) a house with floors raised half a storey at the rear.

backstroke *n* (*swimming*) a stroke using backward circular sweeps of the arms whilst lying face upward.

backward *adj* turned toward the rear or opposite way; shy; slow or retarded. * *adv* backwards.—**backwardness** *n*.

backwards *adv* towards the back; with the back foremost; in a way opposite the usual; into a less good or favorable state or condition; into the past.

backwater *n* a pool of still water fed by a river; a remote, backward place.

backyard *n* a yard at the back of a house.

bacon *n* salted and smoked meat from the back or sides of a pig.

bacteria *npl* (*sing* **bacterium**) microscopic unicellular organisms.—**bacterial** *adj*.

bad *adj* (**worse, worst**) not good; not as it should be; inadequate or unfit; rotten or spoiled; incorrect or faulty; wicked; immoral; mischievous; harmful; ill; sorry, distressed.—**badness** *n*.

bade *see* **bid**.

badge *n* an emblem, symbol or distinguishing mark.

badger *n* a hibernating, burrowing black and white mammal related to the weasel. * *vt* to pester or annoy persistently.

badlands *npl* barren, dry, heavily eroded areas of land in northwestern North America.

badly *adv* poorly; inadequately; unsuccessfully; severely; (*inf*) very much.

badminton *n* a court game for two or four players played with light rackets and a shuttlecock volleyed over a net.

baffle vt to bewilder or perplex; to frustrate; to make ineffectual. * n a plate or device used to restrict the flow of sound, light or fluid.—**bafflement** n.—**baffling** adj.

bag n a usu flexible container of paper, plastic, etc that can be closed at the top; a satchel, suitcase, etc; a handbag; game taken in hunting; a bag-like shape or part; (derog) an old woman; (inf: in pl) plenty (of). * vti (pt **bagged**) to place in a bag; to kill in hunting; (inf) to get; to make a claim on; to hang loosely.

baggage n suitcases; luggage.

baggy adj (**baggier, baggiest**) hanging loosely in folds.—**baggily** adv.—**bagginess** n.

bagpipe n (often pl) a musical instrument consisting of an air-filled bag fitted with pipes.

bail[1] n money lodged as security that a prisoner, if released, will return to court to stand trial; such a release; the person pledging such money. * vt to free a person by providing bail; (with out) to help out of financial or other difficulty.

bail[2] vti (usu with out) to scoop out (water) from (a boat).

bail[3] n (cricket) either of two wooden crosspieces that rest on the three stumps; a bar separating horses in an open stable; a metal bar that holds the paper against the roller of a typewriter.

bailiff n in UK, the agent of a landlord or landowner; a sheriff's officer who serves writs and summonses; a minor official in some US courts; (Cdn) a person who repossesses property for private clients.

bait n food attached to a hook to entice fish or make them bite; any lure or enticement. * vt to put food on a hook to lure; to set dogs upon (a badger, etc); to persecute, worry or tease, esp by verbal attacks; to lure, to tempt; to entice.

bake vt (pottery) to dry and harden by heating in the sun or by fire; (food) to cook by dry heat in an oven. * vi to do a baker's work; to dry and harden in heat; (inf) to be very hot.

bakeapple n (Cdn) cloudberry.

baker n a person who bakes and sells bread, cakes, etc.

bakery n a room or building for baking; a shop that sells bread, cakes, etc; baked goods.

baking powder n a leavening agent containing sodium bicarbonate and an acid-forming substance.

balance n a device for weighing, consisting of two dishes or pans hanging from a pivoted horizontal beam; equilibrium; mental stability; the power to influence or control; a remainder. * vt to weigh; to compare; to equalize the debit and credit sides of an account. * vi to be equal in power or weight, etc; to have the debits and credits equal.

balance sheet n a statement of assets and liabilities.

balcony n a projecting platform from an upper storey enclosed by a railing; an upper floor of seats in a theatre, etc.—**balconied** adj.

bald adj lacking a natural or usual covering, as of hair, vegetation, nap; (tyre) having little or no tread; (truth) plain or blunt; bare, unadorned.—**baldly** adv.—**baldness** n.

bale[1] n a large bundle of goods, as raw cotton, compressed and bound. * vt (hay etc) to make into bales. * vi (with out) to parachute from an aircraft.

bale[2] n great evil; woe.—**baleful** adj.

balk vt to obstruct or foil. * vi to stop and refuse to move and act.—also **baulk**.

ball[1] n a spherical or nearly spherical body or mass; a round object for use in tennis, football, etc; a throw or pitch of a ball; a missile for a cannon, rifle, etc; (pl) testicles; any rounded part or protuberance of the body. * vti to form into a ball.

ball[2] n a formal social dance; (inf) a good time.—**ballroom** n.

ballad n a narrative song or poem; a slow, sentimental, esp pop, song.

ballast n heavy material carried in a ship or vehicle to stabilize it when it is not carrying cargo; crushed rock or gravel, etc used in railway tracks.

ballerina n a female ballet dancer.

ballet n a theatrical representation of a story, set to music and performed by dancers; the troupe of dancers.

ball hockey n (Cdn) a game with the rules of ice hockey, but played in a gymnasium or arena and using a hard plastic ball instead of a puck.

ballicater n (Cdn) in Newfoundland, ice formed along a shoreline from waves and freezing spray.

ballistics n (used as sing) the scientific study of projectiles and firearms.

balloon n a large airtight envelope that rises up when filled with hot air or light gases, usu with a basket for passengers; a small inflatable rubber pouch used as a toy; a balloon-shaped line enclosing speech or thoughts in a strip cartoon. * vti to inflate; to swell, expand; to travel in a balloon.—**balloonist** n.

ballot n a paper used in voting; the process of voting; the number of votes cast. * vi (pt **balloted**) to vote.

ballot box n a secure container for ballot papers.

ballpoint pen n a pen with a tiny ball, which rotates against an inking cartridge, as its writing tip.

balsam n a fragrant, resinous substance or the tree yielding it.

bamboo n any of various, often tropical, woody grasses, used for furniture.

bamboozle vt (inf) to deceive; to mystify.

ban n a condemnation, an official prohibition. * vt (pt **banned**) to prohibit, esp officially; to forbid.

banal adj trite, commonplace.—**banality** n.

banana n a herbaceous plant bearing its fruit in compact, hanging bunches.

banana belt n (Cdn) (inf) a region with a relatively warm climate, such as southwestern Ontario or British Columbia.

band¹ *n* a strip of material used for binding; stripe; (*radio*) a range of wavelengths.

band² *n* a group of people with a common purpose; a group of musicians; (*Cdn*) a First Nations community recognized as an administrative unit by the federal government.. * *vti* to associate together for a particular purpose.

bandage *n* a strip of cloth for binding wounds and fractures. * *vt* to bind a wound.

B and B *abbr* = bed and breakfast; (*Cdn*) bilingualism and biculturalism.

bandit *n* a robber.

bandwagon *n* a wagon for carrying a band in a parade; a movement, idea, etc that is (thought to be) heading for success.

bandy¹ *vt* to pass to and fro; (*often with* about) (*rumours, etc*) to spread freely; to exchange words, esp angrily.

bandy² *adj* (**bandier, bandiest**) having legs curved outward at the knee.—*also* **bandy-legged**.

bang *n* a hard blow; a sudden loud sound. * *vt* to hit or knock with a loud noise; (*door*) to slam. * *vi* to make a loud noise; to hit noisily or sharply. * *adv* with a bang, abruptly; (*inf*) precisely.

bangbelly *n* (*Cdn*) in Newfoundland, a baked or fried dumpling-like pudding, cake, or pancake.

bangle *n* a bracelet worn on the arm or ankle.

banish *vt* to exile from a place; to drive away; to get rid of.—**banishment** *n*.

banister *n* the railing or supporting posts in a staircase.—*also* **bannister**.

banjo *n* (*pl* **banjos**) a stringed musical instrument with a drum-like body and a long fretted neck.

bank¹ *n* a mound or pile; the sloping side of a river; elevated ground in a lake or the sea; a row or series of objects, as of dials, switches. * *vti* to form into a mound; to cover (a fire) with fuel so that it burns more slowly; (*aircraft*) to curve or tilt sideways.

bank² *n* an institution that offers various financial services, such as the safekeeping, lending and exchanging of money; the money held by the banker or dealer in a card game; any supply or store. * *vti* (*cheques, cash, etc*) to deposit in a bank.

banker *n* a person who runs a bank; the keeper of the bank at a gaming table.

banking *n* the activity or occupation of running a bank. * *adj* of or concerning a bank.

banknote *n* a note issued by a bank, which serves as money.

bank rate *n* (*Cdn*) the minimum interest rate set by the central bank on short-term loans to other banks.

bankrupt *n* a person, etc legally declared unable to pay his debts; one who becomes insolvent. * *adj* judged to be insolvent; financially ruined. * *vt* to make bankrupt.—**bankruptcy** *n*.

banner *n* a flag or ensign; a headline running across a newspaper page; a strip of cloth bearing a slogan or emblem carried between poles in a parade.

bannister *see* **banister**.

bannock *n* (*Scot*) a thick flat cake made of oatmeal or barley and baked on a griddle; (*Cdn*) a bread made of flour, water, and fat, cooked over an outdoor fire.

banns *npl* public declaration of intention, esp in church, to marry.

banquet *n* a feast; an elaborate and sometimes formal dinner in honor of a person or occasion. * *vt* to hold a banquet.

bantam *n* a dwarf breed of domestic fowl; a small aggressive person; (*boxing*) a bantamweight; (*Cdn*) a level of amateur sports competition for children aged 13 to 15.

banter *vt* to tease good-humouredly.

baptise, baptize *vt* to immerse in or sprinkle with water, esp as a religious rite; to christen, name.

baptism *n* the sprinkling of water on the forehead, or complete immersion in water, as a rite of admitting a person to a Christian church; an initiating experience.—**baptismal** *adj*.—**baptismally** *adv*.

bar¹ *n* a straight length of wood or metal; a counter where drinks etc are served; a place with such a counter; an oblong piece, as of soap; anything that obstructs or hinders; a band or strip; barristers or lawyers collectively; the legal profession; (*mus*) a vertical line dividing a staff into measures; (*mus*) a measure. * *vt* (*pt* **barred**) to secure or fasten as with a bar; to exclude or prevent; to oppose. * *prep* except for.

bar² *n* a unit of atmospheric pressure.

barachois *n* (*Cdn*) in Atlantic Canada, a shallow coastal lagoon or pond created by the formation of a sand bar.

barbecue *n* a metal frame for grilling food over an open fire; an open-air party where barbecued food is served. * *vt* to cook on a barbecue.

barber *n* a person who cuts hair and shaves beards.

barbiturate *n* a sedative drug.

barbotte *n* (*Cdn*) a large catfish.

bare *adj* without covering; unclothed, naked; simple, unadorned; mere; without furnishings. * *vt* to uncover; to reveal.—**bareness** *n*.

bareback *adj* on a horse with no saddle.—*also adv*.

barefaced *adj* with the face shaven or uncovered; shameless.

barefoot, barefooted *adj* with the feet bare.—*also adv*.

barely *adv* openly; merely; scarcely.

bargain *n* an agreement laying down the conditions of a transaction; something sold at a price favorable to the buyer. * *vt* to make a bargain, haggle.

barge *n* a flat-bottomed vessel, used to transport freight along rivers and canals; a large boat for excursions or pleasure trips. * *vi* to lurch clumsily; (*with* in) to interrupt (a conversation) rudely; (*with* into) to enter abruptly.

baritone *n* the adult male voice ranging between

bass and tenor; a singer with such a voice.

bark[1] *n* the harsh or abrupt cry of a dog, wolf, etc; a similar sound, such as one made by a person. * *vi* to make a loud cry like a dog; to speak sharply.

bark[2] *n* the outside covering of a tree trunk. * *vt* to remove the bark from; (*inf*) to scrape; to skin (the knees, etc).

barley *n* a grain used in making beer and whisky, and for food.

barmaid *n* a woman serving alcohol in a bar.

barman *n* a man serving alcohol in a bar.

barmy *adj* (**barmier, barmiest**) (*sl*) crazy.

barn *n* a farm building used for storing grain, hay, etc.

barnacle *n* a hard-shelled marine animal that attaches itself to rocks and ship-bottoms.

Barnardo boy *n* (*Cdn*) (*hist*) one of the orphaned or homeless boys who were sent from Britain to Canada to serve as farm or domestic workers.

barn raising *n* a gathering of people who put up the framework of a neighbour's barn, often followed by a party.

barometer *n* an instrument for measuring atmospheric pressure and imminent changes in the weather; anything that marks change.—**barometric** *adj*.

baron *n* a member of a rank of nobility, the lowest in the British peerage; a powerful businessman.—**baroness** *nf*.

barracks *n* (*used as sing*) a building for housing soldiers.

barrage *n* a man-made dam across a river; heavy artillery fire; (*of protests*) continuous and heavy delivery.

barrel *n* a cylindrical container, usu wooden, with bulging sides held together with hoops; the amount held by a barrel; a tubular structure, as in a gun. * *vt* (*pt* **barrelled**) to put into barrels.

barrel-jumping *n* (*Cdn*) a sport in which a skater jumps over a line of barrels lying on their sides.

barrel organ *n* a mechanical piano or organ played by a revolving cylinder with pins that operate the keys or valves to produce sound.

barren *adj* infertile; incapable of producing offspring; unable to bear crops; unprofitable.

barrens *npl* (*Cdn*) an expanse of flat land that may support shrubs and bushes but not trees, especially (*cap*) a large, treeless, sparsely populated area in northern Canada.

barricade *n* a barrier or blockade used in defence to block a street; an obstruction. * *vt* to block with a barricade.

barrier *n* anything that bars passage, prevents access, controls crowds, etc.

barrister *n* a qualified lawyer who has been called to the bar in England; (*Cdn*) a lawyer who pleads cases in a court of law. The term is used mainly by the Canadian legal profession as all Canadian lawyers are both barristers and solicitors.

barrister and solicitor *n* (*Cdn*) a lawyer.

barrow *n* a wheelbarrow or hand-cart used for carrying loads.

barter *vt* to trade commodities or services without exchanging money. * *vi* to haggle or bargain. * *n* trade by the exchanging of commodities.

base[1] *n* the bottom part of anything; the support or foundation; the fundamental principle; the centre of operations (eg military); (*baseball*) one of the four corners of the diamond. * *vt* to use as a basis; to found (on).—**basal** *adj*.

base[2] *adj* low in morality or honor; worthless; menial.—**basely** *adv*.—**baseness** *n*.

baseball *n* the US national game, involving two teams that score runs by hitting a ball and running round four bases arranged in a diamond shape on the playing area.

basement *n* the part of a building that is partly or wholly below ground level.

bash *vt* (*inf*) to hit hard.

bashful *adj* easily embarrassed, shy.—**bashfully** *adv*.

basic *adj* fundamental. * *n* (*often pl*) a basic principle, factor, etc.—**basically** *adv*.

basil *n* a plant with aromatic leaves used for seasoning food.

basin *n* a wide shallow container for liquid; its contents; any large hollow, often with water in it; a tract of land drained by a river.

basis *n* (*pl* **bases**) a base or foundation; a principal constituent; a fundamental principle or theory.

bask *vi* to lie in sunshine or warmth; to enjoy someone's approval.

basket *n* a container made of interwoven cane, wood strips, etc; the hoop through which basketball players throw the ball to score.

basketball *n* a game in which two teams compete to score by throwing the ball through an elevated net basket or hoop; this ball.

bass[1] *n* (*mus*) the range of the lowest male voice; a singer or instrument with this range. * *adj* of, for or in the range of a bass.

bass[2] *n* any of numerous freshwater food and game fishes.

bassoon *n* an orchestral, deep-toned woodwind instrument.—**bassoonist** *n*.

bastard *n* a person born of unmarried parents; (*offensive*) an unpleasant person; (*inf*) a person (*lucky bastard*). * *adj* illegitimate (by birth); false; not genuine.—**bastardy** *n*.

baste[1] *vt* to drip fat over (roasting meat, etc).

baste[2] *vt* to sew with long loose stitches as a temporary seam.

bat[1] *n* a wooden club used in cricket, baseball, etc; one who bats; a paddle used in table tennis. * *vb* (*pt* **batted**) *vt* to hit as with a bat. * *vi* to take one's turn at bat.

bat[2] *n* a mouse-like flying mammal with forelimbs modified to form wings.

bat[3] *vt* (*pt* **batted**) (*one's eyelids*) to wink or flutter.

batch *n* the quantity of bread, etc produced at one time; one set, group, etc; an amount of work for processing by a computer in a single run.

bath *n* water for washing the body; a bathing; a tub for bathing; (*pl*) a building with baths for public use; a municipal swimming pool. * *vti* to give a bath to; to bathe.

bathe *vt* to dampen with any liquid. * *vi* to have a bath; to go swimming; to become immersed.—**bather** *n*.

bathroom *n* a room with a bath or shower and usually a toilet and washbasin.

baton *n* a staff serving as a symbol of office; a thin stick used by the conductor of an orchestra to beat time; a hollow cylinder carried by each member of a relay team in succession; a policeman's truncheon.

battalion *n* an army unit consisting of three or more companies; a large group.

batter *vt* to beat with repeated blows; to wear out with heavy use. * *vi* to strike heavily and repeatedly. * *n* a mixture of flour, egg, and milk or water used in cooking.

battery *n* a set of heavy guns; a small unit of artillery; an electric cell that supplies current; unlawful beating.

battle *n* a combat or fight between two opposing individuals or armies; a contest. * *vti* to fight; to struggle.

battlefield *n* the land on which a battle is fought.

battlement *n* a parapet or wall with indentations, from which to shoot.

battleship *n* a large, heavily armoured warship.

baulk *see* **balk**.

bawdy *adj* (**bawdier, bawdiest**) humorously indecent; obscene, lewd.—**bawdily** *adv*.—**bawdiness** *n*.

bawl *vti* to shout; to weep loudly. * *n* a loud shout; a noisy weeping.—**bawler** *n*.—**bawling** *n*.

bay[1] *n* a type of laurel tree.

bay[2] *n* a wide inlet of a sea or lake; an inward bend of a shore.

bay[3] *n* an alcove or recess in a wall; a compartment used for a special purpose.

bay[4] *vti* to bark (at). * *n* the cry of a hound or a pursuing pack; the position of one forced to turn and fight.

bay[5] *adj* reddish brown. * *n* a horse of this color.

bay boat *n* in Newfoundland, a ship that carries passengers, mail and supplies to coastal communities.

bayman *n* (*Cdn*) a person who lives beside or near a bay.

bayonet *n* a blade for stabbing attached to the muzzle of a rifle. * *vt* (*pt* **bayoneted** *or* **bayonetted**) to kill or stab with a bayonet.

bay window *n* a window projecting from the outside wall of a house.

bazaar *n* a market-place; a street full of small shops; a benefit sale for a church, etc.

BBC *abbr* = British Broadcasting Corporation.

BC *abbr* = Before Christ; British Columbia.

be *vi* (*pres t* **am, are, is,** *pt* **was, were,** *pp* **been**) to exist; to live; to take place.

beach *n* a flat, sandy shore of the sea. * *vi* to bring (a boat) up on the beach from the sea.

beacon *n* a light for warning or guiding.

bead *n* a small ball pierced for stringing; (*pl*) a string of beads; (*pl*) a rosary; a bubble or droplet of liquid; the sight of a rifle.—**beaded** *adj*.

beading *n* moulding or edging in the form of a series of beads; a wooden strip, rounded on one side, used for trimming.—*also* **beadwork**.

beak *n* a bird's bill; any projecting part; the nose.—**beaked** *adj*.

beaker *n* a large drinking cup, or the amount it holds; a cylindrical vessel with a pouring lip used by chemists and pharmacists.

beam *n* a long straight piece of timber or metal; the crossbar of a balance; a ship's breadth at its widest point; a slender shaft of light, etc; a radiant look, smile, etc; a steady radio or radar signal for guiding aircraft or ships. * *vt* (*light, etc*) to send out; to smile with pleasure.

bean *n* a plant bearing kidney-shaped seeds; a seed or pod of such a plant; any bean-like seed.

bear[1] *vb* (*pt* **bore,** *pp* **borne**) *vt* to carry; to endure; to support, to sustain; to conduct (oneself); to produce or bring; (*with* **out**) to confirm. * *vi* to be productive; (*with* **down**) to press or weigh down; to overwhelm; (*with* **on** *or* **upon**) to have reference to; (*with* **up**) to endure with courage.

bear[2] *n* a large mammal with coarse fur, short legs, strong claws and feeding mainly on fruit and insects; a gruff or ill-mannered person; a teddy bear; a speculator who sells stock in anticipation of a fall in price.

bearable *adj* endurable.—**bearably** *adv*.

beard *n* hair covering a man's chin; similar bristles on an animal or plant. * *vt* to defy, oppose openly.—**bearded** *adj*.

bearer *n* a person who bears or presents; a person who carries something (a coffin, etc).

bearing *n* demeanour; conduct; a compass direction; (*followed by* **to** *or* **upon**) relevance; a machine part on which another part slides, revolves, etc.

bearpaw *n* (*Cdn*) an almost circular type of snowshoe.

beast *n* a large, wild, four-footed animal; a brutal, vicious person; (*inf*) something difficult, an annoyance.

beastly *adj* (**beastlier, beastliest**) (*inf*) disagreeable. * *adv* (*inf*) very (*beastly cold*).

beat *vb* (*pt* **beat,** *pp* **beaten**) *vt* to strike, dash or pound repeatedly; to flog; to overcome or counteract; to find too difficult for; (*mus*) to mark (time) with a baton, etc; (*eggs, etc*) to mix by stirring vigorously; (*esp wings*) to move up and down; (*a path, way, etc*) to form by repeated trampling; (*sl*) to baffle. * *vi* to hit, pound, etc repeatedly; to throb; (*naut*) to sail against the wind. * *n* a recurrent stroke, pulsation, as in a heartbeat or clock ticking; rhythm in music or poetry; the area patrolled by a police officer.

beater *n* an implement for beating, such as an attachment for an electric food mixer.

beating *n* the act of striking or thrashing; throbbing, pulsation; a defeat.

beautician *n* one who offers cosmetic treatments.

beautiful *adj* having beauty; very enjoyable.—**beautifully** *adv*.

beauty *n* the combination of qualities in a person or object that cause delight or pleasure; an attractive woman or girl; good looks.

beaver *n* a large semi-aquatic dam-building rodent; its fur; a hat made from beaver fur. * *vi* (*often with* **away**) to work hard (at).

beaver dam *n* a dam of mud and sticks built by beavers across a narrow body of water.

beaver fever *n* (*Cdn*) an intestinal infection leading to diarrhea, often caused by drinking water contaminated by wildlife feces.

became *see* **become**.

because *conj* since; for the reason that.

beckon *vti* to summon by a gesture.

become *vb* (*pt* **became**, *pp* **become**) *vi* to come or grow to be. * *vt* to be suitable for.

becoming *adj* appropriate; seemly; suitable to the wearer.—**becomingly** *adv*.

bed *n* a piece of furniture for sleeping on; a plot of soil where plants are raised; the bottom of a river, lake, etc; any flat surface used as a foundation; a stratum. * *vt* (*pt* **bedded**) to put to bed; to embed; to plant in a bed of earth; to arrange in layers.

bedraggle *vt* to make untidy or dirty by dragging in the wet or dirt.—**bedraggled** *adj*.

bedridden *adj* confined to bed through illness.

bedroom *n* a room for sleeping in. * *adj* suggestive of sexual relations; inhabited by commuters.

bedside *n* the space beside a bed. * *adj* situated or conducted at the bedside; suitable for someone bedridden.

bedsit, bedsitter, bedsitting room *n* a single room with sleeping and cooking facilities.

bee *n* a social, stinging four-winged insect that is often kept in hives to make honey; any of numerous insects that also feed on pollen and nectar and are related to wasps.

beech *n* a tree with smooth silvery-grey bark; its wood.

beef *n* the meat of a full-grown cow, steer, etc; (*inf*) muscular strength; (*inf*) a complaint, grudge; (*pl* **beeves**) cows, ox, steers, etc bred for their meat. * *vt* (*with* **up**) to add weight, strength or power to.

beeline *n* a direct line or course.

been *see* **be**.

beer *n* an alcoholic drink made from malt, sugar, hops and water fermented with yeast.

beer parlour *n* (*Cdn*) a room in a hotel or tavern where beer is sold and consumed.

beetle *n* any of an order of insects having hard wing covers.

beetroot *n* the fleshy root of beet used as a vegetable, in salads, etc.

befall *vti* (*pt* **befell**, *pp* **befallen**) to happen or occur to.

before *prep* ahead of; in front of; in the presence of; preceding in space or time; in preference to; rather than. * *adv* beforehand; previously; until now. * *conj* earlier than the time that; rather than.

befriend *vt* to be a friend to, to favor.

beg *vti* (*pt* **begged**) to ask for money or food; to ask earnestly; to implore.

began *see* **begin**.

beggar *n* a person who begs or who lives by begging; a pauper; (*inf*) a person. * *vt* to reduce to poverty; (*description*) to render inadequate.

begin *vti* (*pr p* **beginning**, *pt* **began**, *pp* **begun**) to start doing, acting, etc; to originate.

beginner *n* one who has just started to learn or do something; a novice.

beginning *n* source or origin; commencement.

begrudge *vt* to grudge; to envy.

begun *see* **begin**.

behalf *n*: **in** *or* **on behalf of** in the interest of; for.

behave *vti* to act in a specified way; to conduct (oneself) properly.

behaviour, behavior (*US*) *n* way of behaving; conduct or action.—**behavioural** *adj*.

beheld *see* **behold**.

behind *prep* at the rear of; concealed by; later than; supporting. * *adv* in the rear; slow; late.

behold *vb* (*pt* **beheld**) *vt* to look at; to observe. * *vi* to see.—**beholder** *n*.

beige *n* a very light brown.

being *n* life; existence; a person or thing that exists; nature, substance.

belated *adj* coming late.—**belatedly** *adv*.

belch *vti* to expel gas from the stomach by the mouth; to eject violently from inside.—*also n*.

belfry *n* the upper part of a tower in which bells are hung.

belie *vt* to show to be a lie; to misrepresent; to fail to live up to (a hope, promise).

belief *n* a principle or idea considered to be true; religious faith.

believe *vt* to accept as true; to think; to be convinced of. * *vi* to have religious faith.—**believer** *n*.

belittle *vt* (*a person*) to make feel small; to disparage.

bell *n* a hollow metal object which rings when struck; anything bell-shaped; the sound made by a bell.

belligerent *adj* at war; of war; warlike; ready to fight or quarrel.—**belligerence** *n*.

bellow *vi* to roar; to make an outcry. * *vt* to utter loudly. * *n* the roar of a bull; any deep roar.

bellows *n* (*used as pl or sing*) a device for creating and directing a stream of air by compression of its collapsible sides.

belly *n* the lower part of the body between the chest and the thighs; the abdomen; the stomach; the underside of an animal's body; the deep interior, as of a ship. * *vti* to swell out; to bulge.

belong *vi* to have a proper place; to be related (to); (*with* **to**) to be a member; to be owned.

belongings *npl* personal effects, possessions.

beloved *adj* dearly loved. * *n* one who is dearly loved.

below prep lower than; unworthy of. * adv in or to a lower place; beneath; later (in a book, etc).

belt n a band of leather, etc worn around the waist; any similar encircling thing; a continuous moving strap passing over pulleys and so driving machinery; a distinctive region or strip; (sl) a hard blow. * vt to surround, attach with a belt; to thrash with a belt; (sl) to deliver a hard blow; (sl) to hurry; (with out) (sl) to sing or play loudly; (with up) (inf) to fasten with a belt. * vi (with up) (sl: often imper) to be quiet.

bench n a long hard seat for two or more persons; a long table for working at; the place where judges sit in a court of law; the status of a judge; judges collectively; (sport) the place where reserves, etc, sit during play.

bend vb (pt, pp bent) vt to form a curve; to make crooked; to turn, esp from a straight line; to adapt to one's purpose, distort. * vi to turn, esp from a straight line; to yield from pressure to form a curve; (with over or down) to curve the body; to give in. * n a curve, turn; a bent part; (pl) decompression sickness.

beneath prep underneath; below; unworthy. * adv in a lower place; underneath.—also adj.

benefactor n a patron.

beneficial adj advantageous.—**beneficially** adv.

benefit n advantage; anything contributing to improvement; (often pl) allowances paid by a government, employer, etc; a public performance etc, whose proceeds are to help some person or cause. * vb (pt benefited) vt to help. * vi to receive advantage.

benevolence n inclination to do good; kindness; generosity.—**benevolent** adj.—**benevolently** adv.

Bennett buggy n (Cdn) (hist) a motor vehicle hitched to horses or oxen, used during the economic depression of the 1930s by drivers who could not afford gasoline.

bent¹ see bend.

bent² n aptitude; inclination of the mind. * adj curved or crooked; (with on) strongly determined; (sl) dishonest.

Beothuk n a member of an extinct Indian people of Newfoundland; the language of this people. * adj of or pertaining to this people or their language.

bequeath vt (property, etc) to leave by will; to pass on to posterity.

bequest n act of bequeathing; something that is bequeathed, a legacy.

bereave vt to deprive (of) a loved one through death.—**bereaved** adj.—**bereavement** n.

beret n a flat, round, soft cap.

berry n any small, juicy, stoneless fruit (eg blackberry, holly berry).

berry ground n in Newfoundland, a high, treeless area where wild berries can be picked.

berserk adj frenzied; destructively violent.— also adv.

berth n a place in a dock for a ship at mooring; a built-in bed. * vt to put into or furnish with a berth; to moor a ship. * vi to occupy a berth.

beseech vt (pt besought) to implore, to entreat; to beg earnestly for.

beset vt (pr p besetting, pt beset) to surround or hem in; to attack from all sides; to harass.

beside prep at, by the side of, next to; in comparison with; in addition to; aside from.

besides prep other than; in addition; over and above. * adv in addition; except for that mentioned; moreover.

besiege vt to hem in with armed forces; to close in on; to overwhelm; harass.

besought see beseech.

best adj (superl of good) most excellent; most suitable, desirable, etc; largest; above all others. * n one's utmost effort; the highest state of excellence. * adv (superl of well) in or to the highest degree. * vt to defeat, outdo.

best man n the principal attendant of the bridegroom at a wedding.

bestow vt to present as a gift.—**bestowal** n.

best seller n a book or other commodity that sells in vast numbers; the author of such a book.—**best-selling** adj.

bet n a wager or stake; the thing or sum staked; a person or thing likely to bring about a desired result. * vti (pt bet or betted) to declare as in a bet; to stake (money, etc) in a bet (with someone).

betray vt to aid an enemy; to expose treacherously; to be a traitor to; to reveal unknowingly.—**betrayal** n.—**betrayer** n.

better¹ adj (compar of good) more excellent; more suitable; improved in health; larger. * adv (compar of well) in a more excellent manner; in a higher degree; more. * n a person superior in position, etc; a more excellent thing, condition, etc. * vt to outdo; to surpass.

better² n someone who bets.

between prep the space, time, etc separating (two things); (bond, etc) connecting from one or the other.

beverage n a drink, esp one other than water.

beverage room n (Cdn) a bar or other establishment where alcoholic drinks are sold and consumed.

beware vti to be wary or careful (of).

bewilder vt to perplex; to confuse hopelessly.— **bewilderment** n.

bewitching adj fascinating, enchanting.

beyond prep further on than; past; later than; outside the reach of (beyond help). * adv further away.

BGen abbr = (Cdn) Brigadier General.

BIA abbr (Cdn) = Business Improvement Association.

bi and bi abbr (Cdn) = bilingualism and biculturalism.

bias n a slanting or diagonal line, cut or sewn across the grain in cloth; partiality; prejudice. * vt (pt biased or biassed) to prejudice.

bib *n* a cloth or plastic cover tied around a baby or child to prevent food spillage on clothes; the upper part of dungarees or an apron.

Bible *n* the sacred book of the Christian Church; the Old and New Testaments.

bicker *vi* to squabble, quarrel.—*also n.*

bicultural *adj* with or involving two cultures, esp, in Canada, French and English.—**biculturalism** *n.*

bicycle *n* a vehicle consisting of a metal frame on two wheels, driven by pedals and having handlebars and a seat. * *vti* to ride or travel on a bicycle.—**bicyclist** *n.*

bid¹ *n* an offer of an amount one will pay or accept; (*cards*) a statement of the number of tricks that a player intends to win. * *vi* (*pr p* **bidding**, *pt* **bid**) to make a bid.—**bidder** *n.*

bid² *vt* (*pr p* **bidding**, *pt* **bade** *or* **bid**, *pp* **bidden** *or* **bid**) to command or ask; (*farewell, etc*) to express.

bide *vi* to wait; to dwell.

bier *n* a portable framework on which a coffin is put.

big *adj* (**bigger, biggest**) large; of great size; important; grown-up; boastful.—**bigness** *n.*

bigamy *n* the act of marrying a second time when one is already legally married.—**bigamous** *adj.*—**bigamously** *adv.*

Bigfoot *n* Sasquatch.

bighouse *n* a communal dwelling used by some Indian peoples of the Pacific Northwest coast of North America; *sl* a prison.

bigot *n* an intolerant person who blindly supports a particular political view or religion.—**bigoted** *adj.*—**bigotry** *n.*

bike *n* (*inf*) a bicycle; a motorcycle.

bikini *n* (*pl* **bikinis**) a scanty two-piece swimsuit for women.

bile *n* a thick bitter fluid secreted by the liver; bad temper.—**bilious** *adj.*—**biliousness** *n.*

bilingual *adj* written in two languages; able to speak two languages.

bill¹ *n* a bird's beak.

bill² *n* a statement for goods supplied or services rendered; a list, as a menu or theatre programme; a poster or handbill; a draft of a proposed law, to be discussed by a legislature; a bill of exchange; a piece of paper money; (*law*) a written declaration of charges and complaints filed. * *vt* to make out a bill of (items); to present a statement of charges to; to advertise by bills; (*performer*) to book.

billet *n* a written order to provide lodging for military personnel; the lodging; a position or job. * *vt* (*pt* **billeted**) to assign to lodging by billet.

billiards *n* a game in which hard balls are driven by a cue on a felt-covered table with raised, cushioned edges.

billion *n* a thousand millions, the numeral 1 followed by 9 zeros; (UK) a million million.—**billionaire** *n.*

bin *n* a box or enclosed space for storing grain, coal, etc; a dustbin.

bind *vb* (*pt* **bound**) *vt* to tie together, as with rope; to hold or restrain; to encircle with a belt, etc; (*often with* **up**) to bandage; to fasten together the pages of (a book) and protect with a cover; to obligate by duty, love, etc; to compel, as by oath or legal restraint. * *vi* to become tight or stiff; to stick together; to be obligatory. * *n* anything that binds; (*inf*) a difficult situation.

binding *n* the covering of a book holding the pages together.

bingo *n* a game of chance in which players cover numbers on their cards according to the number called aloud.

binoculars *npl* a viewing device for use with both eyes, consisting of two small telescope lenses joined together.

biochemistry *n* the chemistry of living organisms.—**biochemical** *adj.*—**biochemist** *n.*

biography *n* an account of a person's life written by another; biographical writings in general.—**biographer** *n.*—**biographical** *adj.*

biology *n* the study of living organisms.—**biological** *adj.*—**biologically** *adv.*—**biologist** *n.*

birch *n* a tree with a smooth white bark and hard wood; a bundle of birch twigs used for thrashing. * *vt* to flog.

bird *n* any class of warm-blooded, egg-laying vertebrates with a feathered body, scaly legs, and forelimbs modified to form wings; (*sl*) a woman.

bird course *n* (*Cdn*) (*sl*) a school or university course requiring little effort.

birth *n* the act of being born; childbirth; the origin of something; ancestry.

birth control *n* the use of contraceptive drugs or devices to limit reproduction.

birthday *n* the day of birth; the anniversary of the day of birth.

birth rate *n* the number of births per thousand of population per year.

biscuit *n* a small baked cake made with shortening and leavened with baking powder or soda; (*Brit*) a small, flat, dry, sweet or plain cake baked from dough. * *adj* pale brown in color.

bishop *n* a high-ranking clergyman governing a diocese or church district; a chessman that can move in a diagonal direction.

bit¹ *n* a small amount or piece; a small part in a play, film, etc.

bit² *n* a metal mouthpiece in a bridle used for controlling a horse; a cutting or boring attachment for use in a brace, drill, etc.

bit³ *n* (*comput*) a unit of information equivalent to either of two digits, 0 or 1.

bitch *n* a female dog or wolf; (*sl*) a spiteful woman; (*inf*) an unpleasant or difficult situation. * *vi* (*inf*) to grumble.

bite *vti* (*pt* **bit**, *pp* **bitten**) to grip or tear with the teeth; to sting or puncture, as an insect; to cause to smart; to take the bait. * *vi* to press or snap the teeth (into, at, etc). * *n* the act of biting with the teeth; a sting or puncture by an insect.

biting *adj* severe; critical, sarcastic.

bitter *adj* having an acrid or sharp taste; sorrowful; harsh; resentful; cynical.—**bitterly** *adj.*—**bitterness** *n.*

bivouac *n* a temporary camp, esp one without tents. * *vi* (*pt* **bivouacked**) to spend the night in a bivouac.

bizarre *adj* odd, unusual.

blab *vti* (*pt* **blabbed**) to reveal (a secret); to gossip. * *n* a gossip.—**blabber** *n.*

black *adj* of the darkest color, like coal or soot; having dark-colored skin and hair, esp Negro; without light; dirty; evil, wicked; sad, dismal; sullen. * *n* black color; (*often with cap*) a Negro, Australian Aborigine; black clothes, esp as mourning; (*chess, draughts*) black pieces. * *vt* to make black; to blacken; (*shoes*) to polish; to boycott; (*with out*) (*lights*) to extinguish, obliterate; (*broadcast*) to prevent transmission. * *vi* (*with out*) to lose consciousness or vision.—**blackness** *n.*

blackberry *n* a woody bush with thorny stems and berry-like fruit; its black or purple edible fruit. * *vt* to gather blackberries.

black blizzard *n* (*Cdn*) a dust storm of soil blown by high winds.

blackboard *n* a black or dark green board written on with chalk.

black duck *n* a wild duck of North America, mainly dark brown with a purple patch on its wings.

blacken *vt* to make black; to defame.

black eye *n* (*inf*) bruising around the eye caused by a blow.

Blackfoot *n* (*pl* same or **Blackfeet**) a member of a First Nations or Native American people in western Canada and Montana. • *adj* of or pertaining to these peoples or their languages.

blackjack *see* **pontoon**[2].

blacklist *n* a list of those censored, refused employment, etc.—*also vt.*

blackmail *vt* to extort money by threatening to disclose discreditable facts. * *n* the crime of blackmailing.—**blackmailer** *n.*

black market *n* the illegal buying and selling of goods.—**black marketeer** *n.*

blackout *n* the darkness when all lights are switched off; temporary loss of consciousness or electricity.

black robe *n* (*Cdn*) (*hist*) a Roman Catholic priest, esp a Jesuit, who was a missionary among Indian peoples.

black sheep *n* a person regarded as disreputable or a disgrace by their family.

blacksmith *n* a metal worker, esp one who shoes horses.

bladder *n* a sac that fills with fluid, esp one that holds urine flowing from the kidneys; any inflatable bag.

blade *n* the cutting edge of a tool or knife; the broad, flat surface of a leaf; a straight, narrow leaf of grass; the flat part of an oar or paddle; the runner of an ice skate.—**bladed** *adj.*

blame *vt* to hold responsible for; to accuse. * *n* responsibility for an error; reproof.—**blamable, blameable** *adj.*

blameless *adj* innocent; free from blame.—**blamelessly** *adv.*—**blamelessness** *n.*

bland *adj* mild; gentle; insipid.—**blandly** *adv.*—**blandness** *n.*

blank *adj* (*paper*) bearing no writing or marks; vacant; (*mind*) empty of thought; (*denial, refusal*) utter, complete; (*cheque*) signed but with no amount written in. * *n* an empty space, esp one to be filled out on a printed form; an empty place or time; a powder-filled cartridge without a bullet.—**blankly** *adv.*—**blankness** *n.*

blanket *n* a large, soft piece of cloth used for warmth, esp as a bed cover; (*of snow, smoke*) a cover or layer. * *adj* applying to a wide variety of cases. * *vt* (*pt* **blanketed**) to cover.

blanket coat *n* a coat made from a blanket, esp a Hudson's Bay blanket.

blare *vti* to sound harshly or loudly. * *n* a loud, harsh sound.

blasphemy *n* speaking irreverently of God, a divine being or sacred things.

blast *n* a sharp gust of air; the sound of a horn; an explosion; an outburst of criticism. * *vt* to wither; to blow up, explode; to criticize sharply. * *vi* to make a loud, harsh sound; to set off explosives; (*with* **off**) to be launched.

blastoff *n* the launch of a space vehicle or rocket.

blatant *adj* noisy; glaringly conspicuous.—**blatantly** *adv.*

blaze *n* an intensive fire; a bright light; splendour; an outburst (of emotion). * *vi* to burn brightly; to shine with a brilliant light; to be excited, as with anger.

blazer *n* a lightweight jacket, often in a bright color representing membership of a sports club, school, etc.

bleach *vti* to make or become white or colorless. * *n* a substance for bleaching.

bleak *adj* cold; exposed; bare; harsh; gloomy; not hopeful.—**bleakly** *adv.*—**bleakness** *n.*

bleat *vi* to cry as a sheep, goat or calf. * *n* a bleating cry or sound.

bleed *vb* (*pt* **bled**) *vi* to lose blood; to ooze sap, color or dye. * *vt* to remove blood or sap from; (*inf*) to extort money or goods from.

bleep *vi* to emit a high-pitched sound or signal (eg a car alarm). * *n* a small portable electronic radio receiver that emits a bleep to convey a message (—*also* **bleeper**).

blemish *n* a flaw or defect, as a spot. * *vt* to mar; to spoil.

blend *vt* (*varieties of tea, etc*) to mix or mingle; to mix so that the components cannot be distinguished. * *vi* to mix, merge; to shade gradually into each other, as colors; to harmonize. * *n* a mixture.

bless *vt* (*pt* **blessed** *or* **blest**) to consecrate; to praise; to call upon God's protection; to grant happiness; to make the sign of the cross over.

blessed *adj* holy, sacred; fortunate; blissful.—**blessedly** *adv.*—**blessedness** *n.*

blessing *n* a prayer or wish for success or happiness; a cause of happiness; good wishes or approval; a grace said before or after eating.

blew see **blow**[2].

blight n any insect, disease, etc that destroys plants; anything that prevents growth or destroys. * vt to destroy; to frustrate.

blind adj sightless; unable to discern or understand; not directed by reason; (exit) hidden, concealed; closed at one end. * n something that deceives; a shade for a window. * vti to make sightless, to deprive of insight; to dazzle (with facts, a bright light, etc); to deceive.—**blindly** adv.—**blindness** n.

blindfold adj having the eyes covered, so as not to see. * n a cloth or bandage used to cover the eyes.—also vt.

blind spot n a point on the retina of the eye that is insensitive to light; a place where vision is obscured; a subject on which one is ignorant.

blink vi to open and close the eyes rapidly; (light) to flash on and off; (with **at**) to ignore. * vt (with **at**) to be amazed or surprised. * n a glance, a glimpse; a momentary flash.

bliss n supreme happiness; spiritual joy.—**blissful** adj.—**blissfully** adv.

blister n a raised patch on the skin, containing water, as caused by burning or rubbing; a raised bubble on any other surface. * vti to cause or form blisters; to lash with words.

blithe adj happy, cheerful, gay.—**blithely** adv.

blitz n any sudden destructive attack. * vt to subject to a blitz.

blizzard n a severe storm of wind and snow.

bloat vti to swell as with water or air; to puff up, as with pride.—**bloated** adj.

blob n a drop of liquid; a round spot (of color, etc).

block n a solid piece of stone or wood, etc; a piece of wood used as a base (for chopping, etc); a group or row of buildings; a number of things as a unit; the main body of a petrol engine; a building divided into offices; an obstruction. * vt to impede or obstruct; to shape; (often with **out**) to sketch roughly. * vi to obstruct an opponent in sports.

blockade n (mil) the obstruction of an enemy seaport by warships; any strategic barrier.—also vt.

blockage n an obstruction.

block heater n an electric heater that is connected to the engine block of a motor vehicle and allows easier starting in cold weather.

block letter n a handwritten capital letter similar to a printed letter.

bloke n (inf) a man.

blond, blonde adj having light-colored hair and skin; light-colored. * n a blonde person.

blood n the red fluid that circulates in the arteries and veins of animals; the sap of a plant; the essence of life; kinship; descent; hatred; bloodshed.

blood donor n a person who donates blood for transfusion.

blood donor clinic n (Cdn) a temporary location

where people can donate blood.

blood group n any of the classes of human blood.

bloodroot n a woodland plant of eastern North America with white flowers and a red root.

bloodshed n killing.

bloodshot adj (eye) suffused with blood, red and inflamed.

bloodstream n the flow of blood through the blood vessels in the human body.

bloodthirsty adj eager for blood, warlike.—**bloodthirstiness** n.

bloody adj (bloodier, bloodiest) stained with or covered in blood; bloodthirsty; cruel, murderous; (sl) as an intensifier (a bloody good hiding). * vt to cover with blood.

Bloody Caesar n (Cdn) a drink made with vodka and a mixture of tomato and clam juice.

bloody-minded adj (inf) deliberately obstructive.—**bloody-mindedness** n.

bloom n a flower or blossom; the period of being in flower; a period of most health, vigour, etc; a youthful, healthy glow; the powdery coating on some fruit and leaves. * vi to blossom; to be in one's prime; to glow with health etc.

blossom n a flower, esp one that produces edible fruit; a state or time of flowering. * vi to flower; to begin to develop.

blot n a spot or stain, esp of ink; a blemish in reputation. * vt (pt blotted) to spot or stain; to obscure; to disgrace; to absorb with blotting paper.

blotch n a spot or discoloration on the skin; any large blot or stain. * vt to cover with blotches.—**blotched** adj.—**blotchy** adj.

blotting paper n absorbent paper used to dry freshly written ink.

blouse n a shirt-like garment worn by women.

blow[1] n a hard hit, as with the fist; a sudden attack; a sudden misfortune; a setback.

blow[2] vb (pt blew, pp blown) vi to cause a current of air; to be moved or carried (by air, the wind, etc); (mus) to make a sound by forcing in air with the mouth; (often with **out**) to burst suddenly; to breathe hard; (with **out**) to become extinguished by a gust of air; (gas or oil well) to erupt out of control. * vt to move along with a current of air; to make a sound by blowing; to inflate with air; (a fuse, etc) to melt; (inf) to spend (money) freely; (sl) to bungle; (with **out**) to extinguish by a gust; (storm) to dissipate (itself) by blowing; (with **over**) to pass over or pass by; (with **up**) to burst by an explosion; to enlarge a photograph; (inf) to lose one's temper.

blowlamp, blowtorch n a gas-powered torch that produces a hot flame for welding, etc.

blowout n (inf) a festive social event; a bursting of (a tyre) by pressure on a weak spot; an uncontrolled eruption of a gas or oil well.

blubber[1] n whale fat; excessive fat on the body.

blubber[2] vi to weep loudly.

bludgeon n a short, heavy stick used for striking. * vti to strike with a bludgeon; to bully or coerce.

blue adj (bluer, bluest) of the color of the

clear sky; depressed; (*film*) indecent, obscene. * *n* the color of the spectrum lying between green and violet; (*with* **the**) the sky, the sea; (*pl: with* **the**) (*inf*) a depressed feeling; a style of vocal and instrumental jazz.

bluebottle *n* a large fly.

blue box *n* (*Cdn*) a blue container for discarded household items that are picked up for recycling.

blue jay *n* a crested jay of eastern and central North America with a large tail and blue, black and white plumage.

blue line *n* in ice hockey, one of two lines on the ice surface between the centre and the goals.

Bluenose, Bluenoser *n* (*Cdn*) (*inf*) a Nova Scotian.

blueprint *n* a blue photographic print of plans; a detailed scheme, template of work to be done.

bluff¹ *adj* rough in manner; abrupt, outspoken.—**bluffness** *n*.

bluff² *vti* to mislead or frighten by a false, bold front.* *n* deliberate deception.—**bluffer** *n*.

bluff³ *n* a broad, steep cliff or bank or cliff; (*Cdn*) in western Canada, a grove or clump of leafy trees. * *adj* ascending steeply with a flat front

blunder *vi* to make a foolish mistake; to move about clumsily. * *n* a foolish mistake.—**blunderer** *n*.

blunt *adj* not having a sharp edge or point; rude, outspoken. * *vti* to make or become dull.—**bluntly** *adv*.—**bluntness** *n*.

blur *n* a stain, smear; an ill-defined impression. * *vti* (*pt* **blurred**) to smear; to make or become indistinct in shape, etc; to dim.

blurt *vt* (*with* **out**) to utter impulsively.

blush *n* a red flush of the face caused by embarrassment; any rosy color. * *vi* (*with* **for, at**) to show embarrassment, modesty, joy, etc, involuntarily by blushing; to become rosy.

bluster *vi* to make a noise like the wind; to bully. * *n* a blast, as of the wind; bullying or boastful talk.—**blusterer** *n*.—**blustery** *adj*.—**blusteringly, blusterously** *adv*.

boar *n* a male pig, a wild hog.

board *n* meals, esp when provided regularly for pay; a long, flat piece of sawed wood, etc; a flat piece of wood, etc for some special purpose; a council; a group of people who supervise a company; the side of a ship. * *vt* to provide with meals and lodging at fixed terms; to come onto the deck of (a ship); to get on (a train, bus, etc). * *vi* to provide room and/or meals, regularly for pay; (*with* **up**) to cover with boards.

boarding house *n* a house where board is provided.

boardroom *n* a room where meetings of a company's board are held.

boast *vi* to brag. * *vt* to speak proudly of; to possess with pride. * *n* boastful talk.—**boaster** *n*.—**boastful** *adj*.—**boastfully** *adv*.

boat *n* a small, open, waterborne craft; a ship. * *vi* to travel in a boat, esp for pleasure.

boater *n* a stiff flat straw hat.

boating *n* rowing, sailing, etc.

bob *vb* (*pt* **bobbed**) *vi* to move abruptly up and down; to curtsey. * *vt* (*hair*) to cut short. * *n* a jerking motion up and down; the weight on a pendulum, plumb line, etc; a woman's or girl's short haircut.

bobbin *n* a reel or spool on which yarn or thread is wound.

bobby clip *n* a grip for holding hair in position.

bobsleigh, bobsled (*US*) *n* a long racing sledge. * *vi* to ride or race on a bobsleigh.

bodice *n* the upper part of a dress.

bodily *adj* physical; relating to the body. * *adv* in the flesh; as a whole; altogether.

body *n* the whole physical substance of a person, animal, or plant; the trunk of a person or animal; a corpse; the principal part of anything; a distinct mass; substance or consistency, as of liquid; a richness of flavor; a person; a distinct group. * *vt* to give shape to.

bodyguard *n* a person or persons assigned to guard someone.

bog *n* wet, spongy ground; quagmire.—**boggy** *adj*.

boggle *vi* to be surprised; to hesitate (at). * *vt* to confuse (the imagination, mind, etc).

bogus *adj* counterfeit, spurious.

boil¹ *vi* to change rapidly from a liquid to a vapour by heating; to bubble when boiling; to cook in boiling liquid; to be aroused with anger; (*with* **down**) to reduce by boiling; to condense; (*with* **over**) to overflow when boiling; to burst out in anger. * *vt* to heat to boiling point; to cook in boiling water.

boil² *n* an inflamed, pus-filled, painful swelling on the skin.

boiler *n* a container in which to boil things; a tank in which water is heated and steam generated; a device for providing central heating and hot water.

boisterous *adj* wild, noisy; stormy; loud and exuberant.—**boisterously** *adv*.

bold *adj* daring or courageous; fearless; impudent; striking to the eye.—**boldly** *adv*.—**boldness** *n*.

bollard *n* a strong post on a wharf around which mooring lines are secured; one of a line of posts closing off a street to traffic; an illuminated marker on a traffic island.

bolster *n* a long narrow pillow; any bolster-like object or support. * *vt* (*often with* **up**) to support or strengthen.

bolt *n* a bar used to lock a door, etc; a type of arrow; a flash of lightning; a threaded metal rod used with a nut to hold parts together; a roll (of cloth, paper, etc); a sudden dash. * *vt* to lock with a bolt; to eat hastily; to say suddenly; to blurt (out); to abandon (a party, group, etc). * *vi* (*horse*) to rush away suddenly * *adv* erectly upright.

bomb *n* a projectile containing explosives, incendiary material, or chemicals used for destruction; (*sl*) a lot of money. * *vt* to attack with bombs.

bombard *vt* to attack with bombs or artillery; to

attack verbally.—**bombardment** n.

bombast n pretentious or boastful language.—**bombastic** adj.

bomber n a person who bombs; an aeroplane that carries bombs.

bombshell n a shocking surprise.

bona fide adj in good faith; genuine or real.

bond n anything that binds, fastens, or unites; (pl) shackles; an obligation imposed by a contract, promise, etc; the status of goods in a warehouse until taxes are paid; an interest-bearing certificate issued by the government or business, redeemable on a specified date; surety against theft, absconding, etc. * vt to join, bind, or otherwise unite; to provide a bond for; to place or hold (goods) in bond. * vi to hold together by means of a bond.

bone n the hard material making up the skeleton; any constituent part of the skeleton. * vti to remove the bones from, as meat; (with up) (inf) to study hard.—**boneless** adj.

bonnet n a hat with a chin ribbon, a cap.

bonus n an amount paid over the sum due as interest, dividend, or wages.

bony adj (**bonier, boniest**) of or resembling bones; having large or prominent bones; full of bones.

booby trap n a trap for playing a practical joke on someone; a camouflaged explosive device triggered by an unsuspecting victim.

book n a bound set of printed or blank pages; a literary composition of fact or fiction; (pl) written records of accounts. * vt to make a reservation in advance; to note a person's name and address for an alleged offence. * vi to make a reservation.

bookcase n a piece of furniture with shelves for books.

book-keeping n the systematic recording of business accounts.—**book-keeper** n.

booklet n a small book, usu with a paper cover; a pamphlet.

bookmaker n a person who takes bets on horse races, etc, and pays out winnings.

boom[1] n a spar on which a sail is stretched; a barrier across a harbour; a long pole carrying a microphone; (Cdn) a raft of limber or logs fastened together for transportation across a body of water..

boom[2] vi to make a deep, hollow sound. * n a resonant sound, as of the sea.

boom[3] vi to flourish or prosper suddenly. * n a period of vigorous growth (eg in business, sales, prices).

boomerang n a curved stick that, when thrown, returns to the thrower; an action that unexpectedly rebounds and harms the agent.—also vi.

booming ground n (Cdn) a section of a body of water where logs are collected into booms.

boon n something useful or helpful.

boondoggle n (Cdn) (inf) work of little value done merely to appear busy or to provide an income for employees, esp a project funded by a government. • vi do such work.

boost vt (sales etc) to increase; to encourage, to improve; to push. * n a push.

boot n a strong covering for the foot and lower part of the leg; (sl: **with the**) dismissal from employment; the rear compartment of a car used for holding luggage, etc. * vt to kick; (comput) to bring a program from a disc into the memory.

booth n a stall for selling goods; a small enclosure for voting; a public telephone enclosure.

booty n spoils obtained as plunder.

booze vi (inf) to drink alcohol excessively. * n alcohol.—**boozy** adj.

border n the edge, rim, or margin; a dividing line between two countries; a narrow strip along an edge. * vi (with **on, upon**) to be adjacent. * vt to form a border.

borderline n a boundary. * adj on a boundary; doubtful, indefinite.

bore[1] to drill so as to form a hole; to weary, by being dull or uninteresting. * n a hole made by drilling; the diameter of a gun barrel; a dull or uninteresting person.

bore[2] see **bear**[1].

boring adj dull, tedious; making holes.

born adj by birth, natural.

borne see **bear**[1].

borough n a self-governing, incorporated town; an administrative area of a city, as in London or New York.

borrow vt to obtain (an item) with the intention of returning it; (an idea) to adopt as one's own; (loan, money) to obtain from a financial institution at definite rates of interest.—**borrower** n.

bosom n the breast of a human being, esp a woman; the part of a dress that covers it; the seat of the emotions. * adj (friend) very dear, intimate.

boss n (inf) the manager or foreman; a powerful local politician. * vt to domineer.

Boston bluefish n (Cdn) pollack.

botany n the scientific study of plants.—**botanical** adj.—**botanist** n.

botch n a poorly done piece of work. * vt to mend or patch clumsily; to put together without sufficient care.

both adj, pron the two together; the one and the other. * conj together equally.—also adv.

bother vt to perplex or annoy; to take time or trouble. * n worry; trouble; someone who causes problems, etc.

bottle n a glass or plastic container for holding liquids; its contents; (sl) courage, nerve. * vt to put in bottles; to confine as if in a bottle.

bottleneck n a narrow stretch of a road where traffic is held up; a congestion in any stage of a process.

bottom n the lowest or deepest part of anything; the base or foundation; the lowest position (eg in a class); the buttocks; (naut) the part of a ship's hull below water; the seabed. * vt to be based or founded on; to bring to the bottom, to get to the bottom of. * vi to become based; to reach the bottom; (with out) to flatten off after dropping sharply.

bottomless *adj* very deep.

bough *n* a branch of a tree.

bought *see* **buy**.

boulder *n* a large stone or mass of rock rounded by the action of erosion.

boulevard *n* a broad, often tree-lined road; (*Cdn*) a strip of grass between a sidewalk and a roadway; a median in the centre of a road that separates opposite directions of traffic.

bounce *vi* to rebound; to jump up suddenly; (*sl: cheque*) to be returned. * *vt* to cause a ball to bounce; (*sl*) to put (a person) out by force; (*sl*) to fire from a job. * *n* a leap or springiness; capacity for bouncing.

bouncer *n* (*sl*) a man hired to remove people from nightclubs, etc.

bound[1] *see* **bind**.

bound[2] *n* (*usu pl*) the limit or boundary. * *vt* to limit, confine or surround; to name the boundaries of.

bound[3] *n* a jump or leap. * *vi* to jump or leap.

bound[4] *adj* intending to go to, on the way to.

boundary *n* the border of an area; the limit.

boundless *adj* unlimited, vast.

bout *n* a spell, a turn, a period spent in some activity; a contest or struggle.

bovine *adj* relating to cattle; dull, sluggish. * *n* an ox, cow, etc.

bow[1] *vi* to lean the head (and chest) forward as a form of greeting or respect; to submit. * *vt* to bend downwards; to weigh down; to usher in or out with a bow. * *n* a lowering of the head (and chest) in greeting.

bow[2] *n* a weapon for shooting arrows; an implement for playing the strings of a violin; a decorative knot of ribbon, etc. * *vti* to bend, curve.

bow[3] *n* the forward part of a ship.

bowel *n* the intestine; (*pl*) the deep and remote part of anything.

bowl[1] *n* a wooden ball having a bias used in bowling; (*pl*) a game played on a smooth lawn with bowls. * *vti* to play the game of bowls; to send a ball to a batsman; (*cricket*) to dismiss by hitting the wicket with a bowled ball; (*with* **over**) to knock over; (*inf*) to astonish.

bowl[2] *n* a deep, rounded dish; the rounded end of a pipe; a sports stadium.

bowler[1] *n* a person who plays bowls or cricket.

bowler[2] *n* a stiff felt hat.

bowling *n* a game in which a heavy wooden ball is bowled along a bowling alley at ten wooden skittles; the game of bowls.

bowling alley *n* a long narrow wooden lane, usu one of several in a building designed for them.

bowling green *n* a smooth lawn for bowls.

bow tie *n* a tie tied in the shape of a bow.

box[1] *n* a container or receptacle for holding anything; (*theatre*) a compartment with seats; (*inf*) a television set. * *vt* to put into a box; to enclose.

box[2] *vt* to hit using the hands or fists. * *vi* to fight with the fists. * *n* a blow on the head or ear with the fist.

boxer *n* a person who engages in boxing; a breed of dog with smooth hair and a stumpy tail.

boxing *n* the skill or sport of fighting with the fists.

box lacrosse *n* (*Cdn*) a form of lacrosse played indoors.—*also* (*inf*) **boxla**.

box office *n* a theatre ticket office; the popularity of a play, film, etc.—*also adj*.

boy *n* a male child; a son; a lad; a youth. * *interj* an exclamation of surprise or joy.—**boyish** *adj*.

boycott *vt* to refuse to deal with or trade with in order to punish or coerce.—*also n*.

boyfriend *n* a male friend with whom a person is romantically or sexually involved.

BQ *abbr* (*Cdn*) = Bloc Québécois.

bra *n* a woman's undergarment for protecting and supporting the breasts, a brassiere.

brace *n* a prop; a support to stiffen a framework; a hand tool for drilling; (*pl* **brace**) a pair, esp of game; (*pl*) straps for holding up trousers; a dental appliance for straightening the teeth. * *vt* to steady.

bracelet *n* an ornamental chain or band for the wrist.

bracing *adj* refreshing, invigorating.

bracken *n* a large, coarse fern.

bracket *n* a projecting metal support for a shelf; a group or category of people classified according to income; (*pl*) a pair of characters ( ), [ ], { }, used in printing or writing as parentheses. * *vt* (*pt* **bracketed**) to support with brackets; to enclose by brackets; (*people*) to group together.

brag *vti* (*pt* **bragged**) to boast. * *n* a boast or boastful talk.

braid *vt* to weave three or more strands (of hair, straw, etc) together; to make in this way. * *n* a narrow band made for decorating clothing; a plait.

brain *n* nervous tissue contained in the skull of vertebrates that controls the nervous system; intellectual ability; (*inf*) a person of great intelligence; (*often pl*) the chief planner of an organization or enterprise. * *vt* to shatter the skull of; (*sl*) to hit on the head.

brainwash *vt* to change a person's ideas or beliefs by physical or mental conditioning, usu over a long period.—**brainwashing** *n*.

brain wave *n* an electrical impulse in the brain; (*inf*) a bright idea.

braise *vt* (*meat, vegetables, etc*) to fry lightly and cook slowly in liquid in a covered pan.

brake *n* a device for slowing or stopping the motion of a wheel by friction. * *vt* to retard or stop by a brake. * *vi* to apply the brake on a vehicle; to become checked by a brake.

bramble *n* a prickly shrub or vine, esp of raspberries and blackberries.

bran *n* the husks of cereal grain separated from the flour by sieving.

branch *n* an offshoot extending from the trunk or bough of a tree or from the parent stem of a shrub; a separately located subsidiary or office of an enterprise or business; a part of something larger. * vi to possess branches; to divide into branches; to come out (from a main part) as a branch; (with out) to extend one's interests, activities, etc.

branch plant n (Cdn) a factory or business owned by a company based in another country.

brand n an identifying mark on cattle, imprinted with hot iron; a burning piece of wood; a mark of disgrace; a trademark; a particular make (of goods). * vi to burn a mark with a hot iron; to denounce.

brandish (a weapon, etc) vt to wave or flourish in a threatening manner.

brand-new adj entirely new and unused.

brandy n an alcoholic liquor made from distilled wine or fermented fruit juice.

brash adj bold; reckless.—**brashly** adv.—**brashness** n.

brass n an alloy of copper and zinc; (inf) showy; impudent; nerve; cheek; (often pl) the brass instruments of an orchestra or band; (sl) officers or officials of high rank.

brass band n a band that uses brass and percussion instruments.

brasserie n a bar and restaurant.

brassiere n a bra.

brat n an ill-mannered, annoying child.

bravado n pretended confidence; swaggering.

brave adj showing courage; not timid or cowardly; fearless. * vt to confront boldly; to defy. * n a North American Indian warrior.—**bravely** adv.—**bravery** n.

brawl vi to quarrel loudly.—also n.

brawn n strong, well-developed muscles; physical strength.

brawny adj (**brawnier, brawniest**) muscular.

bray n the sound of a donkey; any harsh sound. * vi to make similar sounds.

brazen adj made of brass; shameless. * vt to face a situation boldly and shamelessly.

brazier n a metal container for hot coals.

breach n a break or rupture; violation of a contract, promise etc; a break in friendship. * vt to make an opening in.

bread n a dough, made from flour, yeast and milk, that is baked; nourishment; (sl) money.

breadth n measurement from side to side, width; liberality (eg of interests).

breadwinner n the principal wage-earner of a family.

break vb (pt **broke**, pp **broken**) vt to smash or shatter; to tame; (rules) to violate; to discontinue; to cause to give up a habit; to ruin financially; (news) to impart; to decipher or solve; (with down) to crush or destroy; to analyse; (with in) to intervene; to train. * vi to fall apart; (voice) to assume a lower tone at puberty; to cut off relations with; to suffer a collapse, as of spirit; (news) to become public in a sudden and sensational way; (with down) to fail completely; to succumb emotionally; (with even) to suffer neither profit nor loss (after taking certain action); (with in) to force a way in; (with out) to appear, begin; to erupt; to throw off restraint,

escape; (with up) to disperse; to separate; to collapse. * n a breaking; an interruption; a gap; a sudden change, as in weather; an escape; (snooker, billiards) a continuous run of points; (sl) a fortunate opportunity.

breakable adj able to be broken. * n a fragile object.

breakage n the action of breaking; something broken.

breakdown n a mechanical failure; failure of health; nervous collapse; an analysis.

breakfast n the first meal of the morning; the food consumed. * vi to have breakfast.

break-out n an escape, esp from prison.

breakthrough n the action of breaking through an obstruction; an important advance or discovery.

break-up n separation; collapse; dispersal; (Cdn) the thawing of ice in spring in a frozen river or lake.—also **spring break-up**.

breakwater n a barrier that protects a harbour or area of coast against the force of the waves.

breast n the chest; one of the two mammary glands; the seat of the emotions. * vt to oppose, confront.

breaststroke n a swimming stroke in which both arms are brought out sideways from the chest.

breath n the inhalation and exhalation of air in breathing; the air taken into the lungs; life; a slight breeze.

Breathalyser, Breathalyzer n (trademark) a device for measuring the amount of alcohol in a person's breath.—**breathalyze, breathalyse** vt.

breathe vi to inhale and exhale, to respire air; to take a rest or pause; to exist or live; to speak or sing softly; to whisper. * vt to emit or exhale; to whisper or speak softly.

breather n a pause during exercise to recover one's breath.

breathless adj out of breath; panting; gasping; unable to breathe easily because of emotion.—**breathlessness** n.

breathtaking adj very exciting.

breed vb (pt **bred**) vt to engender; to bring forth; (dogs) to raise; to give rise to. * vi to produce young; to be generated. * n offspring; origin or race; species (of animal).—**breeder** n.

breeze n a light gentle wind. * vi (inf) to move quickly or casually.

breezy adj (**breezier, breeziest**) windy; nonchalant; light-hearted.

brevity n briefness; conciseness.

brew vt to make (beer, ale, etc) from malt and hops by boiling and fermenting; to infuse (tea, etc); to plot, scheme. * vi to be in the process of being brewed. * n a brewed drink.

brewer n a person who brews, usu beer.

brewery n a place where beer, etc is brewed.

bribe n money or gifts offered illegally to gain favor or influence; the gift to do this. * vt to offer or give a bribe to.

bribery n the process of giving or taking bribes.

brick n a baked clay block for building; a similar shaped block of other ma-terial. * vt to lay or wall up with brick.

bricklayer *n* a person who lays bricks.

bridal *adj* relating to a bride or a wedding.

bride *n* a woman about to be married or recently married.

bridegroom *n* a man about to be married or recently married.

bridesmaid *n* a young girl or woman attending the bride during a wedding.

bridge[1] *n* a structure built to convey people or traffic over a river, road, railway line, etc; the platform on a ship where the captain gives directions; the hard ridge of bone in the nose; an arch to raise the strings of a guitar, etc; a mounting for false teeth.—*also vt.*

bridge[2] *n* a card game based on whist.

bridge financing *n* (*Cdn*) bridge loan.

bridge loan *n* a temporary loan made to cover a short period before more permanent financing is arranged.

bridle *n* the headgear of a horse; a restraint or check. * *vt* to put a bridle on (a horse); to restrain or check. * *vi* to draw one's head back as an expression of anger, scorn, etc.

bridle path *n* a trail suitable for horse riding.

brief *n* a summary of a client's case for the instruction of a barrister in a trial at law; an outline of an argument, esp that setting out the main contentions; (*pl*) snug, legless underpants. * *vt* to provide with a precise summary of the facts. * *adj* short, concise.—**briefly** *adv*.—**briefness** *n*.

briefcase *n* a flat case for carrying documents, etc.

brigade *n* an army unit, smaller than a division; a group of people organized to perform a particular function.

bright *adj* clear, shining; brilliant in color or sound; favorable or hopeful; intelligent, illustrious. * *adv* brightly.—**brightly** *adv*.—**brightness** *n*.

brighten *vti* to make or become brighter.

brilliant *adj* sparkling, bright; splendid; very intelligent.—**brilliantly** *adv*.—**brilliance** *n*.

brim *n* the rim of a hollow vessel; the outer edge of a hat. * *vti* (*pt* **brimmed**) to fill or be filled to the brim; (*with* **over**) to overflow.

brin *n* (*Cdn*) in Newfoundland, a burlap bag.

brine *n* salt water.

bring *vt* (*pt* **brought**) to fetch, carry or convey "here" or to the place where the speaker will be; (*rain, relief, etc*) to cause to happen, to result in; to lead to an action or belief; to sell for; (*with* **about**) to induce, to effect; (*with* **down**) to cause to fall by or as if by shooting; (*with* **round, around**) to restore to consciousness; (*with* **up**) to educate, rear; to raise (a matter) for discussion; to vomit.—**bringer** *n*.

brink *n* the verge of a steep place; the point of onset; the threshold of danger.

brisk *adj* alert; vigorous; sharp in tone.—**briskly** *adv*.—**briskness** *n*.

bristle *n* a short, coarse hair. * *vi* to stand up, as bristles; to have the bristles standing up; to show anger or in-dignation; to be thickly

covered (with).

British Columbian *n* a person who lives in or is from British Columbia. * *adj* of British Columbia.

brittle *adj* easily cracked or broken; fragile.—**brittleness** *n*.

broach *vt* (*a topic*) to introduce for discussion; to pierce (a container) and draw out liquid.

broad *adj* of large extent from side to side; wide; spacious; strongly marked in dialect or pronunciation. * *n* (*sl*) a woman.—**broadly** *adv*.

broadcast *n* a programme on radio or television. * *vti* (*pt* **broadcast**) to transmit on radio or television; to make known widely.—**broadcaster** *n*.

broaden *vti* to grow or make broad.

brochure *n* a booklet.

broil *vti* to cook by exposure to direct heat; to grill.

broke *pt* of **break**. * *adj* (*inf*) hard up, having no money.

broken *pp* of **break**. * *adj* splintered, fractured; violated; ruined; tamed; disconnected, interrupted; (*speech*) imperfect.—**brokenly** *adv*.

broken-down *adj* extremely infirm; worn out.

broker *n* an agent who negotiates contracts of purchase and sale; a power broker.

bronchitis *n* inflammation of the lining of the windpipe.—**bronchitic** *adj*.

bronze *n* a copper and tin alloy, sometimes other elements; any object cast in bronze; a reddish-brown color. * *adj* made of, or like, bronze.

brooch *n* an ornament held by a pin or a clasp and usu worn near the neck.

brood *vi* to incubate or hatch (eggs); to ponder over or worry about. * *n* a group having a common nature or origin, esp the children in a family; the number produced in one hatch.

brook[1] *n* a freshwater stream.

brook[2] *vt* to tolerate.

broom *n* a bundle of fibres or twigs attached to a long handle for sweeping.

broomball *n* a game similar to ice hockey in which players run rather than skate and use brooms or broom handles to propel a large ball.

broomstick *n* the handle of a broom.

broth *n* a thin soup made by boiling meat, etc in water.

brothel *n* a house where prostitutes work.

brother *n* a male sibling; a friend who is like a brother; a fellow member of a group, profession or association; a lay member of a men's religious order; (*pl* **brethren**) used chiefly in formal address or in referring to the members of a society or sect.

brother-in-law *n* the brother of a husband or wife; the husband of a sister.

brotherly *adj* like a brother; kind; affectionate.—**brotherliness** *n*.

brought *see* **bring**.

brow *n* the forehead; the eyebrows; the top of a cliff; the jutting top of a hill.

browbeat vt (pt **browbeat**, pp **browbeaten**) to intimidate with threats, to bully.

brown adj having the color of chocolate, a mixture of red, black and yellow; tanned. * n a brown color. * vti to make or become brown.—**brownish** adj.

brown cow n (Cdn) a drink made from a mixture of coffee liqueur and milk or cream.

brownie n a square of flat, rich chocolate cake; a friendly helpful elf; (with cap) a junior member of the Girl Guides or Girl Scouts.

browse vti to nibble, graze; to examine casually.

bruise vt to injure and discolor (body tissue) without breaking the skin; to break down (as leaves and berries) by pounding; to inflict psychological pain on. * vi to inflict a bruise; to undergo bruising. * n contusion of the skin; a similar injury to plant tissue; an injury, esp to the feelings.

brunette n a girl or woman with black or dark-brown hair, often with dark eyes and complexion.—also adj.

brunt n the main force or shock of a blow; the hardest part.

brush n a device made of bristles set in a handle, used for grooming the hair, painting or sweeping; a fox's, etc bushy tail; a light stroke or graze, made in passing. * vt to groom or sweep with a brush; to remove with a brush. * vi to touch lightly or graze.

brush-off n a curt dismissal.

Brussels sprout n a plant with a small edible green head.

brutal adj inhuman; savage, violent; severe.—**brutality** n.—**brutally** adv.

brute n any animal except man; a brutal person; (inf) an unpleasant or difficult person or thing. * adj (force) sheer.

bubble n a film of liquid forming a ball around air or gas; a tiny ball of gas or air in a liquid or solid; a transparent dome; a scheme that collapses. * vi to boil; to rise in bubbles; to make a gurgling sound.

buck n the male of animals such as the deer, hare, rabbit, antelope; (inf) a dashing young man; (sl) a dollar. * vti (horse) to rear upward quickly; (inf) to resist; (with up) (inf) to make or become cheerful; to hurry up.

bucket n a container with a handle for carrying liquids, etc.

buckle n a fastening or clasp for a strap or band; a bend or bulge. * vti to fasten with a buckle; to bend under pressure, etc; (with down) (inf) to apply oneself.

bud n an embryo shoot, flower, or flower cluster of a plant; an early stage of development. * vi (pt **budded**) to produce buds; to begin to develop.

Buddha n the state of perfect enlightenment; an image of Siddharta Gautama, founder of Buddhism.—**Buddhist** adj, n.

budding adj being in an early stage of development; promising.

buddy n (inf) a friend; a term of informal address.

budge vti to shift or move.

budgerigar n a small Australian parrot.—also (coll) **budgie**.

budget n an estimate of income and expenditure within specified limits; the total amount of money for a given purpose; a stock or supply. * vb (pt **budgeted**) vi to make a budget. * vt to put on a budget; to plan.

buff n a heavy, soft, brownish-yellow leather; a dull brownish yellow; (inf) a devotee, fan; (inf) a person's bare skin. * adj made of buff; of a buff color. * vt to clean or shine, orig with leather or a leather-covered wheel.

buffer n anything that lessens shock, as of collision; something that serves as a protective barrier; a temporary storage area in a computer.

buffet[1] n a blow with the hand or fist. * vb (pt **buffeted**) vt to hit with the hand or fist; to batter (as of the wind). * vi to make one's way esp under difficult conditions.

buffet[2] n a counter where refreshments are served; a meal at which guests serve themselves food.

buffoon n a clown, a jester.

bug[1] n a continuing source of irritation.

bug[2] n an insect with sucking mouth parts; any insect; (inf) a germ or virus; (sl) a defect, as in a machine; (sl) a hidden microphone. * vt (sl) to plant a hidden microphone; (sl) to annoy, anger, etc.

bugbear n an object that causes great fear and anxiety.

bugle n a valveless brass instrument like a small trumpet, used esp for military calls. * vti to signal by blowing a bugle.—**bugler** n.

build vb (pt **built**) vt to make or construct, to establish, base; (with up) to create or develop gradually. * vi to put up buildings; (with up) to grow or intensify; (health, reputation) to develop. * n the way a thing is built or shaped; the shape of a person.—**builder** n.

building adj the skill or occupation of constructing houses, boats, etc; something built with walls and a roof.

building society n a company that pays interest on deposits and issues loans to enable people to buy their own houses.

built-in adj incorporated as an integral part of a main structure; inherent.

built-up adj made higher, stronger, etc with added parts; having many buildings on it.

bulb n the underground bud of plants such as the onion and daffodil; a glass bulb in an electric light.—**bulbous** adj.

bulge n a swelling; a rounded projected part. * vti to swell or bend outward.—**bulgy** adj.

bulk n magnitude; great mass; volume; the main part. * adj total, aggregate; not packaged.

bulkhead n a wall-like partition in the interior of a ship, aircraft or vehicle.

bulky adj (**bulkier**, **bulkiest**) large and unwieldy.—**bulkiness** adj.

bull[1] n an adult male bovine animal; a male whale or elephant; a speculator who buys in anticipation of reselling at a profit; the bull's-eye; (sl) nonsense. * adj male; rising in price.

bull² n an official edict issued by the pope, with the papal seal on it.

bulldozer n an excavator with caterpillar tracks for moving earth.

bullet n a small metal missile fired from a gun or rifle.

bulletin n an announcement; a short statement of news or of a patient's progress.

bullfighting n the sport of goading and then killing bulls, popular in Spain, etc.—**bullfighter** n.

bullion n gold or silver in mass before coinage.

bullock n a gelded bull; steer.

bull's-eye n (darts, archery) the centre of a target; something resembling this; a direct hit.

bully n a person, esp a child, who hurts or intimidates others weaker than himself. * vt to intimidate, oppress or hurt.

bum n (inf) a tramp; (inf) a devotee, as of skiing, etc; (sl) buttocks or anus.

bumblebee n a large, furry bee.

bumbleberry pie n (Cdn) a pie with a filling of mixed berries.

bump vi to knock with a jolt. * vt to hurt by striking or knocking; (with off) (sl) to murder. * n a jolt; a knock; a swelling or lump.

bumper n a shock-absorbing bar fixed to the front and rear of a motor vehicle. * adj exceptionally large.

bumptious adj offensively conceited or self-assertive.—**bumptiously** adv. —**bumptiousness** n.

bun n a roll made of bread dough and currants, spices and sugar; a bun-shaped coil of hair at the neck.

bunch n a cluster; a number of things growing or fastened together; (inf) a group of people. * vi to group together. * vt to make into a bunch.

bundle n a number of things fastened together; a fastened package; (sl) a large sum of money. * vt to put together in bundles; to push hurriedly into.

bung n a cork or rubber stopper. * vt to close up with a bung; (sl) to throw, toss.

bungalow n a one-storey house.

bungle vi to mistake or blunder; something carried out clumsily. * vt to spoil something through incompetence or clumsiness.—**bungler** n.

bunion n a lump on the side of the first joint of the big toe.

bunk¹ n a narrow, shelf-like bed.

bunk² n (sl) a hurried departure.

bunker n a large storage container, esp for coal; a sand pit forming an obstacle on a golf course; an underground shelter.

bunkhouse n a building where workers are housed temporarily, esp one for loggers or miners.

bunting n a cotton fabric used for making flags; a line of pennants and decorative flags.

buoy n a bright, anchored, marine float used for mooring. * vt to keep afloat; (usu with **up**) to hearten or raise the spirits of; to mark with buoys.

buoyancy n ability to float or rise; cheerfulness; resilience.—**buoyant** adj.

burden n a load; something worrisome that is difficult to bear; responsibility. * vt to weigh down, to oppress.—**burdensome** adj.

bureau n (pl **bureaus**, **bureaux**) a writing desk; a chest of drawers; a branch of a newspaper, magazine or wire service in an important news centre; a government department.

bureaucracy n a system of government where the administration is organized in a hierarchy; the government collectively; excessive paperwork and red tape.

bureaucrat n an official in a bureaucracy.—**bureaucratic** adj.

burglar n a person who trespasses in a building with the intention of thieving.—**burglary** n.

burgle, **burglarize** vt to commit burglary.

burial n the act of burying.

burly adj (**burlier**, **burliest**) heavily built; sturdy.—**burliness** n.

burn vb (pt **burned** or **burnt**) vt to destroy by fire; to injure by heat. * vi to be on fire; to feel hot; to feel passion; (inf) to suffer from sunburn. * n a mark or injury caused by burning.

burnish vt to make shiny by rubbing; to polish. * n lustre; polish.

burnt see **burn**.

burp vi to belch. * vt to pat a baby on the back to cause it to belch.—also n.

burrow n an underground hide or tunnel dug by a rabbit, badger or fox, etc for shelter. * vi to dig a burrow; to live in a burrow; to hide (oneself).

bursar n a treasurer; a student holding a bursary.

bursary n a scholarship awarded to a student.

burst vb (pt **burst**) vt to break open; to cause to explode. * vi to emerge suddenly; to explode; to break into pieces; to give vent to. * n an explosion; a burst; a volley of shots.

bury vt (bone, corpse) to place in the ground; to conceal, to cover; to blot out of the mind.

bus n a motor coach for public transport. * vti (pt **bused** or **bussed**) to transport or travel by bus.

bush n a low shrub with many branches; a cluster of shrubs forming a hedge; woodland; uncultivated land.

bush camp n (Cdn) the headquarters or living quarters of a mining or logging company in the bush.

bushed adj (inf) tired; exhausted; (Austral) lost in the bush; (Cdn) driven insane because of isolation in the wilderness.

bush fever n (Cdn) a mental disorder resulting from isolation in the wilderness.

bush lot n (Cdn) a woodlot.

bush pilot n (Cdn) a pilot who flies small aircraft into isolated or wilderness areas.

bush plane n (Cdn) a small plane used for flying into isolated or wilderness areas, usu equipped with floats or skis.

bush road n (Cdn) a road cut through bush.

bushworker n (Cdn) a logger.

bushy adj (**bushier, bushiest**) covered with bushes; (hair) thick.—**bushiness** n.

business n trade or commerce; occupation or profession; a firm; one's concern or responsibility; a matter.

businesslike adj efficient, methodical, practical.

businessman n a person who works for an industrial or commercial company.—**businesswoman** nf.

busker n a street entertainer.

bust[1] n the chest or breast of a human being, esp a woman; a sculpture of the head and chest.

bust[2] vti (pt **busted** or **bust**) (inf) to burst or break; to make or become bankrupt or demoted; to hit; to arrest. * n (inf) a failure; financial collapse; a punch; a spree; an arrest.

bustle[1] vi to move or act noisily or fussily. * n noisy activity, stir.

bustle[2] n a pad placed beneath a skirt to cause it to puff up at the back.

busy adj (**busier, busiest**) occupied; active; industrious; (painting) having too much detail; (room, telephone) in use. * vt to occupy; to make or keep busy (esp oneself).—**busily** adv.

busybody n a meddlesome person.

but prep save; except. * conj in contrast; on the contrary, other than. * adv only; merely; just.

butane n a flammable gas used as fuel.

butcher n a person who slaughters meat; a retailer of meat; a ruthless murderer. * vt to slaughter; to murder ruthlessly; to make a mess of or spoil.

butler n a male servant, esp the head servant of a household with several servants.

butt[1] vti to strike or toss with the head or horns, as a bull, etc.—also n.

butt[2] n a large cask for wine or beer.

butt[3] n a mound of earth behind targets; a person who is the target of ridicule or jokes; (pl) the target range.

butt[4] n the thick or blunt end; the stump; (sl) a cigarette; (sl) the buttocks. * vti to join end to end.

butter n a solidified fat made from cream by churning. * vt to spread butter on; (with **up**) (inf) to flatter.

butterfly n an insect with a slender body and four usu brightly colored wings; a swimming stroke.

butter tart n (Cdn) a small tart with a filling of butter, eggs, brown sugar, and raisins.

buttock n one half of the human rump.

button n a disc or knob of metal, plastic, etc used as a fastening; a badge. * vti to fasten with a button or buttons.

buttonhole n the slit through which a button is passed; a flower in the buttonhole. * vt to keep in conversation.

buttress n a projecting structure for strengthening a wall. * vt to support.

buxom adj plump and healthy; (woman) big-bosomed.

buy vt (pt **bought**) to purchase (for money); to bribe, corrupt; to acquire in exchange; (inf) to believe.—**buyer** n.

buzz vi to hum like an insect; to gossip; to hover (about). * vt to spread gossip secretly; (inf) to telephone. * n the humming of bees or flies; a rumour; (sl) a telephone call; (sl) a thrill.

buzzard n a large bird of prey.

buzzer n a device producing a buzzing sound.

by prep beside; next to; via; through the means of; not later than. * adv near to; past; in reserve.

bye-bye interj (inf) goodbye.

by-election, bye-election n an election other than a general election.

bylaw, bye-law n a rule or law made by a local authority or a company.

bypass n a main road avoiding a town; a channel redirecting the flow of something; (med) an operation to redirect the flow of blood into the heart. * vt to go around; to avoid.

by-product n a secondary product in the process of making something else.

bystander n a chance onlooker.

byte n (comput) a set of eight bits treated as a unit.

byword n a familiar saying; a perfect example; an object of derision.

C

C abbr = Celsius, centigrade; (chem symbol) = carbon.

© (symbol) = copyright.

CAA abbr = Canadian Automobile Association; (Brit) Civil Aviation Authority.

cab n a taxicab; the place where the driver sits in a truck, crane, etc.

cabaret n entertainment given in a restaurant or nightclub.

cabbage n a garden plant with thick leaves formed usu into a compact head, used as a vegetable.

cabin n a small house, a hut; a room in a ship; the area where passengers sit in an aircraft.

cabin cruiser n a powerful motorboat with living accommodation.

cabinet n a case with drawers or shelves; a case containing a TV, radio, etc; a body of official advisers to a government.

cabinetmaker n a person who makes fine furniture.

cable n a strong thick rope often of wire strands; an anchor chain; an insulated cord that carries electric current; a cablegram; a bundle of insulated wires for carrying cablegrams, TV signals, etc. * vti to send a message by cablegram.

cable car n a car drawn by a moving cable, as up a steep incline.

cablegram n a message transmitted by telephone line, submarine cable, etc, a cable.

caboose n (Cdn) a portable wooden cabin, esp one on runners that are pulled over snow.

cache *n* a secret hiding place; a store of food left for use by travellers, etc. * *vt* to place in a cache.

cackle *n* the clucking sound of a hen; shrill or silly talk or laughter. * *vti* to utter with a cackle.

cactus *n* (*pl* **cacti, cactuses**) a plant with a fleshy stem that stores water and is often studded with prickles.

caddie, caddy¹ *n* a person who carries a golfer's clubs. * *vi* to perform as a caddie.

caddy² *n* a small box or tin for storing tea.

cadet *n* a student at an armed forces academy.

cadge *vti* to beg or get by begging.—**cadger** *n*.

Caesarean section *n* the removal of a child from the womb by a surgical operation.

CAF *abbr* = Canadian Armed Forces.

café *n* a small restaurant, a coffee bar, a night-club, etc.

cafeteria *n* a self-service restaurant.

caffeine *n* a stimulant present in coffee and tea.

cage *n* a box or enclosure with bars for confin-ing an animal, bird, prisoner, etc; a car for raising or lowering miners. * *vt* to shut in a cage, to confine.

cagey, cagy *adj* (**cagier, cagiest**) (*inf*) wary, secre-tive, not frank.—**cagily** *adv*.—**caginess** *n*.

caisse populaire *n* (*Cdn*) a credit union in Quebec and other French-speaking parts of Canada.

cajole *vti* to persuade or soothe by flattery or deceit.

cake *n* a mixture of flour, eggs, sugar, etc baked in small, flat shapes or a loaf; a small block of compacted or congealed matter. * *vti* to encrust; to form into a cake or hard mass.

calamity *n* a disastrous event, a great misfor-tune; adversity.—**calamitous** *adj*.

calcium *n* the chemical element prevalent in bones and teeth.

calculate *vti* to reckon or compute by math-ematics; to suppose or believe; to plan.—**calculable** *adj*.

calculating *adj* shrewd, scheming.

calculation *n* the act of calculating; the result obtained; an estimate.

calculator *n* a device, esp a small, electronic, hand-held one, for doing mathematical cal-culations rapidly; one who calculates.

calculus *n* (*pl* **calculi, calculuses**) an abnormal, stony mass in the body; (*math*) a mode of calculation using symbols.

calèche *n* (*Cdn*) a two-wheeled, one-horse car-riage, often used to carry tourists.

calendar *n* a system of determining the length and divisions of a year; a chart or table of months, days and seasons; a list of sched-uled events.

calf¹ *n* (*pl* **calves**) the young of a cow, seal, el-ephant, whale, etc; the leather skin of a calf.

calf² *n* (*pl* **calves**) the fleshy back part of the leg below the knee.

Calgarian *n* a person who lives in or is from Calgary, Alberta.

Calgary redeye *n* (*Cdn*) a drink made from beer and tomato juice—*also* **redeye.**

calibre, caliber (*US*) *n* the internal diameter of a gun barrel or tube; capacity, standing, moral weight.

call *vi* to shout or cry out; to pay a short visit; to telephone; (*with* **in**) to pay a brief or infor-mal visit; (*with* **on**) to pay a visit; to ask, to appeal to. * *vt* to summon; to name; to de-scribe as specified; to awaken; to give or-ders for; (*with* **down**) to invoke; (*with* **in**) to summon for advice or help; to bring out of circulation; to demand payment of (a loan); (*with* **off**) to cancel; (*an animal*) to call away in order to stop; (*with* **out**) to cry aloud; (*workers*) to order to strike; (*troops*) to summon to action; (*with* **up**) to telephone; to summon to military action, as in time of war; to recall. * *n* a summons; the note of a bird; a vocation, esp religious; occasion; a need; a demand; a short visit; the use of a telephone; a cry, shout.

call box *n* a telephone box.

caller *n* one who calls, esp by telephone.

call girl *n* a prostitute who is called by telephone to assignations.

callibogus *n* (*Cdn*) a drink made from spruce beer, rum and molasses.

callous *adj* (*skin*) hardened; (*person*) unfeel-ing.—**calloused** *adj*.—**callously** *adv*.—**callous-ness** *n*.

calm *adj* windless; still, unruffled; quiet, peaceful. * *n* the state of being calm; still-ness; tranquillity. * *vti* to become or make calm.—**calmly** *adv*.—**calmness** *n*.

calorie, calory *n* a unit of heat; a measure of food energy.

calve *vti* to give birth to a calf.

camas *n* North American plant of the lily plants with edible bulbs, once consumed by some First Nations or Native American peoples.

camber *n* a slight upward curve in the surface of a road, etc. * *vti* to curve upwards slightly.—**cambered** *adj*.

came *see* **come.**

camel *n* a large four-footed, long-necked animal with a humped back; a fawny-beige color.—*also adj.*

cameo *n* an onyx or other gem carved in relief; an outstanding bit role, esp in a motion pic-ture; a short piece of fine writing.

camera *n* the apparatus used for taking still photographs or television or motion pic-tures; a judge's private chamber.

cameraman *n* a film or television camera opera-tor.

camouflage *n* a method (esp using coloring) of disguise or concealment used to deceive an enemy; a means of putting people off the scent. * *vt* to conceal by camouflage.

camp¹ *n* the ground on which tents or tempo-rary accommodation is erected; the occu-pants of this, such as holiday-makers or troops; the supporters of a particular cause. * *vi* to lodge in a camp; to pitch tents.—**camper** *n*.

camp² *adj* (*sl*) theatrical, exaggerated; effemi-nate.

campaign n a series of military operations; a series of operations with a particular objective, such as election of a candidate or promotion of a product; organized course of action. * vi to take part in or conduct a campaign.—**campaigner** n.

camp site n a camping ground, often with facilities for holiday-makers.

campus n (pl **campuses**) the grounds, and sometimes buildings, of a college or university.

can[1] vt (**could**) to be able to; to have to have the right to; to be allowed to.

can[2] n a container, usu metal, with a separate cover in which petrol, film, etc is stored; a tin in which meat, fruit, drinks, etc, are hermetically sealed; the contents of a can; (sl) jail; (sl) a toilet. * vti (pt **canned**) to preserve (foods) in a can.—**canner** n.

Canada jay n grey jay.

Canada lily n a lily of eastern North America with large yellow, orange or spotted flowers.

Canada mayflower n a woodland lily of eastern North America with white flowers and red berries.

Canadarm n (TM) a mechanical arm on a spacecraft, used to release, retrieve and repair satellites and other equipment.

Canadian football n a form of football resembling American football but with a wider field, three downs and 12 players.

Canadianism n a form of expression peculiar to Canada; a custom peculiar to Canada.

Canadianize vt to render Canadian; to assimilate to the political and social institutions of Canada.—**Canadianization** n.

Canadian whisky n whisky distilled from rye and other grains.

Canadien, Canadienne n a French Canadian.

canal n an artificial waterway cut across land; a duct in the body.

Can-Am adj pertaining to an event, esp in sports, with Canadian and US participants. * n an event with Canadian and US participants.

canary n a small finch, usu greenish to yellow in color, kept as a songbird.

cancel vt (pt **cancelled**) to cross out; to obliterate; to annul, suppress; (reservation, etc) to call off; to countermand.

cancellation n the act of cancelling; annulment; something cancelled; the mark made by cancelling.

Cancer n (astron) the Crab, a northern constellation; (astrol) the 4th sign of the zodiac, operative 21 June-21 July.

cancer n the abnormal and uncontrollable growth of the cells of living organisms, esp a malignant tumour; an undesirable or dangerous expansion of something.—**cancerous** adj.

candela n a unit of luminous intensity.

candid adj frank, outspoken; unprejudiced; (photograph) informal.—**candidly** adv.—**candidness** n.

candidate n a person who has nomination for an office or qualification for membership or award; a student taking an examination.—**candidacy** n.—**candidature** n.

candle n a stick of wax with a wick that burns to give light.

candle ice n ice that has deteriorated into candle-like icicles.

candlelight n the light produced by a candle or candles.

candour, candor (US) n sincerity, openness, frankness.

CANDU n (Cdn) a nuclear reactor that uses fuel bundles and a system that moderates heat with heavy water.

candy n a solid confection of sugar or syrup with flavoring, fruit, nuts, etc, a sweet.

candyfloss n a confection of spun sugar.

cane n the slender, jointed stem of certain plants, as bamboo; a plant with such a stem, as sugar cane; a stick of this used for corporeal punishment (usu with **the**) or supporting plants; strips of this used in furniture making etc; a walking stick. * vt to thrash with a cane; to weave cane into.

canine adj of or like a dog; of the family of animals that includes wolves, dogs and foxes; pertaining to a canine tooth. * n a dog or other member of the same family of animals; in humans, a pointed tooth next to the incisors.

canister n a small box or container for storing tea, flour, etc; a tube containing tear gas which explodes and releases its contents on impact.

CanLit n (Cdn) (inf) Canadian literature.

cannabis n a narcotic drug obtained from the hemp plant; the hemp plant.—also **hashish**, **marijuana**.

canned adj stored in sealed tins; recorded for reproduction; (sl) drunk.

cannibal n a person who eats human flesh; an animal that feeds on its own species. * adj relating to or indulging in this practice.—**cannibalism** n.—**cannibalistic** adj.

cannon n (pl **cannon**) a large mounted piece of artillery; (pl **cannons**) an automatic gun on an aircraft; (billiards) a shot in which the cue ball hits two others successively. * vi to collide with great force (with **into**); to rebound; (billiards) to make a cannon.

cannonball n the heavy, round shot fired from a cannon. * vi to move along at great speed.

cannot = can not.

canoe n a narrow, light boat propelled by paddles.—also vi.—**canoeist** n.

canola n (Cdn) the seeds of a variety of the rape plant, used to make cooking oil.

canon n a decree of the Church; a general rule or standard, criterion; a list of the books of the Bible accepted as genuine; the works of any author recognized as genuine; a member of a cathedral chapter; a part of the mass containing words of consecration; (mus) a round.—**canonical** adj.—**canonically** adv.

canonize vt (RC Church) to officially declare (a person) a saint. —**canonization** n.

canopy n a tent-like covering over a bed,

throne, etc; any roof-like projection.

cant[1] *n* insincere or hypocritical speech; language specific to a group (eg thieves, lawyers); cliched talk, jargon. * *vi* to talk in or use cant.

cant[2] *n* an inclination or tilt; a slanting surface, bevel. * *vti* to slant, to tilt.

can't = can not.

cantaloupe, cantaloup *n* a variety of melon with orange flesh.

cantankerous *adj* ill-natured, bad-tempered, quarrelsome.—**cantankerously** *adv*.—**cantankerousness** *n*.

canteen *n* a restaurant attached to factory, school, etc, catering for large numbers of people; a flask for carrying water; (a box containing) a set of cutlery.

canter *n* a horse's 3-beat gait resembling a slow, smooth gallop.—*also vti.*

cantilever *n* a projecting beam that supports a balcony, etc.

Canuck *n* (*Cdn*) (*inf*) a Canadian.

canvas *n* a strong coarse cloth of hemp or flax, used for tents, sails, etc, and for painting on; sails; a tent or tents; an oil painting on canvas.

canvass *vti* to go through (places) or among (people) asking for votes, opinions, orders, etc.—also *n*.—**canvasser** *n*.

canyon *n* a long, narrow valley between high cliffs.

cap *n* any close-fitting head gear, visored or brimless; a cap-like thing, as an artificial covering for a tooth; a top, a cover; a percussion cap in a toy gun; a type of contraceptive device; (*sport*) the head gear presented to a player chosen for a team. * *vt* (*pt* **capped**) to put a cap on; to cover (the end of); to seal (an oil or gas well); to equal, outdo or top; (*sport*) to choose a player for a team.

capability *n* the quality of being capable; an undeveloped faculty.

capable *adj* able or skilled to do; competent, efficient; susceptible (of); adapted to.—**capably** *adv*.

capacity *n* the power of holding or grasping; cubic content; mental ability or power; character; legal competence; the greatest possible output or content.

cape[1] *n* a headland or promontory running into the sea.

cape[2] *n* a sleeveless garment fastened at the neck and hanging over the shoulders and back.

Cape Bretoner *n* (*Cdn*) a person who lives in or is from the island of Cape Breton, Nova Scotia.

capital[1] *adj* of or pertaining to the head; (*offence*) punishable by death; serious; chief, principal; leading, first-class; of, or being the seat of government; of capital or wealth; relating to a large letter, upper case; (*inf*) excellent. * *n* a city that is the seat of government of a country; a large letter; accumulated wealth used to produce more; stock or money for carrying on a business; a city, town, etc pre-eminent in some special activity.

capital[2] *n* the head or top part of a column or pillar.

capital gain *n* the profit made on the sale of an asset.

capitalism *n* the system of individual ownership of wealth; the dominance of such a system.

capitalist *n* a person who has money invested in business for profit; a supporter of capitalism. * *adj* of or favoring capitalism.—**capitalistic** *adj*.

capital punishment *n* the death penalty for a crime.

capitulate *vi* to surrender on terms; to give in.—**capitulation** *n*.

capote *n* (*Cdn*) (*hist*) a long coat with a hood, tied with a colourful sash.

capricious *adj* unstable, inconstant; unreliable.—**capriciously** *adv*.—**capriciousness** *n*.

Capricorn *n* (*astron*) the Goat, a southern constellation; (*astrol*) the tenth sign of the zodiac, operative 21 December-19 January.

capsize *vti* to upset or overturn.

capstan *n* an upright drum around which cables are wound to haul them in; the spindle in a tape recorder that winds the tape past the head.

capsule *n* a small gelatin case enclosing a drug to be swallowed; a metal or plastic container; (*bot*) a seed case; the orbiting and recoverable part of a spacecraft.

captain *n* a chief, leader; the master of a ship; the pilot of an aircraft; a rank of army, naval and marine officer; the leader of a team, as in sports. * *vt* to be captain of.—**captaincy** *n*.

caption *n* a heading in a newspaper, to a chapter, etc ; a legend or title describing an illustration; a subtitle. * *vti* to provide with a caption.

captivate *vt* to fascinate; to charm.—**captivating** *adj*.—**captivation** *n*.

captivity *n* the state of being a captive; a period of imprisonment.

capture *vt* to take prisoner; (*fortress, etc*) to seize; to catch; to gain or obtain by skill, attraction, etc, to win. * *n* the act of taking a prisoner or seizing by force; anything or anyone so taken.

car *n* a self-propelled motor vehicle, an automobile, a motorcar; the passenger compartment of a train, airship, lift, cable railway, etc; a railway carriage.

carafe *n* an open-topped bottle for serving water or wine at table.

caramel *n* burnt sugar, used in cooking to color or flavor; a type of sweet tasting of this.

carat *n* a measure of weight for precious stones; a measure of the purity of gold.—*also* **karat**.

caravan *n* a large enclosed vehicle equipped to be lived in (—*also* **trailer**); a band of merchants travelling together for safety. * *vi* (*pt* **caravanned**) to travel with a caravan, esp on holiday.

caraway *n* a biennial plant with pungent aromatic seeds used as a flavoring.

carbohydrate *n* a compound of carbon, hydrogen and oxygen, esp in sugars and starches as components of food. * *npl* starchy foods.

carbon *n* a nonmetallic element, a constituent of all organic matter; a duplicate made with carbon paper.

carbon copy *n* a copy of typed or written material made by using carbon paper; an exact copy.

carburettor *n* a device in an internal-combustion engine for making an explosive mixture of air and fuel vapour.

carcass, carcase *n* the dead body of an animal; a framework, skeleton or shell.

card[1] *n* a small piece of cardboard; a piece of this with a figure or picture for playing games or fortune-telling; a piece of this with a person or firm's name, address or with an invitation, greeting, message, etc; (*inf*) an entertaining or eccentric person; a small piece of plastic identifying a person for banking purposes (eg a cheque card, credit card); (*pl*) card games; (*pl*) card playing; (*pl*) employees' documents held by the employer.

card[2] *n* a toothed instrument for combing cotton, wool or flax fibres off. * *vt* (*wool, etc*) to comb.

cardboard *n* thick stiff paper, often with a clay coating. * *adj* made of this; lacking substance.

cardiac *adj* relating to the heart.

cardigan *n* a knitted sweater fastening up the front.

cardinal *adj* of chief importance, fundamental; of a bright red. * *n* an official appointed by the Pope to his councils; bright red.

cardinal numbers *npl* numbers that express how many (1, 2, 3, etc).

care *n* anxiety; concern; serious attention, heed; consideration; charge, protection; the cause or object of concern or anxiety. * *vt* to feel concern; to agree or be willing (to do something). * *vi* (*usu with* **for, about**) to feel affection or regard; to have a desire (for); to provide for, have in one's charge.

career *n* progress through life; a profession, occupation, esp with prospects for promotion. * *vi* to rush rapidly or wildly.

carefree *adj* without cares, lively, light-hearted.

careful *adj* painstaking; cautious; thoughtful.—**carefully** *adv*.—**carefulness** *n*.

careless *adj* not careful; unconcerned, insensitive; carefree.—**carelessly** *adv*.—**carelessness** *n*.

caress *vt* to touch or stroke lovingly.—*also n*.

caretaker *n* a person put in charge of a place or thing; (*government*) one temporarily in control.

cargo *n* (*pl* **cargoes**) the load carried by a ship, truck, aircraft, etc; freight.

Caribbean *adj* of or pertaining to the Caribbean Sea and its islands. * *n* the Caribbean Sea.

caribou *n* a large deer with branched antlers; (*Cdn*) a drink made from red wine and diluted alcohol.

caricature *n* a likeness made ludicrous by exaggeration or distortion of characteristic features. * *vt* to make a caricature of, to parody.—**caricaturist** *n*.

carnal *adj* of the flesh; sexual; sensual; worldly.—**carnally** *adv*.

carnation *n* a garden flower.

carnival *n* public festivities and revelry; a travelling fair with sideshows, etc.

carnivore *n* a flesh-eating mammal.

carnivorous *adj* (*animals*) feeding on flesh; (*plants*) able to trap and digest insects.

carol *n* a joyful song of joy; a Christmas hymn. * *vi* (*pt* **carolled**) to sing carols.

carp[1] *vi* to find fault, esp continually.

carp[2] *n* a brown and yellow freshwater fish.

car park, parking lot (*US*) *n* land or premises intended for parking cars.

carpenter *n* a person skilled in woodwork, esp house building.—**carpentry** *n*.

carpet *n* a woven fabric for covering floors; any thick covering. * *vt* (*pt* **carpeted**) to cover with carpet.

carriage *n* the act of carrying, transport; the cost of this; deportment, bearing; behaviour; a railway coach or compartment; the moving part of a typewriter.

carriageway *n* a road bearing single-line traffic.

carrier *n* one who carries or transports goods, esp for hire; a device for carrying; a person or animal transmitting an infectious disease without being affected by it; an aircraft carrier; a carrier bag.

carrier bag *n* a plastic bag with handles for holding shopping, etc.

carrot *n* a plant grown for its edible, fleshy orange root; an inducement, often illusory.

carry *vt* to convey or transport; to support or bear; to involve, have as a result; to hold (oneself); to extend or prolong; to gain by force; to win over; to stock; (*with* **off**) to cause to die; to remove by force; (*situation*) to handle successfully; (*with* **out**) to perform (a task, etc); to accomplish. * *vi* (*with* **on**) to persevere; to conduct a business, etc; (*inf*) to have an affair; (*inf*) to cause a fuss.

carrycot *n* a baby's portable cot.

carrying place *n* (*Cdn*) a portage.

carry-on *n* (*inf*) a fuss.

carry-out *n* food or drink sold by a restaurant but consumed elsewhere.—*also adj*.

cart *n* a two-wheeled vehicle drawn by horses; any small vehicle for carrying loads. * *vt* to carry in a cart; (*inf*) to transport with effort.

cartilage *n* tough, elastic tissue attached to the bones of animals; gristle.

carton *n* a cardboard box or container.

cartoon *n* a humorous picture dealing with current events; a comic-strip; an animated cartoon; a full-size preparatory sketch for reproduction on a fresco, etc.—**cartoonist** *n*.

cartridge *n* the case that contains the explosive charge and bullet in a gun or rifle; a sealed case of film for a camera; the device containing the stylus on the end of the pick-up arm of a record player.

carve vt to shape by cutting; to adorn with designs; to cut up (meat, etc).

carving n a figure or design carved from wood, stone, etc; the act of carving.

CAS abbr (Cdn) = Children's Aid Society.

cascade n a small, steep waterfall; a shower, as of sparks, etc. * vti to fall in a cascade.

case¹ n a covering; a suitcase; its contents.

case² n an instance; a state of affairs; a condition, circumstance; a lawsuit; an argument for one side; (sl) character; (med) a patient under treatment; (gram) the relationship between nouns, pronouns and adjectives in a sentence.

cash n money in coins or notes; immediate payment, as opposed to that by cheque or on credit; (Cdn) a cash register. * vt to give or get cash for.

cashew n the small, edible nut of a tropical tree.

cashier n a person in charge of the paying and receiving of money in a bank, shop, etc.

cashmere n a fine wool from Kashmir goats; a material made from this.

cash register n an automatic or electronic till that shows and records the amount placed in it.

casing n a protective or outer covering; the material for this.

casino n (pl **casinos**) a room or building where gambling takes place.

cask n a barrel of any size, esp one for liquids; its contents.

casket n a small box or chest for jewels, etc; a coffin.

casse-croûte n (Cdn) in Quebec, a small place of business that sells snacks.

casserole n a covered dish for cooking and serving; the food so cooked and served. * vt to cook in a casserole.

cassette n a usu plastic box that holds an audio or video tape.

cast vb (pt **cast**) vt to throw or fling; to throw off or shed; to record; to direct; to shape in a mould; to calculate; to select actors, etc for a play. * vi to throw, hurl; (with off) to untie a ship from its moorings; (knitting) to loop off stitches from a needle without letting them unravel; (with on) to loop the first row of stitches onto a needle. * n act of casting; a throw; a plaster form for immobilizing an injured limb; a mould for casting; type or quantity; a tinge of color; the actors assigned roles in a play; the set of actors; a slight squint in the eye.

castanets npl hollow shell-shaped pieces of wood held between the fingers and rattled together, esp to accompany Spanish dancing.

castaway n a shipwrecked person.

caste n any of the Hindu hereditary social classes; an exclusive social group.

casting vote n the deciding vote used by the chairman of a meeting when the the votes on each side are equal.

cast iron n iron melted and run into moulds.—also adj.

castle n a fortified building; a chess piece (—also **rook**).

castor n a small container with a perforated top for sprinkling salt, sugar, etc; a small swivelled wheel on a table leg, etc.

castor oil n a vegetable oil used as a purgative and lubricant.

castor sugar n finely ground sugar.

castrate vt to remove the testicles of, to geld.—**castration** n.

casual adj accidental, chance; unplanned; occasional; careless, unmethodical; informal.—**casually** adv.

casualty n a person injured or killed in a war or in an accident; something damaged or destroyed.

cat n a small, domesticated feline mammal kept as a pet; a wild animal related to this; lions, tigers, etc (inf) a spiteful person.

catalogue, catalog (US) n a list of books, names, etc in systematic order. * vti to list, to make a catalogue of.—**cataloguer** n.

catalyst n a substance which accelerates or retards a chemical reaction without itself undergoing any permanent chemical change; a person or thing which produces change.

catapult n a contraption with elastic for shooting small stones (—also **slingshot**); a device for launching aircraft from the deck of an aircraft carrier. * vt to shoot forward as from a catapult.

cataract n a waterfall, esp a large sheet one; a disease of the eye causing dimming of the lens and loss of vision.

catarrh n inflammation of a mucous membrane, esp in the nose.—**catarrhal** adj.

catastrophe n a great disaster.—**catastrophic** adj.—**catastrophically** adv.

catch vb (pt **caught**) vt to take hold of, to grasp; to capture; to ensnare or trap; to be on time for; to detect; to apprehend; to become infected with (a disease); (inf) to see, hear, etc; to grasp (a meaning); (with out) (inf) to detect (a person) in a mistake; (cricket) to catch a ball hit by a batsman before it touches the ground, making him "out." * vi to become entangled; to begin to burn; (with on) (inf) to become popular; to understand; (with up) to reach or come level with (eg a person ahead); to make up for lost time, deal with a backlog. * n the act of catching; a device for fastening; someone worth catching; a hidden difficulty.

catching adj infectious; attractive.

catchment area n a geographic area served by an institution.

catch phrase n a well-known phrase or slogan, esp one associated with a particular group or person.

catchup see **ketchup**.

catchy adj (**catchier, catchiest**) easily remembered, as a tune.

catechism n a simple summary of the principles of religion in question and answer form, used for instruction.

categorical adj unconditional, absolute; positive, explicit.—**categorically** adv.

categorize vt to place in a category.

category *n* a class or division of things.

cater *vi* (*with* **for, to**) to provide with what is needed or desired, esp food and service, as for parties.—**caterer** *n*.

caterpillar *n* the worm-like larvae of a butterfly or moth; the ribbed band in place of wheels on a heavy vehicle; a vehicle (eg tank, tractor) equipped with such tracks.

cathedral *n* the chief church of a diocese. * *adj* of a cathedral.

Catholic *n* a member of the Roman Catholic Church. * *adj* relating to the Roman Catholic Church; embracing the whole body of Christians.—**Catholicism** *n*.

catholic *adj* universal, all-embracing; broadminded, liberal; general, not exclusive.

catsup *see* ketchup.

cattle *npl* domesticated bovine mammals such as bulls and cows.

caught *see* catch.

cauliflower *n* a kind of cabbage with an edible white flower-head used as a vegetable.

cause *n* that which produces an effect; reason, motive, justification; a principle for which people strive; a lawsuit. * *vt* to bring about, to effect; to make (to do something).

causeway *n* a raised road across wet ground or water.

caustic *adj* burning tissue, etc by chemical action; corrosive; sarcastic, cutting. * *n* a caustic substance.—**caustically** *adv*.—**causticity** *n*.

caution *n* care for safety, prudence; warning. * *vt* to warn (against); to admonish.

cautious *adj* careful, circumspect.—**cautiously** *adv*.—**cautiousness** *n*.

cavalry *n* combat troops originally mounted on horseback.

cave *n* a hollow place inside the earth open to the surface. * *vti* (*with* **in**) to collapse or make collapse.

caveman *n* a prehistoric cave dweller; (*inf*) a person who acts in a primitive or crude manner.

cavern *n* a cave, esp a large cave.—**cavernous** *adj*.

caviar, caviare *n* pickled roe of the sturgeon.

cavity *n* a hole; a hollow place, esp in a tooth.

cavort *vi* to frolic, prance.

CAW *abbr* = Canadian Auto Workers.

CB *abbr* = Cape Breton (Island).

CBA *abbr* = Canadian Bar Association; Canadian Booksellers' Association.

CBC *abbr* = Canadian Broadcasting Corporation.

CBI *abbr* = Confederation of British Industry; Central Bureau of Investigation

cc *abbr* = carbon copy; cubic centimetre(s).

CC *abbr* = Companion of the Order of Canada.

CDIC *abbr* = Canada Deposit Insurance Corporation.

Cdn *abbr* = Canadian.

cease *vti* to stop, to come to an end; to discontinue.

ceasefire *n* a period of truce in a war, uprising, etc.

ceaseless *adj* without ceasing; incessant.—**ceaselessly** *adv*.

cedar *n* a large coniferous evergreen tree; its wood.—**cedarwood** *n*.

cede *vt* to yield to another, give up, esp by treaty; to assign or transfer the title of.

CEGEP *abbr* = in Quebec, a college that prepares students for university and offers training in professions and trades.

ceiling *n* the inner roof of a room; the lining of this; an upper limit; the highest altitude a particular aircraft can fly.

celebrate *vt* to make famous; to praise, extol; to perform with proper rites; to mark with ceremony; to keep (festival).—**celebrant** *n*.

celebrated *adj* famous.

celebration *n* the act of celebrating; an observance or ceremony to celebrate anything.

celebrity *n* fame; a famous or well-known person.

celery *n* a vegetable with long juicy edible stalks.

celestial *adj* in or of the sky; heavenly; divine.

celibacy *n* the unmarried state; complete sexual abstinence.

cell *n* a small room for one in a prison or monastery; a small cavity as in a honeycomb; a device that converts chemical energy into electricity; a microscopic unit of living matter; a small group of people bound by common aims within an organization or political party.—**cellular** *adj*.

cellar *n* a basement; a stock of wines.

cello *n* (*pl* **cellos**) a large bass instrument of the violin family.—**cellist** *n*.

cellophane *n* a thin transparent paper made from cellulose.

cellulose *n* a starch-like carbohydrate forming the cell walls of plants, used in making paper, textiles, film, etc.

Celtic *adj* of or relating to the Celts; the language of the Celts, including Scots or Irish Gaelic, Manx, Welsh, Cornish and Breton.

cement *n* a powdered substance of lime and clay, mixed with water, etc to make mortar or concrete, which hardens upon drying; any hard-drying substance. * *vt* to bind or glue together with or as if with cement; to cover with cement.

cemetery *n* a place for the burial of the dead.

cenotaph *n* a monument to a person who is buried elsewhere.

censor *n* an official with the power to examine literature, mail, etc and remove or prohibit anything considered obscene, objectionable, etc. * *vt* to act as a censor.—**censorship** *n*.

censure *n* an expression of disapproval or blame. * *vt* to condemn as wrong; to reprimand.—**censurable** *adj*.

cent *n* a hundredth of a dollar; (*inf*) a negligible amount of money.

centenary *n* a hundredth anniversary or its celebration. * *adj* of a hundred years.

centi- *prefix* one hundredth.

centigrade *adj* of a scale of a hundred degrees, of the Celsius scale. * *n* a hundredth part of a grade.

centimetre, centimeter (*US*) *n* one hundredth of a metre.

centipede *n* a a crawling creature with a long body divided into numerous segments each with a pair of legs.

central *adj* in, at, from or forming the centre; main, principal; important.—**centrally** *adv*.—**centrality** *n*.

central heating *n* a system of heating by pipes carrying hot water from a central boiler.

centralize *vt* to draw to the centre; to place under the control of a central authority, esp government.—**centralization** *n*.

centre, center (*US*) *n* the approximate middle point or part of anything, a pivot; interior; point of concentration, source; political moderation; (*sport*) a player at the centre of the field, etc, a centre-forward. * *adj* of or at the centre. * *vt* (*pr p* **centring**, *pt* **centred**) to place in the centre; to concentrate; to be fixed; (*football, hockey*) to kick or hit the ball into the centre of the pitch.

centre forward *n* (*football, hockey*) the central player in the forward attack.

centre ice *n* the central area of a rink on which ice hockey is played or the exact spot in the centre where the puck is dropped during faceoffs at the start of each period and after a goal is scored.

centrifugal *adj* moving away from the centre of rotation.

century *n* a period of a hundred years; a set of a hundred; (*cricket*) 100 runs made by a batsman in a single innings; a company of a Roman legion.

century home *n* (*Cdn*) a house that is about a hundred years old.

ceramic *adj* of earthenware, porcelain, or brick. * *n* something made of ceramic; (*pl*) the art of pottery.

cereal *n* a grass grown for its edible grain, e.g. wheat, rice; the grain of such grasses; a breakfast food made from such grains. * *adj* of corn or edible grain.

ceremony *n* a sacred rite; formal observance or procedure; behaviour that follows rigid etiquette.

certain *adj* sure, positive; unerring, reliable; sure to happen, inevitable; definite, fixed; some; one.

certainly *adv* without doubt; yes.

certainty *n* something undoubted, inevitable; the condition of being certain.

certificate *n* a document formally attesting a fact; a testimonial of qualifications or character.—**certificated** *adj*.

certify *vt* to declare in writing or attest formally; to endorse with authority.

cervix *n* the neck of the womb.

cessation *n* a stoppage; a pause.

cesspit, cesspool *n* a covered cistern for collecting liquid waste or sewage.

cf. *abbr* = compare (Latin *confer*).

CF *abbr* = Canadian Forces.

CFB *abbr* = Canadian Forces Base.

CFL *abbr* = Canadian Football League.

CGA *abbr* = Certified General Accountant.

chafe *vti* to restore warmth by rubbing; to make or become sore by rubbing; to irritate; to feel irritation, to fret.

chaffinch *n* a European songbird.

chain *n* a series of connected links or rings; a continuous series; a series of related events; a bond; a group of shops, hotels, etc owned by the same company; a unit of length equal to 66 feet. * *vt* to fasten with a chain or chains.

chain reaction *n* a process in which a chemical, atomic or other reaction stimulates further reactions, eg combustion or nuclear fission; a series of events, each of which stimulates the next.

chain-smoke *vti* to smoke (cigarettes) one after the other.—**chain-smoker** *n*.

chain store *n* one of a series of shops owned by one company.

chair *n* a separate seat for one; a seat of authority; a chairman; a professorship; the electric chair. * *vt* to preside as chairman of.

chair lift *n* a series of seats suspended from a cable for carrying sightseers or skiers uphill.

chairman *n* a person who presides at a meeting; the president of a board or committee.—**chairwoman** *nf*.—*also* **chairperson**.

chalet *n* a Swiss hut; any similar building used in a holiday camp, as a ski lodge, etc.

chalice *n* a large cup with a base; a communion cup.

chalk *n* calcium carbonate, a soft white limestone; such a stone or a substitute used for drawing or writing. * *vt* to write, mark or draw with chalk; (*with* **up**) (*inf*) to score, get, achieve; to charge or credit.—**chalky** *adj*.

challenge *vt* to summon to a fight or contest; to call in question; to object to; to hail and interrogate. * *n* the act of challenging; a summons to a contest; a calling in question; a problem that stimulates effort.—**challenger** *n*.—**challenging** *adj*.

chamber *n* a room, esp a bedroom; a deliberative body or a division of a legislature; a room where such a body meets; a compartment; a cavity in the body of an organism; (*pl*) a judge's office.

chambermaid *n* a woman employed to clean bedrooms in a hotel, etc.

chamber music *n* music for performance by a small group, as a string quartet.

chamois *n* a small antelope found in Europe and Asia; a piece of chamois leather.

chamois leather *n* soft, pliable leather formerly made from chamois skin, and now obtained from sheep, goats and deer.

champagne *n* a sparkling white wine; a pale straw color.

champion *n* a person who fights for another; one who upholds a cause; a competitor successful against all others. * *adj* first-class; (*inf*) excellent. * *vt* to defend; to uphold the cause of.

championship *n* the act of championing; the process of determining a champion; a contest held to find a champion.

chance n a course of events; fortune; an accident, an unexpected event; opportunity; possibility; probability; risk. * vti to risk; to happen. * adj accidental, not planned.

chancel n the part of a church around the altar, for the clergy and the choir.

chancellor n a high government official, as, in certain countries, a prime minister; in some universities, the president or other executive officer.—**chancellorship** n.

chandelier n an ornamental hanging frame with branches for holding lights.

change vt to make different, to alter; to transform; to exchange; to put fresh clothes on. * vi to become different, to undergo alteration; to put on fresh clothes; to continue one's journey by leaving one station, etc, or mode of transport and going to and using another. * n alteration, modification; substitution; variety; a fresh set, esp clothes; money in small units; the balance of money returned when given in a larger denomination as payment.

changeable adj able to be changed; altering rapidly between different conditions; inconstant.

channel n the bed or the deeper part of a river, harbour, etc; a body of water joining two larger ones; a navigable passage; a means of passing or conveying; a band of radio frequencies reserved for a particular purpose, eg television station; a path for an electrical signal; a groove or line along which liquids, etc may flow. * vt (pt **channelled**) to form a channel in; to groove; to direct.

chant vti to sing; to recite in a singing manner; to sing or shout (a slogan) rhythmically. * n sacred music to which prose is sung; singsong intonation; a monotonous song; a rhythmic slogan, esp as sung or shouted by sports fans, etc.

chaos n utter confusion, muddle.

chaotic adj completely without order or arrangement.—**chaotically** adv.

chap[1] n (pt **chapped**) (skin) to make or become split or rough in cold weather. * n a chapped place in the skin.

chap[2] n (inf) a man.

chapel n a building for Christian worship, not as large as a church; an association of printers in a printing office.

chaperon, chaperone n a woman who accompanies a girl at social occasions for propriety. * vt to attend as a chaperon.

chaplain n a clergyman serving in a religious capacity with the armed forces, or in a prison, hospital, etc.—**chaplaincy** n.

chapter n a main division of a book; the body or meeting of canons of a cathedral or members of a monastic order; a sequence of events; an organized branch of a society or association.

char[1] n a charwoman. * vt (pt **charred**) to work as a charwoman.

char[2] vb (pt **charred**) vt to burn to charcoal or carbon. * vti to scorch.

char[3] n (sl) tea.

character n the combination of qualities that distinguishes an individual person, group or thing; moral strength; reputation; disposition; a person of marked individuality; a person in a play or novel; a guise, role; a letter or mark in writing, printing, etc.

characteristic adj marking or constituting the particular nature (of a person or thing). * n a characteristic feature.

characterize vt to describe in terms of particular qualities; to designate; to be characteristic of, mark.—**characterization** n.

charade n a game of guessing a word from the acted representation of its syllables and the whole; a travesty; an absurd pretence.

charcoal n the black carbon matter obtained by partially burning wood and used as fuel, as a filter or for drawing.

charge vt to ask as the price; to record as a debt; to load, to fill, saturate; to lay a task or trust on; to burden; to accuse; to attack at a run; to build up an electric charge (in). * n a price charged for a good or service; a buildup of electricity; the amount which a receptacle can hold at one time; the explosive required to fire a weapon; trust, custody; a thing or person entrusted; a task, duty; accusation; an attack.

chariot n a two-wheeled vehicle driven by two or more horses in ancient warfare, races, etc.—**charioteer** n.

charitable adj of or for charity; generous to the needy; benevolent; lenient in judging others, kindly.—**charitably** adv.

charity n leniency or tolerance towards others; generosity in giving to the needy; a benevolent fund or institution.

charm n an alluring quality, fascination; a magic verse or formula; something thought to possess occult power; an object bringing luck; a trinket on a bracelet. * vt to delight, captivate; to influence as by magic.—**charmer** n.

chart n a map, esp for use in navigation; an information sheet with tables, graphs, etc; a table, graph, etc; (pl with **the**) a list of the most popular music recordings. * vt to make a chart of; to plan (a course of action).

charter n a document granting rights, privileges, ownership of land, etc; the hire of transportation; (with cap) (Cdn) the Charter of Rights and Freedoms, part of the constitution of Canada. * vt to grant by charter; to hire.

chartered accountant n an accountant who has qualified by passing the examinations of the Institute of Chartered Accountants.

charwoman n a woman employed to clean a house.

chase vt to pursue; to run after; to drive (away); to hunt; (inf: usu with **up**) to pursue in a determined manner. * n pursuit; a hunt; a quarry hunted; a steeplechase.

chasm n a deep cleft, an abyss, a gaping hole; a wide difference in opinions, etc.

chassis n (pl **chassis**) the frame of a car, aeroplane or other vehicle.

chastity *n* sexual abstinence; virginity.

chat *vi* (*pt* **chatted**) to talk in an easy or familiar way. * *n* informal conversation.

chateau *n* (*Cdn*) (*hist*) in French Canada, the residence of a seigneur or governor. * *adj* (*Cdn*) (*cap*) in the architectural style of such a residence.

chatter *vi* to talk aimlessly and rapidly; (*animal, etc*) to utter rapid cries; (*teeth*) to rattle together. * *n* idle rapid talk; the sound of chattering.— **chatterer** *n*.

chatterbox *n* an incessant talker.

chatty *adj* (**chattier, chattiest**) talkative, full of gossip.—**chattily** *adv*.—**chattiness** *n*.

chauffeur *n* a person who drives a car for someone else. * *vt* to drive as a chauffeur.— **chauffeuse** *nf*.

chautauqua *n* (*hist*) a public cultural entertainment in North America that included music, lectures and theatre.

cheap *adj* low-priced, inexpensive; good value; of little worth, inferior.—**cheaply** *adv*.— **cheapness** *n*.

cheapen *vti* to make or become cheap.

cheat *vti* to defraud; to swindle; to deceive; to play unfairly. * *n* a fraud, deception; a person who cheats.—**cheater** *n*.

check *vti* to bring or come to a stand; to restrain or impede; to admonish, reprove; to test the accuracy of, verify; (*with* **out**) to settle the bill and leave a hotel; to investigate. * *n* repulse; stoppage; a pattern of squares; a control to test accuracy; a tick against listed items; a bill in a restaurant; a cheque; (*chess*) a threatening of the king.

checker[1] *n* a cashier in a supermarket (esp in US); a cloakroom attendant.

checker[2] *see* **draughtsman**[2].

checkers *n* the game of draughts.

checkmate *n* (*chess*) the winning position when the king is threatened and unable to move; defeat. * *vt* (*chess*) to place in checkmate; to defeat, foil.

checkroom *n* a left luggage office.

cheechako *n* a newcomer or neophyte, esp in the Canadian North and Alaska.

cheek *n* the side of the face below the eye; (*sl*) buttock; impudence; (*Cdn*) the edible cheek of a fish, esp cod.

cheeky *adj* (**cheekier, cheekiest**) disrespectful, impudent.—**cheekily** *adv*.—**cheekiness** *n*.

cheer *n* a shout of applause or welcome; a frame of mind, spirits; happiness. * *vt* to gladden; to encourage; to applaud.

cheerful *n* in good spirits; happy.—**cheerfully** *adv*.—**cheerfulness** *n*.

cheese *n* the curds of milk pressed into a firm or hard mass.

chef *n* a professional cook.

chemical *n* a substance used in, or arising from, a chemical process. * *adj* of, used in, or produced by chemistry.—**chemically** *adv*.

chemist *n* a pharmacy; a manufacturer of medicinal drugs; a person skilled in chemistry.

chemistry *n* the science of the properties of substances and their combinations and reactions; chemical structure.

cheque, check (*US*) *n* a money order to a bank.

chequebook, checkbook (*US*) *n* a book containing blank cheques to be drawn on a bank.

chequered, checkered (*US*) *adj* marked with a variegated pattern; having a career of fluctuating fortunes.

cherish *vt* to tend lovingly, foster; to keep in mind.

cherry *n* a small red, pitted fruit; the tree bearing it; a bright red color.

chess *n* a game played by two people with 32 pieces on a chessboard.

chessboard *n* a board chequered with 64 squares used for playing chess or draughts.

chessman *n* any of the 16 pieces used by each player in chess.

chest *n* a large strong box; the part of the body enclosed by the ribs, the thorax.

chestnut *n* a tree or shrub of the beech family; the edible nut of a chestnut; the wood of the chestnut; a horse with chestnut coloring. * *adj* of the color of a chestnut, a deep reddish brown.

chest of drawers *n* a piece of furniture containing several drawers.

chew *vt* to grind between the teeth, to masticate; to ponder, think over. * *n* the act of chewing; something to chew, as a sweet.

chewing gum *n* a flavored gum made from chicle, for chewing.

chic *n* elegance, style. * *adj* stylish.

chick *n* a young bird; (*sl*) a youthful person.

chicken *n* a young, domestic fowl; its flesh. * *adj* cowardly, timorous.

chicken feed *n* poultry food; (*inf*) a trifling amount.

chickenpox *n* a contagious viral disease that causes a rash of red spots on the skin.

chicory *n* a salad plant; its dried, ground, roasted root used to flavor coffee.

chief *adj* principal, most important. * *n* a leader; the head of a tribe or clan.

chiefly *adv* especially; mainly; for the most part.

chiffon *n* a thin gauzy material.

chilblain *n* an inflamed swelling on the hands, etc, due to cold.

child *n* (*pl* **children**) a young human being; a son or daughter; offspring.

childbirth *n* the process of giving birth to children.

childhood *n* the period between birth and puberty in humans.

childish *adj* of, like or suited to a child; foolish.—**childishly**.—**childishness** *n*.

childlike *adj* like a child; innocent, simple, candid.

child minder *n* a person employed to look after children.

chill *n* a sensation of coldness; an illness caused by exposure to cold and marked by shivering; anything that dampens or depresses. * *adj* shivering with cold; feeling cold; unemotional, formal. * *vti* to make or become cold; to harden by cooling; to depress.

chilly *adj* (**chillier, chilliest**) cold; unfriendly.—

chilliness n.

chime n the harmonious sound of a bell; accord; harmony; (pl) a set of bells or metal tubes, etc tuned in a scale; their ringing. * vi to ring (a bell); (with with) to agree. * vt to indicate the hour by chiming, as a clock.

chimney n (pl chimneys) a passage for smoke, hot air or fumes, a funnel.

chimo interj (Cdn) used to give a friendly greeting, esp in the Canadian North.

chimpanzee n an African anthropoid ape.

chin n the part of the face below the mouth.

china n fine porcelain; articles made from this.

chink[1] n a narrow opening; a crack or slit.

chink[2] n the sound of coins clinking together.

Chinook jargon n (hist) a pidgin language made up of English, French and Indian languages, used by traders on the Pacific Northwest coast of North America.

chip vt (pt chipped) to knock small pieces off; to shape or make by chipping. * n a small piece cut or broken off; a thin strip of fried potato; a potato crisp; a counter used in games; a tiny piece of semi-conducting material, such as silicon, printed with a microcircuit and used as part of an integrated circuit.

Chipewyan n a member of a First Nations people in the northern Canadian Prairies and subarctic Northwest Territories; the Athapaskan language of this people. • adj of or pertaining to this people or their language.

chip wagon n (Cdn) a mobile vehicle that sells French fries and other snacks.

chirp n the sharp, shrill note of some birds or a grasshopper. * vi to make this sound.

chisel n a tool with a square cutting end. * vt (pt chiselled) to cut or carve with a chisel; (sl) to defraud.

chit[1] n a voucher or a sum owed for drink, food, etc; a note; a requisition.

chit[2] n a child; (derog) an impudent girl.

chivalry n the medieval system of knighthood; knightly qualities, bravery, courtesy, respect for women.—chivalrous adj.—chivalrously.

chive, chives n a plant whose onion-flavored leaves are used in cooking and salads.

chloride n any compound containing chlorine.

chlorine n a non-metallic element, a yellowish-green poisonous gas used in bleaches, disinfectants, and in industry.

chock n a block of wood or other material used as a wedge. * vt to secure with a chock.

chock-a-block, chock-full adj completely full.

chocolate n a powder or edible solid made of the roasted, pounded cacao bean; a drink made by dissolving this powder in boiling water or milk; a sweet with a centre and chocolate coating. * adj flavored or coated with chocolate; dark reddish brown.

choice n act of choosing; the power to choose; selection; alternative; a thing chosen; preference; the best part. * adj of picked quality, specially good; fastidious.

choir n an organized group of singers, esp a church; the part of a church used by them.

choke vti to stop the breath of, stifle; to throttle; to suffocate; to block (up). * n a fit of choking; a choking sound; a valve that controls the flow of air in a carburettor.

cholera n a severe, infectious intestinal disease.

choose vt (pt chose, pp chosen) to select (one thing) rather than another. * vi to decide, to think fit.—chooser n.

chop vt (pt chopped) to cut by striking; to cut into pieces. * n a cut of meat and bone from the rib, loin, or shoulder; a downward blow or motion.

choppy adj (choppier, choppiest) (sea) running in rough, irregular waves; jerky.—choppiness n.

chopsticks n a pair of wooden or plastic sticks used in Asian countries to eat with.

choral adj relating to, sung by, or written for, a choir or chorus.

chord[1] n (mus) three or more notes played simultaneously.

chord[2] n a straight line joining the ends of an arc.

chore n a piece of housework; a regular or tedious task.

choreography n the art of devising ballets or dances.—choreographer n.—choreographic adj.

chorister n a member of a choir.

chortle vi to chuckle exultantly.—also n.

chorus n a group of singers and dancers in the background to a play, musical, etc; a group of singers, a choir; music sung by a chorus; a refrain; an utterance by many at once. * vt to sing, speak or shout in chorus.

chose, chosen see choose.

Christ n Jesus of Nazareth, regarded by Christians as the Messiah. * interj (taboo) an oath expressing annoyance.

christen vt to enter the Christian Church by baptism; to give a name to; (inf) to use for the first time.—christening n.

Christian n a person who believes in Christianity. * adj relating to, believing in, or based on the doctrines of Christianity; kind, gentle, humane.

Christianity n the religion based on the teachings of Christ.

Christian name n a name given when one is christened; (loosely) any forename.

Christmas n an annual festival (25 December) in memory of the birth of Christ.

Christmas tree n an evergreen tree decorated at Christmas; an imitation tree.

chrome n chromium; a chromium pigment; something plated with an alloy of chromium.

chromium n a hard metallic element used in making steel alloys and electroplating to give a tough surface.

chromosome n any of the microscopic rod-shaped bodies bearing genes.

chronic adj (disease) long-lasting; (sl) bad, extremely unpleasant.—chronically adv.

chronicle n a record of events in chronological

order; an account; a history. * vt to record in a chronicle.—**chronicler** n.

chronological adj arranged in order of occurrence.—**chronologically** adv.

chrysanthemum n a plant with a brightly colored flower head.

chubby adj (**chubbier, chubbiest**) plump.—**chubbiness** n.

chuck[1] vt to throw, to toss; (inf) to stop, to give up.

chuck[2] n a device on a lathe, etc, that holds the work or drill; a cut of beef from the neck to the ribs.

chuck[3] n on the Pacific Northwest coast of North America, a large body of water.

chuckle vt to laugh softly; to gloat. * n a quiet laugh.

chum[1] n (inf) a close friend, esp of the same sex.

chum[2] n a salmon of the Pacific Northwest coast of North America.

chunk n a short, thick piece or lump, as wood, bread, etc.—**chunky** adj.

church n a building for public worship, esp Christian worship; the clerical profession; a religious service; (with cap) all Christians; (with the) a particular Christian denomination.

churchyard n the yard around a church often used as a burial ground.

churn n a large metal container for milk; a device that can be vigorously turned to make milk or cream into butter. * vt to agitate in a churn; to make (butter) this way; to stir violently.

chute n an inclined trough or a passage for sending down water, logs, rubbish, etc; a fall of water, a rapid.

CI abbr (Cdn) = Collegiate Institute.

CID abbr = Criminal Investigation Department.

cider n fermented apple juice as a drink.

cigar n a compact roll of tobacco leaf for smoking.

cigarette n shredded tobacco rolled in fine paper for smoking.

cinch n (sl) a firm hold, an easy job.

cinder n a tiny piece of partly burned wood, etc; (pl) ashes from wood or coal.

cine- prefix motion picture or cinema, as cinecamera, cinefilm.

cinema n a place where motion pictures are shown; film as an industry or art form.

cinnamon n a tree of the laurel family; its aromatic edible bark; a spice made from this; a yellowish brown color.—also adj.

cipaille n (Cdn) a pie made up of alternating layers of meat and vegetables.

cipher n the numeral 0, zero; any single Arabic numeral; a thing or person of no importance, a nonentity; a method of secret writing. * vt to convert (a message) into cipher.—also **cypher**.

circle n a perfectly round plane figure; the line enclosing it; the curved seating area above the stalls in a theatre; a group, set or class (of people); extent, scope, as of influence.

* vti to encompass; to move in a circle; to revolve (round).

circuit n a distance round; a route or course; an area so enclosed; the path of an electric current; a visit to an area by a judge to hold courts; the area itself; a chain or association.

circuitous adj roundabout, indirect.

circular adj shaped like a circle, round; (argument) using as evidence the conclusion which it is seeking to prove; moving round a circle. * n an advertisement, etc addressed to a number of people.

circulate vti to pass from hand to hand or place to place; to spread or be spread about; to move round, finishing at the starting point.—**circulatory** adj.

circulation n the act of circulating; a movement to and fro; the number of copies sold of a newspaper, etc; currency.

circumcise vt to cut off the foreskin of (a male) or the clitoris of (a female), esp as a religious rite.—**circumcision** n.

circumference n the line bounding a circle, a ball, etc; the length of this line.

circumstance n an occurrence, an incident; a detail; ceremony; (pl) a state of affairs; condition in life.

circus n a large arena for the exhibition of games, feats of horsemanship etc; a travelling show of acrobats, clowns, etc; a company of people travelling round giving displays.

cisco n (pl **ciscoes**) (Cdn) a North American freshwater whitefish.

cistern n a tank or reservoir for storing water, esp in a toilet.

cite vt to summon officially to appear in court; to quote; to give as an example or authority.

citizen n a member of a city, state or nation.—**citizenship** n.

Citizenship Court n (Cdn) a federal court that awards Canadian citizenship.

citrus n a genus of trees including the lemon, orange, etc; the fruit of these.

city n an important or cathedral town; a town created a city by charter; the people of a city; business circles, esp financial services.

civic adj of a city, citizen or citizenship. * npl the principles of good citizenship; the study of citizenship.

civic holiday n (Cdn) a public holiday held in most Canadian provinces, usually on the first Monday in August.

civil adj of citizens or the state; not military or ecclesiastical; polite, obliging; (law) relating to crimes other than criminal ones or to private rights.

civil engineer n an engineer who designs and constructs roads, bridges, etc.

civilian n a person who is not a member of the armed forces.

civilization, civilisation n the state of being civilized; the process of civilizing; an advanced stage of social culture; moral and cultural refinement.

civil service *n* those employed in the service of a state apart from the military.

civil war *n* a war between citizens of the same state or country.

claim *vt* to demand as a right; to call for; to require; to profess (to have); to assert. * *n* the act of claiming; a title, right to something; a thing claimed, esp a piece of land for mining.

claimant *n* one who makes a claim.

clam *n* an edible marine bivalve mollusc.

clamber *vi* to climb with difficulty, using the hands as well as the feet. * *n* a climb performed in this way.—**clamberer** *n*.

clammy *adj* (**clammier**, **clammiest**) damp and sticky.—**clamminess** *n*.

clamp *n* a device for gripping objects tightly together. * *vt* to grip with a clamp; to attach firmly.

clan *n* a group of people with a common ancestor, under a single chief; people with the same surname; a party or clique.

clang *n* a loud metallic sound. * *vti* to make or cause to make a clang.

clap[1] *vti* (*pt* **clapped**) to strike (the hands) together sharply; to applaud in this way; to slap; to put or place suddenly or vigorously. * *n* the sound of hands clapping; a sudden sharp noise; a sudden sharp slap.

clap[2] *n* (*vulg*) venereal disease, gonorrhoea.

claret *n* a dry red wine of Bordeaux in France.

clarify *vti* to make or become clear or intelligible; to free or become free from impurities.—**clarification** *n*.

clarinet *n* an orchestral woodwind instrument.—**clarinettist** *n*.

clarity *n* clearness.

clash *n* a loud noise of striking weapons, cymbals, etc; a contradiction, disagreement; a collision. * *vti* to make or cause to make a clash by striking together; to conflict; to collide; to be at variance (with).

clasp *n* a hold, an embrace; a catch or buckle. * *vt* to grasp firmly, to embrace; to fasten with a clasp.

class *n* a division, a group; a kind; a set of students who are taught together; a grade of merit or quality; standing in society, rank. * *vt* to put into a class.

classic *adj* of the highest class or rank, esp in literature; of the best Greek and Roman writers; of music conforming to certain standards of form, complexity, etc; traditional; authoritative. * *n* a work of literature, art, cinema, etc, of the highest excellence; a definitive work of art.

classical *adj* influenced by, of or relating to ancient Roman and Greek art, literature and culture; traditional; serious; refined.—**classically** *adv*.

classical college *n* (*Cdn*) (*hist*) in Quebec, a private school that offered an eight-year program leading to a university undergraduate degree.

classification *n* the organization of knowledge into categories; a category or a division of a category into which knowledge or information has been put.

classify *vt* to arrange in classes, to categorize; to restrict for security reasons.

classmate *n* a member of the same class in a school, college, etc.

classroom *n* a room where pupils or students are taught.

clatter *n* a rattling noise; noisy talk. * *vti* to make or cause a clatter.

clause *n* a single article or stipulation in a treaty, law, contract, etc; (*gram*) a short sentence; a part of a sentence.

claustrophobia *n* a morbid fear of confined spaces.—**claustrophobic** *adj*.

claw *n* the sharp hooked nail of an animal or bird; the pointed end or pincer of a crab, etc; a claw-like thing. * *vti* to seize or tear with claws or nails; to clutch (at).

clay *n* a sticky ductile earthy material.

CLC *abbr* = Canadian Labour Congress.

clean *adj* free from dirt or impurities; unsoiled; morally or ceremonially pure; complete, decisive. * *adv* entirely; outright; neatly. * *vti* to remove dirt from.—**cleanness** *n*.

cleaner *n* a substance or device used for cleaning; a person employed to clean; (*pl*) a dry cleaner.

cleanse *vt* to make clean or pure.

cleanser *n* something that cleanses, esp a detergent, face cream, etc.

clear *adj* bright, not dim; transparent; without blemish; easily seen or heard; unimpeded, open; free from clouds; quit (of); plain, distinct, obvious; keen, discerning; positive, sure. * *adv* plainly; apart from. * *vti* to make or become clear; to rid (of), remove; to to free from suspicion, vindicate; to disentangle; to pass by or over without touching; to make as a profit.—**clearness** *n*.

clearance *n* the act of clearing; permission, authority to proceed; the space between two objects in motion.

clearing *n* a tract of land cleared of trees, etc for cultivation.

clearly *adv* in a clear manner; evidently.

clearway *n* a main road where it is illegal for vehicles to stop.

clef *n* a sign on a music stave that indicates the pitch of the notes.

clench *vt* (*teeth, fist*) to close tightly; to grasp. * *n* a firm grip.

clergy *n* ministers of the Christian church collectively.

clergyman *n* a member of the clergy.

clerical *adj* of or relating to the clergy or a clergyman; of or relating to a clerk or a clerk's work.

clerk *n* an office worker who types, keeps files, etc; a layman with minor duties in a church; a public official who keeps the records of a court, town, etc.

clever *adj* able; intelligent; ingenious; skilful, adroit.—**cleverly** *adv*.—**cleverness** *n*.

cliché *n* a hackneyed phrase; something that has become commonplace.—**cliché'd**, **clichéd** *adj*.

click *n* a slight, sharp sound. * *vi* to make such a sound.

client *n* a person who employs another professionally; a customer.

clientele *n* clients, customers.

cliff *n* a high steep rock face.

climate *n* the weather characteristics of an area; the prevailing attitude, feeling, atmosphere.—**climatic** *adj*.

climax *n* the highest point; a culmination; sexual orgasm. * *vti* to reach, or bring to a climax.—**climactic** *adj*.

climb *vti* to mount with an effort; to ascend; (*plants*) to grow upwards by clinging onto walls, fences or other plants. * *n* an ascent.

climber *n* a mountaineer or rock climber; a climbing plant.

clinch *vt* (*argument, etc*) to confirm or drive home. * *vi* (*boxing*) to grip the opponent with the arms to hinder his punching. * *n* the act of clinching; (*inf*) an embrace.

cling *vi* (*pt* **clung**) to adhere, to be attached (to); to keep hold by embracing or entwining.

clinic *n* a place where outpatients are given medical care or advice; a place where medical specialists practice as a group; a private or specialized hospital; the teaching of medicine by treating patients in the presence of students.

clinical *adj* of or relating to a clinic; based on medical observation; plain, simple; detached, cool, objective.—**clinically** *adv*.

clink¹ *n* a slight metallic ringing sound. * *vti* to make or cause to make such a sound.

clink² *n* (*sl*) prison.

clip¹ *vt* (*pt* **clipped**) to cut or trim with scissors or shears; to punch a small hole in, esp a ticket; (*words*) to shorten or slur; (*inf*) to hit sharply. * *n* the piece clipped off; a yield of wool from sheep; an extract from a film; (*inf*) a smart blow; speed.

clip² *vt* (*pt* **clipped**) to hold firmly; to secure with a clip. * *n* any device that grips, clasps or hooks; a magazine for a gun; a piece of jewellery held in place by a clip.

clique *n* a small exclusive group, a set.—**cliquey** *adj*.—**cliquish** *adj*.

cloak *n* a loose sleeveless outer garment; a covering; something that conceals, a pretext. * *vt* to cover as with a cloak; to conceal.

cloakroom *n* a room where overcoats, etc, may be left.

clock *n* a device for measuring time; any timing device with a dial and displayed figures. * *vt* to time (a race, etc) using a stopwatch or other device; (*inf*) to register a certain speed; (*sl*) to hit.

clockwise *adv* moving in the direction of a clock's hands.—*also adj*.

clockwork *n* the mechanism of a clock or any similar mechanism with springs and gears. * *adj* mechanically regular.

clog *n* a wooden-soled shoe. * *vt* (*pt* **clogged**) to cause a blockage in; to impede, obstruct.

cloister *n* a roofed pillared walk, usu with one side open, in a convent, college, etc; a religious retreat. * *vt* to confine or keep apart as if in a convent.

close¹ *adj* near; reticent, secret; nearly alike; nearly even or equal; dense, compact; sultry, airless; narrow; restricted. * *adv* closely; near by. * *n* a courtyard; the entrance to a courtyard; the precincts of a cathedral.—**closely** *adv*.—**closeness** *n*.

close² *vt* to make closed; to stop up (an opening); to draw together; to conclude; to shut. * *vi* to come together; to complete; to finish. * *n* a completion, end.

closed *adj* shut up; with no opening; restricted; not open to question or debate; not open to the public, exclusive.

closet *n* a small room or a cupboard for clothes, supplies, etc; a small private room. * *vt* (*pt* **closeted**) to enclose in a private room for a confidential talk.

close-up *n* a film or television shot taken from very close range; a close examination.

closure *n* closing; the condition of being closed; something that closes; (*parliament, etc*) a decision to end further debate and move to an immediate vote.

clot *n* a thickened mass, esp of blood; (*sl*) an idiot. * *vti* (*pt* **clotted**) to form into clots, to curdle, coagulate.

cloth *n* woven, knitted or pressed fabric from which garments, etc are made; a piece of this; a tablecloth; clerical dress.

clothe *vt* (*pt* **clothed** *or* **clad**) to cover with a garments; to dress; to surround, endow (with).

clothes *npl* garments, apparel.

clothesline *n* a rope on which washing is hung to dry.

clothespeg, clothespin *n* a plastic, wooden or metal clip for attaching washing to a line.

clothing *n* clothes.

cloud *n* a visible mass of water vapour floating in the sky; a mass of smoke, etc; a threatening thing, a gloomy look; a multitude. * *vt* to darken or obscure as with clouds.—**cloudless** *adj*.

cloudberry *n* a low-growing North American plant of the raspberry family with amber-coloured fruit.

cloudburst *n* a sudden rainstorm.

cloudy *adj* (**cloudier, cloudiest**) of or full of clouds; not clear; gloomy.—**cloudiness** *n*.

clout *n* a blow; (*sl*) power, influence.

clove¹ *n* a segment of a bulb, as garlic.

clove² *n* the dried flower bud of a tropical tree, used as a spice.

clover *n* a low-growing plant with three leaves used as fodder; a trefoil; (*inf*) luxury.

clown *n* a person who entertains with jokes, antics, etc, esp in a circus; a clumsy or boorish person. * *vi* to act the clown, behave comically or clumsily.—**clownish** *adj*.

club *n* a heavy stick used as a weapon; a stick with a head for playing golf, etc; an association of people for athletic, social, or common purposes; its premises; a suit of playing cards with black clover-like markings. * *vt* to beat with or use as a club. * *vi* to form into a club for a common purpose.

clubhouse *n* premises used by a club.

cluck *n* the call of a hen. * *vi* to make such a noise.

clue *n* a guide to the solution of a mystery or problem. * *vt* (*pt* **clued**) to provide with helpful information.

clump *n* a cluster of trees; a lump; (*of hair*) a handful; the sound of heavy footsteps.

clumsy *adj* (**clumsier, clumsiest**) unwieldy; awkward; lacking tact, skill or grace.—**clumsily** *adv*.—**clumsiness** *n*.

clung *see* **cling**.

cluster *n* a bunch; a swarm; a group. * *vti* to form or arrange in a cluster.

clutch[1] *vt* to seize, to grasp tightly; to snatch at. * *n* a tight grip; a device for throwing parts of a machine into or out of action; the pedal operating this device.

clutch[2] *n* a nest of eggs; a brood of chicks.

clutter *n* a disordered mess; confusion. * *vti* to litter; to put into disorder.

CM *abbr* = Member of the Order of Canada.

CMA *abbr* = Canadian Medical Association; Canadian Management Accountant.

CMHC *abbr* = Canada Mortgage and Housing Corporation.

CN *abbr* = Canadian National (Railways).

CNIB *abbr* = Canadian National Institute for the Blind.

Co. *abbr* = Company; County.

c/o *abbr* = care of.

coach *n* a long-distance bus; a railway carriage; a large, covered four-wheeled horse-drawn carriage; a sports instructor; a tutor in a specialized subject. * *vti* to teach or train.

coagulate *vti* to change from a liquid to partially sold state, to clot, curdle.—**coagulation** *n*.

coal *n* a black mineral used for fuel; a piece of this; an ember.

coalfield *n* a region yielding coal.

coalition *n* a temporary union of parties or states.

coarse *adj* rough; large in texture; rude, crude; inferior.—**coarsely** *adv*.—**coarseness** *n*.

coast *n* an area of land bordering the sea; the seashore. * *vi* to sail along a coast; to travel down a slope without power; to proceed with ease.—**coastal** *adj*.

coastguard *n* an organization which monitors the coastline and provides help for ships in difficulties, prevents smuggling, etc.

coast-to-coast-to-coast *adj, adv* (*Cdn*) between the coasts of the Atlantic, Pacific and Arctic oceans.

coat *n* a sleeved outer garment; the natural covering of an animal; a layer. * *vt* to cover with a layer or coating.

coating *n* a surface coat; material for coats.

coat of arms *n* the heraldic bearings of a family, city, institution, etc.

coax *vt* to persuade gently; to obtain by coaxing.—**coaxingly** *adv*.

cobble[1] *n* a cobblestone, a rounded stone used for paving. * *vt* to pave with cobblestones.

cobble[2] *vt* to repair, to make (shoes); to put together roughly or hastily.

cobra *n* a venomous hooded snake of Africa and India.

cobweb *n* a spider's web; a flimsy thing; an entanglement.

cocaine *n* an intoxicating addictive drug obtained from coca leaves, used in anaesthesia.

cock *n* the adult male of the domestic fowl; the male of other birds; a tap or valve; the hammer of a gun; a cocked position; (*vulg*) the penis. * *vt* to set erect, to stick up; to set at an angle; to bring the hammer (of gun) to firing position.

cockerel *n* a young cock.

cockeyed *adj* (*inf*) having a squint; slanting; daft, absurd.

cockle *n* an edible shellfish with a rounded shell.

cockney *n* a person born in the East End of London; the dialect of this area.

cockpit *n* the compartment of a small aircraft for the pilot and crew, the flight deck; an arena for cock fighting; the driver's seat in a racing car.

cockroach *n* a nocturnal beetle-like insect.

cocktail *n* an alcoholic drink containing a mixture of spirits or other liqueurs; an appetizer, usu containing shellfish, served as the first course of a meal.

cocoa *n* a powder of ground cacao seeds; a drink made from this.

coconut *n* the fruit of the coconut palm.

cocoon *n* a silky case spun by some insect larvae for protection in the chrysalis stage; a cosy covering. * *vt* to wrap in a cocoon.

cod *n* a large edible fish of the North Atlantic.

code *n* a system of letters, numbers or symbols used to transmit secret messages, or to simplify communication; a systematic body of laws; a set of rules or conventions; (*comput*) a set of program instructions. * *vt* to put into code.

codify *vt* to collect or arrange (laws, rules, regulations, etc) into a system.—**codifier** *n*.—**codification** *n*.

cod tongue *n* (*Cdn*) the tongue of a codfish, fried in pork fat.

coeducation *n* the teaching of students of both sexes in the same institution.—**coeducational** *adj*.

coerce *vt* to compel; to force by threats.—**coercion** *n*.

coexist *vi* to exist together at the same time; to live in peace together.—**coexistence** *n*.—**coexistent** *adj*.

coffee *n* a drink made from the seeds of the coffee tree; the seeds, or the shrub; a light-brown color.

coffee table *n* a low table for holding drinks, books, etc. * *adj* (*book*) large and for looking at, not reading.

coffin *n* a chest for a dead body to be buried in.

cog *n* a tooth-like projection on the rim of a wheel.

cogent *adj* persuasive, convincing.—**cogently** *adv*.—**cogency** *n*.

cogwheel *n* a wheel with a toothed rim for gearing.

coherent *adj* cohering; capable of intelligible speech; consistent.— **coherently** *adv*.— **coherence** *n*.

coil *vti* to wind in rings or folds; to twist into a circular or spiral shape. * *n* a coiled length of rope; a single ring of this; (*elect*) a spiral wire for the passage of current; an intra-uterine contraceptive device.

coin *n* a piece of legally stamped metal used as money. * *vt* to invent (a word, phrase); to make into money, to mint.

coinage *n* the act of coining; the issue of coins, currency; a coined word.

coincide *vi* to occupy the same portion of space; to happen at the same time; to agree exactly, to correspond.

coincidence *n* the act of coinciding; the occurrence of an event at the same time as another without apparent connection.

coke¹ *n* coal from which gas has been expelled. * *vt* to convert (coal) into coke.

coke² *n* (*sl*) cocaine.

colander *n* a bowl with holes in the bottom for straining cooked vegetables, pasta, etc.

cold *adj* lacking heat or warmth; lacking emotion, passion or courage; unfriendly; (*scent*) faint; (*sl*) unconscious. * *n* absence of heat; the sensation caused by this; cold weather; a virus infection of the respiratory tract.— **coldly** *adv*.— **coldness** *n*.

cold feet *n* (*inf*) fear.

coleslaw *n* raw shredded cabbage in a dressing, used in salads.

collaborate *vi* to work jointly or together, esp in literature; to side with the invaders of one's country.— **collaboration** *n*.— **collaborator** *n*.

collage *n* art made up from scraps of paper, material and other odds and ends pasted onto a hard surface.

collapse *vi* to fall down; to come to ruin, to fail; to break down physically or mentally. * *n* the act of collapsing; a breakdown, prostration.

collapsible *adj* designed to fold compactly.

collar *n* the band of a garment round the neck; a decoration round the neck, a choker; a band of leather or chain put round an animal's neck. * *vt* to put a collar on; (*inf*) to seize.

collarbone *n* one of the two bones that connect the shoulder blades with the breast bone, the clavicle.

colleague *n* an associate in the same profession or office; a fellow worker.

collect *vti* to bring together, gather or assemble; to regain command of (oneself); to concentrate (thoughts, etc). * *n* a short prayer for a particular occasion.

collected *adj* self-possessed, cool.— **collectedly** *adv*.

collection *n* act of collecting; an accumulation; money collected at a meeting, etc; a group of things collected for beauty, interest, rarity or value; the periodic showing of a designer's fashions.

collector *n* a person who collects things, eg

stamps, butterflies, as a hobby or so as to inspect them, as tickets.

college *n* an institution of higher learning; a school offering specialized knowledge; the buildings housing a college; an organized body of professionals.

collegiate institute *n* (*Cdn*) a secondary school that chiefly prepares students for university.

collide *vi* to come into violent contact (with); to dash together; to conflict.

colliery *n* a coal mine and its associated buildings.

collision *n* state of colliding together; a violent impact of moving bodies, a crash; a clash of interests, etc.

colloquial *adj* used in familiar but not formal talk, not literary.— **colloquially** *adv*.

colon¹ *n* the part of the large intestine from the caecum to the rectum.— **colonic** *adj*.

colon² *n* a punctuation mark (:) between the semicolon and the full stop.

colonel *n* a commissioned officer junior to a brigadier but senior to a lieutenant colonel.

colonial *adj* of or pertaining to a colony or colonies; (*with cap*) pertaining to the thirteen British colonies that became the US. * *n* a person who takes part in founding a colony, a settler.

colonize *vt* to establish a colony in; to settle in a colony.

colony *n* an area of land acquired and settled by a distant state and subject to its control; a community of settlers; a group of people of the same nationality or interests living in a particular area; a collection of organisms in close association.

color *n* the eye's perception of wavelengths of light with different colors corresponding to different wavelengths; the attribute of objects to appear different according to their differing ability to absorb, emit, or reflect light of different wavelengths; color of the face or skin; pigment; dye; paint; (*literature*) use of imagery, vividness; (*mus*) depth of sound; (*pl*) a flag. * *vt* to give color to, paint; to misrepresent; to influence. * *vi* to emit color; to blush.— **coloration** *n*.

color bar *n* discrimination based on race, esp by white races against other races.

color-blind *adj* unable to distinguish colors, esp red and green.

colored *adj* possessing color; biased, not objective; of a darker skinned race. * *n* a person of a darker skinned race.

colorful *adj* full of color; vivid.— **colorfully** *adv*.

colossal *adj* gigantic, immense; (*inf*) amazing, wonderful.

colt *n* a young male horse.

column *n* a round pillar for supporting or decorating a building; something of this shape; a vertical division of a page; a narrow-fronted deep formation of troops; a feature article appearing regularly in a newspaper, etc.

columnist *n* a journalist who contributes a regular column.

coma *n* deep prolonged unconsciousness.

comb *n* a toothed instrument for separating hair, wool, etc; a part of a machine like this; the crest of a cock; a honeycomb. * *vt* to arrange (hair) or dress (wool) with a comb; to seek for thoroughly.

combat *vti* (*pt* **combated**) to strive against, oppose; to do battle. * *n* a contest; a fight; struggle.

combination *n* the act of combining; a union of separate parts; persons allied for a purpose; a sequence of numbers which opens a combination lock.

combine *vti* to join together; to unite intimately; to possess together; to cooperate; (*chem*) to form a compound with. * *n* an association formed for commercial or political purposes; a machine for harvesting and threshing grain.

combustible *adj* capable of burning; easily set alight; excitable. * *n* a combustible thing. —**combustibility** *n*.

combustion *n* the process of burning; the process in which substances react with oxygen in air to produce heat.

come *vi* (*pt* **came**, *pp* **come**) to approach; to arrive; to reach; to happen (to); to originate; to turn out (to be); to occur in a certain order; to be derived or descended; to be caused; to result; to be available; (*sl*) to experience a sexual orgasm.

comeback *n* (*inf*) a return to a career or to popularity; (*inf*) a witty answer.

comedian *n* an actor of comic parts; an entertainer who tells jokes; a person who behaves in a humorous manner.

comedy *n* an amusing play or film; drama consisting of amusing plays; an amusing occurrence; humour.

comet *n* a celestial body that travels round the sun, with a visible nucleus and a luminous tail.

comfort *vti* to bring consolation to; to soothe; to cheer. * *n* consolation; relief; bodily ease; (*pl*) things between necessities and luxuries.

comfortable *adj* promoting comfort; at ease; adequate; (*inf*) financially well off.—**comfortably** *adv*.

comic *adj* of comedy; causing amusement. * *n* a comedian; an entertaining person; a paper or book with strip cartoons.

comical *adj* funny, laughable; droll, ludicrous.—**comically** *adv*.

comic strip *n* a series of drawings that depict a story in stages.

coming *adj* approaching next; of future importance.

comma *n* a punctuation mark (,) indicating a pause or break in a sentence, or separating items in a list.

command *vti* to order; to bid; to control; to have at disposal; to evoke, compel; to look down over; to be in authority (over), to govern. * *n* an order; control; disposal; position of authority; something or someone commanded; an instruction to a computer; (*with cap*) (*Cdn*) one of the three main branches of the Canadian armed forces.

commandeer *vt* to seize for military purposes; to appropriate for one's own use.

commander *n* a person who commands, a leader; a naval officer ranking next below a captain.

commando *n* (*pl* **commandos**) a member of an elite military force trained to raid enemy territory.

commemorate *vt* to keep in the memory by ceremony or writing; to be a memorial of.—**commemoration** *n*.—**commemorative** *adj*.

commence *vti* to begin.

commend *vt* to speak favorably of, to praise; to recommend; to entrust.—**commendable** *adj*.

commendation *n* the act of com-mending, praise; an award.

commensurate *adj* having the same extent or measure; proportionate.

comment *n* a remark, observation, criticism; an explanatory note; talk, gossip. * *vi* to make a comment (upon); to annotate.

commentary *n* a series of explanatory notes or remarks.

commentator *n* one who reports and analyses events, trends, etc, as on TV.

commerce *n* trade in goods and services on a large scale between nations or individuals.

commercial *adj* of or engaged in commerce; sponsored by an advertiser; intended to make a profit. * *n* a broadcast advertisement.

commercialize *vt* to put on a business basis; to exploit for profit.—**commercialization** *n*.

commiserate *vti* to sympathize (with); to feel pity for.—**commiseration** *n*.

commission *n* authority to act; a document bestowing this; appointment as a military officer of the rank of lieutenant or above; a body of people appointed for specified duties; business committed to someone; a percentage on sales paid to a salesman or agent; brokerage. * *vt* to empower or appoint by commission; to employ the service of; to authorize.

commissionaire *n* a uniformed attendant at the entrance to an office building, shop, etc.

commissioner *n* a person empowered by a commission; various types of civil servant; a member of a commission.

commit *vti* (*pt* **committed**) to entrust; to consign (to prison); to do, to perpetrate; to pledge, to involve.

commitment *n* the act of committing; an engagement that restricts freedom; an obligation; an order for imprisonment or confinement in a mental institution.—**committal** *n*.

committee *n* a body of people appointed from a larger body to consider or manage some matter.

commodity *n* an article of trade; a useful thing; (*pl*) goods.

common *adj* belonging equally to more than one; public; usual, ordinary; widespread; familiar; frequent; easily obtained, not rare; low, vulgar; (*noun*) applying to any of a class. * *n* a tract of open public land; (*pl*) the common people; the House of Commons.—**commonly** *adv.*—**commonness** *n*.

commoner *n* an ordinary person, not a member of the nobility.

common law *n* the body of law based on custom and judicial precedent, as distinct from statute law. * *adj* denoting a marriage recognized in law not by an official ceremony, but after a couple have cohabited for a number of years.

commonplace *adj* ordinary, unremarkable. * *n* a platitude; an ordinary thing.

common sense *n* ordinary, practical good sense.—**common-sense** *adj*.

commonwealth *n* a political community; a sovereign state, republic; a federation of states; (*with cap*) an association of sovereign states and dependencies ruled or formerly ruled by Britain.

commotion *n* a violent disturbance; agitation; upheaval.

communal *adj* of a commune or community; shared in common.—**communally** *adv*.

commune[1] *n* a group of people living together and sharing possessions; the smallest administrative division in several European countries.

commune[2] *vi* to converse intimately; to communicate spiritually.

communicate *vti* to impart, to share; to succeed in conveying information; to be connected.

communication *n* the act of communicating; information; a connecting passage or channel; (*pl*) connections of transport; (*pl*) means of imparting information, as in newspapers, TV.

communication cord *n* a cord, by pulling which a passenger can stop a train in an emergency.

communion *n* common possession, sharing; fellowship; union in a religious body; (*with cap*) Holy Communion, the Christian sacrament of the Eucharist when bread and wine are consecrated and consumed.

communiqué *n* an official communication, esp to the press or public.

communism *n* a social system under which private property is abolished and the means of production are owned by the people; (*with cap*) a political movement seeking the overthrow of capitalism based on the writings of Karl Marx; the system as instituted in the former USSR and elsewhere.—**communist** *n, adj*.

community *n* an organized political or social body; a body of people in the same locality; the general public, society; any group having work, interests, etc in common; joint ownership; common character.

community hall *n* a hall in a community that is used for local events such as dances and suppers.

commute *vti* to travel daily from a suburban home to a city office; to exchange (for); to change (to); to reduce (a punishment) to one less severe.—**commutation** *n*.

commuter *n* a person who commutes to and from work.

commutershed *n* the area from which it is possible to commute to a large city.

compact[1] *n* an agreement; a contract, a treaty.

compact[2] *adj* closely packed; condensed; terse. * *vt* to press or pack closely; to compose (of). * *n* a small cosmetic case, usu containing powder and a mirror.—**compactly** *adv.*—**compactness** *n*.

companion *n* an associate in an activity; a partner; a friend; one of a pair of matched things.—**companionship** *n*.

company *n* any assembly of people; an association of people for carrying on a business, etc; a society; a military unit; the crew of a ship; companionship, fellowship.

comparable *adj* able or suitable to be compared (*with* with); similar.—**comparably** *adv.*—**comparability** *n*.

comparative *adj* estimated by comparison; relative, not absolute; (*gram*) expressing more.—**comparatively** *adv*.

compare *vt* to make one thing the measure of another; to observe similarity between, to liken; to bear comparison; (*gram*) to give comparative and superlative forms of (an adjective). * *vi* to make comparisons; to be equal or alike.

comparison *n* the act of comparing; an illustration; (*gram*) the use of *more* or *er* with an adjective.

compartment *n* a space partitioned off; a division of a railway carriage; a separate section or category.—**compartmental** *adj*.

compass *n* a circuit, circumference; an extent, area; the range of a voice; an instrument with a magnetic needle indicating north, south, east, west; (*often pl*) a two-legged instrument for drawing circles, etc.

compassion *n* sorrow for another's sufferings; pity.

compassionate *adj* showing compassion; merciful.—**compassionately** *adv*.

compatible *adj* agreeing or fitting in (with); consistent.—**compatibly** *adv.*—**compatibility** *n*.

compel *vt* (*pt* compelled) to force, constrain; to oblige; to obtain by force.

compendium *n* (*pl* compendiums, compendia) an abridgement; a summary; a collection.

compensate *vti* to counterbalance; to make up for; to recompense.—**compensatory** *adj*.

compensation *n* the act of compensating; a sum given to compensate.

compere, compère *n* a person who introduces cabaret performers, television acts, etc. * *vt* to act as a compere (for).

compete *vi* to strive; to contend; to take part in a competition.

competence *n* the quality of being capable; sufficiency; capacity; an adequate income to live on.

competent *adj* fit, capable; adequate; legally qualified.—**competently** *adv*.

competition *n* act of competing; rivalry; a contest in skill or knowledge; a match.

competitive *adj* of, or involving, competition; of sufficient value in terms of price or quality to ensure success against rivals.—**competitively** adv.—**competitiveness** n.

competitor n a person who competes; an opponent; a rival.

compile vt to collect or make up from various sources; to amass; (comput) to translate high-level programme instructions into machine code using a compiler.—**compilation** n.

complacent adj self-satisfied.—**complacently** adv.—**complacency** n.

complain vi to find fault, to grumble; to be ill; (poet) to express grief, to make a mourning sound.

complaint n a statement of some grievance; a cause of distress or dissatisfaction; an illness.

complement n something making up a whole; a full allowance (of equipment or number). * vt to make complete.

complementary adj completing; together forming a balanced whole.

complete adj entire; free from deficiency; finished; thorough. * vt to make complete; to finish.—**completeness** n.

completely adv entirely, utterly.

completion n the act of completing; accomplishment; fulfilment.

complex adj having more than one part; intricate, not simple; difficult. * n a complex whole; a collection of interconnected parts, buildings or units; a group of mostly unconscious impulses, etc strongly influencing behaviour.—**complexity** n.

complexion n a color, texture and look of the skin; aspect, character.

compliance n the act of complying with another's wishes; acquiescence.

compliant adj yielding, submissive.—**compliantly** adv.

complicate vt to make intricate or involved; to mix up.

complicated adj intricately involved; difficult to understand.

complication n a complex or intricate situation; a circumstance that makes (a situation) more complex; (med) a condition or disease following an original illness.

compliment n a polite expression of praise, a flattering tribute; (pl) a formal greeting or expression of regard. * vt to pay a compliment to, to flatter; to congratulate (on).

complimentary adj conveying or expressing a compliment; given free of charge.

comply vi to act in accordance (with); to yield, to agree.

component adj going to the making of a whole, constituent. * n a component part.

compose vt to make up, to form; to construct in one's mind, to write; to arrange, to put in order; to settle, to adjust; to tranquillize; (print) to set up. * vi to create musical works, etc.

composed adj calm, self-controlled.—**composedly** adv.

composer n a person who composes, esp music.

composition n the act or process of composing; a work of literature or music, a painting; a short written essay; the general make-up of something; a chemical compound.

compost n a mixture of decomposed organic matter for fertilizing soil.

composure n the state of being composed, calmness.

compound[1] n a substance or thing made up of a number of parts or ingredients, a mixture; a compound word. * vt to combine (parts, ingredients) into a whole, to mix; to intensify by adding new elements; to settle (debt) by partial payment. * vi to become joined in a compound; to come to terms of agreement. * adj compounded or made up of several parts; not simple.

compound[2] n an enclosure in which a building stands.

compound fracture n a fracture in which the bone pierces the skin.

compound interest n interest paid on the principal sum of capital and the interest that it has accrued.

comprehend vt to grasp with the mind, to understand; to include, to embrace.—**comprehension** n.

comprehensive adj wide in scope or content, including a great deal. * n a comprehensive school.—**comprehensively** adv.—**comprehensiveness** n.

comprehensive school n in Britain, a secondary school for local pupils of all abilities.

compress vt to press or squeeze together; to bring into a smaller bulk; to condense. * n a soft pad for compressing an artery, etc; a wet bandage to for relieving inflammation.

compression n the act of compressing; the increase in pressure in an engine to compress the gases so that they explode.

comprise vt to consist of, to include.

compromise n a settlement of a dispute by mutual concession; a middle course or view between two opposed ones. * vti to adjust by compromise; to lay open to suspicion, disrepute, etc.

compulsion n the act of compelling; something that compels; an irresistible urge.

compulsive adj compelling; acting as if compelled.—**compulsively** adv.

compulsory adj enforced, obligatory, required by law, etc; involving compulsion; essential.—**compulsorily** adv.

computer n an electronic device that processes data in accordance with programmed instructions.

computerize vt to equip with computers; to control or perform (a process) using computers; to store or process data using a computer.—**computerization** n.

comrade n a companion; a fellow member of a Communist party.—**comradely** adv.—**comradeship** n.

con[1] vt (pt **conned**) (inf) to swindle, trick. * n (inf) a confidence trick.

con[2] n against, as in **pro and con**.

con[3] prep with.

Conc. *abbr* (*Cdn*) = concession.

concave *adj* curving inwards, hollow. * *n* a concave line or surface.—**concavity** *n*.

conceal *vt* to hide, to keep from sight; to keep secret.—**concealment** *n*.

concede *vt* to grant; to admit to be true, to allow.

conceit *n* an over-high opinion of oneself; vanity; a far-fetched comparison, a quaint fancy.

conceited *adj* full of conceit, vain.—**conceitedly** *adv*.

conceivable *adj* capable of being imagined or believed.—**conceivably** *adv*.

conceive *vti* to become pregnant (with); to form in the mind; to think out, to imagine; to understand; to express.

concentrate *vt* to bring or converge together to one point; to direct to a single object or purpose; to collect one's thoughts or efforts; (*chem*) to increase the strength of by diminishing bulk, to condense. * *n* a concentrated product, esp a food reduced in bulk by eliminating fluid; a foodstuff relatively high in nutrients.

concentration *n* the act or process of concentrating; the direction of attention to a single object.

concern *vt* to relate or apply to; to fill with anxiety; to interest (oneself) in; to take part, to be mixed up (in). * *n* a thing that concerns one; anxiety, misgiving; interest in or regard for a person or thing; a business or firm.

concerned *adj* troubled, worried; interested.—**concernedly** *adv*.

concerning *prep* about; regarding.

concert *n* a musical entertainment; harmony; agreement or union.

concerted *adj* planned or arranged by mutual agreement; combined; (*mus*) arranged in separate parts for musicians or singers.

concertina *n* a hexagonal musical instrument, which produces sound by squeezing bellows that pass air over metal reeds. * *vi* to collapse or fold like the bellows of a concertina.

concerto *n* (*pl* **concertos**) a musical composition for a solo instrument and orchestra.

concession *n* the act of conceding; something conceded; a grant of rights, land, etc by a government, corporation, or individual; a reduction in price (of admission, travel, etc) for certain people; (*Cdn*) a tract of surveyed farmland that is subdivided into individual lots.—**concessionary** *adj*.

conciliate *vt* to win over from hostility; to make friendly; to appease; to reconcile.—**conciliation** *n*.—**conciliator** *n*.—**conciliatory** *adj*.

concise *adj* brief, condensed, terse.—**concisely** *adv*.—**conciseness** *n*.

conclave *n* a private or secret meeting; a meeting of cardinals in seclusion to choose a pope; the meeting place.

conclude *vti* to bring or come to an end, to finish; to effect, to settle; to infer; to resolve.

conclusion *n* concluding; the end or close; an inference; a final opinion; (*logic*) a proposition deduced from premises.

conclusive *adj* decisive; convincing.—**conclusively** *adv*.

concoct *vt* to make by combining ingredients; to devise, to plan; to invent (a story).

concourse *n* an open space or hall where crowds gather, eg a railway or airport terminal.

concrete *adj* having a material existence; (*gram*) denoting a thing, not a quality, not abstract; made of concrete. * *n* anything concrete; a mixture of sand, cement, etc, used in building. * *vti* to form into a mass, to solidify; to cover with concrete.

concur *vi* (*pt* **concurred**) to happen together, to coincide; to cooperate; to be of the same opinion, to agree.—**concurrence** *n*.

concurrent *adj* existing, acting or occurring at the same time; coinciding.—**concurrently** *adv*.

concussion *n* the violent shock of an impact or explosion; loss of consciousness caused by a violent blow to the head.

condemn *vt* to express strong disapproval of; to find guilty; to blame or censure; to declare unfit for use.—**condemnation** *n*.—**condemnatory** *adj*.

condense *vt* to reduce to a smaller compass, to compress; to change from a gas into a liquid; to concentrate; to express in fewer words. * *vi* to become condensed.—**condenser** *n*.—**condensation** *n*.

condensed milk *n* milk that has been reduced by evaporation and sweetened.

condescend *vi* to waive one's superiority; to deign, to stoop; to act patronizingly.—**condescension** *n*.

condiment *n* a seasoning or relish.

condition *n* anything required for the performance, completion or existence of something else; physical state of health; an abnormality, illness; a prerequisite; (*pl*) attendant circumstances. * *vt* to be essential to the happening or existence of; to stipulate; to agree upon; to make fit; to make accustomed (to).—**conditioner** *n* a person or thing that conditions; a creamy substance for bringing the hair into a glossy condition.

conditional *adj* depending on conditions; not absolute; (*gram*) expressing condition. * *n* a conditional clause or conjunction.—**conditionally** *adv*.

condolence *n* sympathy.

condone *vt* to overlook, to treat as non-existent.

conducive *adj* leading or helping to cause or produce.

conduct *vti* to lead; to convey; to direct (an orchestra); to carry on or manage (a business); to transmit (electricity, heat); to behave (oneself). * *n* management, direction; behaviour.

conductor *n* a person who conducts an orchestra; one in charge of passengers on a train, or who collects fares on a bus; a substance that conducts heat or electricity.—**conductress** *nf*.

conduit *n* a channel or pipe that carries water, etc.

cone *n* a solid figure with a circular or

elliptical base; any cone-shaped object; the scaly fruit of the pine, fir, etc.

confectionery *n* sweets.

confederation *n* the act or state of confederating; an alliance of individuals, organizations or states; (*with cap*) the political union of most British colonies in North America in 1867 to form the Dominion of Canada, subsequently expanded to include the present provinces and territories.

confer *vt* (*pt* **conferred**) to grant or bestow; to compare views or take counsel; to consult.

conference *n* a meeting for discussion or consultation.

confess *vt* to acknowledge or admit; to disclose (sins) to a confessor; (*priest*) to hear confession of. * *vi* to make or hear a confession.

confession *n* admission or acknowledgement of a fault or sin, esp to a confessor; a thing confessed; a statement of one's religious beliefs, creed.

confessional *n* an enclosure in a church where a priest hears confessions.

confessor *n* a priest who hears confessions and grants absolution; one who confesses.

confetti *npl* bits of colored paper thrown at weddings.

confide *vti* to put confidence (in); to entrust; to impart.

confidence *n* firm trust, faith; belief in one's own abilities; boldness; something revealed confidentially.

confidence trick *n* the persuading of a victim to hand over valuables as proof of confidence.

confident *adj* full of confidence; positive, assured.—**confidently** *adv*.

confidential *adj* spoken or written in confidence, secret; entrusted with secrets.—**confidentially** *adv*.—**confidentiality** *n*.

confine *vt* to restrict, to keep within limits; to keep shut up, as in prison, a sickbed, etc; to imprison. * *n* (*pl*) borderland, edge, limit.

confined *adj* narrow, enclosed.

confinement *n* a being confined; the period of childbirth.

confirm *vt* to make stronger; to establish firmly; to make valid, to ratify; to corroborate; to administer rite of confirmation to.

confirmation *n* the act of confirming; convincing proof; the rite by which people are admitted to full communion in Christian churches.

confirmed *adj* habitual; have undergone the rite of confirmation.

confiscate *vt* to appropriate to the state as a penalty; to seize by authority. —**confiscation** *n*.

conflict *n* a fight; a contest; strife, quarrel; emotional disturbance. * *vi* to be at variance; to clash (with); to struggle.

conform *vi* to comply, to be obedient (to); to act in accordance with. * *vt* to adapt; to make like.

conformist *n* one who conforms to established rules, standards, etc; compliance with the rites and doctrines of an established church.—**conformism** *n*.

confound *vt* to mix up, to obscure; to perplex, to astound; to overthrow; to mistake one thing for another.

confounded *adj* astonished; confused; annoying; (*inf*) damned.—**confoundedly** *adv*.

confront *vt* to stand in front of, face; to bring face to face (with); to encounter; to oppose.—**confrontation** *n*.

confuse *vt* to throw into disorder; to mix up; to mistake one thing for another; to perplex, to disconcert; to embarrass; to make unclear.—**confusedly** *adv*.

confusion *n* the act or state of being confused; disorder; embarrassment, discomfiture; lack of clarity.

congeal *vti* to change from a liquid to a solid by cooling, to jell.—**congealment** *n*.

congenial *adj* of a similar disposition or with similar tastes, kindred; suited, agreeable (to).—**congenially** *adv*.—**congeniality** *n*.

congenital *adj* existing or dating since birth, as in certain defects.—**congenitally** *adv*.

conger eel *n* a large marine eel.

congestion *n* an overcrowding; (*med*) an excessive accumulation of blood in any organ; an accumulation of traffic causing obstruction.

congratulate *vt* to express sympathetic pleasure at success or good fortune of, to compliment.—**congratulation** *n*.—**congratulatory** *adj*.

congratulations *npl* an expression of joy or pleasure.

congregate *vti* to flock together, to assemble; to gather into a crowd or mass.

congregation *n* a gathering, an assembly; a body of people assembled for worship.

congress *n* an association or society; an assembly or conference, esp for discussion and action on some question; (*with cap*) the legislature of the US, comprising the Senate and the House of Representatives.

Congressman *n* a member of Congress.—**Congresswoman** *nf*.

conic, conical *adj* of a cone; cone-shaped.

conifer *n* any evergreen trees and shrubs with true cones (as pines) and other (as yews).—**coniferous** *adj*.

conjecture *n* a guess, guesswork. * *vt* to make a conjecture, to guess, surmise.—**conjectural** *adj*.

conjugal *adj* of or relating to marriage.—**conjugally** *adv*.

conjunction *n* (*gram*) a word connecting words, clauses or sentences; a union; a simultaneous occurrence of events; the apparent proximity of two or more planets.

conjunctivitis *n* inflammation of the membrane (conjunctiva) that covers the eyeball and inner eyelid.

conjure *vti* to practise magical tricks; to call up (spirits) by invocation.—**conjurer, conjuror** *n*.

conk *n* (*sl*) the nose or head. * *n* a blow to the nose or head.

con man *n* (*inf*) a swindler, one who defrauds by means of a confidence trick.

connect *vti* to fasten together, to join; to relate together, to link up; (*trains, buses, etc*) timed to arrive as another leaves so that passengers can continue their journey; to establish a link by telephone.—**connector, connecter** n.

connection, connexion n the act of connecting; the state of being connected; a thing that connects; a relationship, bond; a train, bus, etc timed to connect with another; an opportunity to transfer between trains, buses, etc; context; a link between components in an electric circuit; a relative; (pl) clients, customers.

connive vi to permit tacitly; to wink (at); to plot.—**connivance** n.

connoisseur n a trained discriminating judge, esp of the fine arts.

connotation n a consequential meaning, an implication—**connotative** adj.

conquer vt to gain victory (over), to defeat; to acquire by conquest; to overcome, to master. * vi to be victor.—**conqueror** n.

conquest n conquering; the winning of a person's affection; a person or thing conquered.

Cons. abbr = Conservative.

conscience n the knowledge of right and wrong that affects action and behaviour; the sense of guilt or virtue induced by actions, behaviour, etc; an inmost thought; conscientiousness.

conscientious adj following the dictates of the conscience; scrupulous; careful, thorough.—**conscientiously** adv.—**conscientiousness** n.

conscientious objector n a person who refuses to serve in the military forces on moral or religious grounds.

conscious adj aware (of); awake to one's surroundings; (action) realized by the person who does it.—**consciously** adv.

consciousness n the state of being conscious; perception; the whole body of a person's thoughts and feelings.

conscript adj enrolled into service by compulsion; drafted. * n a conscripted person (as a military recruit). * vt to enlist compulsorily.—**conscription** n.

consecrate vt to set apart as sacred, to sanctify; to devote (to).—**consecration** n.

consecutive adj following in regular order without a break; successive; (gram) expressing consequence.—**consecutively** adv.

consensus n an opinion held by all or most; general agreement, esp in opinion.

consent vi to agree (to); to comply; to acquiesce * n agreement, permission; concurrence.

consequence n a result, an outcome; importance; (pl) a game in which each player writes part of a story without knowing what has gone before.

consequent adj occurring as a result.—**consequently** adv.

conservation n conserving; preservation of the environment and natural resources.—**conservationist** n.

conservative adj traditional; cautious; moderate. * n a conservative person; (with cap) a member of the Conservative Party in Britain and other countries.—**conservatively** adv.

conservatory n a greenhouse attached to a house; a conservatoire.

conserve vt to keep from loss or injury; to preserve (food) with sugar. * n a type of jam using whole fruit.

consider vti to reflect (upon), to contemplate; to examine, to weigh the merits of; to take into account; to regard as; to be of the opinion.

considerable adj a fairly large amount; worthy of respect.—**considerably** adv.

considerate adj careful of the feelings of others.—**considerately** adv.

consideration n the act of considering; deliberation; a point of importance; an inducement; thoughtfulness; deference.

considering prep in view of. * adv all in all. * conj seeing that.

consign vt to hand over, to commit; to send goods addressed (to).

consignment n consigning; goods, etc consigned.

consist vi to be made up (of); to be comprised (in).

consistency n degree of density, esp of thick liquids; the state of being consistent.

consistent adj compatible, not contradictory; uniform in thought or action.—**consistently** adv.

consolation n someone or something that offers comfort in distress.

console[1] vt to bring consolation to, to cheer in distress.—**consolable** adj.

console[2] n a desk containing the controls of an electronic system; the part of an organ containing the pedals, stops, etc; an ornamental bracket supporting a shelf or table.

consolidate vti to solidify; to establish firmly, to strengthen; to combine into a single whole.—**consolidation** n.

consolidated school n (Cdn) a school that replaces several existing schools in an area.

consonant n a letter of the alphabet that is not a vowel; the sound representing such a letter. * adj consistent, in keeping (with).

consortium n (pl consortia) an international banking or financial combination.

conspicuous adj easily seen, prominent; outstanding, eminent.—**conspicuousness** n.—**conspicuously** adv.

conspiracy n a secret plan for an illegal act; the act of conspiring.

conspire vti to combine secretly for an evil purpose; to plot, to devise.

constable n a policeman or policewoman of the lowest rank.

constant adj fixed; unchangeable; faithful; continual.—**constancy** n.

constellation n a group of fixed stars.

consternation n surprise and alarm; shock; dismay.

constipation n infrequent and difficult movement of the bowels.

constituency n a body of electors; the voters in a particular district.

constituent adj forming part of a whole, component; having the power to revise the constitution. * *n* a component part; a member of an elective body; a voter in a district.

constitute *vt* to set up by authority, to establish; to frame, to form; to appoint; to compose, to make up.

constitution *n* fundamental physical condition; disposition; temperament; structure, composition; the system of basic laws and principles of a government, society, etc; a document stating these specifically.

constitutional *adj* of or pertaining to a constitution; authorized or limited by a constitution, legal; inherent, natural. * *n* a walk for the sake of one's health.—**constitutionally** *adv*.—**constitutionality** *n*.

constrain *vt* to compel, to force; to hinder by force; to confine, to imprison.

constrained *adj* enforced; embarrassed, inhibited; showing constraint.

constraint *n* compulsion; forcible confinement; repression of feeling; embarrassment.

constrict *vt* to draw together, to squeeze, to compress.

construct *vt* to make, to build, to fit together; to compose. * *n* a structure; an interpretation; an arrangement, esp of words in a sentence.—**constructible** *adj*.—**constructor, constructer** *n*.

construction *n* constructing; anything constructed; a structure, building; interpretation, meaning; (*gram*) two or more words grouped together to form a phrase, clause or sentence.—**constructional** *adj*.

construction holiday *n* (*Cdn*) in Quebec, a compulsory holiday for all construction workers during the last two weeks of July, often taken by other workers.

constructive *adj* helping to improve, promoting development.—**constructively** *adv*.

construe *vti* to translate word for word; to analyse grammatically; to take in a particular sense, to interpret.

consul *n* a person appointed to live in a foreign city to attend to the interests of his country's citizens and business there.—**consular** *adj*.

consulate *n* the official residence of a consul; the office of a Roman consul.

consult *vti* to seek advice from, esp a doctor or lawyer; to deliberate, to confer.

consultant *n* a specialist who gives professional or technical advice; a senior physician or surgeon in a hospital; a person who consults another.—**consultancy** *n*.

consultation *n* the act of consulting; a conference, esp with a doctor or lawyer.—**consultative** *adj*.

consume *vti* to destroy; to use up; to eat or drink up; to waste away; to utilize economic goods.—**consumable** *adj*.

consumer *n* a person who uses goods and services, the end user.

consummate[1] *vt* to bring to perfection, to be the crown of; (*marriage*) to complete by sexual intercourse.—**consummation** *n*.

consummate[2] *adj* complete, perfect.

consumption *n* the act of consuming; the state of being consumed or used up; (*econ*) expenditure on goods and services by consumers; tuberculosis.

contact *n* touch, touching; connection; an acquaintance, esp in business; a connection allowing the passage of electricity; (*med*) a person who has been in contact with a contagious disease.* *vti* to establish contact with.

contact lens *n* a thin correctional lens placed over the cornea of the eye.

contagious *adj* (*disease*) spread by contact; capable of spreading disease by contact; (*influence*) catching, infectious.

contain *vt* to hold, to enclose; to comprise, to include; to hold back or restrain within fixed limits.

container *n* a receptacle, etc designed to contain goods or substances; a standardized receptacle used to transport commodities.

contaminate *vt* to render impure, to pollute.—**contaminant** *n*.—**contamination** *n*.—**contaminator** *n*.

contemplate *vti* to look at steadily; to reflect upon, to meditate; to have in view, to intend.—**contemplation** *n*.

contemporary *adj* living or happening at the same time; of about the same age; present day. * *n* a person living at the same time; a person of the same age.

contempt *n* the feeling one has toward someone or something considered low, worthless etc; the condition of being despised.

contemptible *adj* deserving contempt.—**contemptibly** *adv*.—**contemptibility** *n*.

contemptuous *adj* showing or feeling contempt; disdainful.—**contemptuously** *adv*.—**contemptuousness** *n*.

contend *vti* to take part in a contest, to strive (for); to quarrel; to maintain (that), to assert.—**contender** *n*.

content[1] *n* (*usu pl*) what is in a container; (*usu pl*) what is in a book; substance or meaning.

content[2] *adj* satisfied (with), not desiring more; willing (to); happy; pleased. * *n* satisfaction. * *vt* to make content; to satisfy.—**contentment** *n*.

contention *n* contending, struggling, arguing; a point in dispute; an assertion in an argument.

contest *vti* to call in question, to dispute; to fight to gain, to compete for; to strive. * *n* a struggle, an encounter; a competition; a debate; a dispute.

contestant *n* a competitor in a contest; a person who contests.

context *n* the parts of a written work or speech that precede and follow a word or passage, contributing to its full meaning; associated surroundings, setting.—**contextual** *adj*.

continent[1] *n* one of the six or seven main divisions of the earth's land; (*with cap*) the mainland of Europe, excluding the British Isles; a large extent of land.

continent[2] *adj* able to control urination and defecation; practising self-restraint; chaste.—

continence n.

continental adj of a continent; (with cap) of or relating to Europe, excluding the British Isles; of or relating to the former 13 British colonies later forming the USA. * n an inhabitant of the Continent.

contingency n a possibility of a future event or condition; something dependent on a future event.

contingent adj possible, that may happen; chance; dependent (on); incidental (to). * n a possibility; a quota of troops.—contingently adv.

continual adj frequently repeated, going on all the time.—continually adv.

continuation n a continuing; prolongation; resumption; a thing that continues something else, a sequel, a further instalment.

continue vt to go on (with); to prolong; to extend; to resume, to carry further. * vi to remain, to stay; to last; to preserve.

continuity n continuousness; uninterrupted succession; a script or scenario in a film or broadcast.

continuous adj continuing; occurring without interruption.—continuously adv.—continuousness n.

contort vti to twist out of a normal shape, to pull awry.—contortion n.

contortionist n a person who can twist his or her body into unusual postures.

contour n the outline of a figure, land, etc; the line representing this outline; a contour line.

contour line n a line on a map that passes through all points at the same altitude.

contra- prefix against.

contraband n smuggled goods; smuggling. * adj illegal to import or export.

contraception n the deliberate prevention of conception, birth control.

contraceptive n a contraceptive drug or device.—also adj.

contract vt to draw closer together; to confine; to undertake by contract; (debt) to incur; (disease) to become infected by; (word) to shorten by omitting letters. * vi to shrink; to become smaller or narrower; to make a contract. * n a bargain; an agreement to supply goods or perform work at a stated price; a written agreement enforceable by law.

contraction n the act of contracting; the state of being contracted; a contracted word; a labour pain in childbirth.

contractor n a person who makes a business contract, esp a builder.

contractual adj of a contract.—contractually adv.

contradict vti to assert the contrary or opposite of; to deny; to be at variance (with).

contradiction n the act of contradicting; a denial.—contradictory adj.

contralto n (pl contraltos) a singing voice having a range between tenor and mezzo-soprano; a person having this voice.

contraption n (inf) a device, a gadget.

contrary adj opposed; opposite in nature; wayward, perverse. * n the opposite. * adv in opposition to; in conflict with.—contrarily adv.—contrariness n.

contrast vi to show marked differences. * vt to compare so as to point out the differences. * n the exhibition of differences; difference of qualities shown by comparison; the degree of difference between colors or tones.

contravene vt to infringe (a law), to transgress; to conflict with, to contradict.—contravention n.

contribute vti to give to a common stock or fund; to write (an article) for a magazine, etc; to furnish ideas, etc.—contributory adj.

contribution n the act of contributing; something contributed; a literary article; a payment into a collection.

contributor n a person who contributes, esp the writer of a newspaper article, etc; a contributing factor.

contrite adj deeply repentant, feeling guilt.—contritely adv.—contrition n.

contrivance n something contrived, esp a mechanical device, invention; inventive ability; an artificial construct; a stratagem.

contrive vt to plan ingeniously; to devise, to design, to manage; to achieve, esp by some ploy; to scheme.—contriver n.

control n restraint; command, authority; a check; a means of controlling; a standard of comparison for checking an experiment. * vt (pt controlled) to check; to restrain; to regulate; to govern; (experiment) to verify by comparison.

controversial adj causing controversy, open to argument.

controversy n a discussion of contrary opinions; dispute, argument.

convalesce vi to recover health and strength after an illness; to get better. —convalescence n.

convalescent adj recovering health; aiding the recovery of full health. * n a patient recovering after an illness.

convector n a heater that circulates warm air.

convene vti to call together for a meeting.—convener n.

convenience n what suits one; a useful appliance; a public lavatory.

convenience store n a small store open for extended hours that sells packaged, canned, or bottled foods and drinks as well as common household items.

convenient adj handy; suitable; causing little or no trouble.—conveniently adv.

convent n a house of a religious order, esp an establishment of nuns.

convention n a political or ecclesiastical meeting; an agreement between nations, a treaty; established usage, social custom.

conventional adj of or based on convention or social custom; not spontaneous; following accepted rules; (weapons) non-nuclear.—conventionality n —conventionally adj.

converge vti to come or bring together.—convergence n.—convergent adj.

conversant *adj* well acquainted; proficient; familiar (with).

conversation *n* informal talk or exchange of ideas, opinions, etc between people.—**conversational** *adj.*—**conversationally** *adv.*

converse¹ *vi* to engage in conversation (with). * *n* familiar talk, conversation.

converse² *adj* opposite, contrary. * *n* something that is opposite or contrary.—**conversely** *adv.*

conversion *n* change from one state, or from on religion, to another; something converted from one use to another; an alteration to a building undergoing a change in function; (*rugby*) a score after a try by kicking the ball over the crossbar.

convert *vt* to change from one thing, condition or religion to another; to alter; to apply to a different use; (*rugby*) to make a conversion after a try. * *n* a converted person, esp one who has changed religion.—**convertibility** *n.*

convertible *adj* able to be converted. * *n* a car with a folding or detachable roof.

convex *adj* curving outward like the surface of a sphere.—**convexly** *adv.*—**convexity** *n.*

convey *vt* to transport; to conduct; to transmit; to make known, to communicate; (*law*) to make over (property). —**conveyable** *adj.*—**conveyor** *n.*

conveyor belt *n* a continuous moving belt or linked plates for moving objects in a factory.

convict *vt* to prove or pronounce guilty. * *n* a convicted person serving a prison sentence.

conviction *n* act of convicting; a settled opinion; a firm belief.

convince *vt* to persuade by argument or evidence; to satisfy by proof.

convincing *adj* compelling belief.—**convincingly** *adv.*

convivial *adj* sociable, jovial.—**conviviality** *n.*—**convivially** *adv.*

convulse *vt* to agitate violently; to shake with irregular spasms. * *vi* (*inf*) to cause to shake with uncontrollable laughter.—**convulsive** *adj.*—**convulsively** *adv.*

convulsion *n* a violent involuntary contraction of a muscle or muscles; an agitation, tumult; (*pl*) a violent fit of laughter.

cook *vt* to prepare (food) by heat; (*inf*) to fake (accounts, etc); to subject to great heat. * *vi* to be a cook; to under go cooking. * *n* a person who cooks; one whose job is to cook.

cookbook, cookery book *n* a book of recipes and other information for preparing food.

cooker *n* an electric or gas appliance for cooking.

cookery *n* the art or practice of cooking.

cookie *n* a biscuit.

cool *adj* moderately cold; calm; indifferent. * *vti* to make or become cool. * *n* coolness; composure.—**cooler** *n.*—**coolly** *adv.*—**coolness** *n.*

coop¹ *n* a small pen for poultry. * *vt* to confine as in a coop.

coop², co-op *n* a cooperative society or shop run by a cooperative society.

cooperate, co-operate *vi* to work together, to act jointly.—**cooperation, co-operation** *n.*—**cooperator, co-operator** *n.*

cooperative, co-operative *adj* willing to cooperate; helpful. * *n* an organization or enterprise owned by, and operated for the benefit of, those using its services.—**cooperatively, co-operatively** *adv.*

coordinate, co-ordinate *vt* to integrate (different elements, etc) into an efficient relationship; to adjust to; to function harmoniously. * *n* an equal person or thing; any of a series of numbers that, in a given frame of reference, locate a point in space; (*pl*) separate items of clothing intended to be worn together. * *adj* equal in degree or status.—**coordinately, co-ordinately** *adv.*

coordination, co-ordination *n* the act of coordinating; the state of being coordinated; balanced and harmonious movement of the body.

coot *n* a European water-bird with dark plumage, similar to a duck.

cop *vb* (*pt* **copped**) *vt* (*sl*) to arrest, catch. * *vi* (*with* **out**) (*sl*) to fail to perform, to renege. * *n* (*sl*) capture; a policeman.

cope *vi* to deal successfully with; to contend on even terms (with).

copilot *n* a second pilot in an aircraft.

copious *adj* plentiful, abundant.—**copiously** *adv.*

copper¹ *n* a reddish ductile metallic element; a bronze coin. * *adj* made of, or of the color of, copper.

copper² *n* (*sl*) a police officer.

copulate *vi* to have sexual intercourse.—**copulation** *n.*—**copulative** *adj.*

copy *n* a reproduction; a transcript; a single specimen of a book; a model to be copied; a manuscript for printing; text for an advertisement; subject matter for a writer. * *vt* to make a copy of, to reproduce; to take as a model, to imitate.

copyright *n* the exclusive legal right to the publication and sale of a literary, dramatic, musical, or artistic work in any form. * *adj* protected by copyright.

copywriter *n* a writer of advertising or publicity copy.—**copywriting** *n.*

coral *n* the hard skeleton secreted by certain marine polyps. * *adj* made of or like coral.

cord *n* a thick string or thin rope; something that binds; a slender electric cable; a ribbed fabric, esp corduroy; (*pl*) corduroy trousers.

cordial *adj* hearty, warm; friendly; affectionate. * *n* a fruit-flavored drink.—**cordiality** *n.*—**cordially** *adv.*

cordon *n* a chain of police or soldiers preventing access to an area; a piece of ornamental cord or ribbon given as an award. * *vt* (*with* **off**) (*area*) to prevent access to.

corduroy *n* a strong cotton fabric with a velvety ribbed surface; (*pl*) trousers of this.

core *n* the innermost part, the heart; the inner part of an apple, etc containing seeds; the region of a nuclear reactor containing the fissile material; (*comput*) a form of magnetic memory used to store one bit of information. * *vt* to remove the core from.

cork *n* the outer bark of the cork oak used esp for stoppers and insulation; a stopper for a bottle, esp made of cork. * *adj* made of cork. * *vt* to stop up with a cork; to give a taste of cork to (wine).

corkage *n* a charge made by a restaurant for serving wine, esp when brought in by the customer from outside.

corkscrew *n* a tool for drawing corks from wine bottles. * *adj* resembling a corkscrew.

cormorant *n* a large voracious sea bird with dark plumage and webbed feet.

corn[1] *n* a grain or seed of a cereal plant; plants that yield grain; maize; (*sl*) something corny.

corn[2] *n* a small hard painful growth on the foot.

corn cob *n* the central part of an ear of maize to which the corn kernels are attached.

cornea *n* the transparent membrane in front of the eyeball.—**corneal** *adj*.

corner *n* the point where sides or streets meet; an angle; a secret or confined place; a difficult or dangerous situation; (*football, hockey*) a free kick from the corner of the pitch; a monopoly over the supply of a good or service giving control over the market price; one of the opposite angles in a boxing ring. * *vt* to force into a corner; to monopolize supplies of (a commodity). * *vi* to turn round a corner; to meet at a corner or angle.

cornerstone *n* the principal stone, esp one at the corner of a foundation; an indispensable part.

cornet *n* a tapering valved brass musical instrument; a cone-shaped wafer for ice cream.

cornflour *n* a type of maize flour used for thickening sauces.

cornice *n* a plaster moulding round a ceiling or on the outside of a building.

corny *adj* (**cornier, corniest**) (*inf*) hackneyed; banal; trite; overly sentimental.—**cornily** *adv*.—**corniness** *n*.

corollary *n* an additional inference from a proposition already proved; a result.

coronary *adj* pertaining to the arteries supplying blood to the heart. * *n* a coronary artery.

coronation *n* the act or ceremony of crowning a sovereign.

coroner *n* a public official who inquires into the causes of sudden or accidental deaths.

coronet *n* a small crown; an ornamental headdress.

corporal[1] *n* a non-commissioned officer below the rank of sergeant.

corporal[2] *adj* of or relating to the body; physical, not spiritual.—**corporally** *adv*.

corporal punishment *n* physical punishment, such as beating.

corporate *adj* legally united into a body; of or having a corporation; united.—**corporately** *adv*.

corporation *n* a group of people authorized by law to act as one individual; a city council.

corps *n* (*pl* **corps**) an organized subdivision of the military establishment; a group or organization with a special function (*medical corps*).

corpse *n* a dead body.

corpuscle *n* a red or white blood cell.—*also* **corpuscule.**—**corpuscular** *adj*.

corral *n* a pen for livestock; an enclosure with wagons; a strong stockade. * *vt* (*pt* **corralled**) to form a corral; to put or keep in a corral.

correct *vt* to set right, to remove errors from; to reprove, to punish; to counteract, to neutralize. * *adj* free from error; right, true, accurate; conforming to a fixed standard; proper.—**correctly** *adv*.—**correctness** *n*.

correction *n* the act of correcting; punishment.—**correctional** *adj*.

correlate *vti* to have or to bring into mutual relation; to correspond to one another.—**correlation** *n*.—**correlative** *adj*.

correspond *vi* to answer, to agree; to be similar (to); to communicate by letter.

correspondence *n* communication by writing letters; the letters themselves; agreement.

correspondent *n* a person who writes letters; a journalist who gathers news for newspapers, radio or television from a foreign country. * *adj* similar, analogous.

corridor *n* a long passage into which compartments or rooms open.

corroborate *vt* to confirm; to make more certain; to verify.—**corroboration** *n*.—**corroborative** *adj*.—**corroborator** *n*.

corrode *vti* to eat into or wear away gradually, to rust; to disintegrate.—**corrosion** *n*.

corrugated iron *n* sheet iron pressed in alternate parallel ridges and grooves and galvanized.

corrupt *adj* dishonest; taking bribes; depraved; rotten, putrid. * *vti* to make or become corrupt; to infect; to taint.—**corruptly** *adv*.—**corruptness** *n*.

corset *n* a close-fitting undergarment, worn to support the torso.

cortege, cortège *n* a train of attendants; a retinue; a funeral procession.

cosmetic *n* a preparation for improving the beauty, esp of the face. * *adj* beautifying or correcting faults in the appearance.—**cosmetically** *adv*.

cosmetic bag *n* a small, zippered, waterproof bag for holding cosmetics and related items.

cosmonaut *n* a Russian astronaut.

cosmopolitan *adj* of all parts of the world; free from national prejudice; at home in any part of the world.—**cosmopolitanism** *n*.

cosmos *n* the universe as an ordered whole; any orderly system.

cosset *vt* (*pt* **cosseted**) to make a pet of; to pamper.

cost *vt* (*pt* **cost**) to involve the payment, loss, or sacrifice of; to have as a price; (*pt* **costed**) to fix the price of. * *n* a price; expenditure of time, labour, etc; (*pl*) the expenses of a lawsuit.

costly *adj* (**costlier, costliest**) expensive; involving great sacrifice.—**costliness** *n*.

costume *n* a style of dress, esp belonging to a particular period, fashion, etc; clothes of an unusual or historical nature, as worn by actors in a play, etc.

costume jewellery *n* imitation gems or cheap jewellery worn for decorative effect.

cosy, cozy (*US*) *adj* (**cosier, cosiest**) warm and comfortable; snug.

cot *n* a child's box-like bed; a narrow collapsible bed.

cottage *n* a small house, esp in the country.

cottage cheese *n* a soft cheese made from loose milk curds.

cotton *n* soft white fibre of the cotton plant; fabric or thread made of this; thread. * *adj* made of cotton.

cotton batting, cotton batten *n* (*Cdn*) a form of cotton wool used in first aid and for crafts.

cotton wool *n* raw cotton that has been bleached and sterilized for use as a dressing, etc; a state of being protected.

couch *n* a piece of furniture, with a back and armrests, for seating several persons; a bed, esp as used by psychiatrists for patients. * *vt* to express in words in a particular way.

cough *vi* to expel air from the lungs with a sudden effort and noise. * *n* the act of coughing; a disease causing a cough.

could *see* **can¹**.

council *n* an elected or appointed legislative or advisory body; a central body uniting a group of organizations; an executive body whose members are equal in power and authority.

councillor, councilor (*US*) *n* a member of a council.

counsel *n* advice; consultation, deliberate purpose or design; a person who gives counsel, a lawyer or a group of lawyers; a consultant. * *vb* (*pt* **counselled**) *vt* to advise; to recommend. * *vi* to give or take advice.

counsellor, counselor (*US*) *n* an adviser; a lawyer.

count¹ *n* a European noble.

count² *vt* to number, add up; to reckon; to consider to be; to call aloud (beats or time units); to include or exclude by counting. * *vi* to name numbers or add up items in order; to mark time; to be of importance; to rely (upon). * *n* act of numbering or reckoning; the total counted; a separate and distinct charge in an indictment; rhythm.

countdown *n* the descending count backwards to zero, eg to the moment a rocket lifts off.

countenance *n* the whole form of the face; appearance; support. * *vt* to favor, give approval to.

counter¹ *n* one who or that which counts; a disc used for scoring, a token; a table in a bank or shop across which money or goods are passed.

counter² *adv* contrary; adverse; in an opposite direction; in the wrong way. * *adj* opposed; opposite. * *n* a return blow or parry; an answering move. * *vti* to oppose; to retort; to give a return blow; to retaliate.

counteract *vt* to act in opposition to so as to defeat or hinder; to neutralize.—**counteraction** *n*.—**counteractive** *adj*.

counterattack *n* an attack in response to an attack. * *vt* to make a counterattack.

counterbalance *n* a weight balancing another. * *vt* to act as a counterbalance; to act against with equal power.

counterespionage *n* spying on or exposing enemy spies.

counterfeit *vt* to imitate; to forge; to feign, simulate. * *adj* made in imitation, forged; feigned, sham. * *n* an imitation, a forgery.

counterfoil *n* a detachable section of a cheque or ticket, kept as a receipt or record.

counterpart *n* a thing exactly like another, a duplicate; a corresponding or complementary part or thing.

countess *n* a woman with the rank of count or earl; the wife or widow of an earl or count.

countless *adj* innumerable.

country *n* a region or district; the territory of a nation; a state; the land of one's birth or residence; rural parts; country-and-western. * *adj* rural.

countryman *n* a person who lives in the country; a person from the same country as another.—**countrywoman** *nf*.

countryside *n* a rural district.

county *n* an administrative subdivision for local government.—*also adj.*

coup *n* a sudden telling blow; a masterstroke; a coup d'état.

coup d'état *n* a sudden and unexpected bold stroke of policy; the sudden overthrow of a government.

coupé *n* a closed, four-seater, two-door car with a sloping back.

couple *n* two of the same kind connected together; a pair; a husband and wife; a pair of equal and parallel forces. * *vt* to link or join together. * *vi* to copulate.

couplet *n* two consecutive lines of verse that rhyme with each other.

coupling *n* a device for joining parts of a machine or two railway carriages.

coupon *n* a detachable certificate on a bond, presented for payment of interest; a certificate entitling one to a discount, gift, etc; an entry form, as for a competition.

courage *n* bravery; fortitude; spirit.—**courageous** *adj*.—**courageously** *adv*.—**courageousness** *n*.

coureur de bois (*pl* **coureurs de bois**) *n* (*Cdn*) (*hist*) a French or Metis fur trader.

courier *n* a messenger; a tourist guide; a carrier of illegal goods between countries.

course *n* a race; a path or track; a career; a direction or line of motion; a regular sequence; the portion of a meal served at one time; conduct; behaviour; the direction a ship is steered; a continuous level range of brick or masonry of the same height; the chase of a hare by greyhounds; a series of studies; any of the studies. * *vt* to hunt. * *vi* to move swiftly along an indicated path; to chase with greyhounds.

court *n* an uncovered space surrounded by buildings or walls; a short street; a playing space, as for tennis, etc; a royal palace; the retinue of a sovereign; (*law*) a hall of justice; the judges, etc engaged there; address; civility; flattery. * *vt* to seek the friendship of; to woo; to flatter; to solicit. * *vi* to carry on a courtship.

courteous *adj* polite; obliging.—**courteously** *adv.*—**courteousness** *n.*

courtesan, courtezan *n* (*formerly*) a prostitute, or mistress of a courtier.

courtesy *n* politeness and kindness; civility; a courteous manner or action.

courthouse *n* a public building that houses law courts or local authority offices.

courtier *n* one in attendance at a royal court.

court martial *n* (*pl* **courts martial**) a court of justice composed of naval or military officers for the trial of disciplinary offences.

court-martial *vt* (*pt* **court-martialled**) to try by court martial.

cousin *n* the son or daughter of an uncle or aunt.

cove *n* a small sheltered bay or inlet in a body of water; a curved moulding at the juncture of a wall and ceiling (—*also* **coving**).

covenant *n* a written agreement; a solemn agreement of fellowship and faith between members of a church. * *vt* to promise by a covenant. * *vt* to enter into a formal agreement.—**covenanted** *adj.*

cover *vt* to overspread the top of anything with something else; to hide; to save from punishment; to shelter; to clothe; to understudy; to insure against damage, loss, etc; to report for a newspaper; (*male animal*) to copulate. * *vi* to spread over, as a liquid does; to provide an excuse (for). * *n* that which is laid on something else; a shelter; a covert; an understudy; something used to hide one's real actions, etc; insurance against loss or damage; a place laid at a table for a meal.

coverage *n* the amount, extent, etc covered by something; the amount of reporting of an event for newspaper, television, etc.

cover charge *n* a charge made by a restaurant over and above the cost of the food and service.

covet *vt* (*pt* **coveted**) to desire earnestly; to lust after; to long to possess (what belongs to another).—**covetous** *adj.*—**covetousness** *n.*

coving *see* cove.

cow[1] *n* the mature female of domestic cattle; the mature female of various other animals, as the whale, elephant, etc; (*sl*) a disagreeable woman.

cow[2] *vt* to take the spirit out of, to intimidate.

coward *n* a person lacking courage; one who is afraid.

cowardice *n* lack of courage.

cowardly *adj* of, or like, a coward.—**cowardliness** *n.*

cowboy *n* a person who tends cattle or horses.—*also* **cowhand.**

cower *vi* to crouch or sink down through fear, etc; to tremble.

coxswain *n* a person who steers a boat, esp in a race.

coy *adj* playfully demure; bashful.—**coyly** *adv.*—

coyness *n.*

cozy *see* cosy.

CP *abbr* = Canadian Pacific; Canadian Press.

CPP *abbr* = Canada Pension Plan.

CPS *abbr* = Canadian Parks Service.

crab *n* any of numerous chiefly marine broadly built crustaceans. * *vi* (*pt* **crabbed**) to fish for crabs; to complain.

crack *vt* to burst, break or sever; to utter a sharp, abrupt cry; to injure; to damage mentally; to open a bottle; (*sl*) to make (a joke); (*inf*) to break open (a safe); to decipher (a code). * *vi* to make a sharp explosive sound; (*inf*) to lose control under pressure; to shift erratically in vocal tone. * *n* a chink or fissure; a narrow fracture; a sharp sound; a sharp resonant blow; an altered tone of voice; a chat, gossip; a wisecrack.

cracker *n* a firework that explodes with a crack; a paper tube that when pulled explodes harmlessly and releases a paper hat, etc; a thin, crisp biscuit.

crackle *vi* to make a slight, sharp explosive noise. * *vt* to cover with a delicate network of minute cracks. * *n* a noise of frequent and slight cracks and reports; a surface glaze on glass or porcelain.—**crackly** *adj.*

crackling *n* the browned crisp rind of roast pork.

cradle *n* a baby's crib or a small bed, often on rockers; infancy; birthplace or origin; a case for a broken limb; a framework of timbers, esp for supporting a boat. * *vt* to rock or place in a cradle; to nurse or train in infancy.

craft *n* manual skill; a skilled trade; the members of a skilled trade; cunning; (*pl* **craft**) a boat, ship, or aircraft.

craftsman *n* a person skilled in a particular craft.—**craftsmanship** *n.*

crag *n* a rough steep rock or cliff.—**craggy** *adj* (**craggier, craggiest**).—**cragginess** *n.*

cram *vt* (*pt* **crammed**) to pack tightly, to stuff; to fill to overflowing; (*inf*) to prepare quickly for an examination. * *vi* to eat greedily.

cramp *n* a spasmodic muscular contraction of the limbs; (*pl*) abdominal spasms and pain; a clamp. * *vt* to affect with muscular spasms; to confine narrowly; to hamper; to secure with a cramp. * *vi* to suffer from cramps.

cramped *adj* restricted, narrow; (*handwriting*) small and irregular.

crampon, crampoon *n* a metal frame with spikes attached to boots for walking or climbing on ice.

cranberry *n* a small red sour berry; the shrub it grows on.

crane *n* a large wading bird with very long legs and neck, and a long straight bill; a machine for raising, shifting, and lowering heavy weights. * *vti* to stretch out (the neck).

cranium *n* (*pl* **craniums, crania**) the skull, esp the part enclosing the brain.—**cranial** *adj.*

crank *n* a right-angled arm attached to a shaft

for turning it; (*inf*) an eccentric person. * *vt* to provide with a crank; to turn or wind.

cranny *n* a fissure, crack, crevice.

crash *n* a loud, sudden confused noise; a violent fall or impact; a sudden failure, as of a business or a computer; a collapse, as of the financial market. * *adj* done with great speed, suddenness or effort. * *vti* to clash together with violence; to make a loud clattering noise; (*aircraft*) to land with a crash; to collapse, to ruin; (*inf*) to intrude into (a party).

crash helmet *n* a cushioned helmet worn by airmen, motorcyclists, etc for protection.

crash-land *vti* (*aircraft*) to make an emergency landing without lowering the undercarriage, or to be landed in this way.—**crash-landing** *n*.

crate *n* an open box of wooden slats, for shipping; (*sl*) an old car or aircraft. * *vt* to pack in a crate.

crater *n* the mouth of a volcano; a cavity caused by the explosion of a bomb, shell, etc; an ancient Greek goblet.

cravat *n* a neckcloth.

crave *vt* to have a strong desire (for); to ask humbly, to beg.—**craving** *n*.

crawl *vi* to move along the ground on hands and knees; to move slowly and with difficulty; to creep; (*inf*) to seek favor by servile behaviour; to swarm (with). * *n* the act of crawling; a slow motion; a racing stroke in swimming.—**crawler** *n*.

crayfish *n* any of numerous freshwater crustaceans; the spiny lobster.

crayon *n* a stick or pencil of colored chalk; a drawing done with crayons. * *vt* to draw with a crayon.

craze *n* a passing infatuation; excessive enthusiasm; a crack in pottery glaze. * *vt* to produce cracks; to render insane.

crazy *adj* (**crazier, craziest**) (*inf*) mad, insane; foolish; ridiculous; unsound; (*paving*) composed of irregular pieces.—**crazily** *adv*.—**craziness** *n*.

creak *vi* to make a shrill grating sound. * *n* such a sound.—**creaky** *adj*.

cream *n* the rich, fatty part of milk; the choicest part of anything; a yellowish white color; a type of face or skin preparation. * *vt* to add or apply cream to; to beat into a soft, smooth consistency; to skim cream from; to remove the best part of. * *vi* to form cream or scum; to break into a creamy froth.—**creamy** *adj*.—**creaminess** *n*.

cream cheese *n* soft cheese made from soured milk or cream.

crease *n* a line made by folding; a marked area in front of the goal in ice hockey or lacrosse. * *vti* to make or form creases; to become creased.

create *vt* to cause to come into existence; to form out of nothing. * *vi* to make something new, to originate; (*sl*) to make a fuss.

creation *n* the act of creating; the thing created; the whole world or universe; a production of the human mind.

creative *adj* of creation; having the power to create; imaginative, original, constructive.—**creatively** *adv*.—**creativeness** *n*.—**creativity** *n*.

creator *n* one who creates, esp God.

creature *n* a living being; a created thing; one dependent on the influence of another.

crèche *n* a day nursery for very young children.

credence *n* belief or trust, esp in the reports or testimony of another.

credentials *npl* documents proving the identity, honesty or authority of a person.

credible *adj* believable; trustworthy.—**credibility** *n*.—**credibly** *adv*.

credit *n* belief; trust; honor; good reputation; trust in a person's ability to pay; time allowed for payment; a sum at a person's disposal in a bank; the entry in an account of a sum received; the side of the account on which this is entered; (*educ*) a distinction awarded for good marks in an examination; (*pl*) a list of those responsible for a film, television programme, etc. * *vt* to believe; to trust; to have confidence in; to attribute to; to enter on the credit side of an account.

creditable *adj* worthy of praise.—**creditably** *adv*.

credit card *n* a card issued by a bank, department store, etc authorizing the purchase of goods and services on credit.

creditor *n* a person to whom money is owed.

Cree *n* a member of a First Nations people living in Canada east of the Rocky Mountains; the Algonquian language of this people. * *adj* of or pertaining to this people or their language.

creed *n* a system of religious belief or faith; a summary of Christian doctrine; any set of principles or beliefs.

creek *n* a natural stream of water smaller than a river.

creep *vi* (*pt* **crept**) to move slowly along the ground, as a worm or reptile; (*plant*) to grow along the ground or up a wall; to move stealthily or slowly; to fawn; to cringe; (*flesh*) to feel as if things were creeping over it. * *n* (*inf*) a dislikable or servile person; (*pl: inf*) shrinking horror.

creeper *n* a creeping or climbing plant.

creepy *adj* (**creepier, creepiest**) making one's flesh crawl; causing fear or disgust.—**creepily** *adv*.—**creepiness** *n*.

cremate *vt* to burn (a corpse) to ashes.—**cremation** *n*.

crematorium *n* (*pl* **crematoriums, crematoria**) a place where bodies are cremated.

creosote *n* an oily substance derived from tar used as a wood preservative. * *vt* to treat with creosote.

crepe, crêpe *n* a thin, crinkled cloth of silk, rayon, wool, etc; thin paper like crepe; a thin pancake.

crept *see* **creep**.

crescendo *adv* (*mus*) gradually increasing in loudness or intensity; moving to a climax. * *n* (*pl* **crescendos**) a crescendo passage or effect.

crescent *n* the figure of the moon in its first or last quarter; a narrow, tapering curve; a curving street. * *adj* crescent-shaped, increasing.

cress *n* any of various plants with pungent leaves, used in salads.

crest *n* a plume of feathers on the head of a bird; the ridge of a wave; the summit of a hill; a distinctive device above the shield on a coat of arms. * *vti* to mount to the top of; to take the form of a crest; to provide or adorn with a crest, to crown.

crestfallen *adj* dejected.

cretons *npl* (*Cdn*) in Quebec, a spread of shredded pork and onions cooked in pork fat and served cold.

crevasse *n* a deep cleft in a glacier; a deep crack.

crevice *n* a crack, a fissure.

crew *n* the people operating a ship or aircraft; a group of people working together. * *vi* to act as a member of the crew of a ship, etc.

crib *n* a rack for fodder, a manger; a child's cot with high sides; a model of the manger scene representing the birth of Jesus; (*inf*) something copied from someone else; (*inf*) a literal translation of foreign texts used (usu illicitly) by students in examinations, etc. * *vti* (*pt* **cribbed**) (*inf*) to copy illegally, plagiarize.

crick *n* a painful stiffness of the muscles of the neck. * *vt* to produce a crick in.

cricket[1] *n* a leaping grasshopper-like insect.

cricket[2] *n* a game played with wickets, bats, and a ball, by eleven players on each side.—**cricketer** *n*.

crime *n* a violation of the law; an offence against morality or the public welfare; wrong-doing; (*inf*) a shame, disappointment.

criminal *adj* of the nature of, or guilty of, a crime. * *n* a person who has committed a crime.

Criminal Code *n* a Canadian federal statute containing most laws concerning crimes and the legal procedures dealing with them.

crimson *n* a deep-red color inclining to purple. * *adj* crimson-colored. * *vti* to dye with crimson; to blush.

cringe *vi* to shrink in fear or embarrassment; to cower; to behave with servility; to fawn.

crinkle *vt* to wrinkle; to corrugate; to crimp. * *vi* to curl; to be corrugated or crimped. * *n* a wrinkle.—**crinkly** *adj*.

cripple *vt* to deprive of the use of a limb; to disable. * *n* a lame or otherwise disabled person. * *adj* lame.

crisis *n* (*pl* **crises**) a turning point; a critical point in a disease; an emergency; a time of serious difficulties or danger.

crisp *adj* dry and brittle; bracing; brisk; sharp and incisive; decided. * *n* a potato snack; in US, a potato chip. * *vt* to make crisp.

criterion *n* (*pl* **criteria**) a standard, law or rule by which a correct judgment can be made.

critic *n* a person skilled in judging the merits of literary or artistic works; one who passes

judgment; a fault-finder; (*Cdn*) a member of an opposition party in a legislature who is responsible for review and criticism of a specific government ministry.

critical *adj* skilled in criticism; censorious; relating to the turning point of a disease; crucial.—**critically** *adv*.

criticism *n* a being critical; a critical comment; a review or analysis of a book, play, work of art, etc, by a critic.

criticize *vt* to pass judgment on; to find fault with; to examine critically.

croak *n* a deep hoarse discordant cry. * *vti* to utter a croak; (*inf*) to die, to kill.

crochet *n* a kind of knitting done with a hooked needle. * *vti* to do this; to make crochet articles.

crockery *n* china dishes, earthenware vessels, etc.

crocodile *n* large amphibious reptile, similar to an alligator; its skin, used to make handbags, shoes, etc; a line of schoolchildren walking in pairs.

crocus *n* a bulbous plant with yellow, purple, or white flowers.

croft *n* a small plot of land with a rented farmhouse, esp in Scotland.—**crofter** *n*.

crokinole *n* (*Cdn*) a game in which wooden discs are flicked toward a central hole in a circular board.

crook *n* a shepherd's hooked staff; a bend, a curve; a swindler, a dishonest person. * *vti* to bend or to be bent into the shape of a hook.

crooked *adj* bent, twisted; dishonest. —**crookedly** *adv*.—**crookedness** *n*.

crop *n* a year's or a season's produce of any cultivated plant; harvest; a pouch in a bird's gullet; a hunting whip; hair cut close or short. * *vti* (*pt* **cropped**) to clip short; to bite off or eat down (grass); (*land*) to yield; to sow, to plant; (*geol*) to come to the surface; to appear unexpectedly; to sprout.

croquet *n* a game played with mallets, balls and hoops.

croquette *n* a ball of minced meat, fish or potato seasoned and fried brown.

cross *n* a figure formed by two intersecting lines; a wooden structure, consisting of two beams placed across each other, used in ancient times for crucifixion; the emblem of the Christian faith; a burden, or affliction; a device resembling a cross; a cross-shaped medal; a hybrid. * *vti* to pass across; to intersect; to meet and pass; to place crosswise; to make the sign of the cross over; to thwart, to oppose; to modify (a breed) by intermixture (with). * *adj* transverse; reaching from side to side; intersecting; out of temper, peevish.—**crossly** *adv*.—**crossness** *n*.

crossbar *n* a horizontal bar, as that across goal posts or as bicycle frame.

crossbreed *vt* (*pt* **crossbred**) to breed animals by mating different varieties. * *n* an animal produced in this way.

cross-country *adj* across fields; denoting cross-country racing or skiing.

cross-examine vt to question closely; (law) to question (a witness) who has already been questioned by counsel on the other side.—**cross-examination** n.

cross-eyed adj squinting.

crossing n an intersection of roads or railway lines; a place for crossing a street.

crossroad n a road crossing another; (pl) where two roads cross; (fig) the time when a decisive action has to be made.

cross section n a cutting at right angles to length; the surface then shown; a random selection of the public.

crossword n a puzzle in which interlocking words to be inserted vertically and horizontally in a squared diagram are indicated by clues.

crotch n the region of the body where the legs fork, the genital area; any forked region.

crotchet n (mus) a note equal to a half-minim.

crotchety adj peevish, whimsical.

crouch vi to squat or lie close to the ground; to cringe.

crouton n a small piece of fried or toasted bread, sprinkled onto soups.

crow n any of various usually large, glossy, black birds; a cawing cry, the shrill sound of a cock. * vi (pt **crowed** or **crew**) to make a sound like a cock; to boast in triumph; to utter a cry of pleasure.

crowbar n an iron bar used to lever.

crowberry n an evergreen shrub with black berries; the edible berry of this shrub.

crowd n a number of people or things collected closely together; a dense multitude, a throng; (inf) a set; a clique. * vti to press closely together; to fill to excess; to push, to thrust; to importune.—**crowded** adj.

crown n a wreath worn on the head; the head covering of a monarch; regal power; the top of the head; a summit; a reward; the part of a tooth above the gum; (cap) the sovereign, considered as the head of state. * vt to invest with a crown; to adorn or dignify; to complete; to reward.

Crown attorney n (Cdn) a lawyer who prosecutes crimes on behalf of the Crown.—also **Crown counsel, Crown prosecutor**.

Crown corporation n (Cdn) a corporation owned by a federal or provincial government.

Crown counsel n Crown attorney.

Crown prosecutor n Crown attorney.

CRTC abbr = Canadian Radio-television and Telecommunications Commission.

crucial adj decisive; severe; critical. —**crucially** adv.

crucifix n a cross with the sculptured figure of Christ.

crucifixion n a form of execution by being nailed or bound to a cross by the hands and feet; (with cap) the death of Christ in this manner.

crucify vt to put to death on a cross; to cause extreme pain to; to utterly defeat in an argument.

crude adj in a natural state; unripe; raw; immature; harsh in color; unfinished, rough; lacking polish; blunt; vulgar. * n crude oil.—**crudely** adv.—**crudity** n.

cruel adj (**crueller, cruellest**) disposed to give pain to others; merciless; hard-hearted; fierce; painful; unrelenting. —**cruelly** adv.—**cruelty** n.

cruet n a small glass bottle for vinegar and oil, used at the table.

cruise vi to sail to and fro; to wander about; to move at the most efficient speed for sustained travel. * vt to cruise over or about. * n a voyage from place to place for military purposes or for pleasure.

crumb n a fragment of bread; the soft part of bread; a little piece of anything.

crumble vt to break into crumbs; to cause to fall into pieces. * vi to disappear gradually, to disintegrate.—**crumbly** adj.

crumpet n a soft cake, usu eaten toasted; (sl) a sexually attractive woman.

crumple vti to twist or crush into wrinkles; to crease; to collapse. * n a wrinkle or crease made by crumpling.

crunch vti to crush with the teeth; to tread underfoot with force and noise; to make a sound like this; to chew audibly. * n the sound or act of crunching.

crusade n a medieval Christian military expedition to recover the Holy Land; a vigorous concerted action defending a cause or advancing an idea. * vi to engage in a crusade.—**crusader** n.

crush vt to press between two opposite bodies; to squeeze; to break by pressure; to bruise; to ruin; to quell. * vi to be pressed out of shape or into a smaller compass. * n a violent compression or collision; a dense crowd; (inf) a large party; a drink made from crushed fruit; (sl) an infatuation.

crust n a hard external coating or rind; the exterior solid part of the earth's surface; a shell or hard covering. * vti to cover or become covered with a crust.—**crusty** adj.—**crustily** adv.—**crustiness** n.

crutch n a staff with a crosswise head to support the weight of a lame person; a prop; the crotch.

crux n (pl **cruxes, cruces**) a difficult problem; the essential or deciding point.

cry vi to call aloud; to proclaim; to exclaim vehemently; to implore; to shed tears. * vt to utter loudly and publicly. * n an inarticulate sound; an exclamation of wonder or triumph; an outcry; clamour; an urgent appeal; a spell of weeping; a battle cry; a catchword.

crypt n an underground chamber or vault, esp under a church, used as a chapel or for burial.

cryptic adj hidden, secret; mysterious.

crystal n very clear, brilliant glass; articles of such glass, as goblets. * adj made of crystal.—**crystalline** adj.

crystallize vti to form crystals; to give definite form.—**crystallization** n.

CSB abbr = Canada Savings Bond.

CSC abbr = Correctional Service of Canada.

Cst. *abbr* = (*Cdn*) Constable.

CTC *abbr* = Canadian Transport Commission.

CTV *abbr* = Canadian Television Network.

cu. *abbr* = cubic.

cub *n* a young carnivorous mammal; a young, inexperienced person; (*with cap*) a Cub Scout.

cube *n* a solid body with six equal square sides or faces; a cube-shaped block; the product of a number multiplied by itself twice. * *vt* to raise (number) to the third power, or cube; to cut into cube-shaped pieces.

cube van *n* (*Cdn*) a truck with a cube-like storage compartment at the rear.

cubic *adj* having the form or properties of a cube; three-dimensional.

cubicle *n* a small separate sleeping compartment in a dormitory, etc.

cuckoo *n* a bird with a dark plumage, a curved bill and a characteristic call that lays its eggs in the nests of other birds.

cuckoo clock *n* a clock that strikes the hours with a cuckoo call.

cucumber *n* a long juicy fruit used in salads and as a pickle; the creeping plant that bears it.

cud *n* the food that a ruminating animal brings back into the mouth to chew again.

cuddle *vt* to embrace or hug closely. * *vt* to nestle together. * *n* a close embrace.

cudgel *n* a short thick stick for beating.

cue[1] *n* the last word of a speech in a play, serving as a signal for the next actor to enter or begin to speak; any signal to do something; a hint. * *vt* (*pr p* **cuing** *or* **cueing**) to give a cue to.

cue[2] *n* a tapering rod used in snooker, billiards, and pool to strike the cue ball.

cuff[1] *n* a blow with the fist or the open hand. * *vt* to strike such a blow.

cuff[2] *n* the end of a sleeve; a covering round the wrist; the turn-up on a trouser leg.

cufflink *n* a decorative clip for fastening the edges of a shirt cuff.

cuisine *n* a style of cooking or preparing food; the food prepared.

cul-de-sac *n* a street blocked off at one end; a blind alley.

culinary *adj* of or relating to cooking.

culminate *vti* to reach the highest point of altitude, rank, power, etc; (*astron*) to reach the meridian; to bring to a head or the highest point.—**culmination** *n*.

culpable *adj* deserving censure; criminal; blameworthy.—**culpably** *adv*.—**culpability** *n*.

culprit *n* a person accused, or found guilty, of an offence.

cult *n* a system of worship; devoted attachment to a person, principle, etc; a religion regarded as unorthodox or spurious; its body of adherents.

cultivate *vt* to till; to improve by care, labour, or study; to seek the society of; to civilize or refine.

cultivation *n* the act of cultivating; the state of being cultivated; tillage; culture.

cultural *adj* pertaining to culture.—**culturally** *adv*.

cultural sovereignty *n* (*Cdn*) the authority of a country to maintain its own culture, rather than another, more dominant one.

culture *n* appreciation and understanding of the arts; the skills, arts, etc of a given people in a given period; the customary beliefs, social forms, and material traits of a religious, social, or racial group; improvement of the mind, manner, etc; a growth of bacteria, etc in a prepared substance. * *vt* to cultivate bacteria for study or use.

cultured *adj* educated to appreciate the arts; having good taste; artificially grown, as cultured pearls.

cumbersome *adj* inconveniently heavy or large, unwieldy.

cunning *adj* ingenious; sly; designing; subtle. * *n* slyness, craftiness.

cup *n* a small, bowl-shaped container for liquids, usu with a handle; the amount held in a cup; an ornamental cup used as a trophy. * *vt* (*pt* **cupped**) to take or put as in a cup; to curve (the hands) into the shape of a cup.

cupboard *n* a closet or cabinet with shelves for cups, plates, utensils, food etc.

cupola *n* a dome.

CUPW *abbr* = Canadian Union of Postal Workers.

curate *n* an assistant of a vicar or rector.

curator *n* a superintendent of a a museum, art gallery, etc.

curb *vt* to to restrain; to check; to keep in subjection. * *n* that which checks, restrains, or subdues; a kerb.

curd *n* the coagulated part of soured milk, used to make cheese.

curdle *vti* to turn into curds; to coagulate.

cure *n* the act or art of healing; a remedy; restoration to health. * *vt* to heal; to rid of; to preserve, as by drying, salting, etc.—**curable** *adj*.

curfew *n* a signal, as a bell, at a fixed evening hour as a sign that everyone must be indoors; the signal or hour.

curio *n* (*pl* **curios**) an item valued as rare or unusual.

curiosity *n* the quality of being curious; inquisitiveness; a rare, strange or interesting object.

curious *adj* anxious to know; prying, inquisitive; strange, remarkable, odd.—**curiously** *adv*.—**curiousness** *n*.

curl *vti* to form into a curved shape, to coil; to twist into ringlets; to proceed in a curve, to bend; to play at curling. * *n* a ringlet of hair; a spiral form, a twist; a bend or undulation.

curler *n* a small pin or roller used for curling the hair; a person who plays curling.

curling *n* a game in which two teams slide large smooth stones on ice into a target circle.

curly *adj* (**curlier, curliest**) full of curls.—**curliness** *n*.

currant *n* a small variety of dried grape; a shrub that yields a red or black fruit.

currency *n* the time during which a thing is current; the state of being in use; the money current in a country.

current adj generally accepted; happening now; presently in circulation. * n a body of water or air in motion, a flow; the transmission of electricity through a conductor; a general tendency.

currently adv at the present time.

curriculum n (pl curricula, curriculums) a prescribed course of study.

curriculum vitae n a brief survey of one's career.

curry n a spicy dish with a hot sauce; curry seasoning. * vt to flavor with curry.

curse n a calling down of destruction or evil; a profane oath; a swear word; a violent exclamation of anger; a scourge. * vti to invoke a curse on; to swear, to blaspheme; to afflict, to torment.

cursor n a flashing indicator on a computer screen indicating position; the transparent slide on a slide-rule.

cursory adj hasty, passing; superficial, careless.—cursorily adv.

curt adj short; abrupt; concise; rudely brief.—curtly adv.—curtness n.

curtail vt to cut short; to reduce; to deprive of part (of).—curtailment n.

curtain n a cloth hung as a screen at a window, etc; the movable screen separating the stage from the auditorium; (pl) (sl) the end. * vt to enclose in, or as with, curtains.

curtsy, curtsey n a formal gesture of greeting, involving bending the knees, made by women and children. * vi to make a curtsy.

curve n a bending without angles; a bent form or thing; (geom) a line of which no part is straight. * vti to form into a curve, to bend.—curvy adj.

cushion n a case stuffed with soft material for resting on; the elastic border around a snooker table; the air mass supporting a hovercraft. * vt to furnish with cushions; to protect by padding.

custard n a sauce mixture of milk, eggs and sugar.

custody n guardianship; imprisonment; security.—custodial adj.—custodian n.

custom n a regular practice; usage; frequent repetition of the same act; business patronage; (pl) duties on imports.

customary adj habitual; conventional; common.—customarily adv.

customer n a person who buys from a shop or business, esp regularly.

cut vb (pr p cutting, pt cut) vb to cleave or separate with a sharp instrument; to make an incision in; to divide; to trim; to intersect; to abridge; to diminish; to pass deliberately without recognition; to wound deeply; to reduce or curtail; to grow a new tooth through the gum; to divide (a pack of cards) at random; (inf) to stay away from class, school, etc. * vi to make an incision; to perform the work of an edged instrument; to grow through the gums; (cinema) to change to another scene, to stop photographing. * n an incision or wound made by a sharp instrument; a gash; a sharp stroke; a sarcastic remark; a passage or channel cut out;

a slice; a block on which an engraving is cut; the fashion or shape of a garment; the deliberate ignoring of an acquaintance; the division of a pack of cards; a diminution in price below another merchant; (sl) a share, as of profits. * adj divided or separated; gashed; having the surface ornamented or fashioned; not wrought or handmade.

cutback n a reduction, esp in expenditure.

cute adj (inf) acute, shrewd; pretty or attractive, esp in a dainty way.—cutely adv.—cuteness n.

cuticle n the skin at the base of the fingernail or toe nail; epidermis.

cutlery n knives, forks, etc for eating and serving food.

cutlet n a neck chop of lamb, etc; a small slice cut off from the ribs or leg; minced meat in the form of a cutlet.

cutthroat n a murderer. * adj merciless; (razor) having a long blade in a handle.

cutthroat trout n a North American trout with a red or orange marking under its jaw.

cutting n a piece cut off or from; an incision; a newspaper clipping; a slip from a plant for propagation; a passage or channel cut out; the process of editing a film or recording; a recording. * adj (remarks) hurtful.

cuttlefish n a marine creature with a flattened body that squirts ink when threatened.

CV abbr = curriculum vitae.

CWB abbr = Canadian Wheat Board.

cwt. abbr = hundredweight.

cyanide n a poison.

cyclamen n a plant of the primrose family, with pink, purple or white flowers.

cycle n a recurring series of events or phenomena; the period of this; a body of epics or romances with a common theme; a bicycle, motorcycle, or tricycle. * vi to go in cycles; to ride a bicycle or tricycle.

cyclic, cyclical adj moving or recurring in cycles.—cyclically adj.

cyclist n a person who rides a bicycle.

cyclone n a violent circular storm; an atmospheric movement in which the wind blows spirally round towards a centre of low barometric pressure.—cyclonic adj.

cygnet n a young swan.

cylinder n a hollow figure or object with parallel sides and circular ends; an object shaped like a cylinder; any machine part of this shape; the piston chamber in an engine.—cylindrical adj.

cymbal n (mus) one of a pair of two brass plates struck together to produce a ringing or clashing sound.—cymbalist n.

cynic n a morose, surly, or sarcastic person; one of a sect of ancient Greek philosophers.—cynicism n.

cynical adj sceptical of or sneering at goodness; shameless in admitting unworthy motives.—cynically adv.

cypher see cipher.

cypress n an evergreen tree with hard wood.

cyst n a closed sac developing abnormally in

the structure of plants or animals.—**cystic** *adj*.

czar *see* **tsar**.

D

dab¹ *vt* (*pt* **dabbed**) to touch lightly with something moist or soft. * *n* a quick light tap; a small lump of anything moist or soft.

dab² *n* a species of European flounder.

dabble *vi* to move hands, feet etc gently in water or another liquid; (*usu with* **at, in, with**) to do anything in a superficial or dilettante way. * *vt* to splash.—**dabbler** *n*.

dad, daddy *n* (*inf*) father.

daddy-longlegs *n* (*inf*) a crane fly; (*inf*) in US, any of various spiders or insects with long, slender legs.

daffodil *n* a yellow spring flower, a narcissus; its pale yellow color.

daft *adj* (*inf*) silly, weak-minded; giddy; mad.—**daftness** *n*.

dagger *n* a short weapon for stabbing; a reference mark used in printing (†).—*also* **obelisk**.

daily *adj*, *adv* (happening) every day; constantly, progressively. * *n* a newspaper published every weekday; (*inf*) a charwoman.

dainty *adj* (**daintier, daintiest**) delicate; choice; nice, fastidious. * *n* a titbit, a delicacy.—**daintily** *adv*.—**daintiness** *n*.

dairy *n* a building or room where milk is stored and dairy products made; a shop selling these; a company supplying them.

daisy *n* any of various plants with a yellow centre and white petals, esp the English daisy.

dale *n* a valley.

Dall sheep, Dall's sheep *n* a wild, thin-horned sheep of the mountainous parts of northwest Canada and Alaska.

dally *vi* to lose time by idleness or trifling; to play or trifle (with); to flirt.

dam¹ *n* an artificial embankment to retain water; water so contained. * *vt* (*pt* **dammed**) to retain (water) with such a barrier; to stem, obstruct, restrict.

dam² *n* the mother of a four-footed animal.

damage *n* injury, harm; loss; (*inf*) price, cost; (*pl*) (*law*) payment in compensation for loss or injury. * *vt* to do harm to, to injure.—**damaging** *adj*.

damn *vt* to condemn, censure; to ruin; to curse; to consign to eternal punishment. * *vti* to prove guilty. * *interj* (*sl*) expressing irritation or annoyance. * *n* (*sl*) something having no value. * *adj*, *adv* damned.—**damnatory** *adj*.

damp *n* humidity, moisture; in mines, poisonous or foul gas. * *adj* slightly wet, moist. * *vt* to moisten; (*with* **down**) to stifle, reduce.—**dampness** *n*.

dampen *vti* to make or become damp. * *vt* to stifle.—**dampener** *n*.

damson *n* a small, dark-purple variety of plum; the color of this; the tree on which this fruit grows.

dance *vti* to move rhythmically, esp to music; to skip or leap lightly; to execute (steps); to cause to dance or to move up and down. * *n* a piece of dancing; a dance performance of an artistic nature; a party with music for dancing; music for accompanying dancing.—**dancer** *n*.

dandelion *n* a common wild plant with ragged leaves, a yellow flower and a fluffy seed head.

dandruff *n* scales of skin on the scalp, under the hair, scurf.

danger *n* exposure to injury or risk; a source of harm or risk.

dangerous *adj* involving danger; unsafe; perilous.—**dangerously** *adv*.

dangle *vi* to hang and swing loosely. * *vt* to carry something so that it hangs loosely; to display temptingly.

dapper *adj* nimble; neat in appearance, spruce.

dare *vti* to be bold enough; to venture, to risk; to defy, to challenge. * *n* a challenge.

daredevil *n* a rash, reckless person. * *adj* daring, bold; courageous.

daring *adj* fearless; courageous; unconventional. * *n* adventurous courage.

dark *adj* having little or no light; of a shade of color closer to black than white; (*person*) having brown or black skin or hair; gloomy; (*inf*) secret, unknown; mysterious. * *n* a dark state or color; ignorance; secrecy.—**darkly** *adv*.—**darkness** *n*.

darken *vti* to make or become dark or darker.

darkroom *n* a room for processing photographs in darkness or safe light.

darling *n* a dearly loved person; a favorite. * *adj* lovable; much admired.

darn¹ *vt* to mend a hole in fabric or a garment with stitches. * *n* an area that has been darned.

darn² *interj* a form of **damn** as a mild oath.—*also* *adj*.

dart *n* a small pointed missile; a sudden movement; a fold sewn into a garment for shaping it; (*pl*) an indoor game in which darts are thrown at a target. * *vti* to move rapidly; to send out rapidly.

dartboard *n* a circular cork or wooden target used in the game of darts.

dash *vti* to fling violently; to rush quickly; (*hopes*) to shatter; (*one's spirits, etc*) to depress, confound; to write quickly. * *n* a short race; a rush; a small amount of something added to food; a tinge; a punctuation mark (—); a dashboard; vigour, verve; display.

dashboard *n* an instrument panel in a car.

dasher *n* one of the boards surrounding a hockey rink.

dashing *adj* spirited, stylish, dapper.

data *npl* (*sing* **datum**) (*often used as sing*) facts, statistics, or information either historical or derived by calculation or experimentation.

data processing *n* the analysis of information stored in a computer for various uses, eg stock control, statistical research, mathematical modelling, etc.

date[1] *n* a day or time of occurrence; a statement of this in a letter, etc; a period to which something belongs; a duration; an appointment, esp with a member of the opposite sex. * *vt* to affix a date to; to note the date of; to reckon the time of; (*inf*) to make a date with; (*inf*) to see frequently a member of the opposite sex. * *vi* to reckon from a point in time; to show signs of belonging to a particular period.

date[2] *n* the sweet fruit of the date palm, a palm tree of tropical regions.

date line *n* the line running north to south along the 180-degree meridian, east of which is one day earlier than west of it; a line on a newspaper story giving the date and place of writing.

daub *vt* to smear or overlay (with clay, etc); to paint incompetently. * *n* a smear; a poor painting.

daughter *n* a female child or descendant.

daughter-in-law *n* the wife of one's son.

dauntless *adj* intrepid.—**dauntlessly** *adv*.

dawdle *vi* to move slowly and waste time, to loiter.—**dawdler** *n*.

dawn *vi* (*day*) to begin to grow light; to begin to appear. * *n* daybreak; a first sign.

day *n* the time when the sun is above the horizon; the twenty-four hours from midnight to midnight; daylight; a particular period of success or influence; (*usu pl*) a period, an epoch.

daybreak *n* the first appearance of daylight, dawn.

daydream *n* a reverie. * *vi* to have one's mind on other things; to fantasize.—**daydreamer** *n*.

daylight *n* the light of the sun; dawn; publicity; a visible gap; the dawning of sudden realization or understanding.

day release *n* (*Cdn*) a release of a jailed prisoner during the day or for a short period of time in order to hold a job or to attend school.

daytime *n* the time of daylight.

daze *vt* to stun, to bewilder. * *n* confusion, bewilderment.

dazzle *vt* to confuse the sight of or be partially blinded by strong light; to overwhelm with brilliance. * *n* an overpoweringly strong light; bewilderment. —**dazzler** *n*.—**dazzling** *adj*.—**dazzlingly** *adv*.

dead *adj* without life; inanimate, inert; no longer used; lacking vegetation; emotionally or spiritually insensitive; without motion; (*fire, etc*) extinguished; (*limb, etc*) numb; (*color, sound etc*) dull; (*a ball*) out of play; complete, exact; unerring. * *adv* in a dead manner; completely; utterly. * *n* a dead person; the quietest time.

deaden *vt* to render numb or insensible; to deprive of vitality; to muffle.

dead-end *n* a cul-de-sac; a hopeless situation.

deadhead *n* a sunken or submerged log, esp one that is a hazard to water traffic.

dead heat *n* a race in which two or more finish equal, a tie.

deadline *n* the time by which something must be done.

deadlock *n* a clash of interests making progress impossible; a standstill.—*also vt*.

deadly *adj* (**deadlier, deadliest**) fatal; implacable; (*inf*) tedious. * *adv* death-like; intensely.

deadpan *adj* (*inf*) deliberately expressionless or emotionless.—*also adv*.

deaf *adj* unable to hear; hearing badly; not wishing to hear.—**deafness** *n*.

deafen *vt* to deprive of hearing.—**deafeningly** *adv*.

deal[1] *vb* (*pt* **dealt**) *vt* (*a blow*) to deliver, inflict; (*cards, etc*) to distribute; (*with* **with**) to do business with; (*problem, task*) to solve. * *vi* to do business (with); to trade (in). * *n* a portion, quantity; (*inf*) a large amount; a dealing of cards; a business transaction.

deal[2] *n* fir or pine wood.—*also adj*.

dealer *n* a trader; a person who deals cards; (*sl*) a seller of illegal drugs.

dealings *npl* personal or business transactions.

dean *n* the head of a cathedral chapter; a college fellow in charge of discipline; the head of a university or college faculty.

dear *adj* loved, precious; charming; expensive; a form of address in letters. * *n* a person who is loved. * *adv* at a high price.—**dearly** *adv*.—**dearness** *n*.

dearth *n* scarcity, lack.

death *n* the end of life, dying; the state of being dead; the destruction of something.

deathbed *n* the bed in which a person dies or is about to die.

death certificate *n* an official document with details of the date, place and cause of a person's death.

death duties *npl* taxes paid on an inheritance after a death.

deathly *adj* like death, pale still; deadly.—*also adv*.

debar *vt* (*pt* **debarred**) to exclude, bar. —**debarment** *n*.

debase *vt* to lower in character or value; (*coinage*) to degrade.—**debasement** *n*.

debatable, debateable *adj* open to question, disputed.

debate *n* a formal argument; a discussion, esp in parliament. * *vt* to consider, contest. * *vi* to discuss thoroughly; to join in debate.—**debater** *n*.

debauchery *n* depraved over-indulgence; corruption; profligacy.

debit *n* the entry of a sum owed, opposite to the credit; the left side of a ledger used for this. * *vt* to charge to the debit side of a ledger.

debris, débris *n* broken and scattered remains, wreckage.

debt *n* a sum owed; a state of owing; an obligation.

debtor *n* a person, company, etc who owes money to another.

debut *n* a first appearance as a public performer or in society.

decade *n* a period of ten years; a group of ten.

decadence, decadency *n* a state of deterioration in standards, esp of morality.

decadent *adj* deteriorating; self-indulgent.

decay *vti* to rot, decompose; to deteriorate, wither. * *n* the act or state of decaying; a decline, collapse.

decease *n* death. * *vi* to die.

deceased *adj* dead. * *n* the dead person.

deceit *n* the act of deceiving; cunning; treachery; fraud.

deceitful *adj* treacherous; insincere; misleading.—**deceitfully** *adv.*—**deceitfulness** *n.*

deceive *vt* to cheat; to mislead; to delude; to impose upon.—**deceiver** *n.*

December *n* the twelfth and last month of the year with 31 days.

decency *n* being decent; conforming to accepted standards of behaviour.

decent *adj* respectable, proper; moderate; not obscene; (*inf*) quite good; (*inf*) kind, generous.—**decently** *adv.*

decentralize *vt* (*government, organization*) to divide among local centres. —**decentralization** *n.*

deception *n* the act of deceiving or the state of being deceived; illusion; fraud.

deceptive *adj* apt to mislead; ambiguous; unreliable.—**deceptively** *adv.*—**deceptiveness** *n.*

decibel *n* a unit for measuring sound level.

decide *vti* to determine, to settle; to give a judgment on; to resolve.

decided *adj* unhesitating; clearly marked.

decidedly *adv* definitely, certainly.

deciduous *adj* (*trees, shrubs*) shedding all leaves annually, at the end of the growing season.

decimal *adj* of tenths, of numbers written to the base 10.

decimal point *n* a dot written before the numerator in a decimal fraction (eg 0.5 = °).

decimate *vt* to kill every tenth person; to reduce by one tenth; to kill a great number.—**decimation** *n.*

decipher *vt* to decode; to make out (indistinct writing, meaning, etc).—**decipherable** *adj.*—**decipherment** *n.*

decision *n* a settlement; a ruling; a judgment; determination, firmness.

decisive *adj* determining the issue, positive; conclusive, final.—**decisively** *adv.*

deck *n* the floor on a ship, aircraft, bus or bridge; a pack of playing cards; the turntable of a record-player; the playing mechanism of a tape recorder; (*sl*) the ground, the floor. * *vt* to cover; to adorn.

deck chair *n* a folding chair made of canvas suspended in a frame.

declare *vt* to affirm, proclaim; to admit possession of (dutiable goods). * *vi* (*law*) to make a statement; (*with* **against, for**) to announce one's support; (*cricket*) to choose to close an innings before ten wickets have fallen.—**declaration** *n.*—**declarative** *adj.*—**declaratory** *adj.*

decline *vi* to refuse; to move down; to deteriorate, fall away; to fail; to diminish; to draw to an end; to deviate. * *vt* to reject, to

refuse; (*gram*) to give the cases of a declension. * *n* a diminution; a downward slope; a gradual loss of physical and mental faculties.

decode *vt* to translate a code into plain language.—**decoder** *n.*

decompose *vti* to separate or break up into constituent parts, esp as part of a chemical process; to resolve into its elements. * *vi* to decay.—**decomposition** *n.*

decontaminate *vt* to free from (radioactive, etc) contamination.—**decontamination** *n.*

décor, decor *n* general decorative effect, eg of a room; scenery and stage design.

decorate *vt* to ornament; to paint or wallpaper; to honor with a badge or medal.

decoration *n* decorating; an ornament; a badge or an honor.

decorative *adj* ornamental, pretty to look at.—**decoratively** *adv.*

decorator *n* a person who decorates, esp houses.

decoy *vt* to lure into a trap. * *n* anything intended to lure into a snare.

decrease *vti* to make or become less. * *n* a decreasing; the amount of diminution.

decree *n* an order, edict or law; a judicial decision. * *vt* (*pt* **decreed**) to decide by sentence in law; to appoint.

decrepit *adj* worn out by the infirmities of old age; in the last stage of decay.—**decrepitude** *n.*

dedicate *vt* to consecrate (to some sacred purpose); to devote wholly or chiefly; to inscribe (to someone) —**dedication** *n.*—**dedicator** *n.*—**dedicatory** *adj.*

deduce *vt* to derive (knowledge, a conclusion) from reasoning; infer.—**deducible** *adj.*

deduct *vt* to take (from); to subtract.

deduction *n* deducting; the amount deducted; deducing; a conclusion that something is true because it necessarily follows from a set of general premises known to be valid.—**deductive** *adj.*

deed *n* an act; an exploit; a legal document recording a transaction.

deep *adj* extending or placed far down or far from the outside; fully involved; engrossed; profound, intense; heartfelt; penetrating; difficult to understand; secret; cunning; sunk low; low in pitch; (*color*) of high saturation and low brilliance. * *adv* in a deep manner; far in, into. * *n* that which is deep; the sea.—**deeply** *adv.*—**deepness** *n.*

deepen *vt* to make deeper in any sense; to increase. * *vi* to become deeper.

deepfreeze *n* a refrigerator in which food is frozen and stored.

deep-freeze *vt* to freeze (food) so that it keeps for a long period of time. * *n* a freezer.

deer *n* (*pl* **deer, deers**) a four-footed animal with antlers, esp on the males, including stag, reindeer, etc.

deface *vt* to disfigure; to obliterate. —**defacement** *n.*

default *n* neglect to do what duty or law requires; failure to fulfil a financial obligation; (*comput*) a basic setting or instruction to which a program reverts. * *vi* to fail in one's duty (as honoring a financial obligation, appearing in court).—**defaulter** *n*.

defeat *vt* to frustrate; to win a victory over; to baffle. * *n* a frustration of plans; overthrow, as of an army in battle; loss of a game, race, etc.

defeatism *n* disposition to accept defeat.—**defeatist** *n*.

defect *n* a deficiency; a blemish, fault. * *vi* to desert one's country or a cause.

defective *adj* having a defect; faulty; incomplete. * *n* a person defective in physical or mental powers.—**defectively** *adv*.—**defectiveness** *n*.

defence, defense (*US*) *n* resistance or protection against attack; a means of resisting an attack; protection; vindication; (*law*) a defendant's plea; the defending party in legal proceedings; (*sport*) defending (the goal, etc) against the attacks of the opposing side; the defending players in a team.—**defenceless** *adj*.

defend *vt* to guard or protect; to maintain against attack; (*law*) to resist, as a claim; to contest (a suit).

defendant *n* a person accused or sued in a lawsuit.

defensive *adj* serving to defend; in a state or posture of defence.—**defensively** *adv*.

defer[1] *vt* (*pt* deferred) to put off to another time; to delay.—**deferment, deferral** *n*.—**deferrable, deferable** *adj*.

defer[2] *vi* (*pt* deferred) to yield to another person's wishes, judgment or authority.

deference *n* a deferring or yielding in judgment or opinion; polite respect.

defiance *n* the act of defying; wilful disobedience; a challenge.—**defiant** *adj*.

deficiency *n* being deficient; lack, shortage; deficit.

deficient *adj* insufficient, lacking.

deficit *n* the amount by which an amount falls short of what is required; excess of expenditure over income, or liabilities over assets.

defile[1] *vt* to pollute or corrupt.

defile[2] *n* a long, narrow pass or way, through which troops can pass only in single file. * *vt* to march in single file.

define *vt* to fix the bounds or limits of; to mark the limits or outline of clearly; to describe accurately; to fix the meaning of.—**definable** *adj*.

definite *adj* defined; having distinct limits; fixed; exact; clear.—**definitely** *adv*.

definition *n* a description of a thing by its properties; an explanation of the exact meaning of a word, term, or phrase; sharpness of outline.

definitive *adj* defining or limiting; decisive, final.—**definitively** *adv*.

deflate *vt* to release gas or air from; to reduce in size or importance; to reduce the money supply, restrict credit, etc to reduce infla-

tion in the economy. —**deflation** *n*.—**deflationary** *adj*.

deflect *vti* to turn or cause to turn aside from a line or proper course.—**deflection** *n*.—**deflector** *n*.

deform *vt* to spoil the natural form of; to put out of shape.—**deformation** *n*.

deformity *n* the condition of being deformed; a deformed part of the body; a defect.

defraud *vt* to remove (money, rights, etc) from a person by cheating or deceiving.—**defrauder** *n*.

defray *vt* to provide money (to pay expenses, etc).—**defrayal, defrayment** *n*.

defrost *vt* to unfreeze; to free from frost or ice.—*also vi*.

deft *adj* skilful, adept; nimble.—**deftly** *adv*.—**deftness** *n*.

defunct *adj* no longer being in existence or function or in use.

defuse *vt* to disarm an explosive (bomb or mine) by removing its fuse; to decrease tension in a (crisis) situation.

defy *vt* to resist openly and without fear; to challenge (a person) to attempt something considered dangerous or impossible; to resist attempts at, to elude.

degenerate *adj* having declined in physical or moral qualities; sexually deviant. * *vi* become or grow worse. * *n* a degenerate person.—**degeneracy** *n*.—**degeneration** *n*.

degrading *adj* humiliating.

degree *n* a step in a series; a stage in intensity; the relative quantity in intensity; a unit of measurement in a scale; an academic title awarded as of right or as an honor.

dehydrate *vt* to remove water from. * *vi* to lose water, esp from the bodily tissues.—**dehydration** *n*.

de-ice *vt* to prevent the formation of or to remove ice from a surface.—**de-icer** *n*.

deign *vi* to condescend; to think it worthy to do (something).

deity *n* a god or goddess; the rank or essence of a god; (*with cap and* **the**) God.

dejected *adj* morose, depressed.—**dejectedly** *adv*.

dejection *n* depression; lowness of spirits.

deke *n* a fake shot or movement in ice hockey, esp to draw an opponent out of position. * *vti* to deceive an opponent with a fake shot or movement.

delay *vt* to postpone; to detain, obstruct. * *vi* to linger. * *n* a delaying or being delayed; the time period during which something is delayed.

delayed penalty *n* a penalty in ice hockey that has been signalled by the referee but for which play has not yet been stopped.

delectable *adj* delightful, delicious.—**delectably** *adv*.

delegate *vt* to appoint as a representative; to give powers or responsibilities to (an agent or assembly). * *n* a deputy or an elected representative.

delegation *n* the act of delegating; a group of people empowered to represent others.

delete *vt* to strike out (something written or printed); to erase.—**deletion** *n*.

deliberate *vt* to consider carefully. * *vi* to discuss or debate thoroughly; to consider. * *adj* well thought out; intentional; cautious.—**deliberately** *adv*.

delicacy *n* delicateness; sensibility; a luxurious food.

delicate *adj* fine in texture; fragile, not robust; requiring tactful handling; of exquisite workmanship; requiring skill in techniques.—**delicately** *adv*. —**delicateness** *n*.

delicatessen *n* a store selling prepared foods, esp imported delicacies.

delicious *adj* having a pleasurable effect on the senses, esp taste; delightful.—**deliciously** *adv*.—**deliciousness** *n*.

delight *vt* to please greatly. * *vi* to have or take great pleasure (in). * *n* great pleasure; something that causes this.

delightful *adj* giving great pleasure.—**delightfully** *adv*.

delinquent *adj* negligent; guilty of an offence. * *n* a person guilty of a misdeed, esp a young person who breaks the law.—**delinquency** *n*.

delirium *n* a state of mental disorder, esp caused by a feverish illness; wild enthusiasm.—**delirious** *adj*.

deliver *vt* (*goods, letters, etc*) to transport to a destination; to distribute regularly; to liberate, to rescue; to give birth; to assist at a birth; (*blow*) to launch; (*baseball*) to pitch; (*speech*) to utter.—**deliverer** *n*.

delivery *n* act of delivering; anything delivered or communicated; the manner of delivering (a speech, etc); the manner of bowling in cricket, etc; the act of giving birth.

delta *n* the fourth letter of the Greek alphabet; an alluvial deposit at the mouth of a river.

delude *vt* to mislead, to deceive.

deluge *n* a flood; anything happening in a heavy rush. * *vt* to inundate.

delusion *n* a false belief; a persistent false belief that is a symptom of mental illness.—**delusive** *adj*.—**delusory** *adj*.

delve *vti* to search deeply; to dig.

demagogue, demagog *n* a political orator who derives power from appealing to popular prejudices.—**demagogic** *adj*.—**demagogy** *n*.

demand *vt* to ask for in an authoritative manner. * *n* a request or claim made with authority for what is due; an urgent claim; desire for goods and services shown by consumers.

demanding *adj* constantly making demands; requiring great skill, concentration or effort.

demarcation, demarkation *n* the act of marking off a boundary or setting a limit to; a limit; the strict separation of the type of work done by members of different trade unions.

demean *vt* to lower in dignity.—**demeaning** *adj*.

demeanour, demeanor (*US*) *n* behaviour; bearing.

demented *adj* crazy, insane.—**dementedly** *adv*.

demise *n* (*formal*) death; termination, end.

demobilize *vt* to discharge from the armed forces.—**demobilization** *n*.

democracy *n* a form of government by the people through elected representatives; a country governed by its people; political, social or legal equality.

democrat *n* a person who believes in or promotes democracy; (*with cap*) a member of the Democratic Party in the US.

democratic *adj* of, relating to, or supporting the principles of democracy; favoring or upholding equal rights.—**democratically** *adv*.

demolish *vt* (*a building*) to pull down or knock down; (*an argument*) to defeat; (*inf*) to eat up.—**demolition** *n*.

demonstrate *vt* to indicate or represent clearly; to provide certain evidence of, to prove; to show how something (a machine, etc) works. * *vi* to show one's support for a cause, etc by public parades and protests; to act as a demonstrator of machinery, etc.—**demonstrator** *n*.

demonstration *n* proof by evidence; a display or exhibition; a display of feeling; a public manifestation of opinion, as by a mass meeting, march, etc; a display of armed force.

demonstrative *adj* displaying one's feelings openly and unreservedly; indicative; conclusive; (*gram*) describing an adjective or pronoun indicating the person or thing referred to.—**demonstratively** *adv*.—**demonstrativeness** *n*.

demoralize *vt* to lower the morale of, discourage.—**demoralization** *n*.

demote *vt* to reduce in rank or position.—**demotion** *n*.

demur *vi* (*pt* **demurred**) to raise objections.

den *n* a cave or lair of a wild beast; a place where people gather for illegal activities; a room in a house for relaxation or study.

Dene *n* (*Cdn*) a member of a First Nations people in the Canadian north. * *adj* of or pertaining to this people.

denial *n* the act of denying; a refusal of a request, etc; a refusal or reluctance to admit the truth of something.

denigrate *vt* to disparage the character of; to belittle.—**denigration** *n*.

denim *n* a hard-wearing cotton cloth, esp used for jeans; (*pl*) denim trousers or jeans.

denomination *n* a name or title; a religious group comprising many local churches, larger than a sect; one of a series of related units, esp monetary.—**denominational** *adj*.

denominator *n* the part of a fractional expression written below the fraction line.

denote *vt* to indicate, be the sign of; to mean.—**denotation** *n*.

denounce *vt* to condemn or censure publicly; to inform against; to declare formally the ending of (treaties, etc). —**denouncement** *n*.

dense *adj* difficult to see through; massed closely together; dull-witted, stupid.—**densely** *adv*.—**denseness** *n*.

density *n* the degree of denseness or concentration; stupidity; the ratio of mass to volume.

dent *n* a depression made by pressure or a blow. * *vti* to make a dent or become dented.

dental *adj* of or for the teeth.

dentifrice *n* toothpowder or toothpaste.

dentist *n* a person qualified to treat tooth decay, gum disease, etc.—**dentistry** *n*.

denture *n* (*usu pl*) a set of artificial teeth.

deny *vt* to declare to be untrue; to repudiate; to refuse to acknowledge; to refuse to assent to a request, etc.

deodorant *n* a substance that removes or masks unpleasant odours.

dépanneur *n* (*Cdn*) in Quebec, a small store with extended hours that sells food and other items.

depart *vi* to go away, leave; to deviate (from).

department *n* a unit of specialized functions into which an organization or business is divided; a province; a realm of activity.—**departmental** *adj*.

department store *n* a large shop divided into various departments selling different types of goods.

departure *n* departing; deviating from normal practice; a new venture, course of action, etc.

depend *vi* to be determined by or connected with anything; to rely (on), put trust (in); to be reliant on for support, esp financially.

dependable *adj* able to be relied on.—**dependably** *adv*.—**dependability** *n*.

dependant *n* a person who is dependent on another, esp financially.

dependence, dependance *n* the state of being dependent; reliance, trust; a physical or mental reliance on a drug, person, etc.

dependent *adj* relying on another person, thing etc for support, money, etc; contingent; subordinate.

depict *vt* to represent pictorially; to describe.—**depiction** *n*.

deplete *vt* to use up a large quantity of. —**depletion** *n*.

deplorable *adj* shocking; extremely bad.—**deplorably** *adv*.

deplore *vt* to regret deeply; to complain of; to deprecate.

deploy *vt* (*military forces*) to distribute and position strategically. * *vi* to adopt strategic positions within an area.—**deployment** *n*.

depopulate *vt* to reduce the population of.—**depopulation** *n*.

deport *vt* to expel (an undesirable person) from a country; to behave (in a certain manner).—**deportation** *n*.

deportment *n* manners; behaviour.

depose *vt* to remove from power; to testify, esp in court.

deposit *vt* to place or lay down; to pay money into a bank or other institution for safekeeping, to earn interest, etc; to pay as a first instalment; to let fall, leave. * *n* something deposited for safekeeping; money put in a bank; money given in part payment or security; material left in a layer, eg sediment.

depositor *n* a person who deposits money in a bank, etc.

depot *n* a warehouse, storehouse; a place for storing military supplies; a military train-

ing centre; a bus or railway station.

deprave *vt* to pervert; to corrupt morally.—**depravation** *n*.—**depraved** *adj*.

depravity *n* moral corruption; extreme wickedness.

depreciate *vti* to make or become lower in value.

depreciation *n* a fall in value, esp of an asset through wear and tear; an allowance for this deducted from gross profit; disparagement.

depress *vt* to push down; to sadden, dispirit; to lessen the activity of.—**depressing** *adj*.—**depressingly** *adv*.

depression *n* excessive gloom and despondency; an abnormal state of physiological inactivity; a phase of the business cycle characterized by stagnation, widespread unemployment, etc; a falling in or sinking; a lowering of atmospheric pressure, often signalling rain.

deprive *vt* to take a thing away from; to prevent from using or enjoying.—**deprivation** *n*.

deprived *adj* lacking the essentials of life, such as adequate food, shelter, education, etc.

depth *n* deepness; the distance downwards or inwards; the intensity of emotion or feeling; the profundity of thought; intensity of color; the mid point of the night or winter; the lowness of sound or pitch; the quality of being deep.

depth-charge *n* a bomb designed to explode under water, used against submarines.

deputation *n* a person or group appointed to represent others.

deputize *vi* to act as deputy.

deputy *n* a delegate, representative, or substitute.

deputy minister *n* (*Cdn*) a civil servant who acts as a deputy to the head of a government department or ministry.

derail *vti* (*train*) to cause to leave the rails.—**derailment** *n*.

derange *vt* to throw into confusion; to disturb; to make insane.—**derangement** *n*.

derelict *adj* abandoned, deserted and left to decay; negligent. * *n* a person abandoned by society; a wrecked ship or vehicle.

deride *vt* to scorn, mock.

derision *n* ridicule.

derisive *adj* full of derision; mocking, scornful.

derisory *adj* showing or deserving of derision.

derivation *n* the tracing of a word to its root; origin; descent.

derivative *adj* derived from something else; not original. * *n* something that is derived; a word formed by derivation; (*math*) the rate of change of one quantity with respect to another.

derive *vt* to take or receive from a source; to infer, deduce (from). * *vi* to issue as a derivative (from).

derogatory *adj* disparaging; deliberately offensive.

derrick *n* any crane-like apparatus; a tower over an oil well, etc, holding the drilling machinery.

descend *vi* to come or climb down; to pass from

a higher to a lower place or condition; (*with* **on, upon**) to make a sudden attack upon, or visit unexpectedly; to sink in morals or dignity; to be derived. * *vt* to go, pass, or extend down.

descendant *n* a person who is descended from an ancestor; something derived from an earlier form.

descent *n* a descending; a downward motion or step; a way down; a slope; a raid or invasion; lineage, ancestry.

describe *vt* to give a verbal account of; to trace out.

description *n* a verbal or pictorial account; sort, kind.

descriptive *adj* tending to or serving to describe.

desecrate *vt* to violate a sacred place by destructive or blasphemous behaviour.—**desecration** *n*.

desert[1] *n* (*often pl*) a deserved reward or punishment.

desert[2] *vt* to leave, abandon, with no intention of returning; to abscond from the armed forces without permission.—**deserter** *n*.—**desertion** *n*.

desert[3] *n* a dry, barren region, able to support little or no life; a place lacking in some essential quality.

deserve *vt* to merit or be suitable for (some reward, punishment, etc).—**deservedly** *adv*.

deserving *adj* worthy of support, esp financially.

design *vt* to plan; to create; to devise; to make working drawings for; to intend. * *n* a working drawing; a mental plan or scheme; the particular form or disposition of something; a decorative pattern; .purpose; (*pl*) dishonest intent.

designate *vt* to indicate, specify; to name; to appoint to or nominate for a position, office. * *adj* (*after noun*) appointed to office but not yet installed.

designation *n* the act of designating; nomination; a distinguishing name or title.

designer *n* a person who designs things; a person who is renowned for creating high-class fashion clothes. * *adj* (*inf*) trendy, of the latest, esp expensive, fashion.

desirable *adj* arousing (sexual) desire; advisable or beneficial; worth doing.—**desirably** *adv*.—**desirability** *n*.

desire *vt* to long or wish for; to request, to ask for. * *n* a longing for something regarded as pleasurable or satisfying; a request; something desired; sexual craving.—**desirous** *adj*.

desk *n* a piece of furniture with a writing surface and usu drawers; a counter behind which a cashier, etc sits; the section of a newspaper responsible for a particular topic.

desolate *adj* solitary, lonely; devoid of inhabitants; laid waste.

desolation *n* destruction, ruin; a barren state; loneliness; wretchedness.

despair *vi* to have no hope. * *n* utter loss of hope; something that causes despair.

despatch *see* **dispatch.**

desperate *adj* (almost) hopeless; reckless through lack of hope; urgently requiring (money, etc); (*remedy*) extreme, dangerous.—**desperately** *adv*.

desperation *n* loss of hope; recklessness from despair.

despicable *adj* contemptible, worthless.—**despicably** *adv*.

despise *vt* to regard with contempt or scorn; to consider as worthless, inferior.

despite *prep* in spite of.

despondent *adj* dejected; lacking hope.—**despondence, despondency** *n*.—**despondently** *adv*.

dessert *n* the sweet course at the end of a meal.

dessertspoon *n* a spoon in between a teaspoon and a tablespoon in size, used for eating desserts.

destination *n* the place to which a person or thing is going.

destine *vt* to set aside for some specific purpose; to predetermine; intend.

destiny *n* the power supposedly determining the course of events; the future to which any person or thing is destined; a predetermined course of events.

destitute *adj* (*with* **of**) lacking some quality; lacking the basic necessities of life, very poor.

destream *vt* (*Cdn*) to teach students in an undivided group, rather than according to categories based on their academic abilities.—**destreaming** *n*.

destroy *vt* to demolish, ruin, to put an end to; to kill.

destroyer *n* a fast small warship.

destructible *adj* able to be destroyed.

destruction *n* the act or process of destroying or being destroyed; ruin.

destructive *adj* causing destruction; (*with* **of** *or* **to**) ruinous; (*criticism*) intended to discredit, negative.—**destructively** *adv*.—**destructiveness** *n*.

detach *vt* to release; to separate from a larger group; (*mil*) to send off on special assignment.

detachable *adj* able to be detached.

detached *adj* separate; (*house*) not joined to another; aloof; free from bias or emotion.

detachment *n* indifference; freedom from emotional involvement or bias; the act of detaching; a thing detached; a body of troops detached from the main body and sent on special service ; (*Cdn*) the office or headquarters of a police force in a district.

detail *vt* to describe fully; (*mil*) to set apart for a particular duty. * *n* an item; a particular or minute account; (*art*) treatment of smaller parts; a reproduction of a smaller part of a picture, statue, etc; a small detachment for special service.

detailed *adj* giving full details; thorough.

detain *vt* to place in custody or confinement; to delay.

detect *vt* to discover the existence or presence of; to notice.

detection *n* a discovery or being discovered; the job or process of detecting.

detective *n* a person or a police officer employed to find evidence of crimes.

detector *n* a device for detecting the presence of something.

detention *n* the act of detaining or withholding; a being detained; confinement; being kept in (school after hours) as a punishment.

deter *vt* (*pt* **deterred**) to discourage or prevent (from acting).—**determent** *n*.

detergent *n* a cleaning agent—*also adj*.

deteriorate *vt* to make or become worse.—**deterioration** *n*.

determination *n* the act or process of making a decision; a decision resolving a dispute; firm intention; resoluteness.

determine *vt* to fix or settle officially; to find out; to regulate; to impel. * *vi* to come to a decision.

determined *adj* full of determination, resolute.—**determinedly** *adv*.

deterrent *n* something that deters; a nuclear weapon that deters attack through fear of retaliation. * *adj* deterring.—**deterrence** *n*.

detest *vt* to dislike intensely.—**detestation** *n*.

detestable *adj* intensely disliked, abhorrent.—**detestably** *adv*.

detonate *vti* to explode or cause to explode rapidly and violently.—**detonation** *n*.

detonator *n* a device that sets off an explosion.

detour *n* a deviation from an intended course, esp one serving as an alternative to a more direct route. * *vti* to make or send by a detour.

detract *vt* to take away. * *vi* to take away (from).—**detraction** *n*.—**detractor** *n*.

detriment *n* (a cause of) damage or injury.—**detrimental** *adj*.

devalue, devaluate *vt* to reduce the exchange value of (a currency).—**devaluation** *n*.

devastate *vt* to lay waste; to destroy; to overwhelm.—**devastation** *n*.

develop *vt* to evolve; to bring to maturity; to show the symptoms of (eg a habit, a disease); to treat a photographic film or plate to reveal an image; to improve the value of. * *vi* to grow (into); to become apparent.

developer *n* a person who develops; a person or organization that develops property; a reagent for developing photographs.

developing country *n* a poor country that is attempting to improve its social conditions and encourage industrial growth.

development *n* the process of growing or developing; a new situation that emerges; a piece of land or property that has been developed.

deviate *vi* to diverge from a course, topic, principle, etc.—**deviation** *n*.

device *n* a machine, implement, etc for a particular purpose; an invention; a scheme, a plot.

devil *n* (*with cap*) in Christian and Jewish theology, the supreme spirit of evil, Satan; any evil spirit; an extremely wicked person; (*inf*) a reckless, high-spirited person; (*inf*) someone or something difficult to deal with; (*inf*) a person. * *vb* (*pt* **devilled**) *vt* to cook food with a hot seasoning. * *vi* to act as a drudge to someone; to do research for an author or barrister.

devilish *adj* fiendish; mischievous. * *adv* (*inf*) very.

devious *adj* indirect; not straightforward; underhand, deceitful.—**deviously** *adv*.—**deviousness** *n*.

devise *vt* to invent, contrive; to plan.—**deviser, devisor** *n*.

devoid *adj* lacking (*with* of); free from.

devote *vt* to give or use for a particular activity or purpose.

devoted *adj* zealous; loyal; loving. —**devotedly** *adv*.

devotion *n* given to religious worship; piety; strong affection or attachment (to); ardour; (*pl*) prayers. —**devotional** *adj*.

devour *vt* to eat up greedily; to consume; to absorb eagerly by the senses or mind.

devout *adj* very religious, pious; sincere, dedicated.—**devoutly** *adv*.—**devoutness** *n*.

dew *n* air moisture, deposited on a cool surface, esp at night.

dexterity *n* manual skill, adroitness.

DFO *abbr* (*Cdn*) = Department of Fisheries and Oceans.

DHS *abbr* (*Cdn*) = District High School.

diabetes *n* a medical disorder marked by the persistent and excessive discharge of urine.

diabetic *adj* suffering from diabetes.—*also n*.

diagnose *vt* to ascertain by diagnosis.

diagnosis *n* (*pl* **diagnoses**) the identification of a disease from its symptoms; the analysis of the nature or cause of a problem.—**diagnostic** *adj*.—**diagnostician** *n*.

diagonal *adj* slanting from one corner to an opposite corner of a polygon. * *n* a straight line connecting opposite corners.—**diagonally** *adv*.

diagram *n* a figure or plan drawn in outline to illustrate the form or workings of something.—**diagrammatic** *adj*.

dial *n* the face of a watch or clock; a graduated disc with a pointer used in various instruments; the control on a radio or television set indicating wavelength or station; the numbered disc on a telephone used to enter digits to connect calls; an instrument for telling the time by the sun's shadow. * *vt* (*pt* **dialled**) to measure or indicate by a dial; to make a telephone connection by using a dial or numbered keypad.

dialect *n* the form of language spoken in a particular region or social class.

dialogue, dialog (*US*) *n* a conversation, esp in a play or novel; an exchange of opinions, negotiation.

diameter *n* a straight line bisecting a circle; the length of this line.

diamond *n* a valuable gem, a crystallized form of pure carbon; (*baseball*) the playing field, esp the infield; a suit of playing cards denoted by a red lozenge. * *adj* composed of, or set with diamonds; shaped like a diamond.

diaper *n* a nappy.

diaphragm n the midriff, a muscular structure separating the chest from the abdomen; any thin dividing membrane; a device for regulating aperture of a camera lens; a contraceptive cap covering the cervix; a thin vibrating disc used in a telephone receiver, microphone, etc.

diarrhoea, diarrhea (US) n excessive looseness of the bowels.

diary n a daily record of personal thoughts, events, or business appointments; a book for keeping a daily record.

dice n (the pl of **die**² but used as sing) a small cube with numbered sides used in games of chance. * vt to gamble using dice; to cut (food) into small cubes.

dictate vt to say or read for another person to write or for a machine to record; to pronounce, order with authority. * vi to give dictation; to give orders (to). * n an order, rule, or command; (usu pl) an impulse, ruling principle.—**dictation** n.

dictator n a ruler with absolute authority, usu acquired by force.

dictatorship n the office or government of a dictator; a country governed by a dictator; absolute power.

diction n a way of speaking, enunciation; a person's choice of words.

dictionary n a reference book containing the words of a language or branch of knowledge alphabetically arranged, with their meanings, pronunciation, origin, etc.

did see **do**.

die¹ vi (pr p **dying**, pt **died**) to cease existence; to become extinct; to stop functioning; to feel a deep longing.

die² n a dice.

die³ n an engraved stamp for pressing coins; a casting mould.

diesel n a vehicle driven by diesel engine.

diesel engine n an internal combustion engine in which ignition is produced by the heat of highly compressed air alone.

diet¹ n food selected to adjust weight, to control illness, etc; the food and drink usually consumed by a person or animal. * vt to put on a diet. * vi to eat according to a special diet.—**dieter** n.

diet² n a legislative assembly in some countries.

differ vi to be unlike, distinct (from); to disagree.

difference n the act or state of being unlike; disparity; a distinguishing feature; the amount or manner of being different; the result of the subtraction of one quantity from another; a disagreement or argument.

different adj distinct, separate; unlike, not the same; unusual.—**differently** adv.

differential adj of or showing a difference; (math) relating to increments in given functions. * n something that marks the difference between comparable things; the difference in wage rates for different types of labour, esp within an industry.

differentiate vt to make different; to become specialized; to note differences; (math) to calculate the derivative of.—**differentiation** n.

difficult adj hard to understand; hard to make, do, or carry out; not easy to please.

difficulty n being difficult; a problem, etc that is hard to deal with; an obstacle; a troublesome situation; a disagreement.

diffident adj shy, lacking self-confidence, not assertive.—**diffidence** n.—**diffidently** adv.

diffuse¹ vt to spread widely in all directions. * vti (gases, fluids, particles) to intermingle.—**diffuser, diffusor** n.

diffuse² adj spread widely, not concentrated; wordy, not concise.—**diffusely** adv.

dig vt (pr p **digging**, pt **dug**) to use a tool or hands, claws, etc in making a hole in the ground; to unearth by digging; to excavate; to investigate; to thrust (into); to nudge; (sl) to understand, approve. * n (sl) a thrust; an archaeological excavation; a cutting remark.

digest¹ vt to convert (food) into assimilable form; to reduce (facts, laws, etc) to convenient form by classifying or summarizing; to form a clear view of (a situation) by reflection. * vi to become digested.

digest² n an abridgment of any written matter; a periodical synopsis of published or broadcast material.

digestible adj capable of being digested.—**digestibility** n.

digestion n the act or process of digesting.

digit n any of the basic counting units of a number system, including zero; a human finger or toe.

digital adj of or using digits.—**digitally** adv.

dignified adj possessing dignity; noble; serious.

dignitary n a person in a high position or rank.

dignity n noble, serious, formal in manner and appearance; sense of self-respect, worthiness; a high rank, eg in the government.

digress vi to stray from the main subject in speaking or writing.—**digression** n.

digs npl (inf) lodgings.

dilapidated adj in a state of disrepair; shabby.

dilate vti to enlarge or become enlarged.—**dilation** n.—**dilator, dilater** n.

dilatory adj tardy; causing or meant to cause delay.—**dilatorily** adv.—**dilatoriness** n.

dilemma n a situation where each of two alternative courses is undesirable; any difficult problem or choice.

diligent adj industrious; done with proper care and effort.—**diligently** adv.—**diligence** n.

dilute vt to thin down, esp by mixing with water; to weaken the strength of. * adj diluted.—**dilution** n.

dim adj (**dimmer, dimmest**) faintly lit; not seen, heard, understood, etc clearly; gloomy; unfavorable; (inf) stupid. * vti to make or cause to become dark.—**dimly** adv.—**dimness** n.

dime n a US or Canadian coin worth ten cents.

dimension n any linear measurement of width, length, or thickness; extent; size.—**dimensional** adj.

diminish *vti* to make or become smaller in size, amount, or importance.

diminutive *adj* very small. * *n* a word formed by a suffix to mean small (eg *duckling*) or to convey affection (eg *Freddie*).

dimple *n* a small hollow, usu on the cheek or chin. * *vti* to make or become dimpled; to reveal dimples.

din *n* a loud persistent noise. * *vt* (*pt* **dinned**) to make a din; (*with* **into**) to instil by continual repetition.

dine *vi* to eat dinner. * *vt* to entertain to dinner.

dinghy *n* a small open boat propelled by oars or sails; a small inflatable boat.

dingy *adj* (**dingier, dingiest**) dirty-looking, shabby.—**dinginess** *n*.

dinner *n* the principal meal of the day; a formal meal in honor of a person or occasion.

dinner jacket *n* a man's usu black jacket for semi-formal evening wear.

diocese *n* the district over which a bishop has authority.—**diocesan** *adj*.

dip *vt* (*pt* **dipped**) to put (something) under the surface (of a liquid) and lift quickly out again; to immerse (sheep) in an antiseptic solution. * *vi* to go into water and come out quickly; to drop down or sink out of sight; to read superficially; to slope downward. * *n* a dipping of any kind; a sudden drop; a mixture in which to dip something.

diphtheria *n* an acute infectious disease causing inflammation of the throat and breathing difficulties.

diphthong *n* the union of two vowel sounds pronounced in one syllable; a ligature.

diploma *n* a certificate given by a college or university to its graduating students.

diplomacy *n* the management of relations between nations; skill in handling affairs without arousing hostility.

diplomat *n* a person employed or skilled in diplomacy.

diplomatic, diplomatical *adj* of diplomacy; employing tact and conciliation; tactful.—**diplomatically** *adv*.

dipper *n* (*Cdn*) a small lidless saucepan.

dipstick *n* a rod with graduated markings to measure fluid level.

dire *adj* dreadful; ominous; desperately urgent.

direct *adj* straight; in an unbroken line, with nothing in between; frank; truthful. * *vt* to manage, to control; to tell or show the way; to point to, to aim at; (*a letter or parcel*) to address; to carry out the organizing and supervision of; to train and lead performances; to command. * *vi* to determine a course; to act as a director.—**directness** *n*.

direct current *n* an electric current that flows in one direction only.

direct debit *n* (*Cdn* and *Brit*) a pre-arranged regular debit of a bank account, usu to make a recurring payment.

direct deposit *n* (*US*) the transfer of money, electronically, from one bank account to another.

direction *n* management, control; order, command; a knowing or telling what to do, where to go, etc; any way in which one may face or point; (*pl*) instructions.

directly *adv* in a direct manner; immediately; in a short while.

director *n* person who directs, esp the production of a show for stage or screen; one of the persons directing the affairs of a company or an institution. —**directorial** *adj*.—**directorship** *n*.

directory *n* an alphabetical or classified list, as of telephone numbers, members of an organization, charities, etc.

dirt *n* filth; loose earth; obscenity; scandal.

dirt-cheap *adj* (*inf*) very cheap.

dirty *adj* (**dirtier, dirtiest**) filthy; unclean; dishonest; mean; (*weather*) stormy; obscene. * *vti* to make or become dirty.—**dirtily** *adv*.—**dirtiness** *n*.

Dirty Thirties *n* (*Cdn*) (*inf*) the economic depression of the 1930s.

disability *n* a lack of physical, mental or social fitness; something that disables, a handicap.

disabled *adj* having a physical handicap.

disadvantage *n* an unfavorable condition or situation; loss, damage. * *vt* to put at a disadvantage.

disadvantageous *adj* causing disadvantage.

disagree *vi* to differ in opinion; to quarrel; (*with* **with**) to have a bad effect on.—**disagreement** *n*.

disagreeable *adj* nasty, bad tempered. —**disagreeably** *adv*.

disallow *vt* to refuse to allow or to accept the truth or value of.

disappear *vi* to pass from sight completely; to fade into nothing.—**disappearance** *n*.

disappoint *vt* to fail to fulfil the hopes of (a person).—**disappointed** *adj*.—**disappointing** *adj*.—**disappointingly** *adv*.

disappointment *n* the frustration of one's hopes; annoyance due to failure; a person or thing that disappoints.

disapprove *vti* to express or have an unfavorable opinion (of).—**disapproval** *n*.

disarm *vt* to deprive of weapons or means of defence; to defuse (a bomb); to conciliate. * *vi* to abolish or reduce national armaments.

disarmament *n* the reduction or abolition of a country's armed forces and weaponry.

disaster *n* a devastating and sudden misfortune; utter failure.—**disastrous** *adj*.—**disastrously** *adv*.

disband *vt* to disperse; to break up and separate.—**disbandment** *n*.

disc *n* any flat, thin circular body; something resembling this, as the sun; a cylindrical pad of cartilage between the vertebrae; a gramophone record; (*comput*) a variant spelling of **disk**.

discard *vti* to cast off, get rid of; (*cards*) to throw away a card from one's hand. * *n* something discarded; (*cards*) a discarded card.

disc brake *n* one in which two flat discs press against a central plate on the wheel hub.

discern *vt* to perceive; to see clearly. —discernible *adj*.—discernibly *adv*.

discerning *adj* discriminating; perceptive.—discernment *n*.

discharge *vt* to unload; to send out, emit; to release, acquit; to dismiss from employment; to shoot a gun; to fulfil, as duties. * *vi* to unload; (*gun*) to be fired; (*fluid*) to pour out. * *n* the act or process of discharging; something that is discharged; an authorization for release, acquittal, dismissal, etc.

disciple *n* a person who believes in and helps to spread another's teachings, a follower; one of the twelve apostles of Christ.

disciplinary *adj* of or for discipline.

discipline *n* a field of learning; training and conditioning to produce obedience and self-control; punishment; the maintenance of order and obedience as a result of punishment; a system of rules of behaviour. * *vt* to punish to enforce discipline; to train by instruction; to bring under control.

disc jockey *n* (*inf*) a person who announces records on a programme of broadcast music, or in discotheques.

disclaim *vi* to deny connection with; to renounce all legal claim to.

disclose *vt* to bring into the open, to reveal.—disclosure *n*.

disco *n* (*inf*) a discotheque.

discolor *vti* to ruin the color of; to fade, stain.—discoloration *n*.

discomfort *n* uneasiness; something causing this. * *vt* to make uncomfortable; to make uneasy.

disconcert *vt* to confuse; to upset.

disconnect *vt* to separate or break the connection of.

disconnected *adj* disjointed; incoherent.

disconsolate *adj* miserable; dejected. —disconsolately *adv*.

discontent *n* lack of contentment, dissatisfaction.—discontentment *n*.

discontented *adj* feeling discontent; unhappy, unsatisfied.

discontinue *vti* to stop or come to a stop; to give up.—discontinuance *n*.

discord *n* lack of agreement, strife; (*mus*) a lack of harmony; harsh clashing sounds.—discordance *n*.—discordant *adj*.—discordantly *adv*.

discotheque *n* an occasion when people gather to dance to recorded pop music; a club or party, etc where this takes place; equipment for playing such music.

discount *n* a reduction in the amount or cost; the percentage charged for doing this. * *vt* to deduct from the amount, cost; to allow for exaggeration; to disregard; to make less effective by anticipation. * *vi* to make and give discounts.

discourage *vt* to deprive of the will or courage (to do something); to try to prevent; to hinder.—discouraging *adj*.—discouraged *adj*.—discouragement *n*.

discourteous *adj* lacking in courtesy, rude.—discourteously *adv*.—discourtesy *n*.

discover *vt* to see, find or learn of for the first time.—discoverable *adj*.—discoverer *n*.

discovery *n* the act of discovering or being discovered; something discovered.

discredit *n* damage to a reputation; doubt; disgrace; lack of credibility. * *vt* to damage the reputation of; to cast doubt on the authority or credibility of.

discreet *adj* wisely cautious, prudent; unobtrusive.—discreetly *adv*.—discreetness *n*.

discrepancy *n* difference; a disagreement, as between figures in a total.

discretion *n* the freedom to judge or choose; prudence; wise judgment; skill.

discriminate *vi* to be discerning in matters of taste; to make a distinction; to treat differently, esp unfavorably due to prejudice.—discrimination *n*.—discriminatory *adj*.

discriminating *adj* judicious; discerning; discriminatory.

discus *n* a heavy disc with a thickened middle, thrown by athletes.

discuss *vt* to talk over; to investigate by reasoning or argument.—discussion *n*.

disdain *vt* to scorn, treat with contempt. * *n* scorn; a feeling of contemptuous superiority.—disdainful *adj*.—disdainfully *adv*.

disease *n* an unhealthy condition in an organism caused by infection, poisoning, etc; sickness; a harmful condition or situation.—diseased *adj*.

disembark *vti* to land from a ship, debark.—disembarkation *n*.

disembodied *adj* (*soul, spirit, etc*) free of the body.

disembowel *vt* (*pt* disembowelled) to remove the entrails of; to remove the substance of.

disenchant *vt* to disillusion.—disenchantment *n*.

disengage *vt* to separate or free from engagement or obligation; to detach, to release.—disengaged *adj*.—disengagement *n*.

disentangle *vt* to untangle; to free from complications.—disentanglement *n*.

disfavor *n* dislike; disapproval. * *vt* to treat with disfavor.

disfigure *vt* to spoil the beauty or appearance of.—disfigurement *n*.

disgrace *n* a loss of trust, favor, or honor; something that disgraces. * *vt* to bring disgrace or shame upon.

disgraceful *adj* causing disgrace, shameful.—disgracefully *adv*.

disgruntled *adj* dissatisfied, resentful.

disguise *vt* to hide what one is by appearing as something else; to hide what (a thing) really is. * *n* the use of a changed appearance to conceal identity; a false appearance.

disgust *n* sickening dislike. * *vt* to cause disgust in.—disgustedly *adv*.

dish *n* any of various shallow concave vessels to serve food in; the amount of food served in a dish; the food served; a shallow concave object, as a dish aerial; (*inf*) an attractive person.

dishcloth *n* a cloth for washing dishes.

dishearten *vt* to discourage.

dishevelled, disheveled (*US*) *adj* rumpled, untidy.—**dishevelment** *n*.

dishonest *adj* not honest.—**dishonestly** *adv*.—**dishonesty** *n*.

dishonor, dishonor (*US*) *n* loss of honor; disgrace, shame. * *vt* to bring shame on, to disgrace; to refuse to pay, as a cheque.

dishonorable, dishonorable (*US*) *adj* lacking honor, disgraceful.—**dishonorably** *adv*.

dishwasher *n* an appliance for washing dishes; a person employed to wash dishes.

disillusion *vt* to free from (mistaken) ideals or illusions. * *n* the state of being disillusioned.—**disillusionment** *n*.

disinfect *vt* to destroy germs.—**disinfection** *n*.

disinfectant *n* any chemical agent that inhibits the growth of or destroys germs.

disintegrate *vti* to break or cause to break into separate pieces.—**disintegration** *n*.

disinterested *adj* impartial; objective. —**disinterestedly** *adv*.

disjointed *adj* incoherent, muddled, esp of speech or writing.

disk *n* an alternative spelling of **disc**; (*comput*) a storage device in a computer, either floppy or hard.

dislike *vt* to consider unpleasant. * *n* aversion, distaste.—**dislikable, dislikeable** *adj*.

dislocate *vt* to put (a joint) out of place, to displace; to upset the working of.—**dislocation** *n*.

dislodge *vt* to force or move out of a hiding place, established position, etc. —**dislodgement, dislodgment** *n*.

dismal *adj* gloomy, miserable, sad; (*inf*) feeble, worthless. —**dismally** *adv*.

dismantle *vt* to pull down; to take apart.

dismay *n* apprehension, discouragement. * *vt* to fill with dismay.

disobedient *adj* failing or refusing to obey.—**disobediently** *adv*.—**disobedience** *n*.

disobey *vt* to refuse to follow orders.

disorder *n* lack of order; untidiness; a riot; an illness or interruption of the normal functioning of the body or mind. * *vt* to throw into confusion; to upset.—**disorderly** *adj*.

disorganize *vt* to confuse or disrupt an orderly arrangement.—**disorganization** *n*.

disown *vt* to refuse to acknowledge as one's own.

disparage *vt* to belittle.—**disparagingly** *adv*.—**disparagement** *n*.

disparity *n* essential difference; inequality.

dispassionate *adj* unemotional; impartial.—**dispassionately** *adv*.

dispatch *vt* to send off somewhere; to perform speedily; to kill. * *n* a sending off (of a letter, a messenger etc); promptness; haste; a written message, esp of news.—*also* **despatch**.

dispel *vt* (*pt* **dispelled**) to drive away and scatter.

dispensary *n* a place in a hospital, a chemist shop, etc where medicines are made up and dispensed.

dispense *vt* to deal out, distribute; to prepare and distribute medicines; to administer.

disperse *vt* to scatter in different directions.

* *vi* to separate, become dispersed.—**dispersal** *n*.

dispirited *adj* depressed, discouraged.

displace *vt* to take the place of, to oust; to remove from a position of authority.—**displacement** *n*.

display *vt* to show, expose to view; to exhibit ostentatiously. * *n* a displaying; an eye-catching arrangement, exhibition; a computer monitor for presenting visual information.

displease *vt* to cause offence or annoyance to.

displeasure *n* a feeling of being displeased; dissatisfaction.

disposable *adj* designed to be discarded after use; available for use. * *n* something disposable, eg a baby's nappy.

disposal *n* a disposing of something; order, arrangement.

dispose *vt* to place in order, arrange; to influence. * *vi* to deal with or settle; to give, sell or transfer to another; to throw away.

disposed *adj* inclined (towards something).

disposition *n* a natural way of behaving towards others; tendency; arrangement.

disproportionate *adj* out of proportion.—**disproportionately** *adv*.

disprove *vt* to prove (a claim, etc) to be incorrect.

dispute *vt* to make the subject of an argument or debate; to query the validity of. * *vi* to argue. * *n* an argument; a quarrel.

disqualify *vt* to make ineligible because of a violation of rules; to make unfit or unsuitable, to disable.—**disqualification** *n*.

disquiet *n* anxiety, worry.—*also vt.*—**disquieting** *adj*.—**disquietude** *n*.

disregard *vt* to pay no attention to; to consider as of little or no importance. * *n* lack of attention, neglect.

disrepair *n* a worn-out condition through neglect of repair.

disreputable *adj* of bad reputation.

disrespect *n* lack of respect, rudeness. —**disrespectful** *adj*.—**disrespectfully** *adv*.

disrupt *vti* to break up; to create disorder or confusion; to interrupt.—**disruption** *n*.

dissect *vt* to cut apart (a plant, animal, etc) for scientific examination; to analyse and interpret in fine detail.—**dissection** *n*.—**dissector** *n*.

disseminate *vt* to spread or scatter (ideas, information, etc) widely.—**dissemination** *n*.

dissent *vi* to hold a different opinion; to withhold assent. * *n* a difference of opinion.—**dissenter** *n*.

dissident *adj* disagreeing. * *n* a person who disagrees strongly with government policies, esp one who suffers harassment or imprisonment as a result.—**dissidence** *n*.

dissipate *vt* to scatter, dispel; to waste, squander (money, etc). * *vi* to separate and vanish.

dissipated *adj* dissolute, indulging in excessive pleasure; scattered, wasted.

dissociate *vti* to separate or cause to separate the association of (people, things, etc) in consciousness; to repudiate a connection with.—**dissociation** n.

dissolute adj lacking moral discipline.

dissolve vt to cause to pass into solution; to disperse (a legislative assembly); to melt; (partnership, marriage) to break up legally, annul. * vi to become liquid; to fade away; to be overcome by emotion.

dissuade vt to prevent or discourage by persuasion.—**dissuasion** n.—**dissuasive** adj.

distance n the amount of space between two points or things; a distant place or point; remoteness, coldness of manner. * vt to place at a distance, physically or emotionally; to outdistance in a race, etc.

distant adj separated by a specific distance; far-off in space, time, place, relation, etc; not friendly, aloof.—**distantly** adv.

distaste n aversion; dislike.

distasteful adj unpleasant, offensive. —**distastefully** adv.

distemper n an infectious and often fatal disease of dogs and other animals; a type of paint made by mixing color with egg or glue instead of oil; a painting made with this.

distend vti to swell or cause to swell, esp from internal pressure.

distil, **distill** (US) vti (pt **distilled**) to treat by, or cause to undergo, distillation; to purify; to extract the essence of; to let or cause to fall in drops.

distillery n a place where distilling, esp of alcoholic spirits, is carried on.

distinct adj different, separate (from); easy to perceive by the mind or senses.—**distinctly** adv.—**distinctness** n.

distinction n discrimination, separation; a difference seen or made; a distinguishing mark or characteristic; excellence, superiority; a mark of honor.

distinctive adj clearly marking a person or thing as different from another; characteristic.

distinguish vt to see or recognize as different; to mark as different, characterize; to see or hear clearly; to confer distinction on; to make eminent or known. * vi to perceive a difference. —**distinguishable** adj.

distinguished adj eminent, famous; dignified in appearance or manners.

distort vt to pull or twist out of shape; to alter the true meaning of, misrepresent.—**distortion** n.

distract vt to draw (eg the mind or attention) to something else; to confuse.

distracted adj bewildered, confused.

distraction n something that distracts the attention; an amusement; perplexity; extreme agitation.

distraught adj extremely distressed.

distress n physical or emotional suffering, as from pain, illness, lack of money, etc; a state of danger, desperation. * vt to cause distress to.

distribute vt to divide and share out; to spread, disperse throughout an area.—**distribution** n.

distributor n an agent who sells goods, esp wholesale; a device for distributing current to the spark plugs in an engine.

district n a territorial division defined for administrative purposes; a region or area with a distinguishing character.

district municipality n (Cdn) in British Columbia, an administrative unit for a thinly-populated area.

distrust n suspicion, lack of trust.—also vt.—**distrustful** adj.

disturb vt to interrupt; to cause to move from the normal position or arrangement; to destroy the quiet or composure of.

disturbance n a disturbing or being disturbed; an interruption; an outbreak of disorder and confusion.

ditch n any long narrow trench dug in the ground. * vt to make a ditch in; (sl) to drive (a car) into a ditch; (sl) to make a forced landing of (an aircraft); (sl) to get rid of.

dither vi to hesitate, vacillate.—**ditherer** n.

ditto n the same again, as above—used in written lists and tables to avoid repetition. * vt to repeat.

divan n a long couch without back or sides; a bed of similar design.

dive vi (pt **dived** or **dove**) to plunge headfirst into water; (aircraft) to descend or fall steeply; (diver, submarine) to submerge; to plunge (eg the hand) suddenly into anything; to dash headlong, lunge. * n a headlong plunge; a submerging of a submarine, etc; a sharp descent; a steep decline; (sl) a disreputable public place.

diver n a person who dives; a person who works or explores underwater from a diving bell or in a diving suit; any of various aquatic birds.

diverge vi to branch off in different directions from a common point; to differ in character, form, etc; to deviate from a path or course.—**divergent** adj.—**divergence** n.

diverse adj different; assorted, various.

diversify vt to vary; to invest in a broad range of securities to lessen risk of loss. * vi to engage in a variety of commercial operations to reduce risk.—**diversification** n.

diversion n turning aside from a course; a recreation, amusement; a drawing of attention away from the principal activity; a detour when a road is temporarily closed to traffic.—**diversionary** adj.

diversity n variety.

divert vt to turn aside from one course onto another; to entertain, amuse.

divide vt to break up into parts; to distribute, share out; to sort into categories; to cause to separate from something else; to separate into opposing sides; (Parliament) to vote or cause to vote by division; (math) to ascertain how many times one quantity contains another. * vi to become separated; to diverge; to vote by separating into two sides. * n a watershed; a split.

dividend n a number which is to be divided; the money earned by a company and divided among the shareholders; a bonus derived from some action.

divine *adj* of, from, or like God or a god; (*inf*) excellent. * *n* a clergyman; a theologian. * *vt* to foretell the future by supernatural means; to discover intuitively; to dowse. * *vi* to practise divination.—**divinely** *adv*.—**diviner** *n*.

diving board *n* a platform or springboard for diving from.

divinity *n* any god; theology; the quality of being God or a god.

division *n* a dividing or being divided; a partition, a barrier; a portion or section; a military unit; separation; (*Parliament*) a separation into two opposing sides to vote; a disagreement; (*math*) the process of dividing one number by another.—**divisional** *adj*.

divorce *n* the legal dissolution of marriage; separation. * *vt* to terminate a marriage by divorce; to separate.

divorcé, divorcee *n* a divorced person.—**divorcée** *nf*.

divulge *vt* to tell or reveal.—**divulgence** *n*.

DIY *abbr* = do-it-yourself.

dizzy *adj* (**dizzier, dizziest**) confused; causing giddiness or confusion; (*sl*) silly; foolish. * *vt* to make dizzy; to confuse.—**dizzily** *adv*.

DJ *abbr* = disc jockey; dinner jacket.

DM *abbr* (*Cdn*) = Deputy Minister.

DND *abbr* (*Cdn*) = Department of National Defence.

do *vt* (*pres t* **does**, *pt* **did**, *pp* **done**) to perform; to work; to end, to complete; to make; to provide; to arrange, to tidy; to perform; to cover a distance; to visit; (*sl*) to serve time in prison; (*sl*) to cheat, to rob; (*sl*) to assault. * *vi* to act or behave; to be satisfactory; to manage. * *n* (*pl* **dos, do's**) (*inf*) a party; (*inf*) a hoax. *Do* has special uses where it has no definite meaning, as in asking questions (*Do you like milk?*), emphasizing a verb (*I do want to go*), and standing for a verb already used (*My dog goes where I do*).

docile *adj* easily led; submissive.—**docilely** *adv*.—**docility** *n*.

dock[1] *vt* (*an animal's tail*) to cut short; (*wages, etc*) to deduct a portion of.

dock[2] *n* a wharf; an artificial enclosed area of water for ships to be loaded, repaired, etc; (*pl*) a dockyard. * *vt* to come or bring into dock; to join (spacecraft) together in space.

dock[3] *n* an enclosed area in a court of law reserved for the accused.

docker *n* a labourer who works at the docks.

dockyard *n* an area with docks and facilities for repairing and refitting ships.

doctor *n* a person qualified to treat diseases or physical disorders; the highest academic degree; the holder of such a degree. * *vt* to treat medically; (*machinery, etc*) to patch up; to tamper with, falsify; (*inf*) to castrate or spay.—**doctoral** *adj*.

doctrine *n* a principle of belief.—**doctrinal** *adj*.

document *n* a paper containing information or proof of anything. * *vt* to provide or prove with documents.—**documentation** *n*.

documentary *adj* consisting of documents; presenting a factual account of an event or activity. * *n* a non-fiction film.

dodge *vi* to move quickly in an irregular course. * *vt* to evade (a duty) by cunning; to avoid by a sudden movement or shift of position; to trick. * *n* a sudden movement; (*inf*) a clever trick.—**dodger** *n*.

DOE *abbr* (*Cdn*) = Department of the Environment.

dog *n* a canine mammal of numerous breeds, commonly kept as a domestic pet; the male of the wolf or fox; a despicable person; a device for gripping things. * *vt* (*pt* **dogged**) to pursue relentlessly.—**dog-like** *adj*.

dogan *n* (*Cdn*) (*hist sl*) a Roman Catholic, especially one who is Irish.

dog-collar *n* (*inf*) a clerical collar.

dog-eared *adj* (*book*) having the corners of the pages turned down; worn, shabby.

dogma *n* a belief taught or held as true, esp by a church; a doctrine.

dogmatic, dogmatical *adj* pertaining to a dogma; forcibly asserted as if true; overbearing.—**dogmatically** *adv*.

doings *npl* things done; actions.

doldrums *npl* inactivity; depression; boredom; the regions of the ocean about the equator where there is little wind.

dole *n* (*inf*) money received from the state while unemployed; a small portion. * *vt* to give (out) in small portions.

doleful *adj* sad, gloomy.—**dolefully** *adv*.

doll *n* a toy in the form of a human figure; a ventriloquist's dummy; (*sl*) a woman

dollar *n* the unit of money in the US, Canada, Australia and many other countries.

Dolly Varden *n* a brightly spotted trout of western North America; a large hat lop-sided hat worn by women; a sponge cake made with spices and dried fruit.

dolphin *n* a marine mammal with a beak-like snout, larger than a porpoise but smaller than a whale.

domain *n* an area under the control of a ruler or government; a field of thought, activity, etc.

dome *n* a large, rounded roof; something high and rounded.—*also vt*.

dome fastener *n* a small fastener for articles of clothing or other items that has a rounded portion that snaps into a socket.

domesday *see* **doomsday**.

domestic *adj* belonging to the home or family; not foreign; (*animals*) tame. * *n* a servant in the home.—**domestically** *adv*.

domesticate *vt* to tame; to make home-loving and fond of household duties.—**domestication** *n*.

domicile *n* a house; a person's place of residence.—**domiciliary** *adj*.

dominant *adj* commanding, prevailing over others; overlooking from a superior height. * *n* (*mus*) the fifth note of a diatonic scale.—**dominance** *n*.

dominate *vt* to control or rule by strength; to

hold a commanding position over; to overlook from a superior height.—**domination** n.

dominion n a territory with one ruler or government; the power to rule, authority.

Dominion Day n former name for Canada Day.

domino n (pl **dominoes, dominos**) a flat oblong tile marked with up to six dots; (pl) a popular game usu using a set of 28 dominoes; a loose cloak, usu worn with an eye mask, at masquerades.

don[1] vt (pt **donned**) to put on.

don[2] n a head, fellow or tutor at Oxford or Cambridge universities; (loosely) any university teacher.

donate vt to give as a gift or donation, esp to a charity.—**donator** n.

donation n donating; a contribution.

done see **do**.

donkey n a small animal resembling a horse.

donor n a person who donates something, a donator; a person who gives blood, organs, etc, for medical use.

don't = do not.

donut n (inf) a doughnut.

doom n a grim destiny; ruin. * vt to condemn to failure, destruction, etc.

doomsday n the day of God's Last Judgment of mankind.—also **domesday**.

door n a movable barrier to close an opening in a wall; a doorway; a means of entry or approach.

doorman n a uniformed attendant stationed at the entrance to large hotels, offices, etc.

doormat n a mat placed at the entrance to a doorway for wiping one's feet; (inf) a submissive or easily bullied person.

dope n a thick pasty substance used for lubrication; (inf) any illegal drug, such as cannabis or narcotics; (sl) a stupid person; (sl) information. * vt to treat with dope. * vi to take addictive drugs.

dopey, dopy adj (**dopier, dopiest**) (sl) stupid; (inf) half asleep.—**dopiness** n.

doré n (Cdn) a walleye (fish).

dormant adj sleeping; quiet, as if asleep; inactive.—**dormancy** n.

dormitory n a large room with many beds, as in a boarding school.

dormouse n (pl **dormice**) a small mouse-like creature that hibernates in winter.

Dorset n a member of an extinct Indian people living in the Eastern Arctic prior to their being displaced by the Inuit.

dose n the amount of medicine, radiation, etc administered at one time; a part of an experience; (sl) a venereal disease. * vt to administer a dose (of medicine) to.—**dosage** n.

dosshouse n (sl) a cheap lodging house.

dot n a small round speck, a point; the short signal in Morse code. * vt (pt **dotted**) to mark with a dot; to scatter (about).

DOT abbr = Department of Transport; Department of Transportation.

dote vi (with **on** or **upon**) to show excessive affection.

double adj twice as large, as strong, etc; designed or intended for two; made of two similar parts; having two meanings, characters, etc; (flowers) having more than one circle of petals. * adv twice; in twos. * n a number or amount that is twice as much; a person or thing identical to another; (film) a person closely resembling an actor and who takes their place to perform stunts, etc; (pl) a game between two pairs of players. * vti to make or become twice as much or as many; to fold, to bend; to bend sharply backwards; to sail around; to have an additional purpose.—**doubly** adv.

double bass n the largest instrument of the violin family.

double-breasted adj (suit) having one half of the front overlap the other.

double-cross vt to betray an associate, to cheat.—also n.

double-park vt to park alongside a car which is already parked beside the kerb.

doubt vi to be uncertain or undecided. * vt to hold in doubt; to distrust; to be suspicious of. * n uncertainty; (often pl) lack of confidence in something, distrust.—**doubter** n.

doubtful adj feeling doubt; uncertain; suspicious.—**doubtfully** adv.

doubtless adv no doubt.

dough n a mixture of flour and water, milk, etc used to make bread, pastry, or cake; (inf) money.—**doughy** adj.

doughnut n small, fried, usu ring-shaped, cake.

dove[1] see **dive**.

dove[2] n a small bird of the pigeon family; (politics, diplomacy) an advocate of peace or a peaceful policy.

dovetail n a wedge-shaped joint used in woodwork. * vt to fit or combine together.

dowdy adj (**dowdier, dowdiest**) poorly dressed, not stylish.—**dowdily** adv.—**dowdiness** n.

down[1] n soft fluffy feathers or fine hairs.

down[2] adv toward or in a lower physical position; to a lying or sitting position; toward or to the ground, floor, or bottom; to a source or hiding place; to or in a lower status or in a worse condition; from an earlier time; in cash; to or in a state of less activity. * adj occupying a low position, esp lying on the ground; depressed, dejected. * prep in a descending direction in, on, along, or through. * n a low period (as in activity, emotional life, or fortunes); (inf) a dislike, prejudice; in Canadian and US football, one of a series of attempts by the team on offence to advance the ball ten yards. * vti to go or cause to go or come down; to defeat; to swallow.

downcast adj dejected; (eyes) directed downwards.

downfall n a sudden fall (from power, etc); a sudden or heavy fall of rain, etc.

download vt copy or transfers software or data from one storage device or computer to another; (Cdn) shift responsibilities or costs from one level of government to a lower one. * n a transfer of software or data.

down payment n a deposit.

downpour *n* a heavy fall of rain.

downright *adj* frank; absolute. * *adv* thoroughly.

downtown *n* the main business district of a town or city.—*also adj.*

downward[1] *adj* moving from a higher to a lower level, position or condition. * *adv* downwards.

downwards, downward[2] *adv* towards a lower place, position, etc; from an earlier time to a later.

dowry *n* the money or possessions that a woman brings to her husband at marriage.

doze *vi* to sleep lightly. * *n* a light sleep, a nap.—**dozer** *n.*

dozen *n* a group of twelve.—**dozenth** *adj.*

Dr *abbr* = Doctor; debtor.

drab *adj* (**drabber, drabbest**) dull, un-interesting.—**drably** *adv.*—**drabness** *n.*

draft *n* a rough plan, preliminary sketch; an order for the payment of money by a bank; a smaller group selected from a larger for a specific task; in US, conscription; a draught. * *vt* to draw a rough sketch or outline of; to select for a special purpose; in US, to conscript.

drain *vt* to draw off liquid gradually; to make dry by removing liquid gradually; to exhaust physically or mentally; to drink the entire contents of a glass * *vi* to flow away gradually; to become dry as liquid trickles away. * *n* a sewer, pipe, etc by which water is drained away; something that causes exhaustion or depletion.

drainage *n* a draining; a system of drains; something drained off.

draining-board *n* a sloping, usu grooved, surface beside a sink for draining washed dishes.

drainpipe *n* a pipe that carries waste liquid, sewage, etc out of a building.

drama *n* a play for the stage, radio or television; dramatic literature as a genre; a dramatic situation or a set of events.

dramatic *adj* of or resembling drama; exciting, vivid.—**dramatically** *adv.*

dramatist *n* a person who writes plays.

drank *see* drink.

drape *vt* to cover or hang with cloth; to arrange in loose folds; to place loosely or untidily. * *n* a hanging cloth or curtain; (*pl*) curtains.

draper *n* a seller of cloth.

drastic *adj* acting with force and violence.—**drastically** *adv.*

draught, draft (*US*) *n* a current of air, esp in annenclosed space; the pulling of a load using an animal, etc; something drawn; a dose of medicine or liquid; an act of swallowing; the depth of water required to float a ship; beer, wine, etc stored in bulk in casks; a flat counter used in the game of draughts.

draughts *n* a board game for two players using 24 round pieces.—*also* **checkers.**

draughtsman[1], **draftsman** (*US*) *n* a person who makes detailed drawings or plans.—**draughtsmanship** *n.*

draughtsman[2] *n* a flat counter used in the game of draughts.—*also* **checker.**

draw *vti* (*pt* **drew**, *pp* **drawn**) to haul, to drag; to cause to go in a certain direction; to pull out; to attract; to delineate, to sketch; to receive (as a salary); to bend (a bow) by pulling back the string; to leave (a contest) undecided; to write up, to draft (a will); to produce or allow a current of air; to draw lots; to get information from; (*ship*) to require a certain depth to float. * *n* the act of drawing; (*inf*) an event that attracts customers, people; the drawing of lots; a drawn game.

drawback *n* a hindrance, handicap.

drawbridge *n* a bridge (eg over a moat) designed to be drawn up.

drawer *n* a person who draws; a person who draws a cheque; a sliding box-like compartment (in a table, chest, or desk); (*pl*) knickers, underpants.

drawing *n* a figure, plan, or sketch drawn by using lines.

drawing pin *n* a flat-headed pin used for fastening paper, drawings, etc, to a board.

drawing room *n* a room where visitors are entertained, a living room.

drawl *vt* to speak slowly and with elongated vowel sounds.—*also n.*

drawn *pp of* draw. * *adj* looking strained because of tiredness or worry.

dread *n* great fear or apprehension. * *vt* to fear greatly.—**dreadful** *adj.*—**dreadfully** *adv.*

dream *n* a stream of thoughts and images in sleep; a day-dreaming state, a reverie; an ambition; an ideal. * *vb* (*pt* **dreamt** *or* **dreamed**) *vi* to have a dream in sleep; to fantasize. * *vt* to dream of; to imagine as a reality.—**dreamer** *n.*

dreamy *adj* (**dreamier, dreamiest**) given to dreaming, unpractical; (*inf*) attractive, wonderful.

dreary *adj* (**drearier, dreariest**) dull; cheerless.—**drearily** *adv.*—**dreariness** *n.*

dredge[1] *n* a device for scooping up material from the bottom of a river, harbour, etc.—*also vt.*

dredge[2] *vt* to coat (food) by sprinkling.

dredger[1] *n* a vessel fitted with dredging equipment.

dredger[2] *n* a container with a perforated lid for sprinkling.

dregs *npl* solid impurities that settle on the bottom of a liquid; residue; (*inf*) a worthless person or thing.

drench *vt* to soak, saturate.

dress *n* clothing; a one-piece garment worn by women and girls comprising a top and skirt; a style or manner of clothing. * *vt* to put on or provide with clothing; to decorate; (*wound*) to wash and bandage; (*animal*) to groom; to arrange the hair; to prepare food (eg poultry, fish) for eating by cleaning, gutting, etc. * *vi* to put on clothes; to put on formal wear for an occasion.

dress circle *n* the first tier of seats in a theatre above the stalls.

dresser *n* a person who assists an actor to dress; a type of kitchen sideboard.

dressing *n* a sauce or stuffing for food; manure spread over the soil; dress or clothes; the bandage, ointment, etc applied to a wound.

dressing-down *n* a severe scolding.

dressing-gown *n* a loose garment worn when one is partially clothed.

dress rehearsal *n* rehearsal in full costume.

drew *see* draw.

dribble *vi* to flow in a thin stream or small drips; to let saliva to trickle from the mouth. * *vt* (*soccer, basketball, hockey*) to move (the ball) along little by little with the foot, hand, stick, etc. * *n* the act of dribbling; a thin stream of liquid.—**dribbler** *n*.

drier *see* dryer.

drift *n* a heap of snow, sand, etc deposited by the wind; natural course, tendency; the general meaning or intention (of what is said); the extent of deviation (of an aircraft, etc) from a course; an aimless course; the action or motion of drifting. * *vt* to cause to drift. * *vi* to be driven or carried along by water or air currents; to move along aimlessly; to be piled into heaps by the wind.

drill[1] *n* an implement with a pointed end that bores holes; the training of soldiers, etc; repetitious exercises or training as a teaching method; (*inf*) correct procedure or routine. * *vt* to make a hole with a drill; to instruct or be instructed by drilling.

drill[2] *n* a machine for planting seeds in rows; a furrow in which seeds are planted; a row of seeds planted in this way.—*also vt*.

drink *vb* (*pt* **drank**, *pp* **drunk**) *vt* to swallow (a liquid); to take in, absorb; to join in a toast. * *vi* to consume alcoholic liquor, esp to excess. * *n* liquid to be drunk; alcoholic liquor; (*sl*) the sea.—**drinker** *n*.

drip *vti* (*pt* **dripped**) to fall or let fall in drops. * *n* a liquid that falls in drops; the sound of falling drops; (*med*) a device for injecting a fluid slowly and continuously into a vein; (*inf*) a weak or ineffectual person.

drip-dry *adj* (*clothing*) drying easily and needing little ironing.—*also vti*.

dripping *n* fat that drips from meat during roasting.

drive *vb* (*pt* **drove**, *pp* **driven**) *vt* to urge, push or force onward; to direct the movement or course of; to convey in a vehicle; to carry through strongly; to impress forcefully; to propel (a ball) with a hard blow. * *vi* to be forced along; to be conveyed in a vehicle; to work, to strive (at). * *n* a trip in a vehicle; a stroke to drive a ball (in golf, etc); a driveway; a military attack; an intensive campaign; dynamic ability; the transmission of power to machinery.

driver *n* one who or that which drives; a chauffeur; (*golf*) a wooden club used from the tee.

drive shed *n* (*Cdn*) a large shed for storing vehicles or farm machinery.

driveway *n* a road for vehicles, often on private property.

drizzle *n* fine light rain.—*also vi*.—**drizzly** *adj*.

droke *n* (*Cdn*) in the Atlantic Provinces, a grove of trees; a steep-sided valley.

droll *adj* oddly amusing; whimsical. —**drolly** *adv*.

dromedary *n* a one-humped camel.

drone *n* a male honey-bee; a lazy person; a deep humming sound; a monotonous speaker or speech; an aircraft piloted by remote control. * *vi* to make a monotonous humming sound; to speak in a monotonous manner.

drool *vi* to slaver, dribble; to show excessive enthusiasm for.

droop *vi* to bend or hang down; to become weak or faint. * *n* the act or an instance of drooping.—**droopy** *adj*.

drop *n* a small amount of liquid in a roundish shape; something shaped like this; a tiny quantity; a sudden fall; the distance down. * *vb* (*pt* **dropped**) *vi* to fall in drops; to fall suddenly; to go lower, to sink; to come (in); (*with* **in**) to visit (with) informally; (*with* **out**) to abandon or reject (a course, society, etc). * *vt* to let fall, to cause to fall; to lower or cause to descend; to set down from a vehicle; to mention casually; to cause (the voice) to be less loud; to give up (as an idea).—**dropper** *n*.

dropout *n* a student who abandons a course of study; a person who rejects normal society.—*also vi*.

droppings *npl* animal dung.

dross *n* a surface scum on molten metal; rubbish, waste matter.

drought[1] *see* drive.

drove[1] *see* drive.

drove[2] *n* a group of animals driven in a herd or flock, etc; a large moving crowd of people.

drown *vti* to die or kill by suffocation in water, etc. * *vt* to flood; to drench; to become immersed in some activity; to blot out (a sound) with a louder noise; to remove (sorrow, etc) with drink.

drowse *vi* to be nearly asleep.

drowsy *adj* (**drowsier, drowsiest**) sleepy.—**drowsily** *adv*.—**drowsiness** *n*.

drudge *vi* to do boring or very menial work.—*also n*.—**drudgery** *n*.

drug *n* any substance used in medicine; a narcotic. * *vt* (*pt* **drugged**) to administer drugs to; to stupefy

druggist *n* a pharmacist.

drugstore *n* a retail store in the US selling medicines and other miscellaneous articles such as cosmetics, film, etc.

drum *n* a round percussion instrument, played by striking a membrane stretched across a hollow cylindrical frame; the sound of a drum; anything shaped like a drum, as a container for liquids. * *vb* (*pt* **drummed**) *vi* to play a drum; to beat or tap rhythmically. * *vt* (*with* **in**) to instil (knowledge) into a person by constant repetition; (*with* **up**) to summon as by drum.

drummer *n* a person who plays a drum.

drunk[1] *see* drink.

drunk[2] *adj* intoxicated with alcohol. * *n* a drunk person.

drunkard *n* an habitual drunk.

drunken *adj* intoxicated; caused by excessive drinking.—**drunkenly** *adv*.—**drunkenness** *n*.

dry *adj* (**drier, driest**) free from water or liquid; thirsty; marked by a matter-of-fact, ironic or terse manner of expression; uninteresting, wearisome; (*bread*) without butter, etc; (*wine*) not sweet; not selling alcohol. * *vti* to make or become dry.—**drily, dryly** *adv*. —**dryness** *n*.

dry-clean *vt* to clean with solvents as opposed to water.—**dry-cleaner** *n*.—**dry-cleaning** *n*.

dryer *n* a device for drying, as a tumble-drier; a clothes horse.—*also* **drier.**

dry rot *n* decay of timber caused by a fungus; any form of moral decay or corruption.

dual *adj* double; consisting of two.—**duality** *n*.

dubious *adj* doubtful (about, of); uncertain as to the result; untrustworthy. —**dubiously** *adv*.

duchess *n* the wife or widow of a duke; a woman having the same rank as a duke in her own right.

duck[1] *vt* to dip briefly in water; to lower the head suddenly, esp to avoid some object; to avoid, dodge. * *vi* to dip or dive; to move the head or body suddenly; to evade a duty, etc. * *n* a ducking movement.

duck[2] *n* a water bird related to geese and swans; the female of this bird; its flesh used as food.

duckish *n* (*Cdn*) in Newfoundland, twilight or the time between sunset and darkness.

duct *n* a channel or pipe for fluids, electric cable, etc; a tube in the body for fluids to pass through.

dud *n* (*sl*) anything worthless.—*also adj*.

due *adj* owed as a debt; immediately payable; fitting, appropriate; appointed or expected to do or arrive. * *adv* directly, exactly. * *n* something due or owed; (*pl*) fees.

duel *n* combat with weapons between two persons over a matter of honor, etc; conflict of any kind between two people, sides, ideas, etc. * *vi* (*pt* **duelled**) to fight in a duel.—**duellist** *n*.

duet *n* a musical composition for two performers.

dug *see* **dig.**

duke *n* the highest order of British nobility; the title of a ruler of a European duchy.—**dukedom** *n*.

dull *adj* not sharp or pointed; not bright or clear; stupid; boring; not active. * *vti* to make or become dull.—**dully** *adv*.—**dullness** *n*.

duly *adv* properly; suitably.

dumb *adj* not able to speak; silent; (*inf*) stupid.—**dumbly** *adv*.—**dumbness** *n*.

dumbfound, dumfound *vti* to astonish, surprise.

dummy *n* a figure of a person used to display clothes; (*sl*) a soother or pacifier for a baby; a stupid person; an imitation; (*bridge*) the exposed cards of the dealer's partner.

dump *vt* to drop or put down carelessly in a heap; to deposit as rubbish; to abandon or get rid of; to sell goods abroad at a price lower than the market price abroad. * *n* a place for refuse; a temporary store; (*inf*) a dirty, dilapidated place.

dumpling *n* a rounded piece of dough cooked by boiling or steaming; a short, fat person.

dunce *n* a person who is stupid or slow to learn.

dune *n* a hill of sand piled up by the wind.

dung *n* excrement; manure.

dungarees *npl* overalls or trousers made from a coarse cotton cloth.

dungeon *n* an underground cell for prisoners.

Duo-Tang *n* (*Cdn*) (*TM*) a folder of light cardboard that has three flexible metal fasteners to be inserted through the holes of looseleaf paper.

dupe *n* a person who is cheated. * *vt* to deceive; to trick.

duplicate *adj* in pairs, double; identical; copied exactly from an original. * *n* one of a pair of identical things; a copy. * *vt* to make double; to make an exact copy of; to repeat.—**duplication** *n*.

durable *adj* enduring, resisting wear, etc.—**durability** *n*.—**durably** *adv*.

duration *n* the time in which an event continues.

duress *n* compulsion by use of force or threat; unlawful constraint; imprisonment.

during *prep* throughout the duration of; at a point in the course of.

dusk *n* (the darker part of) twilight.

dusky *adj* (**duskier, duskiest**) having a dark color.—**duskiness** *n*.

dust *n* fine particles of solid matter. * *vt* to free from dust; to sprinkle with flour, sugar, etc.

dustbin *n* a container for household refuse.

dust jacket *n* a paper cover for a book.

dustman *n* a person employed to empty dustbins.

Dutch *adj* pertaining to Holland, its people, or language. * *n* the Dutch language.

duty *n* an obligation that must be performed for moral or legal reasons; respect for one's elders or superiors; actions and responsibilities arising from one's business, occupation, etc; a tax on goods or imports, etc.

duty-free *adj* free from tax or duty.

dwarf *n* (*pl* **dwarfs**) a person, animal, plant of abnormally small size. * *vt* to stunt; to cause to appear small.

dwell *vi* (*pt* **dwelt** *or* **dwelled**) to live (in a place); (*with* **on**) to focus the attention on; to think, talk, or write at length about.—**dweller** *n*.

dwelling *n* the house, etc where one lives, habitation.

dwindle *vi* to shrink, diminish; to become feeble.

dye *vt* (*pr p* **dyeing**, *pt* **dyed**) to give a new color to. * *n* a coloring substance, esp in solution; a color or tint produced by dyeing.

dynamic *adj* relating to force that produces motion; (*person*) forceful, energetic.—**dynamically** *adv*.

dynamics *n* (*used as sing*) the branch of science that deals with forces and their effect on the motion of bodies.

dynamite *n* a powerful explosive; a potentially dangerous situation; (*inf*) an energetic person or thing. * *vt* to blow up with dynamite.

dynamo *n* (*pl* **dynamos**) a device that generates electric current.

dynasty *n* a line of hereditary rulers or leaders

of any powerful family or similar group.—
dynastic adj.

dysentery n painful inflammation of the large intestine with associated diarrhoea.

E

E. abbr = east; eastern.

each adj every one of two or more.

eager adj enthusiastically desirous (of); keen
(for); marked by impatient desire or interest.—**eagerly** adv.—**eagerness** n.

eagle n a bird of prey with keen eyes and
powerful wings; (golf) a score of two
strokes under par.

ear[1] n (the external part of) the organ of hearing; the sense or act of hearing; attention;
something shaped like an ear.

ear[2] n the part of a cereal plant (eg corn, maize)
that contains the seeds.

earache n a pain in the ear.

eardrum n the membrane within the ear that vi-
brates in response to sound waves.

earl n a member of the British nobility ranking
between a marquis and a viscount.—**countess** nf.

early adj (**earlier, earliest**) before the expected or
normal time; of or occurring in the first part
of a period or series; of or occurring in the
distant past or near future.—also adv.—**ear-
liness** n.

earmark vt to set aside for a specific use; to put
an identification mark on. * n a distinguishing mark.

earn vt to gain (money, etc) by work or service;
to acquire; to deserve; to earn interest (on
money invested, etc).

earnest adj sincere in attitude or intention.—
earnestly adv.—**earnestness** n.

earnings npl wages or profits; something
earned.

earring n an ornament worn on the ear lobe.

earth n the world that we inhabit; solid ground,
as opposed to sea; soil; the burrow of a
badger, fox, etc; a connection between an
electric device or circuit with the earth;
(inf) a large amount of money. * vt to cover
with or bury in the earth; to connect an
electrical circuit or device to earth.

earthenware n pottery, etc made from baked clay.

earthquake n a violent tremor of the earth's
crust.

earthy adj (**earthier, earthiest**) of or resembling
earth; crude.—**earthiness** n.

earwig n a small insect with a pincer-like appendage at the end of its body.

ease n freedom from pain, discomfort or disturbance; rest from effort or work; effortlessness; lack of inhibition or restraint,
naturalness. * vt to relieve from pain, trouble, or anxiety; to relax, make less tight, release; to move carefully and gradually. * vi
(often with **off**) to become less active, intense, or severe.

easel n a supporting frame, esp one used by
artists to support their canvases while
painting.

easily adv with ease; by far; probably.

east n the direction of the sunrise; the compass
point opposite west; (with cap and **the**) the
area of the world east of Europe. * adj, adv
in, towards, or from the east.

Easter n the Christian festival observed on a
Sunday in March or April in commemoration of the resurrection of Christ.

easterly adj situated towards or belonging to
the east, coming from the east. * n a wind
from the east.

eastern adj of or in the east.

Eastern Canadian n a person who lives in or is
from Ontario, Quebec, or one of the provinces east of them. * adj of or pertaining to
such a person.

eastward adj towards the east.—**eastwards** adv.

easy adj (**easier, easiest**) free from pain, trouble,
anxiety; not difficult or requiring much ef-
fort; (manner) relaxed; lenient; compliant;
unhurried; (inf) open to all alternatives.
* adv with ease.—**easiness** n.

easy chair n a comfortable chair.

easygoing adj placid, tolerant, relaxed.

eat vt (pt **ate**, pp **eaten**) to take into the mouth,
chew and swallow as food; to have a meal;
to consume, to destroy bit by bit; (also with
into) to corrode; (inf) to bother, cause anxiety to; (pl: inf) food.—**eater** n.

eatable adj suitable for eating; fit to be eaten.
* n (pl) food.

eaves npl the overhanging edge of a roof.

eavesdrop vi (pt **eavesdropped**) to listen secretly
to a private conversation.—**eavesdropper**
n.

ebb n the flow of the tide out to sea; a decline.
* vi (tide water) to flow back; to become
lower, to decline.

ebony n a hard heavy wood. * adj black as ebony.

ebullient adj exuberant, enthusiastic; boiling.—
ebullience, ebulliency n. —**ebulliently** adv.

EC abbr = (formerly) European Community;
East Central.

eccentric adj deviating from a usual pattern; unconventional in manner or appearance,
odd; (circles) not concentric; off centre. * n
an eccentric person.—**eccentrically** adv.—**eccentricity** n.

ecclesiastic[1] n a member of the clergy.

ecclesiastic[2], **ecclesiastical** adj of or relating to the
Christian Church or clergy.

echo n (pl **echoes**) a repetition of sound caused
by the reflection of sound waves; imitation;
the reflection of a radar signal by an object.
* vb (pr p **echoing**, pt **echoed**) vi to resound; to
produce an echo. * vt to repeat; to imitate;
to send back (a sound) by an echo.

eclipse n the obscuring of the light of the sun or
moon by the intervention of the other; a
decline into obscurity, as from overshadow-
ing by others. * vt to cause an eclipse of; to
overshadow, darken; to surpass.

ecology n (the study of) the relationships between living things and their environments.—**ecological** adj.—**ecologist** n.

economic adj pertaining to economics or the economy; (business, etc) capable of producing a profit.

economical adj thrifty.—**economically** adv.

economics n (used as sing) the social science concerned with the production, consumption and distribution of goods and services; (as pl) financial aspects.—**economist** n.

economize vti to spend money carefully; to save; to use prudently.—**economization** n.

economy n careful use of money and resources to minimize waste; an instance of this; the management of the finances and resources, etc of a business, industry or organization; the economic system of a country.

ecstasy n intense joy; (sl) a synthetic amphetamine-based drug that reduces social and sexual inhibitions. —**ecstatic** adj.—**ecstatically** adv.

ecumenical adj of the whole Christian Church; seeking Christian unity worldwide.—**ecumenicalism** n.

eczema n inflammation of the skin causing itching and the formation of scaly red patches.—**eczematous** adj.

EDC abbr (Cdn) = Export Development Corporation.

eddy n a swiftly revolving current of air, water, fog, etc. * vi to move round and round.

edge n the border, brink, verge, margin; the sharp cutting side of a blade; sharpness, keenness; force, effectiveness. * vt to supply an edge or border to; to move gradually.

edgeways, edgewise adv with the edge forwards; sideways.

edgy adj (edgier, edgiest) irritable.—**edginess** n.

edible adj fit or safe to eat.

edict n a decree.

edifice n a substantial building; any large or complex organization or institution.

edit vt to prepare (text) for publication; to be in charge of a publication; (cinema) to prepare a final version of a film by selection and arrangement of sequences.

edition n a whole number of copies of a book, etc printed at a time; the form of a particular publication.

editor n a person in charge of a newspaper or other publication; a person who edits written material for publication; one who prepares the final version of a film; a person in overall charge of the form and content of a radio or television programme.

editorial adj of or produced by an editor. * n an article expressing the opinions of the editor or publishers of a newspaper or magazine.—**editorially** adv.

educate vt to train the mind, to teach; to provide schooling for.—**educator** n.

education n the process of learning and training; instruction as imparted in schools, colleges and universities; a course or type of instruction; the theory and practice of teaching.—**educational** adj.—**educationally** adv.

EEC abbr = (formerly) European Economic Community.

eel n a snake-like fish.

eerie adj (eerier, eeriest) causing fear; weird.—**eerily** adv.—**eeriness** n.

effect n the result of a cause or action by some agent; the power to produce some result; the fundamental meaning; an impression on the senses; an operative condition; (pl) personal belongings; (pl: theatre, cinema) sounds, lighting, etc to accompany a production. * vt to bring about, to accomplish.—**effectible** adj.

effective adj producing a specified effect; forceful, striking in impression; actual, real; operative.—**effectively** adv.—**effectiveness** n.

effeminate adj (man) displaying what are regarded as feminine qualities.—**effeminately** adv.—**effeminacy** n.

efficacious adj achieving the desired result.—**efficacy** n.

efficiency unit n (Cdn) a hotel room or temporarily let small apartment that has some cooking and washing facilities.

efficient adj achieving results without waste of time or effort; competent.—**efficiently** adv.—**efficiency** n.

effigy n a sculpture or portrait; a crude figure of a person, esp for exposure to public contempt and ridicule.

effort n exertion; an attempt, try; a product of great exertion.

effortless adj done with little effort, or seemingly so.—**effortlessly** adv.—**effortlessness** n.

effrontery n impudent boldness, insolence.

e.g., eg, eg. abbr = for example (Latin exempli gratia).

egalitarian adj upholding the principle of equal rights for all.—also n.—**egalitarianism** n.

egg[1] n the oval hard-shelled reproductive cell laid by birds, reptiles and fish; the egg of the domestic poultry used as food; ovum.—**eggy** adj.

egg[2] vt (with on) to incite (someone to do something).

eggplant n a plant producing a smooth, dark-purple fruit; this fruit used as a vegetable, aubergine.

eggshell n the hard outer covering of an egg. * adj fragile; (paint) having a slight sheen.

ego n the self; self-image, conceit.

eiderdown n the down of the eider duck used for stuffing quilts, etc; a thick quilt with a soft filling.

eight n, adj one more than seven; the symbol for this (8, VIII, viii); (the crew of) an eight-oared rowing boat.

eighteen n, adj one more than seventeen; the symbol for this (18, XVIII, xviii).—**eighteenth** adj.

eighth adj, n one after seventh; one of eight equal parts.

eighty n eight times ten; the symbol for this (80, LXXX, lxxx); (pl) the numbers from 80 to 89.—**eightieth** adj, n.

either adj, n the one or the other of two; each of two. * conj correlative to or.

eject *vt* to turn out, to expel by force. * *vi* to escape from an aircraft or spacecraft using an ejector seat.—**ejection** *n*.—**ejector** *n*.

ejector seat *n* an escape seat, esp in combat aircraft, that can be ejected with its occupant in an emergency by means of explosive bolts.

eke *vt* (*with* **out**) to supplement; to use (a supply) frugally; to make (a living) with difficulty.

elaborate *adj* highly detailed; planned with care and exactness. * *vt* to work out, explain in detail.—**elaborately** *adv*.—**elaboration** *n*.

elapse *vi* (*time*) to pass by.

elastic *adj* returning to the original size and shape if stretched or squeezed; springy; adaptable. * *n* fabric, tape, etc incorporating elastic thread.—**elastically** *adv*.—**elasticity** *n*.

elbow *n* the joint between the forearm and upper arm; the part of a piece of clothing covering this; any sharp turn or bend, as in a pipe. * *vt* to shove away rudely with the elbow; to jostle.

elder[1] *n* a tree or shrub with flat clusters of white or pink flowers.

elder[2] *n* an older person; an office bearer in some churches.

elderly *adj* quite old.

eldest *n* oldest, first born.

elect *vti* to choose by voting; to make a selection (of); to make a decision on. * *adj* chosen for an office but not installed.

election *n* the public choice of a person for office, esp a politician.

elector *n* a person who has a vote at an election.

electoral *adj* of elections or electors.

electoral officer *n* a public official who oversees the running of an election.

electorate *n* the whole body of qualified electors.

electric *adj* of, producing or worked by electricity; exciting, thrilling. * *npl* electric fittings.

electrical *adj* of or relating to electricity.—**electrically** *adv*.

electric blanket *n* a blanket heated by an internal electric element.

electrician *n* a person who installs and repairs electrical devices.

electricity *n* a form of energy comprising certain charged particles; an electric current.

electrify *vt* to charge with electricity; to modify or equip for the use of electric power; to astonish or excite.—**electrification** *n*.

electrode *n* a conductor through which an electric current enters or leaves a gas discharge tube, etc.

electromagnetic *adj* having electric and magnetic properties.—**electromagnetism** *n*.

electron *n* a negatively charged elementary particle that forms the part of the atom outside the nucleus.

electronic *adj* of or worked by streams of electrons flowing through devices, vacuum or gas; of or concerned with electrons or electronics. —**electronically** *adv*.

electronics *n* (*used as sing*) the study, development and application of electronic devices; (*as pl*) electronic circuits.

elegant *adj* graceful; refined; dignified, tasteful in manner and appearance.—**elegantly** *adv*.—**elegance** *n*.

element *n* a constituent part; any of the 105 known substances composed of atoms with the same number of protons in their nuclei; a favorable environment for a plant or animal; a wire that produces heat in an electric cooker, kettle, etc; any of the four substances (earth, air, fire, water) that in ancient and medieval thought were believed to constitute the universe; (*pl*) atmospheric conditions (wind, rain, etc); (*pl*) the basic principles, rudiments.

elementary *adj* concerned with the basic principles of a subject.

elephant *n* a large heavy mammal with a long trunk, thick skin, and ivory tusks.

elevate *vt* to lift up; to raise in rank; to improve in intellectual or moral stature.

elevation *n* a raised place; the height above the earth's surface or above sea level; the angle to which a gun is aimed above the horizon; a drawing that shows the front, rear, or side view of something.

elevator *n* a cage or platform for moving something from one level to another; a moveable surface on the tailplane of an aircraft to produce motion up and down; a lift; a building for storing grain.

eleven *adj, n* one more than ten; the symbol for this (11, XI, xi); (*cricket, football, etc*) a team of eleven players.—**eleventh** *adj, n*.

elevenses *npl* (*inf*) a light snack taken around mid-morning.

elf *n* (*pl* **elves**) a mischievous fairy. —**elfin** *adj*.—**elfish** *adj*.

elicit *vt* to draw out (information, etc).

eligible *adj* suitable to be chosen, legally qualified; desirable, esp as a marriage partner.—**eligibility** *n*.

eliminate *vt* to expel, get rid of; to eradicate completely; (*sl*) to kill; to exclude (eg a competitor) from a competition, usu by defeat.—**elimination** *n*.—**eliminator** *n*.

elite, élite *n* a superior group; (*typewriting*) a letter size having twelve characters to the inch.

ellipse *n* (*geom*) a closed plane figure formed by the plane section of a right-angled cone; a flattened circle.

elm *n* a tall deciduous shade tree with spreading branches and broad top; its hard heavy wood.

elocution *n* skill in public speaking.—**elocutionary** *adj*.—**elocutionist** *n*.

elongate *vti* to make or become longer.—**elongation** *n*.

elope *vi* to run away secretly with a lover, esp to get married.

eloquence *n* skill in the use of words; speaking with fluency, power or persuasiveness.

eloquent *adj* (*speaking, writing, etc*) fluent and powerful.

else *adv* besides; otherwise.

elucidate vt to make clear, to explain. —**elucidation** n.—**elucidatory** adv.

elude vt to avoid stealthily; to escape the understanding or memory of a person.

elusive adj escaping; baffling; solitary, difficult to contact.

emanate vi to issue from a source.—**emanation** n.

emancipate vt to liberate, esp from bondage or slavery.—**emancipation** n.—**emancipator** n.

embalm vt to preserve (a dead body) with drugs, chemicals, etc.—**embalmment** n.

embankment n an earth or stone mound made to hold back water or to carry a roadway.

embargo n (pl **embargoes**) an order of a government forbidding ships to enter or leave its ports; any ban or restriction on commerce by law; a prohibition, ban. * vt to lay an embargo on; to requisition.

embark vti to put or go on board a ship or aircraft to begin a journey; to make a start in any activity or enterprise.—**embarkation** n.

embarrass vt to make (a person) feel confused, uncomfortable or disconcerted.—**embarrassment** n.

embassy n a person or group sent abroad as ambassadors; the official residence of an ambassador.

embed vt (pt **embedded**) to fix firmly in surrounding matter.

embellish vt to decorate, to adorn.—**embellishment** n.

ember n a piece of glowing coal or wood in fire; (pl) the smouldering remains of a fire.

embezzle vt to steal (money, securities, etc entrusted to one's care).—**embezzlement** n.—**embezzler** n.

embitter vt to cause to feel bitter.—**embitterment** n.

emblem n a symbol; a figure adopted and used as an identifying mark.

embody vt to express in definite form; to incorporate in a single book, law, system, etc.—**embodiment** n.

emboss vt to ornament with a raised design.—**embossment** n.

embrace vt to take and hold tightly in the arms as a sign of affection; to accept eagerly (eg an opportunity); to adopt (eg a religious faith); to include.—also n.

embroider vt to ornament with decorative stitches; to embellish (eg a story).

embroidery n decorative needlework; elaboration or exaggeration.

embryo n (pl **embryos**) an animal during the period of its growth from a fertilized egg up to the third month; a human product of conception up to about the second month of growth; a thing in a rudimentary state.

emerald n a rich green gemstone; its color.

emerge vi to appear up out of, to come into view; to be revealed as the result of investigation; * n (Cdn) (inf) a section of a hospital that handles emergencies.—**emergence** n.—**emergent** adj.

emergency n an unforeseen situation demanding immediate action; a serious medical condition requiring instant treatment.

emery n a hard granular mineral used for grinding and polishing; a hard abrasive powder.

emery board n a nailfile made from cardboard covered with crushed emery.

emery paper n a stiff paper covered with powdered emery.

emetic n a medicine that induces vomiting.—also adj.

emigrant n a person who emigrates.

emigrate vi to leave one's country for residence in another.—**emigration** n.

eminence, eminency n high rank or position; a person of high rank or attainments; (with cap: RC Church) the title for a cardinal; a raised piece of ground, a high place.

eminent adj famous; conspicuous; distinguished.—**eminently** adv.

emit vt (pt **emitted**) to send out (light, heat, etc); to put into circulation; to express, to utter.—**emission** n.—**emissive** adj.—**emitter** n.

emotion n a strong feeling of any kind.

emotional adj of emotion; inclined to express excessive emotion.—**emotionally** adv.—**emotionalism** n.

emotive adj characterized by or arousing emotion.

emperor n the sovereign ruler over an empire.—**empress** nf.

emphasis n (pl **emphases**) particular stress or prominence given to something; force or vigour of expression; clarity of form or outline.

emphasize vt to place stress on.

emphatic adj spoken, done or marked with emphasis; forceful, decisive.—**emphatically** adv.

empire n a large state or group of states under a single sovereign, usu an emperor; nations governed by a single sovereign state; a large and complex business organization.

empirical adj based on observation, experiment or experience only, not theoretical.—**empirically** adv.

employ vt to give work and pay to; to make use of.

employee n a person who is hired by another person for wages.

employer n a person, business, etc that employs people.

employment n an employing; a being employed; occupation or profession.

empower vt to give official authority to.

empress n the female ruler of an empire; the wife or widow of an emperor.

empty adj (**emptier, emptiest**) containing nothing; not occupied; lacking reality, substance, or value; hungry. * vt to make empty; to transfer or discharge (the contents of something) by emptying. * vi to become empty; to discharge contents. * n empty containers or bottles.—**emptily** adv.—**emptiness** n.

emulate vt to try to equal or do better than; to imitate; to rival or compete.—**emulation** n.—**emulative** adj.—**emulator** n.

emulsion n a mixture of mutually insoluble

liquids in which one is dispersed in droplets throughout the other; a light-sensitive substance on photographic paper or film.

enable vt to give the authority or means to do something; to make easy or possible.

enamel n a glasslike substance used to coat the surface of metal or pottery; the hard outer layer of a tooth; a usu glossy paint that forms a hard coat. * vt (pt **enamelled**) to cover or decorate with enamel.

enamour, enamor (US) vt to inspire with love.—**enamoured** adj.

enchant vt to bewitch, to delight.—**enchanter** n.—**enchantment** n.—**enchantress** nf.

encircle vt to surround; to move or pass completely round.—**encirclement** n.

enclose vt to shut up or in; to put in a wrapper or parcel, usu together with a letter.

enclosure n an enclosing; an enclosed area; something enclosed with a letter in a parcel, etc.

encore interj once more! * n a call for the repetition of a performance.—also vt.

encounter vt to meet, esp unexpectedly; to fight, engage in battle with; to be faced with (problems, etc). * n a meeting; a conflict, battle.

encourage vt to inspire with confidence or hope; to urge, incite; to promote the development of.—**encouragement** n.

encroach vi to infringe another's territory, rights, etc; to advance beyond an established limit.—**encroachment** n.

encyclopaedia, encyclopedia n a book or books containing information on all branches of knowledge, or treating comprehensively a particular branch.

end n the last part; the place where a thing stops; purpose; result, outcome. * vt to bring to an end; to destroy. * vi to come to an end; to result (in). * adj final; ultimate.

endanger vt to put in danger.

endear vt to make loved or more loved.—**endearing** adj.

endeavour, endeavor (US) vi to try or attempt (to). * n an attempt.

ending n reaching or coming to an end; the final part.

endless adj unending; uninterrupted; extremely numerous.

endorsation n (Cdn) endorsement.

endorse vt to write one's name, comment, etc, on the back of to approve; to record an offence on a driving licence; to support.—**endorsement** n.

endow vt to give money or property to provide an income for; to provide with a special power or attribute.

endurance n the ability to withstand pain, hardship, strain, etc.

endure vt to undergo, tolerate (hardship, etc) esp with patience. * vi to continue in existence, to last out.—**endurable** adj.—**endurably** adv.

enemy n a person who hates or dislikes and wishes to harm another; a military opponent; something harmful or deadly.

energetic adj lively, active; done with energy.—**energetically** adv.

energy n capacity of acting or being active; vigour, power; (physics) capacity to do work.

enforce vt to compel obedience by threat; to execute with vigour.—**enforceable** adj.—**enforcement** n.

engage vt to pledge as security; to promise to marry; to keep busy; to hire; to attract and hold, esp attention or sympathy; to cause to participate; to bring or enter into conflict; to begin or take part in a venture; to connect or interlock, to mesh.

engaged adj entered into a promise to marry; reserved, occupied or busy.

engagement n the act or state of being engaged; a pledge; an appointment agreed with another person; employment; a battle.

engaging adj pleasing, attractive.

engender vt to bring to existence.

engine n a machine by which physical power is applied to produce a physical effect; a locomotive; (formerly) a mechanical device, such as a large catapult, used in war.

engineer n a person trained in engineering; a person who operates an engine, etc; a member of a military group devoted to engineering work; a designer or builder of engines. * vt to contrive, plan, esp deviously.

engineering n the art or practice of constructing and using machinery; the art and science by which natural forces and materials are utilized in structures or machines.

English adj of, relating to, or characteristic of, England, the English people, or the English language. * n the language of the British people, the US and other areas; English language and literature as a subject of study.

engrained see **ingrained**.

engrave vt to produce by cutting or carving a surface; to cut to produce a representation that may be printed from; to lodge deeply (in the mind, etc).—**engraver** n.

engraving n a print made from an engraved surface.

engulf vt to flow over and enclose; to overwhelm.

enhance vt to increase in value, importance, attractiveness, etc; to heighten.—**enhancement** n.

enigma n someone or something that is puzzling or mysterious.—**enigmatic** adj.—**enigmatically** adv.

enjoy vt to get pleasure from, take joy in; to use or have the advantage of; to experience.—**enjoyment** n.

enjoyable adj giving enjoyment.—**enjoyably** adv.

enlarge vti to make or grow larger; to reproduce (a photograph) in a larger form; to speak or write at length (on).

enlargement n an act, instance, or state of enlarging; a photograph, etc that has been enlarged.

enlighten vt to instruct; to inform.—**enlightenment** n.

enlightened *adj* well-informed, tolerant, unprejudiced.

enlist *vt* to engage for service in the armed forces; to secure the aid or support of. * *vi* to register oneself for the armed services.—**enlistment** *n*.

enmity *n* hostility, esp mutual hatred.

enormity *n* great wickedness; a serious crime; huge size, magnitude.

enormous *adj* extremely large.—**enormously** *adv*.

enough *adj* adequate, sufficient. * *adv* so as to be sufficient; very; quite. * *n* a sufficiency. * *interj* stop!

enquire *see* inquire.

enrich *vt* to make rich or richer; to ornament; to improve in quality by adding to.—**enrichment** *n*.

enrol, enroll (*US*) *vti* (*pt* **enrolled**) to enter or register on a roll or list; to become a member of a society, club, etc; to admit as a member.—**enrolment** *n*.

ensign *n* a flag; the lowest commissioned officer in the US Navy.

enslave *vt* to make into a slave; to subjugate.—**enslavement** *n*.

ensue *vi* to occur as a consequence or in time.

ensure *vt* to make certain, sure or safe.

entail *vt* to involve as a result; to restrict the inheritance of property. * *n* the act of entailing or the estate entailed.

enter *vi* to go or come in or into; to come on stage; to begin, start; (*with* for) to register as an entrant. * *vt* to come or go into; to pierce, penetrate; (*organization*) to join; to insert; (*proposal, etc*) to submit; to record (an item) in a diary, etc.

enterprise *n* a difficult or challenging undertaking; a business project; readiness to engage in new ventures.

entertain *vt* to show hospitality to; to amuse, please (a person or audience); to have in mind; to consider.

entertainer *n* a person who entertains in public, esp professionally.

entertainment *n* entertaining; amusement; an act or show intended to amuse and interest.

enthusiasm *n* intense interest or liking; something that arouses keen interest.

enthusiast *n* a person filled with enthusiasm for something.

enthusiastic *adj* filled with enthusiasm.—**enthusiastically** *adv*.

entice *vt* to attract by offering some pleasure or reward.—**enticement** *n*.

entire *adj* whole; complete.—**entirely** *adv*.

entirety *n* completeness; the total.

entitle *vt* to give a title to; to give a right (to).—**entitlement** *n*.

entrance[1] *n* the act of entering; the power or authority to enter; a means of entering; an admission fee.

entrance[2] *vt* to put into a trance; to fill with great delight.—**entrancement** *n*.—**entrancing** *adj*.

entrant *n* a person who enters (eg a competition, profession).

entreat *vt* to request earnestly; to implore, beg.—**entreaty** *n*.

entrench *vt* to dig a trench as a defensive perimeter; to establish (oneself) in a strong defensive position.—**entrenchment** *n*.

entrust *vt* (*with* with) to confer as a responsibility, duty, etc; (*with* to) to place something in another's care.

entry *n* the act of entering; a place of entrance; an item recorded in a diary, journal, etc; a person or thing taking part in a contest.

entwine *vt* to twine together or around.

enumerate *vt* to count; to list.—**enumeration** *n*.—**enumerator** *n*.

enunciate *vt* to state definitely; to pronounce clearly.—**enunciation** *n*.

envelop *vt* (*pt* **enveloped**) to enclose completely (as if) with a covering.—**envelopment** *n*.

envelope *n* something used to wrap or cover, esp a gummed paper container for a letter.

envious *adj* filled with envy.—**enviously** *adv*.

environment *n* external conditions and surroundings, esp those that affect the quality of life of plants, animals and human beings.—**environmental** *adj*.

envisage *vt* to have a mental picture of.

envoy *n* a diplomatic agent; a representative.

envy *n* resentment or discontent at another's achievements, possessions, etc; an object of envy. * *vt* to feel envy of.

enzyme *n* a complex protein, produced by living cells, that induces or speeds chemical reactions in plants and animals.

ephemeral *adj* existing only for a very short time.

epic *n* a long poem narrating the deeds of a hero; any literary work, film, etc in the same style. * *adj* relating to or resembling an epic.

epidemic *adj, n* (a disease) attacking many people at the same time in a community or region.

epilepsy *n* a disorder of the nervous system marked typically by convulsive attacks and loss of consciousness.—**epileptic** *adj, n*.

epilogue *n* the concluding section of a book or other literary work; a short speech addressed by an actor to the audience at the end of a play.

epiphany *n* a moment of sudden revelation or insight; (*with cap*) a festival of the Christian Church in commemoration of the coming of the Magi to Christ.

episode *n* a piece of action in a dramatic or literary work; an incident in a sequence of events.

epistle *n* (*formal*) a letter; (*with cap*) a letter written by one of Christ's Apostles.

epitaph *n* an inscription in memory of a dead person, usu on a tombstone.

epitome *n* a typical example; a paradigm; personification; a condensed account of a written work.

epitomize *vt* to be or make an epitome of.

epoch *n* a date in time used as a point of reference; an age in history associated with certain characteristics; a unit of geological time.—**epochal** *adj*.

equable *adj* level, uniform; (*climate*) free from

extremes of hot and cold; even-tempered.—**equably** adv.

equal adj the same in amount, size, number, or value; impartial, regarding or affecting all objects in the same way; capable of meeting a task or situation. * n a person that is equal. * vt (pt **equalled**) to be equal to, esp to be identical in value; to make or do something equal to.—**equality** n.—**equally** adv.

equalization payment n (Cdn) a transfer of funds from the federal government to a poorer province to ensure that all provinces have about the same level of public services and taxation.

equalize vti to make or become equal; (games) to even the score.—**equalization** n.

equanimity n evenness of temper; composure.

equate vt to make, treat, or regard as comparable. * vi to correspond as equal.

equation n an act of equalling; the state of being equal; (logic, math) a usu formal statement of equivalence with the relations denoted by the sign =; (chem) an expression representing a reaction in symbols.

equator n an imaginary circle passing round the globe, equidistant from the poles.—**equatorial** n.

equilibrium n (pl **equilibriums**, **equilibria**) a state of balance of weight, power, force, etc.

equinox n the two times of the year when night and day are equal in length (around 21 March and 23 September).—**equinoctial** adj.

equip vt (pt **equipped**) to provide with all the necessary tools or supplies.

equipment n the tools, supplies and other items needed for a particular task, expedition, etc.

equitable adj just and fair; (law) pertaining to equity as opposed to common or statute law.—**equitably** adv.

equity n fairness; (law) a legal system based on natural justice developed into a body of rules supplementing the common law; (pl) ordinary shares in a company.

equivalent adj equal in amount, force, meaning, etc; virtually identical, esp in effect or function. * n an equivalent thing.

equivocal adj ambiguous; uncertain; questionable; arousing suspicion.—**equivocally** adv.

era n an historical period typified by some special feature; a chronological order or system of notation reckoned from a given date as a basis.

eradicate vt to obliterate.—**eradication** n.—**eradicator** n.

erase vt to rub out, obliterate; to remove a recording from magnetic tape; to remove data from a computer memory or storage medium.

erect adj upright; not leaning or lying down; (sexual organs) rigid and swollen with blood from sexual stimulation. * vt to construct, set up.—**erecter**, **erector** n.—**erectness** n.

erection n construction; something erected, as a building; swelling, esp of the penis, due to sexual excitement.

ermine n (pl **ermines**, **ermine**) the weasel in its winter coat; the white fur of the winter coat; a rank or office whose official robe is edged with ermine.

Ermite n a creamy blue-veined cheese made in Quebec.

erode vt to eat or wear away gradually.—**erosion** n.—**erosive** adj.

erotic adj of sexual love; sexually stimulating.—**erotically** adv.

eroticism n erotic nature; sexually arousing themes in literature and art; sexual desire.

err vi to be or do wrong.

errand n a short journey to perform some task, usu on behalf of another; the purpose of this journey.

erratic adj capricious; irregular; eccentric; odd.—**erratically** adv.

erroneous adj incorrect; mistaken.—**erroneously** adv.

error n a mistake, an inaccuracy; a mistaken belief or action.

erudite adj scholarly, having great knowledge.—**erudition** n.

erupt vi to burst forth; to break out into a rash; (volcano) to explode, ejecting ash and lava into the air.—**eruption** n.—**eruptive** adj.

escalate vi to increase rapidly in magnitude or intensity.—**escalation** n.

escalator n a motorized set of stairs arranged to ascend or descend continuously.

escapade n a wild or mischievous adventure.

escape vt to free oneself from confinement, etc; to avoid, remain unnoticed; to be forgotten. * vi to achieve freedom; (gas, liquid) to leak. * n an act or instance of escaping; a means of escape; a leakage of liquid or gas; a temporary respite from reality.—**escaper** n.

escort n a person, group, ship, aircraft, etc accompanying a person or thing to give protection, etc. * vt to attend as escort.

espionage n spying or the use of spies to obtain information.

esquire n a general courtesy title used instead of Mr in addressing letters.

essay n a short prose work usu dealing with a subject from a limited or personal point of view; an attempt. * vt to try, to attempt.

essence n that which makes a thing what it is; a substance extracted from another substance and having the special qualities of the original; a perfume.

essential adj of or containing the essence of something; indispensable, of the greatest importance. * n (often pl) indispensable elements or qualities.—**essentially** adv.

establish vt to set up (eg a business) permanently; to settle (a person) in a place or position; to get generally accepted; to place beyond dispute, prove as a fact.

establishment n the act of establishing; a commercial organization or other large institution; the staff and resources of an organization; a household; (with cap) those in power who work to preserve the status quo.

estate n landed property; a large area of residential or industrial development; a person's total possessions, esp at their death; a social or political class.

estate agent n a person whose business is selling and leasing property.

estate car n a car with extra carrying space reached through a rear door.

esteem vt to value or regard highly; to consider or think. * n high regard, a favorable opinion.

estimate vt to judge the value, amount, significance of; to calculate approximately. * n an approximate calculation; a judgment or opinion; a preliminary calculation of the cost of a particular job.

estimation n estimating; an opinion, judgment; esteem.

estuary n an arm of the sea at the mouth of a river.

etching n the art or process of producing designs on and printing from etched plates; an impression made from an etched plate.

eternal adj continuing forever without beginning or end, everlasting; unchangeable; (inf) seemingly endless. —**eternally** adv.

eternity n infinite time; the timelessness thought to constitute life after death; (inf) a very long time.

ether n (chem) a light flammable liquid used as an anaesthetic or solvent; the upper regions of space.

ethic n a moral principle or set of principles. * adj ethical.

ethical adj of or pertaining to ethics; conforming to the principles of proper conduct, as established by society, a profession, etc; (med) legally available only on prescription. —**ethically** adv.

ethics n (used as sing) the philosophical analysis of human morality and conduct; system of conduct or behaviour; moral principles.

ethnic adj of races or large groups of people classed according to common traits and customs. —**ethnically** adv.

etiquette n the form of conduct or behaviour prescribed by custom or authority to be observed in social, official or professional life.

EU abbr = European Union.

eulogy n a speech or piece of writing in praise or celebration of someone or something.

euphemism n a mild or inoffensive word substituted for a more unpleasant or offensive term; the use of such words. —**euphemistic** adj. —**euphemistically** adv.

Euro-Canadian n a Canadian of European origin or descent. * adj pertaining to Canadians of European origin or descent.

euthanasia n the act or practice of killing painlessly, esp to relieve incurable suffering.

evacuate vti to move (people, etc) from an area of danger to one of safety; to leave or make empty; to discharge wastes from the body. —**evacuation** n.

evade vt to manage to avoid, esp by dexterity or slyness. —**evadable, evadible** adj. —**evader** n.

evaluate vt to determine the value of; to assess. —**evaluation** n. —**evaluator** n.

evangelist n a person who preaches the gospel;

one of the writers of the four Gospels. —**evangelistic** adj.

evaporate vti to change into a vapour; to remove water from; to give off moisture; to vanish; to disappear. —**evaporation** n.

evasion n the act of evading; a means of evading, esp an equivocal reply or excuse. —**evasive** adj. —**evasively** adv. —**evasiveness** n.

eve n the evening or the whole day, before a festival; the period immediately before an event; (formerly) evening.

even adj level, flat; smooth; regular, equal; balanced; exact; divisible by two. * vti to make or become even; (with up) to balance (debts, etc). * adv exactly; precisely; fully; quite; at the very time; used as an intensive to emphasize the identity of something (he looked content, even happy), to indicate something unexpected (she refused even to look at him), or to stress the comparative degree (she did even better). —**evenly** adv. —**evenness** n.

even-handed adj impartial, fair.

evening n the latter part of the day and early part of the night.

event n something that happens; a social occasion; contingency; a contest in a sports programme.

eventful adj full of incidents; momentous

eventual adj happening at some future unspecified time; ultimate. —**eventually** adv.

eventuality n a possible occurrence.

ever adv always, at all times; at any time; in any case.

evergreen adj (plants, trees) having foliage that remains green all year. —also n.

everlasting adj enduring forever; (plants) having flowers that may be dried without loss of form or color. —**everlastingly** adv.

every adj being one of the total.

everybody, everyone pron every person.

everyday adj happening daily; commonplace; worn or used on ordinary days.

everything pron all things, all; of the utmost importance.

everywhere adv in every place.

evict vt to expel from land or from a building by legal process; to expel. —**eviction** n.

evidence n an outward sign; proof, testimony, esp matter submitted in court to determine the truth of alleged facts. * vt to demonstrate clearly; to give proof or evidence for.

evident adj easy to see or understand. —**evidently** adv.

evil adj wicked; causing or threatening distress or harm. * n a sin; a source of harm or distress. —**evilly** adv.

evoke vt to call forth or up. —**evocation** n. —**evocative** adj.

evolution n a process of change in a particular direction; the process by which something attains its distinctive characteristics; a theory that existing types of plants and animals have developed from earlier forms. —**evolutionary** adj.

evolve vi to develop by or as if by evolution. —**evolvement** n.

ewe *n* a female sheep.

ex[1] *n* (*inf*) a former husband, wife, etc.

ex[2] *prep* out of, from.

ex- *prefix* out, forth; quite, entirely; formerly.

exact *adj* without error, absolutely accurate; detailed. * *vt* to compel by force, to extort; to require.—**exactness** *n*.

exacting *adj* greatly demanding; requiring close attention and precision.

exactitude *n* (the state of) being exact.

exactly *adv* in an exact manner; precisely. * *interj* quite so!

exactor *n* (*Cdn*) a bet on the first-and second-place finishers in a horse race, specifying their order of finishing.

exaggerate *vt* to enlarge (a statement, etc) beyond what is really so or believable.—**exaggeration** *n*.

exalt *vt* to raise up, esp in rank, power, or dignity.—**exaltation** *n*.

exam *n* (*inf*) an examination.

examination *n* an examining, close scrutiny; a set of written or oral questions designed as a test of knowledge; the formal questioning of a witness on oath.

examination for discovery *n* (*Cdn*) a meeting before the start of a trial in civil law to disclose what evidence will be presented.

examine *vt* to look at closely and carefully, to investigate; to test, esp by questioning.—**examiner** *n*.

example *n* a representative sample; a model to be followed or avoided; a problem to be solved in order to show the application of some rule; a warning to others.

exasperate *vt* to annoy intensely.—**exasperation** *n*.

excavate *vt* to form a hole or tunnel by digging; to unearth; to expose to view (remains, etc) by digging away a covering.—**excavation** *n*.—**excavator** *n*.

exceed *vt* to be greater than or superior to; to go beyond the limit of.

exceedingly *adv* very, extremely.

excellence *n* that in which one excels; superior merit or quality; (*with cap*) a title of honor given to certain high officials (—*also* **Excellency**).

excellent *adj* very good, outstanding.—**excellently** *adv*.

except *vt* to exclude, to take or leave out. * *prep* not including; other than.

exception *n* the act of excepting; something excepted; an objection.

exceptional *adj* unusual, forming an exception; superior.

excerpt *n* an extract from a book, film, etc.

excess *n* the exceeding of proper established limits; the amount by which one thing or quantity exceeds another; (*pl*) overindulgence in eating or drinking; unacceptable conduct.

excessive *adj* greater than what is acceptable, too much.—**excessively** *adv*.

exchange *vt* to give and take (one thing in return for another); to give to and receive from another person. * *n* the exchanging of one thing for another; the thing exchanged; the conversion of money from one currency to another; the system of settling commercial debts between foreign governments; a place where things and services are exchanged, esp a marketplace for securities; a centre or device in which telephone lines are interconnected.—**exchangeable** *adj*.

exchequer *n* (*with cap*) the British governmental department in charge of finances; (*inf*) personal finances.

excise[1] *n* a tax on the manufacture, sale, or use of certain articles within a country.

excise[2] *vt* to remove by cutting out.—**excision** *n*.

excitable *adj* easily excited.—**excitability** *n*.

excite *vt* to arouse the feelings of, esp to generate feelings of pleasurable anticipation; to cause to experience strong emotion; to stir up, agitate; to rouse to activity; to stimulate a response, eg in a bodily organ.

excited *adj* experiencing or expressing excitement.—**excitedly** *adv*.

excitement *n* a feeling of strong, esp pleasurable, emotion; something that excites.

exciting *adj* causing excitement; stimulating.

exclaim *vti* to shout out or utter suddenly and with strong emotion.

exclamation *n* a sudden crying out; a word or utterance exclaimed.

exclamation mark, exclamation point *n* the punctuation mark (!) placed after an exclamation.

exclude *vt* to shut out, to keep out; to reject or omit; to eject.—**exclusion** *n*.

exclusive *adj* excluding all else; reserved for particular persons; snobbishly aloof; fashionable, high-class, expensive; unobtainable or unpublished elsewhere; sole, undivided. —**exclusively** *adv*.—**exclusiveness** *n*.—**exclusivity** *n*.

excommunicate *vt* to bar from association with a church; to exclude from fellowship.—**excommunication** *n*.

excrement *n* waste matter discharged from the bowels.—**excremental** *adj*.

excruciating *adj* intensely painful or distressful; (*inf*) very bad.

excursion *n* a pleasure trip; a short journey.

excuse *vt* to pardon; to forgive; to give a reason or apology for; to be a reason or explanation of; to let off.—*also n.*

execute *vt* to carry out, put into effect; to perform; to produce (eg a work of art); to make legally valid; to put to death by law.

execution *n* the act or process of executing; the carrying out or suffering of a death sentence; the style or technique of performing, eg music.

executioner *n* a person who executes a death sentence upon a condemned prisoner.

executive *n* a person or group concerned with administration or management of a business or organization; the branch of government with the power to put laws, etc into effect. * *adj* having the power to execute decisions, laws, decrees, etc.

exemplary *adj* deserving imitation; serving as a warning.

exemplify *vt* to illustrate by example; to be

an instance or example of.—**exemplification** n.

exempt adj not liable, free from the obligations required of others.—also vt.—**exemption** n.

exercise n the use or application of a power or right; regular physical or mental exertion; something performed to develop or test a specific ability or skill; (often pl) manoeuvres for military training. * vt to use, exert, employ; to engage in regular physical activity; to train (troops) by drills and manoeuvres; to engage the attention of; to perplex.

exert vt to bring (eg strength, influence) into use.

exhaust vt to use up completely; to make empty; to use up, tire out; (subject) to deal with or develop completely. * n the escape of waste gas or steam from an engine; the device through which these escape. — **exhausted** adj.—**exhaustible** adj. —**exhausting** adj.

exhaustion n the act of exhausting or being exhausted; extreme weariness.

exhaustive adj comprehensive, thorough.—**exhaustively** adv.

exhibit vt to display, esp in public; to present to a court in legal form. * n an act or instance of exhibiting, something exhibited; something produced and identified in court for use as evidence.—**exhibitor** n.

exhibition n a showing, a display; a public show; (Cdn) a large fair that includes agricultural exhibits and craft displays.

exhilarate vt to make very happy; to invigorate.—**exhilaration** n.

exhort vt to urge or advise strongly. —**exhortation** n.—**exhortative** adj.—**exhortatory** adj.

exile n prolonged absence from one's own country, either through choice or as a punishment; an exiled person.—also vt.

exist vi to have being; to just manage a living; to occur in a specific place under specific conditions.

existence n the state or fact of existing; continuance of life; everything that exists.

exit n a way out of an enclosed space; death; a departure from a stage. * vi to leave, withdraw; to go offstage.

exonerate vt to absolve from blame; to relieve from a responsibility, obligation.—**exoneration** n.

exorcise vt to expel an evil spirit (from a person or place) by ritual and prayer.—**exorcism** n.—**exorcist** n.

exotic adj foreign; strange; excitingly different or unusual.—**exotically** adv.

expand vt to increase in size, bulk, extent, importance; to describe in fuller detail. * vi to become larger; to become more genial and responsive.

expanse n a wide area of land, etc; the extent of a spread-out area.

expansion n the act of expanding or being expanded; something expanded; the amount by which something expands; the fuller development of a theme, etc.

expatriate adj living in another country; self-exiled or banished. * n an expatriate person.

* vti to exile (oneself) or banish (another person).—**expatriation** n.

expect vt to anticipate; to regard as likely to arrive or happen; to consider necessary, reasonable or due; to think, suppose.

expectant adj expecting, hopeful; filled with anticipation; pregnant.—**expectantly** adv.—**expectancy** n.

expectation n the act or state of expecting; something that is expected to happen; (pl) prospects for the future, esp of inheritance.

expediency, expedience n fitness, suitability; an inclination towards expedient methods.

expedient adj suitable or desirable under the circumstances. * n a means to an end; a means devised or used for want of something better.—**expediently** adv.

expedite vt to carry out promptly; to facilitate.—**expediter, expeditor** n.

expedition n a journey to achieve some purpose, as exploration, etc; the party making this journey; speedy efficiency, promptness.

expel vt (pt **expelled**) to drive out, to eject; to banish.

expend vt to spend (money, time, energy, etc); to use up, consume.

expenditure n the act or process of expending money, etc; the amount expended.

expense n a payment of money for something, expenditure; a cause of expenditure; (pl) money spent on some business activity; reimbursement for this.

expense account n an account of expenses to be repaid to an employee.

expensive adj causing or involving great expense; costly.—**expensively** adv.—**expensiveness** n.

experience n observation or practice resulting in or tending towards knowledge; knowledge gained by seeing and doing; a state of being affected from without (as by events); an affecting event. * vt to have experience of.

experienced adj wise or skilled through experience.

experiment n any test or trial to find out something; a controlled procedure carried out to discover, test, or demonstrate something. * vi to carry out experiments.—**experimentation** n.

experimental adj of, derived from, or proceeding by experiment; empirical; provisional.—**experimentalism** n.

expert adj thoroughly skilled; knowledgeable through training and experience. * n a person with special skills or training in any art or science.—**expertly** adv.

expertise n expert knowledge or skill.

expire vti to come to an end; to lapse or become void; to breathe out; to die.—**expiration** n.

explain vt to make plain or clear; to give a reason for, account for.

explanation n an act or process of explaining; something that explains, esp a statement.

explanatory adj serving as an explanation.

explicit adj clearly stated, not merely implied; outspoken, frank; graphically detailed.—**explicitly** adv.—**explicitness** n.

explode *vti* to burst or cause to blow up with a loud noise, as in the detonation of a bomb; (*emotions*) to burst out; (*population*) to increase rapidly; to expose (a theory, etc) as false.

exploit *n* a bold achievement. * *vt* to utilize, develop (raw materials, etc); to take unfair advantage of, esp for financial gain.—**exploitation** *n*.

exploratory, explorative *adj* for the purpose of exploring or investigating.

explore *vti* to examine or inquire into; to travel through (a country) for the purpose of discovery; to examine minutely.—**exploration** *n*.—**explorer** *n*.

explosion *n* an act or instance of exploding; a sudden loud noise caused by this; an outburst of emotion; a rapid increase or expansion.

explosive *adj* liable to or able to explode; liable or threatening to burst out with violence and noise. * *n* an explosive substance.—**explosively** *adv*.

exponent *n* a person who explains or interprets something; a person who champions, advocates, or exemplifies; (*math*) an index of the power to which an expression is raised.

export *vt* to send out (goods) of one country for sale in another. * *n* the act of exporting; the article exported.—**exportable** *adj*.—**exportation** *n*.—**exporter** *n*.

expose *vt* to deprive of protection or shelter; to subject to an influence (as light, weather); to display, reveal; to uncover or disclose.

exposure *n* an exposing or state of being exposed; time during which light reaches and acts on a photographic film, paper or plate; publicity.

expound *vt* to explain or set forth in detail.

express *vt* to represent in words; to make known one's thoughts, feelings, etc; to represent by signs, symbols, etc; to squeeze out. * *adj* firmly stated, explicit; (*train, bus, etc*) travelling at high speed with few or no stops. * *adv* at high speed, by express service. * *n* an express train, coach, etc; a system or company for sending freight, etc at rates higher than standard.

expression *n* an act of expressing, esp by words; a word or phrase; a look; intonation; a manner of showing feeling in communicating or performing (eg music); (*math*) a collection of symbols serving to express something. —**expressionless** *adj*.

expressive *adj* serving to express; full of expression.

expressly *adv* explicitly; for a specific purpose.

expulsion *n* the act of expelling or being expelled.—**expulsive** *adj*.

exquisite *adj* very beautiful, refined; sensitive, showing discrimination; acutely felt, as pain or pleasure.—**exquisitely** *adv*.

extend *vt* to stretch or spread out; to stretch fully; to prolong in time; to cause to reach in distance, etc; to enlarge, increase the scope of; to hold out (eg the hand); to accord, grant; to give, offer, (eg sympathy).

* *vi* to prolong in distance or time; to reach in scope.

extension *n* act of extending or state of being extended; extent, scope; an added part, eg to a building; an extra period; a programme of extramural teaching provided by a college, etc; an additional telephone connected to the principal line.

extensive *adj* large; having a wide scope or extent.—**extensively** *adv*.—**extensiveness** *n*.

extent *n* the distance over which a thing is extended; the range or scope of something; the limit to which something extends.

exterior *adj* of, on, or coming from the outside; external; (*paint, etc*) suitable for use on the outside. * *n* the external part or surface; outward manner or appearance.

exterminate *vt* to destroy completely.—**extermination** *n*.—**exterminator** *n*.

external *adj* outwardly perceivable; of, relating to, or located on the outside or outer part. * *n* an external feature. —**externally** *adv*.

extinct *adj* (*animals*) not alive, no longer existing; (*fire*) not burning, out; (*volcano*) no longer active.—**extinction** *n*.

extinguish *vt* to put out (a fire, light, etc); to bring to an end.

extinguisher *n* a device for putting out a fire.

extort *vt* to obtain (money, promises, etc) by force or improper pressure.—**extortion** *n*.—**extortioner** *n*.

extortionate *adj* excessively high in price.

extra *adj* additional. * *adv* unusually; in addition. * *n* something extra or additional, esp a charge; a special edition of a newspaper; a person who plays a non-speaking role in a film.

extra- *prefix* outside, beyond.

extra-billing *n* (*Cdn*) the charging of fees by a doctor to a patient in excess of what a public health insurance pays.

extract *vt* to take or pull out by force; to withdraw by chemical or physical means; to abstract. * *n* the essence of a substance obtained by extraction; a passage taken from a book, play, film, etc.

extraction *n* the act of extracting; lineage; something extracted.

extradite *vt* to surrender (an alleged criminal) to the country where the offence was committed.—**extradition** *n*.

extramarital *adj* occurring outside marriage, esp sexual relationships.

extraneous *adj* coming from outside; not essential.—**extraneously** *adv*.

extraordinary *adj* not usual or regular; remarkable, exceptional.—**extraordinarily** *adv*.

extravagant *adj* lavish in spending; (*prices*) excessively high; wasteful; (*behaviour, praise, etc*) lacking in restraint, flamboyant, profuse.—**extravagantly** *adv*.—**extravagance** *n*.

extravert *see* **extrovert**.

extreme *adj* of the highest degree or intensity; excessive, immoderate, unwarranted; very severe, stringent; outermost. * *n* the highest or furthest limit or degree; (*often pl*) either of the two points marking the ends of a scale or range.—**extremely** adv.

extremist n a person of extreme views, esp political.—**extremism** n.

extremity n the utmost point or degree; the most remote part; the utmost violence, vigour, or necessity; the end; (pl) the hands or feet.

extricate vt to release from difficulties; to disentangle.—**extrication** n.

extrovert n a person more interested in the external world than his own feelings. —also **extravert**.

exuberant adj lively, high-spirited; profuse.—**exuberantly** adv.—**exuberance** n.

exude vt to cause or allow to ooze through pores or incisions, as sweat, pus; to display (confidence, emotion) freely.—**exudation** n.

exult vi to rejoice greatly.—**exultation** n.

eye n the organ of sight; the iris; the faculty of seeing; the external part of the eye; something resembling an eye. * vt (pr p **eyeing** or **eying**, pt **eyed**) to look at; to observe closely.

eyeball n the ball of the eye. * vt (sl) to stare at.

eyebrow n the hairy ridge above the eye.

eye-catching adj attractive or striking in appearance.

eyelash n the fringe of fine hairs along the edge of each eyelid.

eyelid n the lid of skin and muscle that moves to cover the eye.

eye-opener n something that comes as a shock or surprise.

eye-shadow n a colored powder applied to accentuate or decorate the eyelids.

eyesight n the faculty of seeing.

eyesore n anything offensive to the sight.

eye-witness n a person who sees an event.

eyrie n the nest of an eagle or other bird of prey; any high inaccessible place or position.

F

F abbr = Fahrenheit; (chem symbol) fluorine.

fable n a story, often with animal characters, conveying a moral; a lie, fabrication; a story involving mythical, legendary or supernatural characters or events.

fabric n cloth made by knitting, weaving, etc; framework, structure.

fabulous adj told in fables; incredible, astonishing; (inf) very good.—**fabulously** adv.

façade, facade n the main front or face of a building; an outward appearance, esp concealing something.

face n the front part of the head containing the eyes, nose, etc; facial expression; the front or outer surface of anything; external show or appearance; dignity, self-respect; impudence, effrontery; a coal face. * vt to be confronted by (a problem, etc); to deal with (an opponent, etc) resolutely; to be opposite to; to turn (a card) face upwards; to cover with a new surface. * vi to turn the face in a certain direction; to be situated in or have a specific direction.

face-lift n plastic surgery to smooth and firm the face; an improvement or renovation, esp to the outside of a building.

faceoff n the act of starting or restarting play in hockey or lacrosse by dropping or placing the puck or ball between two opposing players' sticks; a direct confrontation.

facet n a small plane surface (as on a cut gem); an aspect of character, a problem, issue, etc.

facetious adj joking, esp in an inappropriate manner.—**facetiously** adv.—**facetiousness** n.

facia see fascia.

facial adj of or pertaining to the face. * n a beauty treatment for the face.—**facially** adv.

facile adj easy to do; superficial.

facilitate vt to make easier.

facility n the quality of being easily done; aptitude, dexterity; something, eg a service or equipment, that makes it easy to do something.

facsimile n an exact copy of a book, document, etc; a method of transmitting printed matter through the telephone system.—also **fax**.

fact n a thing known to have happened or to exist; reality; a piece of verifiable information; (law) an event, occurrence, etc as distinguished from its legal consequences.

faction[1] n a small group of people in an organization working together in a common cause against the main body; dissension within a group or organization.—**factional** adj.—**factionally** adv.—**factious** adj.

faction[2] n a book, film, etc based on facts but presented as a blend of fact and fiction.

factor n any circumstance that contributes towards a result; (math) any of two or more numbers that, when multiplied together, form a product; a person who acts for another; a company that buys invoices at a discount and then collects payments on them; (Cdn) (hist) a person in charge of a fur-trading post.

factory n a building or buildings where things are manufactured; (Cdn) (hist) a large fur-trading post.

factual adj based on, or containing, facts; actual.—**factually** adv.

faculty n any natural power of a living organism; special aptitude; a teaching department of a college or university, or the staff of such a department.

fad n a personal habit or idiosyncrasy; a craze.—**faddish, faddy** adj.

fade vi to lose vigour or brightness of color gradually; to vanish gradually. * vt to cause (an image or a sound) to increase or decrease in brightness or intensity gradually.—also n.

fag vti (pt **fagged**) to become or cause to be tired by hard work. * n (formerly) a British public schoolboy who performs chores for senior pupils; (inf) drudgery; (sl) a homosexual; (sl) a cigarette.

fag-end n the useless remains of anything; (sl) a cigarette-end.

fail *vi* to weaken, to fade or die away; to stop operating; to fall short; to be insufficient; to be negligent in duty, expectation, etc; (*exam, etc*) to be unsuccessful; to become bankrupt. * *vt* to disappoint the expectations or hopes of; to be unsuccessful in an exam, etc; to leave, to abandon; to grade (a candidate) as not passing a test, etc. * *n* failure in an examination.

failing *n* a fault, weakness. * *prep* in default or absence of.

failure *n* failing, non-performance, lack of success; the ceasing of normal operation of something; a deficiency; bankruptcy; an unsuccessful person or thing.

faint *adj* dim, indistinct; weak, feeble; timid; on the verge of losing consciousness. * *vi* to lose consciousness temporarily from a decrease in the supply of blood to the brain, as from shock. * *n* an act or condition of fainting.—**faintly** *adv*.—**faintness** *n*.

faint-hearted *adj* lacking courage and resolution.

fair[1] *adj* pleasing to the eye; clean, unblemished; (*hair*) light-colored; (*weather*) clear and sunny; (*handwriting*) easy to read; just and honest; according to the rules; moderately large; average. * *adv* in a fair manner; squarely.—**fairness** *n*.

fair[2] *n* a gathering for the sale of goods, esp for charity; a competitive exhibition of farm, household, or manufactured goods; a funfair.

fairly *adv* in a fair manner; justly; moderately.

fairy *n* an imaginary supernatural being, usu in human form; (*sl*) a male homosexual.

fairy story, fairy tale *n* a story about fairies; an incredible story; a fabrication.

faith *n* trust or confidence in a person or thing; a strong conviction, esp a belief in a religion; any system of religious belief; fidelity to one's promises, sincerity.

faithful *adj* loyal; true; true to the original, accurate.—**faithfully** *adv*.

fake *vt* to make (an object) appear more real or valuable in order to deceive; to pretend, simulate. * *n* a faked article, a forgery; an impostor. * *adj* counterfeit, not genuine.—**faker** *n*.

falcon *n* a type of hawk trained for use in falconry.

fall *vi* (*pt* **fell**, *pp* **fallen**) to descend by force of gravity; to come as if by falling; to collapse; to drop to the ground; to become lower, weaker, less; to lose power, status, etc; to lose office; to slope downwards; to be wounded or killed in battle; to pass into a certain state; to become pregnant; to take place, happen; to be directed by chance; to come by inheritance; (*with* **back**) to retreat; (*with* **out**) to quarrel; to leave one's place in a military formation. * *n* act or instance of falling; something which falls; the amount by which something falls; a decline in status, position; overthrow; a downward slope; a decrease in size, quantity, value; in US, autumn;

(*wrestling*) a scoring move by pinning both shoulders of an opponent to the floor at once.

fallacy *n* a false idea; a mistake in reasoning.

fallible *adj* liable to make mistakes.—**fallibly** *adv*.— **fallibility** *n*.

fall-out *n* a deposit of radioactive dust from a nuclear explosion; a by-product.

fallow[1] *adj* (*lan d*) ploughed and left unplanted for a season or more.

fallow[2] *adj* yellowish-brown.

false *adj* wrong, incorrect; deceitful; artificial; disloyal, treacherous; misleading, fallacious.—**falsely** *adv*.—**falseness** *n*.

falsehood *n* a being untrue; the act of deceiving; a lie.

falter *vi* to move or walk unsteadily, to stumble; to hesitate or stammer in speech; to be weak or unsure, to waver.

fame *n* the state of being well known; good reputation.—**famed** *adj*.

Fameuse *n* (*Cdn*) snow apple.

familiar *adj* well-acquainted; friendly; common; well-known; too informal, presumptuous. * *n* a spirit or demon supposed to aid a witch, etc; an intimate. —**familiarly** *adv*.—**familiarity** *n*.

familiarize *vt* to make well known or acquainted; to make (something) well known.—**familiarization** *n*.

family *n* parents and their children; a person's children; a set of relatives; the descendants of a common ancestor; any group of persons or things related in some way; a group of related plants or animals; a unit of a crime syndicate (as the Mafia).

family allowance *n* (*Cdn*) formerly, a monthly payment by the federal government to mothers who had children who were under 18 years of age; (*Brit*) formerly, the name for child benefit.

famine *n* an acute scarcity of food in a particular area; an extreme scarcity of anything.

famous *adj* renowned; (*inf*) excellent.—**famously** *adv*.

fan[1] *n* a handheld or mechanical device used to set up a current of air. * *vt* (*pt* **fanned**) to cool, as with a fan; to ventilate; to stir up, to excite; to spread out like a fan.

fan[2] *n* an enthusiastic follower of some sport, hobby, person, etc.

fanatic *n* a person who is excessively enthusiastic about something.—**fanatical** *adj*.—**fanatically** *adv*.

fan belt *n* the belt that drives the cooling fan in a car engine.

fanciful *adj* not factual, imaginary; indulging in fancy; elaborate or intricate in design.—**fancifully** *adv*.

fancy *n* imagination; a mental image; a whim; fondness. * *adj* (**fancier, fanciest**) not based on fact, imaginary; elegant or ornamental. * *vt* to imagine; to have a fancy or liking for; (*inf*) to be sexually attracted to.

fancy dress *n* a costume worn at masquerades or parties, usu representing an animal, historical character, etc.

fang n a long sharp tooth, as in a canine; the long hollow tooth through which venomous snakes inject poison.

fan hitch n (Cdn) in the North, a method of harnessing a dog sled in which the lead dog is on a long trace, with the other dogs arranged in a fan-shaped pattern.

fanlight n a semicircular window with radiating bars like the ribs of a fan.

fantastic adj unrealistic, fanciful; unbelievable; imaginative; (inf) wonderful.—**fantastically** adv.

fantasy n imagination; a product of the imagination, esp an extravagant or bizarre notion or creation; an imaginative poem, play or novel.

far adj (**farther, farthest** or **further, furthest**) remote in space or time; long; (political views, etc) extreme * adv very distant in space, time, or degree; to or from a distance in time or position, very much.

faraway adj distant, remote; dreamy.

farce n a style of light comedy; a drama using such comedy; a ludicrous situation.—**farcical** adj.

fare n money paid for transportation; a passenger in public transport; food. * vi to be in a specified condition.

farewell interj goodbye.—also n.

far-fetched adj unlikely.

farm n an area of land (with buildings) on which crops and animals are raised. * vt to grow crops or breed livestock; to cultivate, as land; to breed fish commercially; (with **out**) to put out (work, etc) to be done by others, to subcontract.

farmer n a person who manages or operates a farm.

farmer's sausage n (Cdn) a sausage of seasoned, coarsely grown raw pork, bound in a casing but not in links.

farmhouse n a house on a farm.

farmyard n a yard close to or surrounded by farm buildings.

far-reaching adj having serious or widespread consequences.

far-seeing adj having foresight.

fart vi (vulg) to expel wind from the anus.—also n.

farther adj at or to a greater distance. * adv to a greater degree.

farthest adj at or to the greatest distance. * adv to the greatest degree.

fascia n (pl **fasciae**) the instrument panel of a motor vehicle, the dashboard; the flat surface above a shop front, with the name, etc.—also **facia**.

fascinate vt to hold the attention of, to attract irresistibly.—**fascination** n.

fashion n the current style of dress, conduct, speech, etc; the manner or form of appearance or action. * vt to make in a particular form; to suit or adapt.

fashionable adj conforming to the current fashion; attracting or frequented by people of fashion.—**fashionably** adv.

fast[1] adj swift, quick; (clock) ahead of time; firmly attached, fixed; (color, dye) non-fading; wild, promiscuous. * adv firmly, thoroughly, rapidly, quickly.

fast[2] vi to go without all or certain foods. * n a period of fasting.

fasten vti to secure firmly; to attach; to fix (the eyes, attention) steadily.

fastener, fastening n a clip, catch, etc for fastening.

fastidious adj hard to please; daintily refined; over-sensitive.—**fastidiously** adv.—**fastidiousness** n.

fat adj (**fatter, fattest**) plump; thick; fertile; profitable. * n an oily or greasy material found in animal tissue and plant seeds; the richest or best part of anything; a superfluous part.—**fatness** n.

fatal adj causing death; disastrous (to); fateful.—**fatally** adv.

fatalism n belief that all events are predetermined by fate and therefore inevitable; acceptance of this doctrine.—**fatalist** n.—**fatalistic** adj.

fatality n a death caused by a disaster or accident; a person killed in such a way; a fatal power or influence.

fate n the ultimate power that predetermines events, destiny; the ultimate end, outcome; misfortune, doom, death.

fateful adj having important, usu unpleasant, consequences.—**fatefully** adv.

father n a male parent; an ancestor; a founder or originator; (with cap) God; a title of respect applied to monks, priests, etc. * vt to be the father of; to found, originate.—**fatherhood** n.

father-in-law n the father of one's husband or wife.

fathom n a nautical measure of 6 feet (1.83 m). * vt to measure the depth of; to understand.

fatigue n tiredness from physical or mental effort; the tendency of a material to break under repeated stress; any of the menial or manual tasks performed by military personnel; (pl) the clothing worn on fatigue or in the field. * vti to make or become tired.

fatten vt to make fat or fleshy; to make abundant.—**fattening** adj.

fatty adj (**fattier, fattiest**) resembling or containing fat. * n (inf) a fat person.

fatuous adj foolish, idiotic.—**fatuously** adv.—**fatuousness** n.—**fatuity** n.

faucet n a fixture for draining off liquid (as from a pipe or cask); a tap.

fault n a failing, defect; a minor offence; (tennis, etc) an incorrect serve or other error; a fracture in the earth's crust causing displacement of strata. * vt to find fault with, blame. * vi to commit a fault.

faultless adj without fault.—**faultlessly** adv.—**faultlessness** n.

faulty adj (**faultier, faultiest**) imperfect.—**faultily** adv.—**faultiness** n.

fauna n (pl **faunas, faunae**) the animals of a region, period, or specific environment.

favor n goodwill; approval; a kind or helpful act; partiality; a gift given out at a party; (usu pl) a privilege conceded, esp sexual. * vt to regard or treat with favor; to show support for; to oblige (with); to afford advantage to, facilitate.

favorable adj expressing approval; pleasing; propitious; conducive (to).—**favorably** adv.

favorite n a favored person or thing; a competitor expected to win. * adj most preferred.

favoritism n the showing of unfair favor.

fawn[1] n a young deer; a yellowish-brown color. * adj fawn-colored.

fawn[2] vi (dogs, etc) to crouch to show affection; to flatter obsequiously.—**fawner** n.—**fawning** n.

fax see **facsimile**.

FD abbr (Cdn) = Forest District.

fear n an unpleasant emotion excited by danger, pain, etc; a cause of fear; anxiety; deep reverence. * vt to feel fear, be afraid of; to be apprehensive, anxious; to be sorry. * vi to be afraid or apprehensive.—**fearless** adj.—**fearlessly** adv.—**fearlessness** n.

fearful adj causing intense fear; timorous; apprehensive (of); (inf) very great, very bad.—**fearfully** adv.

feasible adj able to be done or implemented, possible.—**feasibly** adv.—**feasibility** n.

feast n an elaborate meal prepared for a special occasion; something that gives abundant pleasure; a periodic religious celebration. * vi to have or take part in a feast. * vt to entertain with a feast.

feat n an action of remarkable strength, skill, or courage.

feather n any of the light outgrowths forming the covering of a bird, a hollow central shaft with a vane of fine barbs on each side; a plume; something resembling a feather; the water thrown up by the turn of the blade of an oar. * vt to ornament with feathers; to turn (a blade) so that the edge is foremost.—**feathering** n.—**feathery** adj.

feature n any of the parts of the face; a characteristic trait of something; a special attraction or distinctive quality of something; a prominent newspaper article, etc; the main film in a cinema programme. * vti to make or be a feature of (something).

featureless adj lacking prominent or distinctive features.

February n the second month of the year, having 28 days (or 29 days in leap years).

federal adj designating, or of a union of states, etc, in which each member surrenders some of its power to a central authority; of a central government of this type.—**federalism** n.—**federalist** n.—**federally** adv.

federation n a union of states, groups, etc, in which each subordinates its power to a central authority; a federated organization.

fee n the price paid for the advice or service of a professional; a charge for some privilege, as membership of a club; (law) an inheritance in land.

feeble adj weak, ineffective.—**feebly** adv.—**feebleness** n.

feeble-minded adj mentally defective; of low intelligence.

feed vb (pt **fed**) vt to give food to; to give as food to; to supply with necessary material; to gratify. * vi to consume food. * n food for animals; material fed into a machine; the part of a machine supplying this material.

feedback n a return to the input of part of the output of a system; information about a product, service, etc returned to the supplier for evaluation.

feel vb (pt **felt**) vt to perceive or explore by the touch; to find one's way by cautious trial; to be conscious of, experience; to have a vague or instinctual impression of; to believe, consider. * vi to be able to experience the sensation of touch; to be affected by; to convey a certain sensation when touched. * n the sense of touch; feeling; a quality as revealed by touch.

feeler n a tactile organ (as a tentacle or antenna) of an animal; a tentative approach or suggestion to test another person's reactions.

feeling n the sense of touch; mental or physical awareness; a physical or mental impression; a state of mind; sympathy; emotional sensitivity; a belief or opinion arising from emotion; (pl) emotions, sensibilities.

feet see **foot**.

feign vt to invent; to pretend.

fell[1] see **fall**.

fell[2] vt to cut, beat, or knock down; to kill, to sew (a seam) by folding one raw edge under the other.

fell[3] n a skin, hide, pelt.

fell[4] adj (poet) cruel, fierce, bloody, deadly.

fellow n an associate; a comrade; an equal in power, rank, or position; the other of a pair, a mate; a member of the governing body in some colleges and universities; a member of a learned society; (inf) a man or boy. * adj belonging to the same group or class.

fellowship n companionship; a mutual sharing; a group of people with the same interests; the position held by a college fellow.

felony n (formerly) a grave crime.

felt[1] see **feel**.

felt[2] n a fabric made from woollen fibres, often mixed with fur or hair, pressed together. * vti to make into or become like felt.

female adj of the sex that produces young; of a woman or women; (pipe, plug, etc) designed with a hollow part for receiving an inserted piece. * n a female animal or plant.

feminine adj of, resembling, or appropriate to women; (gram) of that gender to which words denoting females belong.—**femininity** n.

feminism n the movement to win political, economic and social equality for women.—**feminist** adj. n.

fence n a barrier put round land to mark a boundary, or prevent animals, etc from escaping; a receiver of stolen goods. * vt to surround with a fence; to keep (out) as by a fence. * vi to practise fencing; to make evasive answers; to act as a fence for stolen goods.—**fencer** n.

fencing n fences; material for making fences; the art of fighting with foils or other types of sword.

fend vi (with **for**) to provide a livelihood for.

fender n anything that protects or fends off something else, as old tyres along the side of a vessel, or the part of a car body over the wheel.

ferment n an agent causing fermentation, as yeast; excitement, agitation. * vti to (cause to) undergo fermentation; to (cause to) be excited, agitated.

fermentation n the breakdown of complex molecules in organic components caused by the influence of yeast or other substances.

fern n any of a large class of non-flowering plants having roots, stems, and fronds, and reproducing by spores.—**ferny** adj.

ferocious adj savage, fierce.—**ferociously** adv.—**ferocity** n.

ferry vt to convey (passengers, etc) over a stretch of water; to transport from one place to another, esp along a regular route. * n a boat used for ferrying; a ferrying service; the location of a ferry.—**ferryman** n.

fertile adj able to bear offspring; (land) easily supporting plants and vegetation; (animals) capable of breeding; (eggs) able to grow and develop; prolific; (mind, brain) inventive.—**fertility** n.

fertilize vt to make (soil) fertile by adding nutrients; to impregnate; to pollinate.—**fertilization** n.

fertilizer n natural organic or artificial substances used to enrich the soil.

fervent, fervid adj passionate; zealous.—**fervently, fervidly** adv.—**fervency** n.

fester vti to become or cause to become infected; to suppurate; to rankle.

festival n a time of celebration; performances of music, plays, etc given periodically.

festive adj merry, joyous.

fetch vt to go for and bring back; to cause to come; (goods) to sell for (a certain price); (inf) to deal (a blow, slap, etc).

fetching adj attractive.

fête, fete n a festival; a usu outdoor sale, bazaar or entertainment in aid of charity. * vt to honor or entertain (as if) with a fête.

Fête nationale n (Cdn) in Quebec, official name of St Jean Baptiste Day.

fetish n an object believed by primitive peoples to have magical properties; any object or activity regarded with excessive devotion.

fetus, n (pl **fetuses**) the unborn young of an animal, esp in its later stages; in humans, the offspring in the womb from the fourth month until birth.—also **foetus** (pl **foetuses**).—**fetal, foetal** adj.

feud n a state of hostilities, esp between individuals, families, or clans; a dispute.—also vi.

feudal adj pertaining to feudalism; (inf) old-fashioned, redundant.

feudalism n the economic and social system in medieval Europe, in which land, worked by serfs, was held by vassals in exchange for military and other services to overlords.

fever n an abnormally increased body temperature; any disease marked by a high fever; a state of restless excitement.—**fevered** adj.

feverish adj having a fever; indicating a fever; restlessly excited.—**feverishly** adv.—**feverishness** n.

few adj, n a small number, not many.—**fewness** n.

fiancé n a person engaged to be married.—**fiancée** nf.

fiasco n (pl **fiascos, fiascoes**) a complete and humiliating failure.

fib n a lie about something unimportant.—also vi.—**fibber** n.

fibre, fiber (US) n a natural or synthetic thread, eg from cotton, nylon, which is spun into yarn; a material composed of such yarn; texture; strength of character; a fibrous substance, roughage.—**fibrous** adj.

fibreglass, fiberglass (US) n glass in fibrous form, often bonded with plastic, used in making various products.

fickle adj inconstant; capricious.—**fickleness** n.

fiction n an invented story; any literary work with imaginary characters and events, as a novel, play, etc; such works collectively.—**fictional** adj.—**fictionally** adv.

fictitious adj imaginary, not real; feigned.—**fictitiously** adv.

fiddle n (inf) a violin; (sl) a swindle. * vt (inf) to play on a violin; (sl) to swindle; to falsify. * vi to handle restlessly, to fidget.—**fiddler** n.

fidelity n faithfulness, loyalty; truthfulness; accuracy in reproducing sound.

fidget vi to (cause to) move restlessly.—also n.—**fidgety** adj.

field n an area of land cleared of trees and buildings, used for pasture or crops; an area rich in a natural product (eg gold, coal); a battlefield; a sports ground; an area affected by electrical, magnetic or gravitational influence, etc; the area visible through an optical lens; a division of activity, knowledge, etc; all competitors in a contest; (comput) a section of a record in a database. * vt (cricket, baseball, etc) to catch or stop and return the ball as a fielder; to put (eg. a team) into the field to play; (inf) to handle (eg questions) successfully.

field glasses npl small, portable binoculars for use outdoors.

fieldwork n research done outside the laboratory or place of work by scientists, archaeologists, social workers, etc. —**fieldworker** n.

fiend *n* an evil spirit; an inhumanly wicked person; (*inf*) an avid fan.—**fiendish** *adj.*—**fiendishly** *adv.*

fierce *adj* ferociously hostile; angry, violent; intense; strong, extreme.—**fiercely** *adv.*—**fierceness** *n.*

fiery *adj* (**fierier, fieriest**) like or consisting of fire; the color of fire; intensely hot; spicy; passionate, ardent; impetuous; irascible.—**fierily** *adv.*—**fieriness** *n.*

fifteen *adj, n* one more than fourteen; the symbol for this (15, XV, xv); the first point scored by a side in a game of tennis.—**fifteenth** *adj, n.*

fifth *adj, n* last of five; being one of five equal parts.

fifty *adj, n* five times ten; the symbol for this (50, L, l).—**fiftieth** *adj.*

fig *n* a tree yielding a soft, pear-shaped fruit; a thing of little or no importance.

fight *vb* (*pt* **fought**) *vi* to engage in battle in war or in single combat; to strive, struggle (for). * *vt* to engage in or carry on a conflict with; to achieve (one's way) by fighting; to strive to overcome. * *n* fighting; a struggle or conflict of any kind; a boxing match.

fighter *n* a person who fights; a person who does not yield easily; an aircraft designed to destroy enemy aircraft.

figment *n* something imagined or invented.

figurative *adj* metaphorical; using figures of speech.—**figuratively** *adv.*

figure *n* a character representing a number; a number; value or price; bodily shape or form; a graphic representation of a thing, person or animal; a design; a geometrical form; a statue; appearance; a personage; (*dancing, skating*) a set of steps or movements; (*pl*) arithmetic. * *vt* to represent in a diagram or outline; to imagine; (*inf*) to consider; (*inf*) to believe. * *vi* to take a part (in), be conspicuous (in); to calculate.

figurehead *n* a carved figure on the bow of a ship; a nominal head or leader.

filament *n* a slender thread or strand; a fibre; the fine wire in a light bulb.

file[1] *n* a container for keeping papers, etc, in order; an orderly arrangement of papers; a line of persons or things; (*comput*) a collection of related data under a specific name. * *vt* to dispatch or register; to put on public record. * *vi* to move in a line; to apply.

file[2] *n* a tool, usu steel, with a rough surface for smoothing or grinding. * *vt* to cut or smooth with, or as with, a file; to polish, improve.

filing *n* a particle rubbed off with a file.

fill *vt* to put as much as possible into; to occupy wholly; to put a person into (a position or job, etc); to supply the things called for (in an order, etc); to close or plug (holes, etc). * *vi* to become full. * *n* enough to make full or to satisfy; anything that fills.

fillet *n* a thin boneless strip of meat or fish; a ribbon, etc worn as a headband; (*archit*) a narrow band used between mouldings. * *vt* to bone and slice (fish or meat).

filling *n* a substance used to fill a tooth cavity; the contents of a sandwich, pie, etc. * *adj* (*meal, etc*) substantial.

filling station *n* a place where petrol is sold to motorists, a service station.

fillip *n* a blow with the nail of the finger; a stimulus.

film *n* a fine, thin skin, coating, etc; a flexible cellulose material covered with a light-sensitive substance used in photography; a haze or blur; a motion picture. * *vti* to cover or be covered as with a film; to photograph or make a film (of).

filter *n* a device or substance straining out solid particles, impurities, etc, from a liquid or gas; a device for removing or minimizing electrical oscillations, or sound or light waves, of certain frequencies; a traffic signal that allows cars to turn left or right while the main lights are red. * *vti* to pass through or as through a filter; to remove with a filter.

filth *n* dirt; obscenity.

filthy *adj* (**filthier, filthiest**) dirty, disgusting; obscene; (*inf*) extremely unpleasant.—**filthily** *adv.*—**filthiness** *n.*

fin *n* an organ by which a fish, etc steers itself and swims; a rubber flipper used for underwater swimming; any fin-shaped object used as a stabilizer, as on an aircraft or rocket.

final *adj* of or coming at the end; conclusive. * *n* (*often pl*) the last of a series of contests; a final examination.—**finally** *adv.*

finale *n* the concluding part of any public performance; the last section in a musical composition.

finalist *n* a contestant in a final.

finalize *vt* to make complete, to bring to an end.—**finalization** *n.*

finance *n* the management of money; (*pl*) money resources. * *vt* to supply or raise money for.—**financial** *adj.*—**financially** *adv.*

financier *n* a person skilled in finance.

find *vb* (*pt* **found**) *vt* to discover by chance; to come upon by searching; to perceive; to recover (something lost); to reach, attain; to decide and declare to be. * *vi* to reach a decision (as by a jury). * *n* a discovery, something found.

finding *n* a discovery; the conclusion reached by a judicial enquiry.

fine[1] *adj* very good; with no impurities, refined; (*weather*) clear and bright; not heavy or coarse; very thin or small; sharp; subtle; elegant. * *adv* in a fine manner; (*inf*) very well.—**finely** *adv.*—**fineness** *n.*

fine[2] *n* a sum of money imposed as a punishment. * *vt* to punish by a fine.

fine arts *npl* painting, sculpture, music, etc valued for their aesthetic qualities.

finery *n* elaborate clothes, jewellery, etc.

finesse *n* delicacy or subtlety of performance; skilfulness, diplomacy in handling a situation; (*bridge*) an attempt to take a trick with a card lower than a higher card held by an opponent. * vt to achieve by finesse; to play (a card) as a finesse.

finger n one of the digits of the hand, usu excluding the thumb; anything shaped like a finger; (inf) the breadth of a finger. * vt to touch with fingers; (mus) to use the fingers in a certain way when playing.

fingernail n the nail on a finger.

fingerprint n the impression of the ridges on a fingertip, esp as used for purposes of identification.—also vt.

finicky, finicking adj too particular, fussy.

finish vt to bring to an end, to come to the end of; to consume entirely; to perfect; to give a desired surface effect to. * vi to come to an end. * n the last part, the end; anything used to finish a surface; the finished effect; means or manner of completing or perfecting; polished manners, speech, etc.—finisher n.

finite adj having definable limits; (verb form) having a distinct grammatical person and number.

fiord see fjord.

fir n a kind of evergreen, cone-bearing tree; its timber.

fire n the flame, heat and light of combustion; something burning; burning fuel in a grate to heat a room; an electric or gas fire; a destructive burning; a strong feeling; a discharge of firearms. * vti to ignite; to supply with fuel; to bake (bricks, etc) in a kiln; to excite or become excited; to shoot (a gun, etc); to hurl or direct with force; to dismiss from a position.

fire alarm n a device that uses a bell, hooter, etc to warn of a fire.

firearm n a handgun.

fire brigade n an organization of men trained and equipped to fight fires.

fire escape n a means of exit from a building, esp a stairway, for use in case of fire.

fire hall n (Cdn) a fire station.

fireman n a member of a fire brigade; a person employed to tend furnaces.

fireplace n a place for a fire, esp a recess in a wall; the surrounding area.

fireside n the area in a room nearest the fireplace; home.

firework n a device packed with explosive and combustible material to produce noisy and colorful displays; (pl) such a display; (pl) a fit of temper, an outburst of emotions.

firing squad n a detachment with the task of firing a salute at a military funeral or carrying out an execution.

firm¹ adj securely fixed; solid, compact; steady; resolute; definite. * vti to make or become firm.—firmly adv.—firmness n.

firm² n a business partnership; a commercial company.

first adj before all others in a series; 1st; earliest; foremost, as in rank, quality, etc. * adv before anyone or anything else; for the first time; sooner. * n any person or thing that is first; the beginning; the winning place, as in a race; low gear; the highest award in a university degree.

first aid n emergency treatment for an injury, etc, before regular medical aid is available.

first-class adj of the highest quality, as in accommodation, travel.—also n.

firsthand adj obtained directly.

First Lady n the wife of the US president.

firstly adv in the first place.

First Ministers npl (Cdn) the Prime Minister and the premiers of the provinces.

First Nations npl (Cdn) Indian peoples or their communities, not including the Inuit or Metis peoples. * adj of or pertaining to such a people or community.

First Peoples npl the aboriginal peoples of a country, in Canada including First Nations, Inuit, and Metis peoples.

first-rate adj, adv of the best quality; (inf) excellent.

fiscal adj of or relating to public revenue; financial. * n a prosecuting official in some countries.

fish n (pl fish, fishes) any of a large group of cold-blooded animals living in water, having backbones, gills and fins; the flesh of fish used as food. * vi to catch or try to catch fish; (with for) to try to obtain by roundabout methods. * vt (often with out) to grope for, find, and bring to view.

fish and brewis n (Cdn) a dish of salt cod and hardtack soaked in water and then cooked with fried salt pork.

fisherman n a person who fishes for sport or for a living; a ship used in fishing.

fishery n the fishing industry; an area where fish are caught.

fish finger n a small oblong piece of fish covered in breadcrumbs.

fish flake n (Cdn) a large rack on which to dry fish.

fishing stage n (Cdn) a shed used for preparing freshly caught fish before they are dried.

fishmonger n a shop that sells fish.

fishway n (Cdn) a lock built to assist fish in passing a waterfall or other obstacle on their way upstream to spawn.

fishy adj (fishier, fishiest) like a fish in odour, taste, etc; (inf) creating doubt or suspicion.—fishily adv.—fishiness n.

fission n a split or cleavage; the reproductive division of biological cells; the splitting of the atomic nucleus resulting in the release of energy, nuclear fission.—fissionable adj.

fissure n a narrow opening or cleft.—also vti.

fist n the hand when tightly closed or clenched.

fit¹ adj (fitter, fittest) suited to some purpose, function, etc; proper, right; healthy; (sl) inclined, ready. * n the manner of fitting. * vb (pt fitted) vt to be suitable to; to be the proper size or shape for; to adjust so as to fit; to equip, to outfit. * vi to be suitable or proper; to have the proper size or shape. —

fitly *adv.*—**fitness** *n.*

fit² *n* any sudden, uncontrollable attack, as of coughing; an outburst, as of anger; a short period of impulsive activity; a seizure involving convulsions or loss of consciousness.

fitful *adj* marked by intermittent activity; spasmodic.—**fitfully** *adv.*—**fitfulness** *n.*

fitment *n* a piece of equipment, esp fixed furniture.

fitter *n* a person who specializes in fitting clothes; a person skilled in the assembly and operation of a particular piece of machinery.

fitting *adj* appropriate. * *n* an act of one that fits, esp a trying on of altered clothes; a small often standardized electrical part.—**fittingly** *adv.*

five *adj, n* one more than four; the symbol for this (5, V, v).

fiver *n* (*inf*) a £5 note.

fix *vt* to fasten firmly; to set firmly in the mind; to direct (one's eyes) steadily at something; to make rigid; to make permanent; to establish (a date, etc) definitely; to set in order; to repair; to prepare (food or meals); (*inf*) to influence the result or action of (a race, jury, etc) by bribery; (*inf*) to punish. * *vi* to become fixed; (*inf*) to prepare or intend. * *n* the position of a ship, etc, determined from the bearings of two known positions; (*inf*) a predicament; (*inf*) a situation that has been fixed; (*inf*) something whose supply becomes continually necessary or greatly desired, as a drug, activity, etc.

fixture *n* what is fixed to anything, as to land or to a house; a fixed article of furniture; a firmly established person or thing; a fixed or appointed time or event.

fizz *vi* to make a hissing or sputtering sound. * *n* this sound; any effervescent drink.—**fizzy** *adj.*—**fizziness** *n.*

fizzle *vi* to make a weak fizzing sound; (*with* out) (*inf*) to end feebly, die out, esp after a promising start.

fjord *n* a long, narrow inlet of the sea between high cliffs, esp in Norway. —*also* **fiord.**

F/L *abbr* (*Cdn*) = Flight Lieutenant.

flabbergast *vt* (*inf*) to astonish, startle.

flabby *adj* (**flabbier, flabbiest**) fat and soft; weak and ineffective.—**flabbiness** *n.*

flag¹ *vi* (*pt* **flagged**) to grow limp; to become weak, listless.

flag² *n* a piece of cloth, usu with a design, used to show nationality, party, a particular branch of the armed forces, etc, or as a signal. * *vt* (*pt* **flagged**) to decorate with flags; to signal to (as if) with a flag; (*usu with* down) to signal to stop.

flag³ *n* a hard, flat stone used for paving, a flagstone. * *vt* (*pt* **flagged**) to pave.

flagon *n* a pottery or metal container for liquids with a handle and spout and often a lid.

flagrant *adj* conspicuous, notorious.—**flagrantly** *adv.*—**flagrancy** *n.*

flair *n* natural ability, aptitude; discernment; (*inf*) stylishness, sophistication.

flake *n* a small piece of snow; a small thin layer chipped from a larger mass of something. * *vi* to form into flakes.—**flaky** *adj.*

flamboyant *adj* brilliantly colored; ornate; strikingly elaborate; dashing, exuberant.—**flamboyantly** *adv.*—**flamboyance** *n.*

flame *n* the burning gas of a fire, appearing as a tongue of light; the state of burning with a blaze; a thing like a flame; an intense emotion; (*inf*) a sweetheart. * *vi* to burst into flame; to become bright red with emotion.

flamingo *n* any of several wading birds with rosy-white plumage and long legs and neck.

flammable *adj* easily set on fire.—**flammability** *n.*

flan *n* an open case of pastry or sponge cake with a sweet or savory filling.

flange *n* a projecting or raised edge.

flank *n* the fleshy part of the side from the ribs to the hip; the side of anything; the right or left side of a formation of troops. * *vt* to attack the flank of; to skirt the side of; to be situated at the side of.

flannel *n* a soft light cotton or woollen cloth; a small cloth for washing the face and hands; (*sl*) nonsense, equivocation; (*pl*) trousers of such cloth. * *vt* (*pt* **flannelled**) to wash with a flannel; (*inf*) to flatter.

flannelette *n* a soft cotton fabric.

flap *vi* (*pt* **flapped**) to move up and down, as wings; to sway loosely and noisily; to move or hang like a flap; (*inf*) to get into a fluster. * *n* the motion or noise of a flap; anything broad and flexible, either hinged or hanging loose; a light blow with a flat object; (*inf*) agitation, panic.

flare *vi* to burn with a sudden, bright, unsteady flame; to burst into emotion, esp anger; to widen out gradually. * *n* an unsteady flame; a sudden flash; a bright light used as a signal or illumination; a widened part or shape.

flare-up *n* a sudden burst of fire; (*inf*) a sudden burst of emotion.

flash *n* a sudden, brief light; a brief moment; a sudden brief display; (*TV, radio*) a sudden brief news item on an important event; (*photog*) a device producing a brief intense light; a sudden onrush of water. * *vi* to emit a sudden, brief light; to sparkle; to come or pass suddenly; (*sl*) to expose the genitals indecently. * *vt* to cause to flash; to send (news, etc) swiftly; (*inf*) to show off. * *adj* (*inf*) flashy.—**flasher** *n.*

flashback *n* an interruption in the continuity of a story, etc, by telling or showing an earlier episode.

flashbulb *n* a small bulb giving an intense light used in photography.

flashlight *n* a torch.

flashy *adj* (**flashier, flashiest**) pretentious; showy, gaudy.

flask *n* a slim-necked bottle; a vacuum flask.

flat *adj* (**flatter, flattest**) having a smooth level surface; lying spread out; broad, even, and thin; not fluctuating; (*tyre*) deflated; dull, tedious; (*drink*) not fizzy; (*battery*) drained of electric current. * *adv* in a flat manner or position; exactly; (*mus*) below true pitch. * *n* anything flat, esp a surface, part, or expanse; a flat tyre; a set of rooms on one floor of a building.—**flatly** *adv.*—**flatness** *n.*

flatten *vti* to make or become flat.

flatter *vt* to praise excessively or insincerely, esp to win favor; to display to advantage; to represent as more attractive, etc than reality; to gratify the vanity of; to encourage falsely.—**flatterer** *n.*—**flattery** *n.*

flaunt *vi* to move or behave ostentatiously; (*flag*) to wave in the wind. * *vt* to display.

flavor *n* the taste of something in the mouth; a characteristic quality. * *vt* to give flavor to.

flavoring *n* any substance used to give flavor to food.

flaw *n* a defect; a crack. * *vti* to make or become flawed.—**flawless** *adj.*

flax *n* a blue-flowered plant cultivated for its fibre and seed; its fibre.

flaxen *adj* made of flax; pale yellow.

flea *n* a small wingless jumping bloodsucking insect.

fledge *vt* (*birds*) to rear until ready to fly; to cover or provide with feathers.

fledgling *n* a young bird just fledged; an inexperienced person, a trainee.

flee *vti* (*pt* **fled**) to run away from danger, etc; to pass away quickly, to disappear.

fleece *n* the woollen coat of sheep or similar animal. * *vt* to remove wool from; to defraud.—**fleecy** *adj.*

fleet[1] *n* a number of warships under one command; (*often with cap*) a country's navy; any group of cars, ships, buses, etc, under one control.

fleet[2] *adj* swift moving; nimble.—**fleetly** *adv.*— **fleetness** *n.*

fleeting *adj* brief, transient.

flesh *n* the soft substance of the body, esp the muscular tissue; the pulpy part of fruits and vegetables; meat; the body as distinct from the soul; all mankind; a yellowish-pink color. * *vt* to give substance to (*usu with* **out**). —**fleshy** *adj.*

flexible, flexile *adj* easily bent; adaptable, versatile; docile.—**flexibly** *adv.* — **flexibility** *n.*

flick *n* a light stroke or blow; (*inf*) a cinema film. * *vt* to strike or propel with a flick; a flicking movement.

flicker *vi* to burn unsteadily, as a flame; to move quickly to and fro. * *n* a flickering moment of light or flame; a flickering movement.

flier *see* **flyer**.

flight[1] *n* the act, manner, or power of flying; distance flown; a group of creatures or things flying together; an aircraft scheduled to fly a certain trip; a trip by aircraft; a set of stairs, as between landings; a mental act of soaring beyond the ordinary; a set of feathers on a dart or arrow.

flight[2] *n* an act or instance of fleeing.

flimsy *adj* (**flimsier, flimsiest**) weak, insubstantial; light and thin; (*excuse etc*) unconvincing.—**flimsily** *adv.*—**flimsiness** *n.*

flinch *vi* to draw back, as from pain or fear; to wince.

fling *vb* (*pt* **flung**) *vt* to cast, throw aside, esp with force; to put or send suddenly or without warning. * *vi* to kick out violently; to move or rush quickly or impetuously. * *n* the act of flinging; a lively dance; a period of pleasurable indulgence.

flint *n* a very hard rock that produces sparks when struck with steel; an alloy used for producing a spark in lighters.

flip[1] *n* a drink made from any alcoholic beverage sweetened and mixed with beaten egg.

flip[2] *vb* (*pt* **flipped**) *vt* to toss with a jerk, to flick; to snap (a coin) in the air with the thumb; to turn or turn over. * *vi* to move jerkily; (*inf*) to burst into anger.

flippant *adj* impertinent; frivolous.—**flippancy** *n.*—**flippantly** *adv.*

flipper pie *n* (*Cdn*) a pie with a filling of seal flippers and vegetables.

flirt *vi* to make insincere amorous approaches; to trifle or toy (eg with an idea). * *n* a person who toys amorously with the opposite sex.—**flirtation** *n.*

flit *vi* (*pt* **flitted**) to move lightly and rapidly; to vacate (a premises) stealthily.—*also n.*

float *vi* to rest on the surface of or be suspended in a liquid; to move lightly; to wander aimlessly. * *vt* to cause to float; to put into circulation; to start up a business, esp by offering shares for sale. * *n* anything that floats; a cork or other device used on a fishing line to signal that the bait has been taken; a low flat vehicle decorated for exhibit in a parade; a small sum of money available for cash expenditures.

flock[1] *n* a group of certain animals as birds, sheep, etc, living and feeding together; a group of people or things. * *vi* to assemble or travel in a flock or crowd.

flock[2] *n* a tuft of wool or cotton fibre; woollen or cotton waste used for stuffing furniture.

flog *vt* (*pt* **flogged**) to beat harshly with a rod, stick or whip; (*sl*) to sell.—**flogging** *n.*

flood *n* an overflowing of water on an area normally dry; the rising of the tide; a great outpouring, as of words. * *vt* to cover or fill, as with a flood; to put too much water, fuel, etc on or in. * *vi* to gush out in a flood; to become flooded.

floodlight *n* a strong beam of light used to illuminate a stage, sports field, stadium, etc. * *vt* (*pt* **floodlit**) to illuminate with floodlights.

floor *n* the inside bottom surface of a room; the bottom surface of anything, as the ocean; a storey in a building; the area in a legislative assembly where the members debate; the lower limit, the base. * *vt* to provide with a floor; to knock down (a person) in a fight; (*inf*) to defeat; (*inf*) to shock, to confuse.

floorboard *n* one of the boards making up a floor.

flop *vi* (*pt* **flopped**) to sway or bounce loosely; to move in a heavy, clumsy or relaxed manner; (*inf*) to fail. * *n* a flopping movement; a collapse; (*inf*) a complete failure.

floppy *adj* (**floppier, floppiest**) limp, hanging loosely.—**floppiness** *n*.

flora *n* (*pl* **floras, florae**) the plants of a region or a period.

floral *adj* pertaining to flowers.

florid *adj* flowery; elaborate; (*complexion*) ruddy.

florist *n* a person who sells or grows flowers and ornamental plants.

flotation *n* the act or process of floating; a launching of a business venture.

flounce[1] *vi* to move in an emphatic or impatient manner.—*also n*.

flounce[2] *n* a frill of material sewn to the skirt of a dress. * *vt* to add flounces to.

flounder[1] *vi* to move awkwardly and with difficulty; to be clumsy in thinking or speaking.

flounder[2] *n* a small flatfish used as food.

flour *n* the finely ground powder of wheat or other grain. * *vt* to sprinkle with flour.—**floury** *adj*.

flourish *vi* (*plants*) to grow luxuriantly; to thrive, prosper; to live and work at a specified time. * *vt* to brandish dramatically. * *n* embellishment; a curve made by a bold stroke of a pen; a sweeping gesture; a musical fanfare.

flout *vt* to treat with contempt, to disobey openly.—**flouter** *n*.—**floutingly** *adv*.

flow *vi* (*liquids*) to move (as if) in a stream; (*tide*) to rise; to glide smoothly; (*conversation, etc*) to continue effortlessly; to be characterized by smooth and easy movement; to hang free or loosely; to be plentiful. * *n* a flowing; the rate of flow; anything that flows; the rising of the tide.

flow chart *n* a diagram representing the sequence of and relationships between different steps or procedures in a complex process, eg manufacturing.

flower *n* the seed-producing structure of a flowering plant, blossom; a plant cultivated for its blossoms; the best or finest part. * *vt* to cause to bear flowers. * *vi* to produce blossoms; to reach the best stage.

flowery *adj* full of or decorated with flowers; (*language*) full of elaborate expressions.

flown *see* **fly**.

flu *n* (*inf*) influenza.

fluctuate *vi* (*prices, etc*) to be continually varying in an irregular way.—**fluctuation** *n*.

fluent *adj* able to write and speak a foreign language with ease; articulate, speaking and writing easily and smoothly; graceful.—**fluency** *n*.—**fluently** *adv*.

fluff *n* soft, light down; a loose, soft mass, as of hair; (*inf*) a mistake, bungle. * *vt* to pat or shake until fluffy; (*inf*) to bungle.

fluffy *adj* (**fluffier, fluffiest**) like fluff; feathery.—**fluffiness** *n*.

fluid *n* a substance able to flow freely, as a liquid or gas does. * *adj* able to flow freely; able to change rapidly or easily.—**fluidity** *n*.

fluke[1] *n* a flatfish; a flattened parasitic worm.

fluke[2] *n* the part of an anchor that fastens in the sea bed, river bottom, etc; the barbed end of a harpoon; one of the lobes of a whale's tail.

fluke[3] *n* a stroke of luck.—**fluky** *adj*.

flung *see* **fling**.

fluoride *n* any of various compounds of fluorine.

flurry *n* a sudden gust of wind, rain, or snow; a sudden commotion. * *vti* to (cause to) become flustered.

flush[1] *n* a rapid flow, as of water; sudden, vigorous growth; a sudden excitement; a blush; a sudden feeling of heat, as in a fever. * *vi* to flow rapidly; to blush or glow; to be washed out by a sudden flow of water. * *vt* to wash out with a sudden flow of water; to cause to blush; to excite. * *adj* level or in one plane with another surface; (*inf*) abundant, well-supplied, esp with money.

flush[2] *vt* to make game birds fly away suddenly.

flush[3] *n* (*poker, etc*) a hand of cards all of the same suit.

fluster *vti* to make or become confused. * *n* agitation or confusion.

flute *n* an orchestral woodwind instrument in the form of a straight pipe (with finger holes and keys) held horizontally and played through a hole located near one end; a decorative groove. * *vi* to play or make sounds like a flute; to cut grooves in.

flutter *vi* (*birds*) to flap the wings; to wave about rapidly; (*heart*) to beat irregularly or spasmodically. * *vt* to cause to flutter. * *n* rapid, irregular motion; nervous excitement; commotion, confusion; (*inf*) a small bet.—**fluttery** *adj*.

flux *n* a continual flowing or changing; a substance used to help metals fuse together, as in soldering.

fly[1] *n* a two-winged insect; a natural or imitation fly attached to a fish-hook as bait.

fly[2] *vb* (*pt* **flew**, *pp* **flown**) *vi* to move through the air, esp on wings; to travel in an aircraft; to control an aircraft; to take flight, flee; to pass quickly; (*inf*) to depart quickly. * *vt* to cause to fly, as a kite; to escape, flee from; to transport by aircraft. * *n* a flap that hides buttons, a zip, etc on trousers; material forming the outer roof of a tent; a device for regulating machinery, a flywheel.

fly[3] *adj* (*inf*) sly, astute.

flyer *n* something that flies or moves very fast; a pilot.—*also* **flier**.

flying *adj* capable of flight; fleeing; fast-moving. * *n* the act of flying an aircraft, etc.

flying saucer *n* an unidentified flying disc-shaped object, purportedly from outer space.

flying start *n* a start in a race when the competitor is already moving at the starting line; a promising start.

flyover *n* a bridge that carries a road or railway over another; a fly-past.

fly-past *n* a processional flight of aircraft.

flywheel *n* a heavy wheel which stores energy by inertia, used to regulate machinery.

foal *n* the young of a horse or related animal.
* *vti* to give birth to a foal.

foam *n* froth or fine bubbles on the surface of liquid; something like foam, as frothy saliva; a rigid or springy cellular mass made from liquid rubber, plastic, etc. * *vi* to cause or emit foam.—**foamy** *adj.*

fob[1] *n* the chain or ribbon for attaching a watch to a waistcoat; any object attached to a watch chain; a small pocket in a waistcoat for a watch.

fob[2] *vt* (*pt* **fobbed**) (*with* **off**) to cheat; to put off; to palm off (upon).

focal *adj* of or pertaining to a focus.

focus *n* (*pl* **focuses, foci**) a point where rays of light, heat, etc meet after being bent by a lens, curved mirror, etc; correct adjustment of the eye or lens to form a clear image; a centre of activity or interest. * *vt* (*pt* **focused** *or* **focussed**) to adjust the focus of; to bring into focus; to concentrate.

fodder *n* dried food for horses, etc.

foe *n* an enemy, an adversary.

foetus *see* **fetus.**

fog *n* (a state of poor visibility caused by) a large mass of water vapour condensed to fine particles just above the earth's surface; a state of mental confusion; (*photog*) cloudiness on a developed photograph. * *vti* (*pt* **fogged**) to make or become foggy.

foggy *adj* (**foggier, foggiest**) thick with fog; mentally confused; indistinct, opaque.—**fogginess** *n.*

foible *n* a slight weakness or failing; an idiosyncrasy.

foil[1] *vt* to defeat; to frustrate.

foil[2] *n* a very thin sheet of metal; anything that sets off or enhances another by contrast.

foil[3] *n* a long, thin blunted sword used for fencing.

fold[1] *vt* to cover by bending or doubling over so that one part covers another; to wrap up, envelop; to interlace (one's arms); to clasp (one's hands); to embrace; to incorporate (an ingredient) into a food mixture by gentle overturnings. * *vi* to become folded; to fail completely; to collapse, esp to go out of business. * *n* something folded, as a piece of cloth; a crease or hollow made by folding.

fold[2] *n* a pen for sheep; a group of people or institutions having a common belief, etc. * *vt* to pen in a fold.

folder *n* a folded cover or large envelope for holding loose papers.

foliage *n* leaves, as of a plant or tree.

folk *n* a people of a country or tribe; people in general, esp those of a particular area; relatives; folk music. * *adj* of or originating among the ordinary people.

folklore *n* the traditional beliefs, legends, etc of a people.

folk song *n* a traditional song.

follow *vt* to go or come after; to pursue; to go along (a path, road, etc); to copy; to obey; to adopt, as an opinion; to watch fixedly; to

focus the mind on; to understand the meaning of; to monitor the progress of; to come or occur after in time; to result from; (*with* **through**) to pursue (an aim) to a conclusion; (*with* **up**) to pursue a question, inquiry, etc, that has been started. * *vi* to go or come after another; to result; (*with* **on**) (*cricket*) to take a second innings immediately after a first; (*with* **through**) (*sport*) to continue a stroke or motion of a bat, club, etc after the ball has been struck.

follower *n* a disciple or adherent; a person who imitates another.

following *n* a body of adherents or believers. * *adj* next after; now to be stated.

folly *n* a lack of sense; a foolish act or idea; an extravagant and fanciful building which serves no practical purpose.

fond *adj* loving, affectionate; doting, indulgent; (*with* **of**) having a liking for. —**fondly** *adv.*—**fondness** *n.*

fondle *vt* to caress.

font[1] *n* a receptacle for baptismal water; a receptacle for holy water.

font[2] *see* **fount**[1].

food *n* any substance, esp a solid, taken in by a plant or animal to enable it to live and grow; anything that nourishes.

foodstuff *n* a substance used as food.

fool *n* a person lacking wisdom or common sense; (*Middle Ages*) a jester; a dupe; a cold dessert of whipped cream and fruit purée. * *vt* to deceive, make a fool of. * *vi* to act jokingly; to spend time idly; to tease or meddle with.—**foolery** *n.*

foolhardy *adj* foolishly bold; rash.—**foolhardiness** *n.*

foolish *adj* unwise; ridiculous; ill-judged.—**foolishly** *adv.*—**foolishness** *n.*

foolproof *adj* proof against failure; easy to understand; easy to use.

foot *n* (*pl* **feet**) the end part of the leg, on which one stands; anything resembling foot, as the lower part of a chair, table, etc; the lower part or edge of something, bottom; a measure of length equal to 12 inches (30.48 cm); the part of a garment that covers the foot; an attachment on a sewing machine that grips the fabric; a group of syllables serving as a unit of metre in verse. * *vi* to dance. * *vt* to walk, dance over or on; to pay the entire cost of (a bill).

foot-and-mouth disease *n* a contagious diasease of cattle.

football *n* a field game played with an inflated leather ball by two teams; the ball used.—**footballer** *n.*

footbridge *n* a narrow bridge for pedestrians.

foothill *n* a hill at the foot of higher hills.

foothold *n* a ledge, etc, for placing the foot when climbing, etc; a place from which further progress may be made.

footing *n* the basis upon which something rests; status, relationship; a foothold.

footlights *npl* a row of lights in front of a stage floor.

footman n a liveried servant.

footnote n a note or comment at the foot of a page.

footpath n a narrow path for pedestrians.

footsore adj having painful feet from excessive walking.

footwear n shoes and socks, etc.

for prep because of, as a result of; as the price of, or recompense of; in order to be, to serve as; appropriate to, or adapted to; in quest of; in the direction of; on behalf of; in place of; in favor of; with respect to; notwithstanding, in spite of; to the extent of; throughout the space of; during. * conj because.

forage n food for domestic animals, esp when taken by browsing or grazing; a search for provisions. * vi to search for food.—**forager** n.

foray n a sudden raid. * vti to plunder.

forbade see **forbid**.

forbear vb (pt **forbore**, pp **forborne**) vi to endure, to avoid. * vt to hold oneself back from.—**forbearance** n.

forbid vt (pt **forbad** or **forbade**, pp **forbidden**) to command (a person) not to do something; to render impossible, prevent.

forbidding adj unfriendly, solemn, strict.—**forbiddingly** adv.

force n strength, power, effort; (physics) (the intensity of) an influence that causes movement of a body or other effects; a body of soldiers, police, etc prepared for action; effectiveness; violence, compulsion; legal or logical validity. * vt to compel or oblige by physical effort, superior strength, etc; to achieve by force; to press or drive against resistance; to produce with effort; to break open, penetrate; to impose, inflict; to cause (plants, animals) to grow faster than normal.

forceful adj powerful, effective.—**forcefully** adv.—**forcefulness** n.

forceps n an instrument for grasping and holding firmly, or exerting traction upon objects, esp by jewellers and surgeons.

ford n a shallow crossing place in a river, etc.—also vt.—**fordable** adj.

fore adj in front. * n the front. * adv in, at or towards the front. * interj (golf) a warning cry to anybody who may be hit by the ball.

forearm[1] n the arm between the elbow and the wrist.

forearm[2] vt to arm in advance.

forecast vt (pt **forecast** or **forecasted**) to predict (events, weather, etc) through rational analysis; to serve as a forecast of.—also n.

forecourt n an enclosed space in front of a building, as in a filling station.

forefathers npl ancestors.

forefinger n the finger next the thumb.

forego[1] see **forgo**.

forego[2] vt (pt **forewent**, pp **foregone**) to precede.

foregone conclusion n an inevitable result, easily predictable.

foreground n the part of a picture or view nearest the spectator's vision.

forehead n the part of the face above the eyes.

foreign adj of, in, or belonging to another country; involving other countries; alien in character; introduced from outside.

foreigner n a person from another country.

foreman n a person who supervises workers in a factory, etc; the spokesperson of a jury.—**forewoman** nf.

foremost adj first in importance; most advanced in rank or position.

forensic adj belonging to or used in courts of law.—**forensically** adv.

forensic medicine n the application of medical expertise to legal and criminal investigations.

forerunner n a person or thing that comes in advance of another; a portent.

foresee vt (pt **foresaw**, pp **foreseen**) to be aware of beforehand.

foresight n foreseeing; the power to foresee; provision for the future.

forest n a thick growth of trees, etc covering a large tract of land; something resembling a forest.

forestall vt to prevent by taking action beforehand; to anticipate.

forestry n the science of planting and cultivating forests.

foretell vt (pt **foretold**) to forecast, to predict.

for ever, forever adv for all future time; continually.

foreword n a preface to a book.

forfeit n something confiscated or given up as a penalty for a fault. * vt to lose or be penalized by forfeiture.—**forfeiture** n.

forgave see **forgive**.

forge[1] n (a workshop with) a furnace in which metals are heated and shaped. * vt to shape (metal) by heating and hammering; to counterfeit (eg a signature). * vi to commit forgery.

forge[2] vt to move steadily forward with effort.

forgery n fraudulently copying; a forged copy.

forget vti (pt **forgot**, pp **forgotten**) to be unable to remember; to overlook or neglect.

forgetful adj apt to forget, inattentive. —**forgetfully** adv.—**forgetfulness** n.

forgive vt (pt **forgave**, pp **forgiven**) to cease to feel resentment against (a person); to pardon. * vi to be merciful or forgiving.—**forgiveness** n.

forgo vt (pt **forwent**, pp **forgone**) to give up, abstain from.—also **forego**.

fork n a small, usu metal, instrument with two or more thin prongs set in a handle, used in eating and cooking; a pronged agricultural or gardening tool for digging, etc; anything that divides into prongs or branches; one of the branches into which a road or river divides; the point of separation. * vi to divide into branches; to follow a branch of a fork in a road, etc. * vt to form as a fork; to dig, lift, etc with a fork.

fork-lift truck n a vehicle with power-operated prongs for raising and lowering loads.

form n general structure; the figure of a person

or animal; a mould; a particular mode, kind, type, etc; arrangement; a way of doing something requiring skill; a conventional procedure; a printed document with blanks to be filled in; a class in school; condition of mind or body; a chart giving information about racehorses; changed appearance of a word to show inflection; (*sl*) a criminal record. * *vt* to shape; to train; to develop (habits); to constitute. * *vi* to be formed.

formal *adj* in conformity with established rules or habits; regular; relating to outward appearance only; ceremonial; punctilious; stiff.—**formally** *adv*.

format *n* the size, form, shape in which books, etc are issued; the general style or presentation of something, eg a television programme; (*comput*) the arrangement of data on magnetic disk, etc for access and storage. * *vt* (*pt* **formatted**) to arrange in a particular form, esp for a computer.

formation *n* form of making or producing; that which is formed; structure; regular array or prearranged order.

formative *adj* pertaining to formation and development; shaping.

former *adj* of or occurring in a previous time; the first mentioned (of two). —**formerly** *adv*.

formidable *adj* causing fear or awe; difficult to defeat or overcome; difficult to handle.—**formidably** *adv*.

formula *n* (*pl* **formulas, formulae**) a set of symbols expressing the composition of a substance; a general expression in algebraic form for solving a problem; a prescribed form; a formal statement of doctrines; a list of ingredients, as for a prescription or recipe; a fixed method according to which something is to be done; a prescribed recipe for baby food.

formulate *vt* to express in a formula; to devise.—**formulation** *n*.

forsake *vt* (*pt* **forsook**, *pp* **forsaken**) to desert; to give up, renounce.

fort *n* a fortified place for military defence.

forte[1] *n* something at which a person excels.

forte[2] *adv* (*mus*) loudly.

forth *adv* forwards; onwards; out.

forthcoming *adj* about to appear; readily available; responsive.

forthright *adv* frank, direct, outspoken.—**forthrightness** *n*.

fortification *n* act or process or fortifying; a wall, barricade, etc built to defend a position.

fortify *vt* to strengthen physically, emotionally, etc; to strengthen against attack, as with forts; to support; (*wine, etc*) to add alcohol to; (*milk*) to add vitamins to.

fortitude *n* courage in adversity.

fortnight *n* a period of two weeks or fourteen consecutive days.

fortnightly *adj, adv* once a fortnight.

fortress *n* a strong fort or fortified town.

fortuitous *adj* happening by chance.—**fortuitously** *adv*.—**fortuitousness** *n*.—**fortuity** *n*.

fortunate *adj* having or occurring by good luck.—**fortunately** *adv*.

fortune *n* the supposed arbitrary power that determines events; luck; destiny; prosperity, success; vast wealth.

fortune-teller *n* a person who claims to foretell a person's future.

forty *n* four times ten, the symbol for this (40, XL, xl).—*also adj*.—**fortieth** *adj*.

forty-ninth parallel *n* (*Cdn*) the parallel of 49° north of the equator, esp as forming the border between Canada and the US.

forty-ouncer (*Cdn*) (*inf*) a forty-ounce bottle of alcoholic liquor.

forum *n* an assembly or meeting to discuss topics of public concern; a medium for public debate, as a magazine; the marketplace and centre of public affairs in ancient Rome.

forward *adj* at, toward, or of the front; advanced; onward; prompt; bold; presumptuous; of or for the future. * *vt* to promote; to send on. * *n* (*sport*) an attacking player in various games. * *adv* toward the front; ahead.—**forwardness** *n*.

forwent *see* **forgo**.

fossil *n* the petrified remains of an animal or vegetable preserved in rock; (*inf*) a thing or person regarded as outmoded or redundant. * *adj* of or like a fossil; dug from the earth.

foster *vt* to encourage; to bring up (a child that is not one's own).

fought *see* **fight**.

foul *adj* stinking, loathsome; extremely dirty; indecent; wicked; (*language*) obscene; (*weather*) stormy; (*sports*) against the rules. * *vt* to make filthy; to dishonor; to obstruct; to entangle (a rope, etc); to make a foul against, as in a game. * *vi* to be or become fouled. * *n* (*sports*) a hit, blow, move, etc that is foul.—**foully** *adv*.

found[1] *see* **find**.

found[2] *vt* to bring into being; to establish (as an institution) often with provision for future maintenance.

found[3] *vt* to melt and pour (metal) into a mould to produce castings.

foundation *n* an endowment for an institution; such an institution; the base of a house, wall, etc; a first layer of cosmetic applied to the skin; an underlying principle, etc; a supporting undergarment, as a corset.

founder[1] *n* one who founds an institution, a benefactor.

founder[2] *n* a person who casts metal.

founder[3] *vi* (*ship*) to fill with water and sink; to collapse; to fail.

found-in *n* (*Cdn*) a person arrested for being discovered in a place where illegal activities go on.

founding people *n* (*Cdn*) the French or English, considered as one of the two peoples that founded the nation-state of Canada.

foundry *n* a workshop or factory where metal castings are produced.

fount[1] *n* a set of printing type or characters of one style and size.—*also* **font**.

fount[2] *n* a source.

fountain n a natural spring of water; a source; an artificial jet or flow of water; the basin where this flows; a reservoir, as for ink. * vti to (cause to) flow or spurt like a fountain.

four n one more than three; the symbol for this (4, IV, iv); the fourth in a series or set; something having four units as members (as a four-cylinder engine).—also adj.

fourteen n, adj four and ten; the symbol for this (14, XIV, xiv).—**fourteenth** adj.

fourth adj next after third. * n one of four equal parts of something.—**fourthly** adv.

fowl n any of the domestic birds used as food, as the chicken, etc; the flesh of these birds. * vi to hunt or snare wildfowl.—**fowling** n.—**fowler** n.

fox n any of various small, alert wild mammals of the dog family; the fur of the fox; a sly, crafty person. * vt to deceive by cunning. * vi (inf) to bemuse, puzzle.

foyer n an anteroom; an entrance hallway, as in a hotel or theatre.

fraction n a small part, amount, etc; (math) a quantity less than a whole, expressed as a decimal or with a numerator and denominator.—**fractional** adj.—**fractionally** adv.

fracture n the breaking of any hard material, esp a bone. * vti to break; to cause or suffer a fracture.

fragile adj easily broken; frail; delicate.—**fragilely** adv.—**fragility** n.

fragment n a piece broken off or detached; an incomplete portion. * vti to break or cause to break into fragments.

fragmentary adj consisting of fragments; incomplete.

fragrance, fragrancy n a pleasant scent, a perfume.

fragrant adj sweet-scented.—**fragrantly** adv.

frail adj physically or morally weak; fragile.

frame vt to form according to a pattern; to construct; to put into words; to enclose (a picture) in a border; (sl) to falsify evidence against (an innocent person). * n something composed of parts fitted together and united; the physical make-up of an animal, esp a human body; the framework of a house; the case enclosing a window, door, etc; an ornamental border, as round a picture; (snooker) a triangular mould for setting up balls before play; (snooker) a single game.—**framer** n.

framework n a structural frame; a basic structure; frame of reference.

franchise n the right to vote in public elections; authorization to sell the goods of a manufacturer in a particular area. * vt to grant a franchise.

francize vt (Cdn) to cause a person or group to adopt French as the official and working language of business, employment, and education.—**francization** n.

Franco-Canadian n (Cdn) a French Canadian. * adj French-Canadian; pertaining to France and Canada.

francophone adj (esp Cdn) French-speaking. * n a person whose first language is French.

frank adj free and direct in expressing oneself; honest, open. * vt to mark letters, etc with a mark denoting free postage. * n a mark indicating free postage.—**frankness** n.

frantic adj violently agitated; furious, wild.—**frantically** adv.

fraternal adj of or belonging to a brother or fraternity; friendly, brotherly.—**fraternally** adv.

fraternity n brotherly feeling; a society of people with common interests.

fraternize vt to associate in a friendly manner.—**fraternization** n.

fraud n deliberate deceit; an act of deception; (inf) a deceitful person; an impostor.

fraudulent adj deceiving or intending to deceive; obtained by deceit.—**fraudulence** n.—**fraudulently** adv.

fraught adj filled or loaded (with).

fray[1] n a fight, a brawl.

fray[2] vti (fabric, etc) to (cause to) wear away into threads, esp at the edge of; (nerves, temper) to make or become irritated or strained.

freak n an unusual happening; any abnormal animal, person, or plant; (inf) a person who dresses or acts in a notably unconventional manner; an ardent enthusiast.—**freakish** adj.

freckle n a small, brownish spot on the skin. * vti to make or become spotted with freckles.—**freckled, freckly** adj.

free adj (freer, freest) not under the control or power of another; having social and political liberty; independent; able to move in any direction; not burdened by obligations; not confined to the usual rules; not exact; generous; frank; with no cost or charge; exempt from taxes, duties, etc; clear of obstruction; not fastened. * adv without cost; in a free manner. * vt (pt freed) to set free; to clear of obstruction, etc.—**freely** adv.

freedom n being free; exemption from obligation; unrestricted use; a right or privilege.

freelance n a person who pursues a profession without long-term commitment to any employer (—also freelancer). * vt to work as a freelance.

Freemason n a member of the secretive fraternity (Free and Accepted Masons) dedicated to mutual aid.

free trade n trade based on the unrestricted international exchange of goods with tariffs used only as a source of revenue.—**freetrader** n.

freeway n in North America, a fast road, a motorway.

freewheel n a device for temporarily disconnecting and setting free the back wheel of a bicycle from the driving gear. * vi to ride a bicycle with the gear disconnected; to drive a car with the gear in neutral.—**freewheeler** n.

free will n voluntary choice or decision; freedom of human beings to make choices that are not determined by prior causes or by divine intervention.

freeze *vb* (*pt* **froze**, *pp* **frozen**) *vi* to be formed into, or become covered by ice; to become very cold; to be damaged or killed by cold; to become motionless; to be made speechless by strong emotion; to become formal and unfriendly. * *vt* to harden into ice; to convert from a liquid to a solid with cold; to make extremely cold; to act towards in a stiff and formal way; to act on usu destructively by frost; to anaesthetize by cold; to fix (prices, etc) at a given level by authority; to make (funds, etc) unavailable to the owners by authority.

freezer *n* a container that freezes and preserves food for long periods.

freezing point *n* the temperature at which a liquid solidifies.

freeze-up *n* (*esp Cdn*) the freezing of a body of water, esp in the autumn.

freight *n* the transport of goods by water, land, or air; the cost for this; the goods transported. * *vt* to load with freight; to send by freight.

freighter *n* a ship or aircraft carrying freight.

French *adj* of France, its people, culture, etc. * *n* the language of France.

French Canada *n* Quebec and other parts of Canada where mainly French is spoken.

French Canadian *n* a Canadian whose first language is French. * *adj.* **French-Canadian** pertaining to French-speaking Canadians.

French French (*Cdn*) (*inf*) French as spoken in France, as distinguished from that spoken in French Canada.

French fries, french fries *npl* thin strips of potato fried in oil, etc, chips.

French immersion *n* (*Cdn*) an educational program in which English-speaking students are taught entirely in French.

French windows, French doors *npl* a pair of floor-length casement windows in an outside wall, opening on to a patio, garden, etc.

frenzy *n* wild excitement; violent mental derangement.—**frenzied** *adj.*—**frenziedly** *adv.*

frequency *n* repeated occurrence; the number of occurrences, cycles, etc in a given period.

frequent *adj* coming or happening often. * *vi* to visit often; to resort to.—**frequently** *adv.*

fresco *n* (*pl* **frescos, frescoes**) a picture painted on walls covered with damp freshly laid plaster.

fresh *adj* recently made, grown, etc; not salted, pickled, etc; not spoiled; lively, not tired; not worn, soiled, faded, etc; new, recent; inexperienced; cool and refreshing; (*wind*) brisk; (*water*) not salt; (*inf*) presumptuous, impertinent.—**freshly** *adv.*—**freshness** *n.*

freshen *vi* to make or become fresh.—**freshener** *n.*

freshwater *adj* of a river; not sea-going.

fret[1] *vti* (*pt* **fretted**) to make or become worried or anxious; to wear away or roughen by rubbing.

fret[2] *n* a running design of interlacing small

bars. * *vt* (*pt* **fretted**) to furnish with frets.

fret[3] *n* any of a series of metal ridges along the finger-board of a guitar, banjo, etc used as a guide for depressing the strings.

friar *n* a member of certain Roman Catholic religious orders.

friction *n* a rubbing of one object against another; conflict between differing opinions, ideas, etc; the resistance to motion of things that touch.—**frictional** *adj.*

Friday *n* the sixth day of the week.

fridge *n* (*inf*) a refrigerator.

fried *see* **fry**[1].

friend *n* a person whom one knows well and is fond of; an ally, supporter —**friendless** *adj.*—**friendship** *n.*

friendly *adj* (**friendlier, friendliest**) like a friend; kindly; favorable. * *n* a sporting game played for fun, not in competition.—**friendliness** *n.*

frieze *n* a decorative band along the top of the wall of a room.

frigate *n* a warship smaller than a destroyer used for escort, anti-submarine, and patrol duties.

fright *n* sudden fear; a shock; (*inf*) something unsightly or ridiculous in appearance.

frighten *vt* to terrify, to scare; to force by frightening.

frightful *adj* terrible, shocking; (*inf*) extreme, very bad.—**frightfully** *adv.*

frigid *adj* extremely cold; not warm or friendly; unresponsive sexually.—**frigidly** *adv.*—**frigidity** *n.*

frill *n* a piece of pleated or gathered fabric used for edging; something superfluous, an affectation. * *vt* to decorate with a frill or frills.—**frilled** *adj.*—**frilly** *adj.*

fringe *n* a decorative border of hanging threads; hair hanging over the forehead; an outer edge; a marginal or minor part. * *vt* to be or make a fringe for. * *adj* at the outer edge; additional; minor; unconventional.

frisk *vi* to leap playfully. * *vt* (*inf*) to search (a person) by feeling for concealed weapons, etc.

frisky *adj* (**friskier, friskiest**) lively, playful.—**friskiness** *n.*

fritter[1] *n* a slice of fruit or meat fried in batter.

fritter[2] *vt* (*with* **away**) to waste; to break into tiny pieces.

frivolity *n* a trifling act, thought, or action.

frivolous *adj* irresponsible; trifling; silly.—**frivolously** *adv.*

fro *adv* away from; backward.

frock *n* a dress.

frog *n* a small tailless web-footed jumping amphibian; a decorative loop used to fasten clothing; (*offensive*) a French person.

frogman *n* a person who wears rubber suit, flippers, oxygen supply, etc and is trained in working underwater.

frolic *n* a lively party or game; merriment, fun. * *vi* (*pt* **frolicked**) to play happily.

from *prep* beginning at, starting with; out of; originating with; out of the possibility or use of.

front n outward behaviour; (inf) an appearance of social standing; etc; the part facing forward; the first part; a forward or leading position; the promenade of a seaside resort; the advanced battle area in warfare; a person or group used to hide another's activity; an advancing mass of cold or warm air. * adj at, to, in, on, or of the front. * vti to face; to serve as a front (for).

frontal adj of or belonging to the front; of or pertaining to the forehead. * n a decorative covering for the front of an altar.

frontier n the border between two countries; the limit of existing knowledge of a subject.

frost n temperature at or below freezing point; a coating of powdery ice particles; coldness of manner. * vt to cover (as if) with frost or frosting; to give a frost-like opaque surface to (glass).

frostbite n injury to a part of the body by exposure to cold.

frosting n icing.

frosty adj (frostier, frostiest) cold with frost; cold or reserved in manner.—**frostily** adv.—**frostiness** n.

froth n foam; foaming saliva; frivolity. —also vi.—**frothily** adv.—**frothy** adj.

frown vi to contract the brow as in anger or thought; (with upon) to regard with displeasure or disapproval.—also n.

froze, frozen see **freeze**.

frugal adj economical, thrifty; inexpensive, meagre.—**frugally** adv.—**frugality** n.

fruit n the seed-bearing part of any plant; the fleshy part of this used as food; the result or product of any action. * vti to bear or cause to bear fruit.

fruitful adj producing lots of fruit; productive.—**fruitfulness** n.

fruition n a coming to fulfilment, realization.

fruit machine n a coin-operated gambling machine, using symbols of fruit to indicate a winning combination.

frustrate vt to prevent from achieving a goal or gratifying a desire; to discourage, to irritate, to tire.—**frustration** n.

fry[1] vti (pt **fried**) to cook over direct heat in hot fat. * n a dish of things fried.

fry[2] n recently hatched fishes.

f-stop see **stop**.

ft. abbr = foot or feet.

FTA abbr = Free Trade Agreement.

fuchsia n any of a genus of decorative shrubs.

fudge n a soft sweet made of butter, milk, sugar, flavoring, etc. * vi to refuse to commit oneself; to cheat. * vt to fake; to fail to come to grips with.

fuel n material burned to supply heat and power, or as a source of nuclear energy; anything that serves to intensify strong feelings. * vti (pt **fuelled**) to supply with fuel.

fugitive n a person who flees. * adj fleeing, as from danger or justice; fleeting, transient.

fugue n a polyphonic musical composition with its theme taken up successively by different voices.—**fugal** adj.

fulfil, fulfill (US) vt (pt **fulfilled**) to carry out (a promise, etc); to achieve the completion of; to satisfy; to bring to an end, complete.—**fulfilment** n.

full adj having or holding all that can be contained; having eaten all one wants; having a great number (of); complete; having reached to greatest size, extent, etc. * n the greatest amount, extent etc. * adv completely, directly, exactly.

fullback n (football, rugby, hockey, etc) one of the defensive players at the back; the position held by this player.

full-stop n the punctuation mark (.) at the end of a sentence.—also **period**.

full time n the finish of a match.

full-time adj working or lasting the whole time.—**full-timer** n.

fully adv thoroughly; at least.

fumble vi to grope about. * vt to handle clumsily; to say or act awkwardly; to fail to catch (a ball) cleanly.—also n.

fume n (usu pl) smoke, gas or vapour, esp if offensive or suffocating. * vi to give off fumes; to express anger.

fumigate vt to disinfect or exterminate (pests, etc) using fumes.—**fumigation** n.

fun n (what provides) amusement and enjoyment.

function n the activity characteristic of a person or thing; the specific purpose of a certain person or thing; an official ceremony or social entertainment. * vi to perform a function; to act, operate.

functional adj of a function or functions; practical, not ornamental.

fund n a supply that can be drawn upon; a sum of money set aside for a purpose; (pl) ready money. * vt to provide funds for.

fundamental adj basic; essential. * n that which serves as a groundwork; an essential.—**fundamentally** adv.

funeral n the ceremony associated with the burial or cremation of the dead; a procession accompanying a coffin to a burial.

fungus n (pl **fungi, funguses**) any of a major group of lower plants, as mildews, mushrooms, yeasts, etc, that lack chlorophyll and reproduce by spores.—**fungal** adj.

funnel n an implement, usually a cone with a wide top and tapering to a narrow tube, for pouring fluids, powders, into bottles, etc; a metal chimney for the escape of smoke, steam, etc. * vti (pt **funnelled**) to (cause) to pour through a funnel.

funny adj (**funnier, funniest**) causing laughter; puzzling, odd; (inf) unwell, queasy.—**funnily** adv.—**funniness** n.

fur n the short, soft, fine hair on the bodies of certain animals; their skins with the fur attached; a garment made of fur; a fabric made in imitation of fur; a fur-like coating, as on the tongue. * vti (pt **furred**) to cover or become covered with fur.

furious *adj* full of anger; intense, violent.—
furiously *adv*.

furlong *n* 220 yards, one-eighth of a mile.

furlough *n* leave of absence from duty, esp for
military personnel. * *vt* to grant a furlough
to.

furnace *n* an enclosed chamber in which heat is
produced to burn refuse, smelt ore, etc.

furnish *vt* to provide (a room, etc) with furniture; to equip with what is necessary; to
supply.

furnishings *npl* furniture, carpets, etc.

furniture *n* the things in a room, etc that equip it
for living, as chairs, etc.

furrow *n* the groove in the earth made by a
plough; a groove or track resembling this; a
wrinkle. * *vti* to make furrows in; to wrinkle.

furry *adj* (**furrier**, **furriest**) like, made of, or covered with, fur.

further *adv* at or to a greater distance or degree;
in addition. * *adj* more distant, remote; additional. * *vt* to help forward, promote.

furthermore *adv* moreover, besides.

furthest *adj* at or to the greatest distance.

furtive *adj* stealthy; sly.—**furtively** *adv*. —**furtive-
ness** *n*.

fury *n* intense rage; a frenzy; a violently angry
person.

fuse *vti* to join or become joined by melting; to
(cause to) melt by the application of heat; to
equip a plug, circuit, etc with a fuse; to
(cause to) fail by blowing a fuse. * *n* a tube
or wick filled with combustible material for
setting off an explosive charge; a piece of
thin wire that melts and breaks when an
electric current exceeds a certain level.

fuselage *n* the body of an aircraft.

fusible *adj* able to be fused.—**fusibly** *adv*.

fusion *n* the act of melting, blending or fusing; a
product of fusion; union, partnership; nuclear fusion.

fuss *n* excited activity, bustle; a nervous state;
(*inf*) a quarrel; (*inf*) a showy display of approval. * *vi* to worry over trifles; to whine,
as a baby.—**fusser** *n*.

fussy *adj* (**fussier**, **fussiest**) worrying over details;
hard to please; fastidious; over-elabo-
rate.—**fussily** *adv*.—**fussiness** *n*.

futile *adj* useless; ineffective.—**futility** *n*.

future *adj* that is to be; of or referring to time
yet to come. * *n* the time to come; future
events; likelihood of eventual success.

futuristic *adj* forward-looking in design, appearance, intention, etc.

fuzzy *adj* (**fuzzier**, **fuzziest**) like fuzz; fluffy;
blurred.—**fuzzily** *adv*.—**fuzziness** *n*.

G

g *abbr* = gallons(s); gram(s); gravity; acceleration due to gravity.

gabble *vti* to talk or utter rapidly or incoher-

ently; to utter inarticulate or animal
sounds.—**gabbler** *n*.

gable *n* the triangular upper part of a wall enclosed by the sloping ends of a pitched
roof.—**gabled** *adj*.

gadget *n* a small, often ingenious, mechanical
or electronic tool or device.

gag *n* something put over or into the mouth to
prevent talking; any restraint of free
speech; a joke. * *vb* (*pt* **gagged**) *vt* to cause to
retch; to keep from speaking, as by stop-
ping the mouth of. * *vi* to retch; to tell
jokes.

gaiety *n* happiness, liveliness; colorful appearance.

gaily *adv* in a cheerful manner; with bright
colors.

gain *vt* to obtain, earn, esp by effort; to win in a
contest; to attract; to get as an addition
(esp profit or advantage); to make an increase in; to reach. * *vi* to make progress;
to increase in weight. * *n* an increase esp
in profit or advantage; an acquisition.

gainful *adj* profitable.—**gainfully** *adv*.

gainsay *vt* (*pt* **gainsaid**) (*formal*) to dispute; to
deny.

gait *n* a manner of walking or running; the sequence of footsteps made by a moving
horse.

gala *n* a celebration, festival.

galaxy *n* any of the systems of stars in the universe; any splendid assemblage; (*with cap*)
the galaxy containing the Earth's solar system; the Milky Way.

gale *n* a strong wind, specifically one between
39 to 46 mph; an outburst.

gallant *adj* dignified, stately; brave; noble;
(*man*) polite and chivalrous to women.—
gallantly *adv*.—**gallantry** *n*.

gall bladder *n* a membranous sac attached to the
liver in which bile is stored.

gallery *n* a covered passage for walking; a long
narrow outside balcony; a balcony running
along the inside wall of a building; (the oc-
cupants of) an upper area of seating in a
theatre; a long narrow room used for a special purpose, eg shooting practice; a room
or building designed for the exhibition of
works of art; the spectators at a golf tournament, tennis match, etc.

galley *n* a long, usu low, ship of ancient or medieval times, propelled by oars; the kitchen of
a ship, aircraft; (*print*) a shallow tray for
holding type; proofs printed from such type
(—*also* **galley proof**).

gallon *n* a unit of liquid measure comprising
277.42 cubic inches (in US, 231 cubic
inches); (*pl*) (*inf*) a large amount.

gallop *n* the fastest gait of a horse, etc; a succession of leaping strides; a fast pace. * *vti*
to go or cause to go at a gallop; to move
swiftly.

gallows *n* (*pl* **gallowses**, **gallows**) a wooden frame
used for hanging criminals.

gallstone *n* a small solid mass in the gall bladder.

gambit *n* (*chess*) an opening in which a piece is

sacrificed to gain an advantage; any action to gain an advantage.

gamble *vi* to play games of chance for money; to take a risk for some advantage. * *vt* to risk in gambling, to bet. * *n* a risky venture; a bet.—**gambler** *n*.

game[1] *n* any form of play, amusement; activity or sport involving competition; a scheme, a plan; wild birds or animals hunted for sport or food, the flesh of such animals. * *vi* to play for a stake. * *adj* (*inf*) brave, resolute; (*inf*) willing.—**gamely** *adv*.—**gameness** *n*.

game[2] *adj* (*limbs*) injured, crippled.

game-breaking *adj* of a play in sports that turns a close game suddenly and decisively in favour of one team.

gamekeeper *n* a person who breeds and takes care of game birds and animals, as on an estate.

game misconduct *n* a penalty in ice hockey that expels a player for the remainder of the game.

gammon *n* cured or smoked ham; meat from the hindquarters of a side of bacon.

gander *n* an adult male goose; (*inf*) a quick look.

gang *n* a group of persons, esp labourers, working together; a group of persons acting or associating together, esp for illegal purposes. * *vti* to form into or act as a gang.

gangrene *n* death of body tissue when the blood supply is obstructed.—**gangrenous** *adj*.

gangster *n* a member of a criminal gang.

gangway *n* a passageway, esp an opening in a ship's side for loading, etc; a gangplank.

gaol, gaoler *see* jail, jailer.

gap *n* a break or opening in something, as a wall or fence; an interruption in continuity, an interval; a mountain pass; a divergence, disparity. * *vt* (*pt* **gapped**) to make a gap in.—**gappy** *adj*.

gape *vi* to open the mouth wide; to stare in astonishment, esp with the mouth open; to open widely. * *n* the act of gaping; a wide opening.

garage *n* an enclosed shelter for motor vehicles; a place where motor vehicles are repaired and serviced, and fuel sold. * *vt* to put or keep in a garage.

garbage *n* food waste; unwanted or useless material; rubbish.

garbage mitt *n* a heavy mitt worn by a garbage collector.

garburator *n* (*Cdn*) a garbage disposal unit for a household.

garden *n* an area of ground for growing herbs, fruits, flowers, or vegetables, usu attached to a house; a fertile, well-cultivated region; a public park or recreation area, usu laid-out with plants and trees. * *vi* to make, or work in, a garden.—**gardener** *n*.—**gardening** *n*.

gargle *vti* to rinse the throat by breathing air from the lungs through liquid held in the mouth. * *n* a liquid for this purpose; the sound made by gargling.

gargoyle *n* a grotesquely carved face or figure, usu acting as a spout to drain water from a gutter; a person with an ugly face.

garish *adj* crudely bright, gaudy.—**garishly** *adv*.

garland *n* a wreath of flowers or leaves worn or hung as decoration. * *vt* to decorate with a garland.

garlic *n* a bulbous herb cultivated for its compound bulbs used in cookery; its bulb.—**garlicky** *adj*.

garment *n* an item of clothing.

garnish *vt* to decorate; to decorate (food) with something that adds color or flavor. * *n* something used to garnish food.—**garniture** *n*.

garret *n* an attic.

garrison *n* troops stationed at a fort; a fortified place with troops. * *vt* to station (troops) in (a fortified place) for its defence.

garrulous *adj* excessively talkative.—**garrulity** *n*.—**garrulous** *adv*.—**garrulousness** *n*.

garter *n* an elasticated band used to support a stocking or sock.

gas *n* (*pl* **gases**) an air-like substance with the capacity to expand indefinitely and not liquefy or solidify at ordinary temperatures; any mixture of flammable gases used for lighting or heating; any gas used as an anaesthetic; any poisonous substance dispersed in the air, as in war; (*inf*) empty talk; gasoline. * *vt* (*pt* **gassed**) to poison or disable with gas; (*inf*) to talk idly.

gas bar *n* (*Cdn*) a gas station that consists of pumps and a kiosk only.

gash *n* a long, deep, open cut.—*also vt*.

gasket *n* a piece or ring of rubber, metal, etc sandwiched between metal surfaces to act as a seal.

gas mask *n* a protective breathing device worn over the face, which filters out poisonous gases.

gasoline, gasolene *n* petrol.

gasp *vi* to draw in the breath suddenly and audibly, as from shock; to struggle to catch the breath. * *vt* to utter breathlessly. * *n* the act of gasping.

gaspereau *n* a fish that is a member of the herring family, found mainly off the Atlantic coast of North America.

gastric *adj* of, in, or near the stomach.

gastronomy *n* the art and science of good eating.—**gastronomic** *adj*.

gate *n* a movable structure controlling passage through an opening in a fence or wall; a gateway; a movable barrier; a structure controlling the flow of water, as in a canal; a device (as in a computer) that outputs a signal when specified input conditions are met; the total amount or number of paid admissions to a football match, etc. * *vt* to supply with a gate; to keep within the gates (of a university) as a punishment; (*Cdn*) keep an inmate in prison for the full length of a sentence, by re-arresting the inmate upon release after he or she has served less than the full term.

gate-crasher *n* a person who attends a party, etc without being invited.—**gatecrash** *vi*.

gateway *n* an opening for a gate; a means of entrance or exit.

gather *vt* to bring together in one place or group; to get gradually; to collect (as taxes); to harvest; to draw (parts) together; to pucker fabric by pulling a thread or stitching; to understand, infer. * *vi* to come together in a body; to cluster around a focus of attention; (*sore*) to swell and fill with pus.

gathering *n* the act of gathering or assembling together; an assembly; folds made in a garment by gathering.

gauche *adj* socially inept; graceless, tactless.—**gauchely** *adv*.

gaudy *adj* (**gaudier, gaudiest**) excessively ornamented; tastelessly bright. —**gaudily** *adv*.—**gaudiness** *n*.

gauge, gage (*US*) *n* measurement according to some standard or system; any device for measuring; the distance between rails of a railway; the size of the bore of a shotgun; the thickness of sheet metal, wire, etc. * *vt* to measure the size, amount, etc, of.—**gaugeable** *adj*.—**gauger** *n*.

gaunt *adj* excessively thin as from hunger or age; looking grim or forbidding.—**gauntness** *n*.

gauntlet[1] *n* a knight's armoured glove; a long glove, often with a flaring cuff.

gauntlet[2] *n* (*formerly*) a type of military punishment in which a victim was forced to run between two lines of men who struck him as he passed.

gauze *n* any very thin, loosely woven fabric, as of cotton or silk; a firm woven material of metal or plastic filaments; a surgical dressing.—**gauzy** *adj*.—**gauzily** *adv*.

gave *see* **give**.

gawp *vi* (*inf*) to stare stupidly.

gay *adj* joyous and lively; colorful; homosexual.—**gayness** *n*.

gaze *vi* to look steadily. * *n* a steady look.

gazelle *n* any of numerous small swift Asian or African antelopes.

gazump *vti* to force up a price (esp of a house) after a price has been agreed. —**gazumper** *n*.

GB *abbr* = Great Britain.

GCE *abbr* = General Certificate of Education.

gear *n* clothing; equipment, esp for some task or activity; a toothed wheel for meshing with another; (*often pl*) a system of such gears meshed to transmit motion; a specific adjustment of such a system; a part of a mechanism with a specific function. * *vt* to connect by or furnish with gears; to adapt (one thing) to conform with another.

gearbox *n* a metal case enclosing a system of gears.

gear lever *n* a lever used to engage or change gear, esp in a motor vehicle.

geese *see* **goose**.

gelatin, gelatine *n* a tasteless, odourless substance extracted by boiling bones, hoofs, etc and used in food, photographic film, medicines, etc.

gelignite *n* an explosive consisting of nitroglycerin absorbed in a base of wood pulp mixed with sodium or potassium nitrate.

gem *n* a precious stone, esp when cut and polished for use as a jewel; a person or thing regarded as extremely valuable or beloved.

Gemini *n* the third sign of the zodiac, represented by the twins Castor and Pollux, operative 21 May-20 June.

gender *n* the classification by which words are grouped as feminine, masculine, or neuter; (*inf*) the sex of a person.

general *adj* not local, special, or specialized; of or for a whole genus, relating to or covering all instances or individuals of a class or group; widespread, common to many; not specific or precise; holding superior rank, chief. * *n* something that involves or is applicable to the whole; a commissioned officer above a lieutenant general; a leader, commander; the title of the head of some religious orders.

general election *n* a national election to choose parliamentary representatives in every constituency.

generalize *vti* to form general conclusions from specific instances; to talk (about something) in general terms.—**generalization** *n*.

generally *adv* widely; popularly; usually; not specifically.

general practitioner *n* a non-specialist doctor who treats all types of illnesses in the community.

generate *vt* to bring into existence; to produce.

generation *n* the act or process of generating; a single succession in natural descent; people of the same period; production, as of electric current.

generator *n* one who or that which generates; a machine that changes mechanical energy to electrical energy.

generosity *n* the quality of being generous; liberality; munificence.

generous *adj* magnanimous; of a noble nature; willing to give or share; large, ample.—**generously** *adv*.

genetic *adj* of or relating to the origin, development or causes of something; of or relating to genes or genetics.—**genetically** *adv*.

genial *adj* kindly, sympathetic and cheerful in manner; mild, pleasantly warm.—**genially** *adv*.—**geniality** *n*.

genitals, genitalia *npl* the (external) sexual organs.

genitive *adj* (*gram*) of or belonging to the case of nouns, pronouns and adjectives expressing ownership or relation. * *n* the genitive case.

genius *n* (*pl* **geniuses**) a person possessing extraordinary intellectual power; (*with* **for**) natural ability.

gent *n* (*inf*) a gentleman.

genteel *adj* polite or well-bred; affectedly refined.—**genteelly** *adv*.

gentle *adj* belonging to a family of high social station; refined, courteous; generous; kind;

kindly; patient; not harsh or rough.—**gently** *adv*.

gentleman *n* a man of good family and social standing; a courteous, gracious and honorable man; a polite term of address.—**gentlemanly** *adj*.

gentry *n* people of high social standing; (*formerly*) landed proprietors not belonging to the nobility.

genuine *adj* not fake or artificial; real; sincere.—**genuinely** *adv*.—**genuineness** *n*.

geography *n* the science of the physical nature of the earth, such as land and sea masses, climate, vegetation, etc, and their interaction with the human population; the physical features of a region.—**geographer** *n*.—**geographic, geographical** *adj*.—**geographically** *adv*.

geology *n* the science relating to the history and structure of the earth's crust, its rocks and fossils.—**geologist** *n*.—**geological** *adj*.—**geologically** *adv*.

geometry *n* the branch of mathematics dealing with the properties, measurement, and relationships of points, lines, planes, and solids.—**geometric, geometrical** *adj*.—**geometrically** *adv*.

geranium *n* a garden plant with red, pink or white flowers.

germ *n* a simple form of living matter capable of growth and development into an organism; any microscopic, disease-causing organism; an origin or foundation capable of growing and developing.

German *adj* of or relating to Germany, its people or their language. * *n* a native of Germany.

German measles *n* (*used as sing*) a mild contagious disease similar to measles.—*also* **rubella**.

germinate *vti* to start developing; to sprout, as from a seed.—**germination** *n*.—**germinator** *n*.

gestate *vt* to carry (young) in the womb during pregnancy; to develop (a plan, etc) gradually in the mind.—**gestation** *n*.

gesticulate *vi* to make expressive gestures, esp when speaking.—**gesticulation** *n*.

gesture *n* movement of part of the body to express or emphasize ideas, emotions, etc. * *vi* to make a gesture. —**gestural** *adj*.

get *vb* (*pr p* **getting**, *pt* **got**, *pp* **got** *or* **gotten**) *vt* to obtain, gain, win; to receive; to acquire; to go and bring; to catch; to persuade; to cause to be; to prepare; (*inf*) (*with* **have** *or* **has**) to be obliged to; to possess; (*inf*) to strike, kill, baffle; defeat, etc; (*inf*) to understand; (*with* **out of**) to avoid doing; (*with* **over**) to communicate effectively. * *vi* to come; to go; to arrive; to come to be; to manage or contrive; (*with* **at**) to reach; (*inf*) to imply; (*inf*) to criticize; (*inf*) to corrupt, bribe; (*with* **away**) to escape; (*with* **by**) (*inf*) to manage, to survive; (*with* **off**) to come off, down, or out of; to be acquitted; to depart; (*with* **on**) to go on or into; to put on; to proceed; to grow older; to manage; to succeed; (*with* **on with**) to establish a friendly relationship; (*with* **out**) to go out or away; to take out; to disclose, publish; (*with* **over**) to recover from; to forget; (*with* **through**) to finish; to manage to survive; to succeed; (*with* **up**) to rise to one's feet; to get out of bed; (*inf*) to organize; (*inf*) to dress in a certain style; (*inf*) to be involved in (mischief, etc).

getaway *n* the act of escaping; a start in a race, etc.

get-together *n* (*inf*) an informal social gathering or meeting.

get-up *n* (*inf*) dress, costume.

geyser *n* a natural spring from which columns of boiling water and steam gush into the air at intervals; a water heater.

GG = *abbr* Governor General; (*Cdn*) Governor General's Award.

ghastly *adj* (**ghastlier, ghastliest**) terrifying, horrible; (*inf*) intensely disagreeable; pale, unwell looking.—**ghastliness** *n*.

gherkin *n* a small cucumber used for pickling.

ghetto *n* (*pl* **ghettos**) a section of a city in which members of a minority group live, esp because of social, legal or economic pressure.

ghost *n* the supposed disembodied spirit of a dead person, appearing as a shadowy apparition; a faint trace or suggestion; a false image in a photographic negative.—**ghostly** *adj*.—**ghostliness** *n*.

giant *n* a huge legendary being of great strength; a person or thing of great size, strength, intellect, etc. * *adj* incredibly large.—**giantess** *nf*.

gibberish *n* unintelligible talk, nonsense.

gibe *n* a taunt, sneer. * *vti* to jeer, scoff (at).—*also* **jibe**.

giblets *npl* the edible internal organs of a bird.

giddy *adj* (**giddier, giddiest**) frivolous, flighty; having a feeling of whirling around as if about to lose balance and fall; causing giddiness.—**giddily** *adv*.—**giddiness** *n*.

gift *n* something given; the act of giving; a natural ability. * *vt* to present with or as a gift.

gifted *adj* having great natural ability.

gigantic *adj* exceedingly large.—**gigantically** *adv*.

giggle *vi* to laugh in a nervous or silly manner. * *n* a laugh in this manner; (*inf*) a prank, a joke.—**giggler** *n*.

gild *vt* (*pt* **gilded** *or* **gilt**) to coat with gold leaf; to give a deceptively attractive appearance to.—**gilder** *n*—**gilding** *n*.

gill[1] *n* an organ, esp in fish, for breathing in water.

gill[2] *n* a liquid measure equal to a quarter of a pint.

gills *npl* the fold of skin below the beak of certain birds; one of the radiating plates under the cap of a mushroom; a person's cheeks or jowls.

gilt[1] *see* **gild**.

gilt[2] *n* gilding; a substance used for this.

gimlet *n* a small tool with a screw point for boring holes.

gimmick *n* a trick or device for attracting notice, advertising or promoting a person, product or service. —**gimmickry** n.—**gimmicky** adj.

gin[1] n an alcoholic spirit distilled from grain and flavored with juniper berries.

gin[2] n a trap for catching small animals; a type of crane; a machine for separating seeds from raw cotton.

ginger n a tropical plant with fleshy roots used as a flavoring; spice prepared by drying and grinding; (inf) vigour; a reddish-brown.— **gingery** adj.

ginger ale, ginger beer n a carbonated soft drink flavored with ginger.

gingerbread n a cake flavored with ginger.

gingerly adv with care or caution. * adj cautious.

gingham n a cotton fabric with stripes or checks.

gipsy see **gypsy**.

giraffe n a large cud-chewing mammal of Africa, with very long legs and neck.

girder n a large steel beam for supporting joists, the framework of a building, etc.

girdle n a belt for the waist.

girl n a female child; a young woman; (inf) a woman of any age.—**girlhood** n.—**girlish** adj.

girlfriend n a female friend, esp with whom one is romantically involved.

girth n the thickness round something; a band put around the belly of a horse, etc to hold a saddle or pack.

gist n the principal point or essence of anything.

give vb (pt **gave**, pp **given**) vt to hand over as a present; to deliver; to hand over in or for payment; to pass (regards etc) along; to act as host or sponsor of; to supply; to yield; (advice) to offer; (punishment, etc) to inflict; to sacrifice; to perform; (with **away**) to make a gift of; to give (the bride) to the bridegroom; to sell cheaply; to reveal, betray; (with **in**) to deliver (a document, etc); (with **off**) to emit (fumes, etc); (with **out**) to discharge; to make public; to distribute; (with **over**) to devote time to a specific activity; to cease (an activity); (with **up**) to hand over; to renounce; to cease; to stop trying; to despair of; to devote wholly. * vi to bend, move, etc from force or pressure; (inf) to be happening. * n capacity or tendency to yield to force or strain; the quality or state of being springy; (with **in**) to submit; (with **out**) to become worn out; (with **up**) to surrender.

give-away n (inf) an unintentional revelation.

glacier n a large mass of snow and ice moving slowly down a mountain.

glad adj (**gladder**, **gladdest**) happy; causing joy; very willing; bright.—**gladly** adv.—**gladness** n.

gladden vti to make or become glad.

gladiator n (ancient Rome) a person trained to fight with men or beasts in a public arena.—**gladiatorial** adj.

glamour, glamor (US) n charm, allure; attractiveness, beauty.—**glamorous** adj.—**glamorously** adv.

glance vi to strike obliquely and go off at an angle; to flash; to look quickly. * n a glancing off; a flash; a quick look. —**glancingly** adv.

gland n an organ that separates substances from the blood and synthesizes them for further use in, or for elimination from, the body.—**glandular** adj.

glare n a harsh uncomfortably bright light, esp painfully bright sunlight; an angry or fierce stare. * vi to shine with a steady, dazzling light; to stare fiercely.

glass n a hard brittle substance, usu transparent; glassware; a glass article, as a drinking vessel; (pl) spectacles or binoculars; the amount held by a drinking glass. * adj of or made of glass. * vt to equip, enclose, or cover with glass.

glasshouse n a large greenhouse for the commercial cultivation of plants; (inf) a military prison.

glassware n objects made of glass, esp drinking vessels.

glassy adj (**glassier**, **glassiest**) resembling glass; smooth; expressionless, lifeless.—**glassily** adv.—**glassiness** n.

glaze vt to provide (windows etc) with glass; to give a hard glossy finish to (pottery, etc); to cover (foods, etc) with a glossy surface. * vi to become glassy or glossy. * n a glassy finish or coating.—**glazer** n.

glazier n a person who fits glass in windows.— **glaziery** n.

gleam n a subdued or moderate beam of light; a brief show of some quality or emotion, esp hope. * vi to emit or reflect a beam of light.

glee n joy and gaiety; delight; (mus) a song in parts for three or more male voices.—**gleeful** adj.—**gleefully** adv.

glen n a narrow valley.

glib adj (**glibber**, **glibbest**) speaking or spoken smoothly, to the point of insincerity; lacking depth and substance.—**glibly** adv.—**glibness** n.

glib ice n (Cdn) extremely slippery ice on a roadway.

glide vti to move smoothly and effortlessly; to descend in an aircraft or glider with little or no engine power. * n a gliding movement.

glider n an engineless aircraft carried along by air currents.

gliding n the sport of flying gliders.

glimmer vi to give a faint, flickering light; to appear faintly.—also n.

glimpse n a brief, momentary view. * vt to catch a glimpse of.

glint n a brief flash of light; a brief indication. * vti to (cause to) gleam brightly.

glisten vi to shine, as light reflected from a wet surface.

glitter vi to sparkle; (usu with **with**) to be brilliantly attractive. * n a sparkle; showiness, glamour; tiny pieces of sparkling material used for decoration.—**glittery** adj.

gloaming n twilight.

gloat vi to gaze or contemplate with wicked or malicious satisfaction.

global *adj* worldwide; comprehensive.—**globally** *adv*.

global village *n* the world considered as a single community because of instantaneous communications.

globe *n* anything spherical or almost spherical; the earth, or a model of it.

gloom *n* near darkness; deep sadness. * *vti* to look sullen or dejected; to make or become cloudy or murky.

gloomy *adj* (**gloomier, gloomiest**) almost dark, obscure; depressed, dejected.—**gloomily** *adv*.—**gloominess** *n*.

glorify *vt* to worship; to praise, to honor; to cause to appear more worthy, important, or splendid than in reality.—**glorification** *n*.

glorious *adj* having or deserving glory; conferring glory or renown; beautiful; delightful.—**gloriously** *adv*.

glory *n* great honor or fame, or its source; adoration; great splendour or beauty; heavenly bliss. * *vi* (*with* **in**) to exult, rejoice proudly.

gloss[1] *n* the lustre of a polished surface; a superficially attractive appearance. * *vt* to give a shiny surface to; (*with* **over**) to hide (an error, etc) or make seem right or inconsequential.

gloss[2] *n* an explanation of an unusual word (in the margin or between the lines of a text); a misleading explanation; a glossary. * *vt* to provide with glosses; to give a misleading sense of.

glossary *n* a list of specialized or technical words and their definitions.

glossy *adj* (**glossier, glossiest**) having a shiny or highly polished surface; superficial; (*magazines*) lavishly produced.—**glossily** *adv*.—**glossiness** *n*.

glove *n* a covering for the hand; a baseball player's mitt; a boxing glove. * *vt* to cover (as if) with a glove.

glow *vi* to shine (as if) with an intense heat; to emit a steady light without flames; to be full of life and enthusiasm; to flush or redden with emotion. * *n* a light emitted due to intense heat; a steady, even light without flames; a reddening of the complexion; warmth of emotion or feeling.

glower *vi* to scowl; to stare sullenly or angrily.—*also n*.—**gloweringly** *adv*.

glucose *n* a crystalline sugar occurring naturally in fruits, honey, etc.

glue *n* a sticky, viscous substance used as an adhesive. * *vt* (*pr p* **gluing**, *pt* **glued**) to join with glue.—**gluey** *adj*.

glum *adj* (**glummer, glummest**) sullen; gloomy.—**glumly** *adv*.—**glumness** *n*.

glut *vt* (*pt* **glutted**) to over-supply (the market). * *n* a surfeit, an excess of supply.

glutton *n* a person who eats and drinks to excess; a person who has a tremendous capacity for something (eg for work).—**gluttonous** *adj*.—**gluttony** *n*.

gm *abbr* = gram(s).

gnarled *adj* (*tree trunks*) full of knots; (*hands*) rough, knobbly; crabby in disposition.

gnat *n* any of various small, two-winged insects that bite or sting.

gnaw *vti* (*pp* **gnawed** *or* **gnawn**) to bite away bit by bit; to torment, as by constant pain.

gnome *n* (*folklore*) a dwarf who dwells in the earth and guards its treasure; a small statue of a gnome used as a garden decoration; a small and ugly person; (*sl*) an international banker or financier.

GNWT *abbr* = Government of the Northwest Territories.

go[1] *vb* (*pt* **went**, *pp* **gone**) *vi* to move on a course; to proceed; to work properly; to act, sound, as specified; to result; to become; to be accepted or valid; to leave, to depart; to die; to be allotted or sold; to be able to pass (through); to fit (into); to be capable of being divided (into); to belong; (*with* **about**) to handle (a task, etc) efficiently; to undertake (duties, etc); (*sailing*) to change tack; (*with* **off**) to explode; to become stale; to fall asleep; to take place as planned; to cease to like; (*with* **slow**) to work at a slow rate as part of an industrial dispute. * *vt* to travel along; (*inf*) to put up with. * *n* (*pl* **goes**) a success; (*inf*) a try; (*inf*) energy.

go[2] *n* a Japanese board game.

goad *n* a sharp-pointed stick for driving cattle, etc; any stimulus to action. * *vt* to drive (as if) with a goad; to irritate, nag persistently.

go-ahead *n* (*inf*) permission to proceed. * *adj* (*inf*) enterprising, ambitious.

goal *n* the place at which a race, trip, etc is ended; an objective; the place over or into which (the ball) must go to score in some games; the score made; the position of goalkeeper.

goalkeeper *n* a player who defends the goal.

goat *n* a mammal related to the sheep that has backward curving horns, a short tail, and usu straight hair; a lecherous man.

gobble *vt* to eat greedily; (*often with* **up**) to take, accept or read eagerly. * *vi* to make a gurgling noise, as a turkey.

go-between *n* a messenger, an intermediary.

goblet *n* a large drinking vessel with a base and stem but without a handle.

goblin *n* an evil or mischievous elf.

god *n* any of various beings conceived of as supernatural and immortal, esp a male deity; an idol; a person or thing deified; (*with cap*) in monotheistic religions, the creator and ruler of the universe.

godchild *n* (*pl* **godchildren**) the child a godparent sponsors.

goddess *n* a female god; a lovely woman.

godfather *n* a male godparent; the head of a Mafia crime family or other criminal organization.

god-forsaken *adj* desolate, wretched.

godmother *n* a female godparent.

godparent *n* a person who sponsors a child, as at baptism, taking responsibility for its faith.

godsend *n* anything that comes unexpectedly when needed or desired.

godson *n* a male godchild.

goggle *vi* to stare with bulging eyes. * *npl* large spectacles fitting snugly against the face, to protect the eyes.

going *n* an act or instance of going, a departure; the state of the ground, eg for walking, etc; rate of progress. * *adj* that goes; commonly accepted; thriving; existing.

gold *n* a malleable yellow metallic element used esp for coins and jewellery; a precious metal; money, wealth; a yellow color. * *adj* of, or like, gold.

golden *adj* made of or relating to gold; bright yellow; priceless; flourishing.

golden rule *n* a guiding principle.

goldeye *n* a silvery freshwater of central North America. often smoked for food.—*also* **Winnipeg goldeye.**

goldfish *n* (*pl* **goldfish**) a small gold-colored fish of the carp family, kept in ponds and aquariums.

golf *n* an outdoor game in which the player attempts to hit a small ball with clubs around a turfed course into a succession of holes in the smallest number of strokes.—**golfer** *n*.

golf club *n* a club with a wooden or metal head used in golf; a golf association or its premises.

golf course, golf links *n* a tract of land laid out for playing golf.

gondola *n* a long, narrow, black boat used on the canals of Venice; a cabin suspended under an airship or balloon; an enclosed car suspended from a cable used to transport passengers, esp skiers up a mountain; a display structure in a supermarket, etc.

gone¹ *see* **go¹**.

gone² *adj* departed; dead; lost; (*inf*) in an excited state; (*inf*) pregnant for a specified period.

gong *n* a disk-shaped percussion instrument struck with a usu padded hammer; (*sl*) a medal. * *vi* to sound a gong.

good *adj* (**better, best**) having the right or proper qualities; beneficial; valid; healthy or sound; virtuous, honorable; enjoyable, pleasant, etc; skilled; considerable. * *n* something good; benefit; something that has economic utility; (*with* **the**) good persons; (*pl*) personal property; commodities; (*pl*) the desired or required articles. * *adv* (*inf*) well; fully.

goodbye *interj* a concluding remark at parting; farewell.—*also n*.

Good Friday *n* the Friday before Easter, commemorating the Crucifixion of Christ.

good-looking *adj* handsome.

goodness *n* the state of being good; the good element in something; kindness; virtue. * *interj* an exclamation of surprise.

goods and services tax *n* a federal value-added tax.

goodwill *n* benevolence; willingness; the established custom and reputation of a business.

goose *n* (*pl* **geese**) a large, long-necked, web-footed bird related to swans and ducks; its flesh as food; a female goose as distinguished from a gander; (*inf*) a foolish person.

gooseberry *n* the berry of a shrub related to the currant, used in jams, etc.

goose bumps, goose pimples, goose flesh *n* a roughening of the skin caused usu by cold or fear.

gore¹ *n* (clotted) blood from a wound.

gore² *n* a tapering section of material used to shape a garment, sail, etc.

gore³ *vt* to pierce or wound as with a tusk or horns.

gorge *n* a ravine. * *vt* to swallow greedily; to glut. * *vi* to feed gluttonously.

gorgeous *adj* strikingly attractive; brilliantly colored; (*inf*) magnificent.—**gorgeously** *adv*.—**gorgeousness** *n*.

gorilla *n* an anthropoid ape of western equatorial Africa related to the chimpanzee but much larger.

gorse *n* a spiny yellow-flowered European shrub.

gory *adj* (**gorier, goriest**) bloodthirsty; causing bloodshed; covered in blood. —**gorily** *adv*.—**goriness** *n*.

go-slow *n* a deliberate slowing of the work rate by employees as a form of industrial action.

gospel *n* the life and teachings of Christ contained in the first four books of the New Testament; (*with cap*) one of these books; anything proclaimed or accepted as the absolute truth.

gossamer *n* very fine cobwebs; any very light and flimsy material. * *adj* light as gossamer.

gossip *n* one who chatters idly about others; such talk. * *vi* to take part in or spread gossip.—**gossipy** *adj*.

got, gotten *see* **get**.

gotchie *n* (*Cdn*) (*sl*) boys' or men's underwear.

gout *n* a disease causing painful inflammation of the joints; esp of the great toe.—**gouty** *adj*.

govern *vti* to exercise authority over; to rule, to control; to influence the action of; to determine.

governess *n* a woman employed in a private home to teach children.

government *n* the exercise of authority over a state, organization, etc; a system of ruling, political administration, etc; those who direct the affairs of a state, etc.—**governmental** *adj*.

Government House *n* an official residence of the Crown's representative, esp a Lieutenant-Governor.

governor *n* a person appointed to govern a province, etc; the elected head of any state of the US; the director or head of a governing body of an organization or institution; (*sl*) an employer; a mechanical device for automatically controlling the speed of an engine.

Governor General *n* (*pl* **Governors-General**) the representative of the Crown as head of state in a country in the Commonwealth of Nations.

Gov. Gen. *abbr* = Governor General.

gown *n* a loose outer garment, specifically a woman's formal dress, a nightgown, a long, flowing robe worn by clergymen, judges, university teachers, etc; a type of overall worn in the operating room.

GP *abbr* = general practitioner.

grab *vt* (*pt* **grabbed**) to take or grasp suddenly; to obtain unscrupulously; (*inf*) to catch the interest or attention of. * *n* a sudden clutch or attempt to grasp; a mechanical device for grasping and lifting objects.

grace *n* beauty or charm of form, movement, or expression; good will; favor; a delay granted for payment of an obligation; a short prayer of thanks for a meal. * *vt* to decorate; to dignify.

graceful *adj* having beauty of form, movement, or expression.—**gracefully** *adv.*—**gracefulness** *n.*

gracious *adj* having or showing kindness, courtesy, etc; compassionate; polite to supposed inferiors; marked by luxury, ease, etc. * *interj* an expression of surprise.—**graciously** *adv.*—**graciousness** *n.*

gradation *n* a series of systematic steps in rank, degree, etc; arranging in such stages; a single stage in a gradual progression; progressive change.

grade *n* a stage or step in a progression; a degree in a scale of quality, rank, etc; a group of people of the same rank, merit, etc; the degree of slope; a sloping part; a mark or rating in an examination, etc. * *vt* to arrange in grades; to give a grade to; to make level or evenly sloping.

gradient *n* a sloping road or railway; the degree of slope in a road, etc.

gradual *adj* taking place by degrees. —**gradually** *adv.*

graduate *n* a person who has completed a course of study at a school, college, etc; a receptacle marked with figures for measuring contents. * *adj* holding an academic degree or diploma; of or relating to studies beyond the first or bachelor's degree.

graduation *n* graduating or being graduated; the ceremony at which degrees are conferred by a college or university; an arranging or marking in grades or stages.

graft *n* a shoot or bud of one plant inserted into another, where it grows permanently; the transplanting of skin, bone, etc; the getting of money or advantage dishonestly.

grain *n* the seed of any cereal plant, as wheat, corn, etc; cereal plants; a tiny, solid particle, as of salt or sand; a unit of weight, 0.0648 gram; the arrangement of fibres, layers, etc of wood, leather, etc; the markings or texture due to this; natural disposition. * *vt* to form into grains; to paint in imitation of the grain of wood, etc. * *vi* to become granular.

gram, gramme *n* the basic unit of weight in the metric system, equal to one thousandth of a kilogram (one 28th of an ounce).

grammar *n* the study of the forms of words and their arrangement in sentences; a system of rules for speaking and writing a language; a grammar textbook; the use of language in speech or writing judged with regard to correctness of spelling, syntax, etc.

grammatical *adj* conforming to the rules of grammar.—**grammatically** *adv.*

gramophone *n* a record player, esp an old mechanical model with an acoustic horn.

granary *n* a building for storing grain.

grand *adj* higher in rank than others; most important; imposing in size, beauty, extent, etc; distinguished; illustrious; comprehensive; (*inf*) very good; delightful. * *n* a grand piano; (*inf*) a thousand pounds or dollars. — **grandly** *adv.*—**grandness** *n.*

grandchild *n* the child of a person's son or daughter.

granddad *n* (*inf*) grandfather; an old man.

granddaughter *n* the daughter of a person's son or daughter.

grandfather *n* the father of a person's father or mother.

grandiose *adj* having grandeur; imposing; pompous and showy.—**grandiosity** *n.*

grandmother *n* the mother of a person's father or mother.

grand piano *n* a large piano with a horizontal harp-shaped case.

grandson *n* the son of a person's son or daughter.

grandstand *n* the main structure for seating spectators at a sporting event.

granite *n* a hard, igneous rock consisting chiefly of feldspar and quartz; unyielding firmness of endurance.

granny, grannie *n* (*inf*) a grandmother; (*inf*) an old woman.

grant *vt* to consent to; to give or transfer by legal procedure; to admit as true. * *n* the act of granting; a thing granted, esp a gift for a particular purpose; a transfer of property by deed; the instrument by which such a transfer is made.

granule *n* a small grain or particle.

grape *n* a small round, juicy berry, growing in clusters on a vine; a dark purplish red.

grapefruit *n* a large, round, sour citrus fruit with a yellow rind.

graph *n* a diagram representing successive changes in the value of a variable quantity or quantities.—*also vt.*

graphic, graphical *adj* described in realistic detail; pertaining to a graph, lettering, drawing, painting, etc.

grapple *vt* to seize or grip firmly. * *vi* to struggle hand-to-hand with; to deal or contend with. * *n* a grapnel; an act of grappling, a wrestle; a grip.

grasp *vt* to grip, as with the hand; to seize; to understand. * *vi* to try to clutch, seize; (*with* **at**) to take eagerly. * *n* a firm grip; power of seizing and holding; comprehension.

grasping *adj* greedy, avaricious.

grass *n* any of a large family of plants with jointed stems and long narrow leaves including cereals, bamboo, etc; such plants grown as lawn; pasture; (*sl*) marijuana; (*sl*) an informer. * *vi* to cover with grass; (*sl*) to inform, betray.

grass hockey *n* (*Cdn*) field hockey.

grasshopper *n* any of a group of plant-eating, winged insects with powerful hind legs for jumping.

grassy *adj* (**grassier, grassiest**) abounding in, covered with, or like, grass.—**grassiness** *n*.

grate[1] *n* a frame of metal bars for holding fuel in a fireplace; a fireplace; a grating.

grate[2] *vt* to grind into particles by scraping; to rub against (an object) or grind (the teeth) together with a harsh sound; to irritate. * *vi* to rub or rasp noisily; to cause irritation.

grateful *adj* appreciative; welcome. —**gratefully** *adv*.—**gratefulness** *n*.

grater *n* a metal implement with a jagged surface for grating food.

gratify *vt* to please; to indulge.—**gratification** *n*.

grating[1] *n* a open framework or lattice of bars placed across an opening.

grating[2] *adj* harsh; irritating.—**gratingly** *adv*.

gratitude *n* a being thankful for favors received.

gratuity *n* money given for a service, a tip.

grave[1] *n* a hole dug in the ground for burying the dead; any place of burial, a tomb.

grave[2] *adj* serious, important; harmful; solemn, sombre; (*sound*) low in pitch. * *n* an accent (') over a vowel. —**gravely** *adv*.

gravel *n* coarse sand with small rounded stones. * *vt* (*pt* **gravelled**) to cover, spread with gravel.

gravestone *n* a stone marking a grave, usu inscribed with the name and details of the deceased.

graveyard *n* a burial ground, cemetery.

gravitate *vi* to move or tend to move under the force of gravitation.

gravity *n* importance, esp seriousness; weight; the attraction of bodies toward the centre of the earth, the moon, or a planet.

gravy *n* the juice given off by meat in cooking; the sauce made from this juice; (*sl*) money easily obtained.

graze[1] *vi* to feed on growing grass or pasture. * *vt* to put (animals) to feed on growing grass or pasture.

graze[2] *vt* to touch lightly in passing; to scrape, scratch. * *n* an abrasion, esp on the skin, caused by scraping.

grease *n* melted animal fat; any thick, oily substance or lubricant. * *vt* to smear or lubricate with grease.

greasy *adj* (**greasier, greasiest**) covered with grease; full of grease; slippery; oily in manner.—**greasily** *adv*.—**greasiness** *n*.

great *adj* of much more than ordinary size, extent, etc; much above the average; intense; eminent; most important; more distant in a family relationship by one generation; (*often with* **at**) (*inf*) skilful; (*inf*) excellent; fine.

* *n* (*inf*) a distinguished person.—**greatly** *adv*.—**greatness** *n*.

Great White North (*Cdn*) (*inf*) Canada.

greed *n* excessive desire, esp for food or wealth.

greedy *adj* (**greedier, greediest**) wanting more than one needs or deserves; having too strong a desire for food and drink.—**greedily** *adv*.—**greediness** *n*.

Greek *adj* of Greece, its people, or its language. * *n* a native of Greece; the language used by Greeks; (*inf*) something unintelligible.

green *adj* of the color green; covered with plants or foliage; environmentally conscious; having a sickly appearance; unripe; inexperienced, naive; not fully processed or treated; (*inf*) jealous. * *n* a color between blue and yellow in the spectrum; the color of growing grass; something of a green color; (*pl*) green leafy vegetables, as spinach, etc; a grassy plot, esp the end of a golf fairway.—**greenish** *adj*.—**greeny** *adj*.—**greenly** *adv*.—**greenness** *n*.

Green Chamber *n* (*Cdn*) the Canadian Senate.

greengrocer *n* a dealer in vegetables and fruit.—**greengrocery** *n*.

greenhouse *n* a heated building, mainly of glass, for growing plants.

greet *vt* to address with friendliness; to meet (a person, event, etc) in a specified way; to present itself to.

greeting *n* the act of welcoming with words or gestures; an expression of good wishes; (*pl*) a message of regards.

gregarious *adj* (*animals*) living in flocks and herds; (*people*) sociable, fond of company.—**gregariously** *adv*.

grenade *n* a small bomb thrown manually or projected (as by a rifle or special launcher).

grew *see* **grow**.

grey, gray (*US*) *n* any of a series of neutral colors ranging between black and white; something (as an animal, etc) of a grey color. * *adj* grey in color; having grey hair; darkish; dreary; vague, indeterminate.—**greyish** *adj*.—**greyness** *n*.

greyhound *n* any of a breed of tall and slender dogs noted for its great speed and keen sight.

grey jay *n* (*Cdn*) a North American jay with grey, black and white plumage.—*also* **Canada jay**.

grid *n* a gridiron, a grating; an electrode for controlling the flow of electrons in an electron tube; a network of squares on a map used for easy reference; a national network of transmission lines, pipes, etc for electricity, water, gas, etc.

grid road *n* (*Cdn*) a road that follows the surveyed divisions of an area or community.

grief *n* extreme sorrow caused as by a loss; deep distress.

grievance *n* a circumstance thought to be unjust and cause for complaint.

grieve *vti* to feel or cause to feel grief.

grill *vt* to cook by direct heat using a grill or gridiron; (*inf*) to question relentlessly. * *n* a device on a cooker that radiates heat downward for grilling; a gridiron; grilled food; a grille; a grillroom.

grille, grill n an open grating forming a screen.

grillroom n a restaurant that specializes in grilled food.

grim adj (**grimmer, grimmest**) hard and unyielding, stern; appearing harsh, forbidding; repellent, ghastly in character.—**grimly** adv.— **grimness** n.

grimace n a contortion of the face expressing pain, anguish, humour, etc.—also vi.

grime n soot or dirt, rubbed into a sur-face, as the skin. * vt to dirty, soil with grime.— **grimy** adj.—**griminess** n.

grin vi (pt **grinned**) to smile broadly as in amusement; to show the teeth in pain, scorn, etc. * n a broad smile.

grind vb (pt **ground**) vt to reduce to powder or fragments by crushing; to wear down, sharpen, or smooth by friction; to rub (teeth) harshly together; to oppress, tyrannize; to operate by a crank. * vi to be crushed, smoothed, or sharpened by grinding; to jar or grate; to work monotonously; to rotate the hips erotically. * n the act or sound of grinding; hard monotonous work.

grip n a secure grasp; the manner of holding a bat, club, racket, etc; the power of grasping firmly; mental grasp; mastery; a handle; a small travelling bag. * vt (pt **gripped**) to take firmly and hold fast.

gripe vt to cause sharp pain in the bowels of; (sl) to annoy. * vi (sl) to complain.

grisly adj (**grislier, grisliest**) terrifying; ghastly; arousing horror.

gristle n cartilage, esp in meat.—**gristly** adv.

grit n rough particles, as of sand; firmness of spirit; stubborn courage; (with cap) (Cdn) (inf) a member or supporter of the Liberal Party of Canada. * vt (pt **gritted**) to clench or grind together (eg the teeth); to spread grit on (eg an icy road).

groan vi to utter a deep moan; to make a harsh sound (as of creaking) under sudden or prolonged strain.—also n.

grocer n a dealer in food and household supplies.

groggy adj (**groggier, groggiest**) (inf) weak and unsteady, usu through illness, exhaustion or alcohol.—**groggily** adv.—**grogginess** n.

groin n the fold marking the junction of the lower abdomen and the thighs; the location of the genitals.

groom n one employed to care for horses; a bridegroom. * vt to clean and care for (animals); to make neat and tidy; to train (a person) for a purpose.

groove n a long, narrow channel; a spiral track in a gramophone record for the stylus; a settled routine. * vt to make a groove in.

grope vi to search about blindly as in the dark; to search uncertainly for a solution to a problem. * vt to find by feeling; (sl) to fondle sexually. * n the act of groping.—**gropingly** adv.

gross adj fat and coarse-looking; flagrant, dense, thick; lacking in refinement; earthy; obscene; total, with no deductions. * n (pl **grosses**) an overall total; (pl **gross**) twelve dozen. * vt to earn as total revenue.

grotesque adj distorted or fantastic in appearance, shape, etc; ridiculous; absurdly incongruous. * n a grotesque person or thing; a decorative device combining distorted plant, animal and human forms.— **grotesquely** adv.—**grotesqueness** n.

grotto n (pl **grottoes, grottos**) a cave, esp one with attractive features.

ground n the solid surface of the earth; soil; the background, as in design; the connection of an electrical conductor with the earth; (pl) a basis for belief, action, or argument; the area about and relating to a building; a tract of land; sediment. * vti to set on the ground; to run aground or cause to run aground; to base, found, or establish; to instruct in the first principles of; to prevent (aircraft) from flying.

grounding n basic general knowledge of a subject.

groundsheet n a waterproof sheet placed on the ground in a tent.

groundwork n foundation, basis.

group n a number of persons or things considered as a collective unit; a small musical band of players or singers; a number of companies under single ownership; two or more figures forming one artistic design. * vti to form into a group or groups.

grouse[1] n (pl **grouse**) a game bird; its flesh as food.

grouse[2] vi (inf) to complain.—**grouser** n.

grove n a small wood, generally without undergrowth.

grovel vi (pt **grovelled**) to lie and crawl in a prostrate position as a sign of respect, fear or humility. —**groveller** n.

grow vb (pt **grew**, pp **grown**) vi to come into being; to be produced naturally; to develop, as a living thing; to increase in size, quantity, etc. * vt to cause or let grow; to raise, to cultivate. —**growable** adj.—**grower** n.

growl vi to make a rumbling, menacing sound such as an angry dog makes. * vt to express in a growling manner. * n a growling noise; a grumble.—**growler** n.

growth n the act or process of growing; progressive increase, development; something that grows or has grown; an abnormal formation of tissue, as a tumour.

grub vb (pt **grubbed**) vi to dig in the ground; to work hard. * vt to clear (ground) of roots; to uproot. * n the worm-like larva of a beetle; (sl) food.

grubby adj (**grubbier, grubbiest**) dirty, soiled.— **grubbiness** n.

grudge n a deep feeling of resentment or ill will. * vt to be reluctant to give or admit something.—**grudging** adj. —**grudgingly** adv.

gruelling, grueling (US) adj severely testing, exhausting.

gruesome *adj* causing horror or loathing.

gruff *adj* rough or surly; hoarse.—**gruffly** *adv.*—**gruffness** *n.*

grumble *vti* to mutter in discontent; to make a rumbling sound.—*also n.* —**grumbler** *n.*

grumpy *adj* (**grumpier, grumpiest**) bad-tempered, peevish.—**grumpily** *adv.*—**grumpiness** *n.*

grunt *vi* to make a gruff guttural sound like a pig; to say or speak in such a manner.—*also n.*

GSC *abbr* = Geological Survey of Canada.

GST *abbr* (*Cdn*) = Goods and Services Tax.

GTA *abbr* = Greater Toronto Area.

guarantee *n* a pledge or security for another's debt or obligation; a pledge to replace something substandard, etc; an assurance that something will be done as specified; something offered as a pledge or security; a guarantor. * *vt* to give a guarantee for; to promise.

guaranteed investment certificate *n* (*Cdn*) a certificate issued by a financial institution that guarantees a fixed interest rate on a sum of money for a fixed term.

guarantor *n* a person who gives a guaranty or guarantee.

guard *vt* to watch over and protect; to defend; to keep from escape or trouble; to restrain. * *vi* to keep watch (against); to act as a guard. * *n* defence; protection; a posture of readiness for defence; a device to protect against injury or loss; a person or group that guards; (*boxing, fencing, cricket*) a defensive attitude; an official in charge of a train.

guarded *adj* discreet; cautious.—**guardedly** *adv.*

guardian *n* a custodian; a person legally in charge of a minor or someone incapable of taking care of their own affairs.—**guardianship** *n.*

guerrilla, guerilla *n* a member of a small force of irregular soldiers, making surprise raids.—*also adj.*

guess *vt* to form an opinion of or state with little or no factual knowledge; to judge correctly by doing this; to think or suppose. * *n* an estimate based on guessing.—**guesser** *n.*

guest *n* a person entertained at the home, club, etc of another; any paying customer of a hotel, restaurant, etc; a performer appearing by special invitation.

guesthouse *n* a private home or boarding-house offering accommodation.

guestroom *n* a room kept for guests.

guffaw *n* a crude noisy laugh.—*also vi.*

guidance *n* leadership; advice or counsel.

guide *vt* to point out the way for; to lead; to direct the course of; to control. * *n* a person who leads or directs others; a person who shows and explains points of interest; something that provides a person with guiding information; a device controlling the motion of something; a book of basic instruction; (*with cap*) a member of the girls' organization equivalent to the Scouts.

guidebook *n* a book containing directions and information for tourists.

guided missile *n* a military missile whose course is controlled by radar or internal instruments, etc.

guide dog *n* a dog trained to guide people who are blind.

guild *n* a club, society; an association of people with common interests formed for mutual aid and protection, as craftsmen in the Middle Ages.

guile *n* craftiness, deceit.—**guileful** *adj.*—**guileless** *adj.*

guillotine *n* an instrument for beheading by a heavy blade descending between grooved posts; a device or machine for cutting paper; a rule for limiting time for discussion in a legislature.—*also vt.*

guilt *n* the fact of having done a wrong or committed an offence; a feeling of self-reproach from believing one has done a wrong.

guiltless *adj* innocent.

guilty *adj* (**guiltier, guiltiest**) having guilt; feeling or showing guilt.—**guiltily** *adv.*—**guiltiness** *n.*

guinea *n* a former English gold coin equal to 21 shillings (£1.05).

guinea pig *n* a rodent-like animal commonly kept as a pet, and often used in scientific experiments; a person or thing subject to an experiment.

guise *n* an external appearance, aspect; an assumed appearance, pretence.

guitar *n* a stringed musical instrument with a long, fretted neck, and a flat body, which is plucked with a plectrum or the fingers.—**guitarist** *n.*

gulf *n* a large area of ocean reaching into land; a wide, deep chasm; a vast separation.

gull *n* any of numerous long-winged web-footed sea birds.

gullet *n* the oesophagus; the throat.

gullible *adj* easily deceived.—**gullibility** *n.*—**gullibly** *adv.*

gully *n* a narrow trench cut by running water after rain; (*cricket*) a fielding position between the slips and point. * *vt* to make gullies in.

gulp *vt* to swallow hastily or greedily; to choke back as if swallowing. * *n* a gulping or swallowing; a mouthful.

gum[1] *n* the firm tissue that surrounds the teeth.

gum[2] *n* a sticky substance found in certain trees and plants; an adhesive; chewing gum. * *vb* (*pt* **gummed**) *vt* to coat or unite with gum. * *vi* to become sticky or clogged.

gumboot *n* a rubber, waterproof boot, a wellington.

gumption *n* (*inf*) shrewd practical common sense; initiative.

gun *n* a weapon with a metal tube from which a projectile is discharged by an explosive; the shooting of a gun as a signal or salute; anything like a gun. * *vb* (*pt* **gunned**) *vi* to shoot or hunt with a gun. * *vt* (*inf*) to shoot (a person); (*sl*) to advance the throttle of an engine.

gunboat *n* a small armed ship.

gunman *n* an armed gangster; a hired killer.

gunner *n* a soldier, etc who helps fire artillery; a naval warrant officer in charge of a ship's guns.

gunpowder *n* an explosive powder used in guns, for blasting, etc.

gurgle *vi* (*liquid*) to make a low bubbling sound; to utter with this sound.—*also n.*

gush *vi* to issue plentifully; to have a sudden flow; to talk or write effusively. * *vt* to cause to gush. * *n* a sudden outpouring.—**gushy** *adj.*

gusset *n* a small triangular piece of cloth inserted in a garment to strengthen or enlarge a part.

gust *n* a sudden brief rush of wind; a sudden outburst. * *vi* to blow in gusts. —**gusty** *adj.*—**gustily** *adv.*

gusto *n* great enjoyment, zest.

gut *n* (*often pl*) the bowels or the stomach; the intestine; tough cord made from animal intestines; (*pl*) (*sl*) daring; courage. * *vt* (*pt* **gutted**) to remove the intestines from; to destroy the interior of.

gutter *n* a channel for carrying off water, esp at a roadside or under the eaves of a roof; a channel or groove to direct something (as of a bowling alley); the lowest condition of human life. * *adj* marked by extreme vulgarity or indecency. * *vt* to provide with a gutter. * *vi* to flow in rivulets; (*candle*) to melt unevenly; (*candle flame*) to flutter.—**guttering** *n.*

guttersnipe *n* a dirty child who plays in the streets, esp slum areas.

guttural *adj* formed or pronounced in the throat; harsh-sounding.—**gutturally** *adv.*

guy¹ *n* a rope, chain, etc, for fixing or steadying anything. * *vt* to fix or steady with a guy.

guy² *n* an effigy of Guy Fawkes made from old clothes stuffed with newspapers, etc burnt on the anniversary of the Gunpowder Plot (5 November); (*inf*) a man or boy; (*pl*) (*inf*) men or women; a shabby person. * *vt* to tease.

guzzle *vti* to gulp down food or drink greedily.—**guzzler** *n.*

gym *n* (*inf*) a gymnasium.

gymnasium *n* a room or building equipped for physical training and sports.

gymnast *n* a person skilled in gymnastics.

gymnastics *n* (*used as sing*) training in exercises devised to strengthen the body; (*pl*) gymnastic exercises; (*pl*) feats of dexterity or agility.

gynaecology, gynecology (*US*) *n* the branch of medicine that deals with the diseases and disorders of the female reproductive system.—**gynaecological** *adj.*—**gynaecologist** *n.*

gypsy *n* (*with cap*) a member of a travelling people, orig from India, now spread throughout Europe and North America; a person who looks or lives like a Gypsy.—*also* **gipsy.**

gyrate *vi* to revolve; to whirl or spiral. —**gyration** *n.*—**gyratory** *adj.*

H

haberdasher *n* a dealer in sewing accessories; in US, a dealer in men's clothing.—**haberdashery** *n.*

habit *n* a distinctive costume, as of a nun, etc; a thing done often and hence easily; a usual way of doing things; an addiction, esp to narcotics. * *vt* to clothe.

habitant *n* (*Cdn*) (*hist*) a French settler in rural Quebec.

habitual *adj* having the nature of a habit; regular.—**habitually** *adv.*

hack¹ *vt* to cut or chop (at) violently; to clear (vegetation) by chopping; (*comput*) to gain illegal access to confidential data. * *n* a gash or notch; a harsh, dry cough.

hack² *n* a riding horse for hire; an old worn-out horse; a mediocre or unexceptional writer; a coach for hire; (*inf*) a taxicab. * *vti* to ride a horse cross-country. * *adj* banal, hackneyed.

hackneyed *adj* made trite or banal through overuse.

had *see* **have.**

haddock *n* (*pl* **haddock**) an important Atlantic food fish related to the cod.

haemorrhage, hemorrhage (*US*) *n* the escape of blood from a blood vessel; heavy bleeding. * *vi* to bleed heavily.

haemorrhoids, hemorrhoids (*US*) *npl* swollen or bleeding veins around the anus.—*also* **piles.**

haggard *n adj* having an exhausted, untidy look.

haggle *vi* to bargain; barter.—**haggler** *n.*

Haida *n* a member of a First Nations people on the Pacific Northwest coast of Canada; the language of this people. * *adj* of or pertaining to this people or their language.

hail¹ *vt* to greet; to summon by shouting or signalling, as a taxi; to welcome with approval, to acclaim. * *vi* to originate from. * *interj* an exclamation of tribute, greeting, etc. * *n* a shout to gain attention; a distance within which one can be heard calling.—**hailer** *n.*

hail² *n* frozen raindrops; something, as abuse, bullets, etc, sent forcefully in rapid succession. * *vti* to pour down like hail.

hailstone *n* a pellet of hail.

hair *n* a threadlike growth from the skin of mammals; a mass of hairs, esp on the human head; a threadlike growth on a plant.

haircut *n* a shortening and styling of hair by cutting it; the style of cutting.

hair-do *n* a particular style of hair after cutting, etc.

hairdresser *n* a person who cuts, styles, colors, etc hair.

hairpiece *n* a wig or toupee; an additional piece of hair attached to a person's real hair.

hairpin *n* U-shaped pin used to hold hair in place.

hairpin bend *n* a sharply curving bend in a road,

etc.

hair-raising *adj* terrifying, shocking.

hairstyle *n* the way in which hair is arranged.—**hairstylist** *n*.

hairy *adj* (**hairier, hairiest**) covered with hair; (*inf*) difficult, dangerous.—**hairiness** *n*.

hake *n* (*pl* **hake**) a marine food fish related to the cod.

half *n* (*pl* **halves**) either of two equal parts of something; (*inf*) a half-price ticket for a bus, etc; (*inf*) half a pint. * *adj* being a half; incomplete; partial. * *adv* to the extent of a half; (*inf*) partly.

halfback *n* (*football, hockey*) a player occupying a position between the forwards and the fullbacks; a player in this position in other sports.

half-caste *n* a person whose parents are of different races.

half-hearted *adj* with little interest, enthusiasm, etc.

half-hour *n* 30 minutes; the point 30 minutes after the beginning of an hour.

half-time *n* (*sport*) an interval between two halves of a game.

halfway *adj* midway between two points, etc.

halibut *n* a large marine flatfish used as food.

Haligonian *n* a person who lives in or is from Halifax, Nova Scotia.

hall *n* a public building with offices, etc; a large room for exhibits, gatherings, etc; the main house on a landed estate; a college building, esp a dining room; a vestibule at the entrance of a building; a hallway.

hallmark *n* a mark used on gold, silver or platinum articles to signify a standard of purity, weight, date of manufacture; a mark or symbol of high quality; a characteristic feature. * *vt* to stamp with a hallmark.

hallo *see* **hello**.

hallucination *n* the apparent perception of sights, sounds, etc that are not actually present; something perceived in this manner.—**hallucinatory** *adj*.

halo *n* (*pl* **haloes, halos**) a circle of light, as around the sun; a symbolic ring of light around the head of a saint in pictures; the aura of glory surrounding an idealized person or thing.

halt[1] *n* a temporary interruption or cessation of progress; a minor station on a railway line. * *vti* to stop or come to a stop.

halt[2] *vi* to falter; to hesitate.—**halting** *adj*.

halve *vt* to divide equally into two; to reduce by half; (*golf*) to play one hole in the same number of strokes as one's opponent.

halves *see* **half**.

ham *n* the upper part of a pig's hind leg, salted, smoked, etc; the meat from this area; (*inf*) the back of the upper thigh; (*inf*) an actor who overacts; (*inf*) a licensed amateur radio operator. * *vt* (*pt* **hammed**) to speak or move in an exaggerated manner, to overact.

hamburger *n* ground beef; a cooked patty of such meat, often in a bread roll with pickle, etc.

hamlet *n* a very small village.

hammer *n* a tool for pounding, driving nails, etc, having a heavy head and a handle; a thing like this in shape or use, as the part of the gun that strikes the firing pin; a bone of the middle ear; a heavy metal ball attached to a wire thrown in athletic contests. * *vti* to strike repeatedly, as with a hammer; to drive, force, or shape, as with hammer blows; (*inf*) to defeat utterly.

hammock *n* a length of strong cloth or netting suspended by the ends and used as a bed.

hamper[1] *vt* to hinder; to interfere with; to encumber.

hamper[2] *n* a large, usu covered, basket for storing or transporting food and crockery, etc.

hand *n* the part of the arm below the wrist, used for grasping; a side or direction; possession or care; control; an active part; a promise to marry; skill; handwriting; applause; help; a hired worker; a source; one of a ship's crew; anything like a hand, as a pointer on a clock; the breadth of a hand, four inches when measuring the height of a horse; the cards held by a player at one time; a round of card play; (*inf*) applause. * *adj* of, for, or controlled by the hand. * *vt* to give as with the hand; to help or conduct with the hand. * *vi* (*with* **on**) to pass to the next.

handbag *n* a woman's small bag for carrying personal items.

handbook *n* a book containing useful instructions.

handcuff *n* (*usu pl*) either of a pair of connected steel rings for shackling the wrists of a prisoner. * *vt* to manacle.

handful *n* as much as will fill the hand; a few; (*inf*) a person who is difficult to handle or control.

handicap *n* a mental or physical impairment; a contest in which difficulties are imposed on, or advantages given to, contestants to equalize their chances; such a difficulty or advantage; any hindrance. * *vt* (*pt* **handicapped**) to give a handicap to; to hinder.—**handicapper** *n*.

handicraft *n* a skill involving the hands, such as basketwork, pottery, etc; an item of pottery, etc made by hand.

handkerchief *n* a small cloth for blowing the nose, etc.

handle *vt* to touch, hold, or move with the hand; to manage or operate with the hands; to manage, deal with; to buy and sell (goods). * *vi* to react in a specified way. * *n* a part of anything designed to be held or grasped by the hand.—**handleable** *adj*.—**handling** *n*.

handlebar *n* (*often pl*) the curved metal bar with a grip at each end used to steer a bicycle, etc; a bushy moustache with curved ends.

handmade *adj* made by hand, carefully crafted.

handsome *adj* good-looking; dignified; generous; ample.—**handsomely** *adv*.—**handsomeness** *n*.

handy *adj* (**handier, handiest**) convenient, near; easy to use; skilled with the hands.—**handily**

adv.—**handiness** *n*.

handyman *n* a person who does odd jobs.

hang *vb* (*pt* **hung**) *vt* to support from above, esp by a rope, chain, etc, to suspend; (*door, etc*) to attach by hinges to allow to swing freely; to decorate with pictures, or other suspended objects; (*wallpaper*) to stick to a wall; to exhibit (works of art); to prevent (a jury) from coming to a decision; (*pt* **hanged**) to put to execute or kill by suspending by the neck. * *vi* to be suspended, so as to dangle loosely; to fall or droop; (*clothing, etc*) to fall or flow in a certain direction; to lean, incline, or protrude; to depend; to remain in the air; to be in suspense; (*pt* **hanged**) to die by hanging; (*with* **about, around**) to loiter; (*with* **back**) to hesitate, be reluctant; (*with* **out**) to meet regularly at a particular place. * *n* the way in which anything hangs; (*sl*) a damn.

hangar *n* a shelter for aircraft.

hanger *n* a device on which something is hung.

hanger-on *n* a sycophantic follower.

hang-glider *n* an unpowered aircraft consisting of a metal frame over which a lightweight material is stretched, with a harness for the pilot suspended below.—**hang gliding** *n*.

hangover *n* the unpleasant after-effects of excessive consumption of alcohol; something surviving from an earlier time.

hang-up *n* an emotional preoccupation with something.

hank *n* a coiled or looped bundle of wool, rope, etc.

hanker *vi* (*with* **after, for**) to desire longingly.—**hankering** *n*.

hanky, hankie *n* (*inf*) a handkerchief.

haphazard *adj* not planned; random. * *adv* by chance.—**haphazardly** *adv*.

happen *vi* to take place; to be, occur, or come by chance.

happening *n* an occurrence; an improvisation.

happy *adj* (**happier, happiest**) fortunate; having, expressing, or enjoying pleasure or contentment; pleased; appropriate, felicitous.—**happily** *adv*.—**happiness** *n*.

happy-go-lucky *adj* irresponsible; carefree.

harass *vt* to annoy, to irritate; to trouble (an enemy) by constant raids and attacks.—**harassment** *n*.

harbour, harbor (*US*) *n* a protected inlet for anchoring ships; any place of refuge. * *vt* to shelter or house; (*grudge, etc*) to keep in the mind secretly. * *vi* to take shelter.

hard *adj* firm, solid, not easily cut or punctured; difficult to comprehend; difficult to accomplish; difficult to bear, painful; severe, unfeeling, ungenerous; indisputable, intractable; (*drugs*) addictive and damaging to health; (*weather*) severe; (*currency*) stable in value; (*news*) definite, not speculative; (*drink*) very alcoholic; (*water*) having a high mineral content that prevents lathering with soap; (*color, sound*) harsh. * *adv* with great effort or intensity; earnestly, with concentration; so as to cause hard-

ness; with difficulty; with bitterness or grief; close, near by.—**hardness** *n*.

hardback *n* a book bound with a stiff cover.—*also adj*.

hardboard *n* a stiff board made of compressed wood chips.

hard-boiled *adj* (*eggs*) boiled until solid; (*inf*) unfeeling.

hard cash *n* payment in coins and notes as opposed to cheque, etc.

harden *vti* to make or become hard.—**hardener** *n*.

hardly *adv* scarcely; barely; with difficulty; not to be expected.

hardrock mining *n* mining performed underground in large formations of igneous or metamorphic rock.

hard sell *n* an aggressive selling technique.

hardship *n* something that causes suffering or privation.

hard up *adj* (*inf*) short of money.

hardware *n* articles made of metal as tools, nails, etc; (*comput*) the mechanical and electronic components that make up a computer system.

hardy *adj* (**hardier, hardiest**) bold, resolute; robust; vigorous; able to withstand exposure to physical or emotional hardship.—**hardily** *adv.*—**hardiness** *n*.

hare *n* any of various timid, swift, long-eared mammals, resembling but larger than the rabbit.

harebrained *adj* flighty; foolish.

harelip *n* a congenital deformity of the upper lip in the form of a vertical fissure.

harem, hareem *n* the usu secluded part of a Muslim household where the women live; the women in a harem.

harm *n* hurt; damage; injury. * *vt.* to inflict hurt, damage, or injury upon.

harmful *adj* hurtful.—**harmfully** *adv*.

harmless *adj* not likely to cause harm.—**harmlessly** *adv.*—**harmlessness** *n*.

harmonic *adj* (*mus*) of or in harmony. * *n* an overtone; (*pl*) the science of musical sounds.

harmonica *n* a small wind instrument that produces tones when air is blown or sucked across a series of metal reeds; a mouth-organ.

harmonious *adj* fitting together in an orderly and pleasing manner; agreeing in ideas, interests, etc; melodious. —**harmoniously** *adv*.

harmonium *n* a keyboard musical instrument whose tones are produced by thin metal reeds operated by foot bellows.

harmonize *vi* to be in harmony; to sing in harmony. * *vt* to make harmonious.—**harmonization** *n*.

harmonized sales tax *n* (*Cdn*) a tax on goods and services, combining the federal goods and services tax and the provincial sales tax.

harmony *n* a pleasing agreement of parts in color, size, etc; agreement in action, ideas, etc; the pleasing combination of musical tones in a chord.

harness *n* the leather straps and metal pieces

by which a horse is fastened to a vehicle, plough, etc; any similar fastening or attachment, eg for a parachute, hang-glider. * *vt* to put a harness on; to control so as to use the power of.

harp *n* a stringed musical instrument played by plucking. * *vi* (*with* **on** *or* **upon**) to talk persistently (on some subject).—**harpist** *n*.

harpoon *n* a barbed spear with an attached line, for spearing whales, etc.—*also vt.*

harpsichord *n* a musical instrument resembling a grand piano whose strings are plucked by a mechanism rather than struck.

harrow *n* a heavy frame with spikes, spring teeth, or disks for breaking up and levelling ploughed ground. * *vt* to draw a harrow over (land); to cause mental distress to.—**harrowing** *adj*.

harsh *adj* unpleasantly rough; jarring on the senses or feelings; rigorous; cruel.—**harshly** *adv*.—**harshness** *n*.

harvest *n* (the season of) gathering in the ripened crops; the yield of a particular crop; the reward or product of any exertion or action. * *vti* to gather in (a crop). * *vt* to win by achievement. —**harvester** *n*.

harvest excursion *n* (*Cdn*) (*hist*) an organized, low-priced train excursion for workers travelling to western Canada to harvest grain crops.

has *see* **have.**

hash[1] *n* a chopped mixture of reheated cooked meat and vegetables. * *vt* to chop up (meat or vegetables) for hash; to mix or mess up.

hash[2] *n* (*inf*) hashish.

hashish *n* resin derived from the leaves and shoots of the hemp plant, smoked or chewed as an intoxicant.

haste *n* quickness of motion.

hasten *vt* to accelerate; to cause to hurry. * *vi* to move or act with speed.

hasty *adj* (**hastier, hastiest**) done in a hurry; rash, precipitate.—**hastily** *adv*. —**hastiness** *n*.

hat *n* a covering for the head.

hatch[1] *n* a small door or opening (as on an aircraft or spaceship); an opening in the deck of a ship or in the floor or roof of a building; a lid for such an opening; a hatchway.

hatch[2] *vt* to produce (young) from the egg, esp by incubating; to devise (eg a plot). * *vi* to emerge from the egg; to incubate.

hatch[3] *vt* (*drawing, engraving*) to shade using closely spaced parallel lines or incisions.

hatchback *n* a sloping rear end on a car with a door; a car of this design.

hatchet *n* a small axe with a short handle.

hate *vt* to feel intense dislike for. * *vi* to feel hatred; to wish to avoid. * *n* a strong feeling of dislike or contempt; the person or thing hated.

hateful *adj* deserving or arousing hate.—**hatefully** *adv*.

hatred *n* intense dislike or enmity.

hat trick *n* (*cricket*) the taking of three wickets with three successive bowls; the scoring of three successive goals, points, etc in any game.

haughty *adj* (**haughtier, haughtiest**) having or expressing arrogance.—**haughtily** *adv*.—**haughtiness** *n*.

haul *vti* to move by pulling; to transport by truck, etc. * *n* the act of hauling; the amount gained, caught, etc at one time; the distance over which something is transported.

haulage *n* the transport of commodities; the charge for this.

haulier *n* a person or business that transports goods by road.

haunch *n* the part of the body around the hips; the leg and loin of a deer, sheep, etc.

haunt *vt* to visit often or continually; to recur repeatedly to. * *vi* to linger; to appear habitually as a ghost. * *n* a place often visited.

have *vt* (*pres t* **has**, *pr p* **having**, *pt* **had**) to have in one's possession; to possess as an attribute; to hold in the mind; to experience; to give birth to; to allow, or tolerate; to arrange or hold; to engage in; to cause, compel, or require to be; to be to be obliged; (*sl*) to have sexual intercourse with; to be pregnant with; (*inf*) to hold at a disadvantage; (*inf*) to deceive; to accept or receive; to consume food, drink, etc; to show some quality; to perplex.

haven *n* a place where ships can safely anchor; a refuge.

have-not province *n* (*Cdn*) province that receives equalization payments from the federal government because it does not have sufficient tax revenue.

have province *n* (*Cdn*) a province that has enough tax revenue that it is ineligible to receive equalization payments from the federal government.

haversack *n* a canvas bag similar to a knapsack but worn over one shoulder.

havoc *n* widespread destruction or disorder.

hawk[1] *n* any of numerous birds of prey; a person who advocates aggressive or intimidatory action.—**hawkish** *adj*.

hawk[2] *vti* to clear the throat (of) audibly.

hawk[3] *vt* to offer goods for sale, as in the street.

hawker *n* a person who goes about offering goods for sale.

hay *n* grass cut and dried for fodder.

hay fever *n* an allergic reaction to pollen causing irritation of the nose and eyes.

haystack, hayrick *n* a pile of stacked hay ready for storing.

haywire *adj* (*inf*) out of order; disorganized.

hazard *n* risk; danger; an obstacle on a golf course. * *vt* to risk.

hazardous *adj* dangerous; risky.

haze *n* a thin vapour of fog, smoke, etc in the air; slight vagueness of mind. * *vti* to make or become hazy.

hazy *adj* (**hazier, haziest**) misty; vague .—**hazily** *adv*.—**haziness** *n*.

HBC *abbr* = Hudson's Bay Company.

he *pron* the male person or animal named before; a person (male or female). * *n* a male person or animal.

head *n* the part of an animal or human body containing the brain, eyes, ears, nose and mouth; the top part of anything; the foremost part; the chief person; (*pl*) a unit of counting; the striking part of a tool; mind; understanding; the topic of a chapter, etc; crisis, conclusion; pressure of water, steam, etc; the source of a river, etc; froth, as on beer. * *adj* at the head, top or front; coming from in front; chief, leading.* *vt* to command; to lead; to cause to go in a specified direction; to set out; to travel (in a particular direction); to strike (a football) with the head.—**headless** *adj*.

headache *n* a continuous pain in the head; (*inf*) a cause of worry or trouble.

heading *n* something forming the head, top, or front; the title, topic, etc of a chapter, etc; the direction in which a vehicle is moving.

headland *n* a promontory.

headlight, headlamp *n* a light at the front of a vehicle.

headline *n* printed lines at the top of a newspaper article giving the topic; a brief news summary. * *vt* to give featured billing or publicity to.

headlong *adj* with the head first; with uncontrolled speed or force; rashly.—*also adv*.

headmaster, headmistress *n* the principal of a school.

head-on *adj* with the head or front foremost; without compromise.—*also adv*.

headquarters *n* the centre of operations of one in command, as in an army; the main office in any organization.

headrest *n* a support for the head.

headroom *n* space overhead, as in a doorway or tunnel.

headstrong *adj* determined to do as one pleases.

head waiter *n* the head of the dining-room staff in a restaurant.

headway *n* forward motion; progress.

headwind *n* a wind blowing against the direction of a ship or aircraft.

heady *adj* (**headier, headiest**) (*alcoholic drinks*) intoxicating; invigorating, exciting; impetuous.—**headily** *adv*.—**headiness** *n*.

heal *vti* to make or become healthy; to cure; (*wound, etc*) to repair by natural processes.—**healer** *n*.

health *n* physical and mental well-being; freedom from disease, etc; the condition of body or mind; a wish for health and happiness, as in a toast.

health card *n* (*Cdn*) a card identifying a person as eligible to receive medical services paid by a public insurance plan.

healthy *adj* (**healthier, healthiest**) having or producing good health; beneficial; sound.—**healthily** *adv*.—**healthiness** *n*.

heap *n* a mass or pile of jumbled things; (*pl*) (*inf*) a large amount. * *vt* to throw in a heap; to pile high; to fill (a plate, etc) full or to overflowing.

hear *vb* (*pt* **heard**) *vt* to perceive by the ear; to listen to; to conduct a hearing of (a law case, etc); to be informed of; to learn. * *vi* to be able to hear sounds; (*with* **of** *or* **about**) to be told.—**hearer** *n*.

hearing *n* the sense by which sound is perceived by the ear; an opportunity to be heard; the distance over which something can be heard, earshot.

hearing aid *n* a small electronic amplifier worn behind the ear to improve hearing.

hearsay *n* rumour, gossip.

hearse *n* a vehicle for transporting a coffin to a funeral.

heart *n* the hollow, muscular organ that circulates the blood; the central, vital, or main part; the human heart as the centre of emotions, esp sympathy, courage, etc; a conventional design representing a heart; one of a suit of playing cards marked with such a symbol in red.

heartache *n* sorrow or grief.

heart attack *n* a sudden instance of abnormal heart functioning, esp coronary thrombosis.

heartbeat *n* the rhythmic contraction and dilation of the heart.

heartbreak *n* overwhelming sorrow or grief.—**heartbreaking** *adj*.—**heartbroken** *adj*.

heartburn *n* a burning sensation in the lower chest.

heartfelt *adj* sincere.

hearth *n* the floor of a fireplace and surrounding area; this as symbolic of house and home.

heartily *adv* vigorously, enthusiastically; sincerely.

heartless *adj* unfeeling.—**heartlessly** *adv*.—**heartlessness** *n*.

hearty *adj* (**heartier, heartiest**) warm and friendly; unrestrained, as laughter; strong and healthy; nourishing and plentiful.—**heartiness** *n*.

heat *n* energy produced by molecular agitation; the quality of being hot; the perception of hotness; hot weather or climate; strong feeling, esp anger, etc; a single bout, round, or trial in sports; the period of sexual excitement and readiness for mating in female animals; (*sl*) coercion. * *vti* to make or become warm or hot; to make or become excited.

heated *adj* made hot; excited, impassioned.—**heatedly** *adv*.

heater *n* a device that provides heat; (*sl*) a gun.

heath *n* an area of uncultivated land with scrubby vegetation; any of various shrubby plants that thrive on sandy soil, eg heather.

heathen *n* (*pl* **heathens, heathen**) anyone not acknowledging the God of Christian, Jew, or Muslim belief; a person regarded as irreligious, uncivilized, etc.

heather *n* a common evergreen shrub of northern and alpine regions with small stalkless leaves and tiny usu purplish pink flowers.

heating *n* a system of providing heat, as central heating; the warmth provided.

heat wave n a prolonged period of hot weather.

heave vb vt to lift or move, esp with great effort; to utter (a sigh, etc) with effort; (inf) to throw. * vi to rise and fall rhythmically; to vomit; to pant; to gasp; to haul; (pt **hove**) (with **to**) (ship) to come to a stop. * n the act or effort of heaving.

heaven n (usu pl) the visible sky; (sometimes cap) the dwelling place of God and his angels where the blessed go after death; any place or state of great happiness; (pl) interj an exclamation of surprise.

heavenly adj of or relating to heaven or heavens; divine; (inf) excellent, delightful.—**heavenliness** n.

heavy adj (**heavier, heaviest**) hard to lift or carry; of more than the usual, expected, or defined weight; to an unusual extent; hard to do; stodgy, hard to digest; cloudy; (industry) using massive machinery to produce basic materials, as chemicals and steel; (ground) difficult to make fast progress on; clumsy; dull, serious. * n (theatre) a villain; (sl) a person hired to threaten violence, a thug.—**heavily** adv.—**heaviness** n.

heavyweight n a professional boxer weighing more than 175 pounds (79 kg) or wrestler weighing over 209 pounds (95 kg); (inf) a very influential or important individual.

Hebrew n a member of an ancient Semitic people; an Israelite; a Jew; the ancient Semitic language of the Hebrews; its modern form.—also adj.

heckle vti to harass (a speaker) with questions or taunts.—**heckler** n.

hectic adj involving intense excitement or activity.—**hectically** adv.

he'd = he had, he would.

hedge n a fence consisting of a dense line of bushes or small trees; a barrier or means of protection against something, esp financial loss; an evasive or noncommittal answer or statement. * vt to surround or enclose with a hedge; to place secondary bets as a precaution. * vi to avoid giving a direct answer in an argument or debate.

hedgehog n a small insectivorous mammal with sharp spines on the back.

heed vt to pay close attention (to). * n careful attention.—**heedful** adj.

heedless adj inattentive; thoughtless. —**heedlessly** adv.

heel[1] n the back part of the foot, under the ankle; the part covering or supporting the heel in stockings, socks, etc or shoes; a solid attachment forming the back of the sole of a shoe; (inf) a despicable person. * vt to furnish with a heel; to follow closely; (inf) to provide with money, etc. * vi to follow along at the heels of someone.

heel[2] vti to tilt or become tilted to one side, as a ship.

hefty adj (**heftier, heftiest**) (inf) heavy; large and strong; big.—**heftily** adv.—**heftiness** n.

heifer n a young cow that has not calved.

height n the topmost point; the highest limit; the distance from the bottom to the top; altitude; a relatively great distance above a given level; an eminence; a hill.

heighten vti to make or come higher or more intense.

heir n a person who inherits or is entitled to inherit another's property, title, etc.

heiress n a woman or girl who is an heir, esp to great wealth.

heirloom n any possession handed down from generation to generation.

held see **hold**[1].

helicopter n a kind of aircraft lifted and moved, or kept hovering, by large rotary blades mounted horizontally.

hell n (Christianity) the place of punishment of the wicked after death; the home of devils and demons; any place or state of supreme misery or discomfort; (inf) a cause of this. * interj (inf) an exclamation of anger, surprise, etc.

he'll = he will.

hellish adj of, pertaining to or resembling hell; very wicked; (inf) very unpleasant.

hello interj an expression of greeting. * n the act of saying "hello."—also **hallo, hullo**.

helm n the tiller or wheel used to steer a ship; a position of control or direction, authority.

helmet n protective headgear worn by soldiers, policemen, divers, etc.

helmsman n a person who steers.—**helmswoman** nf.

help vt to make things better or easier for; to aid; to assist; to remedy; to keep from; to serve or wait on. * vi to give aid; to be useful. * n the action of helping; aid; assistance; a remedy; a person that helps, esp a hired person. —**helper** n.

helpful adj giving help; useful.—**helpfully** adv.—**helpfulness** n.

helping n a single portion of food.

helpless adj unable to manage alone, dependent on others; weak and defenceless.—**helplessly** adv.—**helplessness** n.

help-wanted index n (Cdn) a seasonally-adjusted measure of employment, based on jobs that are advertised.

hem n the edge of a garment, etc turned back and stitched or fixed. * vt (pt **hemmed**) to finish (a garment) with a hem; (with **in**) to enclose, confine.—**hemmer** n.

hemisphere n half of a sphere or globe; any of the halves (northern, southern, eastern, or western) of the earth.—**hemispherical** adj.

hemp n a widely cultivated Asian herb of the mulberry family; its fibre, used to mmke rope, sailcloth, etc; a narcotic drug obtained from different varieties of this plant (—also **cannabis, marijuana**).

hen n the female of many birds, esp the chicken.

hence adv from here; from this time; from this reason.

henceforth, henceforward adv from now on.

henchman n a trusted helper or follower.

henpeck *vt* to nag and domineer over (one's husband).—**henpecked** *adj*.

her *pron* the objective case of **she**. * *adj* of or belonging to her.

herald *n* a person who conveys news or messages; a forerunner, harbinger; (*Middle Ages*) an official at a tournament. * *vt* to usher in; to proclaim.

heraldry *n* the study of genealogies and coats of arms; ceremony; pomp. —**heraldic** *adj*.

herb *n* any seed plant whose stem withers away annually; any plant used as a medicine, seasoning, etc.—**herby** *adj*.

herd *n* a large number of animals, esp cattle, living and feeding together. * *vi* to assemble or move animals together. * *vt* to gather together and move as if a herd; to tend, as a herdsman.—**herder** *n*.

here *adv* at or in this place; to or into this place; now; on earth.

hereafter *adv* after this, in some future time or state. * *n* (*with* **the**) the future, life after death.

hereby *adv* by this means.

hereditary *adj* descending by inheritance; transmitted to offspring.

heredity *n* the transmission of genetic material that determines physical and mental characteristics from one generation to another.

heresy *n* a religious belief regarded as contrary to the orthodox doctrine of a church; any belief or opinion contrary to established or accepted theory.

heretic *n* a dissenter from an established belief or doctrine.—**heretical** *adj*.

heritage *n* something inherited at birth; anything deriving from the past or tradition; historical sites, traditions, practices, etc regarded as the valuable inheritance of contemporary society.

hermetic *adj* perfectly closed and airtight.—**hermetically** *adv*.

hermit *n* a person who lives in complete solitude, esp for religious reasons; a recluse.

hernia *n* the protrusion of an organ, esp part of the intestine, through an opening in the wall of the cavity in which it sits; a rupture.—**hernial** *adj*.

hero *n* (*pl* **heroes**) a person of exceptional bravery; a person admired for superior qualities and achievements; the central male character in a novel, play, etc.

heroic *adj* of or like a hero; of or about heroes and their deeds; daring, risky.—**heroically** *adv*.

heroin *n* a powerfully addictive drug derived from morphine.

heroine *n* a woman with the attributes of a hero; the leading female character in a novel, film or play.

heroism *n* the qualities or conduct of a hero.

heron *n* a slim long-necked wading bird.

herring *n* (*pl* **herrings**, **herring**) a small food fish.

herring choker *n* (*Cdn*) (*sl*) a New Brunswicker.

hers *pron* something or someone belonging to her.

herself *pron* the reflexive form of **she** or **her**.

he's = he is; he has.

hesitant *adj* hesitating.—**hesitantly** *adv*.—**hesitancy** *n*.

hesitate *vi* to be slow in acting due to uncertainty or indecision; to be reluctant (to); to falter or stammer when speaking.—**hesitating** *adj*.—**hesitation** *n*.

het-up *adj* (*inf*) agitated, annoyed.

hew *vb* (*pp* **hewed** *or* **hewn**) *vt* to strike or cut with blows using an axe, etc; to shape with such blows. * *vi* to conform (to a rule, principle, etc).—**hewer** *n*.

hexagon *n* a polygon having six sides and six angles.—**hexagonal** *adj*.—**hexagonally** *adv*.

heyday *n* a period of greatest success, happiness, etc.

Hfx. *abbr* = Halifax (Nova Scotia).

hi *interj* an exclamation of greeting.

hibernate *vi* to spend the winter in a dormant condition like deep sleep; to be inactive.—**hibernation** *n*.

hiccup *n* a sudden involuntary spasm of the diaphragm followed by inhalation and closure of the glottis producing a characteristic sound; (*inf*) a minor setback. * *vt* (*pt* **hiccuped** *or* **hiccupped**) to have hiccups.

hide¹ *vb* (*pt* **hid**, *pp* **hidden**, **hid**) *vt* to conceal, put out of sight; to keep secret; to screen or obscure from view. * *vi* to conceal oneself. * *n* a camouflaged place of concealment used by hunters, bird-watchers, etc.

hide² *n* the raw or dressed skin of an animal; (*inf*) the human skin.

hideous *adj* visually repulsive; horrifying.—**hideously** *adv*.

hiding *n* (*inf*) a thrashing.

hierarchy *n* a group of persons or things arranged in order of rank, grade, etc.—**hierarchical** *adj*.

high *adj* lofty, tall; extending upward a (specified) distance; situated at or done from a height; above others in rank, position, etc; greater in size, amount, cost, etc than usual; raised or acute in pitch; (*meat*) slightly bad; (*inf*) intoxicated; (*inf*) under the influence of drugs. * *adv* in or to a high degree, rank, etc. * *n* a high level, place, etc; an area of high barometric pressure; (*inf*) a euphoric condition induced by alcohol or drugs.

High Arctic *n* (*Cdn*) the part of the Arctic within the Arctic Circle.—*also* **High North.**

highbrow *n* (*inf*) an intellectual.—*also adj*.

High Commission *n* a diplomatic mission representing one member country in the Commonwealth of Nations in another.—**High Commissioner** *n*.

high-flyer, high-flier *n* an ambitious person; a person of great ability in any profession.

high-handed *adj* overbearing.

highjack *see* **hijack.**

highlight *n* the lightest area of a painting, etc; the most interesting or important feature; (*pl*) lightening of areas of the hair using a bleach. * *vt* to bring to special attention; to give highlights to.

highly *adv* highly, very much; favorably; at a high level, wage, rank, etc.

highness *n* the state or quality of being high; (*with cap*) a title used in speaking to or of royalty.

High North *n* High Arctic.

high-rise *adj* (*building*) having multiple storeys.—*also n.*

high school *n* a secondary school.

highway *n* a public road; a main thoroughfare.

hijack *vt* to steal (goods in transit) by force; to force (an aircraft) to make an unscheduled flight. * *n* a hijacking.—*also* **highjack.**—**hijacker, highjacker** *n.*

hike *vi* to take a long walk. * *vt* (*inf*) to pull up. * *n* a long walk; a tramp.—**hiker** *n.*

hilarious *adj* highly amusing.—**hilariously** *adv.*—**hilarity** *n.*

hill *n* a natural rise of land lower than a mountain; a heap or mound; an slope in a road, etc.; (*with cap*) (*Cdn*) Parliament Hill.—**hilly** *adj.*

hilt *n* the handle of a sword, dagger, tool, etc.

him *pron* the objective case of **he.**

himself *pron* the reflexive or emphatic form of **he, him.**

hind[1] *adj* (**hinder, hindmost** *or* **hindermost**) situated at the back; rear.

hind[2] *n* (*pl* **hinds, hind**) a female deer.

hinder *vt* to keep back, or prevent the progress of. * *vi* to be an obstacle.—**hinderer** *n.*—**hinderingly** *adv.*

hindrance *n* the act of hindering; an obstacle, impediment.

hinge *n* a joint or flexible part on which a door, lid, etc turns; a natural joint, as of a clam; a small piece of gummed paper for sticking stamps in an album. * *vti* to attach or hang by a hinge; to depend.

hint *n* an indirect or subtle suggestion; a slight mention; a little piece of practical or helpful advice. * *vt* to suggest or indicate indirectly. * *vi* to give a hint.

hip[1] *n* either side of the body below the waist and above the thigh.

hip[2] *n* the fruit of the wild rose.

hip[3] *interj* used as part of a cheer (**hip, hip, hurrah**).

hip[4] *adj* (*sl*) stylish, up-to-date.

hippopotamus *n* (*pl* **hippopotamuses**) a large African water-loving mammal with thick dark skin, short legs, and a very large head and muzzle.

hire *vt* to pay for the services of (a person) or the use of (a thing). * *n* the payment for the temporary use of anything.—**hirer** *n.*

hire-purchase *n* a system by which a person takes possession of an article after paying a deposit and then becomes the owner only after payment of a series of instalments is completed.

his *poss pron* of or belonging to **him.**—*also adj.*

hiss *vi* to make a sound resembling a prolonged *s*; to show disapproval by hissing. * *vt* to say or indicate by hissing. * *n* the act or sound of hissing.

historian *n* a person who writes or studies history.

historic *adj* (potentially) important or famous in history.

historical *adj* belonging to or involving history or historical methods; concerning actual events as opposed to myth or legend; based on history.—**historically** *adv.*

history *n* a record or account of past events; the study, analysis of past events; past events in total; the past events or experiences of a specific person or thing; an unusual or significant past.

hit *vti* (*pt* **hit**) to come against (something) with force; to give a blow (to), to strike; to strike with a missile; to affect strongly; to arrive at; (*with* **on**) to discover by accident or unexpectedly. * *n* a blow that strikes its mark; a collision; a successful and popular song, book, etc; (*inf*) an underworld killing; (*sl*) a dose of a drug.

hit-and-run *n* a motor vehicle accident in which the driver leaves the scene without stopping or informing the authorities.

hitch *vt* to move, pull, etc with jerks; to fasten with a hook, knot, etc; to obtain a ride by hitchhiking. * *vi* to hitchhike. * *n* a tug; a hindrance, obstruction; a kind of knot used for temporary fastening; (*inf*) a ride obtained from hitchhiking.

hitchhike *vt* to travel by asking for free lifts from motorists along the way. —**hitchhiker** *n.*

hive *n* a shelter for a colony of bees; a beehive; the bees of a hive; a crowd of busy people; a place of great activity. * *vt* to gather (bees) into a hive. * *vi* to enter the hive; (*with* **off**) to separate from a group.

HMCS *abbr* = Her Majesty's Canadian Ship.

HMS *abbr* = Her (or His) Majesty's Ship.

hoard *n* an accumulation of food, money, etc stored away for future use. * *vti* to accumulate and store away.—**hoarder** *n.*

hoarding *n* a temporary screen of boards erected around a construction site; a large board used for advertising.

hoarse *adj* (*voice*) rough, as from a cold; (*person*) having a hoarse voice. —**hoarsely** *adv.*—**hoarseness** *n.*

hoax *n* a deception; a practical joke. * *vt* to deceive by a hoax.—**hoaxer** *n.*

hob *n* a ledge near a fireplace for keeping kettles, etc hot; a flat surface on a cooker incorporating hot plates or burners.

hobble *vi* to walk unsteadily, to limp. * *vt* to fasten the legs of (horses, etc) loosely together to prevent straying. * *n* a limp; a rope etc used to hobble a horse.

hobby *n* a spare-time activity carried out for personal amusement.

hock[1] *vt* (*sl*) to give something in security for a loan.

hock[2] *n* the joint bending backward on the hind leg of a horse, etc.

hock[3] *n* a variety of German white wine.

hockey *n* an outdoor game played by two teams

of 11 players with a ball and clubs curved at one end; ice hockey.

hoe *n* a long-handled tool for weeding, loosening the earth, etc. * *vti* (*pr p* **hoeing**, *pt* **hoed**) to dig, weed, till, etc with a hoe.

hog *n* a castrated male pig raised for its meat; (*inf*) a selfish, greedy, or filthy person. * *vt* (*pt* **hogged**) to take more than one's due; to hoard greedily.

Hogtown *n* (*Cdn*) (*sl*) Toronto, Canada.

hoist *vt* to raise aloft, esp with a pulley, crane, etc. * *n* a hoisting; an apparatus for lifting.

hold[1] *vb* (*pt* **held**) *vt* to take and keep in one's possession; to grasp; to maintain in a certain position or condition; to retain; to contain; to own, to occupy; to support, sustain; to remain firm; to carry on, as a meeting; to regard; to believe, to consider; to bear or carry oneself; (*with* **back**) to withhold; to restrain; (*with* **down**) to restrain; (*inf*) to manage to retain one's job, etc; (*with* **forth**) to offer (eg an inducement); (*with* **off**) to keep apart; (*with* **up**) to delay; to hinder; to commit an armed robbery. * *vi* to go on being firm, loyal, etc; to remain unbroken or unyielding; to be true or valid; to continue; (*with* **back**) to refrain; (*with* **forth**) to speak at length; (*with* **off**) to wait, to refrain; (*with* **on**) to maintain a grip on; to persist; (*inf*) to keep a telephone line open. * *n* the act or manner of holding; grip; a dominating force on a person.—**holder** *n*.

hold[2] *n* the storage space in a ship or aircraft used for cargo.

holdall *n* a portable container for miscellaneous articles.

holding *n* (*often pl*) property, esp land, stocks and bonds; the action of illegally blocking or obstructing an opponent in a sports contest.

hold-up *n* a delay; an armed robbery.

hole *n* a hollow place; a cavity; a pit; an animal's burrow; an aperture; a perforation; a small, squalid, dingy place; (*inf*) a difficult situation; (*golf*) a small cavity into which the ball is hit; the tee, the fairway, etc leading to this. * *vti* to make a hole in (something); to drive into a hole; (*with* **up**) to hibernate; (*inf*) to hide oneself.

holey *adj* full of holes.

holiday *n* a period away from work, school, etc for travel, rest or recreation; a day of freedom from work, etc, esp one set aside by law. * *vi* to spend a holiday..

holiday-maker *n* a person on holiday.

holiness *n* sanctity; (*with cap*) the title of the Pope.

hollow *adj* having a cavity within or below; recessed, concave; empty or worthless. * *n* a hole, cavity; a depression, a valley.* *vti* to make or become hollow.—**hollowly** *adv*.

holly *n* an evergreen shrub with prickly leaves and red berries.

holster *n* a leather case attached to a belt for a pistol.

holy *adj* (**holier, holiest**) dedicated to religious use; without sin; deserving reverence.

Holy Ghost *n* the Holy Spirit.

Holy Spirit *n* the Third Person of the Trinity.

homage *n* a public demonstration of respect or honor towards someone or something.

home *n* the place where one lives; the city, etc where one was born or reared; a place thought of as home; a household and its affairs; an institution for the aged, orphans, etc. * *adj* of one's home or country; domestic. * *adv* at, to, or in the direction of home; to the point aimed at. * *vi* (*birds*) to return home; to be guided onto a target; to head for a destination; to send or go home.

home child *n* (*Cdn*) (*hist*) one of the orphaned or homeless children who were sent from Britain to Canada to serve as farm or domestic workers.

home ice *n* the rink or arena where a hockey team or curling rink normally plays when not playing away from home.

homeland *n* the country where a person was born.

homely *adj* (**homelier, homeliest**) simple, everyday; crude; not good-looking.—**homeliness** *n*.

home-made *adj* made, or as if made, at home.

homeopath *n* a medical practitioner of homeopathy.—*also* **homoeopath, homeopathist, homoeopathist.**

homeopathy *n* the system of treating disease by small quantities of drugs that cause symptoms similar to those of the disease.—*also* **homoeopathy.** —**homeopathic, homoeopathic** *adj*.—**homeopathically, homoeopathically** *adv*.

homesick *adj* longing for home.—**homesickness** *n*.

homeward *adj* going towards home. * *adv* homewards.

homework *n* work, esp piecework, done at home; schoolwork to be done outside the classroom; preliminary study for a project.

homicide *n* the killing of a person by another; a person who kills another. —**homicidal** *adj*.

homoeopath, homoeopathy *see* **homeopath, homeopathy.**

homogeneous *adj* composed of parts that are of identical or a similar kind or nature; of uniform structure.—**homogeneity** *n*.

homosexual *adj* sexually attracted towards a person of the same sex. * *n* a homosexual person.—**homosexuality** *n*.

honest *adj* truthful; trustworthy; sincere or genuine; gained by fair means; frank, open.

honestly *adv* in an honest manner; really.

honesty *n* the quality of being honest; a plant that forms transparent seed pods.

honey *n* (*pl* **honeys**) a sweet sticky yellowish substance that bees make as food from the nectar of flowers; sweetness; its color; (*inf*) darling. * *adj* of, resembling honey; much loved.

honey bucket *n* (*sl*) a container for human waste, esp in an outdoor toilet.

honeycomb *n* the structure of six-sided wax cells made by bees to hold their honey, eggs, etc; anything arranged like this. * *vt* to fill with holes like a honeycomb.

honeymoon *n* the vacation spent together by a newly married couple.—*also vi.*—**honeymooner** *n*.

honk *n* (a sound like) the call of the wild goose; the sound made by an old-fashioned motor horn.—*also vti.*

honor *n* high regard or respect; glory; fame; good reputation; integrity; chastity; high rank; distinction; (*with cap*) the title of certain officials, as judges; cards of the highest value in certain card games. * *vt* to respect greatly; to do or give something in honor of; to accept and pay (a cheque when due, etc).

honorable *adj* worthy of being honored; honest; upright; bringing honor; (*with cap*) a title of respect for certain officials, as Members of Parliament, when addressing each other.—**honorably** *adv*.

honorary *adj* given as an honor; (*office*) voluntary, unpaid.

hood[1] *n* a loose covering to protect the head and back of the neck; any hood-like thing as the (folding) top of a car, etc; a car bonnet.

hood[2] *n* (*inf*) a hoodlum.

hoodwink *vt* to mislead by trickery.

hoof *n* (*pl* **hoofs, hooves**) the horny covering on the ends of the feet of certain animals, as horses, cows, etc.

hook *n* a piece of bent or curved metal to catch or hold anything; a fishhook; something shaped like a hook; a strike, blow, etc, in which a curving motion is involved. * *vt* to seize, fasten, hold, as with a hook; (*rugby*) to pass the ball backwards from a scrum.

hooking *n* an illegal check in ice hockey in which a player hooks an opponent with a stick, usu from behind.

hooligan *n* a lawless young person.—**hooliganism** *n*.

hoop *n* a circular band of metal or wood; an iron band for holding together the staves of barrels; anything like this, as a child's toy or ring in a hoop skirt. * *vt* to bind (as if) with hoops.

hoot *n* the sound that an owl makes; a similar sound, as made by a train whistle; a shout of scorn; (*inf*) laughter; (*inf*) an amusing person or thing. * *vi* to utter a hoot; to blow a whistle, etc. * *vt* to express (scorn) of (someone) by hooting.

hooter *n* something that hoots, such as a car horn; (*sl*) a nose.

hooves *see* hoof.

hop[1] *vi* (*pt* **hopped**) to jump up on one leg; to leap with all feet at once, as a frog, etc; (*inf*) to make a quick trip. * *n* a hopping movement; (*inf*) an informal dance; a trip, esp in an aircraft.

hop[2] *n* a climbing plant with small cone-shaped flowers; (*pl*) the dried ripe cones, used for flavoring beer.

hope *n* a feeling that what is wanted will happen; the object of this; a person or thing on which one may base some hope. * *vt* to

want and expect. * *vi* to have hope (for).

hopeful *adj* filled with hope; inspiring hope or promise of success. * *n* a person who hopes to or looks likely to be a success.

hopefully *adv* in a hopeful manner; it is hoped.

hopeless *adj* without hope; offering no grounds for hope or promise of success; impossible to solve; (*inf*) incompetent.—**hopelessly** *adv*.—**hopelessness** *n*.

horde *n* a crowd or throng; a swarm.

horizon *n* the apparent line along which the earth and sky meet; the limit of a person's knowledge, interest, etc.

horizontal *adj* level; parallel to the plane of the horizon.—**horizontally** *adv*.

hormone *n* a product of living cells formed in one part of the organism and carried to another part, where it takes effect; a synthetic compound having the same purpose. —**hormonal** *adj*.

horn *n* a bony outgrowth on the head of certain animals; the hard substance of which this is made; any projection like a horn; a wind instrument, esp the French horn or trumpet; a device to sound a warning.

horned *adj* having horns.

hornet *n* a large wasp with a severe sting.

horny *adj* (**hornier, horniest**) like horn; hard; callous; (*sl*) sexually aroused.

horoscope *n* a chart of the signs and positions of planets, etc, by which astrologers profess to predict future events, esp in the life of an individual.

horrible *adj* arousing horror; (*inf*) very bad, unpleasant, etc.—**horribly** *adv*.

horrid *adj* terrible; horrible.—**horridly** *adv*.

horrify *vt* to fill with horror.

horror *n* the strong feeling caused by something frightful or shocking; strong dislike; a person, thing inspiring horror.

hors-d'oeuvre *n* an appetizer served at the beginning of a meal.

horse *n* four-legged, solid-hoofed herbivorous mammal with a flowing mane and a tail, domesticated for carrying loads or riders, etc; cavalry; a vaulting horse; a frame with legs to support something.

horse chestnut *n* a large tree with large palmate leaves and erect clusters of flowers.

horseman *n* a person skilled in the riding or care of horses; (*Cdn*) (*inf*) a member of the Royal Canadian Mounted Police.—**horsemanship** *n*.

horsepower *n* a unit for measuring the power of engines, etc, equal to 746 watts or 33,000 foot-pounds per minute.

horseradish *n* a tall herb of the mustard family; a sauce or relish made with its pungent root.

horseshoe *n* a flat U-shaped, protective metal plate nailed to a horse's hoof; anything shaped like this.

horticulture *n* the art or science of growing flowers, fruits, and vegetables.—**horticultural** *adj*.—**horticulturist** *n*.

hose[1] *n* a flexible tube used to convey fluids. * *vt* to spray with a hose.

hose[2] *n* (*pl* **hose**) stockings, socks, tights collectively.

hoser n (Cdn) (sl) an ignorant and boorish man, fond of drinking beer.

hosiery n stockings; socks.

hospitable adj offering a generous welcome to guests or strangers; sociable.—**hospitably** adv.

hospital n an institution where the sick or injured are given medical treatment.

hospitality n the act, practice, or quality of being hospitable.

host[1] n a person who receives or entertains a stranger or guest at his house; an animal or plant on or in which another lives; a compere on a television or radio programme. * vti to act as a host (to a party, television programme, etc).

host[2] n a very large number of people or things.

host[3] n the wafer of bread used in the Eucharist or Holy Communion.

hostage n a person given or kept as security until certain conditions are met.

hostel n a lodging place for the homeless, travellers, or other groups.

hostess n a woman acting as a host; a woman who entertains guests at a nightclub, etc.

hostile adj of or being an enemy; unfriendly.—**hostilely** adv.

hostility n enmity, antagonism; (pl) deliberate acts of warfare.

hot adj (**hotter, hottest**) of high temperature; very warm; giving or feeling heat; causing a burning sensation on the tongue; full of intense feeling; following closely; electrically charged; (inf) recent, new; (inf) radioactive; (inf) stolen. * adv in a hot manner.—**hotly** adv.—**hotness** n.

hot dog n a sausage, esp a frankfurter, served in a long soft roll.

hotel n a commercial establishment providing lodging and meals for travellers, etc.

hotelier n the owner or manager of a hotel.

hothead n an impetuous person.—**hot-headed** adj.

hothouse n a heated greenhouse for raising plants; an environment that encourages rapid growth.

hotplate n a heated surface for cooking or keeping food warm; a small portable heating device.

hound n a dog used in hunting; a contemptible person. * vt to hunt or chase as with hounds; to urge on by harassment.—**hounder** n.

hour n a period of 60 minutes, a 24th part of a day; the time for a specific activity; the time; a special point in time; the distance covered in an hour; (pl) the customary period for work, etc.

hourly adj occurring every hour; done during an hour; frequent. * adv at every hour; frequently.

house n a building to live in, esp by one person or family; a household; a family or dynasty including relatives, ancestors and descendants; the audience in a theatre; a business firm; a legislative assembly. * vt to provide accommodation or storage for; to cover, encase.

house arrest n detention in one's own house, as opposed to prison.

houseboat n a boat furnished and used as a home.

housebreaker n a burglar; a person employed to demolish buildings.—**housebreaking** n.

household n all those people living together in the same house. * adj pertaining to running a house and family; domestic; familiar.

housekeeper n a person who runs a home, esp one hired to do so.

housekeeping n the daily running of a household; (inf) money used for domestic expenses; routine maintenance of equipment, records, etc in an organization.

house league n (Cdn) a sports league whose teams are formed from members of the same school or organization.

house warming n a party given to celebrate moving into a new house.

housewife n the woman who keeps house.—**housewifery** n.

housework n the cooking, cleaning, etc involved in running a home.

housing n houses collectively; the provision of accommodation; a casing enclosing a piece of machinery, etc; a slot or groove in a piece of wood, etc to receive an insertion.

housing estate n accommodation, shops, leisure facilities, etc planned as a single unit.

hovel n a small miserable dwelling.

hover vi (bird, etc) to hang in the air stationary; to hang about, to linger.

hovercraft n a land or water vehicle that travels supported on a cushion of air.

how adv in what way or manner; by what means; to what extent; in what condition.

howl vi to utter the long, wailing cry of wolves, dogs, etc; to utter a similar cry of anger, pain, etc; to shout or laugh in pain, amusement, etc. * vt to utter with a howl; to drive by howling. * n the wailing cry of a wolf, dog, etc; any similar sound.

howler n (inf) a stupid mistake.

HP abbr = hire purchase; horsepower; high pressure; Houses of Parliament.

HQ abbr = headquarters.

HST abbr (Cdn) = Harmonized Sales Tax.

hub n the centre part of a wheel; a centre of activity.

hubbub n a confused noise of many voices; an uproar.

huddle vti to crowd together in a confined space; to curl (oneself) up. * n a confused crowd or heap.

Hudson's Bay blanket n (Cdn) a woollen blanket with a creamy white background and a pattern of white coloured stripes.

hue n color; a particular shade or tint of a color.

huff n a state of smouldering resentment. * vi to blow; to puff.—**huffy** adj.—**huffily** adv.

hug vb (pt **hugged**) vt to hold or squeeze tightly

with the arms; to cling to; to keep close to. * *vi* to embrace one another. * *n* a strong embrace.—**huggable** *adj*.

huge *adj* very large, enormous.—**hugely** *adv*.—**hugeness** *n*.

hulk *n* the body of a ship, esp if old and dismantled; a large, clumsy person or thing.

hulking *adj* unwieldy, bulky.

hull *n* the outer covering of a fruit or seed; the framework of a ship. * *vt* to remove the hulls of; to pierce the hull of (a ship, etc).

hullo *see* **hello**.

hum *vb* (*pt* **hummed**) *vi* to make a low continuous vibrating sound; to hesitate in speaking and utter an inarticulate sound; (*inf*) to be lively, busy; (*sl*) to stink. * *vt* to sing with closed lips. * *n* a humming sound; a murmur; (*sl*) a stink.

human *adj* of or relating to human beings; having the qualities of humans as opposed to animals; kind, considerate. * *n* a human being.

humane *adj* kind, compassionate, merciful.—**humanely** *adv*.

humanity *n* the human race; the state or quality of being human or humane; philanthropy; kindness; (*pl*) the study of literature and the arts, as opposed to the sciences.

humble *adj* having a low estimation of one's abilities; modest, unpretentious; servile. * *vt* to lower in condition or rank; to humiliate.—**humbly** *adv*.—**humbleness** *n*.

humbug *n* fraud, sham, hoax; an insincere person; a peppermint-flavored sweet. * *vt* (*pt* **humbugged**) to cheat or impose upon; to hoax.

humdrum *adj* dull, ordinary, boring.

humid *adj* (*air*) moist, damp.

humidex *n* (*Cdn*) a measure of the amount of discomfort caused by a combination of heat and humidity in the air.

humidity *n* (a measure of the amount of) dampness in the air.

humiliate *vt* to cause to feel humble; to lower the pride or dignity of.—**humiliation** *n*.

humility *n* the state of being humble.

humorist *n* a person who writes or speaks in a humorous manner.

humorous *adj* funny, amusing; causing laughter.—**humorously** *adv*.—**humorousness** *n*.

humour, humor (*US*) *n* the ability to appreciate or express what is funny, amusing, etc; the expression of this; temperament, disposition; state of mind; (*formerly*) any of the four fluids of the body (blood, phlegm, yellow and black bile) that were thought to determine temperament. * *vt* to indulge; to gratify by conforming to the wishes of.—**humourless** *adj*.

hump *n* a rounded protuberance; a fleshy lump on the back of an animal (as a camel or whale); a deformity causing curvature of the spine. * *vt* to hunch; to arch.

humpback *n* a hunchback.—**humpbacked** *adj*.

hunch *n* a hump; (*inf*) an intuitive feeling. * *vt*

to arch into a hump. * *vi* to move forward jerkily.

hunchback *n* a person with curvature of the spine.

hundred *adj, n* ten times ten; the symbol for this(100, C, c); the hundredth in a series or set.

hundredweight *n* a unit of weight, equal to 112 pounds in Britain and 100 pounds in the US.

hung *see* **hang**.

hunger *n* (a feeling weak or empty from) a need for food; a strong desire. * *vi* to feel hunger; to have a strong desire (for).

hungry *adj* (**hungrier, hungriest**) desiring food; craving for something; greedy.—**hungrily** *adv*.

hunt *vti* to seek out to kill or capture (game) for food or sport; to search (for); to chase. * *n* a chase; a search; a party organized for hunting.

hunter *n* a person who hunts; a horse used in hunting.—**huntress** *nf*.

hunting *n* the art or practice of one who hunts; a pursuit; a search.

hurdle *n* a portable frame of bars for temporary fences or for jumping over by horses or runners; an obstacle. (*pl*) a race over hurdles.—**hurdler** *n*.

hurl *vt* to throw violently; to utter vehemently.—*also n*.

hurrah *interj* an exclamation of approval or joy.

hurricane *n* a violent tropical cyclone with winds of at least 74 miles per hour.

hurried *adj* performed with great haste.—**hurriedly** *adv*.

hurry *n* rush; urgency; eagerness to do, go, etc. * *vt* to cause to move or happen more quickly. * *vi* to move or act with haste.

hurt *vb* (*pt* **hurt**) *vt* to cause physical pain to; to injure, damage; to offend. * *vi* to feel pain; to cause pain.—**hurtful** *adj*.

hurtle *vti* to move or throw with great speed and force.

husband *n* a man to whom a woman is married. * *vt* to conserve; to manage economically.

hush *vti* to make or become silent. * *n* a silence or calm.

husk *n* the dry covering of certain fruits and seeds; any dry, rough, or useless covering. * *vt* to strip the husk from.

husky[1] *adj* (**huskier, huskiest**) (*voice*) hoarse; rough-sounding; hefty, strong. —**huskily** *adv*.—**huskiness** *n*.

husky[2] *n* an Arctic sled dog.

hustle *vt* to jostle or push roughly or hurriedly; to force hurriedly; (*sl*) to obtain by rough or illegal means. * *vi* to move hurriedly. * *n* an instance of hustling.—**hustler** *n*.

hut *n* a very plain or crude little house or cabin.

hutch *n* a pen or coop for small animals; a hut.

hyacinth *n* a plant of the lily family with spikes of bell-shaped flowers; the orange gemstone jacinth; a light violet to moderate purple.

hyaena *see* **hyena**.

hybrid n the offspring of two plants or animals of different species; a mongrel. * adj crossbred.

hydrant n a large pipe with a valve for drawing water from a main.

hydraulic adj operated by water or other liquid, esp by moving through pipes under pressure; of hydraulics.—**hydraulically** adv.

hydraulics npl (used as sing) the science dealing with the mechanical properties of liquids and their application in engineering.

hydro n (Cdn) electricity, especially hydroelectricity.

hydroelectricity n electricity generated by water power.—**hydroelectric** adj.

hydrogen n a flammable, colorless, odourless, tasteless, gaseous chemical element, the lightest substance known.

hyena n a nocturnal, carnivorous, scavenging mammal like a wolf.—also **hyaena**.

hygiene n the principles and practice of health and cleanliness.—**hygienic** adj.—**hygienically** adv.

hymn n a song of praise to God or other object of worship.

hyphen n a punctuation mark (-) used to join two syllables or words, or to divide words into parts. * vt to hyphenate.

hypnosis n (pl **hypnoses**) a relaxed state resembling sleep in which the mind responds to external suggestion.

hypnotism n the act of inducing hypnosis; the study and use of hypnosis. —**hypnotist** n.

hypnotize vt to put in a state of hypnosis; to fascinate.

hypocrisy n a falsely pretending to possess virtues, beliefs, etc; an example of this.—**hypocrite** n.—**hypocritical** adj.—**hypocritically** adv.

hypothesis n (pl **hypotheses**) something assumed for the purpose of argument; a theory to explain some fact that may or may not prove to be true; supposition; conjecture.

hypothetical adj based on hypothesis, conjectural.—**hypothetically** adv.

hysteria n a mental disorder marked by excitability, anxiety, imaginary organic disorders, etc; frenzied emotion or excitement.

hysteric n a hysterical person; (pl) fits of hysteria.

hysterical adj caused by hysteria; suffering from hysteria; (inf) extremely funny.—**hysterically** adv.

I pron the person who is speaking or writing, used in referring to himself or herself.

ice n water frozen solid; a sheet of this; a portion of ice cream or water ice; (sl) diamonds. * vti (often with **up** or **over**) to freeze; to cool with ice; to cover with icing.

iceberg n a great mass of mostly submerged ice floating in the sea.

icebox n a compartment in a refrigerator for making and storing ice; a refrigerator.

ice bridge n (Cdn) a formation of ice across a body of water strong enough to support motor or other traffic.

ice cream adj a sweet frozen food, made from flavored milk or cream.

ice fishing n the activity of fishing through holes cut in the ice of a lake or river.

ice hockey n indoor or outdoor hockey played on ice by two teams of six skaters with curved sticks and a puck.

ice hole n (Cdn) a hole cut in ice so that people may fish.

ice road n (Cdn) a road built across a frozen body of water.

icicle n a hanging tapering length of ice formed when dripping water freezes.

icing n a semi-solid sugary mixture covering cakes, etc.

icon n an image; (Eastern Church) a sacred image, usu on a wooden panel.

icy adj (**icier, iciest**) full of, made of, or covered with ice; slippery or very cold; cold in manner.—**icily** adv.—**iciness** n.

I'd = I had, I should, I would.

idea n a mental impression of anything; a vague impression, notion; an opinion or belief; a scheme; a supposition; a person's conception of something; a significance or purpose.

ideal adj existing in the mind or as an idea; satisfying an ideal, perfect. * n the most perfect conception of anything; a person, thing regarded as perfect; a standard for attainment or imitation; an aim or principle.—**ideally** adv.

identical adj exactly the same; having the same origin.—**identically** adv.

identification n the act of identifying; the state of being identified; that which identifies.

identify vt to consider to be the same, equate; to establish the identity of; to associate closely; to regard (oneself) as similar to another.—**identifier** n.

identity n the state of being exactly alike; the distinguishing characteristics of a person, personality; the state of being the same as a specified person or thing.

ideology n the doctrines, beliefs or opinions of an individual, social class, political party, etc.—**ideological** adj.—**ideologist, ideologue** n.

idiocy n mental deficiency; stupidity; imbecility; something stupid, foolish.

idiom n an accepted phrase or expression with a different meaning from the literal; the usual way in which the words of a language are used to express thought; the dialect of a people, region, etc; the characteristic style of a school of art, literature, etc—**idiomatic** adj.—**idiomatically** adv.

idiosyncrasy n a type of behaviour or characteristic peculiar to a person or group; a quirk, eccentricity.—**idiosyncratic** adj.

idiot n a severely mentally retarded adult; (inf) a foolish or stupid person.

idiotic *adj* stupid; senseless.—**idiotically** *adv*.

idle *adj* not employed, unoccupied; not in use; averse to work; useless; worthless. * *vt* to waste or spend (time) in idleness. * *vi* to move slowly or aimlessly; (*engine*) to operate without transmitting power.—**idleness** *n*.—**idler** *n*.—**idly** *adv*.

idol *n* an image or object worshipped as a god; a person who is intensely loved, admired or honored.

idolize *vt* to make an idol of, for worship; to love to excess.—**idolization** *n*.

i.e. *abbr* = *id est*, that is.

if *conj* on condition that; in the event that; supposing that; even though; whenever; whether.

igloo *n* an Inuit house built of blocks of snow and ice.

ignite *vti* to set fire to; to catch fire; to burn or cause to burn.

ignition *n* an act or instance of igniting; the starting of an internal combustion engine; the mechanism that ignites an internal combustion engine.

ignorant *adj* lacking knowledge; uninformed, uneducated; resulting from or showing lack of knowledge.—**ignorance** *n*.—**ignorantly** *adv*.

ignore *vt* to disregard; to deliberately refuse to notice someone.

ill *adj* not in good health; harmful; bad; hostile; faulty; unfavorable. * *adv* badly, wrongly; hardly, with difficulty. * *n* trouble; harm; evil.

I'll = I shall, I will.

ill-advised *adj* unwise.

ill at ease *adj* uneasy, embarrassed.

illegal *adj* against the law.—**illegally** *adv*.—**illegality** *n*.

illegible *adj* impossible to read.—**illegibly** *adv*.—**illegibility** *n*.

illegitimate *adj* born of parents not married to each other; contrary to law, rules, or logic.—**illegitimately** *adv*.—**illegitimacy** *n*.

illicit *adj* improper; unlawful.—**illicitly** *adv*.

illiterate *adj* uneducated, esp not knowing how to read or write. * *n* an illiterate person.—**illiterately** *adv*.—**illiteracy** *n*.

ill-natured *adj* spiteful.

illness *n* a state of ill-health; sickness.

illogical *adj* not logical or reasonable.—**illogically** *adv*.—**illogicality** *n*.

ill-treat *vt* to treat unkindly, unfairly, etc.—**ill-treatment** *n*.

illuminate *vt* to give light to; to light up; to make clear; to inform; to decorate as with gold or lights.—**illumination** *n*.—**illuminative** *adj*.

illusion *n* a false idea or conception; an unreal or misleading image or appearance.—**illusional, illusionary** *adj*.

illusory, illusive *adj* deceptive; based on illusion.

illustrate *vt* to explain, as by examples; to provide (books, etc) with explanatory pictures, charts, etc; to serve as an example.—**illustrative** *adj*.—**illustrator** *n*.

illustration *n* the act of illustrating; the state of being illustrated; an example that explains or corroborates; a picture or diagram in a book, etc.

illustrious *adj* distinguished, famous. —**illustriousness** *n*.

ill-will *n* antagonism, hostility.

I'm = I am.

image *n* a representation of a person or thing; the visual impression of something in a lens, mirror, etc; a copy; a likeness; a mental picture; the concept of a person, product, etc held by the public at large. * *vt* to make a representation of; to reflect; to imagine.

imagery *n* the work of the imagination; mental pictures; figures of speech; images in general or collectively.

imaginary *adj* existing only in the imagination.

imagination *n* the image-forming power of the mind, or the power of the mind that modifies the conceptions, esp the higher form of this power exercised in art and poetry; creative ability; resourcefulness in overcoming practical difficulties, etc.

imaginative *adj* having or showing imagination; produced by imagination.—**imaginatively** *adv*.

imagine *vt* to form a mental image of; to believe falsely; (*inf*) to suppose; to guess. * *vi* to employ the imagination.

IMAX *n* (*Cdn*) (*TM*) a form of cinematography in which extra-large film is shot and then projected on a giant screen.

imbalance *n* a lack of balance, as in proportion, emphasis, etc.

imbecile *n* an adult with a mental age of a three- to eight-year-old child; an idiotic person. * *adj* stupid or foolish.—**imbecility** *n*.

imitate *vt* to try to follow as a pattern or model; to mimic humorously, impersonate; to copy, reproduce.—**imitator** *n*.

imitation *n* an act or instance of imitating; a copy; an act of mimicking or impersonation.

immaculate *adj* spotless; flawless; pure, morally unblemished.—**immaculately** *adv*.

immaterial *adj* spiritual as opposed to physical; unimportant.

immature *adj* not mature.—**immaturity** *n*.

immediate *adj* acting or occurring without delay; next, nearest, without intervening agency; next in relationship; in close proximity, near to; directly concerning or touching a person or thing.—**immediacy** *n*.

immediately *adv* without delay; directly; near, close by. * *conj* as soon as.

immense *adj* very large in size or extent; limitless; (*inf*) excellent.—**immensely** *adv*.

immerse *vt* to plunge into a liquid; to absorb or engross; to baptize by total submergence.—**immersible** *adj*.

immersion heater *n* an electric element for heating liquids, esp water in a domestic hot-water tank.

immigrant *n* a person who immigrates; a person recently settled in a country but not born there.

immigrate *vi* to come into a new country, esp to settle permanently.—**immigration** *n.*—**immigratory** *adj.*

imminent *adj* about to happen; impending.—**imminence** *n.*—**imminently** *adv.*

immobilize *vt* to make immobile.—**immobilization** *n.*

immoral *adj* against accepted standards of proper behaviour; sexually degenerate; corrupt; wicked.—**immorally** *adv.*—**immorality** *n.*

immortal *adj* living for ever; enduring; having lasting fame. * *n* an immortal being or person; (*pl*) the gods of classical mythology.—**immortality** *n.*

immortalize *vt* to render immortal; to bestow lasting fame upon.—**immortalization** *n.*

immune *adj* not susceptible to a specified disease through inoculation or natural resistance; conferring immunity; exempt from a certain obligation, tax, duty, etc.

immunize *vt* to make immune, esp against infection.—**immunization** *n.*

impact *n* violent contact; a shocking effect; the force of a body colliding with another. * *vt* to force tightly together. * *vi* to hit with force.—**impaction** *n.*

impair *vt* to make worse, less, etc.—**impairment** *n.*

impaired *adj* (*Cdn*) affected by alcohol or narcotics so as to prevent the safe driving of a motor vehicle.

impale *vt* to fix on, or pierce through, with something pointed.—**impalement** *n.*

impartial *adj* not favoring one side more than another, unbiased.—**impartiality** *n.*—**impartially** *adv.*

impassable *adj* (*roads, etc*) incapable of being travelled through or over.—**impassability** *n.*—**impassably** *adv.*

impatient *adj* lacking patience; intolerant of delay, etc; restless.—**impatience** *n.*—**impatiently** *adv.*

impeach *vt* to question a person's honesty; to try (a public official) on a charge of wrongdoing.—**impeachment** *n.*

impeccable *adj* without defect or error; faultless.—**impeccability** *n.*—**impeccably** *adv.*

impede *vt* to obstruct or hinder the progress of.

impediment *n* something that impedes; an obstruction; a physical defect, as a stammer that prevents fluency of speech.

impend *vi* to be imminent; to threaten.—**impending** *adj.*

imperative *adj* urgent, pressing; authoritative; obligatory; designating or of the mood of a verb that expresses a command, entreaty, etc. * *n* a command; (*gram*) the imperative mood of a verb.

imperceptible *adj* not able to be detected by the mind or senses; slight, minute, gradual.—**imperceptibility** *n.*—**imperceptibly** *adv.*

imperfect *adj* having faults, flaws, mistakes, etc; defective; incomplete; (*gram*) designating a verb tense that indicates a past action or state as incomplete or continuous.

* (*gram*) an imperfect tense.

imperfection *n* the state or quality of being imperfect; a defect, fault.

imperial *adj* of an empire, emperor, or empress; majestic; of great size or superior quality; of the British non-metric system of weights and measures.—**imperially** *adv.*

impersonal *adj* not referring to any particular person; cold, unfeeling; not existing as a person; (*verb*) occurring only in the third person singular, usu with "it" as subject.—**impersonality** *n.*—**impersonally** *adv.*

impersonate *vt* to assume the role of another person as entertainment or for fraud.—**impersonation** *n.*—**impersonator** *n.*

impertinent *adj* impudent; insolent; irrelevant.—**impertinence** *n.*—**impertinently** *adv.*

impervious *adj* incapable of being penetrated, as by water; not readily receptive (to) or affected (by).

impetuous *adj* acting or done suddenly with impulsive energy.—**impetuosity** *n.*—**impetuously** *adv.*

impetus *n* the force with which a body moves against resistance; driving force or motive.

impinge *vi* (*with* **on, upon**) to have an impact; to encroach.—**impingement** *n.*

implausible *adj* not plausible.—**implausibility** *n.*—**implausibly** *adv.*

implement *n* something used in a given activity. * *vt* to carry out, put into effect.—**implementation** *n.*

implicate *vt* to show to have a part, esp in a crime; to imply.

implication *n* an implicating or being implicated; that which is implied; an inference not expressed but understood; deduction.

implicit *adj* implied rather than stated explicitly; unquestioning, absolute.—**implicitly** *adv.*

implore *vt* to request earnestly; to plead, entreat.—**imploringly** *adv.*

imply *vt* to hint, suggest indirectly; to indicate or involve as a consequence.

impolite *adj* not polite, rude.—**impolitely** *adv.*—**impoliteness** *n.*

imponderable *adj* not able to be weighed or measured. * *n* something difficult to measure or assess.

import *vt* to bring (goods) in from a foreign country for sale or use; to mean; to signify. * *vi* to be of importance, to matter. * *n* something imported; meaning; importance.—**importable** *adj.*—**importer** *n.*

importance *n* the quality of being important; a high place in public estimation; high self-esteem.

important *adj* having great significance or consequence; (*person*) having power, authority, etc.—**importantly** *adv.*

impose *vt* to put (a burden, tax, punishment) on or upon; to force (oneself) on others; to lay pages of type or film and secure them. * *vi* (*with* **on** *or* **upon**) to take advantage of; to cheat or defraud.

imposing *adj* impressive because of size, appearance, dignity, etc.—**imposingly** *adv.*

impossibility n the character of being impossible; that which cannot be, or be supposed to be, done.

impossible adj not capable of existing, being done, or happening; (inf) unendurable, outrageous.—**impossibly** adv.

impostor, imposter n a person who acts fraudulently by impersonating another.

impotent adj lacking in necessary strength, powerless; (man) unable to engage in sexual intercourse.—**impotence** n.—**impotently** adv.

impound vt to take legal possession of; to shut up (an animal) in a pound.

impoverish vt to make poor; to deprive of strength.—**impoverishment** n.

impracticable adj not able to be carried out, not feasible.—**impracticability** n.—**impracticably** adv.

impractical adj not practical; not competent in practical skills.—**impracticality** n.—**impractically** adv.

imprecise adj not precise; ill-defined.—**imprecisely** adv.—**imprecision** n.

impregnable adj secure against attack, unyielding.—**impregnability** n.—**impregnably** adv.

impregnate vt to cause to become pregnant, to fertilize; to saturate, soak (with); to pervade.—**impregnation** n.

impresario n the manager of an opera, a concert series, etc.

impress[1] vt to make a strong, usu favorable, impression on; to fix deeply in the mind; to stamp with a mark; to imprint. * n an imprint, a mark.

impress[2] vt to coerce into military service.—**impressment** n.

impression n the effect produced in the mind by an experience; a mark produced by imprinting; a vague idea, notion; the act of impressing or being impressed; a notable or strong influence on the mind or senses; the number of copies of a book printed at one go; an impersonation or act of mimicry.

impressionable n easily impressed or influenced.—**impressionability** n.—**impressionably** adv.

impressive adj tending to impress the mind or emotions; arousing wonder or admiration.—**impressiveness** n.

imprison vt to put in a prison; to confine, as in a prison.—**imprisonment** n.

improbable adj unlikely to be true or to happen.—**improbability** n.—**improbably** adv.

impromptu adj, adv unrehearsed, unprepared. * n something impromptu, as a speech.

improper adj lacking propriety, indecent; incorrect; not suitable or appropriate.—**improperly** adv.

impropriety n the quality of being improper; indecency; an improper act, error.

improve vt to make or become better.—**improvable** adj.—**improver** n.

improvement n the act of improving or being improved; an alteration that improves or adds to the value of something.

improvise vti to compose, perform, recite, etc without preparation; to make or do with whatever is at hand.—**improvisation** n.—**improviser** n.

impulse n a sudden push or thrust; a stimulus transmitted through a nerve or a muscle; a sudden instinctive urge to act.

impulsive adj tending to act on impulse; forceful, impelling; acting momentarily.—**impulsively** adv.—**impulsiveness** n.

impunity n exemption or freedom from punishment or harm.

impure adj unclean; adulterated.

impurity n a being impure; an impure substance or constituent.

in prep inside; within; at; as contained by; during; at the end of; not beyond; affected by; being a member of; wearing; using; because of; into. * adv to or at a certain place; so as to be contained by a certain space, condition, etc; (games) batting, in play. * adj that is in power; inner; inside; gathered, counted, etc; (inf) currently smart, fashionable, etc.

in. abbr = inch(es).

inability n lack of ability.

inaccessible adj not accessible, unapproachable.—**inaccessibility** n.—**inaccessibly** adv.

inaccurate adj not accurate, imprecise.—**inaccuracy** n.—**inaccurately** adv.

inactive adj not active.—**inactively** adv.—**inactivity** n.

inadequate adj not adequate; not capable.— **inadequacy** n.—**inadequately** adv.

inadmissible adj not admissible, esp as evidence.—**inadmissibility** n.

inadvertent adj not attentive or observant, careless; due to oversight.—**inadvertence, inadvertency** n.—**inadvertently** adv.

inadvisable adj not advisable; inexpedient.—**inadvisably** adv.

inane adj lacking sense, silly.—**inanely** adv.—**inanity** n.

inanimate adj not animate; showing no signs of life; dull.—**inanimately** adv.—**inanimation** n.

inappropriate adj unsuitable.—**inappropriately** adv.—**inappropriateness** n.

inarticulate adj not expressed in words; incapable of being expressed in words; incapable of coherent or effective expression of ideas, feelings, etc.—**inarticulately** adv.

inasmuch adv in like degree; (with **as**) seeing that; because.

inattentive adj not attending; neglectful.—**inattention** n.

inaudible adj unable to be heard.—**inaudibility** n.—**inaudibly** adv.

inaugural n of or pertaining to an inauguration; a speech made at an inauguration.

inaugurate vt to admit ceremonially into office; to open (a building, etc) formally to the public; to cause to begin, initiate.—**inauguration** n.

inborn adj present from birth; hereditary.

inbred adj innate; produced by inbreeding.

inbreed vti (pt **inbred**) to breed by continual mating of individuals of the same or closely related stocks.

Inc. *abbr* = Incorporated.

incapable *adj* lacking capability; not able or fit to perform an activity.—**incapability** *n.*—**incapably** *adv.*

incapacitate *vt* to weaken, to disable; to make ineligible.—**incapacitation** *n.*

incarnate *adj* endowed with a human body; personified. * *vt* to give bodily form to; to be the type or embodiment of.—**incarnation** *n.*

incendiary *adj* pertaining to arson; (*bomb*) designed to start fires; tending to stir up or inflame. * *n* a person that sets fire to a building, etc maliciously, an arsonist; an incendiary substance (as in a bomb); a person who stirs up violence, etc.

incense[1] *vt* to make extremely angry.

incense[2] *n* a substance that gives off a fragrant odour when burned; the fumes so produced; any pleasant odour.

incessant *adj* never ceasing; continual, constant.—**incessantly** *adv.*

incest *n* sexual intercourse between persons too closely related to marry legally.

inch *n* a measure of length equal to one twelfth of a foot (2.54 cm); a very small distance or amount. * *vti* to move very slowly, or by degrees.

incidence *n* the degree or range of occurrence or effect.

incidental *adj* happening in connection with something more important; happening by chance. * *npl* miscellaneous items, minor expenses.

incidentally *adv* in passing, as an aside.

incinerator *n* a furnace for burning rubbish.

incipient *adj* beginning to be or appear; initial.—**incipience** *n.*

incision *n* incising; a cut made into something, esp by a surgeon into a body.

incisive *adj* keen, penetrating; decisive; biting.—**incisively** *adv.*—**incisiveness** *n.*

incite *vt* to urge to action; to rouse.—**incitement** *n.*

inclination *n* a propensity or disposition, esp a liking; a deviation from the horizontal or vertical; a slope; inclining or being inclined; a bending movement, a bow.

incline *vi* to lean, to slope; to be disposed towards an opinion or action. * *vt* to cause to bend (the head or body) forwards; to cause to deviate, esp from the horizontal or vertical. * *n* a slope.

include *vt* to enclose, contain; to comprise as part or a larger group, amount, etc.—**inclusion** *n.*

inclusive *adj* comprehensive; including the limits specified.—**inclusively** *adv.*

incognito *adj, adv* under an assumed name or identity. * *n* (*pl* **incognitos**) a person appearing or living incognito; the name assumed by such a person.—**incognita** *nf.*

incoherent *adj* lacking organization or clarity; inarticulate in speech or thought.—**incoher-**

ence *n.*—**incoherently** *adv.*

income *n* the money etc received for labour or services, or from property, investments, etc.

income tax *n* a tax levied on the net income of a person or business.

incoming *adj* coming; accruing. * *n* the act of coming in; that which comes in; income.

incompatible *adj* not able to exist together in harmony; antagonistic; inconsistent.—**incompatibility** *n.* —**incompatibly** *adv.*

incompetent *adj* lacking the necessary ability, skill, etc. * *n* an incompetent person.—**incompetence** *n.*—**incompetently** *adv.*

incomplete *adj* unfinished; lacking a part or parts.—**incompletely** *adv.*—**incompleteness** *n.*

incomprehensible *adj* not to be understood or grasped by the mind; inconceivable.—**incomprehension** *n.*

inconclusive *adj* leading to no definite result; ineffective; inefficient.—**inconclusively** *adv.*—**inconclusiveness** *n.*

incongruous *adj* lacking harmony or agreement of parts; unsuitable; inappropriate.—**incongruity** *n.*—**incongruously** *adv.*

inconsequential, inconsequent *adj* not following logically; irrelevant.—**inconsequentially, inconsequently** *adv.*

inconsiderate *adj* uncaring about others; thoughtless.—**inconsiderately** *adv.*—**inconsiderateness, inconsideration** *n.*

inconsistent *adj* not compatible with other facts; contradictory; irregular, fickle.—**inconsistency** *n.*—**inconsistently** *adv.*

inconspicuous *adj* not conspicuous.—**inconspicuously** *adv.*—**inconspicuousness** *n.*

inconstant *adj* subject to change; unstable; variable; fickle; capricious.—**inconstancy** *n.*

incontinent *adj* unable to control the excretion of bodily wastes; lacking sexual restraint.—**incontinence** *n.*

inconvenience *n* want of convenience; unfitness; that which incommodes; disadvantage. * *vt* to put to inconvenience; to annoy.—**inconvenient** *adj.*

incorrect *adj* faulty; inaccurate; improper.—**incorrectly** *adv.*

incorruptible *adj* incapable of physical corruption, decay or dissolution; incapable of being bribed; not liable to moral perversion or contamination.—**incorruptibly** *adv.*

increase *vti* to make or become greater in size, quality, amount, etc. * *n* increasing or becoming increased; the result or amount by which something increases.—**increasingly** *adv.*

incredible *adj* unbelievable; (*inf*) wonderful.—**incredibly** *adv.*

incredulous *adj* not able or willing to accept as true; unbelieving.—**incredulity** *n.*—**incredulously** *adv.*

increment *n* (the amount of) an increase; an addition.—**incremental** *adj.*

incriminate *vt* to involve in or indicate as involved in a crime or fault.—**incrimination**

n.—**incriminatory** *adj.*

incubator *n* an apparatus in which eggs are hatched by artificial heat; an apparatus for nurturing premature babies until they can survive unaided.

incur *vt* (*pt* **incurred**) to bring upon oneself (something undesirable).

incurable *adj* incapable of being cured; beyond the power of skill or medicine; lacking remedy; incorrigible. * *n* a person diseased beyond cure.—**incurably** *adv.*

incursion *n* an invasion or raid into another's territory, etc.

indebted *adj* in debt; owing gratitude.—**indebtedness** *n.*

indecent *adj* offending against accepted standards of decent behaviour.—**indecency** *n.*—**indecently** *adv.*

indecision *n* not able to make a decision; hesitation.

indecisive *adj* inconclusive; irresolute.—**indecisively** *adv.*—**indecisiveness** *n.*

indeed *adv* truly, certainly. * *interj* expressing irony, surprise, disbelief, etc.

indefinable *adj* that cannot be defined.—**indefinably** *adv.*

indefinite *adj* not certain, undecided; imprecise, vague; having no fixed limits.—**indefinitely** *adv.*—**indefiniteness** *n.*

indelible *adj* not able to be removed or erased; (*pen, ink, etc*) making an indelible mark.—**indelibly** *adv.*

indemnify *vt* to insure against loss, damage, etc; to repay (for damage, loss, etc).—**indemnification** *n.*

indentation *n* a being indented; a notch, cut, inlet, etc; a dent; a spacing in from the margin (—*also* **indention, indent**).

independence *n* the state of being independent.

independent *adj* freedom from the influence or control of others; self-governing; self-determined; not adhering to any political party; not connected with others; not depending on another for financial support. * *n* a person who is independent in thinking, action etc.—**independently** *adv.*

indépendantiste *n* (*Cdn*) a person who supports the political independence of Quebec. * *of* or pertaining to the movement for the political independence of Quebec.

indescribable *adj* unable to be described; too beautiful, horrible, intense, etc for words.

index *n* (*pl* **indexes, indices**) an alphabetical list of names, subjects, items, etc mentioned in a printed book, usu listed alphabetically at the end of the text; a figure showing ratio or relative change, as of prices or wages; any indication or sign; a pointer or dial on an instrument; the exponent of a number. * *vt* to make an index of or for.—**indexer** *n.*

index finger *n* the forefinger.

index-linked *adj* (*salary, pension, etc*) linked directly to changes in the cost-of-living index.

Indian *n* a native of India; an American Indian, the original inhabitants of the continent of America; the language of the people of India; (*Cdn*) one of three categories of aboriginal people (Indians, Inuit and Metis); (*Cdn*) a status Indian. * *adj* of or pertaining to a native of India; of or pertaining to the aboriginal peoples of North and South America.

Indian agent *n* (*Cdn*) a federal government official who administers programs on a First Nations reserve or in a region.

Indian paintbrush *n* a North American plant with flowers hidden by brightly coloured bracts.

Indian pear *n* a North American shrub with white flowers; the edible fruit of this shrub.

indicate *vt* to point out; to show or demonstrate; to be a sign or symptom of; to state briefly, suggest.—**indication** *n.*

indicative *adj* serving as a sign (of); (*gram*) denoting the mood of the verb that affirms or denies.

indicator *n* a thing that indicates or points; a measuring device with a pointer, etc; an instrument showing the operating condition of a piece of machinery, etc; a device giving updated information, such as a departure board in a railway station or airport; a flashing light used to warn of a change in direction of a vehicle.

indict *vt* to charge with a crime; to accuse.

indictable *adj* subject to being indicted; making one liable to indictment.

indictment *n* a formal written statement framed by a prosecuting authority charging a person of a crime.

indifferent *adj* showing no concern, uninterested; unimportant; impartial; average; mediocre.—**indifference** *n.*—**indifferently** *adv.*

indigenous *adj* existing naturally in a particular country, region, or environment; native.

indigestible *adj* difficult or impossible to digest.—**indigestibility** *n.*

indigestion *n* a pain caused by difficulty in digesting food.

indignant *adj* expressing anger, esp at mean or unjust action.—**indignantly** *adv.*

indignation *n* anger at something regarded as unfair, wicked, etc.

indignity *n* humiliation; treatment making one feel degraded, undignified.

indirect *adj* not straight; roundabout; secondary; dishonest.—**indirectly** *adv.*

indiscreet *adj* not discreet; tactless.—**indiscreetly** *adv.*

indiscretion *n* an indiscreet act; rashness.

indiscriminate *adj* not making a careful choice; confused; random; making no distinctions.—**indiscriminately** *adv.*—**indiscrimination** *n.*

indispensable *adj* absolutely essential.—**indispensability** *n.*—**indispensably** *adv.*

indisposed *adj* ill or sick; reluctant; disinclined.

indisputable *adj* unquestionable; certain.—**indisputability** *n.*—**indisputably** *adv.*

indistinct *adj* not clearly marked; dim; not distinct.—**indistinctly** *adv.*—**indistinctness** *n.*

individual *adj* existing as a separate thing or being; of, by, for, or relating to a single person or thing. * *n* a single thing or being; a person.

individualist *n* a person who thinks or behaves with marked independence.—**individualism** *n.*—**individualistic** *adj.*

individuality *n* the condition of being individual; separate or distinct existence; distinctive character.

Indo-Canadian *n* a Canadian born on the Indian subcontinent, esp India. * *adj* pertaining to such Canadians.

indoctrinate *vt* to systematically instruct in doctrines, ideas, beliefs, etc.—**indoctrination** *n.*

indolent *adj* idle; lazy.—**indolently** *adv.*—**indolence** *n.*

indoor *adj* done, used, or situated within a building.

indoors *adv* in or into a building.

indubitable *adj* not capable of being doubted.—**indubitably** *adv.*

induce *vt* to persuade; to bring on; to draw (a conclusion) from particular facts; to bring about (an electric or magnetic effect) in a body by placing it within a field of force.

inducement *n* something that induces; a stimulus; a motive.

induction *n* the act or an instance of inducting, eg into office; reasoning from particular premises to general conclusions; the inducing of an electric or magnetic effect by a field of force.—**inductive** *adj.*

indulge *vt* to satisfy (a desire); to gratify the wishes of; to humour. * *vi* to give way to one's desire.

indulgence *n* indulging or being indulged; a thing indulged in; a favor or privilege; (*RC Church*) a remission of punishment still due for a sin after the guilt has been forgiven.

indulgent *adj* indulging or characterized by indulgence; lenient.—**indulgently** *adv.*

industrial *adj* relating to or engaged in industry; used in industry; having many highly developed industries.—**industrially** *adv.*

industrialist *n* a person who owns or manages an industrial enterprise.

industrialize *vti* to make or become industrial.—**industrialization** *n.*

industrial league *n* (*Cdn*) a sports league, esp for ice hockey, whose teams are sponsored by businesses.

industrious *adj* hard-working.—**industriously** *adv.*—**industriousness** *n.*

industry *n* organized production or manufacture of goods; manufacturing enterprises collectively; a branch of commercial enterprise producing a particular product; any large-scale business activity; the owners and managers of industry; diligence.

inebriated *adj* drunken.—**inebriation** *n.*

inedible *adj* not fit to be eaten.

ineffective *adj* not effective.—**ineffectively** *adv.*

ineffectual *adj* not effectual; futile. —**ineffectually** *adv.*

inefficiency *n* the quality or condition of being inefficient; an instance of inefficiency or incompetence.

inefficient *adj* not efficient.—**inefficiently** *adv.*

ineligible *adj* not eligible.—**ineligibility** *n.*

inept *adj* unsuitable; unfit; foolish; awkward; clumsy.—**ineptitude** *n.*—**ineptly** *adv.*

inequality *n* lack of equality in size, status, etc; unevenness.

inert *adj* without power to move or to resist; inactive; dull; slow; with few or no active properties.—**inertly** *adv.*—**inertness** *n.*

inertia *n* (*physics*) the tendency of matter to remain at rest (or continue in a fixed direction) unless acted on by an outside force; disinclination to act.

inestimable *adj* not to be estimated; beyond measure or price; incalculable; invaluable.—**inestimably** *adv.*

inevitable *adj* sure to happen; unavoidable. * something that is inevitable.—**inevitability** *n.*—**inevitably** *adv.*

inexact *adj* not strictly true or correct.—**inexactitude** *n.*—**inexactly** *adv.*

inexhaustible *adj* not to be exhausted or spent; unfailing; unwearied.—**inexhaustibly** *adv.*

inexorable *adj* unable to be persuaded by persuasion or entreaty, relentless.—**inexorably** *adv.*

inexpensive *adj* cheap.—**inexpensively** *adv.*

inexperience *n* want of experience or of the knowledge that comes by experience.

inexperienced *adj* lacking experience; unpractised; unskilled; unversed.

inexplicable *adj* not to be explained, made plain, or intelligible; not to be interpreted or accounted for.—**inexplicably** *adv.*

inextricable *adj* that cannot be disentangled, solved, or escaped from.—**inextricably** *adv.*

infallible *adj* incapable of being wrong; dependable; reliable.—**infallibility** *n.*—**infallibly** *adv.*

infamous *adj* having a bad reputation; notorious; causing a bad reputation; scandalous.

infamy *n* ill fame; public disgrace; ignominy.

infancy *n* early childhood; the beginning or early existence of anything.

infant *n* a very young child; a baby.

infantile *adj* of infants; like an infant, babyish.

infantry *n* soldiers trained to fight on foot.

infatuate *vt* to inspire with intense, foolish, or short-lived passion.—**infatuated** *adj.*—**infatuation** *n.*

infect *vt* to contaminate with disease-causing microorganisms; to taint; to affect, esp so as to harm.—**infective** *adj.*

infection *n* an infecting or being infected; an infectious disease; a diseased condition.

infectious *adj* (*disease*) able to be transmitted; a disease caused by the spread of bacteria in the body, etc; causing or transmitted by infection; tending to spread to others.

infer *vt* (*pt* **inferred**) to conclude by reasoning from facts or premises, to deduce; to accept as a fact or consequence.—**inferable, inferible** *adj.*

inference *n* an inferring; something inferred or deduced; a reasoning from premises to a conclusion.—**inferential** adj.

inferior adj lower in position, rank, degree, or quality. * n an inferior person.—**inferiority** n.

inferiority complex n (psychol) an acute sense of inferiority expressed by a lack of confidence or in exaggerated aggression.

infernal adj of hell; hellish; fiendish; (inf) irritating, detestable.—**infernally** adv.

inferno n (pl **infernos**) hell; intense heat; a devastating fire.

infertile adj not fertile.—**infertility** n.

infest vt to overrun in large numbers, usu so as to be harmful; to be parasitic in or on.—**infestation** n.

infidelity n unfaithfulness, esp in marriage.

infighting n (boxing) exchanging punches at close quarters; intense competition within an organization.—**infighter** n.

infiltrate vti to filter or pass gradually through or into; to permeate; to penetrate (enemy lines, etc) gradually or stealthily, eg as spies.—**infiltration** n.—**infiltrator** n.

infinite adj endless, limitless; very great; vast.—**infinitely** adv.

infinitive n (gram) the form of a verb without reference to person, number or tense.

infinity n the condition or quality of being infinite; an unlimited number, quantity, or time period.

infirmary n a hospital or place for the treatment of the sick.

infirmity n being infirm; a physical weakness.

inflame vti to arouse, excite, etc or to become aroused, excited, etc; to undergo or cause to undergo inflammation.

inflammable adj able to catch fire, flammable; easily excited.

inflammation n an inflaming or being inflamed; redness, pain, heat, and swelling in the body, due to injury or disease.

inflate vti to fill or become filled with air or gas; to puff up with pride; to increase beyond what is normal, esp the supply of money or credit.—**inflatable** adj.

inflation n an inflating or being inflated; an increase in the currency in circulation or a marked expansion of credit, resulting in a fall in currency value and a sharp rise in prices.

inflexible adj not flexible; stiff, rigid; fixed; unyielding.—**inflexibility** n.—**inflexibly** adv.

inflict vt to impose (pain, a penalty, etc) on a person or thing.—**infliction** n.

influence n the power to affect others; the power to produce effects by having wealth, position, ability, etc; a person with influence. * vt to have influence on.

influential adj having or exerting great influence.—**influentially** adv.

influenza n a contagious feverish virus disease marked by muscular pain and inflammation of the respiratory system.

influx n a sudden inflow of people or things to a place.

inform vt to provide knowledge of something to. * vi to give information to the police, etc,

esp in accusing another.

informal adj not formal; not according to fixed rules or ceremony, etc; casual.—**informally** adv.

informality n the lack of regular, customary, or legal form; an informal act.

information n something told or facts learned; news; knowledge; data stored in or retrieved from a computer.

informative adj conveying information, instructive.

informer n a person who informs on another, esp to the police for a reward.

infrared n (radiation) having a wavelength longer than light but shorter than radio waves; of, pertaining to, or using such radiation.

infrequent adj seldom occurring; rare.—**infrequence, infrequency** n.

infringe vt to break or violate, esp an agreement or a law.—**infringement** n.

infuriate vt to enrage; to make furious.—**infuriating** adj.

ingenious adj clever, resourceful, etc; made or done in an original or clever way.—**ingeniously** adv.—**ingenuity** n.

ingot n a brick-shaped mass of cast metal, esp gold or silver.

ingrained adj (habits, feelings, etc) firmly established; (dirt) deeply embedded.—also **engrained**.

ingratiate vt to bring oneself into another's favor.

ingratitude n absence of gratitude; insensibility to kindness.

ingredient n something included in a mixture; a component.

inhabit vt to live in; to occupy; to reside.

inhabitant n a person or animal inhabiting a specified place.

inhale vti to breathe in.—**inhalation** n.

inherit vt to receive (property, a title, etc) under a will or by right of legal succession; to possess by genetic transmission. * vi to receive by inheritance; to succeed as heir.—**inheritor** n.

inheritance n the action of inheriting; something inherited.

inhibit vt to restrain; to prohibit.—**inhibiter** n.

inhibition n an inhibiting or being inhibited; a mental process that restrains or represses an action, emotion, or thought.

inhospitable adj not hospitable; affording no shelter; barren; cheerless.—**inhospitably** adv.—**inhospitality** n.

inhuman adj lacking in the human qualities of kindness, pity, etc; cruel, brutal, unfeeling; not human.

inimitable adj impossible to imitate; matchless.—**inimitably** adv.

iniquity n wickedness; great injustice.

initial adj of or at the beginning. * n the first letter of each word in a name; a large letter at the beginning of a chapter, etc. * vt (pt **initialled**) to sign with initials.—**initially** adv.

initiate vt to bring (something) into practice or

use; to teach the fundamentals of a subject to; to admit as a member into a club, etc, esp with a secret ceremony. * *n* an initiated person.—**initiation** *n*.—**initiator** *n*.—**initiatory** *adj*.

initiative *n* the action of taking the first step; ability to originate new ideas or methods.

inject *vt* to force (a fluid) into a vein, tissue, etc, esp with a syringe; to introduce (a remark, quality, etc), to interject.

injection *n* an injecting; a substance that is injected.

injure *vt* to harm physically or mentally; to hurt, do wrong to.

injury *n* physical damage; harm.

injustice *n* the state or practice of being unfair; an unjust act.

ink *n* a colored liquid used for writing, printing, etc; the dark protective secretion of an octopus, etc. * *vt* to cover, mark, or color with ink.

inkling *n* a hint; a vague notion.

inlaid *see* inlay.

inland *adj* of or in the interior of a country. * *n* an inland region. * *adv* into or toward this region.

in-law *n* a relative by marriage.

inlay *vt* (*pt* inlaid) to decorate a surface by inserting pieces of metal, wood, etc. * *n* inlaid work; material inlaid.

inlet *n* a narrow strip of water extending into a body of land; an opening; a passage, pipe, etc for liquid to enter a machine, etc.

inmate *n* a person confined with others in a prison or institution.

inn *n* a small hotel; a restaurant or public house, esp in the countryside.

innate *adj* existing from birth; inherent; instinctive.—**innately** *adv*.

inner *adj* further within; inside, internal; private, exclusive. * *n* (*archery*) the innermost ring on a target.

innocent *adj* not guilty of a particular crime; free from sin; blameless; harmless; inoffensive; simple, credulous, naive. * *n* an innocent person, as a child.—**innocence** *n*.—**innocently** *adv*.

innocuous *adj* harmless.—**innocuously** *adv*.—**innocuousness** *n*.

innovate *vi* to introduce new methods, ideas, etc; to make changes.—**innovation** *n*.—**innovative, innovatory** *adj*.

Innu *n* a member of a First Nations people of Labrador and northern Quebec; the language of this people. * *adj* of or pertaining to this people or their language.

innuendo *n* (*pl* innuendoes, innuendos) a hint or sly remark, usu derogatory; an insinuation.

inoculate *vt* to inject a serum or a vaccine into, esp in order to create immunity; to protect as if by inoculation.—**inoculation** *n*.

inopportune *adj* unseasonable; untimely.

inordinate *adj* excessive.—**inordinately** *adv*.

inorganic *adj* not having the structure or characteristics of living organisms; denoting a chemical compound not containing car-

bon.—**inorganically** *adv*.

inpatient *n* a patient being treated while remaining in hospital.

input *n* what is put in, as power into a machine, data into a computer, etc. * *vt* (*pt* input *or* inputted) to put in; to enter (data) into a computer.

inquest *n* a judicial inquiry held by a coroner, esp into a case of violent or unexplained death; (*inf*) any detailed inquiry or investigation.

inquire *vi* to request information about; (*usu with* into) to investigate. * *vt* to ask about.—*also* enquire.—**inquirer, enquirer** *n*.

inquiry *n* the act of inquiring; a search by questioning; an investigation; a question; research.—*also* enquiry.

inquisitive *adj* eager for knowledge; unnecessarily curious; prying.—**inquisitively** *adv*.—**inquisitiveness** *n*.

inroad *n* a raid into enemy territory; an encroachment or advance.

insane *adj* not sane, mentally ill; of or for insane people; very foolish.—**insanely** *adv*.

insanitary *adj* unclean, likely to cause infection or ill-health.

insanity *n* derangement of the mind or intellect; lunacy; madness.

insatiable *adj* not easily satisfied; greedy.—**insatiability** *n*.—**insatiably** *adv*.

inscribe *vt* to mark or engrave (words, etc) on (a surface); to add (a person's name) to a list; to dedicate (a book) to someone; to autograph; to fix in the mind.

inscription *n* an inscribing; words, etc, inscribed on a tomb, coin, etc.

inscrutable *adj* hard to understand, incomprehensible; enigmatic.—**inscrutability** *n*.—**inscrutably** *adv*.

insect *n* any of a class of small arthropods with three pairs of legs, a head, thorax, and abdomen and two or four wings.

insecticide *n* a substance for killing insects.

insecure *adj* not safe; feeling anxiety; not dependable.—**insecurely** *adv*.

insecurity *n* the condition of being insecure; lack of confidence or sureness; instability; something insecure.

insensible *adj* unconscious; unaware; indifferent; imperceptible.—**insensibility** *n*.—**insensibly** *adv*.

inseparable *adj* not able to be separated; closely attached, as romantically.

insert *vt* to put or fit (something) into something else. * *n* something inserted.—**insertion** *n*.

inshore *adj, adv* near or towards the shore.

inside *n* the inner side, surface, or part; (*pl: inf*) the internal organs, stomach, bowels. * *adj* internal; known only to insiders; secret. * *adv* on or in the inside; within; indoors; (*sl*) in prison. * *prep* in or within.

inside out *adj* reversed; with the inner surface facing the outside.

insider *n* a person within a place or group; a person with access to confidential information.

insidious *adj* marked by slyness or treachery; more dangerous than seems evident.—**insidiously** *adv.*—**insidiousness** *n.*

insight *n* the ability to see and understand clearly the inner nature of things, esp by intuition; an instance of such understanding.—**insightful** *adj.*

insignificant *adj* having little or no importance; trivial; worthless; small, inadequate.—**insignificance** *n.*—**insignificantly** *adv.*

insincere *adj* not sincere; hypocritical.—**insincerely** *adv.*—**insincerity** *n.*

insinuate *vt* to introduce or work in slowly, indirectly, etc; to hint.—**insinuation** *n.*

insipid *adj* lacking any distinctive flavor; uninteresting, dull.—**insipidity** *n.*—**insipidly** *adv.*—**insipidness** *n.*

insist *vi* (*often with* **on** *or* **upon**) to take and maintain a stand. * *vt* to demand strongly; to declare firmly.

insistent *adj* insisting or demanding.—**insistence** *n.*—**insistently** *adv.*

insolent *adj* disrespectful; impudent, arrogant; rude.—**insolence** *n.*—**insolently** *adv.*

insoluble *adj* incapable of being dissolved; impossible to solve or explain.—**insolubility** *n.*—**insolubly** *adv.*

insolvent *adj* unable to pay one's debts; bankrupt.—**insolvency** *n.*

insomnia *n* abnormal inability to sleep.

inspect *vt* to look at carefully; to examine or review officially.—**inspection** *n.*

inspector *n* an official who inspects in order to ensure compliance with regulations, etc; a police officer ranking below a superintendent.—**inspectorate** *n.*

inspiration *n* an inspiring; any stimulus to creative thought; an inspired idea, action, etc.—**inspirational** *adj.*

inspire *vt* to stimulate, as to some creative effort; to motivate by divine influence; to arouse (a thought or feeling) in (someone); to cause.—**inspiring** *adj.*

install, instal *vt* (*pt* **installed**) to formally place in an office, rank, etc; to establish in a place; to settle in a position or state.—**installer** *n.*

installation *n* the act of installing or being installed; machinery, equipment, etc that has been installed.

instalment, installment (*US*) *n* a sum of money to be paid at regular specified times; any of several parts, as of a magazine story or television serial.

instance *n* an example; a step in proceeding; an occasion. * *vt* to give as an example.

instant *adj* immediate; (*food*) concentrated or precooked for quick preparation. * *n* a moment; a particular moment.

instantly *adv* immediately.

instead *adv* in place of the one mentioned.

instep *n* the upper part of the arch of the foot, between the ankle and the toes.

instigate *vt* to urge on, goad; to initiate.—**instigation** *n.*—**instigator** *n.*

instil, instill (*US*) *vt* (*pt* **instilled**) to put (an idea,

etc) in or into (the mind) gradually.—**instillation** *n.*—**instilment, instillment** *n.*

instinct *n* the inborn tendency to behave in a way characteristic of a species; a natural or acquired tendency; a knack.

instinctive, instinctual *adj* of, relating to, or prompted by instinct.—**instinctively, instinctually** *adv.*

institute *vt* to organize, establish; to start, initiate. * *n* an organization for the promotion of science, art, etc; a school, college, or department of a university specializing in some field.

institution *n* an established law, custom, etc; an organization having a social, educational, or religious purpose; the building housing it; (*inf*) a long-established person or thing.

instruct *vt* to provide with information; to teach; to give instructions to; to authorize.—**instructor** *n.*—**instructress** *nf.*

instruction *n* an order, direction; the act or process of teaching or training; knowledge imparted; (*comput*) a command in a program to perform a particular operation; (*pl*) orders, directions; detailed guidance.—**instructional** *adj.*

instructive *adj* issuing or containing instructions; giving information, educational.—**instructively** *adv.*

instrument *n* a thing by means of which something is done; a tool or implement; any of various devices for indicating, measuring, controlling, etc; any of various devices producing musical sound; a formal document. * *vt* to orchestrate.

instrumental *adj* serving as a means of doing something; helpful; of, performed on, or written for a musical instrument or instruments.

instrumentalist *n* a person who plays a musical instrument.

insubordinate *adj* not submitting to authority; rebellious.—**insubordination** *n.*

insufferable *adj* intolerable; unbearable.—**insufferably** *adv.*

insufficient *adj* not sufficient.—**insufficiency** *n.*—**insufficiently** *adv.*

insular *adj* of or like an island or islanders; narrow-minded; illiberal.—**insularity** *n.*

insulate *vt* to set apart; to isolate; to cover with a nonconducting material in order to prevent the escape of electricity, heat, sound, etc.—**insulation** *n.*—**insulator** *n.*

insulin *n* a hormone that controls absorption of sugar by the body, secreted by islets of tissue in the pancreas.

insult *vt* to treat with indignity or contempt; to offend. * *n* an insulting remark or act.

insuperable *adj* unable to be overcome.—**insuperability** *n.*—**insuperably** *adv.*

insurable earnings *npl* (*Cdn*) income on which unemployment premiums are paid.

insurance *n* insuring or being insured; a contract purchased to guarantee compensation for a specified loss by fire, death, etc; the amount for which something is insured; the business of insuring against loss.

insure *vt* to take out or issue insurance on; to ensure. * *vi* to contract to give or take insurance.—**insurer** *n*.

insurrection *adj* a rising or revolt against established authority.—**insurrectionist** *n*.

intact *adj* unimpaired; whole.

intake *n* the place in a pipe, etc where a liquid or gas is taken in; a thing or quantity taken in, as students, etc; the process of taking in.

intangible *adj* that cannot be touched, incorporeal; representing value but without material being, as good will; indefinable. * *n* something that is intangible.—**intangibility** *n*.—**intangibly** *adv*.

integral *adj* necessary for completeness; whole or complete; made up of parts forming a whole. * *n* the result of a mathematical integration.—**integrally** *adv*.

integrate *vti* to make whole or become complete; to bring (parts) together into a whole; to remove barriers imposing segregation upon (racial groups); to abolish segregation; (*math*) to find the integral of.—**integration** *n*.

integrity *n* honesty, sincerity; completeness, wholeness; an unimpaired condition.

intellect *n* the ability to reason or understand; high intelligence; a very intelligent person.

intellectual *adj* of, involving, or appealing to the intellect; requiring intelligence. * *n* an intellectual person.

intelligence *n* the ability to learn or understand; the ability to cope with a new situation; news or information; those engaged in gathering secret, esp military, information.

intelligent *adj* having or showing intelligence; clever, wise, etc.—**intelligently** *adv*.

intelligible *adj* able to be understood; clear.—**intelligibility** *n*.—**intelligibly** *adv*.

intemperate *adj* indulging excessively in alcoholic drink; unrestrained; (*climate*) extreme.—**intemperance** *n*.—**intemperately** *adv*.

intend *vt* to mean, to signify; to propose, have in mind as an aim or purpose.

intense *adj* very strong, concentrated; passionate, emotional.—**intensely** *adv*.

intensify *vti* to make or become more intense.—**intensification** *n*.

intensity *n* the state or quality of being intense; density, as of a negative plate; the force or energy of any physical agent.

intensive *adj* of or characterized by intensity; thorough; denoting careful attention given to patients right after surgery, etc.—**intensively** *adv*.

intent *adj* firmly directed; having one's attention or purpose firmly fixed. * *n* intention; something intended; purpose or meaning.—**intently** *adv*.—**intentness** *n*.

intention *n* a determination to act in a specified way; anything intended.

intentional *adj* done purposely.—**intentionally** *adv*.

inter *vt* (*pt* **interred**) to bury.

interact *vi* to act upon each other.—**interaction** *n*.

intercede *vi* to intervene on another's behalf; to mediate.

intercept *vt* to stop or catch in its course. * *n* a point of intersection of two geometric figures; interception by an interceptor.—**interception** *n*.

interchange *vt* to give and receive one thing for another; to exchange, to put (each of two things) in the place of the other; to alternate. * *n* an interchanging; a junction on a motorway designed to prevent traffic intersecting.

interchangeable *adj* able to be interchanged.—**interchangeability** *n*.

intercom *n* (*inf*) a system of intercommunicating, as in an aircraft.

interconnect *vti* to connect by reciprocal links.—**interconnection** *n*.

intercourse *n* a connection by dealings or communication between individuals or groups; sexual intercourse, copulation.

interest *n* a feeling of curiosity about something; the power of causing this feeling; a share in, or a right to, something; anything in which one has a share; benefit; money paid for the use of money; the rate of such payment. * *vt* to excite the attention of; to cause to have a share in; to concern oneself with.

interested *adj* having or expressing an interest; affected by personal interest, not impartial.

interesting *n* engaging the attention.

interfere *vi* to clash; to come between; to intervene; to meddle; to obstruct.

interference *n* an interfering; (*radio, TV*) the interruption of reception by atmospherics or by unwanted signals.

interim *n* an intervening period of time. * *adj* provisional, temporary. * *adv* meanwhile.

interior *adj* situated within; inner; inland; private. * *n* the interior part, as of a room, country, etc.

interjection *n* an interjecting; an interruption; an exclamation.

interlock *vti* to lock or become locked together; to join with one another.

interloper *n* a person who meddles; an intruder.

interlude *n* anything that fills time between two events, as music between acts of a play.

intermarry *vi* (*different races, religions, etc*) to become connected by marriage; to marry within one's close family.—**intermarriage** *n*.

intermediary *n* a mediator. * *adj* acting as a mediator; intermediate.

intermediate *adj* in the middle; in between.

intermission *n* an interval of time between parts of a performance.

intermittent *adj* stopping and starting again at intervals; periodic.—**intermittently** *adv*.

intern *vt* to detain and confine within an area, esp during wartime.—**internment** *n*.

internal *adj* of or on the inside; of or inside the body; intrinsic; domestic.—**internally** *adv*.

international *adj* between or among nations; concerned with the relations between nations; for the use of all nations; of or for people in various nations. * *n* a sporting competition between teams from different countries; a member of an international team of players.—**internationally** adv.

interplay n the action of two things on each other, interaction.

interpret vt to explain; to translate; to construe; to give one's own conception of, as in a play or musical composition. * vi to translate between speakers of different languages.—**interpretation** n.

interpreter n a person who translates orally for persons speaking in different languages; (comput) a program that translates an instruction into machine code.

interrogate vti to question, esp formally.—**interrogation** n.—**interrogator** n.

interrogative adj asking a question. * n a word used in asking a question.—**interrogatively** adv.

interrogatory adj questioning.

interrupt vt to break into (a discussion, etc) or break in upon (a speaker, worker, etc); to make a break in the continuity of. * vi to interrupt an action, talk, etc.—**interrupter** n.—**interruption** n.

intersect vti to cut or divide by passing through or crossing; (lines, roads, etc) to meet and cross.

intersection n an intersecting; the place where two lines, roads, etc meet or cross.

intersperse vt to scatter or insert among other things; to diversify with other things scattered here and there.

intertwine vti to twine or twist closely together.

interval n a space between things; the time between events; (mus) the difference of pitch between two notes.

intervene vi to occur or come between; to occur between two events, etc; to come in to modify, settle, or hinder some action, etc.—**intervention** n.

interview n a meeting in which a person is asked about his or her views, etc, as by a newspaper or television reporter; a published account of this; a formal meeting at which a candidate for a job is questioned and assessed by a prospective employer. * vt to have an interview with.—**interviewer** n.

intestate adj having made no will. * n a person who dies intestate.—**intestacy** n.

intestine n the lower part of the alimentary canal between the stomach and the anus.—**intestinal** adj.

intimacy n close or confidential friendship; familiarity; sexual relations.

intimate adj most private or personal; very close or familiar, esp sexually; deep and thorough. * n an intimate friend. * vt to indicate; to make known; to hint or imply.—**intimately** adv.

intimation n the act of intimating; a notice, announcement.

intimidate vt to frighten; to discourage, silence, etc esp by threats.—**intimidation** n.

into prep to the interior or inner parts of; to the middle; to a particular condition; (inf)

deeply interested or involved in.

intolerable adj unbearable.—**intolerably** adv.

intolerance n lack of toleration of the opinions or practices of others; inability to bear or endure.—**intolerant** adj.

intonation n intoning; variations in pitch of the speaking voice; an accent.

intoxicate vt to make drunken; to elate; to poison.

intoxication n drunkenness; great excitement; poisoning.

intractable adj unmanageable, uncontrollable; (problem, illness, etc) difficult to solve, alleviate, or cure.—**intractability** n.—**intractably** adv.

intransigent adj unwilling to compromise, irreconcilable.—**intransigence** n.

intransitive adj (gram) denoting a verb that does not take a direct object.—**intransitively** adv.

intravenous adj into a vein.—**intravenously** adv.

intrepid adj bold; fearless; brave.—**intrepidity** n.—**intrepidly** adv.

intricate adj difficult to understand; complex, complicated; involved, detailed.—**intricacy** n.—**intricately** adv.

intrigue n a secret or underhand plotting; a secret or underhanded plot or scheme; a secret love affair. * vi to carry on an intrigue. * vt to excite the interest or curiosity of.

intrinsic adj belonging to the real nature of a person or thing; inherent.—**intrinsically** adv.

introduce vt to make (a person) acquainted by name (with other persons); to bring into use or establish; to present (a bill, etc) for consideration or approval (by parliament, etc); to present a radio or television programme; to bring into or insert.

introduction n an introducing or being introduced; the presentation of one person to another; preliminary text in a book; a preliminary passage in a musical composition.

introductory adj serving as an introduction; preliminary.

introspection n examination of one's own mind and feelings, etc.—**introspective** adj.

introvert n a person who is more interested in his or her own thoughts, feelings, etc than in external objects or events. * adj characterized by introversion (—also introverted).—**introversion** n.

intrude vti to force (oneself) upon others unasked.—**intruder** n.

intrusion n the act or an instance of intruding; the forcible entry of molten rock into and between existing rocks.—**intrusively** adv.

intuition n a perceiving of the truth of something immediately without reasoning or analysis; a hunch, an insight.—**intuitively** adv.

Inuk n a member of the Inuit people.

inukshuk n a figure of a human made from stones, used by the Inuit as a marker.

Inuktitut n the language of the Inuit.

inundate vt to cover as with a flood; to deluge.—**inundation** n.

invade vt to enter (a country) with hostile intentions; to encroach upon; to penetrate; to crowd into as if invading.—**invader** *n*.

invalid[1] *adj* not valid.

invalid[2] *n* a person who is ill or disabled. * *vt* to cause to become an invalid; to disable; to cause to retire from the armed forces because of ill-health or injury.

invalidate *vt* to render not valid; to deprive of legal force.—**invalidation** *n*.

invaluable *adj* too valuable to be measured in money.—**invaluably** *adv*.

invariable *adj* never changing; constant.—**invariably** *adv*.

invasion *n* the act of invading with military forces; an encroachment, intrusion.

invective *n* the use of violent or abusive language or writing.

invent *vt* to think up; to think out or produce (a new device, process, etc); to originate; to fabricate (a lie, etc).—**inventor** *n*.

invention *n* something invented; inventiveness.

inventive *adj* pertaining to invention; skilled in inventing.—**inventiveness** *n*.

inventory *n* an itemized list of goods, property, etc, as of a business; the store of such goods for such a listing; a list of the property of an individual or an estate. * *vt* to make an inventory of; to enter in an inventory.

inverse *adj* reversed in order or position; opposite, contrary. * *n* an inverse state or thing.—**inversely** *adv*.

invert *vt* to turn upside down or inside out; to reverse in order, position or relationship.

invertebrate *adj* without a backbone. * *n* an animal without a backbone.

invest *vt* to commit (money) to property, stocks and shares, etc for profit; to devote effort, time, etc on a particular activity; to install in office with ceremony; to furnish with power, authority, etc. * *vi* to invest money.

investigate *vti* to search (into); to inquire, examine.—**investigator** *n*.

investigation *n* the act of investigating; an inquiry; a search to uncover facts, etc.

investiture *n* the act or right of giving legal possession; the ceremony of investing a person with an office, robes, title, etc.

investment *n* the act of investing money productively; the amount invested; an activity in which time, effort or money has been invested.

investor *n* a person who invests money.

inveterate *adj* firmly established, ingrained; habitual.—**inveteracy** *n*.—**inveterately** *adv*.

invidious *adj* tending to provoke ill-will, resentment or envy; (*decisions, etc*) unfairly discriminating.—**invidiously** *adv*.—**invidiousness** *n*.

invigorate *vt* to fill with vigour and energy; to refresh.—**invigorating** *adj*.

invincible *adj* unconquerable.—**invincibility** *n*.—**invincibly** *adv*.

inviolate *adj* not violated; unbroken, unharmed.

invisible *adj* unable to be seen; hidden.—**invis-**ibility *n*.—**invisibly** *adv*.

invitation *n* a message used in inviting.

invite *vt* to ask to come somewhere or do something; to ask for; to give occasion for; to tempt; to entice. * *n* (*inf*) an invitation.

inviting *adj* attractive, enticing.—**invitingly** *adv*.

invoice *n* a list of goods dispatched, usu with particulars of their price and quantity. * *vt* to submit an invoice for or to.

invoke *vt* to call on (God, etc) for help, blessing, etc; to resort to (a law, etc) as pertinent; to implore.

involuntary *adj* not done by choice; not consciously controlled.—**involuntarily** *adv*.—**involuntariness** *n*.

involve *vt* to affect or include; to require; to occupy, to make busy; to complicate; to implicate.—**involvement** *n*.

invulnerable *adj* not capable of being wounded or hurt in any way.—**invulnerability** *n*.

inward *adj* situated within or directed to the inside; relating to or in the mind or spirit. * *adv* inwards.

inwardly *adv* within; in the mind or spirit; towards the inside or centre.

inwards *adv* towards the inside or interior; in the mind or spirit.

iodine *n* a nonmetallic element, found in seawater and seaweed, whose compounds are used in medicine and photography.

iota *n* the ninth letter of the Greek alphabet; a very small quantity; a jot.

IOU *n* a written note promising to pay a sum of money to the holder.

IQ *abbr* = Intelligence Quotient.

irascible *adj* easily angered; hot-tempered.—**irascibility** *n*.—**irascibly** *adv*.

irate *adj* enraged, furious.—**irately** *adv*.

IRB *abbr* (*Cdn*) = Immigration and Refugee Board.

iris *n* (*pl* **irises, irides**) the round, pigmented membrane surrounding the pupil of the eye; (*pl* **irises**) a perennial herbaceous plant with sword-shaped leaves and brightly colored flowers.

Irish *adj* of Ireland or its people. * *n* the Celtic language of Ireland.

irk *vt* to annoy, irritate.

irksome *adj* tedious; tiresome.

iron *n* a metallic element, the most common of all metals; a tool, etc of this metal; a heavy implement with a heated flat underface for pressing cloth; (*pl*) shackles of iron; firm strength; power; any of certain golf clubs with angled metal heads. * *adj* of iron; like iron, strong and firm. * *vti* to press with a hot iron.

ironic, ironical *adj* of or using irony.—**ironically** *adv*.

ironmonger *n* a dealer in metal utensils, tools, etc; a hardware shop.—**ironmongery** *n*.

ironworks *n* a factory where iron is smelted, cast, or wrought.

irony *n* an expression in which the intended meaning of the words is the opposite of their usual sense; an event or result that is the opposite of what is expected.

Iroquoian *n* a speaker of one of a grouping of Indian languages in eastern North America; the language spoken by a people using one of these languages. * *adj* of or pertaining to this people or their language.

Iroquois *n* a member of one of several Indian peoples mainly of Ontario, Quebec, and New York State; the language of one of these peoples. * *adj* of or pertaining to these peoples or their languages.

irrational *adj* not rational, lacking the power of reason; senseless; unreasonable; absurd.—**irrationality** *n*.—**irrationally** *adv*.

irreconcilable *adj* not able to be brought into agreement; incompatible.—**irreconcilably** *adv*.

irredeemable *adj* not able to be redeemed.—**irredeemably** *adv*.

irrefutable *adj* unable to deny or disprove; indisputable.—**irrefutably** *adv*.

irregular *adj* not regular, straight or even; not conforming to the rules; imperfect; (*troops*) not part of the regular armed forces.—**irregularly** *adv*.

irregularity *n* departure from a rule, order or method; crookedness.

irrelevant *adj* not pertinent; not to the point.—**irrelevance** *n*.—**irrelevantly** *adv*.

irreparable *adj* that cannot be repaired, rectified or made good.—**irreparably** *adv*.

irreplaceable *adj* unable to be replaced.—**irreplaceability** *n*.

irrepressible *adj* unable to be controlled or restrained.—**irrepressibly** *adv*.

irreproachable *adj* blameless; faultless.—**irreproachably** *adv*.

irresistible *adj* not able to be resisted; overpowering; fascinating; very charming, alluring.—**irresistibly** *adv*.

irresolute *adj* lacking resolution, uncertain, hesitating.—**irresolutely** *adv*.—**irresoluteness** *n*.—**irresolution** *n*.

irrespective *adj* (*with* **of**) regardless.—**irrespectively** *adv*.

irresponsible *adj* not showing a proper sense of the consequences of one's actions; unable to bear responsibility.—**irresponsibility** *n*.—**irresponsibly** *adv*.

irreverent *adj* not reverent, disrespectful.—**irreverence** *n*.—**irreverently** *adv*.

irrevocable *adj* unable to be revoked, unalterable.

irrigate *vt* to supply (land) with water as by means of artificial ditches, pipes, etc; (*med*) to wash out (a cavity, wound, etc).—**irrigation** *n*.—**irrigator** *n*.

irritable *adj* easily annoyed, irritated, or provoked; (*med*) excessively sensitive to a stimulus.—**irritability** *n*.—**irritably** *adv*.

irritate *vt* to provoke to anger; to annoy; to make inflamed or sore.—**irritation** *n*.

is *see* **be**.

Islam *n* the Muslim religion, a monotheistic religion founded by Mohammed; the Muslim

world.—**Islamic** *adj*.

island *n* a land mass smaller than a continent and surrounded by water; anything like this in position or isolation.

islander *n* a native or inhabitant of an island.

isle *n* an island, esp a small one.

isn't = is not.

isolate *vt* to set apart from others; to place alone; to quarantine a person or animal with a contagious disease; to separate a constituent substance from a compound.—**isolation** *n*.

isolation pay *n* (*Cdn*) a supplement to a salary given as additional compensation for someone who works in a remote area, esp in the North.

isotope *n* any of two or more forms of an element having the same atomic number but different atomic weights.—**isotopic** *adj*.

issue *n* an outgoing; an outlet; a result; offspring; a point under dispute; a sending or giving out; all that is put forth at one time (an issue of bonds, a periodical, etc). * *vi* to go or flow out; to result (from) or end (in); to be published. * *vt* to let out; to discharge; to give or deal out, as supplies; to publish.

isthmus *n* (*pl* **isthmuses, isthmi**) a narrow strip of land having water at each side and connecting two larger bodies of land.

it *pron* the thing mentioned; the subject of an impersonal verb; a subject or object of indefinite sense in various constructions. * *n* the player, as in tag, who must catch another.

Italian *adj* of Italy or its people. * *n* a native of Italy; the Italian language.

italic *adj* denoting a type in which the letters slant upward to the right (*this is italic type*). * *n* (*usu pl*) italic type or handwriting.

itch *n* an irritating sensation on the surface of the skin causing a need to scratch; an insistent desire. * *vi* to have or feel an irritating sensation in the skin; to feel a restless desire.

itchy *adj* (**itchier, itchiest**) pertaining to or affected with an itch.—**itchiness** *n*.

item *n* an article; a unit; a separate thing; a bit of news or information; (*inf*) a couple having an affair.

itemize *vt* to specify the items of; to set down by items.—**itemization** *n*.

itinerant *adj* travelling from place to place. * *n* a traveller.

itinerary *n* a route; a record of a journey; a detailed plan of a journey.

it'll = it will, it shall.

its *poss pron* relating to or belonging to it.

it's = it is, it has.

itself *pron* the reflexive and emphatic form of **it**.

ITV *abbr* = Independent Television.

ivory *n* the hard, creamy-white substance forming the tusks of elephants, etc; any substance like ivory; creamy white. * *adj* of or like ivory; creamy white.

ivy *n* a climbing or creeping vine with a woody stem and evergreen leaves.

J

jab *vti* (*pt* **jabbed**) to poke or thrust roughly; to punch with short, straight blows. * *n* a sudden thrust or stab; (*inf*) an injection with a hypodermic needle.

jabber *vti* to speak or say rapidly, incoherently, or foolishly. * *n* such talk.

jack *n* any of various mechanical or hydraulic devices used to lift something heavy; a playing card with a knave's picture on it, ranking below the queen; a small flag flown on a ship's bow as a signal or to show nationality; (*bowls*) a small white ball used as a target. * *vt* to raise by means of a jack.

jacket *n* a short coat; an outer covering, as the removable paper cover of a book.

jackknife *n* a pocket-knife; a dive in which the diver touches his feet with knees straight and then straightens out. * *vi* (*articulated lorry*) to lose control so that the trailer and cab swing against each other.

jackpot *n* the accumulated stakes in certain games, as poker.

jade *n* a hard, ornamental semiprecious stone; its light green color.

jaded *adj* tired, exhausted; satiated.

jagged *adj* having sharp projecting points; notched or ragged.—**jaggedly** *adv*.

jail *n* a prison. * *vt* to send to or confine in prison.—*also* **gaol**.

jailer *n* a person in charge of prisoners in a jail.—*also* **gaoler**.

jam[1] *n* a preserve made from fruit boiled with sugar until thickened; (*inf*) something easy or desirable.

jam[2] *vb* (*pt* **jammed**) *vt* to press or squeeze into a confined space; to crowd full with people or things; to cause (machinery) to become wedged and inoperable; to cause interference to a radio signal rendering it unintelligible. * *vi* to become stuck or blocked; (*sl*) to play in a jam session. * *n* a crowded mass or congestion in a confined space; a blockage caused by jamming; (*inf*) a difficult situation.

jamb *n* the straight vertical side post of a door, etc.

jangle *vi* to make a harsh or discordant sound, as bells. * *vt* to cause to jangle; to irritate.—*also n*.

janitor *n* a person who looks after a building, doing routine maintenance, etc.—**janitorial** *adj*.

January *n* the first month of the year, having 31 days.

Japanese *adj* of Japan, its people or language. * *n* the language of Japan.

jar[1] *vb* (*pt* **jarred**) *vi* to make a harsh, discordant noise; to have an irritating effect (on one); to vibrate from an impact; to clash. * *vt* to jolt. * *n* a grating sound; a vibration due to impact; a jolt.

jar[2] *n* a short cylindrical glass vessel with a wide mouth; (*inf*) a pint of beer.

jargon *n* the specialized or technical vocabulary of a science, profession, etc; obscure and usu pretentious language.

jasmine *n* any of a genus of climbing shrubs with fragrant white or yellow flowers.

jaundice *n* a condition characterized by yellowing of the skin, caused by excess of bile in the bloodstream; bitterness; resentment; prejudice.

jaundiced *adj* affected with jaundice; jealous, envious, disillusioned.

jaunt *n* a short journey, usu for pleasure. * *vi* to make such a journey.

jaunty *adj* (**jauntier**, **jauntiest**) sprightly or self-confident in manner.—**jauntily** *adv*.—**jauntiness** *n*.

javelin *n* a light spear, esp one thrown some distance in a contest.

jaw *n* one of the bones in which teeth are set; either of two movable parts that grasp or crush something, as in a vice; (*sl*) a friendly chat, gossip. * *vi* (*sl*) to talk boringly and at length.

jaywalk *vi* to walk across a street carelessly without obeying traffic rules or signals.—**jaywalker** *n*.

jazz *n* a general term for American popular music, characterized by syncopated rhythms and embracing ragtime, blues, swing, jive, and bebop; (*sl*) pretentious or nonsensical talk or actions. * *vt* (*sl*) (*with up*) to enliven or embellish.—**jazzy** *adj*.—**jazziness** *n*.

jealous *adj* apprehensive of or hostile towards someone thought of as a rival; envious of, resentful; anxiously vigilant or protective.—**jealously** *adv*.

jealousy *n* suspicious fear or watchfulness, esp the fear of being supplanted by a rival.

jeans *npl* trousers made from denim.

jeep *n* a small robust vehicle with heavy duty tyres and four-wheel drive for use on rough terrain, esp by the military.

jeer *vt* to laugh derisively. * *vi* to scoff (at). * *n* a jeering remark.

jelly *n* a soft, gelatinous food made from fruit syrup or meat juice; any substance like this.—**jellied** *adj*.

jellyfish *n* a sea creature with a nearly transparent body and long tentacles.

jeopardize *vt* to endanger, put at risk.

jeopardy *n* great danger or risk.

jerk[1] *n* a sudden sharp pull or twist; a sudden muscular contraction or reflex; (*inf*) a stupid person. * *vti* to move with a jerk; to pull sharply; to twitch.

jerk[2] *vt* to preserve (meat) by cutting it into long strips and drying it in the sun. * *n* jerked meat (—*also* **jerky**).

jerkin *n* a close-fitting sleeveless jacket.

jerky *adj* (**jerkier**, **jerkiest**) moving with jerks.—**jerkily** *adv*.—**jerkiness** *n*.

jersey *n* any plain machine-knitted fabric of

natural or man-made fibres; a knitted sweater. * adj pertaining to the island of Jersey or its breed of cattle.

jest n a joke; a thing to be laughed at. * vi to jeer; to joke.

jet¹ n a hard, black, compact mineral that can be polished and is used in jewellery; a lustrous black.—**jet-black** adj.

jet² n a stream of liquid or gas suddenly emitted; a spout for emitting a jet; a jet-propelled aircraft. * vti (pt **jetted**) to gush out in a stream; (inf) to travel or convey by jet.

jet engine n an engine, such as a gas turbine, producing jet propulsion.

jetsam n cargo thrown overboard from a ship in distress to lighten its load, esp such cargo when washed up on the shore.

jettison vt to abandon; to throw overboard.

jetty n a wharf; a small pier.

Jew n a person descended, or regarded as descended, from the ancient Hebrews; a person whose religion is Judaism.

jewel n a precious stone; a gem; a piece of jewellery; someone or something highly esteemed; a small gem used as a bearing in a watch.

jeweller, jeweler (US) n a person who makes, repairs or deals in jewellery, watches, etc.

jewellery, jewelry(US) n jewels such as rings, brooches, etc, worn for decoration.

Jewish adj of or like Jews.

jib n a triangular sail extending from the foremast in a ship; the projecting arm of a crane. * vti (pt **jibbed**) to pull (a sail) round to the other side; (sail) to swing round.

jibe see **gibe**.

jiffy, jiff n (inf) a very short time.

jigsaw n a saw with a narrow fine-toothed blade for cutting irregular shapes; a picture on wood or board cut into irregular pieces for re-assembling for amusement.

jilt vt to discard (a lover) unfeelingly, esp without warning.

jingle n a metallic tinkling sound like a bunch of keys being shaken together; a catchy verse or song with easy rhythm, simple rhymes, etc. * vti (to cause) to make a light tinkling sound.

jinx n (inf) someone or something thought to bring bad luck.

jitter vi (inf) to feel nervous or act nervously. * npl (inf) (with **the**) an uneasy nervous feeling; fidgets.

job n a piece of work done for pay; a task; a duty; the thing or material being worked on; work; employment; (sl) a criminal enterprise; (inf) a difficult task. * adj hired or done by the job. * vti (pt **jobbed**) to deal in (goods) as a jobber; to sublet (work, etc).

jobless adj unemployed.

jockey n a person whose job is riding horses in races. * vti to act as a jockey; to manœuvre for a more advantageous position; to swindle or cheat.

jocular adj joking; full of jokes.—**jocularity** n.—

jocularly adv.

joe job n (Cdn) a low-paying or monotonous job.

jog vb (pt **jogged**) vt to give a slight shake or nudge to; to rouse, as the memory. * vi to move up and down with an unsteady motion; to run at a relaxed trot for exercise; (horse) to run at a jog-trot. * n a slight shake or push; a nudge; a slow walk or trot.—**jogger** n.

Johnny Canuck n (inf) a Canadian; Canada.

join vti to bring and come together (with); to connect; to unite; to become a part or member of (a club, etc); to participate (in a conversation, etc); (with **up**) to enlist in the armed forces; to unite, connect. * n a joining; a place of joining.

joiner n a carpenter who finishes interior woodwork; (inf) a person who is involved in many clubs and activities, etc.

joint n a place where, or way in which, two things are joined; any of the parts of a jointed whole; the parts where two bones move on one another in an animal; a division of an animal carcass made by a butcher; (sl) a cheap bar or restaurant; (sl) a gambling or drinking den; (sl) a cannabis cigarette. * adj common to two or more; sharing with another. * vt to connect by a joint or joints; to divide (an animal carcass) into parts for cooking.

jointly adv in common.

joist n any of the parallel beams supporting the floor-boards or the laths of a ceiling.

joke n something said or done to cause laughter; a thing done or said merely in fun; a person or thing to be laughed at. * vi to make jokes.

joker n a person who jokes; (sl) a person; an extra playing card made use of in certain games.

jolly adj (**jollier, jolliest**) merry; full of fun; delightful; (inf) enjoyable. * vti (inf) to try to make (a person) feel good; to make fun of (someone).

jolt vt to give a sudden shake or knock to; to move along jerkily; to surprise or shock suddenly. * n a sudden jar or knock; an emotional shock.

jostle vti to shake or knock roughly; to collide or come into contact (with); to elbow for position.—also n.

jot n a very small amount. * vt (pt **jotted**) to note (down) briefly.

jotter n a notebook.

joual n (Cdn) a form of urban, working-class French in Quebec that has non-standard syntax and many borrowings from English.

journal n a daily record of happenings, as a diary; a newspaper or periodical; (bookkeeping) a book of original entry for recording transactions; that part of a shaft or axle that turns in a bearing.

journalese n a facile style of writing found in many magazines, newspapers, etc.

journalism n the work of gathering news for, or producing a newspaper, magazine or news broadcast.—**journalist** *n*.—**journalistic** *adj*.

journey *n* a travelling or going from one place to another; the distance covered when travelling. * *vi* to make a journey.

jowl *n* the lower jaw; (*usu pl*) the cheek; the loose flesh around the throat; the similar flesh in an animal, as a dewlap.

joy *n* intense happiness; something that causes this.—**joyless** *adj*.—**joylessly** *adv*.—**joylessness** *n*.

joyful *adj* filled with, expressing, or causing joy.—**joyfully** *adv*.—**joyfulness** *n*.

joyous *adj* joyful.—**joyously** *adv*.—**joyousness** *n*.

joy-ride *n* (*inf*) a car ride, often in a stolen vehicle and at reckless speed, just for pleasure.—**joy-rider** *n*.—**joy-riding** *n*.

JP *abbr* = Justice of the Peace.

Jr. *abbr* = Junior.

jubilant *adj* joyful and triumphant; elated; rejoicing.—**jubilation** *n*.

jubilee *n* a 50th or 25th anniversary; a time of rejoicing.

judge *n* a public official with authority to hear and decide cases in a court of law; a person chosen to settle a dispute or decide who wins; a person qualified to decide on the relative worth of anything. * *vti* to hear and pass judgment (on) in a court of law; to determine the winner of (a contest) or settle (a dispute); to form an opinion about; to criticize or censure; to suppose, think.

judgment, judgement *n* a judging; a deciding; a legal decision; an opinion; the ability to come to a wise decision; censure.

judicial *adj* of judges, courts, or their functions; jurisdiction; judges or courts collectively.—**judicially** *adv*.

judicious *adj* possessing or characterized by sound judgment.—**judiciously** *adv*.

judo *n* a Japanese system of unarmed combat, adapted as a competitive sport from jujitsu.

jug *n* a vessel for holding and pouring liquids, with a handle and curved lip; a pitcher; (*sl*) prison. * *vt* (*pt* **jugged**) to stew meat (esp hare) in an earthenware pot; (*sl*) to put into prison.—**jugful** *n*.

juggernaut *n* a terrible, irresistible force; a large heavy truck.

juggle *vi* to toss up balls, etc and keep them in the air. * *vt* to manipulate skilfully; to manipulate so as to deceive. * *n* a juggling.—**juggler** *n*.

juice *n* the liquid part of fruit, vegetables or meat; liquid secreted by a bodily organ; (*inf*) vitality; (*inf*) electric current; (*inf*) petrol.

juicy *adj* (**juicier, juiciest**) full of juice; (*inf*) very interesting; (*inf*) highly profitable.—**juicily** *adv*.—**juiciness** *n*.

jukebox *n* a coin-operated automatic record or CD player.

July *n* the seventh month of the year, having 31 days.

jumble *vt* (*often with* **up**) to mix together in a disordered mass. * *n* items mixed together in a confused mass; articles for a jumble sale.

jumble sale *n* a sale of second-hand clothes, books, etc to raise money for charity.

jumbo *n* (*pl* **jumbos**) something very large of its kind.

jumbo jet *n* a very large jet airliner.

jump *vi* to spring or leap from the ground, a height, etc; to jerk; (*often with* **at**) to act swiftly and eagerly; to pass suddenly, as to a new topic; to rise suddenly, as prices; (*sl*) to be lively. * *vt* to leap or pass over (something); to leap upon; to cause (prices, etc) to rise; to fail to turn up (for trial when out on bail); (*inf*) to attack suddenly; (*inf*) to react to prematurely; (*sl*) to leave suddenly. * *n* a jumping; a distance jumped; a sudden transition; an obstacle; a nervous start.

jumper *n* a knitted garment for the upper body; a sleeveless dress for wearing over a blouse, etc.

jumpy *adj* (**jumpier, jumpiest**) moving in jerks, etc; easily startled, apprehensive.—**jumpily** *adv*.—**jumpiness** *n*.

junction *n* a place or point where things join; a place where roads or railway lines, etc meet, link or cross each other.

juncture *n* a junction; a point of time; a crisis.

June *n* the sixth month of the year, having 30 days.

jungle *n* an area overgrown with dense tropical trees and other vegetation, etc; any scene of wild confusion, disorder, or of ruthless competition for survival.

junior *adj* younger in age; of more recent or lower status; of juniors. * *n* a person who is younger, of lower rank, etc; a young person employed in minor capacity in an office; a member of a junior school; (*inf*) (*with cap*) the younger son, in US often used after the name if the same as the father's.

juniper *n* an evergreen shrub that yields purple berries.

junk[1] *n* a flat-bottomed sailing vessel prevalent in the China Seas.

junk[2] *n* discarded useless objects; (*inf*) rubbish, trash; (*sl*) any narcotic drug, such as heroin. * *vt* (*inf*) to scrap.

junk shop *n* a shop selling miscellaneous second-hand goods.

junta *n* a group of people, esp military, who assume responsibility for the government of a country following a coup d'état or revolution.

jurisdiction *n* the right or authority to apply the law; the exercise of such authority; the limits of territory over which such authority extends.

jurisprudence *n* the science or philosophy of law; a division of law.—**jurisprudential** *adj*.

juror *n* a member of a jury; a person who takes an oath.

jury *n* a body of usu 12 people sworn to hear evidence and to deliver a verdict on a case; a committee or panel that decides winners in a contest.

just *adj* fair, impartial; deserved, merited;

proper, exact; conforming strictly with the facts. * *adv* exactly; nearly; only; barely; a very short time ago; immediately; (*inf*) really; justly, equitably; by right.—**justly** *adv*.—**justness** *n*.

justice *n* justness, fairness; the use of authority to maintain what is just; the administration of law; a judge.

jut *vti* (*pt* **jutted**) to stick out; to project. * *n* a part that juts.

juvenile *adj* young; immature; of or for young persons. * *n* a young person.

juxtapose *vt* to place side by side.—**juxtaposition** *n*.

K

kabloona *n* (*pl* same or **kabloonas**) a person who is not an Inuit, esp a white person.

kaleidoscope *n* a small tube containing bits of colored glass reflected by mirrors to form symmetrical patterns as the tube is rotated; anything that constantly changes. — **kaleidoscopic** *adj*.

kamik *n* an Inuit boot made from caribou hide.

kangaroo *n* an Australian mammal with short forelegs and strong, large hind legs for jumping.

karat *see* **carat**.

keel *n* one of the main structural members of a ship extending along the bottom from stem to stern to which the frame is attached; any structure resembling this. * *vti* (to cause) to turn over.

keen[1] *adj* eager, enthusiastic; intellectually acute, shrewd; having a sharp point or fine edge; (*senses*) perceptive, penetrating; extremely cold and piercing; intense; (*prices*) very low so as to be competitive.—**keenly** *adv*.—**keenness** *n*.

keen[2] *n* a dirge or lament for the dead. * *vi* to lament the dead.

keep *vb* (*pt* **kept**) *vt* to celebrate, observe; to fulfil; to protect, guard; to take care of; to preserve; to provide for; to make regular entries in; to maintain in a specified state; to hold for the future; to hold and not let go. * *vi* to stay in a specified condition; to continue, go on; to refrain or restrain oneself; to stay fresh, not spoil. * *n* food and shelter; care and custody; the inner stronghold of a castle.

keeper *n* one who guards, watches, or takes care of persons or things.

keeping *n* care, charge; observance; agreement, conformity.

keepsake *n* something kept in memory of the giver.

keg *n* a small barrel.

kennel *n* a small shelter for a dog, a doghouse; (*often pl*) a place where dogs are bred or kept. * *vt* (*pt* **kennelled**) to keep in a kennel.

kept *see* **keep**.

kerb *n* a line of raised stone forming the edge of a pavement.—**kerbstone** *n*.

kernel *n* the inner edible part of a fruit or nut; the essential part of anything.

kerosene, kerosine *n* a fuel oil distilled from petroleum, paraffin.

ketchup *n* any of various thick sauces, esp one made from puréed tomato, for meat, fish, etc.—*also* **catchup, catsup**

kettle *n* a container with a handle and spout for boiling water.

kettledrum *n* a musical instrument consisting of a hollow metal body with a parchment head, the tension of which controls the pitch and is adjusted by screws.

key[1] *n* a device for locking and unlocking something; a thing that explains or solves, as the legend of a map, a code, etc; a controlling position, person, or thing; one of a set of parts or levers pressed in a keyboard or typewriter, etc; (*mus*) a system of related tones based on a keynote and forming a given scale; style or mood of expression; a roughened surface for improved adhesion of plaster, etc; an electric circuit breaker. * *vt* to furnish with a key; to bring into harmony. * *adj* controlling; important.

key[2] *n* a low island or reef.

keyboard *n* a set of keys in a piano, organ, computer, etc.

keyhole *n* an opening (in a lock) into which a key is inserted.

keynote *n* the basic note of a musical scale; the basic idea or ruling principle. * *vt* to give the keynote of; to give the keynote speech at.

khaki *adj* dull yellowish-brown. * *n* (*pl* **khakis**) strong, twilled cloth of this color; (*often pl*) a khaki uniform or trousers.

kick *vt* to strike with the foot; to drive, force, etc as by kicking; to score (a goal, etc) by kicking. * *vi* to strike out with the foot; to recoil, as a gun; (*inf*) to complain; (*with* **off**) (*football*) to give the ball the first kick to start play; (*inf*) to start. * *n* an act or method of kicking; a sudden recoil; (*inf*) a thrill; (*inf*) an intoxicating effect.—**kicker** *n*.

kickoff *n* (*football*) a kick putting the ball into play; the beginning or start of proceedings, eg a discussion.

kid *n* a young goat; soft leather made from its skin; (*inf*) a child. * *vti* (*pt* **kidded**) (*inf*) to tease or fool playfully; (*goat*) to bring forth young.

kidnap *vt* (*pt* **kidnapped**) to seize and hold to ransom, as of a person.—**kidnapper** *n*.

kidney *n* (*pl* **kidneys**) either of a pair of glandular organs excreting waste products from the blood as urine; an animal's kidney used as food.

kill *vt* to cause the death of; to destroy; to neutralize (a color); to spend (time) on trivial matters; to turn off (an engine, etc); (*inf*) to cause severe discomfort or pain to. * *n* the act of killing; an animal or animals killed.—

killer n.

killdeer n a large North American plover with a mournful call.

killing adj (inf) tiring; very amusing; causing death, deadly. * n the act of killing, murder; (inf) a sudden (financial) success.

kiln n a furnace or large oven for baking or drying (lime, bricks, pottery, etc).

kilo n kilogram; kilometre.

kilogram, kilogramme n a unit of weight and mass, equal to 1000 grams or 2.2046 pounds.

kilometre, kilometer (US) n a unit of length equal to 1000 metres or 0.62 mile.—kilometric adj.

kilowatt n a unit of electrical power, equal to 1000 watts.

kilt n a knee-length skirt made from tartan material pleated at the sides, worn as part of the Scottish Highland dress for men and women.

kimono n a loose Japanese robe.

kin n relatives; family.

kind¹ n sort; variety; class; a natural group or division; essential character.

kind² adj sympathetic; friendly; gentle; benevolent.—kind-hearted adj.—kindness n.

kindergarten n a class or school for very young children.

kindle vt to set on fire; to excite (feelings, interest, etc). * vi to catch fire; to become aroused or excited.

kindly adj (kindlier, kindliest) kind; gracious; agreeable; pleasant. * adv in a kindly manner; favorably.—kindliness n.

kindred n a person's family or relatives; family relationship; resemblance. * adj related; like, similar.

kinetic adj of or produced by movement.

king n the man who rules a country and its people; a man with the title of ruler, but with limited power to rule; man supreme in a certain sphere; something best in its class; the chief piece in chess; a playing card with a picture of a king on it, ranking above a queen; (draughts) a piece that has been crowned.

kingdom n a country headed by a king or queen; a realm, domain; any of the three divisions of the natural world: animal: vegetable; mineral.

kingfisher n a short-tailed diving bird that feeds chiefly on fish.

king-size, king-sized adj larger than standard size.

kink n a tight twist or curl in a piece of string, rope, hair, etc; a painful cramp in the neck, back, etc; an eccentricity of personality. * vti to form or cause to form a kink or kinks.

kinky adj (kinkier, kinkiest) full of kinks; (inf) eccentric; (inf) sexually bizarre.—kinkily adv.—kinkiness n.

kinnikinnick n (hist) among some Indian peoples, a substitute for tobacco made from dried wild berries and leaves.

kiosk n a small open structure used for selling newspapers, confectionery, etc; a public telephone booth.

kipper n a kippered herring, etc. * vt to cure (fish) by salting and drying or smoking.

kiss vti to touch with the lips as an expression of love, affection or in greeting; to touch the lips with those of another person as a sign of love or desire; to touch lightly. * n an act of kissing; a light, gentle touch.

kit n clothing and personal equipment, etc; tools and equipment for a specific purpose; a set of parts with instructions ready to be assembled. * vt (pt kitted) (usu with out or up) to provide with kit.

kitbag n a strong cylindrical bag carried over one shoulder used for holding kit, esp by military personnel.

kitchen n a place where food is prepared and cooked.

kite n a bird of prey with long narrow wings and a forked tail; a light frame covered with a thin covering for flying in the wind.

kith n friends and relations, now only in kith and kin.

kitten n a young cat; the young of other small mammals. * vti to give birth to kittens.

kitty n the stakes in a game of poker or other gambling game; a shared fund of money.

kleptomania n an uncontrollable impulse to steal.—kleptomaniac n.

knack n an ability to do something easily; a trick; a habit.

knapsack n a bag for carrying equipment or supplies on the back.

knave n (formerly) a tricky or dishonest man; the jack in a pack of playing cards.—knavery n.—knavish adj.

knead vt to squeeze and press together (dough, clay, etc) into a uniform lump with the hands; to make (bread, etc) by kneading; to squeeze and press with the hands.

knee n the joint between the thigh and the lower part of the human leg; anything shaped like a bent knee. * vt (pt kneed) to hit or touch with the knee.

kneecap n the small bone covering and protecting the front part of the knee-joint. * vt (pt kneecapped) to maim by shooting into the kneecap.—kneecapping n.

kneel vi (pt knelt) to go down on one's knee or knees; to remain in this position.

knell n the sound of a bell rung slowly and solemnly at a death or funeral; a warning of death, failure, etc. * vi (bell) to ring a knell; to summon, announce, etc (as if) by a knell.

knelt see kneel.

knew see know.

knickers npl an undergarment covering the lower body and having separate leg holes, worn by women and girls.

knife n (pl knives) a flat piece of steel, etc, with a sharp edge set in a handle, used to cut or as a weapon; a sharp blade forming part of a tool or machine. * vt to cut or stab with a knife.

knight n (Middle Ages) a medieval mounted soldier; a man who for some achievement is given honorary rank entitling him to use "Sir" before his given name; a chessman shaped like a horse's head. * *vt* to make (a man) a knight.—**knighthood** *n*.—**knightly** *adv*.

knit *vb* (*pt* **knitted** *or* **knit**) *vt* to form (fabric or a garment) by interlooping yarn using knitting needles or a machine; to cause (eg broken bones) to grow together; to link or join together closely; to draw (the brows) together. * *vi* to make knitted fabric from yarn by means of needles; to grow together; to become joined or united. * *n* a knitted garment or fabric.—**knitter** *n*.

knitting *n* work being knitted.

knitting needle *n* a long thin eyeless needle, usu made of plastic or steel, used in knitting.

knitwear *n* knitted clothing.

knob *n* a rounded lump or protuberance; a handle, usu round, of a door, drawer, etc.

knock *vi* to strike with a sharp blow; to rap on a door; to bump, collide; (*engine*) to make a thumping noise; (*with* **off**) (*inf*) to finish work. * *vt* to strike; (*inf*) to criticize; (*with* **about, around**) to wander around aimlessly; to treat roughly; (*with* **back**) (*inf*) to drink, swallow quickly; to reject, refuse; (*with* **down**) to indicate a sale at an auction; (*with* **down** *or* **off**) to hit so as to cause to fall; (*with* **off**) (*inf*) to complete hastily; (*inf*) to reduce in price; (*sl*) to steal; (*with* **out**) to make unconscious or exhausted; to eliminate in a knockout competition; (*inf*) to amaze. * *n* a knocking, a hit, a rap.

knockdown *adj* cheap; (*furniture*) easy to dismantle.

knocker *n* a device hinged against a door for use in knocking.

knock-kneed *adj* having inward-curving legs.

knockout *n* a punch or blow that produces unconsciousness; a contest in which competitors are eliminated at each round; (*inf*) an attractive or extremely impressive person or thing.

knot *n* a lump in a thread, etc formed by a tightened loop or tangling; a fastening made by tying lengths of rope, etc; an ornamental bow; a small group, cluster; a hard mass of wood which a branch grows out from a tree, which shows as a roundish, cross-grained piece in a board; a unit of speed of one nautical mile per hour; something that ties closely, esp the bond of marriage. * *vti* (*pt* **knotted**) to make or form a knot (in); to entangle or become entangled.

knotty *adj* (**knottier, knottiest**) full of knots; hard to solve; puzzling.

know *vt* (*pt* **knew,** *pp* **known**) to be well-informed about; to be aware of; to be acquainted with; to recognize or distinguish.

know-how *n* practical skill, experience.

knowing *adj* having knowledge; shrewd; clever; implying a secret understanding.—**knowingly** *adv*.

knowledge *n* what one knows; the body of facts, etc accumulated over time; fact of knowing; range of information or understanding; the act of knowing.

knowledgeable, knowledgable *adj* having knowledge or intelligence; well-informed.

known *see* **know.**

knuckle *n* a joint of the finger, esp at the roots of the fingers; the knee of an animal used as food. * *vi* (*with* **down**) (*inf*) to start to work hard; (*with* **under**) to yield, to give in.

KO *abbr* = knockout.

kokanee *n* (*Cdn*) a form of non-migratory salmon of lakes in western Canada.

Koran *n* the sacred book of the Muslims.

kudlik *n* an Inuit soapstone lamp in which seal oil is burned.

kW *abbr* = kilowatt(s).

l *abbr* = litre(s).

lab *n* (*inf*) laboratory.

Lab. *abbr* = Labrador.

label *n* a slip of paper, cloth, metal, etc attached to anything to provide information about its nature, contents, ownership, etc; a term of generalized classification. * *vt* (*pt* **labelled**) to attach a label to; to designate or classify (as).

laboratory *n* a room or building where scientific work and research is carried out.

laborious *adj* requiring much work; hard-working; laboured.—**laboriously** *adv*.—**laboriousness** *n*.

labour, labor (*US*) *n* work, physical or mental exertion; a specific task; all wage-earning workers; workers collectively; the process of childbirth. * *vi* to work; to work hard; to move with difficulty; to suffer (delusions, etc); to be in childbirth. * *vt* to develop in unnecessary detail.

labour camp *n* a penal colony where forced labour takes place.

Labour Day *n* a public holiday to honour workers, held in Canada and the United States on the first Monday in September, elsewhere on May 1.

labourer, laborer (*US*) *n* a person who labours, esp a person whose work requires strength rather than skill.

Labradorian *n* (*Cdn*) a person who lives in or is from Labrador.

labyrinth *n* a structure containing winding passages through which it is hard to find one's way; a maze.—**labyrinthine** *adj*.

lace *n* a cord, etc used to draw together and fasten parts of a shoe, a corset, etc; a delicate ornamental fabric of openwork design using fine cotton, silk, etc. * *vt* to fasten with a lace or laces; to intertwine, weave; to fortify (a drink, etc) with a dash of spirits.

lack *n* the fact or state of not having any or not having enough; the thing that is needed. * *vti* to be deficient in or entirely without.

lackadaisical *adj* showing lack of energy or interest; listless.—**lackadaisically** *adv*.

laconic *adj* using few words; concise.—**laconically** *adv*.

lacquer *n* a glossy varnish. * *vt* to coat with lacquer, to make glossy.

lad *n* a boy; a young man; a fellow, chap.

ladder *n* a portable metal or wooden framework with rungs between two vertical supports for climbing up and down; something that resembles a ladder in form or use.

laden *adj* loaded with cargo; burdened.

ladle *n* a long-handled, cup-like spoon for scooping liquids; a device like a ladle in shape or use.

lady *n* a polite term for any woman; (*with cap*) a title of honor given to various ranks of women in the British peerage.

ladybird *n* a small, usu brightly-colored beetle.

ladylike *adj* like or suitable for a lady; refined, polite.

lag[1] *vi* (*pt* **lagged**) to fall behind, hang back; to fail to keep pace in movement or development; to weaken in strength or intensity. * *n* a falling behind; a delay.

lag[2] *vt* (*pt* **lagged**) to insulate (pipes, etc) with lagging.

lag[3] *n* (*sl*) a convict; a term of imprisonment.

lager *n* a light beer that has been aged for a certain period.

lagging *n* insulating material used to lag pipes, boilers, etc.

lagoon *n* a shallow lake or pond, esp one connected with a larger body of water; the water enclosed by a circular coral reef.

laid *see* **lay**[2].

laid back *adj* relaxed, easy-going.

lain *see* **lie**[2].

lair *n* the dwelling or resting place of a wild animal; (*inf*) a secluded place, a retreat.

laity *n* laymen, as opposed to clergymen.

lake[1] *n* a large inland body of water.

lake[2] *n* a purplish-red pigment, originally made from lac.

lake boat *n* (*Cdn*) a commercial boat or ship that sails on the Great Lakes.

lakehead *n* (*Cdn*) the area along a lakeshore most distant from the lake's outlet.

lamb *n* a young sheep; its flesh as food; (*inf*) an innocent or gentle person. * *vi* to give birth to a lamb; to tend (ewes) at lambing time.

lame *adj* disabled or crippled, esp in the feet or legs; stiff and painful; weak, ineffectual. * *vt* to make lame.—**lamely** *adv*.—**lameness** *n*.

lament *vti* to feel or express deep sorrow (for); to mourn. * *n* a lamenting; an elegy, dirge, etc mourning some loss or death.

lamentable *adj* distressing, deplorable.—**lamentably** *adv*.

laminated *adj* built in thin sheets or layers.

lamp *n* any device producing light, either by electricity, gas, or by burning oil, etc; a holder or base for such a device; any device for producing therapeutic rays.

lampoon *n* a piece of satirical writing attacking someone. * *vt* to ridicule maliciously in a lampoon.—**lampooner** *n*.—**lampoonery** *n*.—**lampoonist** *n*.

lamppost *n* a post supporting a street lamp.

lance *n* a long wooden spear with a sharp iron or steel head. * *vt* to pierce (as if) with a lance; to open a boil, etc with a lancet.

land *n* the solid part of the earth's surface; ground, soil; a country and its people; property in land. * *vt* to set (an aircraft) down on land or water; to put on shore from a ship; to bring to a particular place; to catch (a fish); to get or secure (a job, prize, etc); to deliver (a blow). * *vi* to go ashore from a ship; to come to port; to arrive at a specified place; to come to rest.

land claim *n* (*Cdn*) a legal claim by a First Nations people to the use or ownership of an area of land.

landed immigrant *n* (*Cdn*) a person granted official status as an immigrant to Canada.

landing *n* the act of coming to shore or to the ground; the place where persons or goods are loaded or unloaded from a ship; a platform at the end of a flight of stairs.

landing stage *n* a platform for landing goods or people from a ship.

landing strip *n* an airstrip.

landlady *n* a woman who owns and rents property; a woman who owns and runs a boarding house, pub, etc.

landlocked *adj* surrounded by land.

landlord *n* a man who owns and rents property; a man who owns and runs a boarding house, pub, etc.

landlubber *n* a person who has had little experience of the sea.

landmark *n* any prominent feature of the landscape distinguishing a locality; an important event or turning point.

Land of the Midnight Sun *n* (*Cdn*) (*inf*) the Arctic.

landowner *n* a person who owns land.

landscape *n* an expanse of natural scenery seen in one view; a picture of natural, inland scenery. * *vt* to make (a plot of ground) more attractive, as by adding lawns, bushes, trees, etc.

landslide *n* the sliding of a mass of soil or rocks down a slope; an overwhelming victory, esp in an election.

lane *n* a narrow road, path, etc; a path or strip specifically designated for ships, aircraft, cars, etc; one of the narrow strips dividing a running track, swimming pool, etc for athletes and swimmers; one of the narrow passages along which balls are bowled in a bowling alley.

laneway *n* (*Cdn*) a lane, esp behind a row of buildings.

language *n* human speech or the written symbols for speech; any means of communicating; a special set of symbols used for programming a computer; the speech of a particular nation, etc; the particular style of verbal expression characteristic of a person, group, profession, etc.

languid *adj* lacking energy or vitality; apathetic, not interested; drooping, sluggish.—**languidly** *adv*.—**languidness** *n*.

languish *vi* to lose strength and vitality; to pine; to suffer neglect or hardship; to assume a pleading or melancholic expression.

lank *adj* tall and thin; long and limp.—**lankly** *adv*.—**lankness** *n*.

lanky *adj* (**lankier, lankiest**) lean, tall, and ungainly.—**lankily** *adv*.—**lankiness** *n*.

lantern *n* a portable transparent case for holding a light; a structure with windows on top of a door or roof to provide light and ventilation; the light-chamber of a lighthouse.

lap[1] *vti* (*pt* **lapped**) to take in (liquid) with the tongue; (*waves*) to flow gently with a splashing sound.

lap[2] *n* the flat area from waist to knees formed by a person sitting; the part of the clothing covering this.

lap[3] *n* an overlapping; a part that overlaps; one complete circuit of a race track. * *vb* (*pt* **lapped**) *vt* to fold (over or on); to wrap. * *vi* to overlap; to extend over something in space or time.

lapel *n* a part of a suit, coat, jacket, etc folded back and continuous with the collar.—**lapelled** *adj*.

lapse *n* a small error; a decline or drop to a lower condition, degree, or state; a moral decline; a period of time elapsed; the termination of a legal right or privilege through disuse. * *vi* to depart from the usual or accepted standard, esp in morals; to pass out of existence or use; to become void or discontinued; (*time*) to slip away.

larceny *n* theft.—**larcenous** *adj*.

lard *n* melted and clarified pig fat. * *vt* to insert strips of bacon or pork fat (in meat) before cooking; to embellish.

larder *n* a room or cupboard where food is stored.

large *adj* great in size, amount, or number; bulky; big; spacious; bigger than others of its kind; operating on a big scale.—**largeness** *n*.

largely *adv* much, in great amounts; mainly, for the most part.

lark[1] *n* any of a family of songbirds.

lark[2] *n* a playful or amusing adventure; a harmless prank. * *vi* (*usu with* **about**) to have fun, frolic.

larva *n* (*pl* **larvae**) the immature form of many animals after emerging from an egg before transformation into the adult state, eg a caterpillar.—**larval** *adj*.

laryngitis *n* inflammation of the larynx.

larynx *n* (*pl* **larynges, larynxes**) the structure at the upper end of the windpipe, containing the vocal cords.

lascivious *adj* lecherous, lustful; arousing sexual desire.—**lasciviously** *adv*.—**lasciviousness** *n*.

laser *n* a device that produces an intense beam of coherent light or other electromagnetic radiation.

lash *vt* to strike forcefully (as if) with a lash; to fasten or secure with a cord, etc; to attack with criticism or ridicule. * *vi* to move quickly and violently; (*rain, waves, etc*) to beat violently against; (*with* **out**) to attack physically or verbally. * *n* the flexible part of a whip; an eyelash; a stroke (as if) with a whip.

lass, lassie *n* a young woman or girl.

lasso *n* (*pl* **lassoes, lassos**) a long rope or leather thong with a running noose for catching horses, cattle, etc. * *vt* (*pr p* **lassoing**, *pt* **lassoed**) to catch (as if) with a lasso.

last[1] *n* a shoemaker's model of the foot on which boots and shoes are made or repaired. * *vt* to shape with a last.

last[2] *vi* to remain in existence, use, etc; to endure. * *vt* to continue during; to be enough for.

last[3] *adj* being or coming after all the others in time or place; only remaining; the most recent; least likely; conclusive. * *adv* after all the others; most recently; finally. * *n* the one coming last.

lasting *adj* enduring.—**lastingly** *adv*.

lastly *adv* at the end, in the last place, finally.

last-minute *adj* at the last possible time when something can be done.

latch *n* a fastening for a door, gate, or window, esp a bar, etc that fits into a notch. * *vti* to fasten with a latch.

latchkey *n* the key of an outer door.

late *adj, adv* after the usual or expected time; at an advanced stage or age; near the end; far on in the day or evening; just prior to the present; deceased; not long past; until lately; out of office.—**lateness** *n*.

lately *adv* recently, in recent times.

latent *adj* existing but not yet visible or developed.—**latency** *n*.

lateral *adj* of, at, from, towards the side.—**laterally** *adv*.

lath *n* a thin narrow strip of wood used in constructing a framework for plaster, etc.

lathe *n* a machine that rotates wood, metal, etc for shaping.

lather *n* a foam made by soap or detergent mixed with water; frothy sweat; a state of excitement or agitation. * *vti* to cover with or form lather.

Latin *adj* of ancient Rome, its people, their language, etc; denoting or of the languages derived from Latin (Italian, Spanish, etc), the peoples who speak them, their countries, etc. * *n* a native or inhabitant of ancient Rome; the language of ancient Rome; a person, as a Spaniard or Italian, whose language is derived from Latin.

latitude *n* the distance from north or south of the equator, measured in degrees; a region with reference to this distance; extent; scope; freedom from restrictions on actions or opinions.—**latitudinal** *adj*.—**latitudinally** *adv*.

latrine *n* a lavatory, as in a military camp.

latter *adj* later; more recent; nearer the end;

being the last mentioned of two.

latterly *adv* recently.

lattice *n* a network of crossed laths or bars.

laudable *adj* praiseworthy.

laugh *vi* to emit explosive inarticulate vocal sounds expressive of amusement, joy or derision. * *vt* to utter or express with laughter. * *n* the act or sound of laughing; (*inf*) an amusing person or thing.—**laughingly** *adv*.

laughable *adj* causing laughter; ridiculous.—**laughably** *adv*.

laughing stock *n* an object of ridicule.

laughter *n* the act or sound of laughing.

launch[1] *vt* to throw, hurl or propel forward; to cause (a vessel) to slide into the water; (*rocket, missile*) to set off; to put into action; to put a new product onto the market. * *vi* to involve oneself enthusiastically. * *n* the act or occasion of launching.

launch[2] *n* an open, or partly enclosed, motor boat.

launching pad, launch pad *n* a platform from which a spacecraft is launched.

launder *vti* to wash and iron clothes. * *vt* to legitimize (money) obtained from criminal activity by passing it through foreign banks, or investing in legitimate businesses, etc.

launderette, laundrette *n* an establishment equipped with coin-operated washing machines and driers for public use.

laundry *n* a place where clothes are washed and ironed; clothes sent to be washed and ironed.

laureate *adj* crowned with laurel leaves as a mark of honor. * *n* a poet laureate.

laurel *n* an evergreen shrub with large, glossy leaves; the leaves used by the ancient Greeks as a symbol of achievement.

lava *n* molten rock flowing from a volcano; the solid substance formed as this cools.

lavatory *n* a sanitary device for the disposal of faeces and urine; a room equipped with this, a toilet.

lavender *n* the fragrant flowers of a perennial shrub dried and used in sachets; a pale purple.

lavish *vt* to give or spend freely. * *adj* abundant, profuse; generous; extravagant.—**lavishly** *adv*.—**lavishness** *n*.

law *n* all the rules of conduct in an organized community as upheld by authority; any one of such rules; obedience to such rules; the study of such rules, jurisprudence; the seeking of justice in courts under such rules; the profession of lawyers, judges, etc; (*inf*) the police; a sequence of events occurring with unvarying uniformity under the same conditions; any rule expected to be observed.

law-abiding *adj* obeying the law.

lawbreaker *n* a person who violates the law.

lawful *adj* in conformity with the law; recognized by law.—**lawfully** *adv*.

lawless *adj* not regulated by law; not in conformity with law, illegal.—**lawlessly** *adv*.—**lawlessness** *n*.

lawn[1] *n* a fine sheer cloth of linen or cotton.

lawn[2] *n* land covered with closely cut grass, esp around a house.

lawn mower *n* a hand-propelled or power-driven machine to cut lawn grass.

lawn tennis *n* tennis played on a grass court.

lawsuit *n* a suit between private parties in a law court.

lawyer *n* a person whose profession is advising others in matters of law or representing them in a court of law.

lax *adj* slack, loose; not tight; not strict or exact.—**laxly** *adv*.—**laxness** *n*.

laxative *n* a substance that promotes emptying of the bowels.—*also adj*.

laxity *n* the state or quality of being lax, laxness.

lay[1] *see* **lie**[2].

lay[2] *vt* (*pt* **laid**) to put down; to allay or suppress; to place in a resting position; to place or set; to place in a correct position; to produce (an egg); (*sl*) to have sexual intercourse with; to devise; to present or assert; to stake a bet; (*with* **off**) to suspend from work temporarily or permanently; (*with* **on**) to supply; (*with* **out**) to plan in detail; to arrange for display; to prepare (a corpse) for viewing; (*inf*) to spend money, esp lavishly. * *vi* (*inf*) to leave (a person or thing) alone. * *n* a way or position in which something is situated; (*sl*) an act of sexual intercourse; a sexual partner.

lay[3] *n* a simple narrative poem, esp as intended to be sung; a ballad.

lay[4] *adj* of or pertaining to those who are not members of the clergy; not belonging to a profession.

layabout *n* a loafer, lazy person.

lay-by *n* a place where motorists can stop at the side of a road without obstructing other traffic.

layer *n* a single thickness, fold, etc. * *vi* to separate into layers; to form by superimposing layers.

layman *n* a person who is not a member of the clergy; a non-specialist, someone who does not possess professional knowledge.

layout *n* the manner in which anything is laid out, esp arrangement of text and pictures on the pages of a newspaper or magazine, etc; the thing laid out.

laze *vti* to idle or loaf.

lazy *adj* (**lazier, laziest**) disinclined to work or exertion; encouraging or causing indolence; sluggishly moving.—**lazily** *adv*.—**laziness** *n*.

lb *abbr* = pound.

LC *abbr* (*Cdn*) = Liquor Commission.

LCBO *abbr* = Liquor Control Board of Ontario.

LCdr *abbr* (*Cdn*) = Lieutenant Commander.

LCol *abbr* (*Cdn*) = Lieutenant Colonel.

L/Cpl *abbr* = Lance Corporal.

lead[1] *vb* (*pt* **led**) *vt* to show the way, esp by going first; to direct or guide on a course; to direct by influence; to be head of (an expedition, orchestra, etc); to be ahead of in a contest; to live, spend (one's life). * vi to show the way, as by going first; (with to) to tend in a certain direction; to be or go first. * n the role of a leader; first place; the amount or distance ahead; anything that leads, as a clue; the leading role in a play, etc; the right of playing first in cards or the card played.

lead² n a heavy, soft, bluish-grey, metallic element; a weight for sounding depths at sea, etc; bullets; a stick of graphite, used in pencils; (print) a thin strip of metal used to space lines of type. * adj of or containing lead. * vt (pt leaded) to cover, weight, or space out with lead.

leaden adj made of lead; very heavy; dull grey; gloomy.

leader n the person who goes first; the principal first violin-player in an orchestra; the director of an orchestra; the inspiration or head of a movement, such as a political party; a person whose example is followed; a leading article in a newspaper.

leadership n the act of leading; the ability to be a leader; the leaders of an organization or movement collectively.

leading¹ adj capable of guiding or influencing; principal; in first position.

leading² n a covering of lead; (print) the body of a type, larger than the size, giving space.

leaf n (pl leaves) any of the flat, thin (usu green) parts growing from the stem of a plant; a sheet of paper; a very thin sheet of metal; a hinged or removable part of a table top. * vi to bear leaves; (with through) to turn the pages of.

leaflet n a small or young leaf; a sheet of printed information (often folded), esp advertising matter distributed free. * vi to distribute leaflets (to).

league¹ n an association of nations, groups, etc for promoting common interests; an association of sports clubs that organizes matches between members; any class or category. * vti to form into a league.

league² n (formerly) a varying measure of distance, averaging about three miles (5km).

leak n a crack or hole through which liquid or gas may accidentally pass; the liquid or gas passing through such an opening; confidential information made public deliberately or accidentally. * vi to (let) escape though an opening; to disclose information surreptitiously.

lean¹ adj thin, with little flesh or fat; spare; meagre. * n meat with little or no fat.—leanness n.

lean² vb (pt leaned or leant) vi to bend or slant from an upright position; to rest supported (on or against); to rely or depend for help (on). * vt to cause to lean.

leaning n inclination, tendency.

leap vb (pt leaped or leapt) vi to jump; (with at) to accept something offered eagerly. * vt to

pass over by a jump; to cause to leap. * n an act of leaping; bound; space passed by leaping; an abrupt transition.

leapfrog n a game in which one player vaults over another's bent back. * vi (pt leap-frogged) to vault in this manner; to advance in alternate jumps.

leap year n a year with an extra day (29 February) occurring every fourth year.

learn vti (pt learnt or learned) to gain knowledge of or skill in; to memorize; to become aware of, realize.—learner n.

learned adj having learning; erudite; acquired by study, experience, etc.—learnedly adv.

learning n a gaining of knowledge; the acquiring of knowledge or skill through study.

lease n a contract by which an owner lets land, property, etc to another person for a specified period. * vt to grant by or hold under lease.

leash n a cord, strap, etc by which a dog or animal is held in check. * vt to hold or restrain on a leash.

least adj smallest in size, degree, etc; slightest. * adv to the smallest degree. * n the smallest in amount.

leather n material made from the skin of an animal prepared by removing the hair and tanning; something made of leather. * vt to cover with leather; to thrash.

leave¹ n permission to do something; official authorization to be absent; the period covered by this.

leave² vb (pt left) vt to depart from; to cause or allow to remain in a specified state; to cause to remain behind; to refrain from consuming or dealing with; to have remaining at death, to bequeath; to have as a remainder; to allow to stay or or continue doing without interference; to entrust or commit to another; to abandon. * vi to depart.

lecherous adj characterized by or encouraging lechery.

lectern n a reading stand in a church; any similar reading support.

lecture n an informative talk to a class, etc; a lengthy reprimand. * vti to give a lecture (to); to reprimand.—lecturer n.

led see lead¹.

ledge n a narrow horizontal surface resembling a shelf projecting from a wall, rock face, etc; an underwater ridge of rocks; a rock layer containing ore.

ledger n a book in which a record of debits, credits, etc is kept.

lee n a shelter; the side or part away from the wind.

leech n a blood-sucking worm; a person who clings to or exploits another.

leek n a vegetable that resembles a greatly elongated green onion.

leer n a sly, oblique or lascivious look.—also vi.

leeway n the distance a ship or aircraft has strayed sideways of its course; freedom of action as regards expenditure of time, money, etc.

left¹ see **leave²**.

left² adj of or on the side that is towards the west when one faces north; worn on the left hand, foot, etc. * n the left side; (often cap) of or relating to the left in politics; the left hand; (boxing) a blow with the left hand.

left-hand adj of or towards the left side of a person or thing; for use by the left hand.

left-handed adj using the left hand in preference to the right; done or made for use with the left hand; ambiguous, backhanded. * adv with the left hand.

left luggage office n a temporary repository for luggage at a railway station, etc.—also **checkroom**.

leftovers npl unused portions of something, esp uneaten food.

left-wing adj of or relating to the liberal faction of a political party, organization, etc.—**left-winger** n.

leg n one of the limbs on which humans and animals support themselves and walk; the part of a garment covering the leg; anything shaped or used like a leg; a branch or limb of a forked object; a section, as of a trip; any of a series of games or matches in a competition.

legacy n money, property, etc left to someone in a will; something passed on by an ancestor or remaining from the past.

legal adj of or based on law; permitted by law; of or for lawyers.—**legally** adv.

legalize vt to make lawful.—**legalization** n.

legation n a diplomatic minister and staff; the headquarters of a diplomatic minister.

legend n a story handed down from the past; a notable person or the stories of his or her exploits; an inscription on a coin, etc; a caption; an explanation of the symbols used on a map.

legendary adj of, based on, or presented in legends; famous, notorious.

leggings npl protective outer coverings for the lower legs; a leg-hugging fashion garment for women.

legible adj able to be read.—**legibly** adv.—**legibility** n.

legion n an infantry unit of the ancient Roman army; a large body of soldiers; a large number, a multitude.

legislate vi to make or pass laws. * vt to bring about by legislation.

legislation n the act or process of lawmaking; the laws themselves.

legislative adj of legislation or a legislature; having the power to make laws.

legislator n a member of a legislative body.

legislature n the body of people who have the power of making laws.

legitimate adj lawful; reasonable, justifiable; conforming to accepted rules, standards, etc; (child) born of parents married to each other.—**legitimacy** n.—**legitimately** adv.

leisure n ease, relaxation, esp freedom from employment or duties. * adj free and unoccupied.—**leisured** adj.

leisurely adj relaxed, without hurry.—**leisureliness** n.

lemon n (a tree bearing) a small yellow oval fruit with an acid pulp; pale yellow; (sl) a person or thing considered disappointing or useless.—**lemony** adj.

lemonade n a lemon-flavored drink.

lend vb (pt lent) vt to give the use of something temporarily in expectation of its return; to provide (money) at interest; to give, impart. * vi to make loans.—**lender** n.

length n the extent of something from end to end, usu the longest dimension; a specified distance or period of time; something of a certain length taken from a larger piece; a long expanse; (often pl) the degree of effort put into some action.

lengthen vti to make or become longer.

lengthways, lengthwise adv in the direction of the length.

lengthy adj (lengthier, lengthiest) long, esp too long.—**lengthily** adv.—**lengthiness** n.

lenient adj not harsh or severe; merciful.—**leniency** n.—**leniently** adv.

lens n a curved piece of transparent glass, plastic, etc used in optical instruments to form an image; any device used to focus electromagnetic rays, sound waves, etc; a similar transparent part of the eye that focuses light rays on the retina.

Lent n the forty weekdays from Ash Wednesday to Easter, observed by Christians as a period of fasting and penitence.—**Lenten** adj.

lentil n any of several leguminous plants with edible seeds; their seed used for food.

Leo n (astrol) the 5th sign of the zodiac, in astrology operative 22 July-21 August; (astron) the Lion, a constellation in the northern hemisphere.

leopard n a large tawny feline with black spots found in Africa and Asia.—also **panther**.

leotard n a skintight one-piece garment worn by dancers and others engaged in strenuous exercise.

leper n a person with leprosy.

leprosy n a chronic infectious bacterial disease of the skin, often resulting in disfigurement.—**leprous** adj.

lesbian n a female homosexual. * adj of or characteristic of lesbians.—**lesbianism** n.

less adj not so much, not so great, etc; fewer; smaller. * adv to a smaller extent. * n a smaller amount. * prep minus.

lessen vti to make or become less.

lesson n something to be learned or studied; something that has been learned or studied; a unit of learning or teaching; (pl) a course of instruction; a selection from the Bible, read as a part of a church service.

lest conj in order, or for fear, that not; that.

let¹ n a stoppage; (tennis) a minor obstruction of the ball that requires a point to be replayed.

let² vb (pr p letting, pt let) vt to allow, permit; to

rent; to assign (a contract); to cause to run out, as blood; as an auxiliary in giving suggestions or commands (*let us go*); (*with* **down**) to lower; to deflate; to disappoint; to untie; to lengthen; (*with* **off**) to allow to leave (a ship, etc); to fire (a gun) or explode (a bomb); to release; to deal leniently with; (*with* **out**) to release; to reveal; to rent out; to make a garment larger; (*with* **up**) to relax; to cease. * *vi* to be rented; (*with* **on**) (*inf*) to pretend; (*inf*) to indicate one's awareness (of a secret, etc). * *n* the letting of property or accommodation.

let-down *n* a disappointment.

lethal *adj* deadly.—**lethality** *n*.—**lethally** *adv*.

lethargy *n* an abnormal drowsiness; sluggishness; apathy.—**lethargic** *adj*.—**lethargically** *adv*.

letter *n* a symbol representing a phonetic value in a written language; a character of the alphabet; a written or printed message; (*pl*) literature; learning; knowledge; literal meaning. * *vt* to mark with letters.

letter bomb *n* an explosive device concealed in an envelope and sent through the post.

letter box *n* a slit in the doorway of a house or building through which letters are delivered; a postbox.

lettering *n* the act or process of inscribing with letters; letters collectively; a title; an inscription.

lettuce *n* a plant with succulent leaves used in salads.

leukaemia, leukemia (*US*) *n* a chronic disease characterized by an abnormal increase in the number of white blood cells in body tissues and the blood.

levee *n* (*Cdn*) a public reception held on New Year's Day by the Governor General or by the Lieutenant-Governor of a province.

level *n* a horizontal line or plane; a position in a scale of values; a flat area or surface; an instrument for determining the horizontal. * *adj* horizontal; having a flat surface; at the same height, rank, position, etc; steady. * *vti* (*pt* **levelled**) to make or become level; to demolish; to raise and aim (a gun, criticism, etc).—**levelly** *adv*.—**leveller** *n*.

level crossing *n* a place where a road and railway or two railway lines cross at the same level.

level-headed *adj* having an even temper and sound judgment.

lever *n* a bar used for prising or moving something; a means to an end; a device consisting of a bar turning about a fixed point; any device used in the same way, eg to operate machinery. * *vt* to raise or move (as with) a lever.

leverage *n* the action of a lever; the mechanical advantage gained by the use of a lever; power, influence.

levity *n* excessive frivolity; lack of necessary seriousness.

levy *vt* to collect by force or authority, as a tax, fine, etc; an amount levied; to enrol or conscript troops; to prepare for or wage war. * *n* a levying; the amount levied.

lewd *adj* indecent; lustful; obscene.—**lewdly** *adv*.—**lewdness** *n*.

LGen *abbr* (*Cdn*) = Lieutenant General.

liability *n* a being liable; something for which one is liable; (*inf*) a handicap, disadvantage; (*pl*) debts, obligations, disadvantages.

liable *adj* legally bound or responsible; subject to; likely (to).

liaison *n* intercommunication as between units of a military force; an illicit love affair; a thickening for sauces, soups, etc, as egg yolks or cream.

liar *n* a person who tells lies.

libel *n* any written or printed matter tending to injure a person's reputation unjustly; (*inf*) any defamatory or damaging assertion about a person. * *vt* (*pt* **libelled**) to utter or publish a libel against.—**libellous** *adj*.

liberal *adj* ample, abundant; not literal or strict; tolerant; (*education*) contributing to a general broadening of the mind, non-specialist; favoring reform or progress. * *n* a person who favors reform or progress.—**liberally** *adv*.

liberate *vt* to set free from foreign occupation, slavery, etc.—**liberation** *n*.—**liberator** *n*.

liberty *n* freedom from slavery, captivity, etc; the right to do as one pleases, freedom; a particular right, freedom, etc granted by authority; an impertinent attitude; authorized leave granted to a sailor.

Libra *n* (*astrol*) the 7th sign of the zodiac, operative 24 September-23 October; a constellation represented as a pair of scales.

librarian *n* a person in charge of a library or trained in librarianship.

library *n* a collection of books, tapes, records, photographs, etc for reference or borrowing; a room, building or institution containing such a collection; (*comput*) a set of, usu general purpose, programs or subroutines for use in programming.

libretto *n* (*pl* **librettos, libretti**) the text to which an opera, oratorio, etc is set.—**librettist** *n*.

lice *see* **louse**.

licence, license (*US*) *n* a formal or legal permission to do something specified; a document granting such permission; freedom to deviate from rule, practice, etc; excessive freedom, an abuse of liberty.

license *vt* to grant a licence to or for; to permit.

licentious *adj* morally unrestrained; lascivious.—**licentiousness** *n*.

lichen *n* any of various small plants consisting of an alga and a fungus living in symbiotic association, growing on stones, trees, etc.

lick *vt* to draw the tongue over, esp to taste or clean; (*flames, etc*) to flicker around or touch lightly; (*inf*) to thrash; (*inf*) to defeat. * *n* a licking with the tongue; (*inf*) a sharp blow; (*inf*) a short, rapid burst of activity.

lid *n* a removable cover as for a box, etc; an eyelid.—**lidded** *adj*.

lido *n* an open air swimming pool and recreational complex for public use.

lie[1] *n* an untrue statement made with intent to

deceive; something that deceives or mis- leads. * *vi* (*pr p* lying, *pt* lied) to speak un- truthfully with an intention to deceive; to create a false impression.

lie² *vi* (*pr p* lying, *pt* lay, *pp* lain) to be or put one- self in a reclining or horizontal position; to rest on a support in a horizontal position; to be in a specified condition; to be situated; to exist. * *n* the way in which something is situated.

lieutenant *n* a commissioned army officer rank- ing below a captain; a naval officer next be- low a lieutenant commander; a deputy, a chief assistant to a superior.—**lieutenancy** *n*.

Lieutenant-Governor (*pl* **Lieutenant-Governors**) *n* (*Cdn*) the representative of the Crown in a province.

life *n* (*pl* **lives**) that property of plants and ani- mals (ending at death) that enables them to use food, grow, reproduce, etc; the state of having this property; living things collec- tively; the time a person or thing exists; one's manner of living; one's animate exist- ence; vigour, liveliness; (*inf*) a life sen- tence; a biography. * *adj* of animate being; lifelong; using a living model; of or relating to or provided by life insurance.

lifebelt *n* an inflatable ring to support a person in the water; a safety belt.

lifeboat *n* a small rescue boat carried by a ship; a specially designed and equipped rescue vessel that helps those in distress along the coastline.

lifeguard *n* an expert swimmer employed to pre- vent drownings.

life jacket *n* a sleeveless jacket or vest of buoy- ant material to keep a person afloat.

lifeless *adj* dead; unconscious; dull.—**lifelessly** *adv*.—**lifelessness** *n*.

lifelike *adj* resembling a real life person or thing.

lifeline *n* a rope for raising or lowering a diver; a rope for rescuing a person, eg as attached to a lifebelt; a vitally important channel of communication or transport.

lifelong *adj* lasting one's whole life.

life preserver *n* a club used as a weapon of self- defence; a lifebelt or life jacket.

lifetime *n* the length of time that a person lives or something lasts.

lift *vt* to bring to a higher position, raise; to raise in rank, condition, etc; (*sl*) to steal; to revoke. * *vi* to exert oneself in raising something; to rise; to go up; (*fog, etc*) to disperse; (*with* off) (*rocket, etc*) to take off. * *n* act or fact of lifting; distance through which a thing is lifted; elevation of mood, etc; elevated position or carriage; a ride in the direction in which one is going; help of any kind; a cage or platform for moving something from one level to another (— *also* **elevator**); upward air pressure maintain- ing an aircraft in flight.

liftoff *n* the vertical thrust of a spacecraft, etc at launching; the time of this.

ligament *n* a band of tissue connecting bones; a unifying bond.

light¹ *n* the agent of illumination that stimulates the sense of sight; electromagnetic radia- tion such as ultraviolet, infrared or X-rays; brightness, illumination; a source of light, as the sun, a lamp, etc; daylight; a thing used to ignite something; a window; knowl- edge, enlightenment; aspect or appear- ance. * *adj* having light; bright; pale in color. * *adv* palely. * *vt* (*pt* lit *or* lighted) to ignite; to cause to give off light; to furnish with light; to brighten, animate.

light² *adj* having little weight; not heavy; less than usual in weight, amount, force, etc; of little importance; easy to bear; easy to di- gest; happy; dizzy, giddy; not serious; mod- erate; moving with ease; producing small products. * *adv* lightly. * *vi* (*pt* lighted *or* lit) to come to rest after travelling through the air; to dismount, to alight; to come or hap- pen on or upon; to strike suddenly, as a blow.—**lightly** *adv*.—**lightness** *n*.

lighten¹ *vti* to make or become light or lighter; to shine, flash.

lighten² *vti* to make or become lighter in weight; to make or become more cheerful; to miti- gate.

lighter¹ *n* a small device that produces a naked flame to light cigarettes.

lighter² *n* a large barge used in loading or un- loading larger ships.

light-headed *adj* dizzy; delirious.

light-hearted *adj* carefree.

lighthouse *n* a tower with a bright light to guide ships.

lighting *n* the process of giving light; equipment for illuminating a stage, television set, etc; the distribution of light on an object, as in a work of art.

lightning *n* a discharge or flash of electricity in the sky. * *adv* fast, sudden.

lightning conductor, lightning rod *n* a metal rod placed high on a building and grounded to divert lightning from the structure.

lightweight *adj* of less than average weight; trivial, unimportant. * *n* a person or thing of less than average weight; a professional boxer weighing 130-135 pounds (59-61 kg); a person of little importance or influence.

light year *n* the distance light travels in one year.

like¹ *adj* having the same characteristics; simi- lar; equal. * *adv* (*inf*) likely. * *prep* similar to; characteristic of; in the mood for; in- dicative of; as for example. * *conj* (*inf*) as; as if. * *n* an equal; counterpart.

like² *vt* to be pleased with; to wish. * *vi* to be so inclined.

likelihood *n* probability.

likely *adj* (**likelier**, **likeliest**) reasonably to be ex- pected; suitable; showing promise of success.* *adv* probably.—**likeliness** *n*.

like-minded *adj* sharing the same tastes, ideas, etc.

liken *vt* to compare.

likewise *adv* the same; also.

liking n fondness; affection; preference.

lilac n a shrub with large clusters of tiny, fragrant flowers; a pale purple. * adj lilac colored.

lily n a bulbous plant having typically trumpet-shaped flowers; its flower.

lily of the valley n a small plant of the lily family with white bell-shaped flowers.

limb n a projecting appendage of an animal body, as an arm, leg, or wing; a large branch of a tree; a participating member, agent; an arm of a cross.

limber[1] adj flexible, able to bend the body easily. * vti to make or become limber.

limber[2] n the detachable wheeled section of a gun carriage.

limbo[1] n (pl limbos) (Christianity) the abode after death assigned to unbaptized souls; a place for lost, unwanted, or neglected persons or things; an intermediate stage or condition between extremes.

limbo[2] n (pl limbos) a West Indian dance that involves bending over backwards and passing under a horizontal bar that is progressively lowered.

lime[1] n a white calcium compound used for making cement and in agriculture. * vt to treat or cover with lime.

lime[2] n a small yellowish-green fruit with a juicy, sour pulp; the tree that bears it; its color.

lime[3] n the linden tree.

limelight n intense publicity; a type of lamp, formerly used in stage lighting, in which lime was heated to produce a brilliant flame.

limerick n a type of humorous verse consisting of five lines.

limestone n a type of rock composed mainly of calcium carbonate.

limit n a boundary; (pl) bounds; the greatest amount allowed; (inf) as much as one can tolerate. * vt to set a limit to; to restrict.

limitation n the act of limiting or being limited; a hindrance to ability or achievement.

limited adj confined within bounds; lacking imagination or originality.

limousine n a large luxury car.

limp[1] vi to walk with or as with a lame leg. * n a lameness in walking.

limp[2] adj not firm; lethargic; wilted; flexible.—**limply** adv.—**limpness** n.

limpet n a mollusc with a low conical shell that clings to rocks.

line[1] vt to put, or serve as, a lining in.

line[2] n a length of cord, rope, or wire; a cord for measuring, making level; a system of conducting fluid, electricity, etc; a thin thread-like mark; anything resembling such a mark, as a wrinkle; edge, limit, boundary; border, outline, contour; a row of persons or things, as printed letters across a page; a succession of persons, lineage; a connected series of things; the course a moving thing takes; a course of conduct, actions, etc; a whole system of transportation; a person's trade or occupation; a field

of experience or interest; (inf) glib, persuasive talk; a verse; the forward combat position in warfare; fortifications, trenches or other defences used in war; a stock of goods; a piece of information; a short letter, note; (pl) all the speeches of a character in a play. * vt to mark with lines; to form a line along; to cover with lines; to arrange in a line. * vi to align.

linear adj of, made of, or using a line or lines; narrow and long; in relation to length only.—**linearity** n.

linen n thread or cloth made of flax; household articles (sheets, cloths, etc) made of linen or cotton cloth.

liner n a large passenger ship or aircraft travelling a regular route.

linesman n an official in certain games who assists the referee in deciding when the ball is out of play, etc.

line-up n an arrangement of persons or things in a line, eg for inspection.

linger vi to stay a long time; to delay departure; to dawdle or loiter; to dwell on in the mind; to remain alive though on the point of death.

lingo n (pl lingoes) (inf) a dialect, jargon, etc.

linguist n a person who is skilled in speaking foreign languages.

linguistic adj of or pertaining to language or linguistics.—**linguistically** adv.

linguistics n (used as sing) the science of language.

lining n a material used to cover the inner surface of a garment, etc; any material covering an inner surface.

link n a single loop or ring of a chain; something resembling a loop or ring or connecting piece; a person or thing acting as a connection, as in a communication system, machine or organization. * vti to connect or become connected.

links npl (also used as sing) flat sandy soil; a golf course, esp by the sea.

link-up n a linking together.

linoleum n a floor covering of coarse fabric backing with a smooth, hard decorative coating.

lint n scraped and softened linen used to dress wounds; fluff.

lintel n the horizontal crosspiece spanning a doorway or window.

lion n a large, flesh-eating feline mammal with a shaggy mane in the adult male; a person of great courage or strength.—**lioness** nf.

lip n either of the two fleshy flaps that surround the mouth; anything like a lip, as the rim of a jug; (sl) insolent talk. * vt (pt lipped) to touch with the lips; to kiss; to utter.

lip service n support expressed but not acted upon.

lipstick n a small stick of cosmetic for coloring the lips; the cosmetic itself.

liqueur n a sweet and variously flavored alcoholic drink.

liquid n a substance that, unlike a gas, does not expand indefinitely and, unlike a solid, flows readily. * *adj* in liquid form; clear; limpid; flowing smoothly and musically, as verse; (*assets*) readily convertible into cash.—**liquidity** *n*.

liquidate *vt* to settle the accounts of; to close a (bankrupt) business and distribute its assets among its creditors; to convert into cash; to eliminate, kill.—**liquidation** *n*.—**liquidator** *n*.

liquidize *vt* to make liquid.

liquor *n* an alcoholic drink; any liquid, esp that in which food has been cooked.

liquor commission *n* (*Cdn*) in some provinces and territories, a government body that regulates the distribution and sales of alcoholic beverages.—*also* **liquor control board**.

liquorice, licorice (*US*) *n* a black extract made from the root of a European plant, used in medicine and confectionery; a liquorice-flavored sweet.

lisp *vi* to substitute the sounds *th* (as in *thin*) for *s* or *th* (as in *then*) for *z*; a speech defect or habit involving such pronunciation; to utter imperfectly. * *vt* to speak or utter with a lisp.—*also* *n*.

list[1] *n* a series of names, numbers, words, etc written or printed in order. * *vt* to make a list of; to enter in a directory, etc.

list[2] *vti* to tilt to one side, as a ship. * *n* such a tilting.

listen *vi* to try to hear; to pay attention, take heed; (*with* **in**) to overhear a conversation, eg on the telephone; to tune into a radio broadcast; to eavesdrop.

listener *n* a person who listens; a person listening to a radio broadcast.

listless *adj* lacking energy or enthusiasm because of illness, dejection, etc; languid.—**listlessly** *adv*.—**listlessness** *n*.

lit *see* **light**[1], **light**[2].

litany *n* a type of prayer in which petitions to God are recited by a priest and elicit set responses by the congregation; any tedious or automatic recital.

literacy *n* the ability to read and write.

literal *adj* in accordance with the exact meaning of a word or text; in a basic or strict sense; prosaic, unimaginative; real.—**literally** *adv*.

literary *adj* of or dealing with literature; knowing much about literature.

literate *adj* able to read and write; educated.—*also* *n*.

literature *n* the writings of a period or of a country, esp those valued for their excellence; of style or form; all the books and articles on a subject; (*inf*) any printed matter.

lithe *adj* supple, flexible.

litigate *vti* to bring or contest in a lawsuit.—**litigation** *n*.

litre, liter (*US*) *n* a measure of liquid capacity in the metric system, equivalent to 1.76 pints.

litter *n* rubbish scattered about; young animals produced at one time; straw, hay, etc used as bedding for animals; a stretcher for carrying a sick or wounded person. * *vt* to make untidy; to scatter about carelessly.

little *adj* not great or big, small in size, amount, degree, etc; short in duration; small in importance or power; narrow-minded. * *n* small in amount, degree, etc. * *adv* less, least, slightly; not much; not in the least.

liturgy *n* the prescribed form of service of a church.—**liturgical** *adj*.—**liturgically** *adv*.

live[1] *vi* to have life; to remain alive; to endure; to pass life in a specified manner; to enjoy a full life; to reside. * *vt* to carry out in one's life; to spend; pass.

live[2] *adj* having life; of the living state or living beings; of present interest; still burning; unexploded; carrying electric current; broadcast during the actual performance.

livelihood *n* employment; a means of living.

lively *adj* (**livelier, liveliest**) full of life; spirited; exciting; vivid; keen. * *adv* in a lively manner.—**liveliness** *n*.

liver *n* the largest glandular organ in vertebrate animals, which secretes bile, etc and is important in metabolism; the liver of an animal used as food; a reddish-brown color.

livery *n* an identifying uniform, as that worn by a servant.

lives *see* **life**.

livestock *n* (farm) animals raised for use or sale.

liveyer *n* (*Cdn*) (*inf*) a permanent resident of Newfoundland or Labrador.

livid *adj* (*skin*) discolored, as from bruising; greyish in color; (*inf*) extremely angry.

living *adj* having life; still in use; true to life, vivid; of life, for living in. * *n* a being alive; livelihood; manner of existence.

living room *n* a room in a house used for general entertainment and relaxation.

living wage *n* a wage sufficient to maintain a reasonable standard of comfort.

lizard *n* a reptile with a slender body, four legs, and a tapering tail.

llama *n* a South American animal, related to the camel, used for carrying loads and as a source of wool.

load *n* an amount carried at one time; something borne with difficulty; a burden; (*often pl*) (*inf*) a great amount. * *vt* to put into or upon; to burden; to oppress; to supply in large quantities; to alter, as by adding a weight to dice or an adulterant to alcoholic drink; to put a charge of ammunition into (a firearm); to put film into (a camera); (*comput*) to install a program in memory. * *vi* to take on a load.

loaded *adj* (*sl*) having plenty of money; drunk; under the influence of drugs.

loaf[1] *n* (*pl* **loaves**) a mass of bread of regular shape and standard weight; food shaped like this; (*sl*) the head.

loaf[2] *vi* to pass time in idleness.—**loafer** *n*.

loam *n* rich and fertile soil.—**loamy** *adj*.

loan *n* the act of lending; something lent, esp money. * *vti* to lend.

loath *adj* unwilling.—*also* **loth**.

loathe *vt* to dislike intensely; to detest.—**loathing** *n*.

lobby *n* an entrance hall of a public building; a person or group that tries to influence legislators. * *vti* to try to influence (legislators) to support a particular cause or take certain action.

lobe *n* a rounded projection, as the lower end of the ear; any of the divisions of the lungs or brain.

lobster *n* any of a family of edible sea crustaceans with four pairs of legs and a pair of large pincers.

lobster supper *n* (*Cdn*) in the Maritime Provinces, a full meal featuring boiled lobsters that is sold and served to the public in a community hall.

local *adj* of or belonging to a particular place; serving the needs of a specific district; of or for a particular part of the body. * *n* an inhabitant of a specific place; (*inf*) a pub serving a particular district.—**locally** *adv*.

locality *n* a neighborhood or a district; a particular scene, position, or place; the fact or condition of having a location in space and time.

locate *vt* to determine or indicate the position of something; to set in or assign to a particular position.

location *n* a specific position or place; a locating or being located; a place outside a studio where a film is (partly) shot; (*comput*) an area in memory where a single item of data is stored.

loch *n* (*Scot*) a lake.

lock[1] *n* a fastening device on doors, etc, operated by a key or combination; part of a canal, dock, etc in which the level of the water can be changed by the operation of gates; the part of a gun by which the charge is fired; a controlling hold, as used in wrestling. * *vt* to fasten with a lock; to shut; to fit, link; to jam together so as to make immovable. * *vi* to become locked; to interlock.

lock[2] *n* a curl of hair; a tuft of wool, etc.

locker *n* a small cupboard, chest, etc that can be locked, esp one for storing possessions in a public place.

locket *n* a small ornamental case, usu holding a lock of hair, photograph or other memento, hung from the neck.

lockjaw *n* tetanus.

lockup *n* (*Cdn*) a period of time in which members of the media are allowed to examine a government budget, but not report on it, while locked in a room just before the budget is released in a legislature.

locomotive *n* an electric, steam, or diesel engine on wheels, designed to move a railway train. * *adj* of locomotion.

locust *n* a type of large grasshopper often travelling in swarms and destroying crops; a type of hard-wooded leguminous tree.

lodge *n* a small house at the entrance to a park or stately home; a country house for seasonal leisure activities; a resort hotel or motel; the local chapter or hall of a fraternal society; a beaver's lair. * *vt* to house temporarily; to shoot, thrust, etc firmly (in); to bring before legal authorities; to confer upon. * *vi* to live in a place for a time; to live as a paying guest; to come to rest and stick firmly (in).

lodger *n* a person who lives in a rented room in another's home.

lodging *n* a temporary residence; (*pl*) accommodation rented in another's house.

loft *n* a space under a roof; a storage area under the roof of a barn or stable; a gallery in a church or hall. * *vt* to send into a high curve.

lofty *adj* (**loftier, loftiest**) (*objects*) of a great height, elevated; (*person*) noble, haughty, superior in manner.—**loftily** *adv*.—**loftiness** *n*.

log *n* a section of a felled tree; a device for ascertaining the speed of a ship; a record of speed, progress, etc, esp one kept on a ship's voyage or aircraft's flight. * *vb* (*pt* **logged**) *vt* to record in a log; to sail or fly (a specified distance). * *vi* (*with* **on, off**) (*comput*) to establish or disestablish communication with a mainframe computer from a remote terminal in a multi-user system.—**logger** *n*.

logbook *n* an official record of a ship's or aircraft's voyage or flight; an official document containing details of a vehicle's registration.

log drive *n* (*Cdn*) the transportation of logs from forests to mills by floating them down rivers.

logic *n* correct reasoning, or the science of this; way of reasoning; what is expected by the working of cause and effect.—**logician** *n*.

logical *adj* conforming to the rules of logic; capable of reasoning according to logic.—**logically** *adv*.—**logicality** *n*.

logistics *n* (*used as sing*) the science of the organization, transport and supply of military forces; the planning and organization of any complex activity.—**logistic** *adj*.

loin *n* (*usu pl*) the lower part of the back between the hipbones and the ribs; the front part of the hindquarters of an animal used for food.

loiter *vi* to linger or stand about aimlessly.—**loiterer** *n*.

loll *vi* to lean or recline in a lazy manner, to lounge; (*tongue*) to hang loosely.

lollipop *n* a flat boiled sweet at the end of a stick.

lone *adj* by oneself; isolated; without companions, solitary.

lonely *adj* (**lonelier, loneliest**) isolated; unhappy at being alone; (*places*) remote, rarely visited.

loner *n* a person who avoids the company of others.

long[1] *adj* measuring much in space or time; having a greater than usual length, quantity, etc; tedious, slow; far-reaching; well-supplied. * *adv* for a long time; from start to finish; at a remote time.

long[2] *vi* to desire earnestly, esp for something not likely to be attained.

long-distance *adj* travelling or communicating over long distances.

longhand *n* ordinary handwriting, as opposed to shorthand.

longhouse *n* among some North American Indian peoples, a traditional dwelling shared by several families.

longing *n* an intense desire.

longitude *n* distance east or west of the prime meridian, expressed in degrees or time.

long jump *n* an athletic event consisting of a horizontal running jump.

long-playing *adj* of or relating to an LP record.

long-range *adj* reaching over a long distance or period of time.

long-sighted *adj* only seeing distant objects clearly.

long-standing *adj* having continued for a long time.

long-suffering *adj* enduring pain, provocation, etc patiently.

long-term *adj* of or extending over a long time.

long wave *n* a radio wave of a frequency less than 300 kHz.

long-winded *adj* speaking or writing at great length; tiresome.

loo *n* (*inf*) a lavatory.

look *vi* to try to see; to see; to search; to appear, seem; to be facing in a specified direction; (*with* in) to pay a brief visit; (*with* up) to improve in prospects. * *vt* to direct one's eyes on; to have an appearance befitting. * *n* the act of looking; a gaze, glance; appearance; aspect; (*with* after) to take care of; (*with* over) to examine; (*with* up) to research (for information, etc) in book; to visit.

look-alike *n* a person that looks like another.

lookout *n* a place for keeping watch; a person assigned to watch.

loom[1] *n* a machine or frame for weaving yarn or thread. * *vt* to weave on a loom.

loom[2] *vi* to come into view indistinctly and often threateningly; to come ominously close, as an impending event.

loonie *n* (*Cdn*) a one-dollar coin.

loop *n* a figure made by a curved line crossing itself; a similar rounded shape in cord, rope, etc crossed on itself; anything forming this figure; (*comput*) a set of instructions in a program that are executed repeatedly; an intrauterine contraceptive device; a segment of film or magnetic tape. * *vt* to make a loop of; to fasten with a loop. * *vi* to form a loop or loops.

loophole *n* a means of evading an obligation, etc; a slit in a wall for looking or shooting through.

loose *adj* free from confinement or restraint; not firmly fastened; not tight or compact; not precise; inexact; (*inf*) relaxed. * *vt* to release; to unfasten; to untie; to detach; (*bullet*) to discharge. * *vi* to become loose.—**loosely** *adv*.—**looseness** *n*.

loosen *vti* to make or become loose or looser.

loot *n* goods taken during warfare, civil unrest, etc; (*sl*) money. * *vti* to plunder, pillage.—

looter *n*.

lop *vt* (*pt* **lopped**) to sever the branches or twigs from a tree; to cut off or out as superfluous.

lopsided *adj* having one side larger in weight, height, or size than the other; badly balanced.

lord *n* a ruler, master or monarch; a male member of the nobility; (*with cap and* **the**) God; a form of address used to certain peers, bishops and judges.

lordly *adj* (**lordlier, lordliest**) noble; haughty; arrogant.

lordship *n* the rank or authority of a lord; rule, dominion; (*with* **his** *or* **your**) a title used in speaking of or to a lord.

lore *n* knowledge; learning, esp of a traditional nature; a particular body of tradition.

lorry *n* a large motor vehicle for transporting heavy loads, a truck.

lose *vb* (*pt* **lost**) *vt* to have taken from one by death, accident, removal, etc; to be unable to find; to fail to keep, as one's temper; to fail to see, hear, or understand; to fail to have, get, etc; to fail to win; to cause the loss of; to wander from (one's way, etc); to squander. * *vi* to suffer (a) loss.—**loser** *n*.

loss *n* a losing or being lost; the damage, trouble caused by losing; the person, thing, or amount lost.

lost *adj* no longer possessed; missing; not won; destroyed or ruined; having wandered astray; wasted.

lot *n* an object, such as a straw, slip of paper, etc drawn from others at random to reach a decision by chance; the decision thus arrived at; one's share by lot; fortune; a plot of ground; a group of persons or things; an item or set of items put up for auction; (*often pl*) (*inf*) a great amount; much; (*inf*) sort.

loth *see* **loath**.

lotion *n* a liquid for cosmetic or external medical use.

lottery *n* a system of raising money by selling numbered tickets that offer the chance of winning a prize; an enterprise, etc which may or may not succeed.

loud *adj* characterized by or producing great noise; emphatic; (*inf*) obtrusive or flashy.—**loudly** *adv*.—**loudness** *n*.

loudspeaker *n* a device for converting electrical energy into sound.

lounge *vi* to move, sit, lie, etc in a relaxed way; to spend time idly. * *n* a room with comfortable furniture for sitting, as a waiting room at an airport, etc; a comfortable sitting room in a hotel or private house.

louse *n* (*pl* **lice**) any of various small wingless insects that are parasitic on humans and animals; any similar but unrelated insects that are parasitic on plants; (*inf*) (*pl* **louses**) a mean, contemptible person.

lousy *adj* (**lousier, lousiest**) infested with lice; (*sl*) disgusting, of poor quality, or inferior; (*sl*) well supplied (with).

lout *n* a clumsy, rude person.—**loutish** *adj*.

lovable, loveable *adj* easy to love or feel affection

for.

love *n* a strong liking for someone or something; a passionate affection for another person; the object of such affection; (*tennis*) a score of zero. * *vti* to feel love (for).

love affair *n* a romantic or sexual relationship between two people.

lovely *adj* (**lovelier, loveliest**) beautiful; (*inf*) highly enjoyable.—**loveliness** *n*.

lover *n* a person in love with another person; a person, esp a man, having an extramarital sexual relationship; (*pl*) a couple in love with each other; someone who loves a specific person or thing.

loving *adj* affectionate.—**lovingly** *adv*.

low[1] *n* the sound a cow makes, a moo. * *vi* to make this sound.

low[2] *adj* not high or tall; below the normal level; less in size, degree, amount, etc, than usual; deep in pitch; depressed in spirits; humble, of low rank; vulgar, coarse; not loud. * *adv* in or to a low degree, level, etc. * *n* a low level, degree, etc; a region of low barometric pressure.

Low Arctic *n* (*Cdn*) the Arctic south of the Arctic Circle.

loyal *adj* firm in allegiance to a person, cause, country, party, etc, faithful; demonstrating unswerving allegiance.—**loyally** *adv*.—**loyalty** *n*.

lozenge *n* a four-sided diamond-shaped figure; a cough drop, sweet, etc, originally diamond-shaped.

LP *n* a long-playing record, usu 12 inches (30.5 cm) in diameter and played at a speed of 33.33 revolutions per minute.

Ltd *abbr* = limited liability (used by private companies only).

lubricant *n* a substance that lubricates.

lubricate *vt* to coat or treat (machinery, etc) with oil or grease to lessen friction; to make smooth, slippery, or greasy. * *vi* to act as a lubricant.—**lubrication** *n*.—**lubricator** *n*.

lucid *adj* easily understood; sane.—**lucidly** *adv*.—**lucidity** *n*.

luck *n* chance; good fortune.

lucky *adj* (**luckier, luckiest**) having or bringing good luck.—**luckily** *adv*.

lucrative *adj* producing wealth or profit; profitable.—**lucrativeness** *n*.

ludicrous *adj* absurd, laughable.—**ludicrously** *adv*.

lug[1] *vt* (*pt* **lugged**) to pull or drag along with effort.

lug[2] *n* an ear-like projection by which a thing is held or supported.

luggage *n* the suitcases and other baggage containing the possessions of a traveller.

lukewarm *adj* barely warm, tepid; lacking enthusiasm.

lull *vt* to soothe, to calm; to calm the suspicions of, esp by deception. * *n* a short period of calm.

lullaby *n* a song to lull children to sleep.

lumbago *n* rheumatic pain in the lower back.

lumber[1] *n* timber, logs, beams, boards, etc, roughly cut and prepared for use; articles of unused household furniture that are stored away; any useless articles. * *vi* to cut down timber and saw it into lumber. * *vt* to clutter with lumber; to heap in disorder.

lumber[2] *vi* to move heavily or clumsily.

lumberjack *n* a person employed to fell trees and transport and prepare timber.

luminous *adj* emitting light; glowing in the dark; clear, easily understood.

lump *n* a small, compact mass of something, usu without definite shape; an abnormal swelling; a dull or stupid person. * *adj* in a lump or lumps. * *vt* to treat or deal with in a mass. * *vi* to become lumpy.

lumpy *adj* (**lumpier, lumpiest**) filled or covered with lumps.—**lumpily** *adv*.—**lumpiness** *n*.

lunacy *n* insanity; utter folly.

lunar *adj* of or like the moon.

lunatic *adj* insane; utterly foolish. * *n* an insane person.

lunch *n* a light meal, esp between breakfast and dinner. * *vi* to eat lunch.

luncheon *n* lunch, esp a formal lunch.

luncheon voucher *n* a voucher, issued to an employee in addition to pay, that can be exchanged for food in certain restaurants.

lung *n* either of the two sponge-like breathing organs in the chest of vertebrates.

lunge *n* a sudden forceful thrust, as with a sword; a sudden plunge forward. * *vti* to move, or cause to move, with a lunge.

lurch *vi* to lean or pitch suddenly to the side.—*also n*.

lure *n* something that attracts, tempts or entices; a brightly colored fishing bait; a device used to recall a trained hawk; a decoy for wild animals. * *vt* to entice, attract, or tempt.

lurid *adj* vivid, glaring; shocking; sensational.—**luridly** *adv*.—**luridness** *n*.

lurk *vi* to lie hidden in wait; to loiter furtively.

luscious *adj* delicious; richly sweet; delighting any of the senses.—**lusciously** *adv*.—**lusciousness** *n*.

lush[1] *adj* tender and juicy; of or showing abundant growth.—**lushly** *adv*.—**lushness** *n*.

lush[2] *n* (*sl*) an alcoholic.

lust *n* strong sexual desire (for); an intense longing for something. * *vi* to feel lust.—**lustful** *adj*.—**lustfully** *adv*.

lustre, luster (*US*) *n* gloss; sheen; brightness; radiance; brilliant beauty or fame; glory.—**lustrous** *adj*.

lusty *adj* (**lustier, lustiest**) strong; vigorous; healthy.—**lustily** *adv*.—**lustiness** *n*.

lute *n* an old-fashioned stringed instrument.

luxuriant *adj* profuse, abundant; ornate; fertile.—**luxuriance** *n*.

luxurious *adj* constituting luxury; indulging in luxury; rich, comfortable.—**luxuriously** *adv*.—**luxuriousness** *n*.

luxury *n* indulgence and pleasure in sumptuous and expensive food, accommodation, clothes, etc; (*often pl*) something that is costly and enjoyable but not indispensable. * *adj* relating to or supplying luxury.

lying *see* **lie¹, lie².**

lynch *vt* to murder (an accused person) by mob action, without lawful trial, as by hanging.

lynx *n* (*pl* **lynxes, lynx**) a wild feline of Europe and North America with spotted fur.

lyre *n* an ancient musical instrument of the harp family.

lyric *adj* denoting or of poetry expressing the writer's emotion; of, or having a high voice with a light, flexible quality. * *n* a lyric poem; (*pl*) the words of a popular song.

lyrical *adj* lyric; (*inf*) expressing rapture or enthusiasm.

M

m *abbr* = metre(s); mile(s); million(s).

MA *abbr* = Master of Arts; Massachusetts.

mac, mack *n* (*inf*) mackintosh.

macaroni *n* pasta in the form of tubes.

mace¹ *n* a staff used as a symbol of authority by certain institutions.

mace² *n* an aromatic spice made from the external covering of the nutmeg.

machine *n* a structure of fixed and moving parts, for doing useful work; an organization functioning like a machine; the controlling group in a political party; a device, as the lever, etc that transmits, or changes the application of energy. * *vt* to shape or finish by machine-operated tools. * *adj* of machines; done by machinery.

machine gun *n* an automatic gun, firing a rapid stream of bullets.—*also vt.*

machinery *n* machines collectively; the parts of a machine; the framework for keeping something going.

machinist *n* one who makes, repairs, or operates machinery.

mackerel *n* (*pl* **mackerel, mackerels**) a common oily food fish.

mackintosh, macintosh *n* a waterproof raincoat.

mad *adj* (**madder, maddest**) insane; frantic; foolish and rash; infatuated; (*inf*) angry.

madam *n* a polite term of address to a woman; a woman in charge of a brothel; (*inf*) a precocious little girl.

madden *vti* to make or become insane, angry, or wildly excited.—**maddening** *adj.*—**maddeningly** *adv.*

made *see* **make**

made-to-measure *adj* (*garment*) made according to the customers individual measurements or requirements.

madly *adv* in an insane manner; at great speed, force; (*inf*) excessively.

madman *n* an insane person.—**madwoman** *nf.*

madness *n* insanity; foolishness; excitability.

magazine *n* a military store; a space where explosives are stored, as in a fort; a supply chamber, as in a camera, a rifle, etc; a periodical publication containing articles, fiction, photographs, etc.

magenta *n* a purplish-red dye; purplish red.—*also adj.*

maggot *n* a wormlike larva, as of the housefly.—**maggoty** *adj.*

magic *n* the use of charms, spells, etc to supposedly influence events by supernatural means; any mysterious power; the art of producing illusions by sleight of hand, etc. * *adj* of or relating to magic; possessing supposedly supernatural powers; (*inf*) wonderful. * *vt* (*pt* **magicked**) to influence, produce or take (away) by or as if by magic.—**magical** *adj.*—**magically** *adv.*

magician *n* one skilled in magic; a conjurer.

magistrate *n* a public officer empowered to administer the law.

magnanimous *adj* noble and generous in conduct or spirit, not petty.—**magnanimously** *adv.*

magnate *n* a very wealthy or influential person.

magnet *n* any piece of iron or steel that has the property of attracting iron; anything that attracts.

magnetic *adj* of magnetism or a magnet; producing or acting by magnetism; having the ability to attract or charm people.—**magnetically** *adv.*

magnetism *n* the property, quality, or condition of being magnetic; the force to which this is due; personal charm.

magnification *n* magnifying or being magnified; the degree of enlargement of something by a lens, microscope, etc.

magnificent *adj* splendid, stately or sumptuous in appearance; superb, of very high quality.—**magnificence** *n.*—**magnificently** *adv.*

magnify *vt* to exaggerate; to increase the apparent size of (an object) as (with) a lens.—**magnifier** *n.*

magnitude *n* greatness of size, extent, etc; importance; (*astron*) the apparent brightness of a star.

magnolia *n* a spring-flowering shrub or tree with evergreen or deciduous leaves and showy flowers.

magpie *n* a black and white bird of the crow family; a person who chatters; an acquisitive person.

mahogany *n* the hard, reddish-brown wood of a tropical tree; a reddish-brown color.

maid *n* a maiden; a woman servant.

maiden *n* a girl or young unmarried woman. * *adj* unmarried or virgin; untried; first; (*cricket*) (*over*) without runs.—**maidenhood** *n.*—**maidenliness** *n.*—**maidenly** *adv.*

maiden name *n* the surname of a woman before marriage.

mail¹ *n* a body armour made of small metal rings or links.

mail² *n* letters, packages, etc transported and delivered by the post office; a postal system. * *vt* to send by mail.

mail order *n* an order for goods to be sent by post.

maim *vt* to cripple; to mutilate.

main *adj* chief in size, importance, etc; principal. * n (often pl but used a sing) a principal pipe in a distribution system for water, gas, etc; the essential point.

mainland n the principal land mass of a continent, as distinguished from nearby islands.

mainstreet v (Cdn) to campaign in an election on the main streets of towns and cities.—**mainstreeter** n.—**mainstreeting** n.

maintain vt to preserve; to support, to sustain; to keep in good condition; to affirm.—**maintainable** adj.

maintenance n upkeep; (financial) support, esp of a spouse after a divorce.

maisonette n a small house; self-contained living quarters, usu on two floors with its own entrance, as part of a larger house.

maize n corn; a light yellow color.

majestic adj dignified; imposing.—**majestically** adv.

majesty n grandeur; (with cap) a title used in speaking to or of a sovereign.

major adj greater in size, importance, amount, etc; (surgery) very serious, life-threatening; (mus) higher than the corresponding minor by half a tone. * vi to specialize (in a field of study). * n in US, an officer ranking just above a captain, in UK, a lieutenant-colonel; (mus) a major key, chord or scale.

majority n the greater number or part of; the excess of the larger number of votes cast for a candidate in an election; full legal age; the military rank of a major.

make vb (pt **made**) vt to cause to exist, occur, or appear; to build, create, produce, manufacture, etc; to prepare for use; to amount to; to have the qualities of; to acquire, earn; to understand; to do, execute; to cause or force; to arrive at, reach; (with **believe**) to imagine, pretend; (with **good**) to make up for, pay compensation; (with **out**) to write out; to complete (a form, etc) in writing; to attempt to understand; to discern, identify; (with **up**) to invent, fabricate, esp to deceive; to prepare; to make complete; to put together; to settle differences between. * vi (with **do**) to manage with what is available; (with **for**) to go in the direction of; to bring about; (with **good**) to become successful or wealthy; (with **off**) to leave in haste; (with **out**) to pretend; to fare, manage; (with **up**) to become reconciled; to compensate for; to put on make-up for the stage. * n style, brand, or origin; manner of production.—**maker** n.

make-believe adj imagined, pretended.—also n.

makeshift adj being a temporary substitute.—also n.

make-up n the cosmetics, etc used by an actor; cosmetics generally; the way something is put together, composition; nature, disposition.

making n the act or process of making, creation; (pl) earnings; (pl) potential; (pl) (sl) the materials for rolling a cigarette.

maladjusted adj poorly adjusted, esp to the social environment.—**maladjustment** n.

malaise n a feeling of discomfort or of uneasiness.

malaria n an infectious disease caused by mosquito bites, and characterized by recurring attacks of fevers and chills.—**malarial** adj.

male adj denoting or of the sex that fertilizes the ovum; of, like, or suitable for men and boys; masculine. * n a male person, animal or plant.

malevolent adj ill-disposed towards others; spiteful, malicious.—**malevolence** n.—**malevolently** adv.

malfunction n faulty functioning. * vi to function wrongly.

malice n active ill will, intention to inflict injury upon another.—**malicious** adj.—**maliciously** adv.—**maliciousness** n.

malign adj harmful; evil. * vt to slander; to defame.—**malignity** n.—**malignly** adv.

malignant adj having a wish to harm others; injurious; (disease) rapidly spreading, resistant to treatment, esp of a tumour.—**malignancy** n.—**malignantly** adv.

malinger vi to feign illness in order to evade work, duty.—**malingerer** n.

malleable adj pliable; capable of being shaped.—**malleability** n.

mallet n a small, usu wooden-headed, short-handled hammer; a long-handled version for striking the ball in the games of polo and croquet.

malnutrition n lack of nutrition.

malpractice n professional misconduct, esp by a medical practitioner.

malt n a cereal grain, such as barley, which is soaked and dried and used in brewing; (inf) malt liquor, malt whisky.—**malty** adj.

mammal n any member of a class of warm-blooded vertebrates that suckle their young with milk.—**mammalian** adj.

mammoth n an extinct elephant with long, curved tusks. * adj enormous.

man n (pl **men**) a human being, esp an adult male; the human race; an adult male with manly qualities, eg courage, virility; a male servant; an individual person; a person with specific qualities for a task, etc; an ordinary soldier, as opposed to an officer; a member of a team, etc; a piece in games such as chess, draughts, etc; a husband. * vt (pt **manned**) to provide with men for work, defence, etc.

Man. abbr = Manitoba.

manage vt to control the movement or behaviour of; to have charge of; to direct; to succeed in accomplishing. * vi to carry on business; to contrive to get along.—**manageable** adj.

management n those carrying out the administration of a business; the managers collectively; the technique of managing or controlling.

manager n a person who manages a company, organization, etc; an agent who looks after the business affairs of an actor, writer, etc; a person who organizes the training of a sports team; a person who manages efficiently.—**managerial** adj.—**managerially** adv.

manageress n a woman who manages a business, shop, etc.

managing adj administering; controlling; having authority.

mandarin n (formerly) a high-ranking bureaucrat of the Chinese empire; any high-ranking official, esp one given to pedantic sometimes obscure public pronouncements; (with cap) the Beijing dialect that is the official pronunciation of the Chinese language; the fruit of a small spiny Chinese tree that has been developed in cultivation (—also **tangerine**).

mandate n an order or command; the authority to act on the behalf of another, esp the will of constituents expressed to their representatives in legislature; (Cdn) the period during which a government is in power. * vt to entrust by mandate.

mandatory adj compulsory.

mandatory supervision n (Cdn) supervision by a parole officer of an inmate for the last third of a prison sentence after the inmate's release on the grounds of good behaviour.

mandolin, mandoline n a stringed instrument similar to a lute, with four or five pairs of strings.

mane n long hair that grows on the back of the neck of the horse, lion, etc.

manful adj showing courage and resolution.—**manfully** adv.

mangle[1] vt to crush, mutilate; to spoil, ruin.

mangle[2] n a machine for drying and pressing sheets, etc between rollers. * vt to smooth through a mangle.

mango n (pl **mangoes**) a yellow-red fleshy tropical fruit with a firm central stone.

mangy adj (**mangier, mangiest**) having mange; scruffy, shabby.—**manginess** n.

manhandle vt to handle roughly; to move by human force.

manhole n a hole through which one can enter a sewer, drain, etc.

manhood n the state or time of being a man; virility; courage, etc.

manhunt n a hunt for a fugitive.—**manhunter** n.

mania n a mental disorder displaying sometimes violent behaviour and great excitement; great excitement or enthusiasm; a craze.

maniac n a madman; a person with wild behaviour; a person with great enthusiasm for something.—**maniacal** adj.

manicure n trimming, polishing etc of fingernails.—also vt.—**manicurist** n.

manifest adj obvious, clearly evident. * vt to make clear; to display, to reveal. * n a list of a ship's or aircraft's cargo; a list of passengers on an aircraft.—**manifestation** n.—**manifestly** adv.

manifesto n (pl **manifestoes, manifestos**) a public printed declaration of intent and policy issued by a government or political party.

manipulate vt to work or handle skilfully; to

manage shrewdly or artfully, often in an unfair way.—**manipulation** n.—**manipulative** adj.—**manipulator** n.

Manitoba maple n a fast-growing North American maple found east of the Rocky Mountains.

Manitoban n (Cdn) a person who lives in or is from Manitoba.

manitou n among some Indian peoples of northeast North America, a good or evil spirit.

mankind n the human race.

manly adj (**manlier, manliest**) appropriate in character to a man; strong; virile.—**manliness** n.

man-made adj manufactured or created by man; artificial, synthetic.

manner n a method of way of doing something; behaviour; type or kind; habit; (pl) polite social behaviour.—**mannerly** adj.

mannerism n an idiosyncrasy.

manoeuvre, maneuver (US) n a planned and controlled movement of troops, warships, etc; a skilful or shrewd move; a stratagem. * vti to perform or cause to perform manoeuvres; to manage or plan skilfully; to move, get, make, etc by some scheme.—**manoeuvrable** adj.,

manor n a landed estate; the main house on such an estate; (sl) a police district.—**manorial** adj.

manpower n power furnished by human strength; the collective availability for work of people in a given area.

mansion n a large, imposing house.

manslaughter n the killing of a human being by another, esp when unlawful but without malice.

mantel n the facing above a fireplace; the shelf above a fireplace.—also **mantelpiece, mantelshelf.**

manual adj of the hands; operated, done, or used by the hand; involving physical skill or hard work rather than the mind. * n a handy book for use as a guide, reference, etc; a book of instructions.—**manually** adv.

manufacture vt to make, esp on a large scale, using machinery; to invent, fabricate. * n the production of goods by manufacturing.—**manufacturer** n.

manure n animal dung used to fertilize soil. * vt to spread manure on.

manuscript n a book or document that is handwritten or typewritten as opposed to printed; an author's original handwritten or typewritten copy as submitted to a publisher before typesetting and printing.

many adj numerous. * n a large number of persons or things.

map n a representation of all or part of the earth's surface, showing either natural features as continents and seas, etc or man-made features as roads, railroads etc. * vt (pt **mapped**) to make a map of.

maple n a tree with two-winged fruits, grown for shade, wood, or sap; its hard light-colored wood; the flavor of the syrup or sugar made from the sap of the sugar maple.

maple butter n (Cdn) a creamy spread made from maple syrup.

maple leaf n (Cdn) the leaf of the maple tree, considered as an emblem of Canada.

mar vt (pt **marred**) to blemish, to spoil, to impair.

marathon n a foot race of 26 miles, 385 yards (42.195 km); any endurance contest.

maraud vi to roam in search of plunder.—**marauder** n.—**marauding** adj.

marble n a hard limestone rock that takes a high polish; a block or work of art made of marble; a little ball of stone, glass, etc; (pl) a children's game played with such balls; (pl) (sl) wits. * adj of or like marble.

March n the third month of the year having 31 days.

march vi to walk with regular steps, as in military formation; to advance steadily. * vt to make a person or group march. * n a steady advance; a regular, steady step; the distance covered in marching; a piece of music for marching.

mare n a mature female horse, mule, donkey.

margarine n a butter substitute made from vegetable and animal fats, etc.

margin n a border, edge; the blank border of a printed or written page; an amount beyond what is needed; provision for increase, error, etc; (commerce) the difference between cost and selling price.

marginal adj written in the margin; situated at the margin or border; close to the lower limit of acceptability; very slight, insignificant; (British politics) denoting a constituency where the sitting MP has only a small majority. * n a marginal constituency.—**marginally** adv.

marigold n a plant with a yellow or orange flower.

marijuana, marihuana n a narcotic obtained by smoking the dried flowers and leaves of the hemp plant.—also **cannabis, pot.**

marina n a small harbour with docks, services, etc for pleasure craft.

marine adj of, in, near, or relating to the sea; maritime; nautical; naval. * n a soldier trained for service on land or sea; naval or merchant ships.

marital adj of marriage, matrimonial.

maritime adj on, near, or living near the sea; of navigation, shipping, etc.

Maritime Command n the Canadian navy.

mark[1] n a spot, scratch, etc on a surface; a distinguishing sign or characteristic; a cross made instead of a signature; a printed or written symbol, as a punctuation mark; a brand or label on an article showing the maker, etc; an indication of some quality, character, etc; a grade for academic work; a standard of quality; impression, influence, etc; a target; (sl) a potential victim for a swindle. * vt to make a mark or marks on; to identify as by a mark; to show plainly; to heed; to grade, rate; (Brit football) to stay close to an opponent so as to hinder his play.

mark[2] n the basic monetary unit of Germany.

marked adj having a mark or marks; noticeable; obvious.—**markedly** adv.

marker n one that marks; something used for marking.

market n a meeting of people for buying and selling merchandise; a space or building in which a market is held; the chance to sell or buy; demand for (goods, etc); a region where goods can be sold; a section of the community offering demand for goods. * vti to offer for sale; to sell, buy domestic provisions.—**marketability** n.—**marketable** adj.

marketing n act of buying or selling; all the processes involved in moving goods from the producer to the consumer.

marksman n one who is skilled at shooting.—**marksmanship** n.

marmalade n a jam-like preserve made from oranges, sugar and water.

maroon[1] n a dark brownish red (—also adj); a type of distress rocket.

maroon[2] vt to abandon alone, esp on a desolate island; to leave helpless and alone.

marquee n a large tent used for entertainment; a canopy over an entrance, as to a theatre.

marquess n (UK) a title of nobility ranking between a duke and an earl.

marquis n (Europe) a nobleman equivalent in rank to a British marquess.

marriage n the legal contract by which a woman and man become wife and husband; a wedding, either religious or civil; a close union.—**marriageable** adj.

marrow n the fatty tissue in the cavities of bones; the best part or essence of anything; a widely grown green fruit eaten as a vegetable.

marry vt to join as wife and husband; to take in marriage; to unite. * vi to get married.

marsh n an area of boggy, poorly drained land.—**marshiness** n.—**marshy** adj.

marshal n in some armies, a general officer of the highest rank; an official in charge of ceremonies, parades, etc. * vt (pt **marshalled**) (ideas, troops) to arrange in order; to guide.

martial adj warlike; military.—**martially** adv.

martial law n rule by military authorities over civilians, as during a war or political emergency.

martyr n a person tortured for a belief or cause; a person who suffers from an illness. * vt to kill as a martyr; to make a martyr of.—**martyrdom** n.

marvel n anything wonderful; a miracle. * vti (pt **marvelled**) to become filled with wonder, surprise, etc.—**marvellous** adj.

Marxism n the theory and practice developed by Karl Marx and Friedrich Engels advocating public ownership of the means of production and the dictatorship of the proletariat until the establishment of a classless society.—**Marxist** adj, n.

marzipan n a paste made from ground almonds,

sugar and egg white, used to coat cakes or make confectionery.

mascara *n* a cosmetic for darkening the eyelashes.

mascot *n* a person, animal or thing thought to bring good luck.

masculine *adj* having characteristics of or appropriate to the male sex; (*gram*) of the male gender.—**masculinity** *n*.

mask *n* a covering to conceal or protect the face; a moulded likeness of the face; anything that conceals or disguises; a respirator placed over the nose and mouth to aid or prevent inhalation of a gas; (*surgery*) a protective gauze placed over the nose and mouth to prevent the spread of germs; (*photog*) a screen used to cover part of a sensitive surface to prevent exposure by light. * *vt* to cover or conceal as with a mask; to disguise one's intentions or character.—**masked** *adj*.

mason *n* a person skilled in working or building with stone; (*with cap*) a Freemason.

masonry *n* stonework.

masquerade *n* a ball or party at which fancy dress and masks are worn; a pretence, false show. * *vi* to take part in a masquerade; to pretend to be what one is not.—**masquerader** *n*.

mass *n* a quantity of matter of indefinite shape and size; a large quantity or number; bulk; size; the main part; (*physics*) the property of a body expressed as a measure of the amount of material contained in it; (*pl*) the common people, esp the lower social classes; (*with cap*) The celebration of the Eucharist. * *adj* of or for the masses or for a large number. * *vti* to gather or form into a mass.

massacre *n* the cruel and indiscriminate killing of many people or animals. * *vt* to kill in large numbers.

massage *n* a kneading and rubbing of the muscles to stimulate the circulation of the blood. * *vt* to give a massage to.

masseur *n* a man who gives a massage professionally.—**masseuse** *nf*.

massive *adj* big, solid, or heavy; large and imposing; relatively large in comparison to normal; extensive.—**massively** *adv*.—**massiveness** *n*.

mass media *npl* newspapers, radio, television, and other means of communication with large numbers of people.

mast *n* a tall vertical pole used to support the sails on a ship; a vertical pole from which a flag is flown; a tall structure supporting a television or radio aerial.

master *n* a man who rules others or has control over something, esp the head of a household; an employer; an owner of an animal or slave; the captain of a merchant ship; a male teacher in a private school; an expert craftsman; a writer or painter regarded as great; an original from which a copy can be made, esp a phonograph record or magnetic tape; (*with cap*) a title for a boy; one holding an advanced academic degree. * *adj* being a master; chief; main; controlling. * *vt* to be for become master of; (*in art, etc*) to become expert.

master corporal *n* a noncommissioned officer in the Canadian army or air force, ranking just below sergeant.

masterly *adj* expert; skilful.—**masterliness** *n*.

mastermind *n* a very clever person, esp one who plans or directs a project. * *vt* to be the mastermind of.

masterpiece *n* a work done with extraordinary skill; the greatest work of a person or group.

master seaman *n* a noncommissioned officer in the Canadian navy, equivalent to a master corporal.

master warrant officer *n* a noncommissioned officer in the Canadian army or air force, ranking just below chief warrant officer.

mastery *n* control as by a master; victory; expertise.

masturbate *vi* to manually stimulate one's sexual organs to achieve orgasm without sexual intercourse.—**masturbation** *n*.

mat[1] *n* a piece of material of woven fibres, etc, used for protection, as under a vase, etc, or on the floor; a thick pad used in wrestling, gymnastics, etc; anything interwoven or tangled into a thick mass. * *vti* (*pt* **matted**) to cover as with a mat; to interweave or tangle into a thick mass.

mat[2] *see* **matt**.

match[1] *n* a thin strip of wood or cardboard tipped with a chemical that ignites under friction.

match[2] *n* any person or thing equal or similar to another; two persons or things that go well together; a contest or game; a mating or marriage. * *vt* to join in marriage; to put in opposition (with, against); to be equal or similar to; (*one thing*) to suit to another. * *vi* to be equal, similar, suitable, etc.

matchbox *n* a small box for holding matches.

matchless *adj* unequalled.—**matchlessly** *adv*.

mate[1] *n* an associate or colleague; (*inf*) a friend; one of a matched pair; a marriage partner; the male or female of paired animals; an officer of a merchant ship, ranking below the master. * *vti* to join as a pair; to couple in marriage or sexual union.

mate[2] *vt* to checkmate.

material *adj* of, derived from, or composed of matter, physical; of the body or bodily needs, comfort, etc, not spiritual; important, essential, etc. * *n* what a thing is, or may be made of; elements or parts; cloth, fabric; (*pl*) tools, etc needed to make or do something; a person regarded as fit for a particular task, position, etc.

materialize *vt* to give material form to. * *vi* to become fact; to make an unexpected appearance.—**materialization** *n*.

maternal *adj* of, like, or from a mother; related through the mother's side of the family.—

maternally *adv.*

maternity *n* motherhood; motherliness. * *adj* relating to pregnancy.

math *n* (*inf*) mathematics.

mathematical, mathematic *adj* of, like or concerned with mathematics; exact and precise.—mathematically *adv.*

mathematics *n* (*used as sing*) the science dealing with quantities, forms, space, etc and their relationships by the use of numbers and symbols; (*sing or pl*) the mathematical operations or processes used in a particular problem, discipline, etc. —mathematician *n.*

maths *n* (*used as sing or pl*) (*inf*) mathematics.

matinée *n* an afternoon performance of a play, etc.

matriarch *n* a woman who heads or rules her family or tribe.—matriarchal *adj.*

matriculate *vti* to enrol, esp as a student.—matriculation *n.*

matrimony *n* the act or rite of marriage; the married state.—matrimonial *adj.*—matrimonially *adv.*

matron *n* a wife or widow, esp one of mature appearance and manner; a woman in charge of domestic and nursing arrangements in a school, hospital or other institution.—matronly *adv.*

matt *adj* without lustre, dull.—*also* mat.

matter *n* what a thing is made of; material; whatever occupies space and is perceptible to the senses; any specified substance; content of thought or expression; a quantity; a thing or affair; significance; trouble, difficulty; pus. * *vi* to be of importance.

matter-of-fact *adj* relating to facts, not opinions, imagination, etc.

matting *n* a coarse material, such as woven straw or hemp, used for making mats.

mattress *n* a casing of strong cloth filled with cotton, foam rubber, coiled springs, etc, used on a bed.

mature *adj* mentally and physically well-developed, grown-up; (*fruit, cheese, etc*) ripe; (*bill*) due; (*plan*) completely worked out. * *vti* to make or become mature; to become due.—maturely *adv.*—matureness *n.*

maturity *n* the state of being mature; full development; the date a loan becomes due.

maudlin *adj* foolishly sentimental; tearfully drunk.

maul *vt* to bruise or lacerate; to paw.

mausoleum *n* a large tomb.

mauve *n* any of several shades of pale purple. * *adj* of this color.

mawkish *adj* maudlin; insipid.—mawkishly *adv.*—mawkishness *n.*

max. *abbr* = maximum.

maxim *n* a concise rule of conduct; a precept.

maximum *n* (*pl* maxima, maximums) the greatest quantity, number, etc. * *adj* highest; greatest possible reached.

May *n* the fifth month of the year having 31 days.

may *vb aux* (*past* might) *expressing* possibility; permission; wish or hope.

maybe *adv* perhaps.

Mayday *n* the international radio-telephone signal indicating a ship or aircraft in distress.

May Day *n* the first day of May, celebrated as a traditional spring festival; observed in many countries as a labour holiday.

mayhem *n* violent destruction, confusion.

mayonnaise *n* a salad dressing made from egg yolks whisked with oil and lemon juice or vinegar.

mayor *n* the chief administrative officer of a municipality.

mayoress *n* the wife of a mayor; a female mayor.

maze *n* a confusing, intricate network of pathways; a confused state.

MB *abbr* = Manitoba.

MCpl *abbr* (*Cdn*) = Master Corporal.

McIntosh *n* a red, medium-sized cooking and eating apple.

McJob *n* (*inf*) a low-paying job with little prospects for advancement.

MDT *abbr* (*Cdn*) = Mountain Daylight Time.

me *pers pron* the objective case of I.

meadow *n* a piece of land where grass is grown for hay; low, level, moist grassland.

meagre, meager (*US*) *adj* thin, emaciated; lacking in quality or quantity.—meagrely *adv.*—meagreness *n.*

meal¹ *n* any of the times for eating, as lunch, dinner, etc; the food served at such a time.

meal² *n* any coarsely ground edible grain; any substance similarly ground.—mealiness *n.*—mealy *adj.*

mealy-mouthed *adj* not outspoken and blunt; euphemistic; devious in speech.

mean¹ *adj* selfish, ungenerous; despicable; shabby; bad-tempered; (*sl*) difficult; (*sl*) expert.—meanly *adv.*—meanness *n.*

mean² *adj* halfway between extremes; average. * *n* what is between extremes.

mean³ *vb* (*pt* meant) *vt* to have in mind; to intend; to intend to express; to signify. * *vi* to have a (specified) degree of importance, effect, etc.

meander *n* a winding path esp a labyrinth; a winding of a stream or river. * *vi* (*river*) to wind; to wander aimlessly.—meandering *adj.*

meaning *n* sense; significance; import. * *adj* significant.—meaningful *adj.*—meaningless *adj.*

meant *see* mean³.

meantime, meanwhile *adv* in or during the intervening time; at the same time. * *n* the intervening time.

measles *n* (*used as sing*) an acute, contagious viral disease, characterized by small red spots on the skin.

measly *adj* (measlier, measliest) (*inf*) slight, worthless; having measles.

measure *n* the extent, dimension, capacity, etc of anything; a determining of this, measurement; a unit of measurement; any standard of valuation; an instrument for measuring; a definite quantity measured out; a course of action; a statute, law; a rhythmical unit. * *vt* to find out the extent, dimensions etc of, esp by a standard; to mark off by measuring; to be a measure of. * *vi* to be of specified measurements.—**measurable** *adj.*—**measurably** *adv.*

measured *adj* set or marked off by a standard; rhythmical, regular; carefully planned or considered.

measurement *n* a measuring or being measured; an extent or quantity determined by measuring; a system of measuring or of measures.

meat *n* animal flesh; food as opposed to drink; the essence of something.

meaty *adj* (**meatier, meatiest**) full of meat; full of substance.

mechanic *n* a person skilled in maintaining or operating machines, cars, etc.

mechanical *adj* of or using machinery or tools; produced or operated by machinery; done as if by a machine, lacking thought or emotion; of the science of mechanics.—**mechanically** *adv.*

mechanics *n* (*used as sing*) the science of motion and the action of forces on bodies; knowledge of machinery; (*pl*) the technical aspects of something.

mechanism *n* the working parts of a machine; any system of interrelated parts; any physical or mental process by which a result is produced.

mechanize *vt* to make mechanical; to equip with machinery or motor vehicles.—**mechanization** *n.*—**mechanized** *adj.*

medal *n* a small, flat piece of inscribed metal, commemorating some event or person or awarded for some distinction.

medallion *n* a large medal; a design, portrait, etc shaped like a medal; a medal worn on a chain around the neck.

medallist, medalist (*US*) *n* one awarded a medal.

meddle *vi* to interfere in another's affairs.—**meddler** *n.*—**meddlesome** *adj.*

media *see* **medium**.

mediaeval *see* **medieval**.

mediate *vt* to intervene (in a dispute); to bring about agreement. * *vi* to be in an intermediate position; to be an intermediary.—**mediation** *n.*—**mediator** *n.*

medical *adj* relating to the practice or study of medicine. * *n* (*inf*) a medical examination.—**medically** *adv.*

medicare *n* a system of public health insurance financed by taxes.

medicine *n* any substance used to treat or prevent disease; the science of preventing, treating or curing disease.—**medicinal** *adj.*—**medicinally** *adv.*

medieval *adj* of or like the Middle Ages.—also **mediaeval**.

mediocre *adj* average; ordinary; inferior.—**mediocrity** *n.*

meditate *vi* to think deeply; to reflect.—**meditative** *adj.*

meditation *n* the act of meditating; contemplation of spiritual or religious matters.

Mediterranean *n* the Mediterranean Sea. * *adj* of, or relating to (the area around) the Mediterranean Sea; denoting a subdivision of the Caucasian race characterized by a slender build and dark complexion; (*climate*) marked by hot, dry summers and warm, wet winters.

medium *n* (*pl* **media, mediums**) the middle state or condition; a substance for transmitting an effect; any intervening means, instrument, or agency; (*pl* **media**) a means of communicating information (eg newspapers, television, radio); (*pl* **mediums**) a person claiming to act as an intermediary between the living and the dead. * *adj* midway; average.

medley *n* (*pl* **medleys**) a miscellany; a musical piece made up of various tunes or passages.

meek *adj* patient, long-suffering; submissive.—**meekly** *adv.*—**meekness** *n.*

meet *vb* (*pt* **met**) *vt* to encounter, to come together; to make the acquaintance of; to contend with, deal with; to experience; to be perceived by (the eye, etc); (*demand, etc*) to satisfy; (*bill, etc*) to pay. * *vi* to come into contact with; to be introduced. * *n* a meeting to hunt or for an athletics competition.

meeting *n* a coming together; a gathering.

megaphone *n* a device to amplify and direct the voice.

melancholy *n* gloominess or depression; sadness. * *adj* sad; depressed.—**melancholia** *n.*—**melancholic** *adj.*

mellow *adj* (*fruit*) sweet and ripe; (*wine*) matured; (*color, light, sound*) soft, not harsh; kind-hearted and understanding. * *vti* to soften through age; to mature.—**mellowness** *n.*

melodrama *n* a play, film, etc filled with overdramatic emotion and action; drama of this genre; sensational events or emotions.—**melodramatic** *adj.*—**melodramatically** *adv.*

melody *n* a tune; a pleasing series of sounds.—**melodic** *adj.*—**melodious** *adj.*

melon *n* the large juicy many-seeded fruit of trailing plants, as the watermelon, cantaloupe.

melt *vti* (*pp* **melted** *or* **molten**) to make or become liquid; to dissolve; to fade or disappear; to soften or be softened emotionally.—**melting** *adj.*—**meltingly** *adv.*

meltdown *n* the melting of the fuel core of a nuclear reactor; the drastic collapse of almost anything.

melting point *n* the temperature at which a solid melts.

member *n* a person belonging to a society or club; a part of a body, such as a limb; a representative in a legislative body; a distinct part of a complex whole.

membership *n* the state of being a member; the number of members of a body; the members collectively.

membrane n a thin pliable sheet or film; the fibrous tissue that covers or lines animal organs.—**membranous, membranaceous** adj.

memento n (pl **mementos, mementoes**) a reminder, esp a souvenir.

memo n (pl **memos**) a memorandum.

memoir n an historical account based on personal experience; (pl) an autobiographical record.

memorable adj worth remembering; easy to remember.—**memorably** adv.

memorandum n (pl **memorandums**) an informal written communication as within an office; (pl **memoranda**) a note to help the memory.

memorial adj serving to preserve the memory of the dead. * n a remembrance; a monument.

memorize vt to learn by heart, to commit to memory.—**memorization** n.

memory n the process of retaining and reproducing past thoughts and sensations; the sum of things remembered; an individual recollection; commemoration; remembrance; the part of a computer that stores information (—also **store**).

men see **man**.

menace n a threat; (inf) a nuisance. * vt to threaten.—**menacing** adj.—**menacingly** adv.

menagerie n a place where wild animals are kept for exhibition; a collection of wild animals.

mend vt to repair; (manners, etc) to reform, improve. * vi to become better. * n the act of mending; a repaired area in a garment, etc.

menial adj consisting of work of little skill; servile. * n a domestic servant; a servile person.

meningitis n inflammation of the membranes enveloping the brain or spinal cord.

menopause n the time of life during which a woman's menstrual cycle ceases permanently.—**menopausal** adj.

menstruation n the monthly discharge of blood from the uterus.—**menstrual** adj.—**menstruate** vi.

mental adj of, or relating to the mind; occurring or performed in the mind; having a psychiatric disorder; (inf) crazy, stupid.—**mentally** adv.

mentality n intellectual power; disposition, character.

mention n a brief reference to something in speech or writing; an official recognition or citation. * vt to refer to briefly; to remark; to honor officially.—**mentionable** adj.

menu n the list of dishes served in a restaurant; a list of options on a computer display.

mercantile adj of merchants or trade.

mercenary adj working or done for money only. * n a soldier hired to fight for a foreign army.

merchandise n commercial goods. * vti to sell, trade.

merchant n a trader; a retailer; (sl) a person fond of a particular activity.

merchant navy n commercial shipping.

merciful adj compassionate, humane.—**mercifulness** n.

merciless adj cruel, pitiless; without mercy.—**mercilessly** adv.—**mercilessness** n.

mercury n a heavy silvery liquid metallic element used in thermometers etc.

mercy n clemency; compassion; kindness; pity.

mere adj nothing more than; simple, unmixed.

merely adv simply; solely.

merge vti to blend or cause to fuse together gradually; to (cause to) combine, unite.

merger n a combining together, esp of two or more commercial organizations.

meridian n the imaginary circle on the surface of the earth passing through the north and south poles.

meringue n a mixture of egg whites beaten with sugar and baked; a small cake or shell made from this, usu filled with cream.

merit n excellence; worth; (pl) (of a case) rights and wrongs; a deserving act. * vt to be worthy of, to deserve.—**meritorious** adj.

mermaid n (legend) a woman with a fish's tale.

merry adj (**merrier, merriest**) cheerful; causing laughter; lively; (inf) slightly drunk.—**merrily** adv.—**merriment** n.

merry-go-round n a revolving platform of hobbyhorses, etc, a carousel, a roundabout.

mesh n an opening between cords of a net, wires of a screen, etc; a net; a network; a snare; (geared wheels, etc) engagement. * vt to entangle, ensnare. * vi to become entangled or interlocked.

mesmerize vt to hypnotize; to fascinate.

mess n a state of disorder or untidiness, esp if dirty; a muddle; an unsightly or disagreeable mixture; a portion of soft and pulpy or semi-liquid food; a building where service personnel dine; a communal meal. * vti to make a mess (of), bungle; to eat in company; to potter (about).

message n any spoken, written, or other form of communication; the chief idea that the writer, artist, etc seeks to communicate in a work.

messenger n a person who carries a message.

messy adj (**messier, messiest**) dirty; confused; untidy.—**messily** adv.—**messiness** n.

met see **meet**.

metabolism n the total processes in living organisms by which tissue is formed, energy produced and waste products eliminated.—**metabolic** adj.

metal n any of a class of chemical elements which are often lustrous, ductile solids, and are good conductors of heat, electricity, etc, such as gold, iron, copper, etc; any alloy of such elements as brass, bronze, etc; anything consisting of metal.—**metalled** adj.

metallic adj of, relating to, or made of metal; similar to metal.

metallurgy n the science of separating metals from their ores and preparing them for use by smelting, refining, etc.—**metallurgical** adj.—**metallurgist** n.

metamorphosis n (pl **metamorphoses**) a complete

change of form, structure, substance, character, appearance, etc; transformation; the marked change in some animals at a stage in their growth, eg chrysalis to butterfly.—**metamorphic** *adj.*—**metamorphose** *vi.*

metaphor *n* a figure of speech in which a word or phrase is used for another of which it is an image.—**metaphorical** *adj.*—**metaphorically** *adv.*

metaphysics *n* (*used as sing*) the branch of philosophy that seeks to explain the nature of being and reality; speculative philosophy in general.—**metaphysical** *adj.*

mete *vt* to allot; to portion (out).

meteor *n* a small particle of matter which travels at great speed through space and becomes luminous through friction as it enters the earth's atmosphere; a shooting star.

meter *n* a device for measuring and recording a quantity of gas, water, time, etc supplied; a parking meter. * *vt* to measure using a meter.

method *n* the mode or procedure of accomplishing something; orderliness of thought; an orderly arrangement or system.

methodical *adj* orderly, systematic.—**methodically** *adv.*

methylated spirit *n* a form of alcohol, adulterated to render it undrinkable, used as a solvent.

meticulous *adj* very precise about small details.—**meticulously** *adv.*—**meticulousness** *n.*

metre¹, meter (*US*) *n* rhythmic pattern in verse, the measured arrangement of syllables according to stress; rhythmic pattern in music.

metre², meter (*US*) *n* the basic unit of length in the metric system, consisting of 100 centimetres and equal to 39.37 inches.

metric *adj* based on the metre as a standard of measurement; of, relating to, or using the metric system.

metrical *adj* of, relating to, or composed in rhythmic metre.

metrication *n* conversion of an existent system of units into the metric system.

metric system *n* a decimal system of weights and measures based on the metre, litre and kilogram.

metronome *n* an instrument that beats musical tempo.

metro *n* a metropolis.

metropolis *n* the main city, often a capital of a country, state, etc; any large and important city.—**metropolitan** *adj.*

mettle *n* courage, spirit.

mew *vi* (*cat*) to emit a high-pitched cry.

mezzanine *n* an intermediate storey between others; a theatre balcony.

MHA *abbr* (*Cdn*) = Member of the House of Assembly.

mice *see* **mouse.**

mickey *n* (*inf*) a half-bottle of alcoholic liquor.

microbe *n* a microscopic organism, esp a disease-causing bacterium.

microfilm *n* film on which documents, etc, are recorded in reduced scale. * *vt* to record on microfilm.

microphone *n* an instrument for transforming sound waves into electric signals, esp for transmission, or recording.—*also* **mike.**

microscope *n* an optical instrument for making magnified images of minute objects by means of a lens or lenses.

microscopic *adj* of, with, like, a microscope; visible only through a microscope; very small.—**microscopically** *adv.*

mid *adj* middle. * *prep* amid.

midday *n* the middle of the day, noon.

middle *adj* halfway between two given points, times, etc; intermediate; central. * *n* the point halfway between two extremes; something intermediate; the waist.

middle age *n* the time between youth and old age.—**middle-aged** *adj.*

Middle Ages *npl* the period of European history between about Ad 500 and 1500.

middle class *n* the class between the lower and upper classes, mostly composed of professional and business people.—**middle-class** *adj.*

middleman *n* a dealer between producer and consumer; an intermediary.

middling *adj* of medium quality, size, etc; second-rate. * *adv* moderately.

midge *n* a small gnat-like insect with a painful bite.

midget *n* a very small person, a dwarf; something small of its kind.—*also adj.*

midnight *n* twelve o'clock at night.

midriff *n* the middle part of the torso between the abdomen and the chest.

midst *n* middle. * *prep* amidst, among.

midway *adv* halfway.

midwife *n* a person trained to assist women before, during, and after childbirth.—**midwifery** *n.*

might¹ *see* **may.**

might² *n* power, bodily strength.

mightn't = might not.

mighty *adj* (**mightier, mightiest**) powerful, strong; massive; (*inf*) very.—**mightily** *adv.*—**mightiness** *n.*

migraine *n* an intense, periodic headache, usu limited to one side of the head.

migrant *n* a person or animal that moves from one region or country to another; an itinerant agricultural labourer. * *adj* migrating.

migrate *vi* to settle in another country or region; (*birds, animals*) to move to another region with the change in season.—**migration** *n.*—**migratory** *adj.*

mike *see* **microphone.**

Mi'kmaq, Micmac *n* a member a First Nations people mainly of the Maritime Provinces of Canada; the language of this people. * *adj* of or pertaining to this people or their language.

mild *adj* (*temper*) gentle; (*weather*) temperate; bland; feeble.—**mildly** *adv.*—**mildness** *n.*

mildew *n* a fungus that attacks some plants or appears on damp cloth, etc as a whitish coating. * *vti* to affect or be affected with mildew.—**mildewy** adj.

mile n a unit of linear measure equal to 5,280 feet (1.61 km); the nautical mile is 6,075 feet (1.85 km).

mileage n total miles travelled; an allowance per mile for travelling expenses; the average number of miles that can be travelled, as per litre of fuel.

milestone n a stone marking the number of miles to a place; an important event in life, history, etc.

milieu n (pl **milieus, milieux**) environment, esp social setting.

militant adj ready to fight, esp for some cause; combative.—also n.—**militancy** n.—**militantly** adv.

military adj relating to soldiers or to war; warlike. * n the armed forces.

militia n an army composed of civilians called out in time of emergency.

milk n a white nutritious liquid secreted by female mammals for feeding their young. * vt to draw milk from; to extract money, etc, from; to exploit.—**milkiness** n.—**milky** adj.

milkman n a person who delivers milk to homes.

milk store n (Cdn) a convenience store.

mill n an apparatus for grinding by crushing between rough surfaces; a building where grain is ground into flour; a factory. * vt to produce or grind in a mill; (coins) to put a raised edge on. * vi to move around confusedly.—**miller** n.

millennium n (pl **millennia, millenniums**) a period of a thousand years.—**millennial** adj.

millet n a cereal grass used for grain and fodder.

milli- prefix a thousandth part.

millimetre, millimeter (US) n a thousandth (0.001) of a metre.

milliner n a designer or seller of women's hats.—**millinery** n.

million n a thousand thousands, the number one followed by six zeros: 1,000,000; (inf) a very large number.—**millionth** adj.

millionaire n a person who owns at least a million of money; one who is extremely rich.

mill rate n the rate at which a property is taxed, expressed as the number of mills of tax for every dollar of assessed value.

millstone n a stone used for grinding corn; a heavy burden.

mime n a theatrical technique using action without words; a mimic. * vi act or express using gestures alone; (singers, musicians) to perform as if singing or playing live to what is actually a prerecorded piece of music.

mimic n a person who imitates, esp an actor skilled in mimicry. * adj related to mimicry; make-believe; sham. * (pt **mimicked**) to imitate or ridicule.

mimicry n practice, art, or way of mimicking.

min. abbr = minimum; minute(s).

minaret n a high, slender tower on a mosque from which the call to prayer is made.

mince vt to chop or cut up into small pieces; to diminish or moderate one's words. * vi to speak or walk with affected daintiness.—**mincing** adj.—**mincingly** adv.

mincemeat n a mixture of chopped apples, raisins, etc used as a pie filling.

mind n the faculty responsible for intellect, thought, feelings, speech; memory; intellect; reason; opinion; sanity. * vt to object to, take offence to; to pay attention to; to obey; to take care of; to be careful about; to care about. * vi to pay attention; to be obedient; to be careful; to object.

mindful adj heedful, not forgetful.—**mindfully** adv.

mindless adj unthinking, stupid; requiring little intellectual effort.—**mindlessly** adv.

mine[1] poss pron belonging to me.

mine[2] n an excavation from which minerals are dug; an explosive device concealed in the water or ground to destroy enemy ships, personnel, or vehicles that pass over or near them; a rich supply or source. * vt to excavate; to lay explosive mines in an area. * vi to dig or work a mine.

mine detector n a device for indicating the whereabouts of explosive mines.

minefield n an area sown with explosive mines; a situation containing hidden problems.

miner n a person who works in a mine.

mineral n an inorganic substance, found naturally in the earth; any substance neither vegetable nor animal. * adj relating to or containing minerals.

mineralogy n the science of minerals.—**mineralogical** adj.—**mineralogically** adv.—**mineralogist** n.

mineral water n water containing mineral salts or gases, often with medicinal properties.

minesweeper n a ship for clearing away explosive mines.—**minesweeping** n.

mingle vti to mix; to combine.

miniature adj minute, on a small scale. * n a painting or reproduction on a very small scale.

minibus n a small bus for carrying up to twelve passengers.

minimal adj very minute; least possible.—**minimally** adv.

minimize vt to reduce to or estimate at a minimum.—**minimization** n.

minimum n (pl **minima, minimums**) the least possible amount; the lowest degree or point reached.

mining n the act, process, or industry of excavating from the earth; (mil) the laying of explosive mines.

mining recorder n (Cdn) a government official who registers mining claims.

minister n a clergyman serving a church; an official heading a government department; a diplomat. * vi to serve as a minister in a church; to give help (to).—**ministerial** adj.—**ministerially** adv.

Minister's Permit n (Cdn) a permit issued by the federal government that permits a person who is otherwise ineligible for immigrant status to remain in the country for a fixed period.

ministry *n* the act of ministering; the clergy; the profession of a clergyman; a government department headed by a minister; the building housing a government department.

mink *n* any of several carnivorous weasel-like mammals valued for its durable soft fur.

minnow *n* a small, slender freshwater fish.

minor *adj* lesser in size, importance, degree, extent, etc; (*mus*) lower than the corresponding major by a semitone. * *n* a person under full legal age.

minority *n* the smaller part or number; a political or racial group smaller than the majority group; the state of being under age.

minstrel *n* a travelling entertainer and musician, esp in the Middle Ages.

mint¹ *n* the place where money is coined; a large amount of money; a source of supply. * *adj* unused, in perfect condition. * *vt* (*coins*) to imprint; to invent.

mint² *n* an aromatic plant whose leaves are used for flavoring.

minuet *n* (the music for) a slow, graceful dance in triple time.

minus *prep* less; (*inf*) without. * *adj* involving subtraction; negative; less than. * *n* a sign (-), indicating subtraction or negative quantity.

minute¹ *n* the sixtieth part of an hour or a degree; a moment; (*pl*) an official record of a meeting. * *vt* to record or summarize the proceedings (of).

minute² *adj* tiny; detailed; exact.—**minutely** *adv.*—**minuteness** *n.*

miracle *n* an extraordinary event attributed to the supernatural; an unusual or astounding event; a remarkable example of something.—**miraculous** *adj.*—**miraculously** *adv.*

mirage *n* an optical illusion in which a distant object or expanse of water seems to be nearby, caused by light reflection from hot air; anything illusory or fanciful.

mirror *n* a smooth surface that reflects images; a faithful depiction. * *vt* (*pt* mirrored) to reflect or depict faithfully.

mirth *n* merriment, esp with laughter.—**mirthful** *adj.*—**mirthless** *adj.*

mis- *prefix* wrong(ly); bad(ly); no, not.

misadventure *n* an unlucky accident; bad luck.

misanthrope, misanthropist *n* a person who hates or distrusts mankind.—**misanthropic** *adj.*—**misanthropically** *adv.*—**misanthropy** *n.*

misapprehension *n* misunderstanding.

misappropriate *vt* to appropriate wrongly or dishonestly; to embezzle.—**misappropriation** *n.*

misbehave *vi* to behave badly.—**misbehaviour** *n.*

miscalculate *vti* to calculate wrongly.—**miscalculation** *n.*

miscarriage *n* the spontaneous expulsion of a foetus prematurely; mismanagement or failure.

miscellaneous *adj* consisting of various kinds; mixed.—**miscellaneously** *adv.*

miscellany *n* a mixed collection; a book comprising miscellaneous writings, etc.

mischief *n* wayward behaviour; damage.

mischievous *adj* harmful, prankish.—**mischievously** *adv.*—**mischievousness** *n.*

misconception *n* a mistaken idea.

misconduct *n* dishonest management; improper behaviour.—*also vt.*

misconstrue *vt* to misinterpret.—**misconstruction** *n.*

misdemeanour, misdemeanor (*US*) *n* (*law*) a minor offence, a misdeed.

miser *n* a greedy, stingy person who hoards money for its own sake.—**miserliness** *n.*—**miserly** *adj.*

miserable *adj* wretched; unhappy; causing misery; bad, inadequate; pitiable.—**miserableness** *n.*—**miserably** *adv.*

misery *n* extreme pain, unhappiness, or poverty; a cause of suffering.

misfire *vi* (*engine, etc*) to fail to ignite, start; to fail to succeed.—*also n.*

misfit *n* something that fits badly; a maladjusted person.—*also vti.*

misfortune *n* ill luck; trouble; a mishap.

misgiving *n* a feeling of misapprehension, mistrust.

misguided *adj* foolish; mistaken.

mishap *n* an unfortunate accident.

misinform *vt* to supply with wrong information.—**misinformation** *n.*

misjudge *vt* to judge wrongly, to form a wrong opinion.—**misjudgment, misjudgement** *n.*

mislay *vt* (*pt* mislaid) to lose something temporarily; to put down or install improperly.

mislead *vt* (*pt* misled) to deceive; to give wrong information to; to lead into wrongdoing.

misleading *adj* deceptive; confusing.

misnomer *n* an incorrect or unsuitable name or description.

misplace *vt* to put in a wrong place; (*trust, etc*) to place unwisely.—**misplacement** *n.*

misprint *vt* to print incorrectly. * *n* an error in printing.

misrepresent *vt* to represent falsely; to give an untrue idea of.—**misrepresentation** *n.*—**misrepresentative** *adj.*

miss¹ *n* (*pl* misses) a girl; (*with cap*) a title used before the surname of an unmarried woman or girl.

miss² *vt* to fail to reach, hit, find, meet, hear; to omit; to fail to take advantage of; to regret or discover the absence or loss of. * *vi* to fail to hit; to fail to be successful; to misfire, as an engine. * *n* a failure to hit, reach, obtain, etc.

missal *n* a book containing the prayers for Mass.

misshapen *adj* badly shaped; deformed.

missile *n* an object, as a rock, spear, rocket, etc, to be thrown, fired, or launched.

missing *adj* absent; lost.

mission *n* a group of people sent by a church, government, etc to carry out a special duty or task; the sending of an aircraft or spacecraft on a special assignment; a vocation.

missionary *n* a person who tries to convert unbelievers to his/her religious faith.—*also adj.*

misspent *adj* wasted, frittered away.

mist *n* a large mass of water vapour, less dense than a fog; something that dims or obscures. * *vti* to cover or be covered, as with mist.—**mistily** *adv.*—**mistiness** *n.*—**misty** *adj.*

mistake *vb* (*pt* **mistook**, *pp* **mistaken**) * *vt* to misunderstand; to misinterpret. * *vi* to make a mistake. * *n* a wrong idea, answer, etc; an error of judgment; a blunder; a misunderstanding.—**mistakable**, **mistakeable** *adj.*

mistaken *adj* erroneous, ill-judged.—**mistakenly** *adv.*

mister *n* (*inf*) sir; (*with cap*) the title used before a man's surname.

mistletoe *n* an evergreen parasitic plant with white berries used as a Christmas decoration.

mistreat *vt* to treat wrongly or badly.—**mistreatment** *n.*

mistress *n* a woman who is head of a household; a woman with whom a man is having a prolonged affair; a female schoolteacher; (*with cap*) the title used before a married woman's surname.

mistrust *n* lack of trust. * *vti* to doubt; to suspect.—**mistrustful** *adj.* —**mistrustfully** *adv*

misunderstand *vt* (*pt* **misunderstood**) to fail to understand correctly.—**misunderstood** *adj.*

misunderstanding *n* a mistake as to sense; a quarrel or disagreement.

misuse *vt* to use for the wrong purpose or in the wrong way; to ill-treat, abuse. * *n* improper or incorrect use.

mitigate *vti* to become or make less severe.—**mitigable** *adj.*—**mitigating** *adj.*—**mitigation** *n.*

mitre, miter (*US*) *n* the headdress of a bishop; a diagonal joint between two pieces of wood to form a corner. * *vt* to join with a mitre corner.

mitt *n* a glove covering the hand but only the base of the fingers; (*sl*) a hand; a boxing glove; a baseball glove.

mitten *n* a glove with a thumb but no separate fingers.

mix *vt* to blend together in a single mass; to make by blending ingredients, as a cake; to combine; (*with* **up**) to make into a mixture; to make disordered; to confuse or mistake. * *vi* to be mixed or blended; to get along together. * *n* a mixture.

mixed *adj* blended; made up of different parts, classes, races, etc; confused.

mixed-up *adj* (*inf*) perplexed, mentally confused.

mixer *n* a device that blends or mixes; a person considered in terms of their ability (good or bad) to get on with others; a soft drink added to an alcoholic beverage.

mixture *n* the process of mixing; a blend made by mixing.

mix-up *n* a mistake; confusion, muddle; (*inf*) a fight.

MLA *abbr* (*Cdn*) = Member of the Legislative Assembly.

MNA *abbr* (*Cdn*) = Member of the National Assembly.

moan *n* a low mournful sound as of sorrow or pain. * *vti* to utter a moan; to complain.—**moaner** *n.*

moat *n* a deep ditch surrounding a fortification or castle, usu filled with water.

mob *n* a disorderly or riotous crowd; a contemptuous term for the masses; (*sl*) a gang of criminals. * *vt* (*pt* **mobbed**) to attack in a disorderly group; to surround.

mobile *adj* movable, not fixed; easily changing; characterized by ease in change of social status; capable of moving freely and quickly; (*inf*) having transport. * *n* a suspended structure of wood, metal, etc with parts that move in air currents.—**mobility** *n.*

Mobile Command *n* the Canadian army.

moccasin *n* a flat shoe based on Amerindian footwear; any soft, flexible shoe resembling this.

mock *vt* to imitate or ridicule; to behave with scorn; to defy; (*with* **up**) to make a model of. * *n* ridicule; an object of scorn. * *adj* false, sham, counterfeit.—**mocking** *n, adj.*—**mockingly** *adv.*

mockery *n* derision, ridicule, or contempt; imitation, esp derisive; someone or something that is mocked; an inadequate person, thing, or action.

mock-up *n* a full-scale working model of a machine, etc.

MOD *abbr* = Ministry of Defence.

mod cons *npl* (*inf*) modern conveniences.

mode *n* a way of acting, doing or existing; a style or fashion; form; (*mus*) any of the scales used in composition; (*statistics*) the predominant item in a series of items; (*gram*) mood.—**modal** *adj.*—**modality** *n.*

model *n* a pattern; an ideal; a standard worth imitating; a representation on a smaller scale, usu three-dimensional; a person who sits for an artist or photographer; a person who displays clothes by wearing them. * *adj* serving as a model; representative of others of the same style. * *vb* (*pt* **modelled**) *vt* (*with* **after, on**) to create by following a model; to display clothes by wearing. * *vi* to serve as a model for an artist, etc.—**modeller** *n.*—**modelling** *n.*

moderate *vti* to make or become moderate; to preside over. * *adj* having reasonable limits; avoiding extremes; mild, calm; of medium quality, amount, etc. * *n* a person who holds moderate views.—**moderately** *adv.*—**moderation** *n.*

modern *adj* of the present or recent times, contemporary; up-to-date.—**modernity** *n.*

modernize *vti* to make or become modern.—**modernization** *n.*

modest *adj* moderate; having a humble opinion of oneself; unpretentious.—**modestly** *adv.*—**modesty** *n.*

modicum *n* a small quantity.

modify *vt* to lessen the severity of; to change or alter slightly; (*gram*) to limit in meaning, to qualify.—**modifiable** *adj*.—**modification** *n*.—**modifier** *n*.

module *n* a unit of measurement; a self-contained unit, esp in a spacecraft.—**modular** *adj*.

mohair *n* the long, fine hair of the Angora goat; the silk cloth made from it.

moist *adj* damp; slightly wet.—**moistly** *adv*.—**moistness** *n*.

moisten *vti* to make or become moist.

moisture *n* liquid in a diffused, absorbed, or condensed state.

moisturize *vt* (*skin, air, etc*) to add moisture to.—**moisturizer** *n*.

molar *n* a back tooth, used for grinding food.

molasses *n* (*used as sing*) the thick brown sugar that is produced during the refining of sugar; treacle.

mole[1] *n* a spot on the skin, usu dark-colored and raised.

mole[2] *n* a small burrowing insectivore with soft dark fur; a spy within an organization.

mole[3] *n* a large breakwater.

mole[4] *n* the basic SI unit of substance.

molecule *n* the simplest unit of a substance, retaining the chemical properties of that substance; a small particle.—**molecular** *adj*.

molest *vt* to annoy; to attack or assault, esp sexually.—**molestation** *n*.—**molester** *n*.

mollusc, mollusk (*US*) *n* an invertebrate animal usu enclosed in a shell, as oysters, etc.

molten *adj* melted by heat.

moment *n* an indefinitely brief period of time; a definite point in time; a brief time of importance.

momentary *adj* lasting only for a moment.

momentous *adj* very important.—**momentously** *adv*.

momentum *n* (*pl* **momenta, momentums**) the impetus of a moving object, equal to the product of its mass and its velocity.

monarch *n* a sovereign who rules by hereditary right.—**monarchic** *adj*.—**monarchical** *adj*.

monarchy *n* a government headed by a monarch; a kingdom.

monastery *n* the residence of a group of monks, or nuns.

monastic *adj* of monks or monasteries. * *n* a monk; a recluse.—**monastically** *adv*.—**monasticism** *n*.

Monday *n* the second day of the week.

monetary *adj* of the coinage or currency of a country; of or relating to money.

money *n* (*pl* **moneys, monies**) coins or paper notes authorized by a government as a medium of exchange; property; wealth.

mongrel *n* an animal or plant of mixed or unknown breed, esp a dog.—*also adj*.

monitor *n* a student chosen to help the teacher; any device for regulating the performance of a machine, aircraft, etc; a screen for viewing the image being produced by a television camera; a display screen connected to a computer. * *vti* (*TV or radio transmissions, etc*) to observe or listen to for political or technical reasons; to watch or check on; to regulate or control, a machine, etc.—**monitory** *adj*.

monk *n* a male member of a religious order living in a monastery.

monkey *n* (*pl* **monkeys**) any of the primates except man and the lemurs, esp the smaller, long-tailed primates; a mischievous child; (*sl*) £500 or $500. * *vi* (*inf*) to play, trifle, or meddle.

monkey nut *n* a peanut.

monkey wrench *n* a large wrench with an adjustable jaw.

mono- *prefix* alone, sole, single.

monochrome *n* a painting, drawing, or print in a single color.

monocle *n* a single eyeglass held in place by the face muscles.

monogram *n* the embroidered or printed initials of one's name on clothing, stationery, etc.—**monogrammed** *adj*.

monologue, monolog *n* a long speech; a soliloquy, a skit, etc for one actor only.

monopolize *vt* to get, have, or exploit a monopoly of; to get full control of.—**monopolization** *n*.

monopoly *n* exclusive control in dealing in a particular commodity or supplying a service; exclusive use or possession; that which is exclusively controlled; such control granted by a government.—**monopolist** *n*.—**monopolistic** *adj*.

monosyllable *n* a word of one syllable.—**monosyllabic** *adj*.

monotone *n* an utterance or musical tone without a change in pitch; a tiresome sameness of style, color, etc.—**monotonous** *adj*.—**monotonously** *adv*.—**monotony** *n*.

monsoon *n* a seasonal wind of southern Asia; the rainy season.

monster *n* any greatly malformed plant or animal; an imaginary beast; a very wicked person; a very large animal or thing. * *adj* very large, huge.—**monstrosity** *n*.

monstrous *adj* abnormally developed; enormous; horrible.—**monstrously** *adv*.

montage *n* a rapid sequence of film shots, often superimposed; the art or technique of assembling various elements, esp pictures or photographs; such an assemblage.

month *n* any of the twelve divisions of the year; a calendar month.

monthly *adj* continuing for a month; done, happening, payable, etc, every month. * *n* a monthly periodical. * *adv* once a month; every month.

monument *n* an obelisk, statue or building that commemorates a person or an event; an exceptional example.

monumental *adj* of, like, or serving as a monument; colossal; lasting.—**monumentally** *adv*.

mood *n* a temporary state of mind or temper; a gloomy feeling; a predominant feeling or spirit; (*gram*) that form of a verb indicating mode of action; (*mus*) mode.

moody *adj* (**moodier, moodiest**) gloomy; temperamental.—**moodily** *adv*.—**moodiness** *n*.

moon *n* the natural satellite that revolves around the earth and shines by reflected sunlight; any natural satellite of another planet; something shaped like the moon. * *vi* to behave in an idle or abstracted way.

moonbeam *n* a ray of moonlight.

moonlight *n* the light of the moon. * *vi* (*inf*) to have a secondary (usu night-time) job.

moonlit *adj* lit by the moon.

moor[1] *n* a tract of open wasteland, usu covered with heather and often marshy.

moor[2] *vti* (*a ship*) to secure or be secured by cable or anchor.

mooring *n* the act of mooring; the place where a ship is moored; (*pl*) the lines, cables, etc by which a ship is moored.

moose *n* (*pl* **moose**) the largest member of the deer family, native to North America.

moose pasture *n* (*Cdn*) (*sl*) a piece of land that is promoted as having valuable mineral deposits but in fact is worthless.

moot *adj* debatable; hypothetical. * *vt* to propose for discussion.

mop *n* a rag, sponge, etc fixed to a handle for washing floors or dishes; a thick or tangled head of hair. * *vt* (*pt* **mopped**) to wash with a mop.

mope *vi* to be gloomy and apathetic.—**mopey** *adj*.

moped *n* a light, motor-assisted bicycle.

moral *adj* of or relating to character and human behaviour, particularly as regards right and wrong; virtuous, esp in sexual conduct; capable of distinguishing right from wrong; probable, although not certain; psychological, emotional. * *n* a moral lesson taught by a fable, event, etc; (*pl*) principles; ethics. —**moralist** *n*.—**moralistic** *adj*.—**morally** *adv*.

morale *n* moral or mental condition with respect to courage, discipline, confidence, etc.

morality *n* virtue; moral principles; a particular system of moral principles.

morality squad *n* (*Cdn*) a unit of a police force dealing with offences related to prostitution, pornography, drugs, or gambling.

morass *n* a bog, marsh.

morbid *adj* diseased, resulting as from a diseased state of mind; gruesome.—**morbidly** *adv*.—**morbidness** *n*.

more *adj* (*superl* **most**) greater; further; additional(—*also compar of* **many, much**). * *adv* to a greater extent or degree; again; further.

moreover *adv* in addition to what has been said before; besides.

morgue *n* a place where the bodies of unknown dead or those dead of unknown causes are temporarily kept prior to burial; a collection of reference materials, eg newspaper clippings.

morning *n* the part of the day from midnight or dawn until noon; the early part of anything.

moron *n* an adult mentally equal to a 8 to 12-year-old child; (*inf*) a very stupid person.—**moronic** *adj*.

morose *adj* sullen, surly; gloomy.—**morosely** *adv*.—**moroseness** *n*.

morphine *n* an alkaloid derived from opium, used as an anaesthetic and sedative.

Morse code *n* a code in which letters are represented by dots and dashes or long and short sounds, and are transmitted by visual or audible signals.

morsel *n* a small quantity of food; a small piece of anything.

mortal *adj* subject to death; causing death, fatal; hostile; very intense. * *n* a human being.—**mortally** *adv*.

mortality *n* state of being mortal; death on a large scale, as from war; number or frequency of deaths in a given period relative to population.

mortar *n* a mixture of cement or lime with sand and water used in building; an artillery piece that fires shells at low velocities and high trajectories; a bowl in which substances are pounded with a pestle.

mortgage *n* a transfer of rights to a piece of property usu as security for the payment of a loan or debt that becomes void when the debt is paid.—*also vt*.

mortify *vti* to subdue by repression or penance; to humiliate or shame; to become gangrenous.—**mortification** *n*.

mortuary *n* a place of temporary storage for dead bodies.

mosaic *n* a surface decoration made by inlaying small pieces (of glass, stone, etc) to form figures or patterns; a design made in mosaic.—*also adj*.

Moslem *see* **Muslim**.

mosque *n* a place of worship for Muslims.

mosquito *n* (*pl* **mosquitoes**) a small two-winged bloodsucking insect.

moss *n* a very small green plant that grows in clusters on rocks, moist ground, etc.—**mossy** *adj*.

most *adj* (*compar* **more**) greatest in number; greatest in amount or degree; in the greatest number of instances(—*also superl of* **many, much**). * *adv* in or to the greatest degree or extent. * *n* the greatest amount or degree; (*with pl*) the greatest number (of).

mostly *adv* for the most part; mainly, usually.

MOT *abbr* = Ministry of Transport.

motel *n* an hotel for motorists with adjacent parking.

moth *n* a four-winged chiefly night-flying insect related to the butterfly.

mothball *n* a small ball of camphor or naphthalene used to protect stored clothes from moths.

moth-eaten *adj* eaten into by moths; dilapidated; outmoded.

mother *n* a female who has given birth to offspring; an origin or source. * *adj* of or like a mother; native. * *vt* to be the mother of or a mother to.—**motherhood** n.

mother-in-law n the mother of one's spouse.

motherly adj of, proper to a mother; like a mother.—**motherliness** n.

mother-of-pearl n the iridescent lining of the shell of the pearl oyster.

motif see **motive**.

motion n activity, movement; a formal suggestion made in a meeting, law court, or legislative assembly; evacuation of the bowels. * vti to signal or direct by a gesture.

motionless adj not moving, still.

motion picture n a film, movie.

motive n something (as a need or desire) that causes a person to act; a recurrent theme in a musical composition (—also **motif**). * adj moving to action; of or relating to motion.

motley adj multicolored; composed of diverse elements.

motor n anything that produces motion; a machine for converting electrical energy into mechanical energy; a motor car. * adj producing motion; of or powered by a motor; of, by or for motor vehicles; of or involving muscular movements. * vi to travel by car.

motorbike n a motorcycle.

motorboat n a boat propelled by an engine or motor.

motorcycle n a two-wheeled motor vehicle.—**motorcyclist** n.

motorist n a person who drives a car.

motor scooter n a small-wheeled motorcycle with an enclosed engine.

motorway n a road with controlled access for fast-moving traffic.—also **freeway** n.

mottled adj marked with blotches of various colors.

motto n (pl **mottoes**, **mottos**) a short saying adopted as a maxim or ideal.

mould[1], **mold** (US) n a fungus producing a furry growth on the surface of organic matter. * vi to become mouldy.—**mouldiness** n.—**mouldy** adj.

mould[2], **mold** (US) n a hollow form in which something is cast; a pattern; something made in a mould; distinctive character. * vt to make in or on a mould; to form, shape, guide.

moult, molt (US) vi to shed hair, skin, horns, etc prior to replacement of new growth.—also n.

mound n an artificial bank of earth or stones; a heap or bank of earth. * vt to form into a mound.

mount[1] n a high hill.

mount[2] vi to increase. * vt to climb, ascend; to get up on (a horse, platform, etc); to provide with horses; (a jewel) to fix on a support; (a picture) to frame. * n a horse for riding; (for a picture) a backing.

mountain n a land mass higher than a hill; a vast number or quantity. * adj of or in mountains.

mountaineer n one who climbs mountains.

mountaineering n the technique of climbing

mountains.

mountainous adj having many mountains; very high; huge.

Mountie n (Cdn) (inf) a member of the Royal Canadian Mounted Police.

mourn vti (someone dead) to grieve for; (something regrettable) to feel or express sorrow for.—**mourner** n.

mournful adj expressing grief or sorrow; causing sorrow.—**mournfully** adv.

mourning adj grieving. * n the expression of grief; dark clothes worn by mourners.

mouse n (pl **mice**) a small rodent with a pointed snout, long body and slender tail; a timid person; a hand-held device used to position the cursor and control software on a computer screen.

moustache, mustache (US) n the hair on the upper lip.

mousy, mousey adj (**mousier, mousiest**) mouse-like; grey-brown in color; quiet, stealthy; timid, retiring.

mouth n (pl **mouths**) the opening in the head through which food is eaten, sound uttered or words spoken; the lips; opening, entrance, as of a bottle, etc. * vt to say, esp insincerely; to form words with the mouth without uttering sound. * vi to utter pompously; to grimace.

mouthful n as much (food) as fills the mouth; a word or phrase that is difficult to say correctly; (sl) a pertinent remark.

mouth organ n a harmonica.

mouthwatering adj appetizing; tasty.

movable, moveable adj that may be moved. * npl personal property.

move vt to shift or change place; to set in motion; to rouse the emotions; to put (a motion) formally. * vi to go from one place to another; to walk, to carry oneself; to change place; to evacuate the bowels; to propose a motion as in a meeting; to change residence; (chess, draughts, etc) to change the position of a piece on the board. * n the act of moving, a movement, esp in board games; one's turn to move; a premeditated action.—**mover** n.

movement n act of moving; the moving part of a machine, esp a clock; the policy and activities of a group; a trend, eg in prices; a division of a musical work; tempo.

movie n a cinema film, motion picture; (pl) the showing of a motion picture; the motion-picture medium or industry.

moving adj arousing the emotions; changing position; causing motion.—**movingly** adv.

mow vti (pt **mowed** or **mown**) (grass, etc) to cut from with a sickle or lawn mower; (with **down**) to cause to fall like cut grass.—**mower** n.

MP abbr = Member of Parliament.

mpg abbr = miles per gallon.

mph abbr = miles per hour.

MPP abbr (Cdn) = Member of the Provincial Parliament.

Mr n (pl **Messrs**) used as a title before a man's

name or an office he holds.

Mrs *n* used as a title before a married woman's name.

Ms *n* the title used before a woman's name instead of Miss or Mrs.

Mtl. *abbr* = Montreal.

MUC *abbr* = Montreal Urban Community.

much *adj* (*compar* **more**, *superl* **most**) plenty. * *adv* considerably; to a great extent.

muck *n* moist manure; black earth with decaying matter; mud, dirt, filth. * *vt* to spread manure; to make dirty; (*with* **out**) to clear of muck. * *vi* to move or load muck; (*with* **about, around**) to engage in useless activity.—**muckiness** *n.*—**mucky** *adj.*

muckamuck, muckymuck *n* (*inf*) an important or self-important person.—*also* **high muckamuck.**

mucus *n* the slimy secretion that keeps mucous membranes moist.

mud *n* soft, wet earth.

muddle *vt* to confuse; to mix up. * *n* confusion, mess.

muddy *adj* (**muddier, muddiest**) like or covered with mud; not bright or clear; confused. * *vti* to make or become dirty or unclear.—**muddily** *adv.*—**muddiness** *n.*

mudguard *n* a screen on a wheel to catch mud splashes.

muff¹ *n* a warm soft fur cover for warming the hands.

muff² *n* a bungling performance; failure to hold a ball when trying to catch it. * *vti* to bungle.

muffin *n* baked yeast roll.

muffle *vt* to wrap up for warmth or to hide; (*sound*) to deaden by wrapping up.

muffler *n* a long scarf; any means of deadening sound; the silencer of a motor vehicle.

mug *n* a cylindrical drinking cup, usu of metal or earthenware; its contents; (*sl*) the face; (*sl*) a fool. * *vb* (*pt* **mugged**) *vt* to assault, usu with intent to rob.

muggy *adj* (**muggier, muggiest**) (*weather*) warm, damp and close.

mukluk *n* a laced winter boot with a heavy rubber sole and a fabric upper portion, modelled after a traditional Inuit boot.

mule¹ *n* the offspring of a male donkey and a female horse; a machine for spinning cotton; an obstinate person.—**mulish** *adj.*—**mulishly** *adv.*—**mulishness** *n.*

mule² *n* a slipper without a heel.

mull¹ *vti* (*inf*) to ponder (over).

mull² *vt* (*wine, etc*) to heat, sweeten and spice.—**mulled** *adj.*

mult-, multi- *prefix* much, many.

multiple *adj* of many parts; manifold; various; complex. * *n* (*math*) a number exactly divisible by another.

multiple sclerosis *n* a disease of the nervous system with loss of muscular coordination, etc.

multiplication *n* the act of multiplying; the process of repeatedly adding a quantity to itself a certain number of times, or any other process which has the same result.

multiply *vti* to increase in number, degree, etc; to find the product (of) by multiplication.

multitude *n* a large number (of people).—**multitudinous** *adj.*

mum¹, mummy *n* (*inf*) mother.

mum² *adj* silent, not speaking.

mumble *vti* to speak indistinctly, mutter. * *n* a mumbled utterance.—**mumbler** *n.*—**mumbling** *adj.*

mummy¹ *see* **mum¹.**

mummy² *n* a carefully preserved dead body, esp an embalmed corpse of ancient Egypt.—**mummification** *n.*—**mummify** *vt.*

mumps *npl* (*used as sing or pl*) an acute contagious virus disease characterized by swelling of the salivary glands.

munch *vti* to chew steadily.

mundane *adj* routine, everyday; banal; worldly.—**mundanely** *adv.*

municipal *adj* of or concerning a city, town, etc or its local government.—**municipally** *adv.*

municipality *n* a city or town having corporate status and powers of self-government; the governing body of a municipality.

munitions *npl* war supplies, esp weapons and ammunition.

mural *adj* relating to a wall. * *n* a picture or design painted directly onto a wall.

murder *n* the intentional and unlawful killing of one person by another; (*inf*) something unusually difficult or dangerous to do or deal with.—*also vt.*—**murderer** *n.*—**murderous** *adj.*—**murderously** *adv.*

murderball *n* (*Cdn*) a game in which players attempt to hit their opponents with a large, inflated ball.

murky *adj* (**murkier, murkiest**) dark, gloomy; darkly vague or obscure.—**murkily** *adv.*—**murkiness** *n.*

murmur *n* a continuous low, indistinct sound; a mumbled complaint; (*med*) an abnormal sound made by the heart. * *vti* to make a murmur; to say in a murmur.—**murmurous** *adj.*

muscle *n* fibrous tissue that contracts and relaxes, producing bodily movement; strength; brawn; power. * *vi* (*inf*) to force one's way (in).—**muscular** *adj.*—**muscularity** *n.*—**muscularly** *adv.*

muse *vti* to ponder, meditate.—**musing** *adj.*

museum *n* a building for exhibiting objects of artistic, historic or scientific interest.

mushroom *n* a fleshy fungus with a capped stalk, some varieties of which are edible. * *vi* to gather mushrooms; to spread rapidly, to increase.

music *n* the art of combining tones into a composition having structure and continuity; vocal or instrumental sounds having rhythm, melody or harmony; an agreeable sound.

musical *adj* of or relating to music or musicians; having the pleasant tonal qualities of music; having an interest in or talent for music. * *n* a play or film incorporating dialogue, singing and dancing.—**musically** adv.

musical ride n (Cdn) a display in which police officers demonstrate choreographed movements to music while on horseback.

musician n one skilled in music, esp a performer.

muskeg n a swamp or bog in northern North America, consisting of water-saturated vegetation, often covered with a layer of mosses.

Muslim n an adherent of Islam.—also adj.

muslin n a fine cotton cloth.

mussel n an edible marine bivalve shellfish.

must aux vb necessity; probability; certainty. *n (inf) something that must be done, had, etc.

mustard n the powdered seeds of the mustard plant used as a condiment; a brownish-yellow color; (sl) zest.

muster vt to assemble or call together, as troops for inspection or duty; to gather. * vi to be assembled, as troops. * n gathering; review; assembly.

musty adj (mustier, mustiest) mouldy, damp; stale.

mute adj silent; dumb; (color) subdued. * n a person who is unable to speak; a device that softens the sound of a musical instrument. * vt to lessen the sound of a musical instrument.—**mutely** adv.—**muteness** n.

mutilate vt to maim; to damage by removing an essential part of.—**mutilation** n.—**mutilator** n.

mutiny vi to revolt against authority in military service.—also n.—**mutineer** n.—**mutinous** adj.—**mutinously** adv.

mutter vti to utter in a low tone or indistinctly; to grumble.—**muttering** n.

mutton n the edible flesh of sheep.

mutual adj given and received in equal amount; having the same feelings one for the other; shared in common.—**mutuality** n.—**mutually** adv.

muzzle n the projecting nose or mouth of an animal; a strap fitted over the jaws to prevent biting; the open end of a gun barrel. * vt to put a muzzle on; to silence or gag.

MVA abbr = market value assessment (for purposes of property taxes).

my poss adj of or belonging to me.

myself pron emphatic and reflexive form of I; in my normal state.

mystery n something unexplained and secret; a story about a secret crime, etc; secrecy.—**mysterious** adj.—**mysteriously** adv.

mystic adj having a meaning beyond normal human understanding; magical. * n one who seeks direct knowledge of God or spiritual truths by self-surrender.—**mysticism** n.

mystify vt to bewilder, confuse.—**mystification** n.

myth n a fable; a fictitious event; a traditional story of gods and heroes, taken to be true.—**mythical** adj.—**mythically** adv.

mythology n myths collectively; the study of myths.—**mythological** adj.—**mythologist** n.

nab vt (pt **nabbed**) (sl) to catch, arrest.

NAFTA abbr = North American Free Trade Agreement.

nag[1] vti (pt **nagged**) to scold constantly; to harass; to be felt persistently. * n a person who nags.

nag[2] (inf) a horse.

nail n a horny plate covering the end of a human finger or toe; a thin pointed metal spike for driving into wood as a fastening or hanging device. * vt to fasten with nails; to fix, secure; (inf) to catch or hit; (inf) to arrest.

naive, naïve adj inexperienced; unsophisticated; (argument) simple.—**naively, naïvely** adv.—**naivety, naiveté, naïveté** n.

naked adj bare, without clothes; without a covering; without addition or ornament; (eye) without optical aid.—**nakedness** n.

name n a word or term by which a person or thing is called; a title; reputation; authority. * vt to give a name to; to call by name; to designate; to appoint to an office; (a date, price, etc) to specify.

name-dropping n the practice of mentioning the names of famous or important people as if they were friends, in order to impress others.—**name-dropper** n.

nameless adj without a name; obscure; anonymous; unnamed; indefinable; too distressing or horrifying to be described.

namely adv that is to say.

namesake n a person or thing with the same name as another.

nanny, nannie n a child's nurse; (inf) a grandmother.

nannyberry n a large shrub of northwest North America with dark blue edible fruit.

nap[1] n a short sleep, doze. * vi (pt **napped**) to take a nap.

nap[2] n a hairy surface on cloth or leather; such a surface.

napalm n a substance added to petrol to form a jelly-like compound used in firebombs and flame-throwers. * vt to attack or burn with napalm.

nape n the back of the neck.

napkin n a square of cloth or paper for wiping fingers or mouth or protecting clothes at table, a serviette; a nappy.

nappy n a piece of absorbent material wrapped around a baby to absorb or retain its excreta.—also diaper, napkin.

narcotic adj inducing sleep. * n a drug, often addictive, used to relieve pain and induce sleep.

narrate vt (a story) to tell, relate; to give an account of; (film, TV) to provide a spoken commentary for.—**narration** n.—**narrator** n.

narrative n a spoken or written account of a sequence of events, experiences, etc; the art or process of narration.—*also adj.*

narrow *adj* small in width; limited; with little margin; (*views*) prejudiced or bigoted. * *n* (*usu pl*) the narrow part of a pass, street, or channel. * *vti* to make or grow narrow; to decrease; to contract.—**narrowly** *adv.*—**narrowness** *n.*

narrow-minded *adj* prejudiced, bigoted; illiberal.—**narrow-mindedness** *n.*

nasal *adj* of the nose; sounded through the nose. * *n* a sound made through the nose.—**nasally** *adv.*

nasty *adj* (*pl* **nastier, nastiest**) unpleasant; offensive; ill-natured; disagreeable; (*problem*) hard to deal with; (*illness*) serious or dangerous.—**nastily** *adv.*—**nastiness** *n.*

nation *n* people of common territory, descent, culture, language, or history; people united under a single government.

national *adj* of a nation; common to a whole nation, general. * *n* a citizen or subject of a specific country.—**nationally** *adv.*

nationalism *n* patriotic sentiments, principles, etc; a policy of national independence or self-government; fanatical patriotism, chauvinism.—**nationalist** *n.*—**nationalistic** *adj.*

nationality *n* the status of belonging to a nation by birth or naturalization; a nation or national group.

nationalize *vt* to make national; to convert into public or government property.—**nationalization** *n.*

nation-state *n* an independent state, most of whose citizens have a common history and culture.

native *adj* inborn; natural to a person; innate; (*language, etc*) of one's place of birth; relating to the indigenous inhabitants of a country or area; occurring naturally. * *n* a person born in the place indicated; a local inhabitant; an indigenous plant or animal; an indigenous inhabitant, esp a non-White under colonial rule.

Native American *n* a member of an Indian people in the United States. * *adj* of or pertaining to such a people or community.

natter *vi* (*inf*) to chat, talk aimlessly.—*also n.*

natural *adj* of or produced by nature; not artificial; innate, not acquired; true to nature; lifelike; normal; at ease; (*mus*) not flat or sharp. * *n* (*inf*) a person or thing considered to have a natural aptitude (for) or to be an obvious choice (for); (*inf*) a certainty; (*mus*) a natural note or a sign indicating one.—**naturalness** *n.*

natural history *n* the study of nature, esp the animal, mineral and vegetable world.

naturalism *n* (*arts*) the theory or practice of describing nature, character, etc, in realistic detail.—**naturalistic** *adj.*

naturalist *n* a person who studies natural history; a person who advocates or practises naturalism.

naturalize *vt* to confer citizenship upon (a person of foreign birth); (*plants*) to become established in a different climate. * *vi* to become established as if native.—**naturalization** *n.*

naturally *adv* in a natural manner, by nature; of course.

natural selection *see* **selection.**

nature *n* the phenomena of physical life not dominated by man; the entire material world as a whole, or forces observable in it; the essential character of anything; the innate character of a person, temperament; kind, class; vital force or functions; natural scenery.

naught *see* **nought.**

naughty *adj* (**naughtier, naughtiest**) mischievous or disobedient; titillating.—**naughtily** *adv.*—**naughtiness** *n.*

nausea *n* a desire to vomit; disgust.

nauseate *vti* to arouse feelings of disgust; to feel nausea or revulsion.—**nauseating** *adj.*

nautical *adj* of ships, sailors, or navigation.

nautical mile *see* **mile.**

naval *adj* of the navy; of ships.

nave *n* the central space of a church, distinct from the chancel and aisles.

navel *n* the small scar in the abdomen caused by severance of the umbilical cord; a central point.

navigable *adj* (rivers, seas) that can be sailed upon or steered through.—**navigability** *n.*

navigate *vti* to steer or direct a ship, aircraft, etc; to travel through or over (*water, air, etc*) in a ship or aircraft; to find a way through, over, etc, and to keep to a course.—**navigator** *n.*

navigation *n* the act, art or science of navigating; the method of calculating the position of a ship, aircraft, etc.

navvy *n* a labourer, esp one who works on roads or railways.

navy *n* (*often* with cap) the warships of a nation; a nation's entire sea force, including ships, men, stores, etc; navy blue.

navy blue *n* an almost black blue.

NCC *abbr* (*Cdn*) = National Capital Commission.

NCdt *abbr* (*Cdn*) = Naval Cadet.

NCM *abbr* (*mil*) = noncommissioned member.

NDP *abbr* (*Cdn*) = New Democratic Party.

NDT *abbr* = Newfoundland Daylight Time.

near *adj* close, not distant in space or time; closely related, intimate; approximate, (*escape, etc*) narrow. * *adv* to or at a little distance; close by; almost. * *prep* close to. * *vti* to approach; to draw close to.—**nearness** *n.*

nearby *adj* neighboring; close by in position.

nearly *adv* almost, closely.

Near North *n* (*Cdn*) the southern edge of subarctic Canada, north of heavily settled areas.

near-sighted *adj* short-sighted, myopic.—**near-sightedness** *n.*

neat *adj* clean and tidy; skilful; efficiently done; well made; (*alcoholic drink*) undiluted; (*sl*) nice, pleasing, etc.—**neatly** *adv.*—**neatness** *n.*

nebulous *adj* indistinct; formless.

necessarily *adv* as a natural consequence.

necessary *adj* indispensable; required; inevitable. * *n* something necessary; (*pl*) essential needs.

necessitate *vt* to make necessary; to compel.

necessity *n* a prerequisite; something that cannot be done without; compulsion; need.

neck *n* the part of the body that connects the head and shoulders; that part of a garment nearest the neck; a neck-like part, esp a narrow strip of land; the narrowest part of a bottle; a strait. * *vti* (*sl*) to kiss and caress.

necklace *n* a string or band, often of precious stones, beads, or pearls, worn around the neck.

née, nee *adj* (*literally*) born: indicating the maiden name of a married woman.

need *n* necessity; a lack of something; a requirement; poverty. * *vt* to have a need for; to require; to be obliged.

needle *n* a small pointed piece of steel for sewing; a larger pointed rod for knitting or crocheting; a stylus; the pointer of a compass, gauge, etc; the thin, short leaf of the pine, spruce, etc; the sharp, slender metal tube at the end of a hypodermic syringe. * *vt* to goad, prod, or tease.

needless *adj* not needed, unnecessary; uncalled for, pointless.—**needlessly** *adv.*—**needlessness** *n.*

needy *adj* (**needier, neediest**) in need, very poor.

negation *n* a negative statement, denial; the opposite or absence of something; a contradiction.

negative *adj* expressing or meaning denial or refusal; lacking positive attributes; (*math*) denoting a quantity less than zero, or one to be subtracted; (*photog*) reversing the light and shade of the original subject, or having the colors replaced by complementary ones; (*elect*) of the charge carried by electrons; producing such a charge. * *n* a negative word, reply, etc; refusal; something that is the opposite or negation of something else; (*in debate, etc*) the side that votes or argues for the opposition; (*photog*) a negative image on transparent film or a plate. * *vt* to refuse assent, contradict; to veto.—**negatively** *adv.*

neglect *vt* to pay little or no attention to; to disregard; to leave uncared for; to fail to do something. * *n* disregard; lack of attention or care.

negligée, negligee *n* a woman's loosely fitting dressing gown.

negligence *n* lack of attention or care; an act of carelessness; a carelessly easy manner.—**negligent** *adj.*—**negligently** *adv.*

negligible *adj* that need not be regarded; unimportant; trifling.

negotiable *adj* able to be legally negotiated; (*bills, drafts, etc*) transferable.—**negotiability** *n.*

negotiate *vti* to discuss, bargain in order to reach an agreement or settlement; to settle by agreement; (*fin*) to obtain or give money value for (a bill); (*obstacle, etc*) to overcome.—**negotiation** *n*—**negotiator** *n.*

Negro *n* (*pl* **Negroes**) a member of the dark-skinned, indigenous peoples of Africa; a member of the Negroid group; a person with some Negro ancestors.—*also adj.*—**Negress** *nf.*

neighbor *n* a person who lives near another; a person or thing situated next to another; a fellow human being.

neighborhood *n* a particular community, area, or district; the people in an area.

neighboring *adj* adjoining, nearby.

neighborly *adj* characteristic of a neighbor, friendly.—*also adv.*—**neighborliness** *n.*

neither *adj, pron* not one or the other (of two); not either. * *conj* not either; also not.

neon *n* an inert gaseous element that gives off a bright orange glow, used in lighting and advertisements.

nephew *n* the son of a brother or sister.

nerve *n* any of the fibres or bundles of fibres that transmit impulses of sensation or of movement between the brain and spinal cord and all parts of the body; courage, coolness in danger; (*inf*) audacity, boldness; (*pl*) nervousness, anxiety. * *vt* to give strength, courage, or vigour to.

nerve-racking, nerve-wracking *adj* straining the nerves, stressful.

nervous *adj* excitable, highly strung; anxious, apprehensive; affecting or acting on the nerves or nervous system.

nervous breakdown *n* a (usu temporary) period of mental illness resulting from severe emotional strain or anxiety.

nest *n* a structure or place where birds, fish, mice, etc, lay eggs or give birth to young; a place where young are nurtured; a swarm or brood; a lair; a cosy place; a set of boxes, tables, etc of different sizes, designed to fit together. * *vi* to make or occupy a nest.

nestle *vti* to rest snugly; to lie snugly, as in a nest; to lie sheltered or half-hidden.

net[1] *n* an openwork material of string, rope, or twine knotted into meshes; a piece of this used to catch fish, to divide a tennis court, etc; a snare. * *vti* (*pt* **netted**) to snare or enclose as with a net; to hit (a ball) into a net or goal.

net[2], **nett** *adj* clear of deductions, allowances or charges. * *n* a net amount, price, weight, profit, etc. * *vt* to clear as a profit.

netball *n* a game for two teams of seven players, in which points are scored by putting a ball through an elevated horizontal ring.

netting *n* netted fabric.

nettle *n* a wild plant with stinging hairs. * *vt* to irritate, annoy.

network *n* an arrangement of intersecting lines; a group of people who co-operate with each other; a chain of interconnected operations, computers, etc; (*radio, TV*) a group of broadcasting stations connected to transmit the same programme simultaneously.

* *vt* to broadcast on a network; (*comput*) to interconnect systems so that information, software, and peripheral devices, such as printers, can be shared.

neurosis *n* (*pl* **neuroses**) a mental disorder with symptoms such as anxiety and phobia.

neurotic *adj* suffering from neurosis; highly strung; of or acting upon the nerves. * *n* someone with neurosis.

neuter *adj* (*gram*) of gender, neither masculine nor feminine; (*biol*) having no sex organs; having undeveloped sex organs in the adult. * *n* a neuter person, word, plant, or animal. * *vt* to castrate or spay.

neutral *adj* nonaligned; not taking sides with either party in a dispute or war; having no distinctive characteristics; (*color*) dull; (*chem*) neither acid nor alkaline; (*physics*) having zero charge. * *n* a neutral state, person, or color; a position of a gear mechanism in which power is not transmitted.— **neutrality** *n*.

never *adv* at no time, not ever; not at all; in no case; (*inf*) surely not.

nevertheless *adv* all the same, notwithstanding; in spite of, however.

new *adj* recently made, discovered, or invented; seen, known, or used for the first time; different, changed; recently grown, fresh; unused; unaccustomed; unfamiliar; recently begun. * *adv* again; newly; recently.

newborn *adj* newly born; reborn.

New Brunswicker *n* (*Cdn*) a person who lives in or is from New Brunswick.

newcomer *n* a recent arrival.

New Democrat *n* (*Cdn*) a member or supporter of the New Democratic Party.

Newfie *n* (*Cdn*) (*inf*) a Newfoundlander.

Newfoundlander *n* a person who lives in or is from Newfoundland.

newly *adv* recently, lately.

new moon *n* the moon when first visible as a crescent.

news *npl* current events; recent happenings; the mass media's coverage of such events; a programme of news on television or radio; information not known before.

newsagent, newsdealer *n* a retailer of newspapers, magazines, etc.

newsflash *n* an important news item broadcast separately and often interrupting other programmes.

newspaper *n* a printed periodical containing news published daily or weekly.

New Year's (Day) *n* the first day of a new year; 1 January, a legal holiday in many countries.

next *adj* nearest; immediately preceding or following; adjacent. * *adv* in the nearest time, place, rank, etc; on the first subsequent occasion.

next of kin *n* the nearest relative of a person.

NF *abbr* = Newfoundland.

NFB *abbr* (*Cdn*) = National Film Board.

Nfld *abbr* = Newfoundland.

NHL *abbr* = National Hockey League.

NHS *abbr* (*Brit*) = National Health Service.

nib *n* a pen point.

nibble *vti* to take small bites at (food, etc); to bite (at) lightly and intermittently.—**nibbler** *n*.

nice *adj* pleasant, attractive, kind, good, etc; particular, fastidious; delicately sensitive.—**nicely** *adv*.—**niceness** *n*.

niche *n* a shallow recess in a wall for a statue, etc; a place, use, or work for which a person or thing is best suited.

nick *n* a small cut, chip, etc, made on a surface; (*slang*) a police station, prison. * *vt* to make a nick in; to wound superficially; (*sl*) to steal; (*sl*) to arrest.

nickel *n* a silvery-white metallic element used in alloys and plating; a US or Canadian coin worth five cents.

nickname *n* a substitute name, often descriptive, given in fun; a familiar form of a proper name. * *vt* to give as a nickname.

nicotine *n* a poisonous alkaloid present in tobacco.

niece *n* the daughter of a brother or sister.

niggling *adj* finicky, fussy; petty; gnawing, irritating.

night *n* the period of darkness from sunset to sunrise; nightfall; a specified or appointed evening.

nightcap *n* a cap worn in bed; (*inf*) an alcoholic drink taken just before going to bed.

nightclub *n* a place of entertainment for drinking, dancing, etc, at night.

nightdress *n* a loose garment worn in bed by women and girls.

nightfall *n* the close of the day.

nightie, nighty *n* (*inf*) a nightdress, nightgown.

nightingale *n* a songbird celebrated for its musical song at night.

nightlife *n* social entertainment at night, esp in towns.

nightly *adj*, *adv* done or happening by night or every night.

nightmare *n* a frightening dream; any horrible experience.—**nightmarish** *adj*.

night school *n* an educational institution where classes are held in the evening.

night-time *n* night.

night watchman *n* the person who guards a building at night.

nil *n* nothing.

nimble *adj* agile; quick.—**nimbly** *adv*.

nine *adj*, *n* one more than eight. * *n* the symbol for this (9, IX, ix); the ninth in a series or set; something having nine units as members.

nineteen *adj*, *n* one more than eighteen. * *n* the symbol for this (19, XIX, xix).—**nineteenth** *adj*.

ninety *adj*, *n* nine times ten. * *n* the symbol for this (90, XC, xc); (*in pl*) **nineties**; the numbers from 90 to 99; the same numbers in a life or century.—**ninetieth** *adj*.

ninth *adj*, *n* next after eighth; one of nine equal parts of a thing.

nip[1] *vt* (*pt* **nipped**) to pinch, pinch off; to squeeze between two surfaces; (*dog*) to give a small bite; to prevent the growth of; (*plants*) to have a harmful effect on because of cold. * *n* a pinch; a sharp squeeze; a bite; severe frost or biting coldness.

nip[2] *n* a small drink of spirits. * *vti* to drink in nips.

nipple *n* the small protuberance on a breast or udder through which the milk passes, a teat; a teat-like rubber part on the cap of a baby's bottle; a projection resembling a nipple.

nippy *adj* (**nippier, nippiest**) (*inf*) quick, nimble; (*weather*) frosty; (*motor car*) small but powerful.

nitrogen *n* a gaseous element forming nearly 78 per cent of air.

No, no[1] *abbr* = number.

no[2] *adv* (*used to express denial or disagreement*) not so, not at all, by no amount. * *adj* not any; not a; not one, none; not at all; by no means. * *n* (*pl* **noes, nos**) a denial; a refusal; a negative vote or voter.

nobility *n* nobleness of character, mind, birth, or rank; the class of people of noble birth.

noble *adj* famous or renowned; excellent in quality or character; of high rank or birth. * *n* a person of high rank in society.—**nobleman** *n*.—**nobly** *adv*.

nobody *n* a person of no importance. * *pron* no person.

nod *vti* (*pt* **nodded**) to incline the head quickly, esp in agreement or greeting; to let the head drop, be drowsy; to indicate by a nod; (*with* **off**) (*inf*) to fall asleep. * *n* a quick bob of the head; a sign of assent or command.

noise *n* a sound, esp a loud, disturbing or unpleasant one; a din; unwanted fluctuations in a transmitted signal; (*pl*) conventional sounds, words, etc made in reaction, such as sympathy. * *vt* to make public.

noisy *adj* (**noisier, noisiest**) making much noise; turbulent, clamorous.—**noisily** *adv*.—**noisiness** *n*.

nomad *n* one of a people or tribe who move in search of pasture; a wanderer.—**nomadic** *adj*.

no-man's-land *n* an unclaimed piece of land; a strip of land, esp between armies, borders; an ambiguous area, subject, etc.

nominal *adj* of or like a name; existing in name only; having minimal real worth, token.—**nominally** *adv*.

nominate *vt* to appoint to an office or position; (*candidate*) to propose for election.—**nominator** *n*.

nomination *n* the act or right of nominating; the state of being nominated.

nominee *n* a person who is nominated.

non- *prefix* not, reversing the meaning of a word.

nonchalant *adj* calm; cool, unconcerned, indifferent.—**nonchalance** *n*.—**nonchalantly** *adv*.

noncommittal *adj* not revealing one's opinion.—**noncommittally** *adv*.

non-confidence, no-confidence *adj* pertaining to a motion or vote in a legislature expressing a lack of majority support for the governing party.

nondescript *adj* hard to classify, indeterminate; lacking individual characteristics. * *n* a nondescript person or thing.

none *pron* no one; not anyone; (*pl verb*) not any; no one. * *adv* not at all.

nonentity *n* a person or thing of no significance.

nonflammable *adj* not easily set on fire.

nonplus *vt* (*pt* **nonplussed**) to cause to be so perplexed that one cannot, go, speak, act further.

nonsense *n* words, actions, etc, that are absurd and have no meaning.—*also adj*.—**nonsensical** *adj*.

non-status Indian *n* (*Cdn*) a person who is not officially registered as a member of a First Nations community.—*see* **status Indian**.

nonstop *adj* (*train, plane, etc*) not making any intermediate stops; not ceasing. * *adv* without stopping or pausing.

noodle[1] *n* (*often pl*) pasta formed into a strip.

noodle[2] *n* (*inf*) a foolish person; (*sl*) the head.

nook *n* a secluded corner, a retreat; a recess.

noon *n* midday; twelve o'clock in the day.

nor *conj* and not; not either.

norm *n* a standard or model, esp the standard of achievement of a large group.—**normative** *adj*.

normal *adj* regular; usual; stable mentally. * *n* anything normal; the usual state, amount, etc.—**normalcy** *n*.—**normality** *n*.—**normally** *adv*.

north *n* one of the four points of the compass, opposite the sun at noon, to the right of a person facing the sunset; the direction in which a compass needle points; (*often with* *cap*) the northern part of one's country or the earth. * *adj* in, of, or towards the north; from the north. * *adv* in or towards the north.

northeast *adj*, *n* (of) the direction midway between north and east.

northern *adj* of or in the north.

northward *adj* towards or in the north.—*also* *adv*.—**northwards** *adv*.

northwest *adj*, *n* (of) the direction midway between north and west.

Norwegian *adj*, *n* (of or relating to) the language, people, etc, of Norway.

nose *n* the part of the face above the mouth, used for breathing and smelling, having two nostrils; the sense of smell; anything like a nose in shape or position. * *vt* to discover as by smell; to nuzzle; to push (away, etc) with the front forward. * *vi* to sniff for; to inch forwards; to pry.

nose dive *n* a swift downward plunge of an aircraft, nose first; any sudden sharp drop, as in prices.—*also vi*.

nosey *see* **nosy**.

nostalgia *n* yearning for past times or places.

nostalgic *adj* feeling or expressing nostalgia; longing for one's youth.—**nostalgically** *adv*.

nostril *n* one of the two external openings of the nose for breathing and smelling.

nosy *adj* (**nosier, nosiest**) (*inf*) inquisitive, snooping.—**nosily** *adv*.—**nosiness** *n*.—*also* **nosey**.

not *adv expressing* denial, refusal, or negation.

notable *adj* worthy of being noted or remembered; remarkable, eminent. * *n* an eminent or famous person.—**notably** *adv*.

notch *n* a V-shaped cut in an edge or surface; (*inf*) a step, degree; a narrow pass with steep sides. * *vt* to cut notches in.

note *n* a brief summary or record, written down for future reference; a memorandum; a short letter; notice, attention; an explanation or comment on the text of a book; a musical sound of a particular pitch; a sign representing such a sound; a piano or organ key; the vocal sound of a bird. * *vt* to notice, observe; to write down; to annotate.

notebook *n* a book with blank pages for writing in.

noted *adj* celebrated, well-known.

notepaper *n* paper for writing letters.

nothing *n* no thing; not anything; nothingness; a zero; a trifle; a person or thing of no importance or value. * *adv* in no way, not at all.

notice *n* an announcement; a warning; a placard giving information; a short article about a book, play, etc; attention, heed; a formal warning of intention to end an agreement at a certain time. * *vt* to observe; to remark upon. * *vi* to be aware of.

noticeable *adj* easily noticed or seen.—**noticeably** *adv*.

notice board *n* a board on which notices, bulletins, etc, are pinned for public information.

notify *vt* to inform; to report, give notice of.

notion *n* a general idea; an opinion; a whim;.

notorious *adj* widely known, esp unfavourably.—**notoriously** *adv*.

notwithstanding *prep* in spite of. * *adv* nevertheless. * *conj* although.

notwithstanding clause *n* (*Cdn*) a section of the Canadian constitution that allows Parliament or a provincial legislature to override certain clauses concerning rights and freedoms.

nougat *n* a chewy sweet consisting of sugar paste with nuts.

nought *n* nothing; a zero.—*also* **naught**.

noun *n* (*gram*) a word that names a person, a living being, an object, action etc; a substantive.

nourish *vt* to feed; to encourage the growth of; to raise, bring up.

nourishing *adj* containing nourishment; health-giving; beneficial.

nourishment *n* food; the act of nourishing.

Nova Scotian *n* (*Cdn*) a person who lives in or is from Nova Scotia.

novel *n* a relatively long prose narrative that is usually fictitious and in the form of a story. * *adj* new and unusual.

novelist *n* a writer of novels.

novelty *n* a novel thing or occurrence; a new or unusual thing; (*pl*) cheap, small objects for sale.

November *n* the eleventh month, having 30 days.

novice *n* a person on probation in a religious order before taking final vows; a beginner.

now *adv* at the present time; by this time; at once; nowadays. * *conj* since; seeing that. * *n* the present time. * *adj* of the present time.

nowadays *adv* in these days; at the present time.

nowhere *adv* not in, at, or to anywhere.

nozzle *n* the spout at the end of a hose, pipe, etc.

NRC *abbr* (*Cdn*) = National Research Council.

NS *abbr* = Nova Scotia.

NST *abbr* = Newfoundland Standard Time.

NT *abbr* = Newfoundland Time.

nuance *n* a subtle difference in meaning, color, etc.

nuclear *adj* of or relating to a nucleus; using nuclear energy; having nuclear weapons.

nuclear energy *n* energy released as a result of nuclear fission or fusion.

nuclear fission *n* the splitting of a nucleus of an atom either spontaneously or by bombarding it with particles.

nuclear fusion *n* the combining of two nuclei to a heavier nucleus, releasing energy in the process.

nuclear power *n* electrical or motive power produced by a nuclear reactor.

nuclear reactor *n* a device in which nuclear fission is maintained and harnessed to produce energy.

nucleus *n* (*pl* **nuclei, nucleuses**) the central part of core around which something may develop, or be grouped or concentrated; the centrally positively charged portion of an atom; the part of an animal or plant cell containing genetic material.

nude *adj* naked; bare; undressed. * *n* a naked human figure, esp in a work of art; the state of being nude.—**nudity** *n*.

nudge *vt* to touch gently with the elbow to attract attention or urge into action; to push slightly.—*also n*.

nuisance *n* a person or thing that annoys or causes trouble.

null *adj* without legal force; invalid.

nullify *vt* to make null, to cancel out.—**nullification** *n*.

numb *adj* deadened; having no feeling (due to cold, shock, etc). * *vt* to make numb.—**numbness** *n*.

number *n* a symbol or word indicating how many; a numeral identifying a person or thing by its position in a series; a single issue of a magazine; a song or piece of music, esp as an item in a performance; (*inf*) an object singled out; a total of persons or things; (*gram*) the form of a word indicating singular or plural; a telephone number; (*pl*) arithmetic; (*pl*) numerical superiority. * *vti* to count; to give a number to; to include or be included as one of a group; to limit the number of; to total.

numbered company *n* (*Cdn*) a corporation whose name is a number, followed by the name of the province in which it is registered.

numberplate *n* a plate on the front or rear of a motor vehicle that displays its registration number.

numeral *n* a symbol or group of symbols used to express a number (eg two = 2 or II, etc).

numerical, numeric *adj* of or relating to numbers; expressed in numbers.

numerous *adj* many, consisting of many items.

nun *n* a woman belonging to a religious order.

nurse *n* a person trained to care for the sick, injured or aged; a person who looks after another person's child or children. * *vt* to tend, to care for; (*baby*) to feed at the breast; (*hatred*) to foster; to tend with an eye to the future.

nursery *n* a room set aside for children; a place where children may be left in temporary care; a place where young trees and plants are raised for transplanting.

nursery rhyme *n* a short traditional poem or song for children.

nursery school *n* a school for young children, usu under five.

nursery slope *n* a gently inclined slope for novice skiers.

nursing *n* the profession of a nurse.

nursing home *n* an establishment providing care for convalescent, chronically ill, or disabled people.

nut *n* a kernel (sometimes edible) enclosed in a hard shell; a usu metallic threaded block screwed on the end of a bolt; (*sl*) a mad person; (*sl*) a devotee, fan.

nutcracker *n* (usu *pl*) a tool for cracking nuts; a bird with speckled plumage.

nutmeg *n* the aromatic kernel produced by a tree, grated and used as a spice.

nutrition *n* the act or process by which plants and animals take in and assimilate food in their systems; the study of the human diet.—**nutritional** *adj*.

nutritious *adj* efficient as food; health-giving, nourishing.

NWT *abbr* = Northwest Territories.

nylon *n* any of numerous strong, tough, elastic, synthetic materials used esp in plastics and textiles; (*pl*) stockings made of nylon.

O

oaf *n* (*pl* **oafs**) a loutish or stupid person.—**oafish** *adj*.—**oafishness** *n*.

oak *n* a tree with a hard durable wood, having acorns as fruits.

OAP *abbr* = old age pensioner.

oar *n* a pole with a flat blade for rowing a boat; an oarsman.

oasis *n* (*pl* **oases**) a fertile place in a desert; a refuge.

oath *n* a solemn declaration to a god or a higher authority that one will speak the truth or keep a promise; a swear word; a blasphemous expression.

oatmeal *n* ground oats; a porridge of this; a pale greyish-brown color.

oats *npl* a cereal grass widely cultivated for its edible grain; the seeds.

obedience *n* the condition of being obedient; observance of orders, instructions, etc; respect for authority.

obedient *adj* obeying; compliant; submissive to authority, dutiful.—**obediently** *adv*.

obelisk *n* a four-sided tapering pillar usu with a pyramidal top.

obey *vti* to carry out (orders, instructions); to comply (with); to submit (to).

obituary *n* an announcement of a person's death, often with a short biography.

object *n* something that can be recognized by the senses; a person or thing towards which action, feeling, etc, is directed; a purpose or aim; (*gram*) a noun or part of a sentence governed by a transitive verb or a preposition. * *vti* to state or raise an objection; to oppose; to disapprove.—**objector** *n*.

objection *n* the act of objecting; a ground for, or expression of, disapproval.

objectionable *adj* causing an objection; disagreeable.—**objectionably** *adv*.

objective *adj* relating to an object; not influenced by opinions or feelings; impartial; having an independent existence of its own, real; (*gram*) of, or appropriate to an object governed by a verb or a preposition. * *n* the thing or placed aimed at; (*gram*) the objective case.—**objectively** *adv*.—**objectivity** *n*.

obligation *n* the act of obligating; a moral or legal requirement; a debt; a favor; a commitment to pay a certain amount of money; the amount owed.

obligatory *adj* binding, not optional; compulsory.

oblige *vt* to compel by moral, legal, or physical force; (*person*) to make grateful for some favor; to do a favor for.

obliging *adj* ready to do favors, agreeable.—**obligingly** *adv*.

oblique *adj* slanting, at an angle; diverging from the straight; indirect, allusive. * *n* an oblique line.—**obliquely** *adv*.

obliterate *vt* to wipe out, to erase, to destroy.—**obliteration** *n*.

oblivion *n* a state of forgetting or being forgotten; a state of mental withdrawal.

oblivious *adj* forgetful, unheeding; unaware (of).

oblong *adj* rectangular. * *n* any oblong figure.

obnoxious *adj* objectionable; highly offensive.—**obnoxiously** *adv*.—**obnoxiousness** *n*.

oboe *n* an orchestral woodwind instrument having a mouthpiece with a double reed.—**oboist** *n*.

obscene *adj* indecent, lewd; offensive to a moral or social standard.—**obscenely** *adv*.

obscenity *n* the state or quality of being obscene; an obscene act, word, etc.

obscure *adj* not clear; dim; indistinct; remote, secret; not easily understood; inconspicuous; unimportant, humble. * *vt* to make unclear, to confuse; to hide.—**obscurely** *adv*.

obscurity *n* the state or quality of being obscure;

an obscure thing or person.

obsequious *adj* subservient; fawning.—**obsequiously** *adv*.

observance *n* the observing of a rule, duty, law, etc; a ceremony or religious rite.

observant *adj* watchful; attentive, mindful.—**observantly** *adv*.

observation *n* the act or faculty of observing; a comment or remark; careful noting of the symptoms of a patient, movements of a suspect, etc prior to diagnosis, analysis or interpretation.

observatory *n* a building for astronomical observation; an institution whose primary purpose is making such observations.

observe *vt* to notice; to perceive; (*a law, etc*) to keep to or adhere to; to arrive at as a conclusion; to examine scientifically. * *vi* to take notice; to make a comment (on).—**observable** *adj*.

observer *n* a person who observes; a delegate who attends a formal meeting but may not take part; an expert analyst and commentator in a particular field.

obsess *vt* to possess or haunt the mind of; to preoccupy.—**obsessive** *adj*, *n*.—**obsessively** *adv*.

obsession *n* a fixed idea, often associated with mental illness; a persistent idea or preoccupation; the condition of obsessing or being obsessed.

obsolescent *adj* becoming obsolete, going out of date.—**obsolescence** *n*.

obsolete *adj* disused, out of date.

obstacle *n* anything that hinders something; an obstruction.

obstacle race *n* a race in which the competitors negotiate various obstacles.

obstetrics *n* (*used as sing*) the branch of medicine concerned with the care and treatment of women during pregnancy and childbirth.—**obstetric** *adj*.—**obstetrician** *n*.

obstinate *adj* stubborn, self-willed; intractable; persistent.—**obstinacy** *n*.—**obstinately** *adv*.

obstreperous *adj* unruly, turbulent, noisy.

obstruct *vt* to block with an obstacle; to impede; to prevent, hinder; to keep (light, etc) from.

obstruction *n* that which obstructs; the act or an example of obstructing; a hindrance, obstacle.

obstructive *adj* tending to obstruct; preventing, hindering.—**obstructively** *adv*.

obtain *vt* to get, to acquire, to gain. * *vi* to be prevalent, hold good.—**obtainable** *adj*.

obtrusive *adj* apt to obtrude, pushy; protruding, sticking out.—**obtrusively** *adv*.—**obtrusiveness** *n*.

obtuse *adj* mentally slow; not pointed; dull, stupid; (*geom*) greater than a right angle.—**obtusely** *adv*.—**obtuseness** *n*.

obviate *vt* to make unnecessary; (*danger, difficulty*) to prevent, clear away.

obvious *adj* easily seen or understood; evident.—**obviously** *adv*.—**obviousness** *n*.

OC *abbr* = Officer of the Order of Canada.

occasion *n* a special occurrence or event; a time when something happens; an opportunity; reason or grounds; a subsidiary cause. * *vt* to cause; to bring about.

occasional *adj* infrequent, not continuous; intermittent; produced for an occasion; (*a cause*) incidental.

occupation *n* the act of occupying; the state of being occupied; employment or profession; a pursuit.—**occupational** *adj*.

occupy *vt* to live in; (*room, office*) to take up or fill; (*a position*) to hold; to engross (one's mind); (*city, etc*) to take possession of.—**occupier** *n*.

occur *vi* (*pt* **occurred**) to happen; to exist; to come into the mind of.

occurrence *n* a happening, an incident, an event; the act or fact of occurring.

ocean *n* a large stretch of sea, esp one of the earth's five oceans; a huge quantity or expanse.

ochre, ocher (*US*) *n* a yellow to orange-colored clay used as a pigment.

o'clock *adv* indicating the hour; indicating a relative direction or position, twelve o'clock being directly ahead or above.

octave *n* (*mus*) the eighth full tone above or below a given tone, the interval of eight degrees between a tone and either of its octaves, or the series of tones within this interval.

October *n* the tenth month of the year, having 31 days.

octopus *n* (*pl* **octopuses**) a mollusc having a soft body and eight tentacles covered with suckers.

odd *adj* eccentric; peculiar; occasional; not divisible by two; with the other of the pair missing; extra or left over. * *npl* probability; balance of advantage in favor of one against another; excess of one number over another, esp in betting; likelihood; disagreement; strife; miscellaneous articles, scraps.—**oddly** *adv*.—**oddness** *n*.

oddity *n* the state of being odd; an odd thing or person; peculiarity.

oddment *n* an odd piece left over, esp of fabric.

ode *n* a lyric poem marked by lofty feeling and dignified style.

odious *adj* causing hatred or offence; disgusting.—**odiously** *adv*.—**odiousness** *n*.

odour, odor (*US*) *n* smell; scent; aroma; a characteristic or predominant quality.

odourless, odorless (*US*) *adj* without odour.

of *prep* from; belonging or relating to; concerning; among; by; during; owing to.

off *adv* away, from; detached, gone; unavailable; disconnected; out of condition; entirely. * *prep* away from; not on. * *adj* distant; no longer operating; cancelled; (*food or drink*) having gone bad; on the right-hand side; (*runners, etc*) having started a race.

offal *n* the entrails of an animal eaten as food.

off-color *adj* unwell; risqué.

offence, offense (*US*) *n* an illegal action, crime; a

sin; an affront, insult; a cause of displeasure or anger.

offend vt to affront, displease; to insult. * vi to break a law.—**offender** n.

offensive adj causing offence; repulsive, disagreeable; insulting; aggressive. * n an attack; a forceful campaign for a cause, etc.—**offensively** adv.—**offensiveness** n.

offer vt to present for acceptance or rejection; to show willingness (to do something); to present for consideration; to bid; (a prayer) to say. * vi to present itself; to declare oneself willing. * n something offered; a bid or proposal.

offering n a gift, present; a sacrifice.

offhand adv impromptu; without thinking. * adj inconsiderate; curt, brusque; unceremonious.

office n a room or building where business is carried out; the people there; (with cap) the location, staff, of authority of a Government department, etc; a task or function; a position of authority; a duty; a religious ceremony, rite.

officer n an official; a person holding a position of authority in a government, business, club, military services, etc; a policeman.

official adj of an office or its tenure; properly authorized; formal. * n a person who holds a public office.—**officially** adv.

officious adj interfering, meddlesome; offering unwanted advice.—**officiously** adv.—**officiousness** n.

offing n the near or foreseeable future.

off-licence n a licence to sell alcohol for consumption off the premises; a place so licensed.

off-peak adj denoting use of a service, etc, in a period of lesser demand.

offset vt (pr p **offsetting**, pt **offset**) to compensate for, counterbalance. * n compensation; a method of printing in which an image is transferred from a plate to a rubber surface and then to paper; a sloping ledge on the face of a wall.

offshore adv at sea some distance from the shore.

offside adj, adv illegally in advance of the ball.

offspring n a child, progeny; a result.

offstage adj, adv out of sight of the audience; behind the scenes.

often adv many times, frequently.

ogle vti to gape at; to make eyes at; to look at lustfully.

OHIP abbr = Ontario Health Insurance Plan.

Ojibwa or **Ojibway** n a member of an Indian people of North America mainly living near Lake Superior; the language of this people. * adj of or pertaining to this people or their language.

oil n a greasy, combustible liquid substance obtained from animal, vegetable, or mineral matter; petroleum; an oil painting; (pl) paint mixed by grinding a pigment in oil. * vt to smear with oil, lubricate.

oilcan n a container with a long spout for releas-

ing oil for lubricating in individual drops.

oilfield n an area on land or under the sea that produces petroleum.

oil painting n a painting in oils; the art of painting in oils; (inf) a good-looking person.

oilskin n fabric made waterproof by treatment with oil; a waterproof garment of oilskin or a plastic-coated fabric.

oil slick n a mass of oil floating on the surface of water.

oil well n a well from which oil is extracted.

oily adj (**oilier, oiliest**) like or covered with oil; greasy; too suave or smooth, unctuous.—**oiliness** n.

ointment n a fatty substance used on the skin for healing or cosmetic purposes; a salve.

OK, okay adj, adv (inf) all right; correct(ly). * n (pl **OK's, okays**) approval.

Oka n (Cdn) a cured, semi-soft cheese made in Quebec.

old adj aged; elderly, not young; having lived or existed for a long time; long used, not new; former; of the past, not modern; experienced; worn out; of long standing.

old age security n (Cdn) a system of pensions paid by the federal government to people who are 65 or older.

old-fashioned adj out of date; in a fashion of an older time.

olive n an evergreen tree cultivated for its edible hard-stoned fruit and oil; its fruit; a yellow-green color. * adj of a yellow-green color.

olive oil n an edible yellow oil obtained from the fruit of the olive by pressing.

Olympic Games, Olympics n (used as sing or pl) an ancient athletic contest revived in 1896 as an international meeting held every four years in a different country.

omelette, omelet (US) n eggs beaten and cooked flat in a pan.

omen n a sign or warning of impending happiness or disaster.

ominous adj relating to an omen; foreboding evil; threatening.—**ominously** adv.

omission n something that has been left out or neglected; the act of omitting.

omit vt (pt **omitted**) to leave out; to neglect to do, leave undone.

omni- prefix all; universally.

on prep in contact with the upper surface of; supported by, attached to, or covering; directed toward; at the time of; concerning; about; using as a basis, condition or principle; immediately after; (sl) using; addicted to. * adv (so as to be) covering or in contact with something; forward; (device) switched on; continuously in progress; due to take place; (actor) on stage; on duty. * adj (cricket) designating the part of the field on the batsman's side in front of the wicket. * n (cricket) the on side.

ON abbr = Ontario.

once adv on one occasion only; formerly; at some time. * conj as soon as. * n one time.

oncoming *adj* approaching.

one *adj* single; undivided, united; the same; a certain unspecified (time, etc). * *n* the first and lowest cardinal number; an individual thing or person; (*inf*) a drink; (*inf*) a joke. * *pron* an indefinite person, used to apply to many people; someone.

oneself *pron reflex form of* one.

one-way *adj* (*traffic*) restricted to one direction; requiring no reciprocal action or obligation.

ongoing *adj* progressing, continuing.

onion *n* an edible bulb with a pungent taste and odour.

onlooker *n* a spectator.

only *adj* alone of its kind; single, sole. * *adv* solely, merely; just; not more than. * *conj* except that, but.

onset *n* a beginning; an assault, attack.

onslaught *n* a fierce attack.

Ont. *abbr* = Ontario.

Ontarian *n* a person who lives in or is from Ontario.

onto *prep* to a position on.

onus *n* responsibility, duty; burden.

onward *adj* advancing, forward. * *adv* onwards.

onwards *adv* to the front, ahead, forward.

onyx *n* a limestone similar to marble with layers of color.

ooze *vti* to flow or leak out slowly; to seep; to exude. * *n* soft mud or slime.

opal *n* a white or bluish stone with a play of iridescent colors.

opaque *adj* not letting light through; neither transparent nor translucent.—**opaquely** *adv*.—**opaqueness** *n*.

open *adj* not closed; accessible; uncovered, unprotected; not fenced; free from trees; spread out, unfolded; public; lacking reserve; (*a person*) forthcoming; generous; readily understood; liable (to); unrestricted; (*syllable*) ending with a vowel; (*consonant*) made without stopping the stream of breath. * *vti* to make or become accessible; to unfasten; to begin; to expand, unfold; to come into view. * *n* a wide space; (*sport*) a competition that any player can enter.—**openness** *n*.

opening *n* a gap, aperture; a beginning; a chance; a job opportunity. * *adj* initial.

openly *adv* frankly; publicly.

open-minded *adj* unprejudiced.—**open-mindedness** *n*.

opera *n* a dramatic work represented through music and song; plural form of **opus**.

operate *vi* to work, to function; to produce a desired effect; to carry out a surgical operation. * *vt* (*a machine*) to work or control; to carry on, run.

operatic *adj* of or relating to opera; exaggerated, overacting.

operation *n* a method of operating; a procedure; a military action; a surgical procedure.

operational *adj* of or relating to an operation; functioning; ready for use; involved in military activity.—**operationally** *adv*.

operative *adj* functioning; in force, effective; of,

by surgery. * *n* a mechanic; a secret agent; a private detective.

operator *n* a person who operates or works a machine, esp a telephone switchboard; a person who owns or runs a business; a person who manipulates.

operetta *n* a short or light opera.

opinion *n* a belief that is not based on proof; judgment; estimation, evaluation; a formal expert judgment; professional advice.

opinionated *adj* unduly confident in one's opinions, dogmatic.

opium *n* a narcotic drug produced from an annual Eurasian poppy.

OPP *abbr* = Ontario Provincial Police.

opponent *n* a person who opposes another; an adversary, antagonist. * *adj* opposing.

opportune *adj* well-timed; convenient.—**opportunely** *adv*.

opportunist *n* a person who forms or adapts his or her views or principles to benefit from opportunities; to seize opportunities as they may arise.—**opportunism** *n*.

opportunity *n* chance; a favorable combination of circumstances.

oppose *vt* to put in front of or in the way of; to place in opposition; to resist; to fight against; to balance against.—**opposer** *n*.

opposite *adj* placed on opposed sides of; face to face; diametrically different; contrary. * *n* a person or thing that is opposite; an antithesis. * *prep, adv* across from.

opposition *n* the act of opposing or the condition of being opposed; resistance; antithesis; hostility; a political party opposing the government; (*astron*) the diametrically opposite position of two heavenly bodies, when 180 degrees apart.

oppress *vt* to treat unjustly; to subjugate; to weigh down in the mind.—**oppressor** *n*.

oppression *n* the act of oppressing; the state of being oppressed; persecution; physical or mental distress.

oppressive *adj* tyrannical; burdensome; (*weather*) sultry, close.—**oppressively** *adv*.—**oppressiveness** *n*.

opt *vi* to choose or to exercise an option.

optical *adj* of or relating to the eye or light; optic; aiding or correcting vision; visual.—**optically** *adv*.

optician *n* a person who makes or sells optical aids.

optimism *n* a tendency to take the most cheerful view of things; hopefulness; the belief that good must ultimately prevail.—**optimist** *n*.—**optimistic** *adj*.—**optimistically** *adv*.

optimum *n* the best, most favorable condition.—*also adj*.

option *n* the act of choosing; the power to choose; a choice; the right to buy, sell or lease at a fixed price within a specified time.

optional *adj* left to choice; not compulsory.—**optionally** *adv*.

opulent *adj* wealthy; luxuriant.—**opulence** *n*.

opus (*pl* **opuses, opera**) an artistic or literary

work; a musical composition.

or *conj denoting* an alternative; the last in a series of choices.

oracle *n* a place in ancient Greece where a deity was consulted; the response given (often ambiguous); a wise adviser; sage advice.—**oracular** *adj*.

oral *adj* of the mouth; (*drugs*) taken by mouth; spoken, not written. * *n* a spoken examination.—**orally** *adv*.

orange *n* a round, reddish-yellow, juicy, edible citrus fruit; the tree bearing it; its color. * *adj* orange-colored.

oration *n* a formal or public speech.

orator *n* an eloquent public speaker.

oratorio *n* (*pl* **oratorios**) a sacred story set to music for voices and instruments.

orb *n* a sphere or globe; an ornamental sphere surmounted by a cross, esp as carried by a sovereign at a coronation.

orbit *n* (*astron*) a curved path along which a planet or satellite moves; a field of action or influence; the eye socket; (*physics*) the path of an electron around the nucleus of an atom. * *vti* to put (a satellite, etc) into orbit; to circle round.—**orbital** *adj*.

orchard *n* an area of land planted with fruit trees.

orchestra *n* a group of musicians playing together under a conductor; their instruments; the space (or pit) in a theatre where they sit; the stalls of a theatre.—**orchestral** *adj*.

orchid *n* a plant with unusually shaped flowers in brilliant colors comprising three petals of uneven size.

ordain *vti* to confer holy orders upon; to appoint; to decree; to order, to command.

ordeal *n* a severe trial or test; an exacting experience.

order *n* arrangement; method; relative position; sequence; an undisturbed condition; tidiness; rules of procedure; an efficient state; a class, group, or sort; a religious fraternity; a style of architecture; an honor or decoration; an instruction or command; a rule or regulation; a state or condition, esp with regard to functioning; a request to supply something; the goods supplied; (*zool*) divisions between class and family or genus. * *vti* to put or keep (things) in order; to arrange; to command; to request (something) to be supplied.

orderly *adj* in good order; well-behaved; methodical. * *n* a hospital attendant; a soldier attending an officer.—**orderliness** *n*.

ordinal *adj* showing position in a series. * *n* an ordinal number.

ordinary *adj* normal, usual; common; plain, unexceptional.—**ordinarily** *adv*.

ordination *n* the act of ordaining or being ordained; admission to the ministry.

ore *n* a substance from which minerals can be extracted.

organ *n* a usu large and complex musical wind instrument with pipes, stops, and a keyboard; a part of an animal or plant that performs a vital or natural function; the means by which anything is done; a medium of information or opinion, a periodical.

organic *adj* of or relating to bodily organs; (disease) affecting a bodily organ; of, or derived from, living organisms; systematically arranged; structural; (*chem*) of the class of compounds that are formed from carbon; (vegetables, etc) grown without the use of artificial fertilizers or pesticides.—**organically** *adv*.

organism *n* an animal or plant, any living thing; an organized body.

organist *n* a person who plays an organ.

organization *n* the act or process of organizing; the state of being organized; arrangement, structure; an organized body or association.

organize *vt* to arrange in an orderly way; to establish; to institute; to persuade to join a cause, group, etc; to arrange for.—**organizer** *n*.

orgasm *n* the climax of sexual excitement.—**orgasmic** *adj*.

orgy *n* a wild party or gathering of people, with excessive drinking and indiscriminate sexual activity; over-indulgence in any activity.

Orient *n* the East, or Asia, esp the Far East.

orient, orientate *vti* to adjust (oneself) to a particular situation; to arrange in a direction, esp in relation to the points of the compass; to face or turn in a particular direction.

oriental *adj* of the Orient, its people or languages.

orifice *n* an opening or mouth of a cavity.

origin *n* the source or beginning of anything; ancestry or parentage.

original *adj* relating to the origin or beginning; earliest, primitive; novel; unusual; inventive, creative. * *n* an original work, as of art or literature; something from which copies are made; a creative person; an eccentric.—**originality** *n*.—**originally** *adv*.

originate *vti* to initiate or begin; to bring or come into being.—**origination** *n*.—**originator** *n*.

ornament *n* anything that enhances the appearance of a person or thing; a small decorative object. * *vt* to adorn, to decorate with ornaments.

ornamental *adj* serving as an ornament; decorative, not useful.—**ornamentally** *adv*.

ornate *adj* richly adorned; (*style*) highly elaborate.—**ornately** *adv*.—**ornateness** *n*.

ornithology *n* the study of birds.—**ornithological** *adj*.—**ornithologist** *n*.

orphan *n* a child whose parents are dead. * *vt* to cause to become an orphan.—*also adj*.

orphanage *n* a residential institution for the care of orphans.

orthodox *adj* conforming with established behaviour or opinions; not heretical; generally accepted, conventional; (*with cap*) of or relating to a conservative political or religious group.

orthopaedics, orthopedics (US) n the study and surgical treatment of bone and joint disorders.—**orthopaedic** adj.—**orthopaedist** n.

OSC abbr = Ontario Securities Commision.

oscillate vi to swing back and forth as a pendulum; to waver, vacillate between extremes of opinion, etc.—**oscillation** n.

ostensible adj apparent; seeming; pretended.— **ostensibly** adv.

ostentation n a showy, pretentious display.—**ostentatious** adj.—**ostentatiously** adv.

osteopathy n the treatment of disease by manipulation of the bones and muscles, often as an adjunct to medical and surgical measures.—**osteopath** n.

ostracize vt to exclude, banish from a group, society, etc.—**ostracism** n.

ostrich n a large, flightless, swift-running African bird.

other adj second; remaining; different; additional. * pron the other one; some other one.

otherwise adv if not, or else; differently.

otter n a fish-eating mammal with smooth fur and a flat tail.

ouaniche n (Cdn) a landlocked form of Atlantic salmon found in lakes in eastern Canada.

ought aux vb expressing obligation or duty; to be bound, to be obliged (to).

ounce n a unit of weight, equal to one sixteenth of a pound or 28.34 grams; one sixteenth of a pint, one fluid ounce.

our poss adj, pron relating or belonging to us.

ours pron belonging to us.

ourselves pron emphatic and reflexive form of we.

oust vt to eject, expel, esp by underhand means; to remove forcibly.

out adv not in; outside; in the open air; to the full extent; beyond bounds; no longer holding office; ruled out, no longer considered; loudly and clearly; no longer included (in a game, fashion, etc); in error; on strike; at an end; extinguished; into the open; published; revealed; (radio conversation) transmission ends. * prep out of; out through; outside. * adj external; outward. * n an exit; means of escape.

outboard adj (engine) outside a ship, etc. * n an engine attached to the outside of a boat.

outbreak n a sudden eruption (of disease, strife, etc).

outburst n a bursting out; a spurt; an explosion of anger, etc.

outcast n a person who is rejected by society.

outclass vt to surpass or excel greatly.

outcome n the result, consequence.

outcry n protest; uproar.

outdo vt (pt outdid, pp outdone) to surpass, to do more than, to excel.

outdoor adj existing, taking place, or used in the open air.

outdoors adv in or into the open air; out of doors. * n the open air, outside world.

outer adj further out or away.

outer space n any region of space beyond the earth's atmosphere.

outfit n the equipment used in an activity; clothes worn together, an ensemble; a group of people associated in an activity. * vt (pt outfitted) to provide with an outfit or equipment.

outfitter n a supplier of equipment or clothes.

outgoing adj departing; retiring; sociable, forthcoming. * n an outlay; (pl) expenditure.

outing n a pleasure trip; an excursion.

outlandish adj unconventional; strange; fantastic.

outlaw vt to declare illegal. * n an outlawed person; a habitual or notorious criminal.

outlay n a spending (of money); expenditure.

outlet n an opening or release; a means of expression; a market for goods or services.

outline n a profile; a general indication; a rough sketch or draft.—also vt.

outlive vt to live longer than, outlast; to live through; to survive.

outlook n mental attitude; view; prospect.

outlying adj detached; remote, distant.

outmoded adj old-fashioned.

out-of-province adj (Cdn) in, from, or pertaining to another province.

outpatient n a person treated at, but not resident in, a hospital.

outport n (Cdn) a small, isolated fishing community, esp in Newfoundland.—**outporter** n

outpost n (mil) a post or detachment at a distance from a main force.

output n the quantity (of goods, etc) produced, esp over a given period; information delivered by a computer, esp to a printer; (elect) the useful voltage, current, or power delivered.—also vt.

outrage n an extremely vicious or violent act; a grave insult or offence; great anger, etc, aroused by this.—also vt.—**outrageous** adj.

outright adj complete, downright, direct. * adv at once; without restrictions.

outset n the start, beginning.

outside n the outer part or surface, the exterior. * adj outer; outdoor; (chance, etc) slight. * adv on or to the outside. * prep on or to the exterior of; beyond.

outsider n a person or thing not included in a set, group, etc, a non-member; a contestant not thought to have a chance in a race.

outsize adj of a larger than usual size.

outskirts npl districts remote from the centre, as of a city.

outspoken adj candid in speech, frank, blunt.

outstanding adj excellent; distinguished, prominent; unpaid; unresolved, still to be done.

outward adj directed towards the outside; external; clearly apparent. * adv outwards.

outwardly adv externally.

outweigh vt to count for more than, to exceed in value, weight, or importance.

outwit vt (pt outwitted) to get the better of, defeat, by wit or cunning.

oval adj egg-shaped; elliptical. * n anything oval.

ovary n one of the two female reproductive or-

gans producing eggs.—**ovarian** *adj*.

ovation *n* enthusiastic applause or public welcome.

oven *n* an enclosed, heated compartment for baking or drying.

over *prep* higher than; on top of; across; to the other side of; above; more than; concerning. * *adv* above; across; in every part; completed; from beginning to end; up and down; in addition; too. * *adj* upper; excessive; surplus; finished; remaining. * *n* (*cricket*) the number of balls bowled before changing ends.

over- *prefix* in excess, too much; above.

overact *vti* to act in an exaggerated manner, to overdo a part.

overall *adj* including everything. * *adv* as a whole; generally. * *n* a loose protective garment; (*pl*) a one-piece protective garment covering body and legs.

overawe *vt* to restrain by awe, to daunt.

overbalance *vti* to fall over; to upset; to outweigh. * *n* a surplus.

overbearing *adj* domineering; overriding.

overboard *adv* over the side of a ship, etc; (*inf*) to extremes of enthusiasm.

overcast *adj* clouded over.

overcharge *vt* (*battery*) to overload; to fill to excess; to demand too high a price (from). * *n* an excessive or exorbitant charge or load.

overcoat *n* a warm, heavy topcoat.

overcome *vti* (*pt* **overcame**, *pp* **overcome**) to get the better of, to prevail; to render helpless or powerless, as by tears, laughter, emotion, etc; to be victorious; to surmount obstacles, etc.

overdo *vt* (*pt* **overdid**, *pp* **overdone**) to do to excess; to overact; to cook (food) too much.—**overdone** *adj*.

overdose *n* an excessive dose —*also vti*.

overdraft *n* an overdrawing, an amount overdrawn, at a bank.

overdraw *vti* (*pt* **overdrew**, *pp* **overdrawn**) to draw in excess of a credit balance; to exaggerate in describing; to make an overdraft.

overestimate *vt* to set too high an estimate on or for.—*also n*.

overflow *vti* (*pp* **overflown**) to flow over, to flood; to exceed the bounds (of); to abound (with emotion, etc). * *n* that which overflows; surplus, excess; an outlet for surplus water, etc.

overgrown *adj* grown beyond the normal size; rank; ungainly.

overhaul *vt* to examine for, or make, repairs; to overtake.—*also n*.

overhead *adj, adv* above the head; in the sky. * *n* (often *pl*) the general, continuing costs of a business, as of rent, light, etc.

overhear *vt* (*pt* **overheard**) to hear without the knowledge of the speaker.

overjoyed *adj* highly delighted.

overland *adj, adv* by, on, or across land.

overlap *vt* (*pt* **overlapped**) to extend over (a thing or each other) so as to coincide in part.—*also n*.

overload *vt* to put too great a burden on; (*elect*) to charge with too much current.

overlook *vt* to fail to notice; to look at from above; to excuse.

overnight *adv* for the night; in the course of the night; suddenly. * *adj* done in the night; lasting the night; sudden.

overpass *n* a road crossing another road, path, etc, at a higher level; the upper level of such a crossing.

overpower *vt* to overcome by superior force, to subdue; to overwhelm.

overpowering *adj* overwhelming; compelling; unbearable.

overrate *vt* to value or assess too highly.

override *vt* (*pt* **overrode**, *pp* **overridden**) to ride over; to nullify; to prevail.

overrule *vt* to set aside by higher authority; to prevail over.

overseas *adj, adv* across or beyond the sea; abroad.

overshadow *vt* to throw a shadow over; to appear more prominent or important than.

overshoot *vt* (*pt* **overshot**) to shoot or send beyond (a target, etc); (*aircraft*) to fly or taxi beyond the end of a runway when landing or taking off.—*also n*.

oversight *n* a careless mistake or omission; supervision.

oversleep *vi* (*pt* **overslept**) to sleep beyond the intended time.

overspill *vi* (*pt* **overspilt** *or* **overspilled**) to spill over, overflow. * *n* that which overspills; excess.—*also adj*.

overt *adj* openly done, unconcealed; (*law*) done with evident intent, deliberate.—**overtly** *adv*.

overtake *vt* (*pt* **overtook**, *pp* **overtaken**) to catch up with and pass; to come upon suddenly.

overthrow *vt* (*pt* **overthrew**, *pp* **overthrown**) to throw over, overturn; (*government, etc*) to bring down by force.—*also n*.

overtime *adv* beyond regular working hours. * *n* extra time worked; payment for this.

overtone *n* an additional subtle meaning; an implicit quality; (*mus*) a harmonic; the color of light reflected (as by a paint).

overture *n* an initiating of negotiations; a formal offer, proposal; (*mus*) an instrumental introduction to an opera, etc.

overturn *vti* to upset, turn over; to overthrow.

overweight *adj* weighing more than the proper amount. * *n* excess weight.

overwhelm *vt* to overcome totally; to submerge; to crush; to overpower with emotion.

overwhelming *adj* irresistible; uncontrollable; vast; vastly superior; extreme.

overwork *vti* to work or use too hard or too long.

overwrought *adj* over-excited; too elaborate.

owe *vti* to be in debt; to be obliged to pay; to feel the need to give, do, etc, as because of gratitude.

owing *adj* due, to be paid; owed; (*with* **to**) because of, on account of.

owl *n* a nocturnal bird of prey with a large head and eyes; a person of nocturnal habits, sol-

emn appearance, etc.—**owlish** *adj*.

own[1] *vti* to possess; to acknowledge, admit; to confess to.

own[2] *adj* belonging to oneself or itself, often used reflexively (*my own, their own*).

owner *n* one who owns, a possessor, a proprietor.—**ownership** *n*.

ox *n* (*pl* **oxen**) a cud-chewing mammal of the cattle family; a castrated bull.

oxide *n* a compound of oxygen with another element.

oxtail *n* the tail of an ox, esp skinned and used for stews, soups, etc.

oxygen *n* a colorless, odourless, tasteless, highly reactive gaseous element forming part of air, water, etc, and essential to life and combustion.

oxygen mask *n* an apparatus worn over the nose and mouth through which oxygen passes from a storage tank.

oxygen tent *n* a canopy over a hospital bed, etc, within which a supply of oxygen is maintained.

oyster *n* an edible marine bivalve shellfish.

oz *abbr* = ounce(s).

ozone *n* a condensed form of oxygen; (*inf*) bracing seaside air.

ozone layer *n* a layer of ozone in the upper atmosphere that absorbs ultraviolet rays from the sun.

P

p *abbr* = page; penny, pence.

p.a. *abbr* = per annum.

Pablum *n* (*TM*) a soft cereal for infants.

pace *n* a single step; the measure of a single stride; speed of movement. * *vti* to measure by paces; to walk up and down; to determine the pace in a race; to walk with regular steps.—**pacer** *n*.

pacemaker *n* a person who sets the pace in a race; an electronic device inserted in the heart, used to regulate heartbeat.

Pacific salmon *n* a salmon of the coastal North Pacific Ocean and its tributaries.

pacify *vt* to soothe; to calm; to restore peace to.—**pacification** *n*.

pack *n* a load or bundle (esp one carried on the back); a set of playing cards; a group or mass; a number of wild animals living together; an organized troop (as of Cub Scouts); a compact mass (as of snow); a small package used as a container for goods for sale. * *vt* to put together in a bundle or pack; (*suitcase*) to fill; to crowd; to press tightly so as to prevent leakage; to carry in a pack; to send (off); (*sl: gun, etc*) to carry; (*sl: punch*) to deliver with force. * *vi* (*snow, ice*) to form into a hard mass; to assemble one's belongings in suitcases or boxes. * *adj* used for carrying packs, loads, etc.—**packer** *n*.

package *n* a parcel, a wrapped bundle; several items, arrangements, etc offered as a unit. * *vt* to make a parcel of; to group together several items, etc.

packet *n* a small box or package; (*sl*) a considerable sum; a vessel carrying mail, etc, between one port and another.

pack ice *n* sea ice formed into a mass by the crushing together of floes, etc.

packing *n* material for protecting packed goods or for making airtight or watertight; the act of filling a suitcase, box, etc.

pact *n* an agreement or treaty.

pad[1] *n* the dull sound of a footstep. * *vi* (*pt* **padded**) to walk, esp with a soft step.

pad[2] *n* a piece of a soft material or stuffing; several sheets of paper glued together at one edge; the cushioned thickening of an animal's sole; a piece of folded absorbent material used as a surgical dressing; a flat concrete surface; (*sl*) one's own home or room. * *vt* (*pt* **padded**) to stuff with soft material; to fill with irrelevant information.

PA day *n* (*Cdn*) professional development day.

padding *n* stuffing; anything unimportant or false added to achieve length or amount.

paddle[1] *vi* to wade about or play in shallow water.

paddle[2] *n* a short oar with a wide blade at one or both ends; a implement shaped like this, used to hit, beat or stir. * *vti* (*canoe, etc*) to propel by a paddle; to beat as with a paddle; to spank.

paddock *n* an enclosed field in which horses are exercised.

paddy *n* threshed unmilled rice; a rice field.

padlock *n* a detachable lock used to fasten doors etc. * *vt* to secure with a padlock.

padre *n* (*sl*) a priest or chaplain.

paediatrics, pediatrics (*US*) *n* the branch of medicine dealing with children and their diseases.—**paediatric** *adj*.—**paediatrician** *n*.

pagan *n* a heathen; a person who has no religion.—*also adj*.—**paganism** *n*.

page[1] *n* a boy attendant at a formal function (as a wedding); a uniformed boy employed to run errands. * *vt* to summon by messenger, loudspeaker, etc.

page[2] *n* a sheet of paper in a book, newspaper etc. * *vt* (*a book*) to number the pages of.—*also* **paginate**.

pageant *n* a spectacular procession or parade; representation in costume of historical events; a mere show.—*also adj*.—**pageantry** *n*.

pageboy *n* a page; a medium-length hairstyle with ends of hair turned under.

paid *see* **pay**.

pail *n* a bucket.

pain *n* physical or mental suffering; hurting; (*pl*) trouble, exertion. * *vt* to cause distress to.

pained *adj* hurt, offended.

painful *adj* giving pain, distressing.—**painfully** *adv*.—**painfulness** *n*.

painkiller *n* (*inf*) a medicine that relieves pain.

painless *adj* without pain.—**painlessly** *adv.*

painstaking *adj* very careful, laborious.—**painstakingly** *adv.*

paint *vt* (*a picture*) to make using oil pigments, etc; to depict with paints; to cover or decorate with paint; to describe. * *vi* to make a picture. * *n* a coloring pigment; a dried coat of paint.

painter¹ *n* a person who paints, esp an artist.

painter² *n* a bow rope for tying up a boat.

painting *n* the act or art of applying paint; a painted picture.

pair *n* a set of two things that are equal, suited, or used together; any two persons or animals regarded as a unit. * *vti* to form a pair (of); to mate.

pal *n* a close friend.—**pally** *adj.*

palace *n* the official residence of a sovereign, president or bishop; a large stately house or public building.

palatable *adj* (*taste*) pleasant; (*fig*) pleasant or acceptable.—**palatably** *adv.*

palate *n* the roof of the mouth; taste; mental relish.

pale¹ *n* a fence stake; a boundary; (*her*) a vertical stripe in the middle of a shield.

pale² *adj* (*complexion*) with less color than usual; (*color, light*) faint, wan, dim. * *vti* to make or become pale.—**paleness** *n.*

palette *n* a small, wooden board on which colored paints are mixed.

pall¹ *n* a heavy cloth over a coffin; (*of smoke*) a mantle.

pall² *vi* to become boring; to become satiated.

pallet¹ *n* a portable platform for lifting and stacking goods.

pallet² *n* a straw bed.

pallid *adj* wan, pale.—**pallidness** *n.*

palm¹ *n* the underside of the hand between fingers and wrist. * *vt* to conceal in or touch with the palm; (*with* off) to pass off by fraud, foist.

palm² *n* a tropical branchless tree with fan-shaped leaves; a symbol of victory.

Palm Sunday *n* the Sunday before Easter.

palpable *adj* tangible; easily perceived, obvious.—**palpably** *adj.*

paltry *adj* almost worthless; trifling.—**paltrily** *adv.*—**paltriness** *n.*

pamper *vt* to overindulge; to coddle, spoil.

pamphlet *n* a thin, unbound booklet; a brochure.

pan¹ *n* a wide metal container, a saucepan; (*of scales*) a tray; the bowl of a lavatory. * *vi* (*pt* panned) (*with* out) (*inf*) to turn out, esp to turn out well; to succeed.

pan² *vt* (*pt* panned) to wash gold-bearing gravel in a pan; (*inf*) to disparage, find fault with.

pan³ *vti* (*pt* panned) (*film camera*) to move horizontally to follow an object or provide a panoramic view.—*also n.*

panacea *n* a cure-all, universal remedy.

pancake *n* a round, thin cake made from batter and cooked on a griddle; a thing shaped thus. * *vi* (*aircraft*) to descend vertically in a level position.

panda *n* a large black and white bear-like herbivore.

pandemonium *n* uproar; chaos.

pander *n* a pimp. * *vi* (*somebody's desires or weaknesses*) to gratify.

pane *n* a sheet of glass in a frame of a window, door, etc.—**paned** *adj.*

panel *n* a usu rectangular section or division forming part of a wall, door, etc; a board for instruments or controls; a lengthwise strip in a skirt, etc; a group of selected persons for judging, discussing, etc. * *vt* (*pt* panelled) to decorate with panels.

panelling, paneling (*US*) *n* panels collectively; sheets of wood, plastic, etc, used for panels.

pang *n* a sudden sharp pain or feeling.

panic *n* a sudden overpowering fright or terror.—*also adj.* * *vti* (*pt* panicked) to affect or be affected with panic.—**panicky** *adj.*

pannier *n* a large basket for carrying loads on the back of an animal or the shoulders of a person; a bag or case slung over the rear wheel of a bicycle or motorcycle.

panorama *n* a complete view in all directions; a comprehensive presentation of a subject; a constantly changing scene.—**panoramic** *adj.*

pansy *n* a garden flower of the violet family, with velvety petals; (*sl*) an effeminate boy or man.

pant *vi* to breathe noisily, gasp; to yearn (for or after something). * *vt* to speak while gasping.

panther *n* a leopard, esp black; a cougar or jaguar.

panties *npl* (*inf*) short underpants.

pantomime *n* a Christmas theatrical entertainment with music and jokes; a drama without words, using only actions and gestures; mime. * *vti* to mime.

pantry *n* a small room or cupboard for storing cooking ingredients and utensils, etc.

pants *npl* trousers; underpants.

panty hose *n* tights.

panzerotto *n* (*Cdn*) a large baked turnover with a pizza-like filling of tomato sauce, cheese, and other ingredients.

papacy *n* the office or authority of the pope; papal system of government.

papal *adj* of the pope or the papacy.

paper *n* the thin, flexible material made from pulped rags, wood, etc which is used to write on, wrap in, or cover walls; a single sheet of this; an official document; a newspaper; an essay or lecture; a set of examination questions; (*pl*) personal documents. * *adj* like or made of paper. * *vt* to cover with wallpaper.—**papery** *adj.*

paperback *n* a book bound in a flexible paper cover.

paperweight *n* a small heavy object for keeping papers in place.

paperwork *n* clerical work of any kind.

papier-mâché *n* a substance made of paper pulp mixed with size, glue, etc, and moulded into various objects when moist.

paprika *n* a mild red condiment ground from the

fruit of certain peppers.

par *n* the standard or normal level; the established value of a currency in foreign-exchange rates; the face value of stocks, shares, etc; (*golf*) the score for a hole by a perfect player; equality.

parable *n* a short story using everyday events to illustrate a religious or moral point.

parachute *n* a fabric umbrella-like canopy used to retard speed of fall from an aircraft. * *vti* to drop, descend by parachute.—**parachutist** *n*.

parade *n* a ceremonial procession; an assembly of troops for review; ostentatious display; public walk, promenade. * *vti* to march or walk through, as for display; to show off; to assemble in military order.

paradise *n* heaven; (*Bible*) the Garden of Eden; any place of perfection.

paradox *n* a self-contradictory statement that may be true; an opinion that conflicts with common beliefs; something with seeming contradictory qualities or phases.—**paradoxical** *adj.*—**paradoxically** *adv.*

paraffin *n* a distilled oil used as fuel.

paragraph *n* a subdivision in a piece of writing used to separate ideas, marked by the beginning of a new line; a brief mention in a newspaper. * *vt* to divide into paragraphs.

parallel *adj* equidistant at every point and extended in the same direction; side by side; never intersecting; similar, corresponding. * *n* a parallel line, surface, etc; a likeness, counterpart; comparison; a line of latitude. * *vt* (*pt* **paralleled**) to make or be parallel; to compare.

paralyse, paralyze (*US*) *vt* to affect with paralysis; to bring to a stop.—**paralytic** *adj, n*.

paralysis *n* (*pl* **paralyses**) a partial or complete loss of voluntary muscle function or sensation in any part of the body; a condition of helpless inactivity.

paramount *adj* of great importance.

paranoia *n* a mental illness characterized by delusions of grandeur and persecution; (*inf*) unfounded fear, suspicion.—**paranoid** *adj, n*.—**paranoiac** *adj, n*.

paraphernalia *npl* personal belongings; accessories; (*law*) what a wife possesses in her own right.

paraphrase *n* expression of a passage in other words in order to clarify meaning. * *vt* to restate.

parasite *n* an organism that lives on and feeds off another without rendering any service in return; a person who sponges off another.—**parasitic** *adj.*—**parasitically** *adv.*

paratroops *npl* troops dropped by parachute into the enemy area.—**paratrooper** *n*.

parcel *n* a tract or plot of land; a wrapped bundle; a package; a collection or group of persons, animals, or things. * *vt* (*pt* **parcelled**) to wrap up into a parcel; (*with* **out**) to apportion.

parch *vti* to make or become hot and dry, thirsty; to scorch, roast.—**parched** *adj.*

parchment *n* the skin of a sheep, etc prepared as a writing material; paper like parchment.

pardon *vt* to forgive; to excuse; to release from penalty. * *n* forgiveness; remission of penalty.—**pardonable** *adj.*

parent *n* a father or a mother; an organism producing another; a source.—**parental** *adj.*—**parenthood** *n*.

parenthesis *n* (*pl* **parentheses**) an explanatory comment in a sentence contained within brackets and set in a sentence, independently of grammatical sequence; the brackets themselves ().—**parenthetical** *adj.*

parish *n* an ecclesiastical area in the charge of one clergyman; the congregation of a church; (*Cdn*) in Quebec and New Brunswick, a subdivision of a county functioning as a political unit.

parishioner *n* an inhabitant of a parish.

parity *n* equality; equality of value at a given ratio between different kinds of money, etc; being at par.

park *n* land kept as a game preserve or recreation area; a piece of ground in an urban area kept for ornament or recreation; an enclosed stadium, esp for ball games; a large enclosed piece of ground attached to a country house. * *vti* (*vehicle*) to leave in a certain place temporarily; (*vehicle*) to manoeuvre into a parking space.

parkade *n* (*Cdn*) a multilevel structure for parking motor vehicles.

park belt *n* parkland.

parkette *n* (*Cdn*) a small urban park.

parking lot *n* a car park.

parking meter *n* a coin-operated machine that registers the purchase of parking time for a motor vehicle.

parkland *n* esp in Canada, open grassland with widely scattered groves of trees.—*also* **park belt**.

parliament *n* a legislative assembly made up of representatives of a nation or part of a nation.—**parliamentarian** *n*.

parliamentary *adj* of, used in, or enacted by a parliament; conforming to the rules of a parliament; having a parliament.

Parliament Hill *n* (*Cdn*) the low hill in Ottawa, Ontario where the parliament of Canada is located; the Canadian federal government.

parlour, parlor (*US*) *n* a room in a house used primarily for conversation or receiving guests; a room or a shop used for business.

parochial *adj* of or relating to a parish; narrow; provincial in outlook.—**parochialism** *n*.

parody *n* a satirical or humorous imitation of a literary or musical work or style. * *vt* to make a parody of.—**parodist** *n*.

parole *n* word of honor; the release of a prisoner before his sentence has expired, on condition of future good behaviour. * *vt* to release on parole.

parquet *n* an inlaid hard wood flooring; the stalls of a theatre.

parrot *n* a tropical or subtropical bird with brilliant plumage and the ability to mimic human speech; one who repeats another's words without understanding. * vt to repeat mechanically.

parry vt to ward off, turn aside. * n a defensive movement in fencing.

parsley n a bright green herb used to flavor or garnish some foods.

parsnip n a long tapered root used as a vegetable.

parson n a priest of a parish, vicar; (inf) any clergyman.

part n a section; a portion (of a whole); an essential, separable component of a piece of equipment or a machine; the role of an actor in a play; a written copy of his/her words; (mus) one of the melodies of a harmony; the music for it; duty, share; one of the sides in a conflict; a parting of the hair; (pl) qualities, talent. * vt to separate; to comb the hair so as to leave a parting. * vi to become separated; to go different ways.

partial adj incomplete; biased, prejudiced; (with to) having a liking or preference for.—**partiality** n.—**partially** adv.

participate vi to join in or take part with others (in some activity).—**participant** n.

participation n the act of participating; the state of being related to a larger whole.

participle n (gram) a verb form used as an adjective.—**participial** adj.

particle n a tiny portion of matter; a speck; a very small part; (gram) a word that cannot be used alone, a prefix, a suffix.

particular adj referring or belonging to a specific person or thing; distinct; exceptional; careful; fastidious. * n a detail, single item; (pl) detailed information.

particularly adv very; especially; in detail.

parting n a departure; a breaking or separating; a dividing line in combing hair. * adj departing, esp dying; separating; dividing.

partisan n a strong supporter of a person, party, or cause.—also adj.—**partisanship** n.

partition n division into parts; that which divides into separate parts; a dividing wall between rooms. * vt to divide.

partly adv in part; to some extent.

partner n one of two or more persons jointly owning a business who share the risks and profits; one of a pair who dance or play a game together; either member of a married or non-married couple. * vt to be a partner (in or of).

partridge n a stout-bodied game bird of the grouse family.

part-time adj working fewer than the full number of hours.—**part time** adv.—**part-timer** n.

party n a group of people united for political or other purpose; a social gathering; a person involved in a contract or lawsuit; a small company, detachment; a person consenting, accessory; (inf) an individual. * vi to attend social parties. * vt to give a party for. * adj of or for a party.

pass vb (pt **passed**) vi to go past; to go beyond or exceed; to move from one place or state to another; (time) to elapse; to go; to die; to happen; (with for) to be considered as; (in exam) to be successful; (cards) to decline to make a bid; (law) to be approved by a legislative assembly. * vt to go past, through, over, etc; (time) to spend; to omit; (law) to enact; (judgment) to pronounce; to excrete; (in test, etc) to gain the required marks; to approve. * n a narrow passage or road; a permit; (in a test, etc) success; transfer of (a ball) to another player; a gesture of the hand; (inf) an uninvited sexual approach.

passable adj fairly good, tolerable; (a river, etc) that can be crossed.—**passably** adv.

passage n act or right of passing; transit; transition; a corridor; a channel; a route or crossing; a lapse of time; a piece of text or music.

passenger n a traveller in a public or private conveyance; one who does not pull his/her weight.

passer-by n (pl **passers-by**) one who happens to pass or go by.

passing adj transient; casual. * n departure, death.

passion n compelling emotion, such as love, hate, envy; ardent love, esp sexual desire; (with cap) the suffering of Christ on the cross; the object of any strong desire.

passionate adj moved by, showing, strong emotion or desire; intense; sensual.—**passionately** adv.

passive adj acted upon, not acting; submissive; (gram) denoting the voice of a verb whose subject receives the action.—**passively** adv.—**passiveness** n.—**passivity** n.

passport n an official document giving the owner the right to travel abroad; something that secures admission or acceptance.

password n a secret term by which a person is recognized and allowed to pass; any means of admission; a sequence of characters required to access a computer system.

past adj completed; ended; in time already elapsed. * adv by. * prep beyond (in time, place, or amount). * n time that has gone by; the history of a person, group, etc; a personal background that is hidden or questionable.

pasta n the flour paste from which spaghetti, noodles, etc is made; any dish of cooked pasta.

paste n a soft plastic mixture; flour and water forming dough or adhesive; a fine glass used for artificial gems. * vt to attach with paste; (sl) to beat, thrash.

pastel n a substance made of chalk, used for drawing; a drawing made with such; a soft, pale color. * adj delicately colored.

pasteurize vt (milk, etc) to sterilize by heat or radiation to destroy harmful organisms.—**pasteurization** n.

pastille n an aromatic or medicated lozenge.

pastime n a hobby; recreation, diversion.

pastoral adj of shepherds or rural life; pertaining to spiritual care, esp of a congregation.—**pastorally** adv.

pastry n dough made of flour, water, and fat used for making pies, tarts, etc; (pl) baked goods.

pasture n land covered with grass for grazing livestock; the grass growing on it. * vt (cattle, etc) to put out to graze in a pasture.—**pasturage** n.

pasty[1] n meat, etc enclosed in pastry and baked; a turnover.

pasty[2] adj (pastier, pastiest) like paste; pallid and unhealthy in appearance.

pat[1] vti (pt patted) to strike gently with the palm of the hand or a flat object; to shape or apply by patting. * n a light tap, usu with the palm of the hand; a light sound; a small lump of shaped butter.

pat[2] adj apt; exact; glib.—also adv.

patch n a piece of cloth used for mending; a scrap of material; a shield for an injured eye; a black spot of silk, etc worn on the face; an irregular spot on a surface; a plot of ground; a bandage; an area or spot. * vt to repair with a patch; to piece together; to mend in a makeshift way.

patchwork n needlework made of pieces sewn together; something made of various bits.

patchy adj (patchier, patchiest) irregular; uneven; covered with patches.—**patchily** adv.—**patchiness** n.

pâté n a spread made of liver, herbs, etc.

patent adj plain; apparent; open to public inspection; protected by a patent. * n a government document, granting the exclusive right to produce and sell an invention, etc for a certain time; the right so granted; the thing protected by such a right. * vt to secure a patent for.

patent leather n leather with a hard, glossy finish.

paternal adj fatherly in disposition; related through the father.—**paternally** adv.

paternity n fatherhood; origin or descent from a father.

path n a way worn by footsteps; a track for people on foot; a direction; a course of conduct.

pathetic adj inspiring pity; (sl) uninteresting, inadequate.—**pathetically** adv.

pathologist n a medical specialist who diagnoses by interpreting the changes in tissue and body fluid caused by a disease.

pathology n the branch of medicine that deals with the nature of disease, esp its functional and structural effects; any abnormal variation from a sound condition.—**pathological** adj.—**pathologically** adv.

pathway n a path; (chem) a sequence of enzyme-catalyzed reactions.

patience n the capacity to endure or wait calmly; a card game for one.

patient adj even-tempered; able to wait or endure calmly; persevering. * n a person receiving medical, dental, etc treatment.—**patiently** adv.

patio n (pl patios) an inner courtyard open to the sky; a paved area adjoining a house, for outdoor lounging, dining, etc.

patriate vt (Cdn) bring a piece of legislation, especially a constitution, under the authority of an independent country that was formerly under the jurisdiction of another.—**patriation** n.

patriot n one who strongly supports and serves his or her country.—**patriotic** adj.—**patriotically** adv.—**patriotism** n.

patrol vti (pt patrolled) to walk around a building or area in order to watch, guard, inspect. * n the act of going the rounds; a unit of persons or vehicles employed for reconnaissance, security, or combat; a subdivision of a Scout or Guide group.

patron n a regular client or customer; a person who sponsors and supports the arts, charities, etc; a protector.

patronage n the support given or custom brought by a patron; clientele; business; trade; the power to grant political favors; such favors.

patronize vt to treat with condescension; to sponsor or support; to be a regular customer of.—**patronizing** adj.—**patronizingly** adv.

patter[1] vi to make quick tapping sounds, as if by striking something; to run with light steps. * n the sound of tapping or quick steps.

patter[2] vi to talk rapidly and glibly. * vt to repeat speech, to gabble. * n glib speech; chatter; lingo.

pattern n a decorative arrangement; a model to be copied; instructions to be followed to make something; a regular way of acting or doing; a predictable route, movement, etc. * vt to make or do in imitation of a pattern.—**patterned** adj.

paunch n the belly, esp a potbelly.

pauper n a very poor person; (formerly) a person dependent on charity.—**pauperism** n.

pause n a temporary stop, esp in speech, action or music. * vi to cease in action temporarily, wait; to hesitate.

pave vt (a road, etc) to cover with concrete to provide a hard level surface.—**paving** n.

pavement n flat slabs, tiles, etc, forming a surface; a paved path adjacent to a road for pedestrians.

pavilion n a building at a sports ground used by players; a temporary building for exhibitions; a domed tent.

paw n a foot of a mammal with claws; (sl) a hand. * vti to touch, dig, hit, etc, with paws; to maul; to handle clumsily or roughly.

pawn[1] n the piece of lowest value in chess; a person used to advance another's purpose.

pawn[2] vt to deposit an article as security for a loan; to wager or risk. * n a thing pawned; the state of being given as a pawn.

pawnbroker n a person licensed to lend money at interest on personal property left with him as security.

pay vti (pt paid) to give (money) to in payment for a debt, goods or services; to give in compensation; to yield a profit; to bear a cost; to suffer a penalty; (homage, attention) to give. * n payment for services or goods; salary, wages.—**paying** adj.—**payer** n.

payable adj that must be paid, due; to be paid on a specified date.

payee n one to whom money is paid.

payment n the act of paying; amount paid; reward.

payroll n a list of employees and their wages; the actual money for paying wages.

pc abbr = per cent; postcard.

PC abbr = personal computer; (Cdn) postal code; (Cdn) Progressive Conservative.

PCO abbr (Cdn) = Privy Council Office.

PD day n (Cdn) professional development day.

PDT abbr = Pacific Daylight Time.

pea n the edible, round, green seed of a climbing leguminous annual plant.

peace n tranquillity, stillness; freedom from contention, violence or war; a treaty that ends a war.

peaceable adj inclined to peace.—**peaceably** adv.

peaceful adj having peace; tranquil; quiet.—**peacefully** adv.—**peacefulness** n.

peach n a round, sweet, juicy, downy-skinned stone-fruit; the tree bearing it; a yellowish pink color; (sl) a well-liked person or thing.

peacock n a male bird with a large brilliantly colored fan-like tail (nf **peahen**); a man who is a show-off.

peak n the summit of a mountain; the highest point; the pointed end of anything; maximum value; the eyeshade of a cap, visor. * vti (politician, actor, etc) to reach or cause to reach the height of power, popularity; (prices) to reach and stay at the highest level.

peal n a reverberating sound as of thunder, laughter, bells, etc; a set of bells, the changes rung on them. * vti to sound in peals, ring out.

peameal bacon n (Cdn) back bacon rolled in a coating of fine cornmeal.

peanut n a leguminous plant with underground pods containing edible seeds; the pod or any of its seeds; (pl: sl) a trifling sum.

peanut butter n a food paste made by grinding roasted peanuts.

pear n a common juicy fruit of tapering oval shape; the tree bearing it.

pearl n the lustrous white round gem produced by oysters; mother-of-pearl; anything resembling a pearl intrinsically or physically; one that is choice and precious; a bluish medium grey.—**pearly** adj.

Peary caribou n a small caribou of the Arctic islands of Canada.

peasant n an agricultural labourer.

peat n decayed vegetable matter from bogs, which is dried and cut into blocks for fuel or used as a fertilizer.—**peaty** adj.

pebble n a small rounded stone; an irregular, grainy surface.—**pebbled** adj.—**pebbly** adj.

peck vt to strike with the beak or a pointed object; to pick at one's food; (inf) to kiss lightly; to nag.—also n.

peckish adj (sl) hungry.

peculiar adj belonging exclusively (to); special; distinct; characteristic; strange.—**peculiarly** adv.

peculiarity n an idiosyncrasy; a characteristic; an oddity.

pecuniary adj of or consisting of money.

pedal n a lever operated by the foot. * vt (pt **pedalled**) to operate, propel by pressing pedals with the foot.

pedant n a person who attaches too much importance to insignificant details.—**pedantic** adj.—**pedantically** adv.

peddle vt to go from place to place selling small goods; (drugs) to sell.

pedestal n the base that supports a column, statue, etc.

pedestrian adj on foot; dull, commonplace. * n a person who walks.

pedigree n a line of descent of an animal; a recorded purity of breed of an individual; a genealogy; lineage; derivation.—also adj.

pedlar n a peddler.

peek vi to look quickly or furtively.—also n.

peel vt to remove skin or rind from; to bare. * vi to flake off, as skin or paint. * n rind, esp that of fruit and vegetables.—**peeling** n.

peep[1] vi to make shrill noises as a young bird. * n a peeping sound.

peep[2] vi to look hastily or furtively; to look through a slit or narrow opening; to be just showing. * n a furtive or hurried glance, a glimpse; (of day) the first appearance.

peer[1] vi to look closely; to look with difficulty; to peep out.

peer[2] n an equal in rank, ability, etc; a nobleman.—**peeress** nf.

peerage n the rank or title of a peer; peers collectively; a book with a list of peers.

peeved adj annoyed, resentful.

peevish adj fretful, irritable.—**peevishly** adv.—**peevishness** n.

peg n a tapered piece (of wood) for securing or hanging things on, for marking position, or for adjusting the strings of an instrument; a predetermined level at which (a price) is fixed; (a fact or opinion) used as a support, pretext, or reason; (mus) one of the movable parts for tuning the string of an instrument. * vti (pt **pegged**) to fasten or mark with a peg; (a price) to keep steady; to work steadily, persevere.

PEI abbr = Prince Edward Island.

pejorative adj disparaging, derogatory.—**pejoratively** adv.

Pekingese, Pekinese n a breed of small dog with long, silky hair, short legs, and a pug nose.

pelican n a large fish-eating waterbird with an expandable pouched bill.

pellet n a small ball, a pill; a piece of shot.

pelmet n a canopy for a window frame to hide rods, etc; a valance.

pelt[1] vt to throw missiles, or words, at. * vi (rain) to fall heavily; to hurry, rush. * n a rush.

pelt[2] n a usu undressed skin of an animal with its hair, wool, or fur.

pelvis *n* the bony cavity that joins the lower limbs to the body; the bones forming this.—**pelvic** *adj*.

pen[1] *n* an implement used with ink for writing or drawing. * *vt* (*pt* **penned**) to write, compose.

pen[2] *n* a small enclosure for cattle, poultry, etc; a small place of confinement. * *vt* (*pt* **penned**) to enclose in a pen, shut up.

penal *adj* relating to, liable to, or prescribing punishment; punitive.—**penally** *adv*.

penalize *vt* to impose a penalty; to put under a disadvantage.—**penalization** *n*.

penalty *n* a punishment attached to an offence; suffering or loss as a result of one's own mistake; a disadvantage imposed for breaking a rule as in football; a fine.

penalty killer *n* a player in ice hockey who specializes in preventing an opposing team from scoring while a teammate has been sent off the ice because of a penalty.

penalty shot *n* a single shot on goal by a player in ice hockey who has been allowed it as a result of an infraction by a member of the opposing team.

penance *n* voluntary suffering to atone for a sin; a sacramental rite consisting of confession, absolution, and penance.

pence *see* **penny**.

pencil *n* a pointed rod-shaped instrument with a core of graphite or crayon for writing, drawing, etc; a set of convergent light rays or straight lines; a fine paintbrush. * *vt* (*pt* **pencilled**) to write, draw, or color with a pencil; (*with* **in**) to commit tentatively.

pendant, pendent *n* a hanging ornament; a complement or match. * *adj* (*usu* **pendent**) hanging; projecting; undecided.

pending *adj* undecided; unfinished; imminent. * *prep* during; until, awaiting.

pendulum *n* a weight suspended from a fixed point so as to swing freely; such a device used to regulate the movement of a clock; something that swings to and fro.

penetrate *vti* to thrust, force a way into or through something; to pierce; to permeate; to understand.—**penetrable** *adj*.—**penetrability** *n*.

penetrating *adj* acute, discerning; (*voice*) easily heard through other sounds.

penetration *n* the capability, act, or action of penetrating; acute insight.

pen friend *n* a friend made and kept through exchanging letters.

penguin *n* a flightless, marine bird with black and white plumage, usu found in the Antarctic.

penicillin *n* an antibiotic produced synthetically from moulds.

peninsula *n* a piece of land almost surrounded by sea.—**peninsular** *adj*.

penis *n* the male copulative organ in mammals and humans.

penitent *adj* feeling regret for sin, repentant, contrite. * *n* a person who atones for sin.—**penitence** *n*.—**penitently** *adv*.

penitentiary *n* a state or federal prison in the US.

penknife *n* a small knife, usually with one folding blade, that fits into the pocket.

pennant *n* a long tapering flag used for identifying vessels and for signalling; such a flag symbolizing a championship.

penniless *adj* having no money; poor.

penny *n* (*pl* **pence** *denoting sum*, **pennies** *denoting separate coins*) a bronze coin of the UK worth one hundredth of a pound; (*formerly*) a bronze coin worth one twelfth of a shilling, or one two hundred and fortieth of a pound; a US or Canadian cent.

pension *n* a periodic payment to a person beyond retirement age, or widowed, or disabled; a periodic payment in consideration of past services. * *vt* to grant a pension to; (*with* **off**) to dismiss or retire from service with a pension.—**pensionable** *adj*.

pensioner *n* a person who receives a pension; a senior citizen.

pensive *adj* thoughtful, musing; wistful, melancholic.—**pensively** *adv*.—**pensiveness** *n*.

pentagon *n* (*geom*) a polygon with five sides; (*with cap*) the US military leadership.—**pentagonal** *adj*.

Pentecost *n* a Christian festival on the seventh Sunday after Easter; Whit Sunday.

penthouse *n* an apartment on the flat roof or in the top floor of a building.

pent-up *adj* (*emotion*) repressed, confined.

penultimate *adj* last but one.

people *n* the body of enfranchised citizens of a state; a person's family, relatives; the persons of a certain place, group, or class; persons considered indefinitely; human beings; (*pl*) all the persons of a racial or ethnic group, typically having a common language, institutions, homes, and folkways. * *vt* to populate with people.

pep *n* (*inf*) energy, vigour.

pepper *n* a sharp, hot condiment made from the fruit of various plants; the fruit of the pepper plant, which can be red, yellow, or green, sweet or hot, and is eaten as a vegetable. * *vt* to sprinkle or flavor with pepper; to hit with small shot; to pelt; to beat.

peppermint *n* a pungent and aromatic mint; its oil used for flavoring; a sweet flavored with peppermint.

pepper squash *n* (*Cdn*) a winter squash with ridged, dark green to orange skin and orange flesh.

pep talk *n* (*inf*) a vigorous talk made with the intention of arousing enthusiasm, increasing confidence, etc.

Péquiste *n* in Quebec, a member or supporter of the Parti Québécois.

per *prep* for or in each; through, by, by means of; (*inf*) according to.

per annum *adv* yearly; each year.

perceive *vt* to become aware of, apprehend, through the senses; to recognize.

per cent *adv* in, for each hundred; (*inf*) percentage.

percentage *n* rate per hundred parts; a proportion; (*inf*) profit, gain.

perceptible *adj* able to be perceived; discernible.—**perceptibility** *n.*—**perceptibly** *adv.*

perception *n* the act or faculty of perceiving; discernment; insight; a way of perceiving, view.

perceptive *adj* able to perceive; observant.—**perceptively** *adv.*—**perceptiveness** *n.*

perch[1] *n* (*pl* **perch**) a spiny-finned chiefly freshwater edible fish.

perch[2] *n* a pole on which birds roost or alight; an elevated seat or position. * *vti* to alight, rest, on a perch; to balance (oneself) on; to set in a high position.

percolator *n* a coffee pot in which boiling water is forced through coffee grounds.

percussion *n* impact, collision; shock, sound, caused by this; (*med*) tapping the body to discover the condition of an organ by the sounds; musical instruments played by striking with sticks or hammers, eg cymbals, drums, etc.—**percussionist** *n.*—**percussive** *adj.*

peremptory *adj* urgent; absolute; dogmatic; dictatorial.—**peremptorily** *adv.*—**peremptoriness** *n.*

perennial *adj* perpetual; lasting throughout the year. * *n* (*bot*) a plant lasting more than two years.—**perennially** *adv.*

perfect *adj* faultless; exact; excellent; complete. * *n* (*gram*) a verb form expressing completed action or designating a present state that is the result of an action in the past. * *vt* to improve; to finish; to make fully accomplished in anything.—**perfectly** *adv.*

perfection *n* the act of perfecting; the quality or condition of being perfect; great excellence; faultlessness; the highest degree; a perfect person or thing.

perfectionist *n* one who demands the highest standard; one who holds that moral perfection may be attained in this world.—**perfectionism** *n.*

perforate *vt* to pierce; to make a hole or row of holes, by boring through.

perforation *n* the act of perforating; the condition of being perforated; a hole; a row of holes to facilitate tearing.

perform *vti* to carry out, do; to put into effect; to act; to execute; to act before an audience; to play a musical instrument.—**performing** *adj.*

performance *n* the act of performing; a dramatic production; an act or action.

performer *n* a person who performs, esp one who entertains an audience.

perfume *n* a pleasing odour; fragrance; a mixture containing fragrant essential oils and a fixative. * *vt* to scent; to put perfume on.

perfunctory *adj* superficial, hasty; done merely as a matter of form, half-hearted; done carelessly; indifferent.—**perfunctorily** *adv.*

perhaps *adv* possibly, maybe.

peril *n* danger, jeopardy; risk, hazard.

perilous *adj* dangerous.— **perilously** *adv.*

perimeter *n* a boundary around an area; (*math*)

the curve or line bounding a closed figure, its length.

period *n* a portion of time; menstruation; an interval of time as in an academic day, playing time in a game, etc; an age or era in history; epoch; a stage in life; (*gram*) a full stop (.); (*astron*) a planet's time of revolution. * *interj* an exclamation used for emphasis.

periodic *adj* relating to a period; recurring at regular intervals, cyclic; intermittent.—**periodically** *adv.*

periodical *adj* periodic. * *n* a magazine, etc issued at regular intervals.

peripheral *adj* incidental, superficial; relating to a periphery.

periphery *n* the outer surface or boundary of an area; the outside surface of anything.

periscope *n* a device with mirrors that enables the viewer to see objects above or around an obstacle or above water, as from a submarine.

perish *vi* to be destroyed or ruined; to die, esp violently.

perishable *adj* (*food*) liable to spoil or decay. * *n* something perishable, esp food.—**perishability** *n.*

perjure *vt* to commit perjury, swear falsely.

perjury *n* (*law*) the crime of giving false witness under oath, swearing to what is untrue.

perk *n* (*inf*) a privilege, gain or profit incidental to regular wages; a tip, gratuity.

perk up *vti* to recover self-confidence; to become lively or cheerful; to prick up, as of a dog's ears; to smarten, trim.—**perky** *adj.*

perm *vt* (*inf*) (*hair*) to give a permanent wave. —*also n.*

permanence *n* the condition or quality of being permanent.

permanent *adj* lasting, or intended to last, indefinitely. * *n* a straightening or curling of hair by use of chemicals or heat lasting through many washings.—**permanently** *adv.*

permeate *vti* to fill every part of, saturate; to pervade, be diffused (through); to pass through by osmosis.—**permeable** *adj.*—**permeability** *n.*

permissible *adj* allowable.

permission *n* authorization; consent.

permissive *adj* allowing permission; lenient; sexually indulgent.—**permissively** *adv.*—**permissiveness** *n.*

permit *vti* (*pt* **permitted**) to allow to be done; to authorize; to give opportunity. * *n* a licence.

permutation *n* any radical alteration; a change in the order of a series; any of the total number of groupings within a group; an ordered arrangement of a set of objects.

pernicious *adj* destructive; very harmful.—**perniciously** *adv.*—**perniciousness** *n.*

perpendicular *adj* upright, vertical; (*geom*) at right angles (to).—*also n.*

perpetrate *vt* (*something evil, criminal, etc*) to do; (*a blunder, etc*) to commit.—**perpetration** *n.*—**perpetrator** *n.*

perpetual *adj* continuous; everlasting; (*plant*)

blooming continuously throughout the season.—**perpetually** adv.

perpetuity n endless duration, eternity; perpetual continuance; an annuity payable forever.

perplex vt to puzzle, bewilder, confuse; to complicate.—**perplexity** n.

persecute vt to harass, oppress, esp for reasons of race, religion, etc; to worry persistently.—**persecution** n.—**persecutor** n.

persevere vi to persist, maintain effort in face of difficulties.—**perseverance, perseveringly** adv.

persist vi to continue in spite of obstacles or opposition; to persevere; to last.—**persistence** n.—**persistency** n.

persistent adj persevering; stubborn.—**persistently** adv.

person n a human being, individual; the body (including clothing) of a human being; (in a play) a character; one who is recognized by law as the subject of rights and duties; (gram) one of the three classes of personal pronouns and verb forms, referring to the person(s) speaking, spoken to, or spoken of.

personable adj pleasing in personality and appearance.

personal adj concerning a person's private affairs, or his/her character, habits, body, etc; done in person; (law) of property that is movable; (gram) denoting person.

personality n one's individual characteristics; excellence or distinction of social and personal traits; a person with such qualities; a celebrity.

personally adv in person; in one's own opinion; as though directed to oneself.

personify vt to think of, represent, as a person; to typify.—**personification** n.

personnel n the employees of an organization or company; the department that hires them.

perspective n objectivity; the art of drawing so as to give an impression of relative distance or solidity; a picture so drawn; relation, proportion, between parts of a subject; vista, prospect.—also adj.

perspire vi to sweat.—**perspiration** n.

persuade vt to convince; to induce by argument, reasoning, advice, etc.

persuasion n the act of persuading; a conviction or opinion; a system of religious beliefs; a group adhering to such a system.

persuasive adj able to persuade; influencing the mind or emotions.—**persuasively** adv.—**persuasiveness** n.

pert adj impudent, cheeky; sprightly.—**pertly** adv.

pertinent adj relevant; to the point.—**pertinence** n.—**pertinently** adv.

perturb vt to trouble; to agitate.

perusal n a careful reading.

pervade vt to permeate or spread through; to be rife among.—**pervasive** adj.

perverse adj deviating from right or truth; persisting in error; wayward; contrary.—**perversely** adv.—**perverseness** n.—**perversity** n.

perversion n an abnormal way of obtaining sexual gratification, eg sadism; a perverted form or usage of something.

pervert vt to corrupt; to misuse; to distort. * n a person who is sexually perverted.

pessimism n a tendency to see in the world what is bad rather than good; a negative outlook that always expects the worst.—**pessimist** n.—**pessimistic** adj.

pest n anything destructive, esp a plant or animal detrimental to man as rats, flies, weeds, etc; a person who pesters or annoys.

pester vt to annoy or irritate persistently.

pesticide n any chemical for killing pests.

pestle n a usu club-shaped tool for pounding or grinding substances in a mortar. * vt to beat, pound, or pulverize with a pestle.

pet n a domesticated animal kept as a companion; a person treated as a favorite. * adj kept as a pet; spoiled, indulged; favorite; particular. * vti (pt petted) to stroke or pat gently; to caress; (inf) to kiss, embrace, etc in making love.

petal n any of the leaf-like parts of a flower's corolla.—**petalled, petaled** adj.

peter out vi to come to an end; to dwindle to nothing.

petite adj (woman) small and trim in figure.

petition n a formal application or entreaty to an authority; a written demand for action by a government, etc, signed by a number of people. * vti to present a petition to; to ask humbly.—**petitionary** adj.—**petitioner** n.—**petitioning** n.

petrol n a liquid fuel or solvent distilled from petroleum.

petroleum n a crude oil occurring naturally in certain rock strata and distilled to yield petrol, paraffin, etc.

petticoat n an underskirt; a slip; (inf) woman.

petty adj (pettier, pettiest) trivial; small-minded; minor.—**pettily** adv.—**pettiness** n.

petty officer n a non-commissioned officer in the navy.

petulant adj showing impatience or irritation; bad-humoured.—**petulance** n.—**petulantly** adv.

pew n a wooden, bench-like seat in a church, often enclosed; (sl) a chair.

pewter n an alloy of tin and lead with a silvery-grey color; dishes, etc, made of pewter.

phantom n a spectre or apparition. * adj illusionary.

pharmacare n (Cdn) a system of health insurance to cover the cost of prescribed drugs, especially a public system financed by taxes.

pharmacist n one licensed to practise pharmacy.

pharmacy n the preparation and dispensing of drugs and medicines; a pharmacist's shop, a drug store.

phase n an amount of the moon's or a planet's surface illuminated at a given time; a characteristic period in a regularly recurring sequence of events or stage in a development. * vt to do by stages or gradually; (with out) (making, using, etc) to stop gradually.

PhD abbr = Doctor of Philosophy.

pheasant n a richly colored game bird.

phenomenon n (pl **phenomena, phenomenons**) anything perceived by the senses as a fact; a fact or event that can be scientifically described; a remarkable thing or person.

phial n a small glass bottle; a vial.

philanthropy n love of mankind, esp as demonstrated by benevolent or charitable actions.—**philanthropic** adj.—**philanthropically** adv.—**philanthropist** n.

philately n the study and collecting of postage and imprinted stamps; stamp collecting.—**philatelic** adj.—**philatelist** n.

philosopher n a person who studies philosophy; a person who acts calmly and rationally.

philosophical adj of, relating to, or according to philosophy; serene; temperate; resigned.—**philosophically** adv.

philosophy n the study of the principles underlying conduct, thought, and the nature of the universe; general principles of a field of knowledge; a particular system of ethics; composure; calmness.

phlegm n a thick mucus discharged from the throat, as during a cold; sluggishness; apathy.

phlegmatic adj unemotional, composed; sluggish.

phobia n an irrational, excessive, and persistent fear of some thing or situation.—**phobic** adj.

phone n, vti (inf) (to) telephone.

phonetics npl (used as sing) the science concerned with pronunciation and the representation of speech sounds.

phonograph n a gramophone or record player.

phony, phoney adj (**phonier, phoniest**) (inf) not genuine. * n a fake; an insincere person.

phosphate n a compound of phosphorus.

phosphorus n a metalloid element; a phosphorescent substance or body, esp one that glows in the dark.

photo see **photograph**.

photo- prefix = light; a photographic process.

photocopy n a photographic reproduction of written or printed work. * vt to copy in this way.—**photocopier** n.

photogenic adj likely to look attractive in photographs; (biol) generating light.—**photogenically** adv.

photograph n an image produced by photography.—also **photo**.

photography n the art or process of recording images permanently and visibly by the chemical action of light on sensitive material, producing prints, slides or film.—**photographer** n.—**photographic** adj.—**photographically** adv.

phrase n a group of words that does not contain a finite verb but which expresses a single idea by itself; a pointed saying; a high-flown expression; (mus) a short, distinct musical passage. * vt to express orally, put in

words; (mus) to divide into melodic phrases.

phrase book n a book containing idiomatic expressions of a foreign language and their translations.

physical adj relating to the world of matter and energy, the human body, or natural science. * n a general medical examination.—**physically** adv.

physician n a doctor of medicine.

physicist n a specialist in physics.

physics n the branch of science concerned with matter and energy and their interactions in the fields of mechanics, acoustics, optics, heat, electricity, magnetism, radiation, atomic structure and nuclear phenomena; the physical processes and phenomena of a particular system.

physiology n the science of the functioning and processes of living organisms.—**physiological** adj.—**physiologically** adv.—**physiologist** n.

physiotherapy n the treatment of disorders and disease by physical and mechanical means (as massage, exercise, water, heat, etc).—**physiotherapist** n.

physique n bodily structure and appearance; build.

pianist n a person who plays the piano.

piano n (pl **pianos**) a large stringed keyboard instrument in which each key operates a felt-covered hammer that strikes a corresponding steel wire or wires.

piccolo n (pl **piccolos**) a small shrill flute.

pick n a heavy tool with a shaft and pointed crossbar for breaking ground; a tool for picking, such as a toothpick or icepick; a plectrum; right of selection; choice; best (of). * vti to break up or remove with a pick; to pluck at; to nibble (at), eat fussily; to contrive; to choose; (fruit, etc) to gather; to steal from a pocket; (lock) to force open; (with up) to lift; to acquire; to call for; to recover; (inf) to make the acquaintance of casually; to learn gradually; to resume; to give a lift to; to increase speed.

pickaxe, pickax (US) n a pick.

picket n a pointed stake; a patrol or group of men selected for a special duty; a person posted by strikes outside a place of work to persuade others not to enter. * vt (pt **picketed**) to tether to a picket; to post as a military picket; to place pickets, or serve as a picket (at a factory, etc).

pickle n vegetables preserved in vinegar; (inf) a plight, mess. * vt to preserve in vinegar.

pickpocket n a person who steals from pockets.

pick-up n the act of picking up; a person or thing picked up; (elect) a device for picking up current; the power to accelerate rapidly; the balanced arm of a record player; a light truck with an enclosed cab and open body.

picnic n a usu informal meal taken on an excursion and eaten outdoors; an outdoor snack; the food so eaten; an easy or agreeable task. * vi (pt **picnicked**) to have a picnic.—**picnicker** n.

pictorial *adj* relating to pictures, painting,or drawing; containing pictures; expressed in pictures; graphic.—**pictorially** *adv*.

picture *n* drawing, painting, photography, or other visual representation; a scene; an impression or mental image; a vivid description; a cinema film. * *vt* to portray, describe in a picture; to visualize.

picturesque *adj* striking, vivid, usually pleasing; making an effective picture.—**picturesquely** *adv*.

pidgin *n* a jargon for trade purposes, using words and grammar from two or more different languages.

pie *n* a baked dish of fruit, meat, etc, with an under or upper crust of pastry, or both.

piebald *adj* covered with patches of two colors. * *n* a piebald horse, etc.

piece *n* a distinct part of anything; a single object; a literary, dramatic, artistic, or musical composition; (*sl*) a firearm; a man in chess or draughts; an opinion, view; a short distance. * *vt* to fit together, join.

piecemeal *adv* gradually; bit by bit.

piecework *n* work paid for according to the quantity produced.

pier *n* a structure supporting the spans of a bridge; a structure built out over water and supported by pillars, used as a landing place, promenade, etc; a heavy column used to support weight.

pierce *vt* to cut or make a hole through; to force a way into; (*fig*) to touch or move. * *vi* to penetrate.

piercing *adj* penetrating; keen; (*cold, pain*) acute.—**piercingly** *adv*.

piety *n* religious devoutness; the characteristic of being pious.

pig *n* a domesticated animal with a broad snout and fat body raised for food; a swine; a greedy or filthy person; an oblong casting of metal poured from the smelting furnace; (*sl*) a policeman. * *vi* (*pt* **pigged**) (*sow*) to give birth; (*inf*) to live in squalor.—**piggish** *adj*.

pigeon *n* a bird with a small head and a heavy body; (*inf*) an object of special concern.

pigeonhole *n* a small compartment for filing papers, etc; a category usu failing to reflect actual complexities. * *vt* to file, classify; to put aside for consideration, shelve.

pigeon-toed *adj* having the toes turned in.

piggy bank *n* a container for coins shaped like a pig.

pigheaded *adj* stupidly stubborn.

piglet *n* a young pig.

pigment *n* paint; a naturally occurring substance used for coloring.—**pigmentation** *n*.

pigmy *see* pygmy.

pigsty *n* a pen for pigs; a dirty hovel.

pigtail *n* a tight braid of hair.

pika *n* a small rodent of mountains and deserts of western North America that has small ears and no tail.

pike *n* a sharp point or spike; the top of a spear; a long-snouted fish, important as a food and game fish.

pike pole *n* (*Cdn*) a long pole with a pointed, hooked metal tip, used for moving logs.

pilchard *n* a fish of the herring family.

pile[1] *n* a heap or mound of objects; a large amount; a lofty building; a pyre; (*sl*) a fortune. * *vt* (*with* **up, on**) to heap or stack; to load; to accumulate. * *vi* to become heaped up; (*with* **up, out, on**) to move confusedly in a mass.

pile[2] *n* a vertical beam driven into (the ground) as a foundation for a building, etc. * *vt* to support with piles; to drive piles into.

pile[3] *n* the nap of a fabric or carpet; soft, fine fur or wool.

pile[4] *n* a haemorrhoid.

pile-up *n* an accumulation of tasks, etc; (*inf*) a collision of several vehicles.

pilgrim *n* a person who makes a pilgrimage.

pilgrimage *n* a journey to a holy place as an act of devotion; any long journey; a life's journey.

pill *n* medicine in round balls or tablet form; (*with cap*) an oral contraceptive.

pillage *n* looting, plunder. * *vti* to plunder, esp during war.—**pillager** *n*.

pillar *n* a slender, vertical structure used as a support or ornament; a column; a strong supporter of a cause.

pillar box *n* a red box for receiving letters for mailing, often columnar.

pillion *n* a seat behind the driver for a passenger on a motorcycle, etc.

pillory *n* (*formerly*) stocks in which criminals were put as punishment. * *vt* to expose to public scorn and ridicule.

pillow *n* a cushion that supports the head during sleep; something that supports to equalize or distribute pressure. * *vti* to rest on, serve as, a pillow.

pillowcase, pillowslip *n* a removable cover for a pillow.

pilot *n* a person who operates an aircraft; one who directs ships in and out of harbour; a guide; a television show produced as a sample of a proposed series. * *vt* to direct the course of, act as pilot; to lead or guide.

pilot light *n* a burning gas flame used to light a larger jet; an electric indicator light.

pimp *n* a prostitute's agent.—*also vt*.

pimple *n* a small, raised, inflamed swelling of the skin.—**pimpled, pimply** *adj*.

pin *n* a piece of metal or wood used to fasten things together; a small piece of pointed wire with a head; an ornament or badge with a pin or clasp for fastening to clothing; (*bowling*) one of the clubs at which the ball is rolled. * *vt* (*pt* **pinned**) to fasten with a pin; to hold, fix; (*with* **down**) to get (someone) to commit himself or herself as to plans, etc; (*a fact, etc*) to establish.

pinafore *n* a sleeveless garment worn over a dress, blouse, etc.

pincers *npl* a tool with two handles and jaws used for gripping and drawing out nails, etc; a grasping claw, as of a crab.

pinch *vti* to squeeze or compress painfully; to

press between the fingers; to nip; (sl) to steal; (sl) to arrest. * n a squeeze or nip; what can be taken up between the finger and thumb, a small amount; a time of stress; an emergency.

pine[1] n an evergreen coniferous tree with long needles and well-formed cones; a tree of the pine family; its wood.

pine[2] vi to languish, waste away through longing or mental stress; (with for) to yearn.

pineapple n a tropical plant; its juicy, fleshy, yellow fruit.

ping n a high-pitched ringing sound. * vti to strike with a ping, emit a ping.

pingo n (pl pingos) a dome-shaped mound of ice covered by soil found in the Arctic.

ping-pong n a name for table tennis; (with caps) a trade name for table tennis equipment.

pink[1] n a garden plant, including carnation, with a fragrant flower; a pale red color; a huntsman's red coat; the highest type. * adj pink-colored; (inf) radical in political views.

pink[2] vt to stab, pierce; (cloth, etc) to cut a zigzag edge on; to perforate with pinking shears.

pink[3] vi (engine) to make a metallic noise like knocking.

pinnacle n a slender tower crowning a roof, etc; a rocky peak of a mountain; the highest point, climax.

pinpoint vt to locate or identify very exactly.

pinstripe n a very narrow stripe in suit fabrics, etc.

pint n a liquid measure equal to half a quart or one eighth of a gallon; (inf) a drink of beer.

pin-up n (sl) a photograph of a naked or partially naked person; a person who has been so photographed; a photograph of a famous person.

pioneer n a person who initiates or explores new areas of enterprise, research, etc.—also vti.

pious adj devout; religious; sanctimonious.—**piously** adv.

pip n the seed in a fleshy fruit, eg apple, orange.

pipe n a tube of wood, metal etc for making musical sounds; (pl) the bagpipes; a stem with a bowl for smoking tobacco; a long tube or hollow body for conveying water, gas, etc. * vt to play on a pipe; (gas, water, etc) to convey by pipe; to lead, summon with the sound of a pipe(s); to trim with piping.

pipeline n a pipe (often underground) used to convey oil, gas, etc; a direct channel for information; the processes through which supplies pass from source to user.

piper n a person who plays a pipe, esp bagpipes.

piping n a length of pipe, pipes collectively; a tube-like fold of material used to trim seams; a strip of icing, cream, for decorating cakes, etc; the art of playing a pipe or bagpipes; a high-pitched sound. * adj making a high-pitched sound.

piping hot adj very hot.

pique n resentment, ill-feeling. * vt to cause resentment in; to offend.

piracy n robbery at sea; the hijacking of a ship or aircraft; infringement of copyright; unauthorized use of patented work.

pirate n a person who commits robbery at sea; a hijacker; one who infringes copyright. * vti to take by piracy; to publish or reproduce in violation of a copyright.

pirouette n a spin on the toes in ballet.—also vi.

Pisces n the Fishes, in astrology the twelfth sign of the zodiac, operative from 19 February - 20 March.

pistol n a small, short-barrelled handgun.

piston n a disc that slides to and fro in a close-fitting cylinder, as in engines, pumps.

pit n a deep hole in the earth; a (coal) mine; a scooped-out place for burning something; a sunken or depressed area below the adjacent floor area; a space at the front of the stage for the orchestra; the area in a securities or commodities exchange in which members do the trading; the scar left by smallpox, etc; the stone of a fruit; a place where racing cars refuel. * vti (pt pitted) to set in competition; to mark or become marked with pits; to make a pit stop.

pitch[1] vti (tent, etc) to erect by driving pegs, stakes, etc, into the ground; to set the level of; (mus) to set in key; to express in a style; to throw, hurl; to fall heavily, plunge, esp forward. * n a throw; height, intensity; a musical tone; a place where a street trader or performer works; distance between threads (of a screw); amount of slope; a sound wave frequency; a sports field; (cricket) the area between the wickets; sales talk.

pitch[2] n the black, sticky substance from distillation of tar, etc; any of various bituminous substances. * vt to smear with pitch.

pitch-black adj black, or extremely dark.

pitch-dark adj completely dark.

pitcher n a large water jug; (baseball) the player who pitches the ball.

pitchfork n a long-handled fork for tossing hay, etc. * vt to lift with this; to thrust suddenly or willy-nilly into.

piteous adj arousing pity; heart-rending.—**piteously** adv.

pitfall n concealed danger; unexpected difficulty.

pith n the soft tissue inside the rind of citrus fruits; the gist, essence; importance.

pithy adj (pithier, pithiest) like or full of pith; concise and full of meaning.—**pithily** adv.—**pithiness** n.

pitiable adj deserving pity, lamentable, wretched.—**pitiably** adv.

pitiful adj causing pity, touching; contemptible, paltry.—**pitifully** adv.

pitiless adj without pity, ruthless.—**pitilessly** adv.—**pitilessness** n.

pittance n a very small quantity or allowance of money.

pity n sympathy with the distress of others; a

cause of grief; a regrettable fact. * vt to feel pity for.

pivot n a pin on which a part turns, fulcrum; a key person upon whom progress depends; a cardinal point or factor. * vt (pt **pivoted**) to turn or hinge (on) a pivot; to attach by a pivot. * vi to run on, or as if on, a pivot.—**pivotal** adj.

pixy, pixie n a fairy or elf.

placard n a poster or notice for public display.

placate vt to appease; to pacify.—**placatory** adj.

place n a locality, spot; a town or village; a building, residence; a short street, a square; space, room; a particular point, part, position, etc; the part of space occupied by a person or thing; a position or job; a seat; rank, precedence; a finishing position in a race. * vt to put; to put in a particular place; to find a place or seat for; to identify; to estimate; to rank; (order) to request material from a supplier. * vi to finish second or among the first three in a race.

place mat n a small mat serving as an individual table cover for a person at a meal.

placid adj calm, tranquil.—**placidity, placidness** n.—**placidly** adv.

plagiarize vt to appropriate writings from another author.—**plagiarism** n.—**plagiarist** n.

plague n a highly contagious and deadly disease; (inf) a person who is a nuisance. * vt to afflict with a plague; (inf) to annoy, harass.

plaice n (pl **plaice**) any of various flatfishes, esp a flounder.

plaid n a long wide piece of woollen cloth used as a cloak in Highland dress; cloth with a tartan or chequered pattern.

plain adj level, flat; understandable; straightforward; manifest, obvious; blunt; unadorned; not elaborate; not colored or patterned; not beautiful; ugly; pure; unmixed. * n a large tract of level country.

plain clothes n ordinary clothes, not uniform, as worn by a policeman on duty.—also adj.

plainly adv clearly, intelligibly.

plaintiff n (law) a person who brings a civil action against another.

plait n intertwined strands of hair, straw, etc; a pigtail.—also vti.

plan n a scheme or idea; a drawing to scale of a building; a diagram, map; any outline or sketch. * vti (pt **planned**) to make a plan of; to design; to arrange beforehand, intend; to make plans.

plane[1] n a tall tree with large broad leaves.

plane[2] n a tool with a steel blade for smoothing level wooden surfaces. * vt to smooth with a plane.

plane[3] n any level or flat surface; a level of attainment; one of the main supporting surfaces of an aeroplane; an aeroplane. * adj flat or level. * vi to fly while keeping the wings motionless; to skim across the surface of water; to travel by aeroplane.

planet n a celestial body that orbits the sun or other star.

plank n a long, broad, thick board; one of the policies forming the platform of a political party. * vt to cover with planks.

plankton n the microscopic organisms that float on seas, lakes, etc.

plant n a living organism with cellulose cell walls, which synthesizes its food from carbon dioxide, water and light; a soft-stemmed organism of this kind, as distinguished from a tree or shrub; the machinery, buildings, etc of a factory, etc; (sl) an act of planting; (sl) something or someone planted. * vt (seeds, cuttings) to put into the ground to grow; to place firmly in position; to found or establish; (sl) to conceal something in another's possession in order to implicate.

plantation n a large cultivated planting of trees; an estate where tea, rubber, cotton, etc, is grown, cultivated by local labour.

plaque n an ornamental tablet or disc attached to or inserted in a surface; a film of mucus on the teeth that harbours bacteria.

plasma n the colorless liquid part of blood, milk, or lymph; a collection of charged particles resembling gas but conducting electricity and affected by a magnetic field.

plaster n an adhesive dressing for cuts; a mixture of sand, lime and water that sets hard and is used for covering walls and ceilings. * vt to cover as with plaster; to apply like a plaster; to make lie smooth and flat; to load to excess.—**plasterer** n.

plastered adj (sl) intoxicated.

plaster of Paris n gypsum and water made into a quick-setting paste.

plastic adj able to be moulded; pliant; made of plastic; (art) relating to modelling or moulding. * n any of various nonmetallic compounds, synthetically produced, that can be moulded, cast, squeezed, drawn, or laminated into objects, films, or filaments.

plastic surgery n surgery to repair deformed or destroyed parts of the body.

plate n a flat sheet of metal on which an engraving is cut; an illustration printed from it; a full-page illustration separate from text; a sheet of metal photographically prepared with text, etc, for printing from; a sheet of glass with sensitized film used as a photographic negative; a trophy as prize at a race; a coating of metal on another metal; utensils plated in silver or gold; plated ware; a flat shallow dish from which food is eaten; a helping of food; the part of a denture that fits the palate; (inf) a denture. * vt (a metal) to coat with a thin film of another metal; to cover with metal plates.

plateau n (pl **plateaux, plateaus**) a flat, elevated area of land; a stable period; a graphic representation showing this.

plate glass n rolled, ground, and polished sheet glass.

platform n a raised floor for speakers, musicians, etc; a stage; a place or opportunity for public discussion; the raised area next to a railway track where passengers board trains; a statement of political aims.

platinum *n* a valuable, silvery-white metal used for jewellery, etc.

platitude *n* a dull truism; a commonplace remark.

platoon *n* a military unit consisting of two or more sections.

platter *n* an oval flat serving dish.

plausible *adj* apparently truthful or reasonable.—**plausibility** *n*.—**plausibly** *adv*.

play *vi* to amuse oneself (with toys, games, etc); to act carelessly or trifle (with somebody's feelings); to gamble; to act on the stage or perform a musical instrument; (*light*) to flicker, shimmer; (*water*) to discharge or direct on. * *vt* to participate in a sport; to be somebody's opponent in a game; to perform a dramatic production; (*instrument*) to produce music on; (*hose*) to direct; (*fish*) to give line to; to bet on. * *n* fun, amusement; the playing of, or manner of playing, a game; the duration of a game; a literary work for performance by actors; gambling; scope, freedom to move.—**playful** *adj*.—**playfully** *adv*.—**playfulness** *n*.

player *n* a person who plays a specified game or instrument; an actor.

playground *n* an area outdoors for children's recreation.

playgroup *n* an organized, regular meeting for the shared supervision of children at play.

playing card *n* one of a set of 52 cards used for playing games, each card having an identical pattern on one side and its own symbol on the reverse.

playing field *n* a place for playing sport.

playpen *n* a portable usu collapsible enclosure in which a young child may be left to play safely.

plaything *n* a toy; a thing or person treated as a toy.

playwright *n* a writer of plays.

plea *n* (*law*) an answer to a charge, made by the accused person; a request; an entreaty.

plead *vti* (*pt* **pleaded, plead** *or* **pled**) to beg, implore; to give as an excuse; to answer (guilty or not guilty) to a charge; to argue (a law case).

pleasant *adj* agreeable; pleasing.—**pleasantly** *adv*.—**pleasantness** *n*.

pleasantry *n* a polite or amusing remark.

please *vti* to satisfy; to give pleasure to; to be willing; to have the wish. * *adv* as a word to express politeness or emphasis in a request; an expression of polite affirmation.—**pleasing** *adj*.—**pleasingly** *adv*.

pleasure *n* enjoyment, recreation; gratification of the senses; preference.—**pleasurable** *adj*.—**pleasurably** *adv*.

pleat *n* a double fold of cloth, etc pressed or stitched in place.—*also vt*.

plebiscite *n* a direct vote of the electorate on a political issue such as annexation, independent nationhood, etc.

plectrum *n* a thin piece of metal, etc for plucking

the strings of a guitar, etc.

pledge *n* a solemn promise; security for payment of a debt; a token or sign; a toast. * *vt* to give as security; to pawn; to bind by solemn promise; to drink a toast to.

plentiful *adj* abundant, copious.

plenty *n* an abundance; more than enough; a great number. * *adv* (*sl*) quite.

pleurisy *n* inflammation of the membranes enclosing the lung.

pliable *adj* easily bent or moulded; easily influenced.—**pliability** *n*.

pliers *npl* a tool with hinged arms and jaws for cutting, shaping wire.

plight[1] *n* a dangerous situation; a predicament.

plight[2] *vt* to pledge, vow solemnly.—*also n*.

plod *vi* (*pt* **plodded**) to walk heavily and slowly, to trudge; to work or study slowly and laboriously.—**plodder** *n*.

plough, plow (*US*) *n* a farm implement for turning up soil; any implement like this, as a snowplough. * *vt* to cut and turn up with a plough; to make a furrow (in), to wrinkle; to force a way through; to work at laboriously; (*with* **into**) to run into; (*with* **back**) to reinvest; (*sl*) to fail an examination.—**ploughman** *n*.

plover *n* a wading bird with a short tail and a bill like a pigeon's.

ploy *n* a tactic or manoeuvre to outwit an opponent; an occupation or job; an escapade.

pluck *vt* to pull off or at; to snatch; to strip off feathers; (*fruit, flowers, etc*) to pick; (*person*) to remove from one situation in life and transfer to another. * *vi* to make a sharp pull or twitch. * *n* a pull or tug; heart, courage; dogged resolution.

plucky *adj* (**pluckier, pluckiest**) brave, spirited.—**pluckily** *adv*.—**pluckiness** *n*.

plug *n* a stopper used for filling a hole; a device for connecting an appliance to an electricity supply; a cake of tobacco; a kind of fishing lure; (*inf*) a free advertisement usu incorporated in other matter. * *vti* (*pt* **plugged**) to stop up with a plug; (*sl*) to shoot or punch; (*inf*) to seek to advertise by frequent repetition; (*inf*) to work doggedly.

plug-in *adj* able to be connected by a plug. * *n* a device or unit able to be connected by a plug; (*Cdn*) an electrical outlet in a garage for plugging in a block heater.

plum *n* an oval smooth-skinned sweet stonefruit; a tree bearing it; a reddish-purple color; a choice thing.

plumb *n* a lead weight attached to a line, for determining depth or verticality; any of various weights. * *adj* perfectly vertical. * *adv* vertically; in a direct manner; (*inf*) entirely. * *vt* to test by a plumb; to examine minutely and critically; to weight with lead; to seal with lead; to supply with or install as plumbing. * *vi* to work as a plumber.

plumber *n* a person who installs and repairs water or gas pipes.

plumbing *n* the system of pipes used in water or gas supply, or drainage; the plumber's craft.

plume *n* a large or ornamental bird's feather; a feathery ornament or thing; something resembling a feather in structure or density. * *vt* (*feathers*) to preen; to adorn with feathers; to indulge (oneself) with an obvious display of self-satisfaction.

plummet *n* a plumb. * *vi* (*pt* **plummeted**) to fall in a perpendicular manner; to drop sharply and abruptly.

plump[1] *adj* rounded, chubby. * *vti* to make or become plump; to swell.—**plumpness** *n*.

plump[2] *vti* to fall, drop or sink, or come into contact suddenly and heavily; (*someone, something*) to favor or give support. * *n* a sudden drop or plunge or the sound of this. * *adv* straight down, straight ahead; abruptly; bluntly.

plunder *vt* to steal goods by force, to loot. * *n* plundering; booty.—**plunderer** *n*.

plunge *vti* to immerse, dive suddenly; to penetrate quickly; to hurl oneself or rush; (*horse*) to start violently forward.

plural *adj* more than one; consisting of o r containing more than one kind or class. * *n* (*gram*) the form referring to more than one person or thing.

plus *prep* added to; in addition to. * *adj* indicating addition; positive. * *n* the sign (+) indicating a value greater than zero; an advantage or benefit; an extra.

plush *n* a velvet-like fabric with a nap. * *adj* made of plush; (*inf*) luxurious.

ply[1] *vti* to work at diligently and energetically; to wield; to subject to persistently; (*goods*) to sell; to go to and fro, run regularly; to keep busy.

ply[2] *n* a layer or thickness, as of cloth, plywood, etc; any of the twisted strands in a yarn, etc. * *vt* to twist together.

plywood *n* a construction material consisting of several thin layers of wood glued together.

PM *abbr* = prime minister.

p.m. *abbr* = post meridiem.

pneumatic *adj* concerning wind, air, or gases; operated by or filled with compressed air.

pneumonia *n* acute inflammation of the lungs.

PO *abbr* = post office; petty officer.

poach[1] *vt* to cook (an egg without its shell, fish, etc) in or over boiling water.

poach[2] *vti* to catch game or fish illegally; to trespass for this purpose; to encroach on, usurp another's rights, etc; to steal another's idea, employee, etc.—**poacher** *n*.—**poaching** *n*.

pocket *n* a small bag or pouch, esp in a garment, for carrying small articles; an isolated or enclosed area; a deposit (as of gold, water, or gas). * *adj* small enough to put in a pocket. * *vt* to put in one's pocket, to steal; (*ball*) to put in a pocket; to envelop; to enclose; (*money*) to take dishonestly; to suppress.—**pocketful** *adj*.

pocketbook *n* a wallet; a woman's purse; monetary resources; a small esp paperback book.

pocketknife *n* a penknife.

pocket money *n* money for occasional expenses; a child's allowance.

pod *n* a dry fruit or seed vessel, as of peas, beans, etc; a protective container or housing; a detachable compartment on a spacecraft. * *vi* (*pt* **podded**) to remove the pod from.

podgy *adj* (**podgier, podgiest**) short and fat, squat.

poem *n* an arrangement of words, esp in metre, often rhymed, in a style more imaginative than ordinary speech; a poetic thing.

poet *n* the writer of a poem; a person with imaginative power and a sense of beauty.

poetic, poetical *adj* of poets or poetry; written in verse; imaginative, romantic, like poetry.—**poetically** *adv*.

poet laureate *n* (*pl* **poets laureate**) the official poet of a nation, appointed to write poems celebrating national events, etc.

poetry *n* the art of writing poems; poems collectively; poetic quality or spirit.

pogey, pogy *n* (*Cdn*) unemployment insurance or welfare benefits.

poignant *adj* piercing; incisive; deeply moving.—**poignantly** *adv*.

point *n* a dot or tiny mark used in writing or printing (eg a decimal point, a full stop); a location; a place in a cycle, course, or scale; a unit in scoring or judging; the sharp end of a knife or pin; a moment of time; one of thirty-two divisions of the compass; a fundamental reason or aim; the tip; a physical characteristic; a railway switch; a unit of size in printing equal to one seventy-second of an inch; a unit used in quoting the prices of stocks, bonds and commodities; a headland or cape. * *vti* to give point to; to sharpen; to aim (at); to extend the finger (at or to); to indicate something; to call attention (to).

point-blank *adj* aimed straight at a mark; direct, blunt.—*also adv*.

point blanket *n* (*Cdn*) a Hudson's Bay blanket with markings of short black lines.

pointed *adj* having a point; pertinent; aimed at a particular person or group; conspicuous.—**pointedly** *adv*.

pointer *n* a rod or needle for pointing; an indicator; a breed of hunting dogs.

pointless *adj* without a point; irrelevant, aimless.—**pointlessly** *adv*.

poise *vt* to balance; to hold supported without motion; (*the head*) to hold in a particular way; to put into readiness. * *vi* to become drawn up into readiness; to hover. * *n* a balanced state; self-possessed assurance of manner; gracious tact; bearing, carriage.—**poised** *adj*.

poison *n* a substance that through its chemical action usu destroys or injures an organism; any corrupt influence; an object of aversion or abhorrence. * *vt* to administer poison in order to kill or injure; to put poison into; to influence wrongfully.—**poisoner** *n*.—**poisonous** *adj*.—**poisonously** *adv*.

poke *vt* to thrust (at), jab or prod; (*hole, etc*) to

make by poking; (*sl*) to hit. * *vi* to jab (at); to pry or search (about or around). * *n* a jab; a prod or nudge; a thrust.

poker[1] *n* a metal rod for poking or stirring fire.

poker[2] *n* a card game in which a player bets that the value of his hand is higher than that of the hands held by others.

poker face *n* an expressionless face, concealing a person's thoughts or feelings.—**poker-faced** *adj.*

poky *adj* (**pokier, pokiest**) small and uncomfortable.

polar *adj* of or near the North or South Pole; of a pole; having positive and negative electricity; directly opposite.

polar bear *n* a large creamy-white bear that inhabits arctic regions.

polarize *vt* (*light waves*) to cause to vibrate in a definite pattern; to give physical polarity to; to break up into opposing factions; to concentrate.—**polarization** *n.*

pole[1] *n* a long slender piece of wood, metal, etc; a flagstaff. * *vt* to propel, support with a pole.

pole[2] *n* either end of an axis, esp of the earth; either of two opposed forces, parts, etc, as the ends of a magnet, terminals of a battery, etc; either of two opposed principles.

polemic *n* a controversy or argument over doctrine; (*pl*) art of controversy.—**polemical** *adj.*

pole vault *n* a field event in which competitors jump over a high bar using a long flexible pole.

police *n* the governmental department for keeping order, detecting crime, law enforcement, etc; the members of such a department; any similar organization. * *vt* to control, protect, etc with police or a similar force.

policeman *n* a member of a police force.—**police-woman** *nf.*

policy[1] *n* a written insurance contract.

policy[2] *n* political wisdom, statecraft; a course of action selected from among alternatives; a high-level overall plan embracing the general principles and aims of an organization, esp a government.

polish *vti* to make or become smooth and shiny by rubbing (with a cloth and polish); (*fig*) to give elegance or culture to; (*with* off) (*inf: meal, job, etc*) to finish completely. * *n* smoothness; elegance of manner; a finish or gloss; a substance, such as wax, used to polish.—**polisher** *n.*

polished *adj* accomplished; smoothly or professionally done or performed; (*of rice*) having had the husk removed.

polite *adj* courteous; well-bred; refined.—**politely** *adv.*—**politeness** *n.*

political *adj* relating to politics or government; characteristic of political parties or politicians.—**politically** *adv.*

politician *n* a person engaged in politics, often used with implications of seeking personal or partisan gain, scheming, etc.

politics *npl* the science and art of government;

political activities, beliefs or affairs; factional scheming for power.

polka *n* a lively dance; the music for this.

polka dot *n* any of a pattern of small round dots on cloth.

poll *n* a counting, listing, etc of persons, esp of voters; the number of votes recorded; an opinion survey; (*pl*) a place where votes are cast. * *vti* to receive the votes (of); to cast a vote; to canvass or question in a poll.

poll captain *n* (*Cdn*) a person responsible for an electoral campaign in one part of a constituency.

pollen *n* the yellow dust, containing male spores, that is formed in the anthers of flowers.

pollination *n* the transfer of pollen from the anthers of a flower to the stigma, esp by insects.— **pollinate** *vti.*

pollute *vt* to contaminate with harmful substances; to make corrupt; to profane.—**polluter** *n.*

pollution *n* the act of polluting; the state of being polluted; contamination by chemicals, noise, etc.

polo *n* a game played on horseback by two teams, using a wooden ball and long-handled mallets.

polo neck *n* a high collar turned over at the top; a sweater with such a collar.

polyester *n* any of a number of synthetic polymeric resins used for adhesives, plastics, and textiles.

polygamy *n* the practice of being married to more than one person at a time.—**polygamist** *n.*—**polygamous** *adj.*

polytechnic *n* a college that provides instruction in many applied sciences and technical subjects.

polythene, polyethylene *n* a light, plastic, multipurpose material.

pomegranate *n* an edible fruit with many seeds; the widely cultivated tropical tree bearing it.

pommel *n* the rounded, upward-projecting front part of a saddle; a knob on the hilt of a sword. * *vt* to pummel.

pomp *n* stately ceremony; ostentation.

pompous *adj* stately; self-important.—**pompously** *adv.*—**pomposity** *n.*—**pompousness** *n.*

pond *n* a body of standing water smaller than a lake.

ponder *vti* to think deeply; to consider carefully.

ponderous *adj* heavy; awkward; dull; lifeless.—**ponderously** *adv.*

pond hockey *n* (*Cdn*) informal ice hockey played on a frozen pond.

pontiff *n* the Pope; a bishop.

pontificate *vi* to speak sententiously, pompously or dogmatically; to officiate at a pontifical mass.

pontoon[1] *n* a boat or cylindrical float forming a support for a bridge.

pontoon[2] *n* a gambling game with cards in which players try to obtain points better than the banker's but not more than 21.—*also* **black-**

jack.

pony *n* a small horse, a bronco, mustang, etc of the western US.

pony tail *n* a style of arranging hair to resemble a pony's tail.

poodle *n* a breed of dog with a solid-colored curly coat of many colors and sizes.

pool[1] *n* a small pond; a puddle; a small collection of liquid; a tank for swimming.

pool[2] *n* a game of billiards played on a table with six pockets; a combination of resources, funds, supplies, people, etc for some common purpose; the parties forming such a combination. * *vti* to contribute to a common fund, to share.

poor *adj* having little money, needy; deserving pity, unfortunate; deficient; disappointing; inferior. * *n* those who have little.—**poorness** *n*.

poorly *adv* insufficiently, badly. * *adj* not in good health.

pop[1] *n* a short, explosive sound, a shot; any carbonated, nonalcoholic beverage. * *vti* (*pt* **popped**) to make or cause a pop; to shoot; to go or come quickly (in, out, up); (*corn, maize*) to roast until it pops; to put suddenly; (*eyes*) to bulge.

pop[2] *adj* in a popular modern style. * *n* pop music; pop art; pop culture.

pop[3] *n* (*inf*) father; (*inf*) a name used to address an old man.

popcorn *n* a kind of corn or maize, which when heated pops or puffs up.

pope *n* bishop of Rome, head of the RC Church.

poplar *n* a slender, quick-growing tree of the willow family.

poplin *n* a sturdy corded fabric.

poppy *n* an annual or perennial plant with showy flowers; a strong reddish color.

populace *n* the common people; the masses; all the people in a country, region, etc.

popular *adj* of the people; well liked; pleasing to many people; easy to understand.—**popularly** *adv*.

popularity *n* the condition or quality of being popular.

popularize *vt* to make popular; to make generally accepted or understood.—**popularization** *n*.

population *n* all the inhabitants or the number of people in an area.

populous *adj* densely inhabited.

porcelain *n* a hard, white, translucent variety of ceramic ware.—*also adj*.

porch *n* a covered entrance to a building; an open or enclosed gallery or room on the outside of a building.

porcupine *n* a large rodent covered with protective quills.

pore[1] *n* a tiny opening, as in the skin, plant leaves, stem, etc, for absorbing and discharging fluids.

pore[2] *vti* to look with steady attention; to study closely.

pork *n* the flesh of a pig used as food.

pornography *n* writings, pictures, films, etc, intended primarily to arouse sexual desire.—

pornographic *adj*.—**pornographer** *n*.

porous *adj* having pores; able to absorb air and fluids, etc.—**porousness** *n*.

porpoise *n* any of several small whales, esp a black blunt-nosed whale of the north Atlantic and Pacific; any of several bottle-nosed dolphins.

porridge *n* a thick food, usu made by boiling oats or oatmeal in water or milk.

port[1] *n* a harbour; a town with a harbour where ships load and unload cargo; airport; a place where goods may be cleared through customs.

port[2] *n* a porthole; an opening, as in a valve face, for the passage of steam, etc; a hole in an armoured vehicle for firing a weapon; a circuit in a computer for inputting or outputting data.

port[3] *n* the left of an aircraft or ship looking forward.—*also adj*.

port[4] *n* a strong, sweet, fortified dark red wine.

portable *adj* capable of being carried or moved about easily.—**portability** *n*.

portal *n* an impressive gate or doorway.

portcullis *n* a grating that can be lowered to bar entrance to a castle.

portent *n* an omen, warning.

porter[1] *n* a doorman or gatekeeper.

porter[2] *n* a person who carries luggage, etc, for hire at a station, airport, etc; a railway attendant for passengers; a dark brown beer.

porthole *n* an opening (as a window) with a cover or closure esp in the side of a ship or aircraft; a port through which to shoot; an opening for intake or exhaust of a fluid.

portico *n* (*pl* **porticoes, porticos**) a covered walkway with columns supporting the roof.

portion *n* a part, a share, esp an allotted part; a helping of food; destiny. * *vt* to share out.

portly *adj* (**portlier, portliest**) dignified; stout.

portrait *n* a painting, photograph, etc, of a person, esp of the face; (*of person*) a likeness; a vivid description.

portray *vt* to make a portrait of; to depict in words; to play the part of in a play, film, etc.— **portrayal** *n*.

pose *n* a position or attitude, esp one held for an artist or photographer; an attitude deliberately adopted for effect. * *vti* to propound, assert; to assume an attitude for effect; to sit for a painting, photograph; to set oneself up (as).

posh *adj* (*inf*) elegant; fashionable.

position *n* place, situation; a position occupied; posture; a job; state of affairs; point of view. * *vt* to place or locate.

positive *adj* affirmative; definite; sure; marked by presence, not absence, of qualities; expressed clearly, or in a confident manner; constructive; empirical; (*elect*) charged with positive electricity; (*math*) greater than zero, plus; (*gram*) of adjective or adverb, denoting the simple form; (*photog*) having light, shade, color as in the original. * *n* a positive quality or quantity; a photographic print made from a negative.

posse *n* a body of people summoned by a sheriff to assist in keeping the peace, etc.

possess *vt* to own, have, keep; to dominate or control the mind of.

possession *n* ownership; something possessed; (*pl*) property.

possessive *adj* of or indicating possession; (*gram*) denoting a case, form or construction expressing possession; having an excessive desire to possess or dominate.—**possessively** *adv*.

possibility *n* the state of being possible; a possible occurrence, a contingency.

possible *adj* that may be or may happen; feasible, practicable; (*inf*) tolerable.—**possibly** *adv*.

post¹ *n* a piece of wood, metal, etc, set upright to support a building, sign, etc; the starting point of a race. * *vt* (*poster, etc*) to put up; to announce by posting notices; (*name*) to put on a posted or published list.

post² *n* a fixed position, esp where a sentry or group of soldiers is stationed; a position or job; a trading post; a settlement. * *vt* to station in a given place.

post³ *n* the official conveyance of letters and parcels, mail; letters, parcels, etc, so conveyed; collection or delivery of post, mail. * *vt* to send a letter or parcel; to keep informed.—**postal** *adj*.

postage *n* the charge for sending a letter, etc, as represented by stamps.

postal code *n* (*Cdn*) a series of six alternating letters and numbers used as part of a postal address to speed the processing of mail.

postcard *n* a card, usu decorative, for sending messages by post.

postdate *vt* to write a future date on a letter or cheque.

poster *n* a usu decorative or ornamental printed sheet for advertising.

poste restante *n* the department of a post office that will hold mail until it is called for.

posterity *n* future generations; all of a person's descendants.

postgraduate *n* a person pursuing study after obtaining a university degree.—*also adj*.

posthumous *adj* (*child*) born after its father's death; (*award, etc*) given after one's death.—**posthumously** *adv*.

postman *n* a person who collects or delivers mail.

postmark *n* the post office mark cancelling the stamp on a letter by showing the date, place of posting.

postmaster *n* the manager of a post office.

postmortem *n* an examination of a corpse to determine the cause of death; an autopsy.—*also adj*.

post office *n* the building where postage stamps are sold and other postal business conducted; (*with caps*) a government department handling the transmission of mail.

postpone *vt* to put off, delay to a future date.—**postponement** *n*.

postscript *n* (*abbr* **PS**) a note added to a letter after completion.

postulate *vt* to assume to be true; to demand or claim. * *n* a position taken as self-evident; (*math*) an unproved assumption taken as basic; an axiom.—**postulation** *n*.

posture *n* a pose; a body position; an attitude of mind; an official stand or position. * *vti* to pose in a particular way; to assume a pose.

posy *n* a small bunch of flowers.

pot¹ *n* a deep, round cooking vessel; an earthenware or plastic container for plants; a framework for catching fish or lobster; (*inf*) a large amount (as of money); (*inf*) all the money bet at a single time. * *vb* (*pt* **potted**) *vt* to put or preserve in a pot. * *vi* to take a pot shot, shoot.

pot² *n* (*sl*) cannabis.

potash *n* potassium carbonate.

potato *n* (*pl* **potatoes**) a starchy, oval tuber eaten as a vegetable.

potency *n* the quality or condition of being potent; power; strength.

potent *adj* powerful; influential; intoxicating; (*a male*) able to have sexual intercourse.—**potently** *adv*.

potential *adj* possible, but not yet actual. * *n* the unrealized ability to do something.—**potentiality** *n*.—**potentially** *adv*.

pothole *n* a hole worn in a road by traffic; (*geol*) a deep hole or cave in rock caused by the action of water.

potholing *n* an activity involving the exploration of deep underground caves.—**potholer** *n*.

potion *n* a mixture of liquids, such as poison.

pot light *n* (*Cdn*) an interior electrical light enclosed in a cylindrical shell and recessed in a ceiling.

pot shot *n* a random or easy shot.

potter¹ *vi* to busy oneself idly; to spend time. —*also* **putter**.

potter² *n* a person who makes earthenware vessels.

pottery *n* earthenware vessels; a workshop where such articles are made.

potty¹ *adj* (**pottier, pottiest**) (*inf*) slightly crazy; trivial, petty.

potty² *n* (*inf*) a chamber pot.

pouch *n* a small bag or sack; a bag for mail; a sacklike structure, as that on the abdomen of a kangaroo, etc, for carrying young.

poultice *n* a hot moist dressing applied to a sore part of the body.

poultry *n* domesticated birds kept for meat or eggs.

pounce *vi* to swoop or spring suddenly (upon) in order to seize; to make a sudden assault or approach.—*also n*.

pound¹ *n* a unit of weight equal to 16 ounces (*abbr* **lb**); a unit of money in the UK and other countries, symbol £.

pound² *vt* to beat into a powder or a pulp; to hit hard. * *vi* to deliver heavy blows repeatedly (at or on); to move with heavy steps; to throb; (*with* **away**) to work hard and continuously.

pound³ *n* a municipal enclosure for stray animals; a depot for holding impounded personal property, eg cars, until claimed; a place or condition of confinement.

pour vti to cause to flow in a stream; to flow continuously; to rain heavily; to serve tea or coffee.—**pourer** n.

pout vti to push out (the lips); to look sulky. * n a thrusting out of the lips; (pl) a fit of pique.

poutine n (Cdn) French fries and cheese curds covered with a sauce, usually gravy.

poverty n the condition of being poor; scarcity.

powder n any substance in tiny, loose particles; a specific kind of powder, esp for medicinal or cosmetic use; fine dry light snow. * vti to sprinkle or cover with powder; to reduce to powder.

powdery adj like powder; easily crumbled.

power n ability to do something; political, social or financial control or force; a person or state with influence over others; legal force or authority; physical force; a source of energy; (math) the result of continued multiplication of a quantity by itself a specified number of times. * adj operated by electricity, a fuel engine, etc; served by an auxiliary system that reduces effort; carrying electricity. * vt to supply with a source of power.—**powered** adj.

powerful adj mighty; strong; influential.—**powerfully** adv.

powerless adj without power; helpless; feeble.—**powerlessly** adv.—**powerlessness** n.

power station, power plant n a building where electric power is generated.

powwow n an American Indian ceremony (as for victory in war); (inf) any conference or get-together. * vi to confer, chat.

pox n a virus disease marked by pustules; (arch) smallpox; syphilis; a plague; a curse.

PQ abbr = Parti Québécois; Province of Quebec.

practicable adj able to be practised; possible, feasible.—**practicability** n.

practical adj concerned with action, not theory; workable; suitable; trained by practice; virtual, in effect.

practical joke n a prank intended to embarrass or to cause discomfort.

practically adv in a practical manner; virtually.

practice n action; habit, custom; repetition and exercise to gain skill; the exercise of a profession.

practise, practice (US) vti to repeat an exercise to acquire skill; to put into practice; to do habitually or frequently; (profession) to work at.

practitioner n a person who practises a profession.

pragmatic adj practical; testing the validity of all concepts by their practical results.—**pragmatically** adv.

prairie n a large area of level or rolling land predominantly in grass; a dry treeless plateau; (pl) the region of western North America that consists of such land; (Cdn) (cap) the provinces of Manitoba, Saskatchewan, and Alberta.

prairie chicken n a grouse of the North American prairies.

prairie crocus n (Cdn) a plant of the buttercup family covered with silky hairs and with purple or white flowers.

prairie lily n a North American lily with upright, spotted reddish-orange flowers.

prairie wool n (Cdn) the natural grassy cover of land on the Prairies.

praise vt to express approval of, to commend; to glorify, to worship. * vi to express praise. * n commendation; glorification.—**praiseworthy** adj.

pram n a four-wheeled carriage for a baby.

prance vi (horse) to spring on the hind legs, bound; (person) to walk or ride in a showy manner; to swagger.—also n.

prank n a mischievous trick or joke; a ludicrous act.

prattle vti to talk in a childish manner; to babble. * n empty chatter.

prawn n an edible marine shrimp-like crustacean.

pray vti to offer prayers to God; to implore.

prayer n supplication, entreaty, praise or thanks to God; the form of this; the act of praying; (pl) devotional services; something prayed for.

preach vi to advocate in an earnest or moralizing way. * vt to deliver a sermon; (patience, etc) to advocate.—**preacher** n.

preamble n an introductory part to a document, speech, or story, stating its purpose.

precarious adj dependent on chance; insecure; dangerous.—**precariously** adv.—**precariousness** n.

precaution n a preventive measure; care taken beforehand; careful foresight.—**precautionary** adj.

precede vti to be, come or go before in time, place, order, rank, or importance.

precedence n priority; the right of higher rank.

precedent n a previous and parallel case serving as an example; (law) a decision, etc, serving as a rule.

preceding adj coming or going before; former.

precept n a rule of moral conduct; a maxim; an order issued by a legally constituted authority to a subordinate.

precinct n (usu pl) an enclosure between buildings, walls, etc; a limited area; an urban area where traffic is prohibited; (pl) environs; in US, a police district or a subdivision of a voting ward.

precious adj of great cost or value; beloved; very fastidious; affected; thoroughgoing. * adv (sl) very.—**preciousness** n.

precipice n a cliff or overhanging rock face.

precipitate vti to throw from a height; to cause to happen suddenly or too soon; (chem) to separate out; to rain; to fall as rain, snow, dew, etc.—**precipitately** adv.

precipitation n the act of precipitating; undue haste; rain, snow, etc; the amount of this.

precipitous adj of or like a precipice; sheer,

steep.—**precipitously** adv.

precis, précis n (pl **precis, précis**) a summary or abstract.—also vt.

precise adj clearly defined, exact; accurate; punctilious; particular.—**precisely** adv.

preclude vt to rule out in advance; to make impossible.—**preclusion** n.—**preclusive** adj.

precocious adj prematurely ripe or developed.—**precociously** adv.

preconceive vt to form an idea or opinion of before actual experience.

precondition n a requirement that must be met beforehand, a prerequisite. * vt (organism, patient) to prepare to behave or react in a certain way under certain conditions.

precursor n a predecessor; a substance from which another substance is formed.—**precursory** adj.

predator n a person who preys, plunders or devours; a carnivorous animal.

predatory adj living on prey, of, or relating to a predator; characterized by hunting or plundering.

predecessor n a former holder of a position or office; an ancestor.

predestine vt to foreordain; to destine beforehand.

predicament n a difficult or embarrassing situation.

predicate vt to state as a quality or attribute; to base (on facts, conditions etc). * n (gram) that which is stated about the subject.

predict vt to foretell; to state (what one believes will happen).—**predictable** adj.—**predictably** adv.

prediction n the act of predicting; that which is predicted; a forecast or prophecy.

predominant adj ruling over, controlling; influencing.—**predominance** n.

predominantly adv mainly.

predominate vt to rule over; to have influence or control over; to prevail; to be greater in number, intensity, etc.

pre-eminent adj distinguished above others; outstanding.—**pre-eminence** n.—**pre-eminently** adv.

pre-empt vt to take action to check other action beforehand; to gain the right to buy (public land) by settling on it; to seize before anyone else can; (scheduled TV, radio programme) to replace; (in bridge) to bid highly to exclude bids from opponents.—**pre-emption** n.—**pre-emptive** adj.

preen vti (birds) to clean and trim the feathers; to congratulate (oneself) for achievement; to groom (oneself); to gloat.

prefab n (inf) a prefabricated building.

preface n an introduction or preliminary explanation; a foreword or introduction to a book; a preamble. * vt to serve as a preface; to introduce.

prefect n a person placed in authority over others; a student monitor in a school; in some countries, an administrative official.

prefer vt (pt **preferred**) to like better; to promote, advance; to put before (a court) for consid-

eration.

preferable adj deserving preference; superior; more desirable.—**preferably** adv.

preference n the act of preferring, choosing, or favoring one above another; that which is chosen or preferred; prior right; advantage given to one person, country, etc, over others.

preferential adj giving or receiving preference.—**preferentially** adv.

prefix vt to put at the beginning of or before; to put as an introduction. * n a syllable or group of syllables placed at the beginning of a word, affecting its meaning.

pregnant adj having a foetus in the womb; significant, meaningful; imaginative; filled (with) or rich (in).—**pregnancy** n.

prehistoric adj of the period before written records began.—**prehistory** n.

prejudge vt to pass judgment on before a trial; to form a premature opinion.—**prejudgment, prejudgement** n.

prejudice n a judgment or opinion made without adequate knowledge; bias; intolerance or hatred of other races, etc; (law) injury or disadvantage due to another's action. * vt to affect or injure through prejudice.—**prejudiced** adj.

preliminary adj preparatory; introductory. * n an event preceding another; a preliminary step or measure; (in school) a preparatory examination.

prelude n an introductory act or event; an event preceding another of greater importance; (mus) a movement which acts as an introduction.—also vt.

premarital adj (sex) taking place before marriage.

premature adj occurring before the expected or normal time; too early, hasty.—**prematurely** adv.—**prematureness, prematurity** n.

premier adj principal; first. * n the head of a government, a prime minister.—**premiership** n.

premiere n the first public performance of a play, film, etc. * vt to give a premiere of. * vi to have a first performance; to appear for the first time as a star performer.

premise n a proposition on which reasoning is based; something assumed or taken for granted; (pl) a piece of land and its buildings. * vt to state as an introduction; to postulate; to base on certain assumptions.

premium n a reward, esp an inducement to buy; a periodical payment for insurance; excess over an original price; something given free or at a reduced price with a purchase; a high value or value in excess of expectation. * adj (goods) high quality.

premonition n a foreboding; a feeling of something about to happen.

preoccupied adj absent-minded, lost in thought; (with **with**) having one's attention completely taken up by.

prep abbr = preparatory school.

preparation n the act of preparing; a preparatory

measure; something prepared, as a medicine, cosmetic, etc.

preparatory *adj* serving to prepare; introductory. * *adv* by way of preparation; in a preparatory manner.

preparatory school *n* a private school that prepares students for an advanced school or college.

prepare *vt* to make ready in advance; to fit out, equip; to cook; to instruct, teach; to put together. * *vi* to make oneself ready.

prepared *adj* subjected to a special process or treatment.

preponderate *vi* to be greater in number, amount, influence, etc; to predominate, prevail; to weigh more.—**preponderance** *n.*—**preponderant** *adj.*

preposition *n* a word used before a noun or pronoun to show its relation to another part of the sentence.—**prepositional** *adj.*

preposterous *adj* ridiculous; laughable; absurd.—**preposterously** *adv.*—**preposterousness** *n.*

prerequisite *n* a condition, etc, that must be fulfilled prior to something else. * *adj* required beforehand.

prerogative *n* a privilege or right accorded through office or hereditary rank.

presbytery *n* a ruling body in presbyterian churches consisting of the ministers and representative elders from congregations within a district; the house of a Roman Catholic priest.

prescribe *vt* to designate; to ordain; (*rules*) to lay down; (*medicine, treatment*) to order, advise.

prescription *n* act of prescribing; (*med*) a written instruction to a pharmacist for the preparation of a drug; (*law*) establishment of a right or title through long use.

presence *n* being present; immediate surroundings; personal appearance and bearing; impressive bearing, personality, etc; something (as a spirit) felt or believed to be present.

presence of mind *n* readiness of resource in an emergency, etc; the ability to say the right thing.

present[1] *adj* being at the specified place; existing or happening now; (*gram*) denoting action or state now or action that is always true. * *n* the time being; now; the present tense.

present[2] *n* a gift.

present[3] *vt* to introduce someone, esp socially; (*a play, etc*) to bring before the public, exhibit; to make a gift or award; to show; to perform; (*law*) to lay a charge before a court; (*weapon*) to point in a particular direction. * *vi* to present a weapon; to become manifest; to come forward as a patient.

presentable *adj* of decent appearance; fit to go into company.

presentation *n* act of presenting; a display or exhibition; style of presenting; something of-

fered or given; a description or persuasive account; (*med*) the position of a fetus in the uterus.

presently *adv* in a short while, soon.

preservation *n* the act of preserving or securing; a state of being preserved or repaired.

preservative *adj* preserving. * *n* something that preserves or has the power of preserving, esp an additive.

preserve *vt* to keep safe from danger; to protect; (*food*) to can, pickle, or prepare for future use; to keep or reserve for personal or special use. * *vi* to make preserves; to raise and protect game for sport. * *n* (*usu pl*) fruit preserved by cooking in sugar; an area restricted for the protection of natural resources, esp one used for regulated hunting, etc; something regarded as reserved for certain persons.

preside *vi* to take the chair or hold the position of authority; to take control or exercise authority.

president *n* the head of state of a republic; the highest officer of a company, club, etc.—**presidency** *n.*—**presidential** *adj.*

press *vt* to act on with steady force or weight; to push against, squeeze, compress, etc; (*clothes, etc*) to iron; to embrace closely; to force, compel; to entreat; to emphasize; to trouble; to urge on; (*record*) to make f r o m a matrix. * *vi* to weigh down; to crowd closely; to go forward with determination. * *n* pressure, urgency, etc; a crowd; a machine for crushing, stamping, etc; a machine for printing; a printing or publishing establishment; the gathering and distribution of news and those who perform these functions; newspapers collectively; any of various pressure devices; an upright closet for storing clothes.

press conference *n* a group interview given to members of the press by a politician, celebrity, etc.

pressing *adj* urgent; calling for immediate attention; importunate. * *n* a number of records made at one time from a master.

pressure *n* the act of pressing; a compelling force; a moral force; compression; urgency; constraint; (*physics*) force per unit of area. * *vt* to pressurize.

pressure group *n* a group of people organized to alert public opinion, legislators, etc, to a particular area of interest.

pressurize *vt* to keep nearly normal atmospheric pressure inside an aeroplane, etc, as at high altitudes; to exert pressure on; to attempt to compel, press.

prestige *n* standing in the eyes of people; commanding position in people's minds.

prestigious *adj* imparting prestige or distinction.

presumably *adv* as may be presumed.

presume *vt* to take for granted, suppose. * *vi* to assume to be true; to act without permission; to take liberties; (*with* **on, upon**) to take advantage of.

presumption n a supposition; a thing presumed; a strong probability; effrontery.

presumptuous adj tending to presume; bold; forward.—**presumptuously** adv.—**presumptuousness** n.

presuppose vt to assume beforehand; to involve as a necessary prior condition.—**presupposition** n.

pretence, pretense (US) n the act of pretending; a hypocritical show; a fraud, a sham.

pretend vti to claim, represent, or assert falsely; to feign, make believe; to lay claim (to).

pretentious adj claiming great importance; ostentatious.—**pretentiously** adv.—**pretentiousness** n.

pretext n a pretended reason to conceal a true one; an excuse.

pretty adj (**prettier, prettiest**) attractive in a dainty, graceful way. * adv (inf) fairly, moderately.—**prettily** adv.—**prettiness** n.

prevail vi to overcome; to predominate; to be customary or in force.

prevailing adj generally accepted, widespread; predominant.

prevalent adj current; predominant; widely practised or experienced.—**prevalence** n.

prevent vt to keep from happening; to hinder.—**preventable, preventible** adj.—**prevention** n.

preventive, preventative adj serving to prevent, precautionary. * n something used to prevent disease.

preview n an advance, restricted showing, as of a film; a showing of scenes from a film to advertise it. * vt to view or show in advance of public presentation; to give a preliminary survey.

previous adj coming before in time or order; prior, former.—**previously** adv.

prey n an animal killed for food by another; a victim. * vi (with **on, upon**) to seize and devour prey; (person) to victimize; to weigh heavily on the mind.

price n the amount, usu in money, paid for anything; the cost of obtaining some benefit; value, worth. * vt to set the price of something; to estimate a price; to deprive by raising prices excessively.

priceless adj very expensive; invaluable; (inf) very amusing, odd, or absurd.

prick n a sharp point; a puncture or piercing made by a sharp point; the wound or sensation inflicted; a qualm (of conscience); (inf) penis; (offensive) a spiteful person usu with authority. * vti to affect with anguish, grief, or remorse; to pierce slightly; to cause a sharp pain to; to goad, spur; (the ears) to erect; (with **out**) to transfer seedlings.

prickle n a thorn, spine or bristle; a pricking sensation. * vti to feel or cause to feel a pricking sensation.

prickly adj having prickles; tingling; irritable.—**prickliness** n.

prickly heat n a skin eruption caused by inflammation of the sweat glands.

pride n feeling of self-worth or esteem; excessive self-esteem; conceit; a sense of one's own importance; a feeling of elation due to success; the cause of this; splendour; a herd (of lions). * vti to be proud of; to take credit for.

priest n in various churches, a person authorized to perform sacred rites; an Anglican, Eastern Orthodox, or Roman Catholic clergyman ranking below a bishop.—**priestliness** n.—**priestly** adj.

priestess n a priest who is a woman; a woman regarded as a leader (as of a movement).

priesthood n the office of priest; priests collectively.

prig n a smug, self-righteous person.—**priggish** adj.

prim adj (**primmer, primmest**) proper, formal and precise in manner; demure.—**primly** adv.—**primness** n.

primarily adv mainly.

primary adj first; earliest; original; first in order of time; chief; elementary. * n a person or thing that is highest in rank, importance, etc; in US, a preliminary election at which candidates are chosen for the final election.

primary school n a school for children up to the age of 11 or 12.

primate n an archbishop or the highest ranking bishop in a province, etc; any of the highest order of mammals, including man.

prime[1] adj first in rank, importance, or quality; chief; (math) of a number, divisible only by itself and 1. * n the best time; the height of perfection; full maturity; full health and strength.

prime[2] vt to prepare or make something ready; to pour liquid into (a pump) or powder into (a firearm); to paint on a primer.

prime minister n the head of the government in a parliamentary democracy.

primer[1] n a simple book for teaching; a small introductory book on a subject.

primer[2] n a detonating device; a first coat of paint or oil.

primeval adj of the first age of the world; primitive.

primitive adj of the beginning or the earliest times; crude; simple; basic. * n a primitive person or thing.—**primitively** adv.

primrose n a perennial plant with pale yellow flowers.

prince n the son of a sovereign; a ruler ranking below a king; the head of a principality; any pre-eminent person.

Prince Edward Islander n (Cdn) a person who lives in or is from Prince Edward Island.

princess n a daughter of a sovereign; the wife of a prince; one outstanding in a specified respect.

principal adj first in rank or importance; chief. * n a principal person; a person who organizes; the head of a college or school; the leading player in a ballet, opera, etc; (law) the person who commits a crime; a person for whom another acts as agent; a capital sum lent or invested; a main beam or rafter.

principality *n* the position of responsibility of a principal; the rank and territory of a prince.

principally *adv* mainly.

Principal Meridian *n* (*Cdn*) a geographical meridian chosen to be the reference point for a land survey.

principle *n* a basic truth; a law or doctrine used as a basis for others; a moral code of conduct; a chemical constituent with a characteristic quality; a scientific law explaining a natural action; the method of a thing's working.

print *vti* to stamp (a mark, letter, etc) on a surface; to produce (on paper, etc) the impressions of inked type, etc; to produce (a book, etc); to write in letters resembling printed ones; to make (a photographic print). * *n* a mark made on a surface by pressure; the impression of letters, designs, etc, made from inked type, a plate, or block; an impression made by a photomechanical process; a photographic copy, esp from a negative.

printer *n* a person engaged in printing; a machine for printing from; a device that produces printout.

printing *n* the activity, skill, or business of producing printed matter; a style of writing using capital letters; the total number of books, etc, printed at one time.

printout *n* a printed record produced automatically (as by a computer).

prior *adj* previous; taking precedence (as in importance). * *n* the superior ranking below an abbot in a monastery; the head of a house or group of houses in a religious community.—**prioress** *nf*.

priority *n* precedence in rank, time, or place; preference; something requiring specified attention.

priory *n* a religious house under a prior or prioress.

prise *vt* to force (open, up) with a lever, etc.

prism *n* (*geom*) a solid whose ends are similar, equal, and parallel plane figures and whose sides are parallelograms; a transparent body of this form usu with triangular ends used for dispersing or reflecting light.—**prismatic** *adj*.

prison *n* a building used to house convicted criminals for punishment and suspects remanded in custody while awaiting trial; a jail.

prisoner *n* a person held in prison or under arrest; a captive; a person confined by a restraint.

pristine *adj* pure; in an original, unspoiled condition.

privacy *n* being private; seclusion; secrecy; one's private life.

private *adj* of or concerning a particular person or group; not open to or controlled by the public; for an individual person; not holding public office; secret. * *n* (*pl*) the genitals; an enlisted man of the lowest military rank in the army.—**privately** *adv*.

privet *n* a white-flowered evergreen shrub used for hedges.

privilege *n* a right or special benefit enjoyed by a person or a small group; a prerogative. * *vt* to bestow a privilege on.

privileged *adj* having or enjoying privileges; not subject to disclosure in a court of law.

privy *adj* private; having access to confidential information. * *n* a lavatory, esp one outside; (*law*) a person with an interest in an action.

Privy Council Office *n* (*Cdn*) a federal administrative office that advises the prime minister and other senior officials and coordinates the activities of the cabinet.

prize *n* an award won in competition or a lottery; a reward given for merit; a thing worth striving for. * *adj* given as, rewarded by, a prize. * *vt* to value highly.

prizefight *n* a professional boxing match.—**prizefighter** *n*.

pro[1] *adv, prep* in favor of. * *n* (*pl* **pros**) an argument for a proposal or motion.

pro[2] *adj, n* professional.

probability *n* that which is probable; likelihood; (*math*) the ratio of the chances in favor of an event to the total number.

probable *adj* likely; to be expected.

probation *n* testing of character or skill; release from prison under supervision by a probation officer; the state or period of being on probation.—**probationary** *adj*.

probe *n* a flexible surgical instrument for exploring a wound; a device, as an unmanned spacecraft, used to obtain information about an environment; an investigation. * *vt* to explore with a probe; to examine closely; to investigate.

probity *n* honesty, integrity, uprightness.

problem *n* a question for solution; a person, thing or matter difficult to cope with; a puzzle; (*math*) a proposition stating something to be done, an intricate unsettled question.

problematic, problematical *adj* presenting a problem; questionable; uncertain.

procedure *n* an established mode of conducting business, esp in law or in a meeting; a practice; a prescribed or traditional course; a step taken as part of an established order of steps.—**procedural** *adj*.

proceed *vi* to go on, esp after stopping; to come from; to continue; to carry on; to issue; to take action; to go to law.

proceeding *n* an advance or going forward; (*pl*) steps, action, in a lawsuit; (*pl*) published records of a society, etc.

proceeds *npl* the total amount of money brought in; the net amount received.

process *n* a course or state of going on; a series of events or actions; a method of operation; forward movement; (*law*) a court summons; the whole course of proceedings in a legal action. * *vt* to handle something following set procedures; (*food, etc*) to prepare by a special process; (*law*) to take action; (*film*) to develop.

procession n a group of people in marching in order, as in a parade.

proclaim vt to announce publicly and officially; to tell openly; to praise.

proclamation n the act of proclaiming; an official notice to the public.

procrastinate vti to defer action, to delay.—**procrastination** n.

procreate vt to bring into being, to engender off-spring.—**procreation** n.

procure vt to obtain by effort; to get and make available for promiscuous sexual intercourse; to bring about. * vi to procure women.—**procurement** n.

prod vt (pt **prodded**) to poke or jab, as with a pointed stick; to rouse into activity. * n the action of prodding; a sharp object; a stimulus.

prodigal adj wasteful; extravagant; open-handed. * n a wastrel; a person who squanders money.

prodigious adj enormous, vast; amazing.—**prodigiously** adv.

prodigy n an extraordinary person, thing or act; a gifted child.

produce vt to bring about; to bring forward, show; to yield; to cause; to manufacture, make; to give birth to; (play, film) to put before the public. * vi to yield something. * n that which is produced, esp agricultural products.

producer n someone who produces, esp a farmer or manufacturer; a person who finances or supervises the putting on of a play or making of a film; an apparatus or plant for making gas.

product n a thing produced by nature, industry or art; a result; an outgrowth; (math) the number obtained by multiplying two or more numbers together.

production n the act of producing; a thing produced; a work presented on the stage or screen or over the air.

productive adj producing or capable of producing; fertile.—**productively** adv.—**productiveness** n.

productivity n the state of being productive; the ratio of the output of a manufacturing business to the input of materials, labour, etc.

profane adj secular, not sacred; showing no respect for sacred things; irreverent; blasphemous; not possessing esoteric or expert knowledge. * vt to desecrate; to debase by a wrong, unworthy or vulgar use.—**profanely** adv.

profess vt to affirm publicly, declare; to claim to be expert in; to declare in words or appearance only.

profession n an act of professing; avowal, esp of religious belief; an occupation requiring specialized knowledge and often long and intensive academic preparation; the people engaged in this; affirmation; entry into a religious order.

professional adj of or following a profession; conforming to the technical or ethical standards of a profession; earning a livelihood in an activity or field often engaged in by amateurs; having a specified occupation as a permanent career; engaged in by persons receiving financial return; pursuing a line of conduct as though it were a profession.—also n.—**professionally** adv.

professional development day n a scheduled day on which teachers or other employees take part in seminars and other activities related to professional development.

professor n a faculty member of the highest academic rank at a university; a teacher at a university, college, etc.—**professorial** adj.—**professorship** n.

proficient adj skilled, competent.—**proficiency** n.—**proficiently** adv.

profile n a side view of the head as in a portrait, drawing, etc; a biographical sketch; a graph representing a person's abilities. * vt to represent in profile; to produce (as by writing, drawing, etc) a profile of.

profit n gain; the excess of returns over expenditure; the compensation to entrepreneurs resulting from the assumption of risk; (pl) the excess returns from a business; advantage, benefit. * vti to be of advantage (to), benefit; to gain.

profitable adj yielding profit, lucrative; beneficial; useful.—**profitability** n.—**profitably** adv.

profiteer vi to make exorbitant profits, esp in wartime.—also n.—**profiteering** n.

profound adj at great depth; intellectually deep; abstruse, mysterious.—**profoundly** adv.

profuse adj abundant; generous; extravagant.—**profusely** adv.—**profuseness** n.

profusion n an abundance.

progeny n offspring; descendants; outcome.

program n a sequence of instructions fed into a computer. * vti (pt **programmed** or **programed**) to feed a program into a computer; to write a program.

programme, program (US) n a printed list containing details of a ceremony, of the actors in a play, etc; a scheduled radio or television broadcast; a curriculum or syllabus for a course of study; a plan or schedule. * vt (pt **programmed**) to prepare a plan or schedule.

progress n a movement forwards or onwards, advance; satisfactory growth or development; a tour from place to place in stages. * vi to move forward, advance; to improve. * vt (project) to take to completion.

progression n progress; advancement by degrees; (math) a series of numbers, each differing from the succeeding according to a fixed law; (mus) a regular succession of chords.

progressive adj advancing, improving; proceeding by degrees; continuously increasing; aiming at reforms. * n a person who believes in moderate political change, esp social improvement by government action.—**progressively** adv.—**progressiveness** n.

prohibit vt to forbid by law; to prevent.—**prohibi-**

tory *adj.*

prohibition *n* the act of forbidding; an order that forbids; a legal ban on the manufacture and sale of alcoholic drinks.—**prohibitionist** *n.*

prohibitive *adj* forbidding; so high as to prevent purchase, use, etc, of something.—**prohibitively** *adv.*

project *n* a plan, scheme; an undertaking; a task carried out by students, etc, involving research. * *vt* to throw forward; (*light, shadow, etc*) to produce an outline of on a distance surface; to make objective or externalize; (*one's voice*) to make heard at a distance; (*feeling, etc*) to attribute to another; to imagine; to estimate, plan, or figure for the future. * *vi* to jut out; to come across vividly; to make oneself heard clearly.

projectile *n* a missile; something propelled by force. * *adj* throwing forward; capable of being thrown forward.

projection *n* the act of projecting or the condition of being projected; a thing projecting; the representation on a plane surface of part of the earth's surface; a projected image; an estimate of future possibilities based on a current trend; a mental image externalized; an unconscious attribution to another of one's own feelings and motives.

projector *n* an instrument that projects images from transparencies or film; an instrument that projects rays of light; a person who promotes enterprises.

proletariat *n* the lowest social or economic class of a community; wage earners; the industrial working class.—**proletarian** *adj.*

proliferate *vi* to grow or reproduce rapidly.—**proliferation** *n.*

prolific *adj* producing abundantly; fruitful.

prologue, prolog (*US*) *n* the introductory lines of a play, speech, or poem; an introductory event.

prolong *vt* to extend or lengthen in space or time; to spin out.

prom *n* a promenade; a dance.

promenade *n* an esplanade; a ball or dance.; a leisurely walk. * *vti* to take a promenade (along, through).

prominence *n* the state of being prominent; a projection; relative importance; celebrity, fame.

prominent *adj* jutting, projecting; standing out, conspicuous; widely and favorably known; distinguished.—**prominently** *adv.*

promiscuous *adj* indiscriminate, esp in sexual liaisons.—**promiscuity** *n.*—**promiscuously** *adv.*—**promiscuousness** *n.*

promise *n* a pledge; an undertaking to do or not to do something; an indication, as of a successful future. * *vti* to pledge; to undertake; to give reason to expect.

promising *adj* likely to turn out well; hopeful.

promontory *n* a peak of high land that juts out into a body of water.

promote *vt* to encourage; to advocate; to raise to a higher rank; (*employee, student*) to advance from one grade to the next higher grade; (*product*) to encourage sales by advertising, publicity, or discounting.

promoter *n* a person who promotes, esp one who organizes and finances a sporting event or pop concert; a substance that increases the activity of a catalyst.

promotion *n* an elevation in position or rank; the furtherance of the sale of merchandise through advertising, publicity, or discounting.—**promotional** *adj.*

prompt *adj* without delay; quick to respond; immediate; of or relating to prompting actors. * *vt* to urge; to inspire; (*actor*) to remind of forgotten words, etc (as in a play). * *n* something that reminds; a time limit for payment of an account; the contract by which this time is fixed.—**promptly** *adv.*

prompter *n* one that prompts, esp a person who sits offstage and reminds actors of forgotten lines.

promptness *n* alacrity in action or decision; quickness; punctuality.

prone *adj* face downwards; lying flat, prostrate; inclined or disposed (to).—**proneness** *n.*

prong *n* a spike of a fork or other forked object.—**pronged** *adj.*

pronoun *n* a word used to represent a noun (eg *I, he, she, it*).

pronounce *vt* to utter, articulate; to speak officially, pass (judgment); to declare formally.—**pronounceable** *adj.*

pronounced *adj* marked, noticeable.

pronouncement *n* a formal announcement, declaration; a confident assertion.

pronunciation *n* articulation; the way a word is pronounced.

proof *n* evidence that establishes the truth; the fact, act, or process of validating; test; demonstration; a sample from type, etc, for correction; a trial print from a photographic negative; the relative strength of an alcoholic liquor. * *adj* resistant; impervious, impenetrable. * *vt* to make proof against (water).

prop[1] *vt* (*pt* **propped**) to support by placing something under or against. * *n* a rigid support; a thing or person giving support.

prop[2] *see* **property.**

prop[3] *abbr* = propeller.

propaganda *n* the organized spread of ideas, doctrines, etc, to promote a cause; the ideas, etc, so spread.—**propagandist** *n, adj.*

propel *vt* (*pt* **propelled**) to drive or move forward.—**propellant, propellent** *n.*

propeller *n* a mechanism to impart drive; a device having two or more blades in a revolving hub for propelling a ship or aircraft.

propensity *n* a natural inclination; disposition, tendency.

proper *adj* own, individual, peculiar; appropriate, fit; correct, conventional; decent, respectable; in the most restricted sense; (*sl*) thorough.

properly *adv* in the right way; justifiably; (*sl*) thoroughly.

property n a quality or attribute; a distinctive feature or characteristic; one's possessions; real estate, land; a movable article used in a stage setting (—also **prop**).

prophecy n a message of divine will and purpose; prediction.

prophesy vti to predict with assurance or on the basis of mystic knowledge; to foretell.

prophet n a religious leader regarded as, or claiming to be, divinely inspired; one who predicts the future.—**prophetess** nf.

prophetic, prophetical adj of a prophet or prophecy; prophesying events.—**prophetically** adv.

proportion n the relationship between things in size, quantity, or degree; ratio; symmetry, balance; comparative part or share; (math) the equality of two ratios; a share or quota; (pl) dimensions. * vt to put in proper relation with something else; to make proportionate (to).

proportional adj of proportion; aiming at due proportion; proportionate.—**proportionality** n.—**proportionally** adv.

proportionate adj in due pro por tion, corresponding in amount. * vt to make proportionate.—**proportionately** adv.

proposal n a scheme, plan, or suggestion; an offer of marriage.

propose vt to present for consideration; to suggest; to intend; to announce the drinking of a toast to; (person) to nominate; to move as a resolution. * vi to make an offer (of marriage).—**proposer** n.

proposition n a proposal for consideration; a plan; a request for sexual intercourse; (inf) a proposed deal, as in business; (inf) an undertaking to be dealt with; (math) a problem to be solved.

proprietor n an owner.—**proprietress** nf.—**proprietorial** adj.

propulsion n the act of propelling; something that propels.

prosaic adj commonplace, matter-of-fact, dull.—**prosaically** adv.

prose n ordinary language without metre. * adj in prose; humdrum, dull.

prosecute vt to bring legal action against; to pursue. * vi to institute and carry on a legal suit or prosecution.

prosecution n the act of prosecuting, esp by law; the prosecuting party in a legal case.

prosecutor n a person who prosecutes, esp in a criminal court.

prospect n a wide view, a vista; (pl) measure of future success; future outlook; expectation; a likely customer, candidate, etc. * vti to explore or search (for).—**prospector** n.

prospective adj likely; anticipated, expected.

prospectus n a printed statement of the features of a new work, enterprise, etc; something (as a condition or statement) that forecasts the course or nature of a situation.

prosper vi to thrive; to flourish; to succeed.

prosperity n success; wealth.—**prosperous** adj.—**prosperously** adv.

prostitute n a person who has sexual intercourse for money; (fig) one who deliberately debases his or her talents (as for money). * vt to offer indiscriminately for sexual intercourse, esp for money; to devote to corrupt or unworthy purposes.

prostrate adj lying face downwards; helpless; overcome; lying prone or supine. * vt to throw oneself down; to lie flat; to humble oneself.—**prostration** n.

protagonist n the main character in a drama, novel, etc; a supporter of a cause.

protect vt to defend from danger or harm; to guard; to maintain the status and integrity of, esp through financial guarantees; to foster or shield from infringement or restriction; to restrict competition through tariffs and trade controls.—**protector** n.

protection n the act of protecting; the condition of being protected; something that protects; shelter; defence; patronage; the taxing of competing imports to foster home industry; the advocacy or theory of this (—also **protectionism**); immunity from prosecution or attack obtained by the payment of money.

protective adj serving to protect, defend, shelter.—**protectively** adv.

protégé n a person guided and helped in his career by another person.—**protégée** nf.

protein n a complex organic compound containing nitrogen that is an essential constituent of food.

protest vi to object to; to remonstrate. * vt to assert or affirm; to execute or have executed a formal protest against; to make a statement or gesture in objection to. * n public dissent; an objection; a complaint; a formal statement of objection.—**protestation** n.—**protester** n.

Protestant n a member or adherent of one of the Christian churches deriving from the Reformation; a Christian not of the Orthodox or Roman Catholic Church, who adheres to the principles of the Reformation.—**Protestantism** n.

protocol n a note, minute or draft of an agreement or transaction; the ceremonial etiquette accepted as correct in official dealings, as between heads of state or diplomatic officials; the formatting of data in an electronic communications system; the plan of a scientific experiment or treatment.

proton n an elementary particle in the nucleus of all atoms, carrying a unit positive charge of electricity.

prototype n an original model or type from which copies are made.

protracted adj extended, prolonged; long-drawn-out.—**protractedly** adv.

protrude vti to thrust outwards or forwards; to obtrude; to jut out, project.—**protrusive** adj.

protuberance n a swelling, prominence.—**protuberant** adj.

proud adj having too high an opinion of oneself; arrogant, haughty; having proper self-respect; satisfied with one's achievements.—**proudly** *adv*.

prove *vti* (*pt* **proved** *or* **proven**) to try out, test, by experiment; to establish or demonstrate as true using accepted procedures; to show (oneself) to be worthy or capable; to turn out (to be), esp after trial or test; to rise.

proverb *n* a short traditional saying expressing a truth or moral instruction; an adage.

proverbial *adj* of or like, a proverb; generally known.—**proverbially** *adv*.

provide *vti* to arrange for; to supply; to prepare; to afford (an opportunity); to make provision for (financially).—**provider** *n*.

provided, providing *conj* on condition (that).

providence *n* foresight, prudence; God's care and protection.

province *n* an administrative district or division of a country; the jurisdiction of an archbishop; (*pl*) the parts of a country removed from the main cities; a department of knowledge or activity.

provincehood *n* (*Cdn*) the quality of status of being a province.

provincial *adj* of a province or provinces; having the way, speech, etc of a certain province; country-like; rustic; unsophisticated. * *n* an inhabitant of the provinces or country areas; a person lacking sophistication.—**provincially** *adv*.

provincialization *n* (*Cdn*) the transfer of government programs or responsibilities to the provinces.

provision *n* a requirement; something provided for the future; a stipulation, condition; (*pl*) supplies of food, stores. * *vt* to supply with stores.

provisional *adj* temporary; conditional.—**provisionally** *adv*.

proviso *n* (*pl* **provisos, provisoes**) a condition, stipulation; a limiting clause in an agreement, etc.

provocation *n* the act of provoking or inciting; a cause of anger, resentment, etc.

provocative *adj* intentionally provoking, esp to anger or sexual desire; (*remark*) stimulating argument or discussion.—**provocatively** *adv*.

provoke *vt* to anger, infuriate; to incite, to arouse; to give rise to; to irritate, exasperate.

prow *n* the forward part of a ship, bow.

prowess *n* bravery, gallantry; skill.

prowl *vi* to move stealthily, esp in search of prey.—*also n*.

prowler *n* one that moves stealthily, esp an opportunist thief.

proximity *n* nearness in place, time, series, etc.

proxy *n* the authority to vote or act for another; a person so authorized.—*also adj*.

prudence *n* the quality of being prudent; caution; discretion; common sense.

prudent *adj* cautious; sensible; managing carefully; circumspect.—**prudently** *adv*.

prune[1] *n* a dried plum.

prune[2] *vti* (*plant*) to remove dead or living parts

from; to cut away what is unwanted or superfluous.

pry *vi* to snoop into other people's affairs; to inquire impertinently.

PS *abbr* = postscript.

PSAC *abbr* = Public Service Alliance of Canada.

psalm *n* a sacred song or hymn, esp one from the Book of Psalms in the Bible.

PST *abbr* = Pacific Standard Time; Provincial Sales Tax.

pseudo *adj* false, pretended.

pseudonym *n* a false named adopted as by an author.—**pseudonymous** *adj*.

psyche *n* the spirit, soul; the mind, esp as a functional entity governing the total organism and its interactions with the environment.

psychiatry *n* the branch of medicine dealing with disorders of the mind, including psychoses and neuroses.—**psychiatric** *adj*.—**psychiatrist** *n*.

psychic, psychical *adj* of the soul or spirit; of the mind; having sensitivity to, or contact with, forces that cannot be explained by natural laws. * *n* a person apparently sensitive to nonphysical forces; a medium; psychic phenomena.

psychoanalysis *n* a method of treating neuroses, phobias, and some other mental disorders by analysing emotional conflicts, repressions, etc.—**psychoanalyse** *vt*.—**psychoanalyst** *n*.

psychology *n* the science that studies the human mind and behaviour; mental state.—**psychological** *adj*.—**psychologically** *adv*.—**psychologist** *n*.

psychopath *n* a person suffering from a mental disorder that results in antisocial behaviour and lack of guilt.—**psychopathic** *adj*.

PTO *abbr* = please turn over.

pub *n* a public house, an inn.

puberty *n* the stage at which the reproductive organs become functional.

public *adj* of, for, or by the people generally; performed in front of people; for the use of all people; open or known to all; acting officially for the people. * *n* the people in general; a particular section of the people, such as an audience, body of readers, etc; open observation.—**publicly** *adv*.

publication *n* public notification; the printing and distribution of books, magazines, etc; something published as a periodical, book, etc.

public house *n* a tavern or bar licensed to sell alcoholic drinks; an inn.

publicity *n* any information or action that brings a person or cause to public notice; work concerned with such promotional matter; notice by the public.

public mischief *n* (*Cdn*) the criminal offence of making a false report or accusation.

public relations *n* relations with the general public of a company, institution, etc, as through publicity.

public school n a school maintained by public money and supervised by local authorities; in England, a private secondary school, usu boarding.

publish vt to make generally known; to announce formally; (book) to issue for sale to the public. * vi to put out an edition; to have one's work accepted for publication.

publisher n a person or company that prints and issues books, magazines, etc.

publishing n the business of the production and distribution of books, magazines, recordings, etc.

puce n, adj (a) purplish brown.

puck n a hard rubber disc used in ice hockey.

pucker vti to draw together in creases, to wrinkle. * n a wrinkle or fold.

pudding n a dessert; a steamed or baked dessert; a suet pie.

puddle n a small pool of water, esp stagnant, spilled, or muddy water.

puerile adj juvenile; childish.

puff n a sudden short blast or gust; an exhalation of air or smoke; a light pastry; a pad for applying powder; a flattering notice, advertisement. * vti to emit a puff; to breathe hard, pant; to put out of breath; to praise with exaggeration; to swell; to blow, smoke, etc, with puffs.

puffin n a sea bird that has a short neck and a brightly colored laterally compressed bill.

puffy adj (**puffier, puffiest**) inflated, swollen; panting.—**puffily** adv.

pugnacious adj fond of fighting, belligerent.—**pugnaciousness** n.—**pugnacity** n.

pull vt to tug at; to pluck; to move or draw towards oneself; to drag; to rip; to tear; (muscle) to strain; (inf) to carry out, perform; (inf) to restrain; (inf: gun, etc) to draw out; (inf) to attract. * vi to carry out the action of pulling something; to be capable of being pulled; to move (away, ahead, etc). * n the act of pulling or being pulled; a tug; a device for pulling; (inf) influence; (inf) drawing power.

pulley n (pl **pulleys**) a wheel with a grooved rim for a cord, etc, used to raise weights by downward pull or change of direction of the pull; a group of these used to increase applied force; a wheel driven by a belt.

pullover n a buttonless garment with or without sleeves pulled on over the head.

pulp n a soft, moist, sticky mass; the soft, juicy part of a fruit or soft pith of a plant stem; ground-up, moistened fibres of wood, rags, etc, used to make paper; a book or magazine printed on cheap paper and often dealing with sensational material. * vti to make or become pulp or pulpy; to produce or reproduce (written matter) in pulp form.—**pulpiness** n.—**pulpy** adj.

pulpit n a raised enclosed platform, esp in a church, from which a clergyman preaches; preachers as a group.

pulsate vi to beat or throb rhythmically; to vibrate, quiver.—**pulsation** n.

pulse[1] n a rhythmic beat or throb, as of the heart; a place where this is felt; an underlying opinion or sentiment or an indication of it; a short radio signal. * vti to throb, pulsate.

pulse[2] n the edible seeds of several leguminous plants, such as beans, peas and lentils; the plants producing them.

pulverize vti to reduce to a fine powder; to demolish, smash; to crumble.—**pulverization** n.

puma n a large tawny American animal of the cat family, a cougar or mountain lion.

pummel vt (pt **pummelled**) to strike repeatedly with the fists, to thump.

pump[1] n a device that forces a liquid or gas into, or draws it out of, something. * vti to move (fluids) with a pump; to remove water, etc, from; to drive air into with a pump; to draw out, move up and down, pour forth, etc, as a pump does; (inf) to obtain information through questioning.

pump[2] n a light low shoe or slipper; a rubber-soled shoe.

pumpkin n a large, round, orange fruit of the gourd family widely cultivated as food.

pun n a play on words of the same sound but different meanings, usu humorous.—also vi.

punch[1] vt to strike with the fist; to prod or poke; to stamp, perforate with a tool; (cattle) to herd. * n a blow with the fist; (inf) vigour; a machine or tool for punching.

punch[2] n a hot, sweet drink made with fruit juices, often mixed with wine or spirits.

punctual adj being on time; prompt.—**punctuality** n.—**punctually** adv.

punctuate vt to use certain standardized marks in (written matter) to clarify meaning; to interrupt; to emphasize. * vi to use punctuation marks.

punctuation n the act of punctuating; the state of being punctuated; a system of punctuation.

puncture n a small hole made by a sharp object; the deflation of a tyre caused by a puncture. * vt to make useless or ineffective as if by a puncture; to deflate. * vi to become punctured.

pundit n a learned person; an expert; a critic, esp a columnist.

pungent adj having an acrid smell or a sharp taste; caustic; bitter.—**pungency** n.—**pungently** adv.

punish vt to subject a person to a penalty for a crime or misdemeanour; to chastise; to handle roughly.

punishable adj liable to legal punishment.

punishment n a penalty for a crime or misdemeanour; rough treatment; the act of punishing or being punished.

punt[1] n a long flat-bottomed square-ended river boat usu propelled with a pole. * vti to propel or convey in a punt.

punt[2] vt to kick a dropped ball before it reaches the ground. * n such a kick.

puny adj (**punier, puniest**) of inferior size, strength, or importance; feeble.

pup *n* a young dog, a puppy; a young fox, seal, rat, etc. * *vi* (*pt* **pupped**) to give birth to pups.

pupil[1] *n* a child or young person taught under the supervision of a teacher or tutor; a person who has been taught or influenced by a famous or distinguished person.

pupil[2] *n* the round, dark opening in the centre of the iris of the eye through which light passes.

puppet *n* a doll moved by strings attached to its limbs or by a hand inserted in its body; a person controlled by another.—*also adj.*—**puppeteer** *n.*—**puppetry** *n.*

puppy *n* a young domestic dog less than a year old.

purchase *vt* to buy; to obtain by effort or suffering. * *n* the act of purchasing; an object bought; leverage for raising or moving loads; means of achieving advantage.—**purchaser** *n.*

pure *adj* clean; not contaminated; not mixed; chaste, innocent; free from taint or defilement; mere; that and that only; abstract and theoretical; (*mus*) not discordant, perfectly in tune.—**pureness** *n.*

pure laine *adj* (*Cdn*) descended as a French-speaking Quebecer from the original settlers of French Canada; of or pertaining to such a person. * *n* a person of such descent.

purge *vt* to cleanse, purify; (*nation, party, etc*) to rid of troublesome people; to clear (oneself) of a charge; to clear out the bowels of. * *n* the act or process of purging; a purgative; the removal of persons believed to be disloyal from an organization, esp a political party.

purify *vti* to make or become pure; to cleanse; to make ceremonially clean; to free from harmful matter.—**purification** *n.*—**purifier** *n.*

purist *n* someone who is a stickler for correctness in language, style, etc.

puritan *adj* a person who is extremely strict in religion or morals; (*with cap*) an extreme Protestant of Elizabethan or Stuart times.—*also adj.*—**puritanic, puritanical** *adj.*

purity *n* the state of being pure.

purl *vt* to knit a stitch by drawing its base loop from front to back of the fabric.—*also n.*

purple *n* a dark, bluish red; crimson cloth or clothing, esp as a former emblem of royalty. * *adj* purple-colored; royal; (*writing style*) over-elaborate.

purport *vt* to claim to be true; to imply; to be intended to seem. * *n* significance; apparent meaning.

purpose *n* objective; intention; aim; function; resolution, determination. * *vti* to intend, design.

purposeful *adj* determined, resolute; intentional.—**purposefully** *adv.*—**purposefulness** *n.*

purr *vi* (*cat*) to make a low, murmuring sound of pleasure.—**purring** *n.*

purse *n* a small pouch or bag for money; finances, money; a sum of money for a present or a prize; a handbag. * *vt* to pucker, wrinkle up.

purser *n* an officer on a passenger ship in charge of accounts, tickets, etc; an airline official responsible for the comfort and welfare of passengers.

pursue *vt* to follow; to chase; to strive for; to seek to attain; to engage in; to proceed with. * *vi* to follow in order to capture.—**pursuer** *n.*

pursuit *n* the act of pursuing; an occupation; a pastime.

pus *n* a yellowish fluid produced by infected sores.

push *vti* to exert pressure so as to move; to press against or forward; to impel forward, shove; to urge the use, sale, etc, of; (*inf*) to approach an age; (*inf*) to sell drugs illegally; to make an effort. * *n* a thrust, shove; an effort; an advance against opposition; (*inf*) energy and drive.

pushchair *n* a wheeled metal and canvas chair for a small child.

pushover *n* (*inf*) something easily done, as a victory over an opposing team; (*inf*) a person easily taken advantage of.

pushy *adj* (**pushier, pushiest**) (*inf*) assertive; forceful; aggressively ambitious.—**pushily** *adv.*—**pushiness** *n.*

puss, pussy *n* an informal name for a cat.

put *vti* (*pr p* **putting**, *pt* **put**) to place, set; to cast, throw; to apply, direct; to bring into a specified state; to add (to); to subject to; to submit; to estimate; to stake; to express; to translate; to propose; (*a weight*) to hurl. * *adj* fixed.

putrid *adj* rotten or decayed and foul-smelling.

putt *vti* (*golf*) to hit (a ball) with a putter. * *n* in golf, a stroke to make the ball roll into the hole.

putter *n* (*golf*) a straight-faced club used in putting.

putty *n* a soft, plastic mixture of powdered chalk and linseed oil used to fill small cracks, fix glass in window frames, etc.

puzzle *vt* to bewilder; to perplex. * *vi* to be perplexed; to exercise one's mind, as over a problem. * *n* bewilderment; a difficult problem; a toy or problem for testing skill or ingenuity; a conundrum.

puzzling *adj* perplexing, bewildering, inexplicable.

pygmy *n* an undersized person.—*also* **pigmy.**

pyjamas, pajamas (*US*) *npl* a loosely fitting sleeping suit of jacket and trousers.

pylon *n* a tower-like structure supporting electric power lines.

pyramid *n* (*geom*) a solid figure having a polygon as base, and whose sides are triangles sharing a common vertex; a huge structure of this shape, as a royal tomb of ancient Egypt; an immaterial structure built on a broad supporting base and narrowing gradually to an apex.

python *n* a large, nonpoisonous snake that kills by constriction.

Q

QC *abbr* = Quebec.

QST *abbr* = Quebec Sales Tax.

quack[1] *n* the cry of a duck. * *vi* to make a sound like a duck.

quack[2] *n* an untrained person who practises medicine fraudulently; one who pretends to have knowledge he does not have.—*also adj*.

quad *n* quadrangle; quadruplet.

quadrangle *n* (*geom*) a plane figure with four sides and four angles, a rectangle; a court enclosed by buildings.—**quadrangular** *adj*.

quadruped *n* a four-footed animal.—**quadrupedal** *adj*.

quadruple *adj* four times as much or as many; made up of or consisting or four; having four divisions or parts. * *vti* to make or become four times as many.

quadruplet *n* one of four children born at birth.

quagmire *n* soft, wet ground; a difficult situation.

quail[1] *vi* to cower, to shrink back with fear.

quail[2] *n* a small American game bird.

quaint *adj* attractive or pleasant in an odd or old-fashioned style.—**quaintly** *adv*.—**quaintness** *n*.

quake *vi* to tremble or shiver, esp with fear or cold; to quiver. * *n* a shaking or tremor; (*inf*) an earthquake.

Quaker *n* a popular name for a member of the Society of Friends, a religious sect advocating peace and simplicity.—**Quakerism** *n*.

qualification *n* qualifying; a thing that qualifies; a quality or acquirement that makes a person fit for a post, etc; modification; limitation; (*pl*) academic achievements.

qualify *vti* to restrict; to describe; to moderate; to modify, limit; to make or become capable or suitable; to fulfil conditions; to pass a final examination; (*gram*) to limit the meaning of.

qualitative *adj* of or depending on quality; determining the nature, not the quality, of components.—**qualitatively** *adv*.

quality *n* a characteristic or attribute; degree of excellence; high standard. * *adj* of high quality.

qualm *n* a doubt; a misgiving; a scruple; a sudden feeling of faintness or nausea.

quandary *n* a predicament; a dilemma.

quantitative, quantitive *adj* capable of being measured; relating to size or amount.—**quantitatively, quantitively** *adv*.

quantity *n* an amount that can be measured, counted or weighed; a large amount; the property by which a thing can be measured; a number or symbol expressing this property.

quarantine *n* a period of isolation imposed to prevent the spread of disease; the time or place of this. * *vt* to put or keep in quarantine.

quarrel *n* an argument; an angry dispute; a cause of dispute. * *vi* (*pt* **quarrelled**) to argue violently; to fall out (with); to find fault (with).

quarrelsome *adj* contentious; apt to quarrel.

quarry[1] *n* an excavation for the extraction of stone, slate, etc; a place from which stone is excavated; a source of information, etc. * *vti* to excavate (from) a quarry; to research.

quarry[2] *n* a hunted animal, prey.

quart *n* a liquid measure equal to a quarter of a gallon or two pints; a dry measure equal to two pints.

quarter *n* a fourth of something; one fourth of a year; one fourth of an hour; (in US) 25 cents, or a coin of this value; any leg of a four-legged animal with the adjoining parts; a particular district or section; (*pl*) lodgings; a particular source; an unspecified person or group; a compass point other than the cardinal points; mercy; (*her*) any of four quadrants of a shield. * *vti* to share or divide into four; to provide with lodgings; to lodge; to range over (an area) in search (of). * *adj* constituting a quarter.

quarterfinal *n* one of four matches held before the semifinals in a tournament.—*also adj*.

quarterly *adj* occurring, issued, or spaced at three-month intervals; (*her*) divided into quarters. * *adv* once every three months; (*her*) in quarters. * *n* a publication issued four times a year.

quartermaster *n* (*mil*) an officer in charge of stores; (*naut*) a petty officer in charge of steering, etc.

quartet, quartette *n* a set or group of four; a piece of music composed for four instruments or voices; a group of four instrumentalists or voices.

quartz *n* a crystalline mineral, a form of silica, usu colorless and transparent.

quash *vt* (*rebellion etc*) to put down; to suppress; to make void.

quasi *adv* seemingly; as if. * *prefix* almost, apparently.

quaver *vi* to tremble, vibrate; to speak or sing with a quivering voice. * *n* a trembling sound or note; (*mus*) a note having half the duration of a crotchet, an eighth note.—**quavery** *adj*.

quay *n* a loading wharf or landing place for vessels.

queasy *adj* (**queasier, queasiest**) nauseous; easily upset; over-scrupulous.—**queasily** *adv*.—**queasiness** *n*.

Quebec heater *n* (*Cdn*) a tall, cylindrical stove that uses coal or wood as cooking or heating fuel.

Quebecer, Quebecker, Québécois *n* (*Cdn*) a person who lives in or is from Quebec.

queen *n* a female sovereign and head of state; the wife or widow of a king; a woman considered pre-eminent; the egg-laying female of bees, wasps, etc; a playing card with a picture of a queen; (*chess*) the most powerful piece; (*sl*) a male homosexual, esp one who ostentatiously takes a feminine role. * *vi* (*with* it) to act like a queen, esp to put on airs. * *vt* (a pawn) to promote to a queen in chess.—**queenly** *adj*.

queen mother *n* a queen dowager who is the mother of a ruling sovereign.

queer *adj* strange, odd, curious; (*inf*) eccentric; (*sl*) homosexual. * *n* a (male) homosexual. * *vt* (*sl*) to spoil the success of.—**queerness** *n*.

quell *vt* to suppress; to allay.

quench *vt* (*thirst*) to satisfy or slake; (*fire*) to put out, extinguish; (*steel*) to cool; to suppress.—**quenchable** *adj*.

query *n* a question; a question mark; doubt. * *vti* to question; to doubt the accuracy of.

quest *n* a search, seeking, esp involving a journey. * *vti* to search (about) for, seek.—**quester** *n*.—**questingly** *adv*.

question *n* an interrogative sentence; an inquiry; a problem; a doubtful or controversial point; a subject of debate before an assembly; a part of a test or examination. * *vti* to ask questions (of); to interrogate intensively; to dispute; to subject to analysis.—**questioner** *n*.

questionable *adj* doubtful; not clearly true or honest.—**questionably** *adv*.

question mark *n* a punctuation mark (?) used at the end of a sentence to indicate a question, or to express doubt about something; something unknown.

questionnaire *n* a series of questions designed to collect statistical information; a survey made by the use of questionnaire.

question period *n* (*Cdn*) a scheduled period of time in a legislature during which members may ask questions of government ministers.

queue *n* a line of people, vehicles, etc awaiting a turn. * *vi* (*pr p* queuing, *pt* queued) to wait in turn.

quibble *n* a minor objection or criticism. * *vi* to argue about trifling matters.

quick *adj* rapid, speedy; nimble; prompt; responsive; alert; eager to learn. * *adv* in a quick manner. * *n* the sensitive flesh below a fingernail or toenail; the inmost sensibilities.—**quickly** *adv*.—**quickness** *n*.

quicken *vti* to speed up or accelerate; to make alive; to come to life; to invigorate.

quicksand *n* loose wet sand easily yielding to pressure in which persons, animals, etc may be swallowed up.

quickstep *n* a ballroom dance in quick time; its music.

quick-witted *adj* mentally alert; quick in repartee.—**quick-wittedness** *n*.

quid *n* (*sl*) a pound (sterling).

quiet *adj* silent, not noisy; still, not moving; gentle, not boisterous; unobtrusive, not showy; placid, calm; monotonous, uneventful; undisturbed. * *n* stillness, peace, repose; an undisturbed state. * *vti* to

quieten.—**quietly** *adv*.—**quietness** *n*.

quieten *vti* to make or become quiet; to calm, soothe.

quill *n* the hollow stem of a feather; anything made of this, as a pen; a stiff, hollow spine of a hedgehog or porcupine.

quilt *n* a thick, warm bedcover; a bedspread; a coverlet of two cloths sewn together with padding between. * *vti* to stitch together like a quilt; to make a quilt.—**quilter** *n*.—**quilting** *n*.

quin *n* a quintuplet.

quinine *n* a bitter crystalline alkaloid used in medicine; one of its salts used esp as an antimalarial and a bitter tonic.

quintet, quintette *n* a set or group of five; a piece of music composed for five instruments or voices; a group of five instrumentalists or voices.

quintuple *adj* fivefold; having five divisions or parts; five times as much or as many. * *vti* to multiply by five. * *n* a number five times greater than another.

quintuplet *n* one of five offspring produced at one birth.

quip *n* a witty remark; a gibe. * *vt* (*pt* quipped) to make a clever or sarcastic remark.

quirk *n* an unexpected turn or twist; a peculiarity of character or mannerism.—**quirky** *adj*.—**quirkiness** *n*.

quit *vti* (*pt* quitted *or* quit) to leave; to stop or cease; to resign; to free from obligation; to admit defeat. * *adj* free from; released from.

quite *adv* completely; somewhat, fairly; really.

quits *adj* even; on equal terms by payment or revenge.

quiver[1] *vi* to shake; to tremble, shiver. * *n* a shiver, vibration.—**quivery** *adj*.

quiver[2] *n* a case for holding arrows.

quiz *n* (*pl* quizzes) a form of entertainment where players are asked questions of general knowledge; a short written or oral test. * *vt* (*pt* quizzed) to interrogate; to make fun of.

quizzical *adj* humorous and questioning.—**quizzically** *adv*.

quoit *n* a ring of metal, plastic, etc thrown in quoits; (*pl*) a game in which rings are thrown at or over a peg.

quorum *n* the minimum number that must be present at a meeting or assembly to make its proceedings valid.

quota *n* a proportional share; a prescribed amount; a part to be contributed.

quotation *n* the act of quoting; the words quoted; an estimated price.

quotation mark *n* a punctuation mark used to indicate the beginning (' *or* ") and the end (' *or* ") of a quoted passage.

quote *vt* to cite; to refer to; to repeat the words of a novel, play, poem, speech, etc exactly; to adduce by way of authority; to set off by quotation marks; to state the price of (something). * *n* (*inf*) something quoted; a quotation mark.—**quotable** *adj*.

R

rabbi *n* (*pl* **rabbis**) the religious and spiritual leader of a Jewish congregation.

rabbit *n* a small burrowing mammal of the hare family with long ears, a short tail, and long hind legs; their flesh as food; their fur.

rabble *n* a disorderly crowd, a mob; the common herd.

rabid *adj* infected with rabies; raging; fanatical.

rabies *n* an acute, infectious, viral disease transmitted by the bite of an infected animal.

raccoon *n* a small nocturnal carnivore of North America that lives in trees; its yellowish grey fur.

race[1] *n* any of the divisions of humankind distinguished esp by color of skin; any geographical, national, or tribal ethnic grouping; a subspecies of plants or animals; distinctive flavor or taste.

race[2] *n* a contest of speed; a rapid current of water. * *vi* to run at top speed or out of control; to compete in a race; (*engine*) to run without a working load. * *vt* to cause to race; to contest against.

racecourse, racetrack (*US*) *n* a track over which races are run, esp an oval track for racing horses.

racehorse *n* a horse bred and trained for racing.

racial *adj* of or relating to any of the divisions of humankind distinguished by color, etc.

racialism, racism *n* a belief in the superiority of some races over others; prejudice against or hatred of other races; discriminating behaviour towards people of another race.— **racist** *n*.

rack *n* a frame for holding or displaying articles; an instrument for torture by stretching; the triangular frame for setting up balls in snooker; a toothed bar to engage with the teeth of a wheel; extreme pain or anxiety. * *vt* (*person*) to stretch on a rack; to arrange in or on a rack; to torture, torment; to move parts of machinery with a toothed rack.

racket[1] *n* a bat strung with nylon, for playing tennis, etc. (*pl*) a game for two or four players played in a four-walled court (—*also* **racquet**).

racket[2] *n* noisy confusion; din; an obtaining of money illegally; any fraudulent business.

racy *adj* lively, spirited; risqué.— **racily** *adv*.

radar *n* a system or device for detecting objects such as aircraft by using the reflection of radio waves.

radiance *n* the condition of being radiant; brilliant light; dazzling beauty.

radiant *adj* shining; beaming with happiness; sending out rays; transmitted by radiation.— **radiantly** *adv*.

radiate *vt* (*light, heat, etc*) to emit in rays; (*happiness, love, etc*) to give forth. * *vi* to spread out as if from a centre; to shine; to emit rays.

radiation *n* radiant particles emitted as energy; rays emitted in nuclear decay; (*med*) treatment using a radioactive substance.

radiator *n* an apparatus for heating a room; a cooling device for a vehicle engine.

radical *adj* of or relating to the root or origin; fundamental; favoring basic change. * *n* a person who advocates fundamental political or social change.— **radicalism** *n*.

radio *n* the transmission of sounds or signals by electromagnetic waves through space, without wires, to a receiving set; such a set; broadcasting by radio as an industry, etc. * *adj* of, using, used in, or sent by radio. * *vti* to transmit, or communicate with, by radio.

radio- *prefix* radial; radio; using radiant energy.

radioactive *adj* giving off radiant energy in the form of particles or rays caused by the disintegration of atomic nuclei.— **radioactivity** *n*.

radiography *n* the production of X-rays for use in medicine, industry, etc.— **radiographer** *n*.

radiology *n* a branch of medicine concerned with the use of radiant energy (as X-rays and radium) in the diagnosis and treatment of disease.— **radiologist** *n*.

radish *n* a pungent root eaten raw as a salad vegetable.

radium *n* a highly radioactive metallic element.

radius *n* (*pl* **radii** *or* **radiuses**) (*geom*) a straight line joining the centre of a circle or sphere to its circumference; a thing like this, a spoke; a sphere of activity; (*anat*) the thicker of the two bones of the forearm.

raffia *n* a kind of palm; fibre from its leaves used in basket-making, etc.

raffle *n* a lottery with prizes. * *vt* to offer as a prize in a raffle.

raft *n* a platform of logs, planks, etc strapped together to float on water.

rafter *n* one of the inclined, parallel beams that support a roof.

rag *n* a torn or waste scrap of cloth; a shred; (*inf*) a sensationalist newspaper; (*pl*) tattered or shabby clothing.

ragbag *n* a bag for scraps; a miscellaneous collection, jumble.

rage *n* violent anger; passion; frenzy; fashion, craze. * *vi* to behave with violent anger; to storm; to spread rapidly; to be prevalent.

ragged *adj* jagged; uneven; irregular; worn into rags; tattered.— **raggedly** *adv*.— **raggedness** *n*.

raid *n* a sudden attack to assault or seize. * *vt* to make a raid on; to steal from.— **raider** *n*.

rail[1] *n* a horizontal bar from one post to another, as in a fence, etc; one of a pair of parallel steel lines forming a track; a railway, railroad.

rail[2] *vi* to speak angrily.

railing *n* a fence of rails and posts; rails collectively.

railroad *n* a railway. * *vt* to force unduly; (*bill, etc*) to push forward fast; to imprison hastily, esp unjustly.

railway, railroad (*US*) *n* a track of parallel steel rails along which carriages are drawn by locomotive engines; a complete system of such tracks.

rain *n* water that falls from the clouds in the form of drops; a shower; a large quantity of anything falling like rain; (*pl*) the rainy season in the tropics. * *vti* (*of rain*) to fall; to fall like rain; (*rain, etc*) to pour down.

rainbow *n* the arc containing the colors of the spectrum formed in the sky by the sun's rays in falling rain or mist. * *adj* many-colored.

raincoat *n* a waterproof coat.

rainfall *n* a fall of rain; the amount of rain that falls on a given area in a specified time.

rainproof *adj* rain-resisting.

rainy *adj* (**rainier, rainiest**) full of rain; wet.

raise *vt* to elevate; to lift up; to set or place upright; to stir up, rouse; to increase in size, amount, degree, intensity, etc; to breed, bring up; (*question, etc*) to put forward; to collect or levy; (*siege*) to abandon. * *n* a rise in wages.

raisin *n* a sweet, dried grape.

raja, rajah *n* an Indian or Malay prince or ruler; an Indian title.

rake[1] *n* a tool with a row of teeth and a handle for gathering, scraping or smoothing. * *vt* to scrape, gather as with a rake; to sweep with gaze or gunshot; (*with* **in**: *money, etc*) to gather a great amount rapidly; (*with* **up**: *past misdemeanours, etc*) to bring to light.

rake[2] *n* the incline or slope of a mast, stern, etc.

rake[3] *n* a dissolute man.

rakish *adj* jaunty, dashing; dissolute. —**rakishly** *adv*.—**rakishness** *n*.

rally *vti* to bring or come together; to recover strength, revive; to take part in a rally. * *n* a large assembly of people; a recovery; (*tennis*) a lengthy exchange of shots; a competitive test of driving and navigational skills.

ram *n* a male sheep; a battering device; a piston; (*with cap*) Aries, the first sign of the zodiac. * *vt* (*pt* **rammed**) to force or drive; to crash; to cram; to thrust violently.

ramble *vi* to wander or stroll about for pleasure; (*plant*) to straggle; to write or talk aimlessly. * *n* a leisurely walk in the countryside.

rambler *n* a person who rambles; a climbing rose.

rambling *adj* spread out, straggling; circuitous; disconnected; disjointed. * *n* the act of walking for pleasure.

ramification *n* a branching out; an offshoot; a consequence.

ramp *n* a sloping walk or runway joining different levels; a wheeled staircase for boarding a plane; a sloping runway for launching boats, as from trailers.

rampage *n* angry or violent behaviour. * *vi* to rush about in an angry or violent manner.

rampant *adj* dominant; luxuriant, unrestrained; violent; rife, prevalent; (*her*) (of a lion) standing on its hind legs.

rampart *n* an embankment surrounding a fortification; a protective wall; (*Cdn*) steep rock walls, esp in a river gorge.

ramshackle *adj* dilapidated.

ran *see* **run**.

ranch *n* a large farm for raising cattle, horses, or sheep; a style of house with all the rooms on one floor. * *vi* to own, manage, or work on a ranch.—**rancher** *n*.

rancid *adj* having an unpleasant smell and taste, as stale fats or oil.—**rancidity, rancidness** *n*.

rancour, rancor (*US*) *n* bitter hate or spite.—**rancorous** *adj*.—**rancorously** *adv*.

random *adj* haphazard; left to chance.

randy *adj* (**randier, randiest**) (*sl*) lustful, sexually aroused.

rang *see* **ring**[2].

range *n* a row; a series of mountains, etc; scope, compass; the distance a vehicle, etc can travel without refuelling; the distance a bullet, etc can travel, or from gun to target; fluctuation; a large open area for grazing livestock; a place for testing rockets in flight; a place for shooting or golf practice; a cooking stove. * *vt* to place in order or a row; to establish the range of; (*livestock*) to graze on a range. * *vi* to be situated in a line; to rank or classify; (*gun*) to point or aim; to vary (inside limits).

ranger *n* a forest or park warden.

rank[1] *n* a line of objects; a line of soldiers standing abreast; high standing or position; status; (*pl*) ordinary members of the armed forces. * *vti* to arrange in a line; to have a specific position in an organization or on a scale; (*with* **with**) to be counted among.

rank[2] *adj* growing uncontrollably; utter, flagrant; offensive in odour or flavor.

rank and file *n* ordinary soldiers; ordinary members, as distinguished from their leaders.

rankle *vi* to fester; to cause continuous resentment or irritation.

ransack *vt* to plunder; to search thoroughly.

ransom *n* the release of a captured person or thing; the price paid for this. * *vt* to secure release of by payment.

rant *vi* to speak loudly or violently; to preach noisily. * *n* loud, pompous talk.

rap *n* a sharp blow; a knock; (*inf*) talk, conversation; (*sl*) arrest for a crime; (*sl*) a song that is rapped. * *vti* (*pt* **rapped**) to strike lightly or sharply; to knock; (*sl*) to criticize sharply; (*with* **out**) to utter abruptly; (*sl*) to speak a song accompanied by an insistent electronic rhythm.

rape[1] *n* the act of forcing a woman to have sexual intercourse against her will; a plundering. * *vti* to commit rape (upon).—**rapist** *n*.

rape[2] *n* a bright yellow plant of the mustard family grown for its leaves and oily seeds.

rape-shield *adj* (*Cdn*) pertaining to laws that limit what questions may be asked an alleged victim of a sexual assault on matters of personal, esp sexual, history.

rapid *adj* at great speed; fast; sudden; steep.
* *npl* a part of a river where the current flows swiftly.—**rapidity** *n*.—**rapidly** *adv*.

rapport *n* a sympathetic relationship; accord.

rapture *n* the state of being carried away with love, joy, etc; intense delight, ecstasy.—**rapturous** *adj*.—**rapturously** *adv*.

rare[1] *adj* unusual; seldom seen; exceptionally good; (*gas*) of low density, thin. *adv*.—**rareness** *n*.

rare[2] *adj* not completely cooked, partly raw; underdone.

rarefy *vti* to make or become less dense; to thin out; to expand without the addition of matter; to make more spiritual or refined.—**rarefied** *adj*.

rarely *adv* almost never; exceptionally, unusually.

rarity *n* rareness; a rare person or thing.

rascal *n* a rogue; a villain; a mischievous person.

rase *see* **raze**.

rash[1] *adj* reckless; impetuous.—**rashly** *adv*.—**rashness** *n*.

rash[2] *n* a skin eruption of spots, etc.

rasher *n* a thin slice of bacon or ham.

rasp *n* a coarse file; a grating sound. * *vt* to scrape with a rasp. * *vi* to produce a grating sound.—**rasping** *n*.

raspberry *n* a shrub with white flowers and red berry-like fruits; the fruit produced; (*inf*) a sound of dislike or derision.

rat *n* a long-tailed rodent similar to a mouse but larger; (*sl*) a sneaky, contemptible person. * *vi* (*pt* **ratted**) to hunt or catch rats; to betray or inform on someone.

ratchet *n* a device with a toothed wheel that moves in one direction only.

rate *n* the amount, degree, etc of something in relation to units of something else; price, esp per unit; degree. * *vt* to fix the value of; to rank; to regard or consider; (*sl*) to think highly of. * *vi* to have value or status.

rather *adv* more willingly; preferably; somewhat; more accurately; on the contrary; (*inf*) yes, certainly.

ratify *vt* to approve formally; to confirm.

rating *n* an assessment; an evaluation, an appraisal, as of credit worthiness; classification by grade, as of military personnel; (*radio, TV*) the relative popularity of a programme according to sample polls.

ratio *n* the number of times one thing contains another; the quantitative relationship between two classes of objects; proportion.

ration *n* (*food, petrol*) a fixed amount or portion; (*pl*) food supply. * *vt* to supply with rations; (*food, petrol*) to restrict the supply of.

rational *adj* of or based on reason; reasonable; sane.—**rationally** *adv*.

rationale *n* the reason for a course of action; an explanation of principles.

rationalize *vti* to make rational; to justify one's reasons for an action; to cut dow150

n on personnel or equipment; to substitute a natural for a supernatural explanation.—**rationalization** *n*.

rat race *n* continual hectic competitive activity.

rattle *vi* to clatter. * *vt* to make a series of sharp, quick noises; to clatter; to recite rapidly; to chatter; (*inf*) to disconcert, fluster.
* *n* a rattling sound; a baby's toy that makes a rattling sound; a voluble talker; the rings on the tail of a rattlesnake.

rattlesnake *n* a venomous American snake with a rattle in its tail.

raucous *adj* hoarse and harsh-sounding; loud and rowdy.

ravage *vt* to ruin, destroy; to plunder, lay waste.
* *n* destruction; ruin; (*pl*) the effects of this.

rave *vi* to speak wildly or as if delirious; (*inf*) to enthuse. * *n* enthusiastic praise.—**raving** *adj*.

raven *n* a large crow-like bird with glossy black feathers. * *adj* of the color or sheen of a raven.

ravenous *adj* very hungry; greedy.—**ravenously** *adv*.

ravine *n* a deep, narrow gorge, a large gully.

ravioli *n* small cases of pasta filled with highly seasoned chopped meat or vegetables.

ravish *vt* to violate; to rape; to captivate.

ravishing *adj* charming, captivating.

raw *adj* uncooked; unrefined; in a natural state, crude; untrained, inexperienced; sore, skinned; damp, chilly; (*inf*) harsh or unfair.—**rawness** *n*.

raw material *n* something out of which a finished article is made; something with a potential for development, improvement, etc.

ray[1] *n* a beam of light that comes from a bright source; any of several lines radiating from a centre; a beam of radiant energy, radioactive particles, etc; a tiny amount.

ray[2] *n* any of various fishes with a flattened body and the eyes on the upper surface.

rayon *n* a textile fibre made from a cellulose solution; a fabric of such fibres.

raze *vt* to demolish; to erase; to level to the ground.—*also* **rase**.

razor *n* a sharp-edged instrument for shaving.

RCL *abbr* = Royal Canadian Legion.

Rd *abbr* = road.

re *prep* concerning, with reference to.

reach *vti* to arrive at; to extend as far as; to make contact with; to pass, hand over; to attain, realize; to stretch out the hand; to extend in influence, space, etc; to carry, as sight, sound, etc; to try to get. * *n* the act or power of reaching; extent; mental range; scope; a continuous extent, esp of water.

react *vi* to act in response to a person or stimulus; to have a mutual or reverse effect; to revolt; (*chem*) to undergo a chemical reaction.

reaction *n* an action in response to a stimulus; a revulsion of feeling; exhaustion after excitement, etc; opposition to new ideas; (*chem*) an action set up by one substance in another.

reactionary adj, n (a person) opposed to political or social change.

reactor n a person or substance that undergoes a reaction; (chem) a vessel in which a reaction occurs; a nuclear reactor.

read vti (pt **read**) to understand something written; to speak aloud (from a book); to study by reading; to interpret, divine; to register, as a gauge; to foretell; (of a computer) to obtain (information) from; (sl) to hear and understand (a radio communication, etc); (with **about, of**) to learn by reading; to be phrased in certain words. * adj well-informed.

reader n a person who reads; one who reads aloud to others; a proofreader; a person who evaluates manuscripts; a textbook, esp on reading; a unit that scans material for computation or storage; a senior lecturer.

readership n all the readers of a certain publication, author, etc.

readily adv in a ready manner; willingly, easily.

reading n the act of one who reads; any material to be read; the amount measured by a barometer, meter, etc; a particular interpretation of a play, etc.

ready adj (**readier, readiest**) prepared; fit for use; willing; inclined, apt; prompt, quick; handy. * n the state of being ready, esp the position of a firearm aimed for firing; (sl) money. * vt to make ready.—**readiness** n.

ready-made adj made in standard sizes, not to measure.

real adj existing, actual, not imaginary; true, genuine, not artificial; (law) immovable, consisting of land or houses. * adv (sl) very; really.

real estate n property; land.

realism n practical outlook; (art, literature) the ability to represent things as they really are; (philos) the doctrine that the physical world has an objective existence.—**realist** n.

realistic adj matter-of-fact, not visionary; lifelike; of or relating to realism.—**realistically** adv.

reality n the fact or condition of being real; an actual fact or thing; truth.

realize vt to become fully aware of; (ambition, etc) to make happen; to cause to appear real; to convert into money, be sold for.—**realization** n.

really adv in fact, in reality; positively, very. * interj indeed.

realm n a kingdom, country; domain, region; sphere.

ream n a quantity of paper varying from 480 to 516 sheets; (pl: inf) a great amount.

reap vti to harvest; to gain (a benefit).

rear[1] n the back part or position, esp of an army; (sl) the rump. * adj of, at, or in the rear.

rear[2] vt to raise; (children) to bring up; to educate, nourish, etc. * vi (horse) to stand on the hind legs.

reason n motive or justification (of an action or belief); the mental power to draw conclusions and determine truth; a cause; moderation; sanity; intelligence. * vti to think logically (about); to analyse; to argue or infer.

reasonable adj able to reason or listen to reason; rational; sensible; not expensive; moderate, fair.—**reasonableness** n.—**reasonably** adv.

reassure vt to hearten; to give confidence to; to free from anxiety.—**reassurance** n.

rebate n a refund of part of an amount paid; discount.

rebel n a person who refuses to conform with convention. * vi (pt **rebelled**) to rise up against authority; to dissent.—**rebellion** n.—**rebellious** adj.

rebound vi to spring back after impact; to bounce back; to recover. * n a recoil; an emotional reaction.

rebuff vt to snub, repulse; to refuse unexpectedly.—also n.

rebuke vt to reprimand, chide. * n censure, a reprimand.

rebut vt (pt **rebutted**) to disprove or refute by argument, etc.—**rebuttal** n.

recall vt to call back; to bring back to mind, remember; to revoke. * n remembrance; a summons to return; the removal from office by popular vote.

recant vti to repudiate or retract a former opinion, declaration, or belief.—**recantation** n.

recap vti (pt **recapped**) to recapitulate. * n (inf) recapitulation.

recapitulate vt to state again, to summarize.—**recapitulation** n.

recapture vt to capture again; (a lost feeling, etc) to discover anew, regain. * n the act of recapturing; a thing or feeling recaptured.

recce n (sl) reconnaissance. * vti (pt **recced** or **recceed**) (sl) to reconnoitre.

recede vi to move back; to withdraw, retreat; to slope backwards; to grow less; to decline in value.

receding adj sloping backwards; disappearing from view; (hair) ceasing to grow at the temples.

receipt n the act of receiving; a written proof of this; (pl) amount received from business. * vt to acknowledge and mark as paid; to write a receipt for.

receive vt to acquire, to be given; to experience, to be subjected to; to admit, to allow; to greet on arrival; to accept as true; (stolen goods) to take in; to transfer electrical signals. * vi to be a recipient; to convert radio waves into perceptible signals.

receiver n a person who receives; equipment that receives electronic signals, esp on a telephone; (law) a person appointed to manage or hold in trust property in bankruptcy or pending a lawsuit.

recent adj happening lately, fresh; not long established, modern.—**recently** adv.

receptacle n a container.

reception n the act of receiving or being received; a welcome; a social gathering; a response, reaction; the quality of the sound or image produced by a radio or TV set.

receptionist *n* a person employed to receive visitors to an office, hotel, hospital, etc.

receptive *adj* able or quick to take in ideas or impressions.

recess *n* a temporary halting of work, a vacation; a hidden or inner place; an alcove or niche. * *vti* to place in a recess; to form a recess in; to take a recess.

recipe *n* a list of ingredients and directions for preparing food; a method for achieving an end.

recipient *n* a person who receives.

reciprocal *adj* done by each to the other; mutual; complementary; interchangeable; (*gram*) expressing a mutual relationship. * *n* (*math*) an expression so related to another that their product is 1.—**reciprocally** *adv*.—**reciprocity** *n*.

reciprocate *vti* to give in return; to repay; (*mech*) to move alternately backwards and forwards.—**reciprocating** *adj*.—**reciprocation** *n*.

recital *n* the act of reciting; a detailed account, narrative; a statement of facts; (*mus*) a performance given by an individual musician.

recite *vti* to repeat aloud from memory; to recount, enumerate; to repeat (a lesson).

reckless *adj* rash, careless, incautious.—**recklessly** *adv*.—**recklessness** *n*.

reckon *vti* to count; to regard or consider; to think; to calculate; (*with* **with**) to take into account.

reckoning *n* a calculation; the settlement of an account.

reclaim *vt* to recover, win back from a wild state or vice; (*wasteland*) to convert into land fit for cultivation; (*plastics, etc*) to obtain from waste materials.—**reclaimable** *adj*.—**reclamation** *n*.

recline *vti* to cause or permit to lean or bend backwards; to lie down on the back or side.—**reclinable** *adj*.

recluse *n* a person who lives in solitude; a hermit.

recognition *n* the act of recognizing; identification; acknowledgment, admission.

recognize *vt* to know again, identify; to greet; to acknowledge formally; to accept, admit.—**recognizable** *adj*.

recoil *vti* to spring back, kick, as a gun; to shrink or flinch. * *n* the act of recoiling, a rebound.

recollect *vti* to recall; to remind (oneself) of something temporarily forgotten; to call something to mind.

recollection *n* the act of recalling to mind; a memory, impression; something remembered; tranquillity of mind; religious contemplation.

recommend *vt* to counsel or advise; to commend or praise; to introduce favorably.—**recommendable** *adj*.—**recommendation** *n*.

recompense *n* to reward or pay an equivalent; to compensate. * *n* reward; repayment; compensation.

reconcile *vt* to re-establish friendly relations; to bring to agreement; to make compatible; to resolve; to settle; to make resigned (to); (*financial account*) to check with another account for accuracy.—**reconcilable** *adj*.—**reconciliation** *n*.

recondition *vt* to repair and restore to good working order.

reconnaissance *n* a survey of an area, esp for obtaining military information about an enemy.

reconnoitre, reconnoiter (*US*) *vti* to make a reconnaisance (of).

reconsider *vt* to consider afresh, review; to modify.—**reconsideration** *n*.

reconstruct *vt* to build again; to build up, as from remains, an image of the original; to supply missing parts by conjecture.—**reconstruction** *n*.

record *vti* to preserve evidence of; to write down; to chart; to register, enrol; to register permanently by mechanical means; (*sound or visual images*) to register on a disc, tape, etc for later reproduction; to celebrate. * *n* a written account; a register; a report of proceedings; the known facts about anything or anyone; an outstanding performance or achievement that surpasses others previously recorded; a grooved vinyl disc for playing on a record player; (*comput*) data in machine-readable form.

recorder *n* an official who keeps records; a machine or device that records; a tape recorder; a wind instrument of the flute family.

recording *n* what is recorded, as on a disc or tape; the record.

record player *n* an instrument for playing records through a loudspeaker.

recount *vt* to narrate the details of, to tell.

re-count *vt* to count again. * *n* a second counting of votes.

recoup *vti* to make good (financial losses); to regain; to make up for something lost.

recourse *n* a resort for help or protection when in danger; that to which one turns when seeking help.

recover *vti* to regain after losing; to reclaim; to regain health or after losing emotional control.—**recoverable** *adj*.

re-cover *vt* to put a new cover on.

recovery *n* the act or process of recovering; the condition of having recovered; reclamation; restoration; a retrieval of a capsule, etc after a space flight.

re-create *vt* to create over again, esp mentally.

recreation *n* relaxation of the body or mind; a sport, pastime or amusement.—**recreational** *adj*.

recruit *n* a soldier newly enlisted; a member newly joined; a beginner. * *vti* to enlist; to increase or maintain the numbers of; to restore, refresh.—**recruitment** *n*.

rectangle *n* a four-sided geometric figure with

all its angles right angles.—**rectangular** adj.

rectify vt to put right, correct; to amend; (chem) to refine by repeated distillation; (elect) to convert to direct current.—**rectifiable** adj.

rector n in some churches, a clergyman in charge of a parish; the head of certain schools, colleges, etc.

rectory n the house of a minister or priest.

recuperate vti to get well again; to recover (losses, etc).—**recuperation** n.

recur vi (pt **recurred**) to be repeated in thought, talk, etc; to occur again or at intervals.—**recurrence** n.—**recurrent** adj.

red adj (**redder, reddest**) of the color of blood; politically left-wing. * n the color of blood; any red pigment; a communist.

red carpet n a strip of red carpet for dignitaries to walk on; a grand or impressive welcome or entertainment.

Red Chamber n (Cdn) the Canadian House of Commons.

Red Cross n a red cross on a white ground, the symbol of the International Red Cross, a society for the relief of suffering in time of war and disaster.

red currant n a cultivated red clustered fruit.

redden vti to make or become red; to blush.

reddish adj tinged with red.—**reddishness** n.

redeem vt to recover by payment; to regain; to deliver from sin; to pay off; to restore to favor; to make amends for.—**redeemable** adj.—**redeemer** n.

redeploy vt (troops, workers) to assign to new positions or activities.—**redeployment** n.

red-handed adj caught in the act of committing a crime.

redhead n a person having red hair.—**redheaded** adj.

red herring n a herring cured to a dark brown color; something that diverts attention from the real issue.

red-hot adj glowing with heat; extremely hot; very excited, angry, etc; very new.

redirect vt to change the direction or course of; to readdress.—**redirection** n.

red light n a warning signal, a cautionary sign; a deterrent.—also adj.

redolent adj having a strong scent, fragrant; reminiscent (of).—**redolence** n.

redouble vti to double again; to make or become twice as much.

red pine n a pine with reddish wood, esp of northeast North America.

redress vt to put right, adjust; to compensate, make up for. * n remedy; compensation.

red tape n rigid adherence to bureaucratic routine and regulations, causing delay.

reduce vt to diminish or make smaller in size, amount, extent, or number; to lower in price; to simplify; to make thin; to subdue; to bring or convert (to another state or form).—**reducible** adj.—**reduction** n.

redundant adj surplus to requirements; (person) deprived of one's job as being no longer necessary; (words) unnecessary to the meaning, excessive.—**redundancy** n.

reed n a tall grass found in marshes; a thin piece of cane in the mouthpiece of a musical instrument; a person or thing too weak to rely on; one easily swayed or overcome.

reef n a ridge of rocks, sand, or coral in water; a hazardous obstruction; a vein of ore.

reek n a strong smell. * vi to give off smoke, fumes or a strong or offensive smell.

reel[1] n a winding device; a spool or bobbin; thread wound on this; a length of film, about 300m (1,000ft). * vt to wind on to a reel; (with in) to draw in (fish, etc) by means of a reel; (with off) to tell, write, etc, with fluency; (with out) to unwind from a reel.

reel[2] vi to stagger or sway about; to be dizzy or in a whirl. * n a staggering motion.

reel[3] n a lively Scottish or Irish dance; the music for it. * vi to dance a reel.

reeve n (Cdn) an elected leader of a town or municipal council.—**reeveship** n.

ref. abbr = with reference to.

refectory n the dining hall of a monastery, college, etc.

refer vti (pt **referred**) to attribute, assign (to); (with to) to direct, have recourse (to); to relate to; to mention or allude to; to direct attention (to).—**referable** adj.

referee n an arbitrator; an umpire; a judge.

reference n the act of referring; a mention or allusion; a testimonial; a person who gives a testimonial; a direction to a passage in a book; a passage referred to.

reference book n a book for reference rather than general reading, eg a yearbook, directory.

referendum n (pl **referenda, referendums**) the submission of an issue directly to the vote of the electorate, a plebiscite.

refill vt to fill again. * n a replacement pack for an empty permanent container; a providing again.

refine vti to purify; to make free from impurities or coarseness; to make or become cultured.

refined adj polished, cultured; affected.

refinement n fineness of manners or taste; an improvement; a fine distinction.

refinery n a plant where raw materials, eg sugar, oil, are refined.

reflect vt (light, heat, etc) to throw back; to bend aside or back; to show an image of, as a mirror; to express. * vi to reproduce to the eye or mind; to mirror; to meditate; (with upon) to ponder; (with on) to discredit, disparage.

reflection, reflexion n a reflecting back, turning aside; the action of changing direction when a ray strikes and is thrown back; reflected heat, light or color; a reflected image; meditation, thought; reconsideration; reproach.

reflector n a disc, instrument, strip or other surface that reflects light or heat.

reflex n an involuntary response to a stimulus. * adj (angle) of more than 180 degrees; (camera) with a full-size viewfinder using the main lens.

reflexive adj (pron, verb) referring back to the

subject.—**reflexively** adv.

reform vti to improve; to make or become better by the removal of faults; to amend; to abolish abuse. * n improvement or transformation, esp of an institution; removal of social ills.—**reformed** adj.

reformer n a person who advocates or works for reform; an apparatus for changing molecular structure.

refrain[1] vi to abstain (from).

refrain[2] n recurring words in a song or poem; a chorus.

refresh vt to revive; to give new energy to; to make cool; to take a drink.

refresher n something that refreshes, esp a drink; a reminder; a training course to renew one's skill or knowledge.

refreshment n the act of refreshing; a restorative; (pl) food and drink; a light meal.

refrigerator n something that refrigerates; a chamber for keeping food, etc, cool; an apparatus for cooling.

refuel vti (pt **refuelled**) to supply with or take on fresh fuel.

refuge n a protection or shelter from danger; a retreat, sanctuary.

refugee n a person who flees to another country to escape political or religious persecution.

refund vti to repay; to reimburse. * n a refunding or the amount refunded.

refusal n the act or process of refusing; the choice of refusing or accepting.

refurbish vt to renovate or re-equip.—**refurbishment** n.

refuse[1] n rubbish, garbage, waste.

refuse[2] vt to decline, reject; to withhold, deny. * vi (horse) to decline to jump.

refute vt to rebut; to disprove.—**refutable** adj.—**refutably** adv.—**refutation** n.

regain vt to get back, recover; to reach again.

regal adj royal; relating to a king or queen.

regalia npl royal badges or prerogatives; the badges of an order, office, or membership; finery.

regard vt to gaze at, observe; to hold in respect; to consider; to heed, take into account. * n a look; attention; reference; respect, esteem; (pl) good wishes, greetings.

regarding prep with reference to, about.

regardless adj having no regard to. * adv (inf) in spite of everything; without heeding the cost, consequences, etc.

regatta n a meeting for yacht or boat races.

regency n the status or authority of a regent; rule by a regent; (with cap) in British history, the period 1810-20.

regent n a person who rules or administers a country during the sovereign's minority, absence, or incapacity; a member of a governing board (as of a university).

regime n a political or ruling system.

regiment n a military unit, smaller than a division, consisting usu of a number of battalions. * vt to organize in a strict manner; to subject to order or conformity.—**regimental** adj.

regimentation n the act of regimenting; excessive orderliness.

region n a large, indefinite part of the earth's surface; one of the zones into which the atmosphere is divided; an administrative area of a country; a part of the body.—**regional** adj.

register n an official list; a written record, as for attendance; the book containing such a record or list; a tone of voice; a variety of language appropriate to a subject or occasion; (comput) a device in which data can be stored and operated on; (print) exact alignment; a device for indicating speed, etc; a plate regulating draught. * vti to record; to enter in or sign a register; to correspond exactly; to entrust a letter to the post with special precautions for safety; to express emotion facially; to make or convey an impression.

registered adj recorded officially; qualified formally or officially.

registrar n a person who keeps records, esp one in an educational institution in charge of student records; a hospital doctor below a specialist in rank.

registration n the act of registering; the condition of having registered.

registry n registration; a place where records are kept; an official record book.

registry office n an office where civil marriages are held, and births and deaths recorded.

regret vt (pt **regretted**) to feel sorrow, grief, or loss; to remember with longing; (with that) to repent of. * n disappointment; sorrow; grief; (pl) polite refusal.—**regretful** adj.—**regretfully** adv.

regrettable adj to be regretted; deserving blame.—**regrettably** adv.

regular adj normal; habitual, not casual; at fixed intervals; according to rule, custom, or practice; uniform, consistent; symmetrical; fully qualified; belonging to a standing army; (inf) thorough, complete; (inf) pleasant, friendly. * n a professional soldier; (inf) a person who attends regularly.—**regularity** n.—**regularly** adv.

regulate vt to control according to a rule; to cause to conform to a standard or needs; to adjust so as to put in good order.—**regulatory** adj.

regulation n the act of regulating; a being regulated; a prescribed rule, decree. * adj normal, standard.

rehabilitate vt (prisoner etc) to help adapt to society after a stay in an institution; to put back in good condition; to restore to rights or privileges; (sick person etc) to help to adjust to normal conditions after illness.—**rehabilitation** n.

rehash n old materials put in a new form. * vt to dish up again.

rehearse vti to practise repeatedly before public performance; to recount, narrate in detail.—**rehearsal** n.

reign *n* the rule of a sovereign; the period of this; influence; domination. * *vi* to rule; to prevail.

reimburse *vt* to repay; to refund (for expense or loss).—**reimbursable** *adj*.—**reimbursement** *n*.

rein *n* the strap of a bridle for guiding or restraining a horse; (*pl*) a means of control or restraint. * *vt* to control with the rein; to restrain.

reincarnation *n* the incarnation of the soul after death in another body.—**reincarnate** *adj*, *vt*.

reindeer *n* a large deer with branched antlers found in northern regions.

reinforce *vt* (*army etc*) to strengthen with fresh troops; (*a material*) to add to the strength of.—**reinforcement** *n*.

reinstate *vt* to restore to a former position, rank, or condition.—**reinstatement** *n*.

reiterate *vt* to repeat; to say or do again or many times.—**reiteration** *n*.

reject *vt* to throw away, to discard; to refuse to accept, to decline; to rebuff. * *n* a thing or person rejected.—**rejection** *n*.

rejoice *vi* to feel joyful or happy.

rejuvenate *vt* to give youthful vigour to.—**rejuvenation** *n*.

relapse *vi* to fall back into a worse state after improvement; to return to a former vice. * *n* the recurrence of illness after apparent recovery.

relate *vt* to narrate, recount; to show a connection. * *vi* to have a formal relationship (with).

related *adj* connected, allied; akin.

relation *n* the way in which one thing stands in respect to another, footing; reference, regard; connection by blood or marriage; a relative; a narration, a narrative; (*pl*) the connections between or among persons, nations, etc; (*pl*) one's family and in-laws.

relationship *n* the tie or degree of kinship or intimacy; affinity; (*inf*) an affair.

relative *adj* having or expressing a relation; corresponding; pertinent; comparative, conditional; respective; meaningful only in relationship; (*gram*) referring to a previous noun, clause, etc. * *n* a person related by blood or marriage.—**relatively** *adv*.

relax *vti* to slacken; to make or become less severe or strict; to make (the muscles) less rigid; to take a rest.

relaxation *n* the act of relaxing; the condition of being relaxed; recreation.

relay *n* a team of fresh horses, men, etc to relieve others; a race between teams, each member of which goes a part of the distance; (*elect*) a device for enabling a weak current to control others; a relayed broadcast. * *vt* (*pt* **relayed**) (*news, etc*) to spread in stages; to broadcast signals.

release *vt* to set free; to let go; to relinquish; (*film, etc*) to issue for public exhibition; (*information*) to make available; (*law*) to make over to another. * *n* a releasing, as from prison, work, etc; a device to hold or release a mechanism; a news item, etc, released to the public; (*law*) a written surrender of a claim.

relegate *vt* to move to an inferior position; to demote; to banish.—**relegation** *n*.

relent *vi* to soften in attitude; to become less harsh or severe.

relentless *adj* pitiless; unremitting.

relevant *adj* applying to the matter in hand, pertinent; to the point.—**relevance** *n*.—**relevancy** *n*.

reliable *adj* dependable, trustworthy.—**reliability** *n*.—**reliably** *adv*.

relic *n* an object, fragment, or custom that has survived from the past; part of a saint's body or belongings; (*pl*) remains of the dead.

relief *n* the sensation following the easing or lifting of discomfort or stress; release from a duty by another person; a person who takes the place of another on duty; that which relieves; aid; assistance to the needy or victims of a disaster; the projection of a carved design from its ground; distinctness, vividness. * *adj* providing relief in disasters etc.

relieve *vt* to bring relief or assistance to; to release from obligation or duty; to ease; (*with* **oneself**) to empty the bladder or bowels. * *vi* to give relief; to break the monotony of; to bring into relief, to stand out.

religion *n* a belief in God or gods; a system of worship and faith; a formalized expression of belief.

relinquish *vt* to give up; to renounce or surrender.—**relinquishment** *n*.

relish *n* an appetizing flavor; a distinctive taste; enjoyment of food or an experience; a spicy accompaniment to food; gusto, zest. * *vt* to like the flavor of; to enjoy, appreciate.

reluctant *adj* unwilling, loath; offering resistance.—**reluctance** *n*.—**reluctantly** *adv*.

rely *vi* to depend on; to trust.

remain *vi* to stay behind or in the same place; to continue to be; to survive, to last; to be left over. * *npl* anything left after use; a corpse.

remainder *n* what is left, the rest; (*math*) the result of subtraction, the quantity left over after division; (*books*) unsold stock; (*law*) the residual interest in an estate.

remand *vt* to send back into custody for further evidence.—*also n*.

remark *vti* to notice; to observe; to pass a comment (upon). * *n* a brief comment.

remarkable *adj* unusual; extraordinary; worthy of comment.—**remarkably** *adv*.

remedial *adj* providing a remedy; correcting; relating to the teaching of people with learning difficulties.

remedy *n* a medicine or any means to cure a disease; anything that puts something else to rights. * *vt* to cure; to put right.

remember *vti* to recall; to bear in mind; to mention (a person) to another as sending regards; to exercise or have the power of memory.

remembrance *n* a reminiscence; a greeting or

gift recalling or expressing friendship or affection; the extent of memory; an honoring of the dead or a past event.

remind vt to cause to remember.

reminder n a thing that reminds, esp a letter from a creditor.

reminisce vi to think, talk, or write about past events.

reminiscence n the recalling of a past experience; (pl) memoirs.

reminiscent adj reminding, suggestive (of); recalling the past.

remission n the act of remitting; the reduction in length of a prison term; the lessening of the symptoms of a disease; pardon, forgiveness.

remit vti (pt **remitted**) to forgive; to refrain from inflicting (a punishment) or exacting (a debt); to abate, moderate; to send payment (by post); (law) to refer to a lower court for reconsideration. * n the act of referring; an area of authority.

remittance n the sending of money or a payment (by post); the payment or money sent.

remnant n a small remaining fragment or number; an oddment or scrap; a trace; an unsold or unused end of piece goods.

remorse n regret and guilt for a misdemeanour; compassion.—**remorseful** adj.—**remorsefully** adv.

remorseless adj ruthless, cruel; relentless.—**remorselessly** adv.—**remorselessness** n.

remote adj far apart or distant in time or place; out of the way; not closely related; secluded; aloof; vague, faint.—**remotely** adv.

remote control n the control of a device or activity from a distance, usu by means of an electric circuit or the making or breaking of radio waves.

removal n the act of removing; a change of home or office; dismissal.

remove vti to take away and put elsewhere; to dismiss, as from office; to get rid of; to kill; to go away. * n a stage in gradation; a degree in relationship.—**removable** adj.

remunerate vt to pay for a service; to reward.—**remuneration** n.

rend vti (pt **rent**) to tear, to wrench (apart); to be torn apart.

render vt (payments, accounts, etc) to submit, as for approval;to give back; to pay back; to perform; to represent as by drawing; to translate, interpret; to cause to be; (fat) to melt down.

rendering n interpretation, translation.

rendezvous n (pl **rendezvous**) an arranged meeting; a place to meet; a popular haunt; the process of bringing two spacecraft together. * vi to meet by appointment.

renegade n a deserter; a person who is faithless to a principle, party, religion, or cause.

renew vti to restore to freshness or vigour; to begin again; to make or get anew; to replace; to grant or obtain an extension of.—**renewable** adj.—**renewal** n.

reno n (Cdn) (inf) a renovated house; renova-

tion.

renounce vt to abandon formally; to give up; to disown.

renovate vt to renew; to restore to good condition; to do up, repair.—**renovation** n.—**renovator** n.

renown n fame, celebrity.

renowned adj famous, illustrious.

rent¹ see **rend**.

rent² n regular payment to another for the use of a house, machinery, etc. * vti to occupy as a tenant; to hire; to let for rent.

rental n an amount paid or received as rent; a house, car, etc, for rent; an act of renting; a business that rents something.

renunciation n the act of renouncing; formal abandonment; repudiation.

re-offer n (Cdn) be a candidate for re-election.

rep abbr = representative; repertory.

repair vt to mend; to restore to good working order; to make amends for. * n the act of repairing; a place repaired; condition as to soundness.

repartee n a witty reply; skill in making such replies.

repay vt (pt **repaid**) to pay back; to refund.—**repayable** adj.—**repayment** n.

repeal vt to annul, to rescind; to revoke.—also n.

repeat vti to say, write, or do again; to reiterate; to recite after another or from memory; to reproduce; to recur. * n a repetition, encore; anything said or done again, as a rebroadcast of a TV programme; (mus) a passage to be repeated; the sign for this.—**repeatable** adj.

repeatedly adv many times, over and over again.

repel vt (pt **repelled**) to drive back; to beat off, repulse; to reject; to hold off; to cause distaste; (water, dirt) to be resistant to.

repellent adj distasteful, unattractive; capable of repelling. * n a substance that repels, esp a spray for protection against insects.

repent vi to wish one had not done something; to feel remorse or regret (for); to regret and change from evil ways.—**repentance** n.—**repentant** adj.

repercussion n a rebound; a reverberation; a far-reaching, often indirect reaction to an event.

repertoire n the stock of plays, songs, etc, that a company, singer, etc, can perform.

repertory n a repertoire; the system of alternating several plays through a season with a permanent acting group.

repetition n the act of repeating; something repeated, a copy.—**repetitive** adj.

replace vt to put back; to take the place of, to substitute for; to supersede.—**replaceable** adj.—**replacement** n.

replenish vt to stock again, refill.—**replenishment** n.

replete adj filled, well provided; stuffed, gorged.

replica n an exact copy; a reproduction.

reply vti to answer, respond; to give as an answer. * n an answer.

report *vti* to give an account of; to tell as news; to take and describe for publication; to make a formal statement of; to complain about or against; to inform against; to present oneself (for duty). * *n* an account of facts; the formal statement of the findings of an investigation; a newspaper, radio or TV account of an event; a rumour; a sharp, loud noise, as of a gun.

reporter *n* a person who gathers and reports news for a newspaper, radio or TV; a person authorized to make statements concerning law decisions or legislative proceedings.

reprehensible *adj* blameworthy, culpable.

represent *vt* to portray; to describe; to typify; to stand for, symbolize; to point out; to perform on the stage; to act as an agent for; to deputize for; to serve as a specimen, example, etc, of.—**representable** *adj*.

representation *n* the act of representing or being represented, as in a parliamentary assembly; a portrait, reproduction; (*pl*) a presentation of claims, protests, views, etc.

representative *adj* typical; portraying; consisting of or based on representation of the electorate by delegates. * *n* an example or type; a person who acts for another; a delegate, agent, salesman, etc.

repress *vt* to suppress, restrain; (*emotions*) to keep under control; to exclude involuntarily from the conscious mind.—**repression** *n*.—**repressive** *adj*.

reprieve *vt* to postpone or commute the punishment of; to give respite to.—*also n*.

reprimand *n* a formal rebuke. * *vt* to reprove formally.

reprisal *n* an act of retaliation for an injury done.

reproach *vt* to accuse of a fault; to blame. * *n* a rebuke; a source of shame or disgrace.—**reproachful** *adj*.

reproduce *vti* to make a copy, duplicate, or likeness of; to produce offspring; to multiply.

reproduction *n* the act of reproducing; the process by which plants and animals breed; a copy or likeness; a representation.—**reproductive** *adj*.

reprove *vt* to rebuke, censure.—**reprovingly** *adv*.

reptile *n* any of a class of cold-blooded, air-breathing vertebrates with horny scales or plates; a grovelling or despised person.—**reptilian** *adj*.

republic *n* a government in which the people elect the head of state and in which the people and their elected representatives have supreme power; a country governed in this way.

republican *adj* of, characteristic of, or supporting a republic. * *n* an advocate of republican government; (*with cap*) a member of the US Republican party.—**republicanism** *n*.

repudiate *vt* to reject, disown; to refuse to acknowledge or pay; to deny.—**repudiation** *n*.

repugnant *adj* distasteful, offensive; contradictory; incompatible.—**repugnance** *n*.

repulse *vt* to drive back; to repel; to reject. * *n* a

rebuff, rejection; a defeat, check.

repulsion *n* a feeling of disgust; aversion; (*physics*) the tendency of bodies to repel each other.

repulsive *adj* disgusting; detestable; exercising repulsion.—**repulsively** *adv*.

reputable *adj* of good repute, respectable.—**reputably** *adv*.

reputation *n* the estimation in which a person or thing is held; good name, honor.

repute *vt* to consider to be, to deem. * *n* reputation.

reputed *adj* generally reported; supposed.

reputedly *adv* in common estimation; by repute.

request *n* an asking for something; a petition; a demand; the thing asked for. * *vt* to ask for earnestly.

requiem *n* a mass for the dead; music for this.

require *vt* to demand; to need, call for; to order, command.

requirement *n* a need or want; an essential condition.

requisite *adj* needed; essential, indispensable. * *n* something required or indispensable.

requisition *n* a formal request, demand, or order, as for military supplies; the taking over of private property, etc for military use. * *vt* to order; to take by requisition.

res *n* (*Cdn*) (*inf*) a school or university residence for students.

rescind *vt* to annul, cancel.

rescue *vt* to save (a person, thing) from captivity, danger, or harm; to free forcibly from legal custody.—*also n*.—**rescuer** *n*.

research *n* a diligent search; a systematic and careful investigation of a particular subject; a scientific study. * *vi* to carry out an investigation; to study.—**researcher** *n*.

resemble *vt* to be like, to have a similarity to.—**resemblance** *n*.

resent *vt* to be indignant about; to begrudge; to take badly.—**resentful** *adj*.—**resentfully** *adv*.—**resentment** *n*.

reservation *n* the act of reserving; (*of tickets, accommodation, etc*) a holding until called for; a limitation or proviso; (*pl*) doubt, scepticism; land set aside for a special purpose.

reserve *vt* to hold back for future use; to retain; to have set aside; (*tickets, hotel room, etc*) to book. * *n* something put aside for future use; land set aside for wild animals; (*Cdn*) an area of land set apart for the use of a First Nations community; (*sport*) a substitute; (*mil*) a force supplementary to a regular army; a restriction or qualification; reticence of feelings; caution.—**reservable** *adj*.

reserved *adj* set apart, booked; uncommunicative, lacking cordiality.—**reservedly** *adv*.

reservoir *n* a tank or artificial lake for storing water; an extra supply or store.

reside *vi* to live in a place permanently; to be vested or present in.

residence *n* the act of living in a place; the period of residing; the house where one lives permanently; the status of a legal resident; a building used as a home.

residential *adj* of or relating to residence; used for private homes.

residential school *n* (*Cdn*) a boarding school for First Nations or Inuit students.

residue *n* a remainder; a part left over; what is left of an estate after payment of debts and legacies.

resign *vti* to give up (employment, etc); to relinquish; to yield to; to reconcile (oneself).

resignation *n* the resigning of office, etc; the written proof of this; patient endurance.

resigned *adj* submissive, acquiescent; accepting the inevitable.

resilient *adj* elastic, springing back; buoyant; (*person*) capable of carrying on after suffering hardship.—**resilience** *n*.—**resiliently** *adv*.

resin *n* a sticky substance exuded in the sap of trees and plants and used in medicines, varnishes, etc; a similar synthetic substance used in plastics.—**resinous** *adj*.

resist *vti* to fight against; to be proof against; to oppose or withstand.

resistance *n* the act of resisting; the power to resist, as to ward off disease; opposition, esp to an occupying force; hindrance; (*elect*) non-conductivity, opposition to a steady current.

resolute *adj* determined; firm of purpose, steadfast.—**resolutely** *adv*.—**resoluteness** *n*.

resolution *n* the act of resolving or the state of being resolved; determination; a fixed intention; the formal decision or opinion of a meeting; analysis, disintegration; (*med*) the dispersion of a tumour, etc; the picture definition in a TV.

resolve *vt* to break into component parts, dissolve; to convert or be converted (into); to analyse; to determine, make up one's mind; to solve, settle; to vote by resolution; to dispel (doubt); to explain; to conclude; (*med: tumour*) to disperse. * *n* a fixed intention; resolution; courage.

resonant *adj* ringing; resounding, echoing.

resort *n* a popular holiday location; a source of help, support, etc; recourse. * *vi* to have recourse to; to turn (to) for help, etc.

resound *vti* to echo; to reverberate; to go on sounding; to be much talked of; to spread (fame).

resounding *adj* echoing; notable; thorough.

resource *n* source of help; an expedient; the ability to cope with a situation; a means of diversion; (*pl*) wealth; assets; raw materials.

resourceful *adj* able to cope in difficult situations; ingenious.—**resourcefulness** *n*.

respect *n* esteem; consideration; regard; (*pl*) good wishes; reference; relation. * *vt* to feel or show esteem or regard to; to treat considerately.

respectable *adj* worthy of esteem; well-behaved; proper, correct, well-conducted; of moderate quality or size.—**respectability** *n*.—**respectably** *adv*.

respective *adj* proper to each, several.

respectively *adv* in the indicated order.

respiration *n* the act or process of breathing.

respite *n* a temporary delay; a period of rest or relief; a reprieve.

resplendent *adj* dazzling, shining brilliantly; magnificent.

respond *vti* to answer; to reply; to show a favorable reaction; to be answerable; (*with* **to**) to react.

response *n* an answer; a reaction to stimulation.

responsibility *n* being responsible; a moral obligation or duty; a charge or trust; a thing one is responsible for.

responsible *adj* having control (over); (*with* **for**) accountable (for); capable of rational conduct; trustworthy; involving responsibility.—**responsibly** *adv*.

responsive *adj* responding; sensitive to influence or stimulus; sympathetic.

rest¹ *n* stillness, sleep; inactivity; the state of not moving; relaxation; tranquillity; a support or prop; a pause in music, etc; a place of quiet. * *vti* to take a rest; to give rest to; to be still; to lie down; to relax; to be fixed (on); to lean, support or be supported; to put one's trust (in).

rest² *n* the remainder; the others. * *vi* to remain.

restaurant *n* a place where meals can be bought and eaten.

restful *adj* peaceful.—**restfully** *adv*.—**restfulness** *n*.

rest home *n* an old people's home; a convalescent home.

restitution *n* the restoring of something to its owner; a reimbursement, as for loss.

restive *adj* impatient; fidgety.

restless *adj* unsettled; agitated.—**restlessly** *adv*.—**restlessness** *n*.

restoration *n* the act of restoring; reconstruction; renovation; (*with cap*) the re-establishment of the monarchy in Britain in 1660 under Charles II.

restore *vt* to give or put back; to re-establish; to repair; to renovate; to bring back to the original condition.—**restorer** *n*.

restrain *vt* to hold back; to restrict; (*person*) to deprive of freedom.

restrained *adj* moderate; self-controlled; without exuberance.

restraint *n* the ability to hold back; something that restrains; control of emotions, impulses, etc.

restrict *vt* to keep within limits, circumscribe.

restricted *adj* affected by restriction; limited; not generally available.

restriction *n* restraint; limitation; a limiting regulation.—**restrictive** *adj*.

rest room *n* a room equipped with toilets, washbowls, etc for the use of the public.

result *vi* to have as a consequence; to terminate in. * *n* a consequence; an outcome; a value obtained by mathematical calculation; (*sport*) the final score; (*pl*) a desired effect.

resume *vti* to begin again; to continue after a stop or pause; to proceed after interruption.—**resumption** n.

resurgence n a revival; a renewal of activity.—**resurgent** adj.

resurrection n a revival; a rising from the dead; (with cap) the rising of Christ from the dead.

resuscitate vti to revive when apparently dead or unconscious.—**resuscitation** n.

retail n selling directly to the consumer in small quantities. * adv at a retail price. * vti to sell or be sold by retail.—also adj.—**retailer** n.—**retailing** n.

retain vt to keep possession of; to keep in the mind, to remember; to keep in place, support; to hire the services of.

retainer n that which returns; (formerly) a servant to a family, a dependant; a fee to retain the services of.

retaliate vti to revenge oneself, usu by returning like for like; to strike back; to cast back (an accusation).—**retaliation** n.—**retaliatory** adj.

retarded adj slow in physical or mental development.

retch vi to heave as if to vomit.

rethink vt (pt **rethought**) to consider or think about again, esp with a change in mind.

reticent adj reserved in speech; uncommunicative.—**reticence** n.

retina n (pl **retinas, retinae**) the innermost part of the eye, on which the image is formed.

retinue n a body of attendants.

retire vi to give up one's work when pensionable age is reached; to withdraw; to retreat; to go to bed. * vt (troops) to withdraw from use; to compel to retire from a position, work, etc.—**retirement** n.

retiring adj unobtrusive; shy.

retort vi to reply sharply or wittily. * n a sharp or witty reply; a vessel with a funnel bent downwards used in distilling; a receptacle used in making gas and steel.

retract vti to draw in or back; to withdraw (a statement, opinion, etc); to recant.—**retractable** adj.—**retraction** n.

retreat vi to withdraw, retire; to recede. * n a withdrawal, esp of troops; a sign for retiring; a quiet or secluded place, refuge; seclusion for religious devotion.

retrial n a second trial.

retribution n deserved reward; something given or exacted in compensation, esp punishment.

retrieve vt to recover; to revive; (a loss) to make good; (comput) to obtain information from data stored in a computer. * vi (dogs) to retrieve game.—**retrievable** adj.—**retrieval** n.

retriever n any of several breeds of dogs capable of being trained for retrieving.

retrospect n a looking back; a mental review of the past.—**retrospection** n.

return vi to come or go back; to reply; to recur. * vt to give or send back; to repay; to yield; to answer; to elect. * n something returned; a recurrence; recompense; (pl)

yield, revenue; a form for computing (income) tax.

reunion n a meeting following separation; a social gathering of former colleagues.

reunite vt to unite again; to reconcile. * vi to become reunited.

rev vt (pt **revved**) (inf) (with **up**) to increase the speed of an engine. * n revolution per minute.

revamp vt to renovate, to rework, remodel; to transform. * n the process of revamping; something revamped.

RevCan n (Cdn) (inf) Revenue Canada.

reveal vt (something hidden or secret) to make known; to expose; to make visible.

reveille n a morning bugle call to wake soldiers.

revel vi (pt **revelled**) (with **in**) to take pleasure or delight in; to make merry. * n (pl) merrymaking; entertainment.—**reveller** n.—**revelry** n.

revelation n the act of revealing; the disclosure of something secret; a communication from God to man; an illuminating experience.

revenge vt to inflict punishment in return for; to satisfy oneself by retaliation; to avenge. * n the act of revenging; retaliation; a vindictive feeling.—**revenger** n.

revengeful adj keen for revenge; vindictive.

revenue n the total income produced by taxation; gross income from a business or investment.

Revenue Canada n (Cdn) the federal government department responsible for collecting taxes.

reverberate vi to rebound, recoil; to be reflected in; to resound, to echo.—**reverberation** n.

reverence n profound respect; devotion; a gesture of respect (such as a bow). * vt to hold in respect.

reverent adj feeling or expressing reverence.—**reverently** adv.

reverie n a daydream; (mus) a dreamy piece.—also **revery**.

reversal n the act or process of reversing.

reverse vti to turn in the opposite direction; to turn outside in, upside down, etc; to move backwards; (law) to revoke or annul. * n the contrary or opposite of something; the back, esp of a coin; a setback; a mechanism for reversing. * adj opposite, contrary; causing movement in the opposite direction.

reversing falls n (Cdn) a set of rapids on a tidal river, the flow of which reverses at intervals because of the pressure of the incoming tide.

reversion n return to a former condition or type; right to future possession.—**reversionary** adj.

revert vi to go back (to a former state); to take up again (a former subject); (biol) to return to a former or primitive type; (law) to go back to a former owner or his heirs.—**revertible** adj.

review n an evaluation; a survey; a reconsideration; a critical assessment; a periodical containing critical essays; an official inspection of ships or troops. * vt to re-examine; to inspect formally; to write an assessment of.

reviewer n a person who writes a review, esp for a newspaper, a critic.

revise vt to correct and amend; to prepare a new, improved version of; to study again (for an examination).—revision n.

revival n the act of reviving; recovery from a neglected or depressed state; renewed performance (of a play); renewed interest in; religious awakening.

revive vti to return to life; to make active again; to take up again.—reviver n.

revoke vt to cancel; to rescind. * vi (cards) to fail to follow suit.—revocable adj.—revocation n.

revolt vt to rebel; to overturn; to shock. * vi to feel great disgust. * n rebellion; uprising; loathing.

revolting adj extremely offensive.—revoltingly adv.

revolution n the act of revolting; a motion round a centre or axis; a single completion of an orbit or rotation; a great change; an overthrow of a government, social system, etc.

revolutionary adj of, advocating revolution; radically new. * n a person who takes part in or favors revolution.

revolutionize vt to cause a complete change in.

revolve vt to travel or cause to travel in a circle or orbit; to rotate.

revolver n a handgun with a magazine that revolves to reload.

revue n a musical show with skits, dances, etc, often satirizing recent events.

revulsion n disgust; aversion; a sudden change or reversal of feeling.

reward n something that is given in return for something done; money offered, as for the capture of a criminal. * vt to give a reward.

rewarding adj (experience, activity, etc) pleasing, profitable.

rewrite vt to write again; to revise. * n something rewritten; revision.

rhapsody n an enthusiastic speech or writing; (mus) an irregular instrumental composition of an epic, heroic or national character.

rhetoric n the art of effective speaking and writing; skill in using speech; insincere language.

rhetorical adj of or relating to rhetoric; high-flown, bombastic. —rhetorically adv.

rheumatic adj of, relating to or suffering from rheumatism. * n a person who has rheumatism.

rheumatism n a disorder causing pain in muscles and joints.

rhinoceros n (pl rhinoceroses, rhinoceros) a large, thick-skinned mammal with one or two horns on the nose.—also rhino.

rhododendron n an evergreen shrub with large flowers.

rhubarb n a plant with large leaves and edible (when cooked) pink stalks; (inf) a noisy quarrel.

rhyme n the repetition of sounds usu at the ends of lines in verse; such poetry or verse; a word corresponding with another in end sound. * vti to form a rhyme (with); to put into rhyme.

rhythm n a regular recurrence of beat, accent or silence in the flow of sound, esp of words and music; a measured flow.—rhythmic, rhythmical adj.—rhythmically adv.

rib n one of the curved bones of the chest attached to the spine; any rib-like structure; a leaf vein; a vein of an insect's wing; a ridge or raised strip, as of knitting; a ridge of a mountain. * vt (pt ribbed) to provide with ribs; to form vertical ridges in knitting; (inf) to tease or ridicule.

ribald adj irreverent; humorously vulgar.

ribbon n silk, satin, velvet, etc, woven into a narrow band; a piece of this; a strip of cloth, etc, inked for use, as in a typewriter; (pl) torn shreds.

rice n an annual cereal grass cultivated in warm climates; its starchy food grain.

rich adj having much money, wealthy; abounding in natural resources, fertile; costly, fine; (food) sweet or oily, highly flavored; deep in color; (inf) full of humour. * n wealthy people collectively; (pl riches) wealth, abundance.—richly adv.—richness n.

rickets n a children's disease marked by softening of the bones, caused by vitamin D deficiency.

rickety adj shaky, unsteady.

rickshaw n a light, two-wheeled man-drawn vehicle, orig used in Japan.

ricochet vi (pt ricocheted or ricochetted) (bullet) to rebound or skip along ground or water. * n a rebound or glancing off; (bullet) a hit made after ricocheting.

rid vt (pt rid or ridded) to free from; to dispose (of).

riddance n clearance; disposal.

ridden[1] see ride.

ridden[2] adj oppressed by; full of.

riddle[1] n a puzzling question; an enigma; a mysterious person or thing.

riddle[2] n a coarse sieve. * vt to sieve or sift; to perforate with holes; to spread through, permeate.

ride vb (pt rode, pp ridden) vti to be carried along or travel in a vehicle or on an animal, bicycle, etc; to be supported or move on the water; to lie at anchor; to travel over a surface; to move on the body; (inf) to continue undisturbed. * vt (horse, bicycle etc); to sit on and control; to oppress, dominate; (inf) to torment. * n a trip or journey in a vehicle or on horseback, on a bicycle, etc; a thing to ride at a fairground.

Rideau Hall n the official residence and office of the Governor General of Canada.

rider n a person who rides; an addition to a document, amending a clause; an additional statement; something used to move along another piece.

ridge n a narrow crest or top; the ploughed

earth thrown up between the furrows; a line where two slopes meet; (*of land etc*) a raised strip or elevation; a range of hills. * *vti* to form into ridges, wrinkle.—**ridged** *adj*.

ridicule *n* mockery, derision. * *vt* to make fun of, to mock.

ridiculous *adj* deserving ridicule; preposterous, silly.—**ridiculously** *adv*.—**ridiculousness** *n*.

riding *n* (*Cdn*) a constituency that elects a member of a legislature.

rife *adj* widespread; prevalent.

riffraff *n* disreputable persons; refuse, rubbish.

rifle[1] *n* a shoulder gun with a spirally grooved bore.

rifle[2] *vti* to steal; to look through (a person's papers or belongings).

rift *n* a split; a cleft; a fissure. * *vti* to split.

rig *vt* (*pt* **rigged**) (*naut*) to equip with sails and tackle; to set up in working order; to manipulate fraudulently. * *n* the way sails, etc, are rigged; equipment or gear for a special purpose; a type of truck.

rigging *n* the ropes for supporting masts and sails; (*in theatre*) a network of ropes and pulleys to support and maintain scenery.

right *adj* correct, true; just or good; appropriate; fit, recovered; opposite to left; conservative; designating the side meant to be seen. * *adv* straight; directly; completely; exactly; correctly, properly; to or on the right side. * *n* that which is just or correct; truth; fairness; justice; privilege; just or legal claim; (*pl*) the correct condition. * *vti* to set or become upright; to correct; to redress.—**rightness** *n*.

right angle *n* an angle of 90 degrees.

righteous *adj* moral, virtuous.—**righteously** *adv*.—**righteousness** *n*.

rightful *adj* legitimate; having a just claim.—**rightfully** *adv*.—**rightfulness** *n*.

right-hand *adj* of or towards the right side of a person or thing; for use by the right hand.

right-handed *adj* using the right hand; done or made for use with the right hand. * *adv* with the right hand.

right-hand man *n* an important and supportive assistant.

rightly *adv* in truth; in the right; with good reason; properly.

right-of-way *n* a public path over private ground; the right to use this; precedence over other traffic.

right-wing *adj* of or relating to the conservative faction of a political party, organization, etc.—**right-winger** *n*.

rigid *adj* stiff, inflexible; severe, strict.—**rigidity** *n*.—**rigidly** *adv*.—**rigidness** *n*.

rigmarole *n* nonsense; a foolishly involved procedure.

rigour, rigor (*US*) *n* harsh inflexibility; severity; strictness.—**rigorous** *adj*.

rim *n* a border or raised edge, esp of something circular; the outer part of a wheel. * *vt* (*pt* **rimmed**) to supply or surround with a rim; to form a rim.

rimless *adj* lacking a rim; (*glasses*) without a frame.

rind *n* crust; peel; bark.

ring[1] *n* a circular band, esp of metal, worn on the finger, in the ear, etc; a hollow circle; a round enclosure; an arena for boxing, etc; a group of people engaged in secret or criminal activity to control a market, etc. * *vt* (*pt* **ringed**) to encircle, surround; to fit with a ring.

ring[2] *vti* (*pt* **rang** *or* **rung**) to emit a bell-like sound; to resound; to peal; to sound a bell; to telephone; (*with* **up**) to total and record esp by means of a cash register; to achieve. * *n* a ringing sound; a resonant note; a set of church bells.

ringette *n* (*Cdn*) a game resembling hockey that is played with a straight stick and a rubber ring.

ringlet *n* a curling lock of hair.

rink *n* an expanse of ice for skating; a smooth floor for roller skating; an alley for bowling.

rink rat *n* (*Cdn*) (*sl*) a young person who frequents a hockey rink, esp one who does chores in exchange for being allowed to skate.

rinse *vt* to wash lightly; to flush under clean water to remove soap. * *n* the act of rinsing; a preparation for tinting the hair.

riot *n* violent public disorder; uproar; unrestrained profusion; (*inf*) something very funny. * *vi* to participate in a riot.—**rioter** *n*.—**rioting** *n*.

riotous *adj* tumultuous, disorderly; luxurious, wanton.—**riotously** *adv*.—**riotousness** *n*.

rip *vti* (*pt* **ripped**) to cut or tear apart roughly; to split; (*with* **off, out**) to remove in a violent or rough manner; (*inf*) to rush, speed; (*with* **into**) to attack, esp verbally. * *n* a tear; a split.

rip cord *n* a cord for releasing a parachute.

ripe *adj* ready to be eaten or harvested; fully developed; mature.—**ripely** *adv*.—**ripeness** *n*.

ripen *vt* to grow or make ripe.

ripple *n* a little wave on the surface of water; the sound of this. * *vti* to have or form little waves on the surface (of).

rise *vi* (*pt* **rose**, *pp* **risen**) to get up; to stand up; to ascend; to increase in value or size; to swell; to revolt; to be provoked; to originate; to tower; to slope up; (*voice*) to reach a higher pitch; to ascend from the grave; (*fish*) to come to the surface. * *n* an ascent; origin; an increase in price, salary, etc; an upward slope.

risk *n* chance of loss or injury; hazard; danger, peril. * *vt* to expose to possible danger or loss; to take the chance of.

risky *adj* (**riskier, riskiest**) dangerous.

risqué *adj* verging on indecency; slightly offensive.

rissole *n* a fried cake of minced meat, egg, and breadcrumbs.

rite *n* a ceremonial practice or procedure, esp religious.

ritual *adj* relating to rites or ceremonies. * *n* a

fixed (religious) ceremony.—**ritually** adv.

rival n one of two or more people, organizations or teams competing with each other for the same goal. * adj competing; having comparable merit or claim. * vt (pt **rivalled**) to strive to equal or excel; to be comparable to; to compete.

rivalry n emulation; competition.

river n a large natural stream of fresh water flowing into an ocean, lake, etc; a copious flow.

riverbed n the channel formed by a river.

riverside n the bank of a river.

rivet n a short, metal bolt for holding metal plates together. * vt (pt **riveted**) to join with rivets; to fix one's eyes upon immovably; to engross one's attention.—**riveter** n.

Riviera n the coast of the northern Mediterranean from southeast France to northwest Italy.

RM abbr (Cdn) = Rural Municipality; Regional Municipality.

road n a surfaced track for travelling on; a highway; a street; a way or route; an anchorage for ships.

road block n a barrier erected across a road to halt traffic.

road hockey n (Cdn) an informal game of hockey played on a road in which a ball rather than a puck is used.—also **street hockey**.

road hog n a car driver who obstructs other vehicles by encroaching on the others' traffic lane.

roadside n the border of a road.—also adj.

roadway n the strip of land over which a road passes; the main part of a road, used by vehicles.

roadworthy adj (vehicle) fit for the road.—**roadworthiness** n.

roam vti to wander about, to travel.

roar vti to make a loud, full, growling sound, as a lion, wind, fire, the sea; to utter loudly, as in a rage; to bellow; to guffaw.—also n.

roaring adj boisterous; noisy; brisk.

roast vti (meat, etc) to cook with little or no moisture, as in an oven; (coffee, etc) to process by exposure to heat; to expose to great heat; (inf) to criticize severely; to undergo roasting. * n roasted meat; a cut of meat for roasting; a picnic at which food is roasted.

rob vb (pt **robbed**) vt to seize forcibly; to steal from; to plunder. * vi to commit robbery.—**robber** n.

robbery n theft from a person by intimidation or by violence.

robe n a long flowing outer garment; the official dress of a judge, academic, etc; a bathrobe or dressing gown; a covering or wrap; (pl) ceremonial vestments. * vti to put on or dress in robes.

robin n a songbird with a dull red breast.

robot n a mechanical device that acts in a seemingly human way; a mechanism guided by automatic controls.

robust adj strong, sturdy; vigorous.—**robustly** adv.—**robustness** n.

rock[1] n a large stone or boulder; a person or thing providing foundation or support; (geol) a natural mineral deposit including sand, clay, etc; a hard sweet; (inf) a diamond, ice; a curling stone.

rock[2] vti to move to and fro, or from side to side; to sway strongly; to shake. * n a rocking motion; rock and roll.

rock and roll n popular music that incorporates country and blues elements and is usu played with a heavily accented beat.

rock bottom n the lowest or most fundamental part or level. * adj very lowest.

rocker n a rocking chair; a curved support on which a cradle, etc rocks.

rockery, rock garden n a garden among rocks for alpine plants.

rocket n any device driven forward by gases escaping through a rear vent. * vi to move in or like a rocket; to soar.

rocking chair n a chair mounted on rockers.

rocking horse n a toy horse fixed on rockers or springs.

rocky adj (**rockier**, **rockiest**) having many rocks; like rock; rugged, hard; shaky, unstable.

rod n a stick; a thin bar of metal or wood; a staff of office; a wand; a fishing rod; (sl) a pistol.

rode see **ride**.

rodent n any of several relatively small gnawing animals with two strong front teeth.

rodeo n (pl **rodeos**) the rounding up of cattle; a display of cowboy skill.

roe[1] n the eggs or sperm of fish.

roe[2] n a small reddish brown deer (—also **roe deer**); the female red deer.

rogue n a scoundrel; a rascal; a mischievous person; a wild animal that lives apart from the herd.—**roguish** adj.—**roguishly** adv.

role n a part in a film or play taken by an actor; a function.

roll n a scroll; anything wound into cylindrical form; a list or register; a turned-over edge; a rolling movement; a small cake of bread; a trill of some birds; an undulation; the sound of thunder; the beating of drumsticks. * vi to move by turning over or from side to side; to move like a wheel; to curl; to move in like waves; to flow. * vt to cause to roll; to turn on its axis; to move on wheels; to press with a roller; (dice) to throw; to beat rapidly, as a drum.

roll call n the reading aloud of a list of names to check attendance.

rolled gold n a thin coating of gold attached to another metal by passing through heavy rollers.

roller n a revolving cylinder used for spreading paint, flattening surfaces; a large wave; (sl) a Rolls Royce car.

roller skate n a four-wheeled skate strapped on to shoes.—**roller skating** n.

rolling pin n a wooden, plastic or stone cylinder for rolling out pastry.

rolling stock n all the vehicles of a railway.

Roman *adj* of or relating to the city of Rome or its ancient empire, or the Latin alphabet; Roman Catholic. * *n* an inhabitant or citizen of Rome; a Roman Catholic.

Roman Catholic *adj* belonging to the Christian church that is headed by the Pope.—*also n.*

romance *n* a prose narrative; a medieval tale of chivalry; a series of unusual adventures; a novel dealing with this; an atmosphere of awe or wonder; a love story; a love affair; a picturesque falsehood. * *vi* to write romantic fiction; to exaggerate.

Roman numerals *npl* the letters I, V, X, L, C, D and M used to represent numbers in the manner of the ancient Romans.

romantic *adj* of or given to romance; strange and picturesque; imaginative; (*art, etc*) preferring passion and imagination to proportion and finish.—**romantically** *adv.*

romp *vi* to play boisterously. * *n* a noisy game; a frolic; an easy win.

rompers *npl* a child's one-piece garment; a jumpsuit.

roof *n* (*pl* **roofs**) the upper covering of a building; the top of a vehicle; an upper limit. * *vt* to provide with a roof, to cover.

roofing *n* materials for a roof.

rook[1] *n* a crow-like bird.

rook[2] *n* (*chess*) a piece with the power to move horizontally or vertically, a castle.

room *n* space; unoccupied space; adequate space; a division of a house, a chamber; scope or opportunity; those in a room; (*pl*) lodgings. * *vi* to lodge.

roommate *n* a person with whom one shares a room or rooms.

roomy *adj* (**roomier, roomiest**) having ample space; wide.—**roominess** *n.*

roost *n* a bird's perch or sleeping-place; a place for resting. * *vi* to rest or sleep on a roost; to settle down, as for the night.

rooster *n* an adult male domestic fowl, a cockerel.

root[1] *n* the part of a plant, usu underground, that anchors the plant, draws water from the soil, etc; the embedded part of a tooth, a hair, etc; a supporting or essential part; an origin or source; (*math*) the factor of a quantity which multiplied by itself gives the quantity; (*mus*) the fundamental note of a chord; (*pl*) plants with edible roots. * *vti* to take root; to become established; (*with* **out**) to tear up, to eradicate.

root[2] *vti* to dig up with the snout; to search about, rummage; (*with* **for**) (*inf*) to encourage a team by cheering.

rope *n* a thick cord or thin cable made of twisted fibres or wires; a string or row of things braided or threaded together; a thickening in a liquid. * *vt* to tie, bind, divide or enclose with a rope; to lasso; (*liquid*) to become ropy.—**ropy** *adj.*

rosary *n* a string of beads for keeping count of prayers; a series of prayers.

rose[1] *see* **rise**.

rose[2] *n* a prickly-stemmed plant with fragrant flowers of many delicate colors; its flower; a rosette; a perforated nozzle; a pinkish red or purplish red.

rosé *n* a pink wine made from skinless red grapes or by mixing white and red wine.

rosemary *n* a fragrant shrubby mint used in cookery and perfumery.

rosette *n* a rose-shaped bunch of ribbon; a carving, etc, in the shape of a rose.

roster *n* a list or roll, as of military personnel; a list of duties.

rostrum *n* (*pl* **rostrums, rostra**) a platform or stage for public speaking.

rosy *adj* (**rosier, rosiest**) of the color of roses; having pink, healthy cheeks; optimistic, hopeful.—**rosily** *adv.*—**rosiness** *n.*

rot *vti* (*pt* **rotted**) to decompose; to decay; to become degenerate. * *n* decay; corruption; several different diseases affecting timber or sheep; (*inf*) nonsense.

rota *n* a turn in succession; a list or roster of duties.

rotary *adj* revolving; turning like a wheel.

rotate *vti* to turn around an axis like a wheel; to follow a sequence.

rotation *n* the action of rotating; a regular succession, as of crops to avoid exhausting the soil.

rotor *n* a rotating part of a machine or engine.

rotten *adj* decayed, decomposed; corrupt; (*inf*) bad, nasty.—**rottenness** *n.*

rotund *adj* rounded; spherical; plump.

rouble *n* a coin and monetary unit of Russia.

rouge *n* a red cosmetic for coloring the cheeks; a red powder for polishing jewellery, etc. * *vti* to color (the face) with rouge.

rough *adj* uneven; not smooth; ill-mannered; violent; rude, unpolished; shaggy; coarse in texture; unrefined; violent, boisterous; stormy; wild; harsh, discordant; crude, unfinished; approximate; (*inf*) difficult. * *n* rough ground; (*golf*) any part of a course with grass, etc, left uncut; a first sketch. * *vt* to make rough; to sketch roughly. * *adv* in a rough manner.—**roughly** *adv.*—**roughness** *n.*

roughing *n* an infraction in ice hockey for using excessive or unnecessary force.

roulette *n* a gambling game played with a revolving disc and a ball; a toothed wheel for making perforations.

round *adj* circular, spherical, or cylindrical in form; curved; plump; (*math*) expressed to the nearest ten, hundred, etc, not fractional; considerable; candid; (*style*) flowing, balanced; (*vowel*) pronounced with rounded lips. * *adv* circularly; on all sides; from one side to another; in a ring; by indirect way; through a recurring period of time; in circumference; in a roundabout way; about; near; here and there; with a rotating movement; in the opposite direction; around. * *prep* encircling; on every side of; in the vicinity of; in a circuit through; around. * *n* anything round; a circuit; (*of shots*) a volley; a unit of ammunition; a series or sequence;

a turn; (*golf*) a circuit of a course; a stage of a contest; (*mus*) a kind of canon. * *vt* to make or become round or plump; (*math*) to express as a round number; to complete; to go or pass around. * *vi* to make a circuit; to turn; to reverse direction.—**roundly** *adv.*—**roundness** *n*.

roundabout *adj* indirect, circuitous. * *n* a circuitous route; a merry-go-round; a crossroad where traffic circulates around a traffic island.

rounded *adj* curved or round; flowing, not angular.

round trip *n* a journey to a place and back again.

roundup *n* a driving together of livestock; (*inf*) the detention of several prisoners; a summary, as of news.

rouse *vti* to provoke; to stir up; to awaken; to wake up; to become active.

rousing *adj* stirring; vigorous.

rout[1] *n* a noisy crowd, a rabble; a disorderly retreat. * *vt* to defeat and put to flight.

rout[2] *vti* to grub up, as a pig; to search haphazardly; to make a furrow in (as wood or metal); to cause to emerge, esp from bed; to come up with; to uncover.

route *n* a course to be taken; the roads travelled on a journey. * *vt* to plan the route of; to send (by a specified route).

routine *n* a procedure that is regular and unvarying; a sequence of set movements, as in a dance, skating, etc.—*also adj*.

row[1] *n* a line of persons or things; a line of seats (in a theatre, etc).

row[2] *vti* to propel with oars; to transport by rowing. * *n* an act or instance of rowing.—**rower** *n*.

row[3] *n* a noisy quarrel or dispute; a scolding; noise, disturbance. * *vi* to quarrel; to scold.

rowdy *adj* (**rowdier, rowdiest**) rough and noisy, disorderly. * *n* a rowdy person, a hooligan.—**rowdiness, rowdyism** *n*.

royal *adj* relating to or fit for a king or queen; regal; under the patronage of a king or queen; founded by a king or queen; of a kingdom, its government, etc. * *n* a type of topsail; a stag with a head of twelve points; (*inf*) a member of a royal family.—**royally** *adv*.

royalist *n* a person who advocates monarchy.

royalty *n* the rank or power of a king or queen; a royal person or persons; a share of the proceeds from a patent, book, song, etc, paid to the owner, author, etc.

rpm *abbr* = revolutions per minute.

RRIF *abbr* (*Cdn*) = Registered Retirement Income Fund.

RRSP *abbr* (*Cdn*) = Registered Retirement Savings Plan.

RSP *abbr* (*Cdn*) = Retirement Savings Plan.

RSVP *abbr* = répondez s'il vous plaît.

rub *vti* (*pt* **rubbed**) to move (a hand, cloth, etc) over the surface of with pressure; to wipe, scour; to clean or polish; (*with* **away, off, out**) to remove or erase by friction; to chafe, grate; to fret; to take a rubbing of; (*with* **along**) to manage somehow; (*with* **down**) to

rub vigorously with a towel; to smooth down. * *n* the act or process of rubbing; a drawback, difficulty.

rubber[1] *n* an elastic substance made synthetically or from the sap of various tropical plants; an eraser.

rubber[2] *n* a group of three games at whist, bridge, etc; the deciding game.

rubber-stamp *vt* (*inf*) to give automatic approval without investigation.

rubbish *n* refuse; garbage, trash; nonsense. * *vt* (*inf*) to criticize.—**rubbishy** *adj*.

rubble *n* rough broken stone or rock; builders' rubbish.

rubby *n* (*pl* **rubbies**) a drunkard who consumes rubbing alcohol, aftershave lotion, or some other cheap intoxicating substance.

ruby *n* a deep red, transparent, valuable precious stone. * *adj* of the color of a ruby.

rucksack *n* a bag worn on the back by hikers.

rudder *n* a flat vertical piece of wood or metal hinged to the stern of a ship or boat or the rear of an aircraft to steer by; a guiding principle.

ruddy *adj* (**ruddier, ruddiest**) reddish pink; (*complexion*) of a healthy, red color.

rude *adj* uncivil, ill-mannered; uncultured, coarse; harsh, brutal; crude, roughly made; in a natural state, primitive; vigorous, hearty.—**rudely** *adv.*—**rudeness** *n*.

rudiment *n* a first stage; a first slight beginning of something; an imperfectly developed organ; (*pl*) elements, first principles.

rudimentary *adj* elementary; imperfectly developed or represented only by a vestige.

rueful *adj* regretful; dejected; showing good-humoured self-pity.—**ruefully** *adv*.

ruff *n* a pleated collar or frill worn round the neck; a fringe of feathers or fur round the neck of a bird or animal.

ruffian *n* a brutal lawless person; a villain.

ruffle *vti* to disturb the smoothness of, to disarrange; to irritate; to agitate; to upset; to swagger about; to be quarrelsome; to flutter. * *n* pleated material used as a trim; a frill; a bird's ruff; a dispute, a quarrel.

rug *n* a thick heavy fabric used as a floor covering; a thick woollen wrap or coverlet.

Rugby *n* a football game for two teams of 15 players played with an oval ball.

rugged *adj* rocky; rough, uneven; strong; stern; robust.—**ruggedly** *adv.*—**ruggedness** *n*.

ruin *n* destruction; downfall; wrecked state; the cause of this; a loss of fortune; (*pl*) the remains of something destroyed, decayed, etc. * *vti* to destroy; to spoil; to bankrupt; to come to ruin.

ruinous *adj* in ruins; causing ruin, disastrous.

rule *n* a straight-edged instrument for drawing lines and measuring; government; the exercise of authority; a regulation, an order; a principle, a standard; habitual practice; the code of a religious order; a straight line. * *vti* to govern, to exercise authority over; to manage; to draw (lines) with a ruler; (*with* **out**) to exclude, to eliminate; to make impossible.

ruler *n* a person who governs; a strip of wood, metal, etc, with a straight edge, used in drawing lines, measuring, etc.

ruling *adj* governing; reigning; dominant. * *n* an authoritative pronouncement.

rum *n* a spirit made from sugar cane.

rumble *vti* to make a low heavy rolling noise; to move with such a sound; (*sl*) to see through, find out. * *n* the dull deep vibrating noise of thunder, etc.

rummage *n* odds and ends; a search by ransacking. * *vti* to search thoroughly; to ransack; to fish (out).

rummage sale *n* a jumble sale.

rumour, rumor (*US*) *n* hearsay, gossip; common talk not based on definite knowledge; an unconfirmed report, story. * *vt* to report by way of rumour.

rump *n* the hindquarters of an animal's body; the buttocks; the back end.

rumpus *n* a commotion; a din.

run *vb* (*pt* **ran**) *vi* to go by moving the legs faster than in walking; to hurry; to flee; to flow; to operate; to be valid; to compete in a race, election, etc; (*colors*), to merge. * *vt* (*a car, etc*) to drive; (*a business, etc*) to manage; (*a story*) to publish in a newspaper; (*temperature*) to suffer from a fever; (*with* **out**) to exhaust a supply; (*inf*) to desert; (*with* **over**) (*vehicle*) to knock down a person or animal; to overflow; to exceed a limit; to rehearse quickly; (*with* **up**) to incur or amass. * *n* an act of running; a trip; a flow; a series; prevalence; a trend; an enclosure for chickens, etc; free and unrestricted access to all parts; (*in tights, etc*) a ladder.

runaway *n* a person or animal that has run away.

rundown *n* a summary.

run-down *adj* dilapidated.

rung[1] *see* **ring**[2].

rung[2] *n* the step of a ladder; the crossbar of a chair.

runner *n* an athlete; a person who runs; a smuggler; a groove or strip on which something glides.

runner bean *n* a climbing plant that produces long green edible pods.

runner-up *n* (*pl* **runners-up**) the competitor who finishes second in a race, contest, etc.

running *n* the act of moving swiftly; that which runs or flows; a racing, managing, etc. * *adj* moving swiftly; kept for a race; being in motion; continuous; discharing pus. * *adv* in succession.

runny *adj* (**runnier, runniest**) tending to flow.

run-of-the-mill *adj* average, mediocre.

runt *n* an unusually small animal, esp the smallest of a litter of pigs; a person of small stature.

runway *n* a landing strip for aircraft.

rupture *n* a breach; a severance, quarrel; the act of bursting or breaking; hernia. * *vti* to cause or suffer a rupture.

rural *adj* relating to the country or agriculture.—**rurally** *adv*.

ruse *n* a trick, deception.

rush[1] *vti* to move, push, drive, etc, swiftly or impetuously; to make a sudden attack (on); to do with unusual haste; to hurry. * *adj* marked by or needing extra speed or urgency. * *n* a sudden surge; a sudden demand; a press, as of business, requiring unusual haste; an unedited film print.

rush[2] *n* a marsh plant; its slender pithy stem; a worthless thing.

rush hour *n* the time at the beginning and end of the working day when traffic is at its heaviest.

rusk *n* a sweet or plain bread sliced and rebaked until dry and crisp.

rust *n* a reddish oxide coating formed on iron or steel when exposed to moisture; a reddish brown color; a red mould on plants; the fungus causing this. * *vti* to form rust (on); to deteriorate, as through disuse.

rustle *n* a crisp, rubbing sound as of dry leaves, paper, etc. * *vti* to make or move with a rustle; to hustle; to steal (cattle); (*with* **up**) (*inf*) to collect or get together.

rusty *adj* (**rustier, rustiest**) coated with rust; rust-colored; faded; out of practice; antiquated.—**rustiness** *n*.

rut[1] *n* a track worn by wheels; an undeviating mechanical routine. * *vt* (*pt* **rutted**) to mark with ruts.

rut[2] *n* the seasonal period of sexual excitement in certain male animals, eg deer. * *vi* (*pt* **rutted**) (*deer, etc*) to be in rut.

ruthless *adj* cruel; merciless.—**ruthlessly** *adv*.—**ruthlessness** *n*.

rye *n* a hardy annual grass; its grain, used for making flour and whiskey; a whiskey made from rye.

S

sabbath *n* a day of rest and worship observed on a Saturday by Jews, Sunday by Christians and Friday by Muslims.

sabbatical *n* a year's leave from a teaching post, often paid, for research or travel.

sabotage *n* deliberate damage of machinery, or disruption of public services, by enemy agents, disgruntled employees, etc, to prevent their effective operation. * *vt* to practise sabotage on; to spoil, disrupt.

saccharin *n* a non-fattening sugar substitute.

saccharine *adj* containing sugar; excessively sweet.

sack[1] *n* a large bag made of coarse cloth used as a container; the contents of this; a loose-fitting dress or coat; (*sl: with* **the**) dismissal. * *vt* to put into sacks; (*sl*) to dismiss.

sack[2] *n* the plunder or destruction of a place. * *vt* to plunder or loot.

sacking *n* the coarse cloth used for sacks; the storming and plundering of a place.

sacrament *n* a religious ceremony forming outward and visible sign of inward and spiritual grace, esp baptism and the Eucharist; the consecrated elements in the Eucharist, esp the bread; a sacred symbol or pledge.—**sacramental** adj.

sacred adj regarded as holy; consecrated to a god or God; connected with religion; worthy of or regarded with reverence, sacrosanct.

sacrifice n the act of offering ceremonially to a deity; the slaughter of an animal (or person) to please a deity; the surrender of something valuable for the sake of something more important; loss without return; something sacrificed, an offering. * vt to slaughter or give up as a sacrifice; to give up for a higher good; to sell at a loss.—**sacrificial** adj.

sacrilege n violation of anything holy or sacred.

sacrosanct adj inviolable; very holy.

sad adj (**sadder, saddest**) expressing grief or unhappiness; sorrowful; deplorable.—**sadly** adv.—**sadness** n.

sadden vti to make or become sad.

saddle n a seat, usu of leather, for a rider on a horse, bicycle, etc; a ridge connecting two mountain peaks; a joint of mutton or venison consisting of the two loins. * vt to put a saddle on; to burden, encumber.

saddlebag n a bag hung from the saddle of a horse or bicycle.

sadism n sexual pleasure obtained from inflicting cruelty upon another; extreme cruelty.—**sadist** n.—**sadistic** adj.

safari n (pl **safaris**) a journey or hunting expedition.

safe adj unhurt; out of danger; reliable; secure; involving no risk; trustworthy; giving protection; prudent; sure; incapable of doing harm. * n a locking metal box or compartment for valuables.—**safely** adv.

safeguard n anything that protects against injury or danger; a proviso against foreseen risks. * vt to protect.

safekeeping n the act or process of keeping safely; protection.

safety n freedom from danger; the state of being safe.

safety belt n a belt worn by a person working at a great height to prevent falling; a seatbelt in a car.

safety pin n a pin with a guard to cover the point.

saffron n a crocus whose bright yellow stigmas are used as a food coloring and flavoring; an orange-yellow color.

sag vi (pt **sagged**) to droop downwards in the middle; to sink or hang down unevenly under pressure.

sage[1] adj wise through reflection and experience. * n a person of profound wisdom.—**sagely** adv.

sage[2] n a herb with leaves used for flavoring food; sagebrush.

Sagittarius n the Archer, ninth sign of the zodiac; in astrology, operative 22 November - 20 December.

sago n a type of Asian palm; its starchy pith used in puddings.

said see **say**.

sail n a piece of canvas used to catch the wind to propel or steer a vessel; sails collectively; anything like a sail; an arm of a windmill; a voyage in a sailing vessel. * vt to navigate a vessel; to manage (a vessel). * vi to be moved by sails; to travel by water; to glide or pass smoothly; to walk in a stately manner.

sailing n the act of sailing; the motion or direction of a ship, etc on water; a departure from a port.

sailing boat, sailboat (US) n a boat that is propelled by a sail or sails.

sailor n a person who sails; one of a ship's crew.

saint n a person who is very patient, charitable, etc; a person who is canonized by the Roman Catholic church.—**sainthood** n.

St Jean Baptiste Day n in Quebec, common and formerly official name of a public holiday celebrated on June 24.

sake n behalf; purpose; benefit; interest.

salad n a dish, usu cold, of vegetables, fruits, meat, eggs, etc; lettuce, etc, used for this.

salad dressing n a cooked or uncooked sauce of oil, vinegar, spices, etc, to put on a salad.

salal n a shrub of western North America with pink or white flowers and edible purple-black berries.

salary n fixed, regular payment for non-manual work, usu paid monthly.

sale n the act of selling; the exchange of goods or services for money; the market or opportunity of selling; an auction; the disposal of goods at reduced prices; the period of this.

saleroom, salesroom n a place where goods are displayed for sale; an auction room.

salesman n a person who sells either in a given territory or in a shop.—**saleswoman** nf.

salient adj projecting outwards; conspicuous; noteworthy; leaping, gushing.

Salishan n a speaker of one of a grouping of Indian languages in the Pacific Northwest coast of North America; the language spoken by a people using one of these languages. * adj of or pertaining to this people or their language.

saliva n the liquid secreted by glands in the mouth that aids digestion.—**salivary** adj.

sallow adj (complexion) an unhealthy yellow color, a pale brown color.—**sallowness** n.

salmon n (pl **salmon**) a large silvery edible fish that lives in salt water and spawns in fresh water; salmon pink.

saloon n a large reception room; a large cabin for the social use of a ship's passengers; a four-seater car with a boot; a place where alcoholic drinks are sold and consumed.

salt n a white crystalline substance (sodium chloride) used as a seasoning or preservative; piquancy, wit; (chem) a compound of an acid and a base; (pl) mineral salt as an aperient. * adj containing or tasting of salt;

preserved with salt; pungent. * vt to flavor, pickle or sprinkle with salt; to give flavor or piquancy to (as a story); (with **away**) to hoard; to keep for the future.—**salty** adj.

salt cellar n a vessel for salt at the table; a saltshaker.

saltchuck n on the Pacific Northwest coast of North America, the ocean or one of its outlets.

salter n someone who or something that salts; (Cdn) a truck that dispenses salt on roads to melt snow and ice.

salutary adj beneficial, wholesome.—**salutarily** adv.—**salutariness** n.

salute n a gesture of respect or greeting; (mil) a motion of the right hand to the head, or of a rifle; a discharge of guns, etc, as a military mark of honor. * vti to make a salute (to); to greet; to kiss; to praise or honor.

salvage n the rescuing of a ship or property from loss at sea, by fire, etc; the reward paid for this; the thing salvaged; waste material intended for further use. * vt to save from loss or danger.

salvation n the act of saving or the state of being saved; in Christianity, the deliverance from evil; a means of preservation.

salvo n (**salvoes, salvos**) a firing of several guns or missiles simultaneously; a sudden burst; a spirited verbal attack.

same adj identical; exactly similar; unchanged; uniform, monotonous; previously mentioned. * pron the same person or thing. * adv in like manner.

sample n a specimen; a small part representative of the whole; an instance. * vt (food, drink)to taste a small quantity of; to test by taking a sample.

sanatorium, sanitarium (US) n (pl **sanatoriums, sanitariums**) an establishment for the treatment of convalescents or the chronically ill.—also

sanctimonious adj pretending to be holy; hypocritically pious or righteous.—**sanctimoniously** adv.

sanction n express permission, authorization; a binding influence; a penalty by which a law is enforced, esp a prohibition on trade with a country that has violated international law. * vt to permit; to give authority.

sanctity n the condition of being holy or sacred.

sanctuary n a sacred place; the part of a church around the altar; a place where one is free from arrest or violence, an asylum; a refuge; an animal reserve.

sand n very fine rock particles; (pl) a desert; a sandy beach. * vt to smooth or polish with sand or sandpaper; to sprinkle with sand.

sandal n a shoe consisting of a sole strapped to the foot; a low slipper or shoe.

sandpaper n a paper coated on one side with sand or another abrasive, used to smooth or polish. * vt to rub with sandpaper.

sandstone n a sedimentary rock of compacted sand.

sandwich n two slices of bread with meat, cheese, or other filling between; anything in a sandwich-like arrangement. * vt to place between two things or two layers; to make such.a place for.

sandy adj (**sandier, sandiest**) of, like, or sprinkled with sand; yellowish grey.—**sandiness** n.

sane adj mentally sound, not mad; reasonable, sensible.—**sanely** adv.—**saneness** n.

sang see **sing**.

sanguine adj confident, hopeful; blood-red; (complexion) ruddy.

sanitary adj relating to the promotion and protection of health; relating to the supply of water, drainage, and sewage disposal; hygienic.

sanitary towel n an absorbent pad worn externally during menstruation.

sanitation n the science and practice of achieving hygienic conditions; drainage and disposal of sewage.

sanity n the condition of being sane; mental health.

sank see **sink**.

Santa Claus n a legendary fat, white-bearded old man who brings presents to children at Christmas.—also **Father Christmas**.

sap n the vital juice of plants; energy and health; (inf) a fool. * vt (pt **sapped**) to drain of sap; to exhaust the energy of; to weaken or undermine.

sapling n a young tree; a youth.

sapphire n a transparent blue precious stone; a deep pure blue.

sarcasm n a scornful or ironic remark; the use of this.—**sarcastic** adj.—**sarcastically** adv.

sardine n a small, edible seafish.

sash[1] n a band of satin or ribbon wor n around the waist or over the shoulder, often as a badge of honor.

sash[2] n a frame for holding the glass of a window, esp one that slides vertically.

Sask. abbr = Saskatchewan.

Saskatchewaner n (Cdn) a person who lives in or is from Saskatchewan.

saskatoon n (Cdn) a shrub of western North America; the sweet purple berry of this shrub.

Sasquatch n a large, hairy, humanlike creature that supposedly inhabits the Pacific Northwest of North America.—also **Bigfoot**.

sat see **sit**.

Satan n the devil, the adversary of God.—**satanic** adj.

satchel n a bag with shoulder straps for carrying school books, etc.

satellite n a planet orbiting another; a man-made object orbiting the earth, moon, etc, to gather scientific information or for communication; a nation economically dependent on a more powerful one.

satin n a fabric of woven silk with a smooth, shiny surface on one side. * adj of or resembling satin.

satire n a literary work in which folly or evil in people's behaviour are held up to ridicule; trenchant wit, sarcasm.—**satirical** adj.—**sa-**

tirically *adv*.

satisfaction *n* the act of satisfying or the condition of being satisfied; that which satisfies; comfort; atonement, reparation.

satisfactory *adj* giving satisfaction; adequate; acceptable; convincing.—**satisfactorily** *adv*.—**satisfactoriness** *n*.

satisfy *vi* to be enough for; to fulfil the needs or desires of. * *vt* to give enough to; (*hunger, desire etc*.) to appease; to please; to gratify; to comply with; (*creditor*) to discharge, to pay in full; to convince; to make reparation to; (*guilt, etc*) to atone for.

saturate *vt* to soak thoroughly; to fill completely.

Saturday *n* the seventh and last day of the week.

sauce *n* a liquid or dressing served with food to enhance its flavor; stewed or preserved fruit eaten with other food or as a dessert; (*inf*) impudence. * *vt* to season with sauce; to make piquant; (*sl*) to cheek.

saucepan *n* a deep cooking pan with a handle and lid.

saucer *n* a round shallow dish placed under a cup; a shallow depression; a thing shaped like a saucer.

saucy *adj* (**saucier, sauciest**) rude, impertinent; sprightly.—**saucily** *adv*.—**sauciness** *n*.

saunter *vi* to walk in a leisurely or idle way. * *n* a stroll.

sausage *n* minced seasoned meat, esp pork, packed into animal gut or other casing.

savage *adj* fierce; wild; untamed; uncivilized; ferocious; primitive. * *n* a member of a primitive society; a brutal, fierce person or animal.—**savagely** *adv*.—**savageness** *n*.

savagery *n* the state of being a savage; an act of violence or cruelty; an uncivilized state.

save *vt* to rescue from harm or danger; to keep, to accumulate; to set aside for future use; to avoid the necessity of; (*energy etc*) to prevent waste of; (*theol*) to deliver from sin. * *vi* to avoid waste, expense, etc; to economize; to store up money or goods; (*sports*) to keep an opponent from scoring or winning. * *n* (*sports*) the act of preventing one's opponent from scoring. * *conj*, prep except, but.

saving *adj* thrifty, economical; (*clause*) containing a reservation; redeeming. * *n* what is saved; (*pl*) money saved for future use. * *prep* except; with apology to.

savings bank *n* a bank receiving small deposits and holding them in interest-bearing accounts.

saviour, savior (*US*) *n* a person who saves another from harm or danger; (*with cap*) Jesus Christ.

savor *n* the flavor or smell of something; a distinctive quality. * *vti* to season; to enjoy; to have a specified taste or smell; to smack (of); to appreciate critically.

savory *adj* having a good taste or smell; spicy, not sweet; reputable. * *n* a savory dish at the beginning or end of dinner; (*pl*) snacks served with drinks.—**savoriness** *n*.

saw[1] *see* **see**[1]

saw[2] *n* a tool with a toothed edge for cutting wood, etc. * *vti* (*pt* **sawed**, *pp* **sawn**) to cut or shape with a saw; to use a saw; to make a to-and-fro motion.

sawdust *n* fine particles of wood caused by sawing.

sawmill *n* a mill where timber is cut into logs or planks.

sawn *see* **saw**[2].

saw-off *n* a compromise reached by competing persons or groups; a tie or stalemate.

saxophone *n* a brass wind instrument with a single reed and about twenty finger-keys.

say *vb* (*pt* **said**) *vt* to speak, to utter; to state in words; to affirm, declare; to recite; to estimate; to assume. * *vi* to tell; to express in words. * *n* the right or opportunity to speak; a share in a decision.

saying *n* a common remark; a proverb or adage.

scab *n* a dry crust on a wound or sore; a plant disease characterized by crustaceous spots; a worker who refuses to join a strike or who replaces a striking worker.—**scabby** *adj*.

scaffold *n* a raised platform for the execution of a criminal; capital punishment; scaffolding.

scaffolding *n* a temporary framework of wood and metal for use by workmen constructing a building, etc; materials for a scaffold.

scald *vt* to burn with hot liquid or steam; to heat almost to boiling point; to immerse in boiling water (to sterilize). * *n* an injury caused by hot liquid or steam.

scale[1] *n* (*pl*) a machine or instrument for weighing; one of the pans or the tray of a set of scales; (*pl with cap*) Libra, the seventh sign of the zodiac. * *vti* to weigh in a set of scales; to have a specified weight on a set of scales.

scale[2] *n* one of the thin plates covering a fish or reptile; a flake (of dry skin); an incrustation on teeth, etc. * *vti* to remove the scales from; to flake off.

scale[3] *n* a graduated measure; an instrument s o marked; (*math*) the basis for a numerical system, 10 being that in general use; (*mus*) a series of tones from the keynote to its octave, in order of pitch; the proportion that a map, etc, bears to what it represents; a series of degrees classified by size, amount, etc; relative scope or size. * *vt* (*wall*) to go up or over; (*model*) to make or draw to scale; to increase or decrease in size.

scallop *n* an edible shellfish with two fluted, fan-shaped shells; one of a series of curves in an edging. * *vt* to cut into scallops.—**scalloped** *adj*.

scalp *n* the skin covering the skull, usu covered with hair. * *vti* to cut the scalp from; to criticize sharply; (*inf*) (*tickets, etc*) to buy and resell at higher prices.

scalpel *n* a short, thin, very sharp knife used esp for surgery.

scamper *vi* to run away quickly or playfully. * *n*

a brisk or playful run or movement.

scan *vb* (*pt* **scanned**) *vt* (*page etc*) to look through quickly; to scrutinize; (*med*) to examine with a radiological device; (*TV*) to pass an electronic beam over; (*radar*) to detect with an electronic beam; (*poem*) to conform to a rhythmical pattern; to check for recorded data by means of a mechanical or electronic device; (*human body*) to make a scan of in a scanner. * *vi* to analyse the pattern of verse. * *n* the act of scanning or an instance of being scanned.

scandal *n* a disgraceful event or action; talk arising from immoral behaviour; a feeling of moral outrage; the thing or person causing this; disgrace; malicious gossip.

scandalize *vt* to shock the moral feelings of; to defame.

scandalous *adj* causing scandal; shameful; spreading slander.

Scandinavia *n* the region comprising Norway, Sweden, and Denmark, and sometimes Iceland.—**Scandinavian** *adj*.

scant *adj* limited; meagre; insufficient; scanty; grudging.

scanty *adj* (**scantier, scantiest**) barely adequate; insufficient; small.—**scantily** *adv*.—**scantiness** *n*.

scapegoat *n* a person who bears the blame for others; one who is the object of irrational hostility.

scar[1] *n* a mark left after the healing of a wound or sore; a blemish resulting from damage or wear. * *vti* (*pt* **scarred**) to mark with or form a scar.

scar[2] *n* a protruding or isolated rock; a precipitous crag; a rocky part of a hillside.

scarce *adj* not in abundance; hard to find; rare.—**scarceness** *n*.

scarcely *adv* hardly, only just; probably not or certainly not.

scarcity *n* the state of being scarce; a dearth, deficiency.

scare *vti* to startle; to frighten or become frightened; to drive away by frightening. * *n* a sudden fear; a period of general fear; a false alarm.

scarecrow *n* a wooden figure dressed in clothes for scaring birds from crops; a thin or tattered person; something frightening but harmless.

scaremonger *n* a person who causes fear or panic by spreading rumours; an alarmist.

scarf *n* (*pl* **scarves**) a rectangular or square piece of cloth worn around the neck, shoulders or head for warmth or decoration.

scarlet *n* a bright red with a tinge of orange; scarlet cloth or clothes. * *adj* scarlet colored; immoral or sinful.

scarlet fever *n* an acute contagious disease marked by a sore throat, fever, and a scarlet rash.

scathing *adj* bitterly critical; cutting, withering.—**scathingly** *adv*.

scatter *vti* to throw loosely about; to sprinkle; to dissipate; to put or take to flight; to dis-

perse; to occur at random. * *n* a scattering or sprinkling.

scatterbrain *n* a frivolous, heedless person.—**scatterbrained** *adj*.

scattered *adj* dispersed widely, spaced out; straggling.

scavenge *vi* to gather things discarded by others; (*animal*) to eat decaying matter.—**scavenger** *n*.

scene *n* the place in which anything occurs; the place in which the action of a play or a story occurs; a section of a play, a division of an act; the stage of a theatre; a painted screen, etc, used on this; an unseemly display of strong emotion; a landscape; surroundings; a place of action; (*inf*) an area of interest or activity (eg *the music scene*).

scenery *n* painted screens, etc, used to represent places, as in a play, film, etc; an aspect of a landscape, esp of beautiful or impressive countryside.

scenic *adj* relating to natural scenery; picturesque; of or used on the stage.—**scenically** *adv*.

scent *n* a perfume; an odour left by an animal, by which it can be tracked; the sense of smell; a line of pursuit or discovery. * *vt* to recognize by the sense of smell; to track by smell; to impart an odour to, to perfume; to get wind of, to detect.

scented *adj* perfumed.

sceptic, skeptic (*US*) *n* a person who questions opinions generally accepted; a person who doubts religious doctrines, an agnostic; an adherent of scepticism.

sceptical, skeptical (*US*) *adj* doubting; questioning.—**sceptically** *adv*.

scepticism, skepticism (*US*) *n* an attitude of questioning criticism, doubt; (*philos*) the doctrine that absolute knowledge is unattainable.

sceptre, scepter (*US*) *n* the staff of office held by a monarch on a ceremonial occasion; sovereignty.

schedule *n* a timetable; a list, inventory or tabulated statement; a timed plan for a project. * *vt* to make a schedule; to plan.

scheme *n* a plan; a project; a systematic arrangement; a diagram; an underhand plot. * *vti* to devise or plot.—**schemer** *n*.

scheming *adj* cunning; intriguing.

schism *n* a division or separation into two parties, esp of a church; the sin of this; discord, disharmony.

schizophrenia *n* a mental disorder characterized by withdrawal from reality and deterioration of the personality; the presence of mutually contradictory qualities or parts.—**schizophrenic** *adj, n*.

scholar *n* a pupil, a student; a learned person; the holder of a scholarship.

scholarly *adj* learned, erudite, academic.

scholarship *n* an annual grant to a scholar or student, usu won by competitive examination; learning, academic achievement.

school[1] *n* a shoal of porpoises, whales, or other

aquatic animals of one kind swimming together.

school² n an educational establishment; its teachers and students; a regular session of teaching; formal education, schooling; a particular division of a university; a place or means of discipline; a group of thinkers, artists, writers, holding similar principles. * vt to train; to teach; to control or discipline.

schoolboy n a boy who attends school.

schoolgirl n a girl who attends school.

schooling n instruction in school.

schoolmaster n a man who teaches in school.

schoolmistress n a woman who teaches in school.

schoolteacher n a person who teaches in school.

schooner n a sailing ship with two or more masts rigged with fore-and-aft sails; a large drinking glass for sherry or beer.

sciatica n pain along the sciatic nerve, esp in the back of the thigh; (loosely) pain in the lower back or adjacent parts.

science n knowledge gained by systematic experimentation and analysis, and the formulation of general principles; a branch of this; skill or technique.

science fiction n highly imaginative fiction typically involving actual or projected scientific phenomena.

scientific adj of or concerned with science; based on or using the principles and methods of science; systematic and exact; having or showing expert skill.—**scientifically** adv.

scientist n a specialist in a branch of science, as in chemistry, etc.

scintillating adj sparkling; amusing.

scissor vt to cut with scissors, to clip. * npl a tool for cutting paper, hair, etc, consisting of two fastened pivoted blades whose edges slide past each other; a gymnastic feat in which the leg movements resemble the opening and closing of scissors.

scoff¹ vti to jeer (at) or mock. * n an expression or object of derision; mocking words, a taunt.

scoff² vt (sl) to eat quickly and greedily. * n (Cdn) (inf) a big meal.

scold vi to reprove angrily; to tell off.

scone n a small, round cake made from flour and fat which is baked and spread with butter, etc.

scoop n a small shovel-like utensil as for taking up flour, ice cream, etc; the bucket of a dredge, etc; the act of scooping or the amount scooped up at one time; (inf) a piece of exclusive news; (inf) the advantage gained in being the first to publish or broadcast this. * vt to shovel, lift or hollow out with a scoop; (inf) to obtain as a scoop; (inf: rival newspaper etc) to forestall with a news item.

scooter n a child's two-wheeled vehicle with a footboard and steering handle; a motor scooter.

scope n the opportunity to use one's abilities; extent; range; an instrument for viewing.

scorch vti to burn or be burned on the surface; to wither from over-exposure to heat; to singe; (inf) to drive or cycle furiously.

scorcher n (inf) a very hot day.

scorching adj (inf: weather) very hot; scathing.

score n the total number of points made in a game or examination; a notch or scratch; a line indicating deletion or position; a group of twenty; a written copy of a musical composition showing the different parts; the music composed for a film; a grievance for settling; a reason or motive; (inf) the real facts; a bill or reckoning; (pl) an indefinite, large number. * vt to mark with cuts; (mus) to arrange in a score, to orchestrate; to gain or record points, as in a game; to evaluate in testing. * vi to make points, as in a game; to keep the score of a game; to gain an advantage, a success, etc; (sl) to be successful in seduction.—**scorer** n.

scorn n extreme contempt or disdain; the object of this. * vt to treat with contempt, to despise; to reject or refuse as unworthy.—**scornful** adj.—**scornfully** adv.

Scorpio n the eighth sign of the zodiac in astrology, operative from 23 October - 21 November.

scorpion n a small, tropical, insect-like animal with pincers and a jointed tail with a poisonous sting.

Scot n a native or inhabitant of Scotland; a member of a Celtic people from Ireland that settled in northern Britain in the 5th and 6th centuries.

Scotch n whisky made in Scotland.

scotch vt (a rumour) to stamp out.

Scots adj of or pertaining to Scotland, its law, money, and people, and the Scots language. * n the dialect of English developed in Lowland Scotland.

Scottish adj of or relating to Scotland and its people.

scoundrel n a rascal; a dishonest person.

scour¹ vt to clean by rubbing with an abrasive cloth; to flush out with a current of water; to purge. * n the act or process of scouring; a place scoured by running water; scouring action; damage done by scouring.

scour² vt to hasten over or along, to range over, esp in search or pursuit.

scourge n a whip; a means of inflicting punishment; a person who harasses and causes widespread and great affliction; a pest. * vt to flog; to punish harshly.

scout n a person, plane, etc, sent to observe the enemy's strength, etc; a person employed to find new talent or survey a competitor, etc; (with cap) a member of the Scouting Association, an organization for young people. * vti to reconnoitre; to go in search of (something).

scowl n a contraction of the brows in an angry or threatening manner; a sullen expression. * vi to make a scowl; to look sullen.

scraggy *adj* (**scraggier, scraggiest**) thin and bony, gaunt.

scram *vi* (*pt* **scrammed**) (*sl*) to get out, to go away at once.

scramble *vi* to move or climb hastily on all fours; to scuffle or struggle for something; to move with urgency or panic. * *vt* to mix haphazardly; to stir (slightly beaten eggs) while cooking; (*trânsmitted signals*) to make unintelligible in transit. * *n* a hard climb or advance; a disorderly struggle; a rapid emergency take-off of fighter planes; a motorcycle rally over rough ground.— **scrambler** *n*.

scrap[1] *n* a small piece; a fragment of discarded material; (*pl*) bits of food. * *adj* in the form of pieces, leftovers, etc; used and discarded. * *vt* (*pt* **scrapped**) to discard; to make into scraps.

scrap[2] *n* (*inf*) a fight or quarrel.—*also vi.*

scrapbook *n* a book for pasting clippings, etc, in.

scrape *vt* to rub with a sharp or abrasive object so as to clean, smooth or remove; to eke out or to be economical; to amass in small portions; to draw along with a grating or vibration; to get narrowly past, to graze; to draw back the foot in making a bow. * *n* the act of scraping; a grating sound; an abrasion, scratch; an awkward predicament.

scraper *n* an instrument for scraping; a grating or edge for scraping mud from boots.

scrapheap *n* a pile of discarded material or things.

scrappy *adj* (**scrappier, scrappiest**) disjointed; fragmentary; full of gaps.—**scrappiness** *n*.

scratch *vt* to mark with a sharp point; to scrape with the nails or claws; to rub to relieve an itch; to chafe; to write awkwardly; (*writing etc*) to strike out; to withdraw from a race, etc. * *vi* to use nails or claws to tear or dig. * *n* the act of scratching; a mark or sound made by this; a slight injury; a starting line for a race; a scribble. * *adj* taken at random, haphazard, impromptu; without a handicap.

scrawl *n* careless or illegible handwriting; a scribble. * *vti* to draw or write carelessly.

scrawny *adj* (**scrawnier, scrawniest**) skinny; bony.

scream *vti* to utter a piercing cry, as of pain, fear, etc; to shout; to shriek. * *n* a sharp, piercing cry; (*inf*) a very funny person or thing.

scree *n* loose shifting stones; a slope covered with these.

screech *n* a harsh, high-pitched cry; (*Cdn*) a dark rum bottled in Newfoundland. * *vti* to utter a screech, to shriek.

screen *n* a movable partition or framework to conceal, divide, or protect; a shelter or shield from heat, danger or view; an electronic display (as in a television set, computer terminal, etc); a surface on which films, slides, etc are projected; the motion picture industry; a coarse wire mesh over a window or door to keep out insects; a sieve. * *vt* to conceal or shelter; to grade by passing through a screen; to separate according to skill, etc; (*a film*) to show on a screen.

screening *n* a showing of a film; a metal or plastic mesh, as for window screens; the refuse matter after sieving.

screw *n* a metal cylinder or cone with a spiral thread around it for fastening things by being turned; any spiral thing like this; a twist or turn of a screw; a twist of paper; pressure; a propeller with revolving blades on a shaft. * *vt* to fasten, tighten etc with a screw; to oppress; to extort, to cheat out of something due; (*sl, vulg*) to have sexual intercourse with; (*with* **up**) to gather (courage, etc). * *vi* to go together or come apart by being turned like a screw; to twist or turn with a writhing movement; (*sl, vulg*) to have sexual intercourse; (*with* **up**) to bungle.

screwdriver *n* a tool like a blunt chisel for turning screws; a drink of vodka and orange juice.

screwy *adj* (*sl*) (**screwier, screwiest**) eccentric, odd.

scribble *vti* to draw or write hastily or carelessly, to scrawl; to be a writer. * *n* hasty writing, a scrawl.—**scribbler** *n*.

script *n* handwriting; a style of writing; the text of a stage play, screenplay or broadcast; a plan of action; (*print*) type that resembles handwriting. * *vt* to write a script (for).

scriptural *adj* of or based on the Bible or Scripture.

scripture *n* any sacred writing; (*with cap, often pl*) the Jewish Bible or Old Testament; the Christian Bible or Old and New Testaments. * *adj* contained in or quoted from the Bible.

scriptwriter *n* a writer of screenplays for films, TV, etc; a screenwriter—**scriptwriting** *n*.

scroll *n* a roll of parchment or paper with writing on it; an ornament like this; (*her*) a ribbon with a motto; a list. * *vti* (*comput*) to move text across a screen; to decorate with scrolls.

scrounge *vti* (*inf*) to seek or obtain (something) for nothing.—**scrounger** *n*.

scrub[1] *n* an arid area of stunted trees and shrubs; such vegetation; anything small or mean. * *adj* small, stunted, inferior, etc.

scrub[2] *vti* (*pt* **scrubbed**) to clean vigorously, to scour; to rub hard; (*inf*) to remove, to cancel. * *n* the act of scrubbing.

scruff *n* the back of the neck, the nape.

scruffy *adj* (**scruffier, scruffiest**) shabby; unkempt.—**scruffily** *adv.*—**scruffiness** *n*.

scrum *n* a scrummage; (*Cdn*) the informal, disorganized questioning of a politician by reporters who crowd around him or her.—*also* **media scrum.**

scrummage *n* (*Rugby football*) a play consisting of a tussle between rival forwards in a compact mass for possession of the ball. * *vi* to form a scrum(mage).

scruncheon *n* a small piece of crisply fried pork used as a garnish.

scruple *n* (*usu pl*) a moral principle or belief

causing one to doubt or hesitate about a course of action. * vti to hesitate owing to scruples.

scrupulous adj careful; conscientious; thorough.—**scrupulously** adv.—**scrupulousness** n.

scrutinize vti to look closely at, to examine narrowly; to make a scrutiny.

scrutiny n a careful examination; a critical gaze; an official inspection of votes cast in an election.

scuff vti to drag the feet, to shuffle; to wear or mark the surface of by doing this.

scuffle n a confused fight; the sound of shuffling. * vi to fight confusedly; to move by shuffling.

scullery n a room for storage or kitchen work, such as washing dishes, etc.

sculptor n a person skilled in sculpture.

sculpture n the art of carving wood or forming clay, stone, etc, into figures, statues, etc; a three-dimensional work of art; a sculptor's work. * vt to carve, adorn or portray with sculptures; to shape, mould or form like sculpture.—**sculptural** adj.

scum n a thin layer of impurities on top of a liquid; refuse; despicable people.

scurrilous adj abusive; grossly offensive.

scurry vi (pt **scurried**) to hurry with quick, short steps, to scamper. * n a bustle; a flurry (as of snow).

scurvy n a disease caused by a deficiency of vitamin C. * adj base; contemptible.

scuttle[1] vi to run quickly; to hurry away. * n a short swift run; a hurried pace.

scuttle[2] n a bucket with a lip for storing coal.

scuttle[3] n (naut) a hatchway, a hole with a cover in a ship's deck or side. * vt to sink a ship by making holes in it.

scythe n a two-handed implement with a large curved blade for cutting grass, etc. * vti to cut with a scythe; to mow down.

sea n the ocean; a section of this; a vast expanse of water; a heavy wave, the swell of the ocean; something like the sea in size; the seafaring life. * adj marine, of the sea.

seaboard n, adj (land) bordering on the sea.

sea breeze n a wind that blows from the sea to the land.

SeaDoo n (Cdn) (TM) a narrow, jet-propelled watercraft for one or two persons, ridden like a motorcycle.

seafood n edible fish or shellfish from the sea.

sea front n the waterfront of a seaside place.

seagoing adj (ship) made for use on the open sea.

seagull n a gull.

seal[1] n an engraved stamp for impressing wax, lead, etc; wax, lead, etc, so impressed; that which authenticates or pledges; a device for closing or securing tightly. * vt to fix a seal to; to close tightly or securely; to shut up; to mark as settled, to confirm.

seal[2] n an aquatic mammal with four webbed flippers; the fur of some seals; a dark brown. * vi to hunt seals.

sealant n a thing that seals, as wax, etc; a substance for stopping a leak, making watertight, etc.

sealer n a person or ship whose business is hunting seals.

sea level n the level of the surface of the sea in relation to the land.

sea lion n a large seal of the Pacific Ocean that has a roar and, in the male, a mane.

seam n the line where two pieces of cloth are stitched together; (geol) a stratum of coal, oil, etc, between thicker ones; a line or wrinkle. * vt to join with a seam; to furrow.

seaman n a sailor; a naval rank.

seamy adj (**seamier, seamiest**) unpleasant or sordid.

seance, séance n a meeting of spiritualists to try to communicate with the dead.

seaplane n an aeroplane with floats that allow it to take off from and land on water.

seaport n a port, harbour or town accessible to oceangoing ships.

search vi to look around to find something; to explore. * vt to examine or inspect closely; to probe into. * n the act of searching; an investigation; a quest.—**searcher** n.

searching adj keen, piercing; examining thoroughly.—**searchingly** adv.

searchlight n a powerful ray of light projected by an apparatus on a swivel; the apparatus.

search warrant n a legal document that authorizes a police search.

seashore n land beside the sea or between high and low water marks; the beach.

seasick adj affected with nausea brought on by the motion of a ship.

seaside n seashore.

season n one of the four equal parts into which the year is divided: spring, summer, autumn, or winter; a period of time; a time when something is plentiful or in use; a suitable time; (inf) a season ticket. * vt (food) to flavor by adding salt, spices, etc; to make mature or experienced; (wood) to dry until ready for use. * vi to become experienced.

seasonal adj of or relating to a particular season.

seasoning n salt, spices, etc, used to enhance the flavor of food; the process of making something fit for use.

season ticket n a ticket or set of tickets valid for a number of concerts, games, journeys, etc, during a specified period.

seat n a piece of furniture for sitting on, such as a chair, bench, etc; the part of a chair on which one sits; the buttocks, the part of the trousers covering them; a way of sitting (on a horse, etc); the chief location, or centre; a part at or forming a base; the right to sit as a member; a parliamentary constituency; a large country house. * vt to place on a seat; to provide with seats; to settle.

seatbelt n an anchored strap worn in a car or aeroplane to secure a person to a seat.

seat sale n (Cdn) a sale of airline tickets at a discount price.

seaweed n a mass of plants growing in or under

water; a sea plant, esp a marine alga.

seaworthy *adj* fit to go to sea; able to withstand sea water, watertight.

sec. *abbr* = second.

secluded *adj* private; sheltered; kept from contact with other people.

seclusion *n* the state of being secluded; privacy, solitude.

second *adj* next after first; alternate; another of the same kind; next below the first in rank, value, etc. * *n* a person or thing coming second; another; an article of merchandise not of first quality; an aid or assistant, as to a boxer, duellist; the gear after low gear; one sixtieth of a minute of time or of an angular degree; (*pl*) (*inf*) another helping of food. * *adv* in the second place, group, etc. * *vt* to act as a second (to); (*a motion, resolution, etc*) to support; (*mil*) to place on temporary service elsewhere.

secondary *adj* subordinate; second in rank or importance; in the second stage; derived, not primary; relating to secondary school. * *n* that which is secondary; a delegate, a deputy.—**secondarily** *adv*.

secondary school *n* a school between elementary or primary school and college or university.

second class *n* the class next to the first in a classification. * *adj* (second-class) relating to a second class; inferior, mediocre; (*seating, accommodation*) next in price and quality to first class; (*mail*) less expensive and handled more slowly (than first class).

second-hand *adj* bought after use by another; derived, not original.—*also adv.*

secondly *adv* in the second place.

second-rate *adj* of inferior quality.

second thought *n* a change in thought or decision after consideration.

secrecy *n* the state of being secret; the ability to keep secret.

secret *adj* not made public; concealed from others; hidden; private; remote. * *n* something hidden; a mystery; a hidden cause.—**secretly** *adv*.

secretariat *n* an administrative office or staff, as in a government.

secretary *n* a person employed to deal with correspondence, filing, telephone calls of another or of an association; the head of a state department.—**secretarial** *adj*.

secretive *adj* given to secrecy; uncommunicative, reticent.—**secretively** *adv.*—**secretiveness** *n*.

sect *n* a religious denomination; a group of people united by a common interest or belief; a faction.

section *n* the act of cutting; a severed or separable part; a division; a distinct portion; a slice; a representation of anything cut through to show its interior; (*geom*) the cutting of a solid by a plane; a plane figure formed by this. * *vti* to cut or separate into sections; to represent in sections; to become separated or cut into parts.

sector *n* (*geom*) a space enclosed by two radii of a circle and the arc they cut off; a distinctive part (as of an economy); a subdivision; (*mil*) an area of activity .

secular *adj* having no connection with religion or the church; worldly.

secularize *vt* to change from religious to civil use or control.—**secularization** *n*.

secure *adj* free from danger, safe; stable; firmly held or fixed; confident, assured (of); reliable. * *vt* to make safe; to fasten firmly; to protect; to confine; to fortify; to guarantee; to gain possession of.—**securely** *adv*.

security *n* the state of being secure; a financial guarantee, surety; a pledge for repayment, etc; a protection or safeguard; a certificate of shares or bonds.

sedate[1] *adj* calm; composed; serious and unemotional.—**sedately** *adv.*—**sedateness** *n*.

sedate[2] *vti* to calm or become calm by the administration of a sedative.

sedation *n* the act of calming or the condition of being calmed, esp by sedatives; the administration of sedatives to calm a patient.

sedative *n* a drug with a soothing, calming effect. * *adj* having a soothing, calming effect.

sediment *n* matter that settles at the bottom of a liquid; (*geol*) matter deposited by water or wind.—**sedimentary** *adj*.

seduce *vt* to lead astray; to corrupt; to entice into unlawful sexual intercourse.—**seducer** *n*.

seduction *n* the act of seducing; temptations; attraction.

seductive *adj* tending to seduce; enticing, alluring.—**seductively** *adv*.

see[1] *vt* (*pt* **saw**, *pp* **seen**) to perceive with the eyes; to observe; to grasp with intelligence; to ascertain; to take care (that); to accompany; to visit to meet; to consult;(*guests*) to receive. * *vi* to have the faculty of sight; to make inquiry; to consider, to reflect; to understand.

see[2] *n* the diocese of a bishop.

seed *n* the small, hard part (ovule) of a plant from which a new plant grows; such seeds collectively; the source of anything; sperm or semen; descendants; (*tennis*) a seeded tournament player. * *vti* to sow (seed); to produce or shed seed; to remove seeds from; (*tennis*) to arrange (a tournament) so that the best players cannot meet until later rounds.

seedling *n* a young plant raised from seed, not from a cutting; a young tree before it is a sapling.

seedy *adj* (**seedier, seediest**) full of seeds; out of sorts, indisposed; shabby; rundown.—**seedily** *adv.*—**seediness** *n*.

seeing *n* vision, sight. * *adj* having sight; observant. * *conj* in view of the fact that; since.

seek *vti* (*pt* **sought**) to search for; to try to find, obtain, or achieve; to resort to; (*with* **to**) to try to, to endeavour; (*with* **out**) to try to secure the society of.—**seeker** *n*.

seem *vi* to appear (to be); to give the impression of; to appear to oneself.

seen *see* **see**[1].

seep *vi* to ooze gently, to leak through.

seer *n* a person who sees visions, a prophet.

seesaw *n* a plank balanced across a central support so that it is tilted up and down by a person sitting on each end; an up-and-down movement like this; vacillation. * *vi* to move up and down; to fluctuate. * *adj, adv* alternately rising and falling.

seethe *vi* to be very angry inwardly; to swarm (with people).

segment *n* a section; a portion; one of the two parts of a circle or sphere when a line is drawn through it. * *vti* to cut or separate into segments.

segregate *vti* to set apart from others, to isolate; to separate racial or minority groups.

seigneur *n* (*Cdn*) (*hist*) a person in French Canada who rented land to tenant farmers.—**seigneurial** *adj*.

seize *vt* to grasp; to capture; to take hold of suddenly or forcibly; to attack or afflict suddenly. * *vi* (*machinery*) to become jammed.—**seizable** *adj*.

seizure *n* the act of seizing; what is seized; a sudden attack of illness, an apoplectic stroke.

seldom *adv* not often, rarely.

select *vti* to choose or pick out. * *adj* excellent; choice; limited (eg in membership); exclusive.

selection *n* the act of selecting; what is or are selected; the process by which certain animals or plants survive while others are eliminated.—*also* **natural selection**.

selective *adj* having the power of selection; highly specific in activity or effect.

self *n* (*pl* **selves**) the identity, character, etc, of any person or thing; one's own person as distinct from all others; one's own interests or advantage. * *adj* (*color*) matching, uniform.

self- *prefix* of itself or oneself; by, for, in relation to, itself or oneself; automatic.

self-assured *adj* confident.—**self-assurance** *n*.

self-catering *adj* catering for oneself.

self-centred, self-centered (*US*) *adj* preoccupied with one's own affairs.—**self-centredness** *n*.

self-colored *adj* of a single color.

self-confident *adj* sure of one's own powers.—**self-confidence** *n*.

self-conscious *adj* embarrassed or awkward in the presence of others, ill at ease.—**self-consciousness** *n*.

self-contained *adj* complete in itself; showing self-control; uncommunicative.

self-control *n* control of one's emotions, desires, etc, by the will.—**self-controlled** *adj*.

self-defence, self-defense (*US*) *n* the act of defending oneself; (*law*) a plea for the justification for the use of force.

self-employed *adj* earning one's living in one's own business or profession, not employed by another; working freelance.

self-evident *adj* evident without proof or explanation.—**self-evidence** *n*.

self-indulgence *n* undue gratification of one's desires, appetites, or whims.—**self-indulgent** *adj*.

self-interest *n* regard to one's own advantage.

selfish *adj* chiefly concerned with oneself; lacking consideration for others.—**selfishly** *adv*.—**selfishness** *n*.

selfless *adj* with no thought of self, unselfish.—**selflessness** *n*.

self-portrait *n* an artist or author's painting or account of himself or herself.

self-possessed *adj* cool and collected.

self-reliant *adj* relying on one's own powers; confident.—**self-reliance** *n*.

self-respect *n* proper respect for oneself, one's standing and dignity.—**self-respecting** *adj*.

self-righteous *adj* thinking oneself better than others; priggish.—**self-righteousness** *n*.

self-sacrifice *n* the sacrifice of one's own interests, welfare, etc, to secure that of others.

self-satisfied *adj* smugly conceited.

self-service *adj* serving oneself in a cafe, shop, filling station, etc.

self-sufficient *adj* independent; supporting oneself (eg in growing food) without the help of others.—**self-sufficiency** *n*.

sell *vb* (*pt* **sold**) *vt* to exchange (goods, services, etc) for money or other equivalent; to offer for sale; to promote; to deal in. * *vi* (*with* **off**) to clear out (stock) at bargain prices; (*with* **out**) to sell off, to betray for money or reward; (*inf*) to disappoint, to trick; to make sales; to attract buyers. * *n* an act or instance of selling; (*inf*) a disappointment, a trick, a fraud.—**seller** *n*.

sellout *n* a show, game, etc, for which all the tickets are sold; (*inf*) a betrayal.

semaphore *n* a system of visual signalling using the operator's arms, flags, etc; a signalling device consisting of a post with movable arms.

semen *n* the fluid that carries sperm in men and male animals.

semi- *prefix* half; not fully; twice in a (specified period).

semibreve *n* (*mus*) a note equal to two minims.

semicircle *n* half of a circle.—**semicircular** *adj*.

semicolon *n* the punctuation mark (;) of intermediate value between a comma and a full stop.

semiconscious *adj* not fully conscious.—**semiconsciousness** *n*.

semi-detached *adj* (*house*) with another joined to it on one side.—*also n*.

semifinal *adj, n* (the match or round) before the final in a knockout tournament.—**semifinalist** *n*.

seminar *n* a group of students engaged in study or research under supervision; any group meeting to pool and disuss ideas.

semiquaver *n* (*mus*) half a quaver.

semiskilled *adj* partly skilled or trained.

semitone *n* (*mus*) an interval equal to half a tone.

semolina *n* coarse particles of grain left after

the sifting of wheat.

senate *n* a legislative or governing body; (*with cap*) the upper branch of a two-body legislature in France, the US, etc; the governing body of some universities.

senator *n* a member of a senate.—**senatorial** *adj*.

send *vti* (*pt* **sent**) to cause or enable to go; to have conveyed, to dispatch (a message or messenger); to cause to move, to propel; to grant; to cause to be; (*sl*) to move (a person) to ecstasy; (*with* **down**) to expel from university; (*with* **for**) to order to be brought, to summon; (*with* **up**) (*inf*) to send to prison; to imitate or make fun of.—**sender** *n*.

send-off *n* a friendly demonstration at a departure; a start given to someone or something.

senile *adj* of or relating to old age; weakened, *esp* mentally, by old age.—**senility** *n*.

senior *adj* higher in rank; of or for seniors; longer in service; older (when used to distinguish between father and son with the same first name). * *n* one's elder or superior in standing; a person of advanced age; a student in the last year of college or high school.

seniority *n* the condition of being senior; status, priority, etc, in a given job.

sensation *n* awareness due to stimulation of the senses; an effect on the senses; a thrill; a state of excited interest; the cause of this.

sensational *adj* of or relating to sensation; exciting violent emotions; melodramatic.—**sensationally** *adv*.

sensationalism *n* the use of sensational writing, language, etc; the doctrine that all knowledge is obtained from sense impressions.—**sensationalist** *n*.

sense *n* one of the five human and animal faculties by which objects are perceived: sight, hearing, smell, taste, and touch; awareness; moral discernment; soundness of judgment; meaning, intelligibility; (*pl*) conscious awareness. * *vt* to perceive; to become aware of; to understand; to detect.

senseless *adj* stupid, foolish; meaningless, purposeless; unconscious.—**senselessly** *adv*.—**senselessness** *n*.

sensibility *n* the capacity to feel; over-sensitiveness; susceptibility; (*pl*) sensitive awareness or feelings.

sensible *adj* having good sense or judgment; reasonable; practical; perceptible by the senses, appreciable; conscious (of); sensitive.—**sensibleness** *n*.—**sensibly** *adv*.

sensitive *adj* having the power of sensation; feeling readily and acutely, keenly perceptive; (*skin*) delicate, easily irritated; (*wound etc*) still in a painful condition; easily hurt or shocked, tender, touchy; highly responsive to slight changes; sensory; (*photog*) reacting to light.—**sensitively** *adj*.—**sensitiveness** *n*.

sensitivity *n* (*pl* **sensitivities**) the condition of being sensitive; awareness of changes or differences; responsiveness to stimuli or feelings, esp to excess.

sensual *adj* bodily, relating to the senses rather than the mind; arousing sexual desire.—**sensuality** *n*.—**sensually** *adv*.

sensuous *adj* giving pleasure to the mind or body through the senses.—**sensuously** *adv*.—**sensuousness** *n*.

sent *see* send.

sentence *n* a court judgment; the punishment imposed; (*gram*) a series of words conveying a complete thought. * *vt* (*a convicted person*) to pronounce punishment upon; to condemn (to).

sentiment *n* a feeling, awareness, or emotion; the thought behind something; an attitude of mind; a tendency to be swayed by feeling rather than reason; an exaggerated emotion.

sentimental *adj* of or arising from feelings; foolishly emotional; nostalgic.

sentry *n* a soldier on guard to give warning of danger and to prevent unauthorized access.

separate *vt* to divide or part; to sever; to set or keep apart; to sort into different sizes. * *vi* to go different ways; to cease to live together as man and wife. * *adj* divided; distinct, individual; not shared. * *n* (*pl*) articles of clothing designed to be interchangeable with others to form various outfits.—**separately** *adv*.

separate school *n* (*Cdn*) a publicly funded school for members of a religious minority, esp Roman Catholics.

separation *n* the act of separating or the state of being separate; a formal arrangement of husband and wife to live apart.

September *n* the ninth month of the year, having 30 days.

septic *adj* infected by micro-organisms; causing or caused by putrefaction.

sequel *n* something that follows, the succeeding part; a consequence; the continuation of a story begun in an earlier literary work, film, etc.

sequence *n* order of succession; a series of succeeding things; a single, uninterrupted episode, as in a film.

sequin *n* a shiny round piece of metal or foil sewn on clothes for decoration.

serenade *n* music sung or played at night beneath a person's window, esp by a lover. * *vt* to entertain with a serenade.

serene *adj* calm; untroubled; tranquil; clear and unclouded; (*with cap*) honored (used as part of certain royal titles).—**serenely** *adv*.—**serenity** *n*.

sergeant *n* a noncommissioned officer ranking above a corporal in the army, air force, and marine corps; a police officer.

serial *adj* of or forming a series; published, shown or broadcast by instalments at regular intervals. * *n* a story presented in regular instalments with a connected plot.

series *n sing, pl* a succession of items or events; a succession of things connected by some likeness; a sequence, a set; a radio or television serial whose episodes have self-contained plots; a set of books issued by one publisher; (*math*) a progression of numbers or quantities according to a certain law.

serious *adj* grave, solemn, not frivolous; meaning what one says, sincere, earnest; requiring close attention or thought; important; critical.—**seriously** *adv*.—**seriousness** *n*.

sermon *n* a speech on religion or morals, esp by a clergyman; a long, serious talk of reproof, esp a tedious one.

serrated *adj* having an edge notched like the teeth of a saw.

serum *n* (*pl* **serums, sera**) the watery part of bodily fluid, esp liquid that separates out from the blood when it coagulates; such fluid taken from the blood of an animal immune to a disease, used as an antitoxin.

servant *n* a personal or domestic attendant; one in the service of another.

serve *vt* to work for; to do military or naval service (for); to be useful to; to meet the needs (of), to suffice; (*a customer*) to wait upon; (*food, etc*) to hand round; (*a sentence*) to undergo; to be a soldier, sailor, etc; (*of a male animal*) to copulate with; (*law*) to deliver (a summons, etc); (*naut*) to bind (a rope) with thin cord to prevent fraying; (*tennis*) to put (the ball) into play. * *vi* to be employed as a servant; to be enough. * *n* the act of serving in tennis, etc.

service *n* the act of serving; the state of being a servant; domestic employment; a department of state employ; the people engaged in it; military employment or duty; work done for others; use, assistance; attendance in a hotel, etc; a facility providing a regular supply of trains, etc; a set of dishes; any religious ceremony; an overhaul of a vehicle; (*tennis*) the act or manner of seving; (*pl*) friendly help or professional aid; a system of providing a utility, as water, gas, etc. * *vt* to provide with assistance; to overhaul.

serviceable *adj* useful; durable.—**serviceably** *adv*.—**serviceableness** *n*.

serviceman *n* a member of the armed services; a person whose work is repairing something.—**servicewoman** *nf*.

serviette *n* a small napkin.

servile *adj* of or like a slave; subservient; submissive; menial.

session *n* the meeting of a court, legislature, etc; a series of such meetings; a period of these; a period of study, classes, etc; a university year; a period of time passed in an activity.

set *vb* (*pr p* **setting**, *pt* **set**) *vt* to put in a specified place, condition, etc; (*trap for animals*) to fix; (*clock etc*) to adjust; (*table*) to arrange for a meal; (*hair*) to fix in a desired style; (*bone*)to put into normal position, etc; to make settled, rigid, or fixed; (*gems*) to mount; to direct; to furnish (an example) for others; to fit (words to music or music

to words); (*type*) to arrange for printing. * *vi* to become firm, hard or fixed; to begin to move (out, forth, off, etc); (*sun*) to sink below the horizon; (*with* **in**) to stitch (a sleeve) within a garment; to become established; (*with* **off**) to show up by contrast; to set in motion; to cause to explode; (*with* **on**) to urge (as a dog) to attack or pursue; to go on, advance; (*with* **up**) to erect; to establish, to found; (*with* **upon**) to attack, usu with violence. * *adj* fixed, established; intentional; rigid, firm; obstinate; ready. * *n* a number of persons or things classed or belonging together; a group, a clique; the way in which a thing is set; direction; the scenery for a play, film, etc; assembled equipment for radio or television reception, etc; (*math*) the totality of points, numbers, or objects that satisfy a given condition; (*tennis*) a series of games forming a unit of a match; a rooted cutting of a plant ready for transplanting; a badger's burrow (—*also* **sett**).

setback *n* misfortune; a reversal.

settee *n* a sofa for two people.

setting *n* a background, scene, surroundings, environment; a mounting, as for a gem; the music for a song, etc.

settle *vti* to put in order; to pay (an account); to clarify; to decide, to come to an agreement; to make or become quiet or calm; to make or become firm; to establish or become established in a place, business, home, etc; to colonize (a country); to take up residence; to come to rest; (*dregs*) to fall to the bottom; to stabilize; to make or become comfortable (for resting); (*bird*) to alight; to bestow legally for life.

settlement *n* the act of settling; a sum settled, esp on a woman at her marriage; an arrangement; a small village; a newly established colony; subsidence (of buildings).

settler *n* a person who settles; an early colonist.

set-up *n* the plan, makeup, etc, of equipment used in an organization; the details of a situation, plan, etc; (*inf*) a contest, etc, arranged to result in an easy win.

seven *adj*, *n* one more than six. * *n* the symbol for this (7, VII, vii); the seventh in a series or set; something having seven units as members.

seventeen *adj*, *n* one more than sixteen. * *n* the symbol for this (17, XVII, xvii).—**seventeenth** *adj*.

seventh *adj*, *n* next after sixth; one of seven equal parts of a thing. * *n* (*mus*) an interval of seven diatonic degrees; the leading note.

seventy *adj*, *n* seven times ten. * *n* the symbol for this (70, LXX, lxx); (in *pl*) **seventies** (70s) the numbers for 70 to 79; the same numbers in a life or century.—**seventieth** *adj*.

sever *vti* to separate, to divide into parts; to break off.—**severance** *n*.

several *adj* more than two but not very many; various; separate, distinct; respective. * *pron* (*with pl vb*) a few. * *n* (*with pl vb*) a small number (of).

severe *adj* harsh, not lenient; very strict; stern; censorious; exacting, difficult; violent, not slight; (*illness*) critical; (*art*) plain, not florid.—**severely** *adv*.—**severity** *n*.

sew *vti* (*pt* sewed, *pp* sewn *or* sewed) to join or stitch together with needle and thread; to make, mend, etc, by sewing; (*with* up) to get full control of; (*inf*) to make sure of success in.—**sewing** *n*.

sewage *n* waste matter carried away in a sewer.

sewer¹ *n* one who sews.

sewer² *n* an underground pipe or drain for carrying off liquid waste matter, etc; a main drain.

sewing machine *n* a machine for sewing or stitching usu driven by an electric motor.

sex *n* the characteristics that distinguish male and female organisms on the basis of their reproductive function; either of the two categories (male and female) so distinguished; males or females collectively; the state of being mal e or female; the attraction between the sexes; (*inf*) sexual intercourse.

sexual *adj* of sex or the sexes; having sex.—**sexually** *adj*.

sexy *adj* (sexier, sexiest) (*inf*) exciting, or intending to excite, sexual desire.

shabby *adj* (shabbier, shabbiest) (*clothes*) threadbare, worn, or dirty; run-down, dilapidated; (*act, trick*) mean, shameful.—**shabbily** *adv*.—**shabbiness** *n*.

shack *n* a small, crudely built house or cabin; a shanty.

shackle *n* a metal fastening, usu in pairs, for the wrists or ankles of a prisoner; a staple; anything that restrains freedom; (*pl*) fetters. * *vt* to fasten or join by a shackle; to hamper, to impede.

shade *n* relative darkness; dimness; the darker parts of anything; shadow; a shield or screen protecting from bright light; a ghost; a place sheltered from the sun; degree of darkness of a color, esp when made by the addition of black; a minute difference; a blind; (*pl*) the darkness of approaching night; (*pl: sl*) sunglasses. * *vti* to screen from light; to overshadow; to make dark; to pass by degrees into another color; to change slightly or by degrees.

shadow *n* a patch of shade; darkness, obscurity; the dark parts of a painting, etc; shelter, protection; the dark shape of an object produced on a surface by intercepted light; an inseparable companion; a person (as a detective, etc) who shadows; an unsubstantial thing, a phantom; a mere remnant, a slight trace; gloom, affliction. * *vt* to cast a shadow over; to cloud; to follow and watch, esp in secret. * *adj* having an indistinct pattern or darker section; (*opposition party*) matching a function or position of the party in power.

shadowy *adj* full of shadows; dim, indistinct; unsubstantial.

shady *adj* (shadier, shadiest) giving or full of shade; sheltered from the sun; (*inf*) of doubtful honesty, disreputable.

shaft *n* a straight rod, a pole; a stem, a shank; the main part of a column; an arrow or spear, or its stem; anything hurled like a missile; a ray of light, a stroke of lightning; a revolving rod for transmitting power, an axle; one of the poles between which a horse is harnessed; a hole giving access to a mine; a vertical opening through a building, as for a lift; a critical remark or attack; (*sl*) harsh or unfair treatment.

shaggy *adj* (shaggier, shaggiest) (*hair, fur, etc*) long and unkempt; rough; untidy.—**shagginess** *n*.

shake *vti* (*pt* shook, *pp* shaken) to move to and fro with quick short motions, to agitate; to tremble or vibrate; to jar or jolt; to brandish; to make or become unsteady; to weaken; to unsettle; to unnerve or become unnerved; to clasp (another's hand) as in greeting; (*with* down) to cause to subside by shaking; to obtain makeshift accommodation; (*sl*) to extort money from; (*with* off) to get rid of; (*with* out) to empty by shaking; to spread (a sail); (*with* up) to shake together, to mix; to upset. * *n* the act of shaking or being shaken; a jolt; a shock; a milkshake; (*inf*) a deal; (*pl inf*) a convulsive trembling.

shake-up *n* an extensive reorganization.

shaky *adj* (shakier, shakiest) unsteady; infirm; unreliable.—**shakily** *adv*.—**shakiness** *n*.

shale *n* a kind of clay rock like slate only softer.

shall *vb aux* (*pt* should) used formally to express the future in the 1st person and determination, obligation or necessity in the 2nd and 3rd person. The more common form is **will**.

shallow *adj* having little depth; superficial, trivial. * *n* a shallow area in otherwise deep water.—**shallowness** *n*.

sham *n* a pretence; a person or thing that is a fraud. * *adj* counterfeit; fake.

shambles *npl* a scene of great disorder.

shame *n* a painful emotion arising from guilt or impropriety; modesty; disgrace, dishonor; the cause of this; (*sl*) a piece of unfairness. * *vti* to cause to feel shame; to bring disgrace on; to force by shame (into); to humiliate by showing superior qualities.

shamefaced *adj* bashful or modest; sheepish; showing shame; ashamed.

shameful *adj* disgraceful; outrageous.

shameless *adj* immodest; impudent, brazen.

shampoo *n* a liquid cleansing agent for washing the hair; the process of washing the hair or a carpet, etc. * *vt* to wash with shampoo.

shamrock *n* a three-leaved cloverlike plant, the national emblem of Ireland.

shandy *n* beer diluted with a non-alcoholic drink (as lemonade).

shanty¹ *n* a crude hut built from corrugated iron or cardboard.

shanty² *n* a rhythmic working song sung by sailors.

shape *n* the external appearance, outline or contour of a thing; a figure; a definite form; an orderly arrangement; a mould or pattern; (*inf*) condition. * *vt* to give shape to; to form; to model, to mould; to determine; (*with* **up**) to develop to a definite or satisfactory form.

shapeless *adj* lacking definite form; baggy.— **shapelessness** *n*.

shapely *adj* (**shapelier, shapeliest**) well-proportioned.—**shapeliness** *n*.

share *n* an allotted portion, a part; one of the parts into which a company's capital stock is divided, entitling the holder to a share of profits. * *vti* to distribute, to apportion (out); to have or experience in common with others; to divide into portions; to contribute or receive a share of; to use jointly.

shareholder *n* a holder of shares in a property, esp a company.

shark *n* a large voracious marine fish; an extortioner, a swindler; (*sl*) an expert in a given activity.

sharp *adj* having a keen edge or fine point; pointed, not rounded; clear-cut; distinct; intense, piercing; cutting, severe; keen, biting; clever, artful; alert, mentally acute; (*mus*) raised a semitone in pitch; out of tune by being too high; (*sl*) smartly dressed. * *adv* punctually; quickly; (*mus*) above the right pitch. * *n* (*mus*) a note that is a semitone higher than the note denoted by the same letter; the symbol for this (?).— **sharply** *adv*.—**sharpness** *n*.

sharpen *vti* to make or become sharp or sharper.

sharpener *n* something that sharpens.

shatter *vti* to reduce to fragments suddenly; to smash; to damage or be damaged severely.

shave *vti* to remove facial or body hair with a razor; to cut away thin slices, to pare; to miss narrowly, to graze. * *n* the act or process of shaving; a narrow escape or miss; a paring.

shaven *adj* shaved.

shaver *n* one who shaves; an instrument for shaving, esp an electrical one.

shaving *n* the act of using a razor or scraping; a thin slice of wood, metal, etc, shaved off.

shawl *n* a large square or oblong cloth worn as a covering for the head or shoulders or as a wrapping for a baby.

she *pron* (*obj* **her**, *poss* **her, hers**) the female person or thing named before or in question. * *n* a female person or animal.

sheaf *n* (*pl* **sheaves**) a bundle of reaped corn bound together; a collection of papers, etc, tied in a bundle.

shear *vti* (*pp* **sheared** *or* **shorn**) to clip or cut (through); to remove (a sheep's fleece) by clipping; to divest; (*metal*) to break off because of a heavy force or twist. * *n* a stress acting sideways on a rivet and causing a break, etc; a machine for cutting metal; (*pl*) large scissors; (*pl*) a tool for cutting hedges, etc.

sheath *n* a close-fitting cover, esp for a blade; a condom; a closefitting dress usu worn without a belt.

shed[1] *n* a hut for storing garden tools; a large roofed shelter often with one or more sides open; a warehouse.

shed[2] *vt* (*pr p* **shedding**, *pt* **shed**) (*tears*) to let fall; (*skin, etc*) to lose or cast off; to allow or cause to flow; to diffuse, radiate. * *n* a parting in the hair.

sheep *n* (*pl* **sheep**) a cud-chewing four-footed animal with a fleece and edible flesh called mutton; a bashful, submissive person.

sheepdog *n* a dog trained to tend, drive, or guard sheep.

sheepish *adj* bashful, embarrassed.—**sheepishly** *adv*.—**sheepishness** *n*.

sheepskin *n* the skin of a sheep, esp with the fleece; a rug, parchment, or leather made from it; a garment made of or lined with sheepskin.

sheer[1] *adj* pure, unmixed; downright, utter; perpendicular, extremely steep; (*fabric*) delicately fine, transparent. * *adv* outright; perpendicularly, steeply.

sheer[2] *vti* to deviate or cause to deviate from a course; to swerve. * *n* the act of sheering; the upward curve of a deck towards bow or stern; a change in a ship's course.

sheet *n* a broad thin piece of any material, as glass, plywood, metal, etc; a large rectangular piece of cloth used as inner bed clothes; a single piece of paper; (*inf*) a newspaper; a broad, flat expanse; a suspended or moving expanse (as of fire or rain).

sheet lightning *n* lightning that has the appearance of a broad sheet due to reflection and diffusion by the clouds and sky.

sheikh *n* an Arab chief.

shelf *n* (*pl* **shelves**) a board fixed horizontally on a wall or in a cupboard for holding articles; a ledge on a cliff face; a reef, a shoal.

shell *n* a hard outside covering of a nut, egg, shellfish, etc; an explosive projectile; an external framework; a light racing boat; outward show; a cartridge. * *vt* to remove the shell from; to bombard (with shells); (*with* **out**) (*inf*) to pay out (money).

shellfish *n* an aquatic animal with a shell, esp an edible one.

shelter *n* a structure that protects, esp against weather; a place giving protection, a refuge; protection. * *vti* to give shelter to, to shield, to cover; to take shelter.

shelve *vti* to place on a shelf; to defer consideration, to put aside; to slope gently, to incline.

shelving *n* material for making shelves; shelves collectively.

shepherd *n* a person who looks after sheep; a pastor. * *vt* to look after, as a shepherd; to manoeuvre or marshal in a particular direction.—**shepherdess** *nf*.

shepherd's pie *n* a dish of minced meat covered with a mashed potato crust.

sheriff *n* in US, the chief law enforcement officer of a county; in Scotland, a judge in an intermediate law court; in England and Wales, the chief officer of the Crown, a ceremonial post.

sherry *n* a fortified wine originally made in Spain.

Shetland pony *n* a breed of small sturdy pony with a shaggy mane.

shield *n* a broad piece of armour carried for defence, usu on the left arm; a protective covering or guard; a thing or person that protects; a trophy in the shape of a shield. * *vti* to defend; to protect; to screen.

shift *vti* (**shiftier, shiftiest**) to change position (of); to contrive, to manage; to remove, to transfer; to replace by another or others; (*gears*) to change the arrangement of. * *n* a change in position; an expedient; a group of people working in relay with others; the time worked by them; a change or transfer; a straight dress.

shifty *adj* artful, tricky; evasive.—**shiftiness** *n*.

shilling *n* a former unit of currency of the UK and other countries, worth one twentieth of a pound.

shillyshally *vi* to vacillate, to hesitate. * *n* the inability to make up one's mind.

shimmer *vi* to glisten softly, to glimmer.—*also n.*

shin *n* the front part of the leg from the knee to the ankle; the shank. * *vi* (*with* up) to climb (a pole, etc) by gripping with legs and hands.

shine *vti* (*pt* **shone**) to emit light; to be bright, to glow; to be brilliant or conspicuous; to direct the light of; to cause to gleam by polishing. * *n* a lustre, a gloss; (*sl*) a liking.

shingle[1] *n* a thin wedge-shaped roof tile; a small signboard.

shingle[2] *n* waterworn pebbles as on a beach; an area covered with these.—**shingly** *adj*.

shingles *npl* a virus disease marked by a painful rash of red spots.

shinny *n* (*Cdn*) an informal game of ice hockey, usu played without a referee or a net.

shiny *adj* (**shinier, shiniest**) glossy, polished; worn smooth.

ship *n* a large vessel navigating deep water; its officers and crew; a spacecraft. * *vti* (*pt* **shipped**) to transport by any carrier; to take in (water) over the side; to lay (oars) inside a boat; to go on board; to go or travel by ship.

shipbuilder *n* a person or company that designs or constructs ships.—**shipbuilding** *n*.

shipment *n* goods shipped; a consignment.

shipping *n* the business of transporting goods; ships collectively.

shipshape *adj* in good order, tidy.

shipwreck *n* the loss of a vessel at sea; the remains of a wrecked ship; ruin, destruction. * *vti* to destroy by or suffer shipwreck; to ruin.

shipyard *n* a yard or shed where ships are built or repaired.

shire *n* in the UK, a county; a strong draft horse.

shirk *vti* to neglect or avoid work; to refuse to face (duty, danger, etc).—**shirker** *n*.

shirt *n* a sleeved garment of cotton, etc, for the upper body, typically having a fitted collar and cuffs and front buttons; (*inf*) one's money or resources.

shiver[1] *n* a small fragment, a splinter.

shiver[2] *vi* to shake or tremble, as with cold or fear, to shudder.—*also n.*—**shivery** *adj*.

shoal[1] *n* a large number of fish swimming together; a large crowd. * *vi* to form shoals.

shoal[2] *n* a submerged sandbank, esp one that shows at low tide; a shallow place; a hidden danger. * *vti* to come to a less deep part; to become shallower.

shock[1] *n* a shaggy mass of hair.

shock[2] *n* a violent jolt or impact; a sudden disturbance to the emotions; the event or experience causing this; the nerve sensation caused by an electrical charge through the body; a disorder of the blood circulation, produced by displacement of body fluids (due to injury); (*sl*) a paralytic stroke. * *vt* to outrage, horrify. * *vi* to experience extreme horror, outrage, etc.

shock absorber *n* a device, as on the springs of a car, that absorbs the force of bumps and jars.

shocking *adj* revolting; scandalous, improper; very bad.—**shockingly** *adv*.

shod *see* shoe.

shoddy *adj* (**shodier, shodiest**) made of inferior material; cheap and nasty, trashy.—**shoddily** *adv*.—**shoddiness** *n*.

shoe *n* an outer covering for the foot not enclosing the ankle; a thing like a shoe, a partial casing; a horseshoe; a drag for a wheel; a device to guide movement, provide contact, or protect against wear or slipping; a dealing box that holds several decks of cards. * *vt* (*pr p* **shoeing**, *pt* **shod**) to provide with shoes; to cover for strength or protection.

shoehorn *n* a curved piece of plastic, metal, or horn used for easing the heel into a shoe.

shoelace *n* a cord that passes through eyelets in a shoe and is tied to keep the shoe on the foot.

shoetree *n* a block of wood, plastic or metal for preserving the shape of a shoe.

shone *see* shine.

shook *see* shake.

shoot *vb* (*pt* **shot**) *vt* to discharge or fire (a gun etc); to hit or kill with a bullet, etc; (*rapids*) to be carried swiftly over; to propel quickly; to thrust out; (*bolt*) to slide home; to variegate (with another color, etc); (*a film scene*) to photograph; (*sport*) to kick or drive (a ball, etc) at goal; (*with* down) to disprove (an argument); (*with* up) to grow rapidly, to rise abruptly. * *vi* to move swiftly, to dart; to emit; to put forth buds, to sprout; to attack or kill indiscriminately; (*sl*) to inject a narcotic into a vein. * *n* a contest, a shooting trip, etc; a new growth or sprout.

shooting *n* the act of firing a gun or letting off an arrow.

shooting star *n* a meteor.

shop *n* a building were retail goods are sold or services provided; a factory; a workshop; the details and technicalities of one's own work, and talk about these. * *vti* (*pt* **shopped**) to visit shops to examine or buy; (*sl*) to inform on (a person) to the police; (*with* **around**) to hunt for the best buy.

shop floor *n* the part of a factory where goods are manufactured; the work force employed there, usu unionized.

shopkeeper *n* a person who owns or runs a shop.—**shopkeeping** *n*.

shoplifting *n* stealing from a shop during shopping hours.—**shoplifter** *n*.

shopper *n* a person who shops; a bag for carrying shopping.

shopping *n* the act of shopping; the goods bought.—*also adj*.

shopping centre *n* a complex of shops, restaurants, and service establishments with a common parking area.

shopsoiled *adj* faded, etc, from being on display in a shop.

shop steward *n* a union member elected to negotiate with management on behalf of his colleagues.

shore¹ *n* land beside the sea or a large body of water; beach.

shore² *n* a prop or beam used for support. * *vt* to prop (up), to support with a shore.

shorn *see* **shear**.

short *adj* not measuring much; not long or tall; not great in range or scope; brief; concise; not retentive; curt; abrupt; less than the correct amount; below standard; deficient; lacking; (*pastry*) crisp or flaky; (*vowel*) not prolonged, unstressed; (*drink*) undiluted, neat. * *n* something short; (*pl*) trousers not covering the knee; (*pl*) an undergarment like these; a short circuit. * *adv* abruptly; concisely; without reaching the end. * *vti* to give less than what is needed; to short-change; to short-circuit.—**shortness** *n*.

shortage *n* a deficiency.

shortbread *n* a rich, crumbly cake or biscuit made with much shortening.

short-circuit *n* the deviation of an electric current by a path of small resistance; an interrupted electric current. * *vti* to establish a short-circuit in; to cut off electric current; to provide with a short cut.

shortcoming *n* a defect or inadequacy.

short cut *n* a shorter route; any way of saving time, effort, etc.

shorten *vt* to make or become short or shorter; to reduce the amount of (sail) spread; to make (pastry, etc) crisp and flaky by adding fat.

shorthand *n* a method of rapid writing using signs or contractions.—*also adj*.

short-lived *adj* not lasting or living for long.

shortly *adv* soon, in a short time; briefly; rudely.

short-sighted *adj* not able to see well at a distance; lacking foresight.—**short-sightedness** *n*.

shortwave *n* a radio wave 60 metres or less in length.

shot¹ *see* **shoot**.

shot² *n* the act of shooting; range, scope; an attempt; a solid projectile for a gun; projectiles collectively; small lead pellets for a shotgun; a marksman; a photograph or a continuous film sequence; a hypodermic injection, as of vaccine; a drink of alcohol.

shotgun *n* a smooth-bore gun for firing small shot at close range.

should *vb aux* used to express obligation, duty, expectation or probability, or a future condition.—*also pt of* **shall**.

shoulder *n* the joint connecting the arm with the trunk; a part like a shoulder; (*pl*) the upper part of the back; (*pl*) the capacity to bear a task or blame; a projecting part; the strip of land bordering a road. * *vt* to place on the shoulder to carry; to assume responsibility; to push with the shoulder, to jostle.

shoulder blade *n* the large flat triangular bone on either side of the back part of the human shoulder.

shout *n* a loud call; a yell. * *vti* to call loudly, to yell.

shove *vti* to drive forward; to push; to jostle. * *n* a forceful push.

shovel *n* an broad tool like a scoop with a long handle for moving loose material. * *vt* (*pt* **shovelled**) to move or lift with a shovel.

show *vti* (*pt* **showed**, *pp* **shown**) to present to view, to exhibit; to demonstrate, to make clear; to prove; to manifest, to disclose; to direct, to guide; to appear, to be visible; to finish third in a horse race; (*inf*) to arrive; (*with* **off**) to display to advantage; to try to attract admiration; to behave pretentiously; (*with* **up**) to put in an appearance, to arrive; to expose to ridicule. * *n* a display, an exhibition; an entertainment; a theatrical performance; a radio or television programme; third place at the finish (as a horse race).

show business *n* the entertainment industry.—*also* **show biz**.

showdown *n* (*inf*) a final conflict; a disclosure of cards at poker.

shower *n* a brief period of rain, hail, or snow; a similar fall, as of tears, meteors, arrows, etc; a great number; a method of cleansing in which the body is sprayed with water from above; a wash in this; a party for the presentation of gifts, esp to a bride. * *vt* to pour copiously; to sprinkle; to bestow (with gifts). * *vi* to cleanse in a shower.

showjumping *n* the competitive riding of horses to demonstrate their skill in jumping.

showroom *n* a room where goods for sale are displayed.

shrank *see* **shrink**.

shrapnel *n* an artillery shell filled with small pieces of metal that scatter on impact.

shred *n* a strip cut or torn off; a fragment, a scrap. * *vt* (*pt* **shredded**) to cut or tear into small pieces.

shrewd *adj* astute, having common sense; keen, penetrating.—**shrewdly** *adv*.—**shrewdness** *n*.

shriek *n* a loud, shrill cry, a scream. * *vti* to screech, to scream.

shrill *adj* high-pitched and piercing in sound; strident.

shrimp *n* a small edible shellfish with a long tail.

shrine *n* a container for sacred relics; a saint's tomb; a place of worship; a hallowed place.

shrink *vti* (*pt* **shrank**, *pp* **shrunk**) to become smaller, to contract as from cold, wetting, etc; to recoil (from), to flinch; to cause (cloth, etc) to contract by soaking. * *n* (*sl*) a psychiatrist.

shrinkage *n* contraction; diminution.

shrivel *vti* (*pt* **shrivelled**) to dry up or wither and become wrinkled; to curl up with heat, etc.

shroud *n* a burial cloth; anything that envelops or conceals; (*naut*) a supporting rope for a mast. * *vt* to wrap in a shroud; to envelop or conceal.

Shrove Tuesday *n* the last day before Lent.

shrub *n* a woody plant smaller than a tree with several stems rising from the same root; a bush.—**shrubby** *adj*.

shrubbery *n* an area of land planted with shrubs.

shrug *vti* (*pt* **shrugged**) to draw up and contract (the shoulders) as a sign of doubt, indifference, etc; (*with* **off**) to brush aside; to shake off; (*a garment*) to remove by wriggling out. * *n* the act of shrugging.

shrunk *see* **shrink**.

shrunken *adj* shrivelled, pinched; reduced.

shudder *vi* to tremble violently, to shiver; to feel strong repugnance. * *n* a convulsive shiver of the body; a vibration.

shuffle *vt* to scrape (the feet) along the ground; to walk with dragging steps; (*playing cards*) to change the order of, to mix; to intermingle, to mix up; (*with* **off**) to get rid of.—*also n*.

shun *vt* (*pt* **shunned**) to avoid scrupulously; to keep away from.

shunt *vti* to move to a different place; to put aside, to shelve; (*trains*) to switch from one track to another; (*sl*) to collide.—*also n*.

shut *vti* (*pr p* **shutting**, *pt* **shut**) to close; to lock, to fasten; to close up parts of, to fold together; to bar; (*with* **down**) to (cause to) stop working or operating; (*with* **in**) to confine; to enclose; to block the view from; (*with* **off**) to check the flow of; to debar; (*with* **out**) to exclude; (*with* **up**) to confine; (*inf*) to stop talking; (*inf*) to silence.

shutdown *n* a stoppage of work or activity, as in a factory.

shutter *n* a movable cover for a window; a flap device for regulating the exposure of light to a camera lens.

shuttle *n* a device in a loom for holding the weft thread and carrying it between the warp threads; a bus, aircraft, etc, making back-and-forth trips over a short route. * *vti* to move back and forth rapidly.

shuttlecock *n* a cork stuck with feathers, or a plastic imitation, hit with a racket in badminton.

shy *adj* (**shyer, shyest** *or* **shier, shiest**) very self-conscious, timid; bashful; wary, suspicious (of); (*sl*) lacking. * *vi* to move suddenly, as when startled; to be or become cautious, etc. * *n* a sudden movement.—**shyly** *adv*.—**shyness** *n*.

Siamese cat *n* a breed of domestic shorthaired cat with a fawn or grey coat, darker ears, paws, tail and face, and blue eyes.

sick *adj* unhealthy, ill; having nausea, vomiting; thoroughly tired (of); disgusted by or suffering from an excess; (*inf*) of humour, sadistic, gruesome.—**sickness** *n*.

sick bay *n* an area in a ship used as a hospital or dispen- sary; a room used for the treatment of the sick.

sicken *vti* to make or become sick or nauseated; to show signs of illness; to nauseate.

sickening *adj* disgusting.

sickle *n* a tool with a crescent-shaped blade for cutting tall grasses; anything shaped like this.

sick leave *n* absence from work due to illness.

sickly *adj* (**sicklier, sickliest**) inclined to be ill; unhealthy; causing nausea; mawkish; pale, feeble.—**sickliness** *n*.

side *n* a line or surface bounding anything; the left or right part of the body; the top or underneath surface; the slope of a hill; an aspect, a direction; a party or faction; a cause; a team; a line of descent; (*sl*) conceit. * *adj* towards or at the side, lateral; incidental. * *vi* to associate with a particular faction.

sideboard *n* a long table or cabinet for holding cutlery, crockery, etc; (*pl*) two strips of hair growing down a man's cheeks (—*also* **sideburns**).

side effect *n* a secondary and usu adverse effect, as of a drug or medical treatment.

sidelight *n* light coming from the side; a light on the side of a car, etc; incidental information.

sideline *n* a line marking the side limit of a playing area; a minor branch of business; a subsidiary interest.

sidelong *adj* oblique, not direct. * *adv* obliquely.

side-saddle *n* a saddle that enables a rider to sit with both feet on the same side of a horse. * *adv* as if sitting on a side-saddle.

sideshow *n* a minor attraction at a fair, etc; a subsidiary event.

sidetrack *vt* to prevent action by diversionary tactics; to shunt aside, to shelve. * *n* a railway siding.

sidewalk *n* a path, usu paved, at the side of a street, pavement.

sideways *adj, adv* towards or from one side; facing to the side.

siding *n* a short line beside a main railway track for use in shunting; a covering as of boards for the outside of a frame building.

sidle *vi* to move sideways, esp to edge along.

siege *n* the surrounding of a fortified place to cut off supplies and compel its surrender;

the act of besieging; a continued attempt to gain something.

sieve *n* a utensil with a meshed wire bottom for sifting and straining; a person who cannot keep secrets. * *vt* to put through a sieve, to sift.

sift *vti* to separate coarser parts from finer with a sieve; to sort out; to examine critically; to pass as through a sieve.

sigh *vti* to draw deep audible breath as a sign of weariness, relief, etc; to make a sound like this; to pine or lament (for); to utter with a sigh.—*also n.*

sight *n* the act or faculty of seeing; what is seen or is worth seeing, a spectacle; a view or glimpse; range of vision; a device on a gun etc to guide the eye in aiming it; aim taken with this; (*inf*) anything that looks unpleasant, odd, etc. * *vti* to catch sight of; to aim through a sight.

sightless *adj* without sight, blind.—**sightlessly** *adv.*

sightseeing *n* the viewing or visitng of places of interest.—**sightseer** *n.*

sign *n* a mark or symbol; a gesture; an indication, token, trace, or symptom (of); an omen; (*math*) a conventional mark used to indicate an operation to be performed; a board or placard with publicly displayed information. * *vi* to append one's signature; to ratify thus. * *vt* to engage by written contract; to write one's name on; to make or indicate by a sign; to signal; to communicate by sign language; (*with* away) to relinquish by signing a deed, etc; (*with* on) to accept employment; to register; (*with* off) to complete a broadcast.

signal *n* a sign, device or gesture to intimate a warning or to give information, esp at a distance; a message so conveyed; a semaphore system used by railways; in radio, etc, the electrical impulses transmitted or received; a sign or event that initiates action. * *vti* (*pt* **signalled**) to make a signal or signals (to); to communicate by signals. * *adj* striking, notable.

signature *n* a person's name written by himself or herself; the act of signing one's own name; a characteristic mark; (*mus*) the flats and sharps after the clef showing the key; (*print*) a mark on the first pages of each sheet of a book as a guide to the binder; such a sheet when folded.

signature tune *n* a tune associated with a performer or a TV, radio programme, etc.

signet ring *n* a ring with a seal set in it.

significant *adj* full of meaning, esp a special or hidden one; momentous, important; highly expressive; indicative (of).—**significance** *n.*—**significantly** *adv.*

silence *n* absence of sound; the time this lasts; refusal to speak or make a sound; secrecy. * *vt* to cause to be silent. * *interj* be silent!

silencer *n* a device for reducing the noise of a vehicle exhaust or gun.

silent *adj* not speaking; taciturn; noiseless;

still.—**silently** *adv.*

silhouette *n* the outline of a shape against light or a lighter background; a solid outline drawing, usu in solid black on white, esp of a profile. * *vt* to show up in outline; to depict in silhouette.

silk *n* a fibre produced by silkworms; lustrous textile cloth, thread or a garment made of silk; (*pl*) silk garments; (*pl*) the colors of a racing stable, worn by a jockey, etc. * *adj* of, relating to or made of silk.

silky *adj* (**silkier, silkiest**) soft and smooth like silk; glossy; suave.—**silkiness** *n.*

silly *adj* (**sillier, silliest**) foolish, stupid; frivolous; lacking in sense or judgment; being stunned or dazed. * *n* a silly person.

silt *n* a fine-grained sandy sediment carried or deposited by water. * *vti* to fill or choke up with silt.

silver *n* a ductile, malleable, greyish-white metallic element used in jewellery, cutlery, tableware, coins, etc; a lustrous, greyish white. * *adj* made of or plated with silver; silvery; (*hair*) grey; marking the 25th in a series * *vt* to coat with silver or a substance resembling silver; to make or become silvery or grey.

silver paper *n* a metallic paper coated or laminated to resemble silver, tinfoil.

silver plate *n* a plating of silver; domestic utensils made of silver or of silver-plated metal.

silversmith *n* a worker in silver.

silver thaw *n* (*Cdn*) a glassy coating of ice on trees or other surfaces caused by freezing rain or a sudden frost.

similar *adj* having a resemblance to, like; nearly corresponding; (*geom*) corresponding exactly in shape if not size.—**similarity** *n.*—**similarly** *adv.*

simile *n* a figure of speech likening one thing to another by the use of like, as, etc.

simmer *vti* to boil gently; to be or keep on the point of boiling; to be in a state of suppressed rage or laughter; (*with* **down**) to abate. * *n* the state of simmering.

simple *adj* single, uncompounded; plain, not elaborate; clear, not complicated; easy to do, understand, or solve; artless, not sophisticated; weak in intellect; unsuspecting, credulous; sheer, mere.—**simpleness** *n.*

simplicity *n* the quality or state of being simple; absence of complications; easiness; lack of ornament, plainness, restraint; artlessness; directness; guilelessness, openness, naivety.

simplify *vt* to make simple or easy to understand.

simply *adv* in a simple way; plainly; merely; absolutely.

simulate *vt* to pretend to have or feel, to feign; (*conditions*) to reproduce in order to conduct an experiment; to imitate.—**simulation** *n.*

simulator *n* a device that simulates specific conditions in order to test actions or reactions.

simultaneous *adj* done or occurring at the same time.—**simultaneously** *adv*.

sin *n* an offence against a religious or moral principle; transgression of the law of God; a wicked act, an offence; a misdeed, a fault. * *vi* (*pt* **sinned**) to commit a sin; to offend (against).

SIN *abbr* (*Cdn*) = Social Insurance Number.

since *adv* from then until now; subsequently; ago. * *prep* during, or continously from (then) until now; after. * *conj* from the time that; because, seeing that.

sincere *adj* genuine, real, not pretended; honest, straightforward.—**sincerely** *adv*.

sincerity *n* the quality or state of being sincere; genuineness, honesty, seriousness.

sinew *n* a cord of fibrous tissue, a tendon; (usu *pl*) the chief supporting force, a mainstay; (*pl*) muscles, brawn.

sinful *adj* guilty of sin, wicked.

sing *vti* (*pt* **sang**, *pp* **sung**) to utter (words) with musical modulations; (*a song*) to perform; to hum, to ring; to write poetry (about), to praise.—**singer** *n*.—**singing** *n*.

singe *vt* (*pr p* **singeing**, *pt* **singed**) to burn slightly; to scorch, esp to remove feathers, etc.—*also* **sing**.

singing *n* the art or an act of singing.

single *adj* one only, not double; individual; composed of one part; alone, sole; separate; unmarried; for one; with one contestant on each side; simple; whole, unbroken; (*tennis*) played between two only; (*ticket*) for the outward journey only. * *n* a single ticket; a game between two players; a hit scoring one; a record with one tune on each side. * *vt* (*with* **out**) to pick out, to select.

single file *n* a single column of persons or things, one behind the other.

single-handed *adj*, *adv* without assistance, unaided.

single-minded *adj* having only one aim in mind.

singlet *n* an undervest.

singly *adv* alone; one by one.

singular *adj* remarkable; exceptional; unusual; eccentric, odd; (*gram*) referring to only one person or thing. * *n* (*gram*) the singular number or form of a word.

sinister *adj* inauspicious; ominous; ill-omened; evil-looking; malignant; wicked; left; (*her*) on the left side of the shield.

sink *vti* (*pt* **sank**, *pp* **sunk** *or* **sunken**) to go under the surface or to the bottom (of a liquid); to submerge in water; to go down slowly; (*wind*) to subside; to pass to a lower state; to droop, to decline; to grow weaker; to become hollow; to lower, to degrade; to cause to sink; to make by digging out; to invest; (*with* **in**) to penetrate; to thrust into; (*inf*) to be understood in full. * *n* a basin with an outflow pipe, usu in a kitchen; a cesspool; an area of sunken land.—**sinking** *n*.

sinner *n* a person who sins.

sinuous *adj* curving; winding; tortuous.—**sinuously** *adv*.

sinus *n* (*pl* **sinuses**) an air cavity in the skull that opens in the nasal cavities.

sip *vti* (*pt* **sipped**) to drink in small mouthfuls. * *n* the act of sipping; the quantity sipped.

siphon *n* a bent tube for drawing off liquids from a higher to a lower level by atmospheric pressure; a bottle with an internal tube and tap at the top for aerated water. * *vti* to draw off, or be drawn off, with a siphon.—*also* **syphon**.

sir *n* a title of respect used to address a man in speech or correspondence; (*with cap*) a title preceding the first name of a knight or baronet. * *vt* to address as "sir".

siren *n* a device producing a loud wailing sound as a warning signal; a fabled sea nymph who lured sailors to destruction with a sweet song; a seductive or alluring woman.

sirloin *n* the upper part of a loin of beef.

sirocco *n* a hot, oppressive wind that blows across southern Europe from North Africa.

sister *n* a female sibling, a daughter of the same parents; a female member or associate of the same race, creed, trade union, etc; a member of a religious sisterhood; one of the same kind, model, etc; a senior nurse. * *adj* (*ship, etc*) belonging to the same type.

sister-in-law *n* the sister of a husband or wife; the wife of a brother.

sisterly *adj* like a sister, kind, affectionate.

sit *vti* (*pr p* **sitting**, *pt* **sat**) to rest oneself on the buttocks, as on a chair; (*bird*) to perch; (*hen*) to cover eggs for hatching; (*legislator, etc*) to occupy a seat; (*court*) to be in session; to pose, as for a portrait; to ride (a horse); to press or weigh (upon); to be located; to rest or lie; to take an examination; to take care of a child, pet, etc, while the parents or owners are away; to cause to sit; to provide seats or seating room for; (*with* **down**) to take a seat; (*with* **for**) to represent in parliament; (*with* **in**) to attend a discussion or a musical session; to participate in a sit-in; (*with* **on**) to hold a meeting to discuss; to delay action on something; (*inf*) to suppress; to rebuke; (*with* **out**) to sit through the whole; to abstain from dancing; (*with* **up**) to straighten the back while sitting; not to go to bed; (*inf*) to be astonished.

site *n* a space occupied or to be occupied by a building; a situation; the place or scene of something. * *vt* to locate, to place.

sit-in *n* a strike in which the strikers refuse to leave the premises; civil disobedience in which demonstrators occupy a public place and refuse to leave voluntarily.

sitting *n* the state of being seated; a period of being seated, as for a meal, a portrait; a session, as of a court; a clutch of eggs. * *adj* that is sitting; being in a judicial or legislative seat; used in or for sitting; performed while sitting.

sitting room *n* a room other than a bedroom or kitchen; a parlour.

situated *adj* having a site, located; placed; provided with money, etc.

situation *n* a place, a position; a state of affairs, circumstances; a job or post.

sit-up *n* an exercise of sitting up from a prone position without using hands or legs.

siwash *n* (*Cdn*) a thick woollen sweater with designs taken from the mythology of First Nations peoples of the northwest coast of North America.

six *adj, n* one more than five. * *n* the symbol for this (6, VI, vi); the sixth in a series or set; something having six units as members.

sixteen *adj, n* one more than fifteen. * *n* the symbol for this (16, XVI, xvi).—**sixteenth** *adj, n.*

sixth *n* one of six equal parts of a thing; (*mus*) an interval of six diatonic degrees; the sixth tone of a diatonic scale.—*also adv.* * *adj* next after fifth.—**sixthly** *adv.*

sixty *n* six times ten. * *n* the symbol for this (60, LX, lx); (in *pl*) sixties (60s), the numbers for 60 to 69; the same numbers in a life or century.—**sixtieth** *adj, adv.*

sizable, sizeable *adj* of some size; large.—**sizably, sizeably** *adv.*—**sizableness, sizeableness** *n.*

size[1] *n* magnitude; the dimensions or proportions of something; a graduated measurement, as of clothing or shoes. * *vt* to sort according to size; to measure; (*with* **up**) (*inf*) to make an estimate or judgment of; to meet requirements.

size[2] *n* a thin pasty substance used to glaze paper, stiffen cloth, etc. * *vt* to treat with size.

sizzle *vti* to make a hissing spluttering noise, as of frying; to be extremely hot; to be very angry; to scorch, sear or fry with a sizzling sound. * *n* a hissing sound.

SK *abbr* = Saskatchewan.

skate[1] *n* a steel blade attached to a boot for gliding on ice; a boot with such a runner; a roller skate. * *vi* to move on skates.—**skater** *n.*

skate[2] *n* an edible fish of the ray family with a broad, flat body and short, spineless tail.

skateboard *n* a short, oblong board with two wheels at each end for standing on and riding.—*also vi.*

skeleton *n* the bony framework of the body of a human, an animal or plant; the bones separated from flesh and preserved in their natural position; a supporting structure, a framework; an outline, an abstract; a very thin person; something shameful kept secret. * *adj* (*staff, crew, etc*) reduced to the lowest possible level.—**skeletal** *adj.*

sketch *n* a rough drawing, quickly made; a preliminary draft; a short literary piece or essay; a short humorous item for a revue, etc; a brief outline. * *vti* to make a sketch (of); to plan roughly.

sketchy *adj* (**sketchier, sketchiest**) incomplete; vague; inadequate.—**sketchily** *adv.*—**sketchiness** *n.*

skewer *n* a long wooden or metal pin on which pieces of meat and vegetables are cooked.

* *vt* to pierce and fasten on a skewer; to transfix.

ski *n* (*pl* **skis**) a long narrow runner of wood, metal or plastic that is fastened to a boot for moving across snow; a water-ski. * *vi* (*pr p* **skiing,** *pt* **skied**) to travel on skis.—**skier** *n.*

skid *vti* (*pt* **skidded**) to slide without rotating; to slip sideways; (*vehicle*) to slide sideways out of control; to cause (a vehicle) to skid. * *n* the act of skidding; a drag to reduce speed; a ship's fender; a movable support for a heavy object; a runner on an aircraft's landing gear.

Ski-Doo *n* (*Cdn*) (*TM*) a snowmobile.

skilful, skillful (*US*) *adj* having skill; proficient, adroit.—**skilfully** *adv.*—**skilfulness** *n.*

skill *n* proficiency; expertness, dexterity; a developed aptitude or ability; a type of work or craft requiring specialist training.

skilled *adj* fully trained, expert.

skim *vti* (*pt* **skimmed**) to remove (cream, scum) from the surface of; to glide lightly over, to brush the surface of; to read superficially.

skimp *vti* to give scant measure (of), to stint; to be sparing or frugal (with).

skimpy *adj* (**skimpier, skimpiest**) small in size; inadequate, scant, meagre.—**skimpily** *adv.*—**skimpiness** *n.*

skin *n* the tissue forming the outer covering of the body; a hide; the rind of a fruit; an outer layer or casing; a film on the surface of a liquid; a vessel for water, etc, made of hide. * *vti* (*pt* **skinned**) to remove the skin from, to peel; to injure by scraping (the knee, etc); to cover or become covered with skin; (*inf*) to swindle.

skin-deep *adj* superficial.

skin diving *n* the sport of swimming underwater with scuba equipment.—**skin-diver** *n.*

skinny *adj* (**skinnier, skinniest**) very thin; emaciated.—**skinniness** *n.*

skip[1] *vti* (*pt* **skipped**) to leap or hop lightly over; to keep jumping over a rope as it is swung under one; to make omissions, to pass over, esp in reading; (*inf*) to leave (town) hurriedly, to make off; (*inf*) to miss deliberately. * *n* a skipping movement; a light jump.

skip[2] *n* a large metal container for holding building debris; a cage or bucket for hoisting workers or materials in a mine, quarry, etc.

skipper *n* the captain of a boat, aircraft, or team. * *vt* to act as skipper; to captain.

skipping rope *n* a light rope, usu with a handle at each end, that is swung over the head and under the feet while jumping.

skirmish *n* a minor fight in a war; a conflict or clash. * *vi* to take part in a skirmish.

skirt *n* a woman's garment that hangs from the waist; the lower part of a dress or coat; an outer edge, a border; (*sl*) a woman. * *vti* to border; to move along the edge (of); to evade.

skirting board *n* a narrow panel of wood at the foot of an interior wall.

skit *n* a short humorous sketch, as in the theatre.

ski tow *n* a motor-driven device that pulls skiers uphill.

skittles *n* a game in which a wooden or plastic bottle-shaped pin is knocked down by a ball.

skookum *adj* in the Pacific Northwest of North America, strong or brave.

skulk *vi* to move in a stealthy manner; to lurk.

skull *n* the bony casing enclosing the brain; the cranium.

skunk *n* a small black-and-white mammal that emits a foul-smelling liquid when frightened; its fur; (*sl*) an obnoxious or mean person.

skunky *adj* (*Cdn*) tasting foul, esp in beer that has been exposed to air too long.

sky *n* the apparent vault over the earth; heaven; the upper atmosphere; weather, climate.

skylight *n* a window in the roof or ceiling.

skyscraper *n* a very tall building.

skyward *adj, adv* towards the sky.—**skywards** *adv*.

slab *n* a flat, broad, thick piece (as of stone, wood, or bread, etc); something resembling this. * *vt* to cut or form into slabs; to cover or support with slabs; to put on thickly.

slack *adj* loose, relaxed, not tight; (*business*) slow, not brisk; sluggish; inattentive, careless. * *n* the part (of a rope, etc) that hangs loose; a dull period; a lull; (*pl*) trousers for casual wear. * *vti* to neglect (one's work, etc), to be lazy; (*with* off) to slacken (a rope, etc).—**slackness** *n*.

slacken *vti* to make or become less active, brisk, etc; to loosen or relax, as a rope; to diminish, to abate.—**slackening** *n, adj*.

slag *n* the waste product from the smelting of metals; volcanic lava.

slam *vti* (*pt* **slammed**) to shut with a loud noise, to bang; to throw (down) violently; (*inf*) to criticize severely. * *n* a sound or the act of slamming, a bang; (*inf*) severe criticism; (*bridge*) the taking of 12 or 13 tricks.

slander *n* a false and malicious statement about another; the uttering of this. * *vt* to utter a slander about, to defame.—**slanderous** *adj*.

slang *n* words or expressions used in familiar speech but not regarded as standard English; jargon of a particular social class, age group, etc. * *adj* relating to slang.

slant *vti* to incline, to slope; to tell in such way as to have a bias. * *n* a slope; an oblique position; a bias, a point of view. * *adj* sloping.—**slantly** *adv*.

slanted *adj* prejudiced, biased; sloping.

slap *n* a smack with the open hand; an insult; a rebuff. * *vt* (*pt* **slapped**) to strike with something flat; to put, hit, etc, with force. * *adv* directly, full.

slapdash *adj* impetuous; hurried; careless; haphazard. * *adv* carelessly.

slapstick *n* boisterous humour of a knockabout kind.

slash *vti* to cut gashes in, to slit; to strike fiercely (at) with a sword, etc; to reduce (prices) sharply. * *n* a cutting blow; a long slit, a gash.

slate¹ *vt* to criticize or punish severely.

slate² *n* a fine-grained rock easily split into thin layers; a flat plate of this or other material used in roofing; a tablet (as of slate) for writing on; a list of proposed candidates. *. *adj* the color of slate, a deep bluish-grey color; made of slate. * *vt* to cover with slates; to suggest as a political candidate.

slaughter *n* the butchering of animals; a wholesale killing, a massacre.—*also vt*.—**slaughterer** *n*.

slaughterhouse *n* a place where animals are slaughtered, an abattoir.

slave *n* a person without freedom or personal rights, who is legally owned by another; a person under domination, esp of a habit or vice; a person who works like a slave, a drudge. * *vti* to toil hard, as a slave.

slavery *n* the condition of being a slave; bondage; drudgery; slave-owning as an institution.

sled, sledge *n* a framework on runners for travelling over snow or ice; a toboggan. * *vti* to go or convey by sledge.

sledgehammer *n* a large, heavy hammer for two hands.

sleek *adj* smooth, glossy; having a prosperous or well-groomed appearance; plausible.

sleep *n* a natural, regularly recurring rest for the body, with little or no consciousness; a period spent sleeping; a state of numbness followed by tingling. * *vti* (*pt* **slept**) to rest in a state of sleep; to be inactive; to provide beds for; (*with* in) to sleep on the premises; to sleep too long in the morning; (*with* on) to have a night's rest before making a decision; (*with* off) to get rid of by sleeping; (*with* over) to pass the night in someone else's house; (*with* with) to have sexual relations with.

sleeper *n* a person or thing that sleeps; a horizontal beam that carries and spreads a weight; a sleeping car; something that suddenly attains prominence or value.

sleeping bag *n* a padded bag for sleeping in, esp outdoors.

sleeping car *n* a railway carriage with berths.

sleeping pill *n* a pill that induces sleep.

sleeping platform *n* a bench or ledge for sleeping inside an igloo.

sleepwalker *n* a person who walks while asleep, a somnambulist.—**sleepwalking** *n*.

sleepy *adj* (**sleepier, sleepiest**) drowsy; tired; lazy, not alert.—**sleepily** *adv*.—**sleepiness** *n*.

sleet *n* snow or hail mixed with rain. * *vi* to rain in the form of sleet.

sleeve *n* the part of a garment enclosing the arm; (*mech*) a tube that fits over a part; an open-ended cover, esp a paperboard envelope for a record.

sleeveless *adj* (*garment*) without sleeves.

sleigh *n* a light vehicle on runners for travelling over snow; a sledge.

sleight of hand n manual dexterity, such as in conjuring or juggling; a deception.

slender adj thin; slim; slight; scanty.—**slenderly** adv.—**slenderness** n.

slept see **sleep**.

slice n a thin flat piece cut from something (as bread, etc); a wedge-shaped piece (of cake, pie, etc); a portion, a share; a broad knife for serving fish, cheese, etc; (golf) a stroke that makes the ball curl to the right. * vti to divide into parts; to cut into slices; to strike (a ball) so that it curves.—**slicer** n —**slicing** adj, n.

slick adj clever, deft; smart but unsound; insincere; wily; (inf) smooth but superficial, tricky, etc. * n a patch or area of oil floating on water. * vt to make glossy; (with **up**) (inf) to make smart, neat, etc.

slide vti (pt **slid**) to move along in constant contact with a smooth surface, as on ice, to glide; to coast over snow and ice; to pass gradually (into); to move (an object) unobtrusively. * n the act of sliding, a glide; a strip of smooth ice for sliding on; a chute; the glass plate of a microscope; a photographic transparency; a landslide.

slide rule n a ruler with a graduated sliding part for making calculations.

sliding scale n a schedule for automatically varying one thing (eg wages) according to the fluctuations of another thing (eg cost of living); a flexible scale.

slight adj small, inconsiderable; trifling; slim; frail, flimsy. * vt to disregard as insignificant; to treat with disrespect, to snub. * n intentional indifference or neglect, discourtesy.

slightly adv to a small degree; slenderly.

slim adj slender, not stout; small in amount, degree, etc; slight. * vti (**slimming**, **slimmed**) to make or become slim; to reduce one's weight by diet, etc.—**slimness** n.

slime n a sticky slippery, half-liquid substance; a glutinous mud; mucus secreted by various animals (eg slugs).

sling n a loop of leather with a string attached for hurling stones; a rope for lifting or hoisting weights; a bandage suspended from the neck for supporting an injured arm. * vt (pt **slung**) to throw, lift, or suspend (as) with a sling; to hurl.

slingshot n a catapult.

slip[1] vti (pt **slipped**) to slide, to glide; to lose one's foothold and slide; to go or put quietly or quickly; to let go, to release; to escape from; (with **up**) to make a slight mistake. * n the act of slipping; a mistake, a lapse; a woman's undergarment; a pillowcase; a slipway.

slip[2] n a small piece of paper; a young, slim person; a long seat or narrow pew; a shoot for grafting, a cutting; a descendant, an offspring.

slipped disc n a ruptured cartilaginous disc between vertebrae.

slipper n a light, soft, shoe worn in the house.

slippery adj so smooth as to cause slipping; difficult to hold or catch; evasive, unreliable, shifty.

slip road n a road that gives access to a main road or motorway.

slipshod adj having the shoes down at heel; slovenly, careless.

slip-up n (inf) an error, a lapse.

slipway n an inclined surface for launching or repairing ships; a sloped landing stage.

slit vt (pr p **slitting**, pt **slit**) to cut open or tear lengthways; to slash or tear into strips. * n a long cut, a slash; a narrow opening.

slither vi to slide, as on a loose or wet surface; to slip or slide like a snake.

slob ice n (Cdn) a sludgy mass of densely packed sea ice.

slog vti (pt **slogged**) to hit hard and wildly; to work laboriously; to trudge doggedly. * n a hard, boring spell of work; a strenuous walk or hike; a hard, random hit.

slogan n a catchy phrase used in advertising or as a motto by a political party, etc.

slop n a puddle of spilled liquid; unappetizing semi-liquid food; (pl) liquid kitchen refuse. * vti (pt **slopped**) to spill or be spilled.

slope n rising or falling ground; an inclined line or surface; the amount or degree of this. * vti to incline, to slant; (inf) to make off, to go.

sloppy adj (**sloppier, sloppiest**) slushy; (inf) maudlin, sentimental; (inf) careless, untidy.—**sloppily** adv.—**sloppiness** n.

slot n a long narrow opening in a mechanism for inserting a coin, a slit. * vt (pt **slotted**) to fit into a slot; to provide with a slot; (inf) to place in a series.

slot machine n a machine operated by the insertion of a coin, used for gambling or dispensing drinks, etc.

slouch vti to sit, stand or move in a drooping, slovenly way. * n a drooping slovenly posture or gait; the downward droop of a hat brim; (inf) a poor performer, a lazy or incompetent person.

slovenly adj untidy, dirty; careless.—**slovenliness** n.

slow adj moving at low speed, not fast; gradual; not quick in understanding; reluctant; backward; dull, sluggish; not progressive; (clock) behind in time; tedious, boring; (surface) causing slowness. * vti (also with **up, down**) to reduce the speed (of).—**slowly** adv.—**slowness** n.

slow-motion adj moving slowly; denoting a filmed or taped scene with the original action slowed down.

sludge n soft mud or snow; sediment; sewage.

slug[1] n a mollusc resembling a snail but with no outer shell.

slug[2] n a small bullet; a disc for inserting into a slot machine; a line of type; (inf) a hard blow; a drink of spirits. * vt (pt **slugged**) (inf) to hit hard with a fist or a bat.

sluice n a gate regulating a flow of water; the water passing through this; an artificial water channel. * *vti* to draw off through a sluice; to wash with a stream of water; to stream out as from a sluice.

slum *n* a squalid, rundown house; (usu *pl*) an overcrowded area characterized by poverty, etc. * *vi* (*pt* **slummed**) to make do with less comfort.

slumber *vi* to sleep. * *n* a light sleep.

slump *n* a sudden fall in value or slackening in demand; (*sport*) a period of poor play. * *vi* to fall or decline suddenly; to sink down heavily; to collapse; to slouch.

slung *see* **sling**.

slur *vti* (*pt* **slurred**) to pronounce or speak indistinctly; (*letters, words*) to run together; (*mus*) to produce by gliding without a break; to make disparaging remarks. * *n* the act of slurring; a stigma, an imputation of disgrace; (*mus*) a curved line over notes to be slurred.

slush *n* liquid mud; melting snow; (*inf*) sentimental language.—**slushy** *adj*.

slut *n* a slovenly or immoral woman.—**sluttish** *adj*.

sly *adj* (**slyer, slyest** *or* **slier, sliest**) secretively cunning, wily; underhand; knowing.—**slyly** *adv*.—**slyness** *n*.

smack[1] *n* a taste; a distinctive smell or flavor; small quantity, a trace. * *vi* to have a smell or taste (of); to have a slight trace of something.

smack[2] *vt* to strike or slap with the open hand; to kiss noisily; to make a sharp noise with the lips.—*also n*.

small *adj* little in size, number, importance, etc; modest, humble; operating on a minor scale; young; petty. * *adv* in small pieces. * *n* the narrow, curving part of the back.

smallpox *n* an acute contagious viral disease, now rare, causing the eruption of pustules which leave the skin scarred and pitted.

small talk *n* light, social conversation.

smart *n* a sudden, stinging pain. * *vi* to have or cause a sharp, stinging pain (as by a slap); to feel distress. * *adj* stinging; astute; clever, witty; fashionable; neatly dressed; (*equipment, etc*) capable of seemingly intelligent action through computer control; (*bombs, missiles*) guided to the target by lasers ensuring pinpoint accuracy.—**smartly** *adv*.—**smartness** *n*.

smarten *vti* to make or become smart.

smash *vti* to break into pieces with noise or violence; to hit, collide, or move with force; to destroy or be destroyed. * *n* a hard, heavy hit; a violent, noisy breaking; a violent collision; total failure, esp in business; (*inf*) a popular success.

smashing *n* (*inf*) excellent.

smattering *n* a slight superficial knowledge; a small number.

smear *vt* to cover with anything greasy or sticky; to make a smudge; to slander. * *n* a smudge; a slanderous attack; a deposit of blood, secretion, etc on a glass slide for examination under a microscope.

smell *n* the sense by which odours are perceived with the nose; a scent, odour, or stench; a trace. * *vti* (*pt* **smelt** *or* **smelled**) to have or perceive an odour.—**smelly** *adj*.

smile *vti* to express amusement, friendship, pleasure, etc, by a slight turning up of the corners of the mouth.—*also n*.

smirk *vi* to smile in an expression of smugness or scorn.—*also n*.

smith *n* a person who works in metal; a blacksmith.

smithy *n* a blacksmith's workshop.

smock *n* a loose shirtlike outer garment to protect the clothes.

smog *n* a mixture of fog and smoke.

smoke *n* a cloud or plume of gas and small particles emitted from a burning substance; any similar vapour; an act of smoking tobacco, etc; (*inf*) a cigar or cigarette. * *vi* to give off smoke; to (habitually) draw in and exhale the smoke of tobacco, etc. * *vt* to fumigate; to cure food by treating with smoke; to darken (eg glass) using smoke.

smoker *n* a person who habitually smokes tobacco; a train compartment where smoking is permitted.

smoky *adj* (**smokier, smokiest**) emitting smoke, esp excessively; filled with smoke; resembling smoke in appearance, flavor, smell, color, etc.

smooth *adj* having an even or flat surface; silky; not rough or lumpy; hairless; of even consistency; calm, unruffled; gently flowing in rhythm or sound. * *vti* to make smooth; to calm; to make easier.—**smoothly** *adv*.—**smoothness** *n*.

smother *vt* to stifle, to suffocate; to put out a fire by covering it to remove the air supply; to cover over thickly; to hold back, suppress. * *vi* to undergo suffocation.—*also n*.

smoulder, smolder (*US*) *vi* to burn slowly or without flame; (*feelings*) to linger on in a suppressed state; to have concealed feelings of anger, jealousy, etc.

smudge *n* a dirty or blurred spot or area; in US, a fire made to produce dense smoke. * *vt* to make a smudge; to smear; to blur; in US, to produce smoke to protect against insects, etc. * *vi* to become smudged.

smug *adj* (**smugger, smuggest**) complacent, self-satisfied.—**smugly** *adv*.—**smugness** *n*.

smuggle *vt* to import or export (goods) secretly without paying customs duties; to convey or introduce secretly.—**smuggler** *n*.

smut *n* a speck or smudge of dirt, soot, etc; indecent talk, writing, or pictures; a fungous disease of crop plants that covers the leaves in sooty spores. * *vti* (*pt* **smutted**) to stain or become stained with smut; (*crops, etc*) to infect or become infected with smut.—**smutty** *adj*.

snack *n* a light meal between regular meals.

snag *n* a sharp point or projection; a tear, as in cloth, made by a snag, etc; an unexpected or hidden difficulty.—*also vti*.

snail *n* a mollusc having a wormlike body and a

spiral protective shell; a slow-moving person or thing.

snake n a limbless, scaly reptile with a long, tapering body, often with salivary glands modified to produce venom; a sly, treacherous person. * vt to twist along like a snake. * vi to crawl silently and stealthily.—**snaky** adj.

snake fence n (Cdn) a fence of roughly split logs arranged in a zigzag pattern.

snap vti (pt **snapped**) (with **at**) to bite or grasp suddenly; (with **at**) to speak or utter sharply; to break suddenly; to make or cause to make a sudden, cracking sound; to close, fasten, etc with this sound. * adj sudden. * n a sharp, cracking sound; a fastener that closes with a snapping sound; a crisp biscuit; a snapshot; a sudden spell of cold weather; (inf) vigour, energy.

snappy adj (**snappier, snappiest**) speaking sharply; brisk; lively; smart, fashionable.—**snappily** adv.

snapshot n a photograph taken casually with a simple camera.

snare n a loop of string or wire for trapping birds or animals; something that catches one unawares, a trap; a loop of gut wound with wire stretched around a snare drum that produces a rattling sound. * vt to trap using a snare.

snarl[1] vi to growl with bared teeth; to speak in a rough, angry manner. * vt to express in a snarling manner.—also n.

snarl[2] vti to make or become entangled or complicated. * n a tangle; disorder.

snatch vt to seize or grasp suddenly; to take as opportunity occurs. * n the act of snatching; a brief period; a fragment; (inf) a robbery.

sneak vti to move, act, give, put, take, etc, secretly or stealthily. * n a person who acts secretly or stealthily; (inf) a person who tells or informs on others. * adj without warning.—**sneaky** adj.

sneer vi to show scorn or contempt by curling up the upper lip.—also n.

sneeze vi to expel air through the nose violently and audibly.—also n.

snide adj malicious; superior in attitude; sneering.

sniff vti to inhale through the nose audibly; to smell by sniffing; to scoff.—also n.

snigger vti to laugh disrespectfully.—also n.

snip vti (pt **snipped**) to cut or clip with a single stroke of the scissors, etc. * n a small piece cut off; the act or sound of snipping; (inf) a bargain; (inf) a certainty, cinch.

snipe n (pl **snipe**) any of various birds with long straight flexible bills. * vi to shoot at individuals from a hidden position; to make sly criticisms of.—**sniper** n.

snippet n a scrap of information.

snob n a person who wishes to be associated with those of a higher social status, whilst acting condescendingly to those whom he or she regards as inferior.—**snobbery** n.—

snobbish adj.

snooker n a game played on a billiard table with 15 red balls, 6 variously colored balls, and a white cue ball; a position in the game where a ball lies directly between the cue ball and target ball. * vt to place in a snooker; (inf) to obstruct, thwart.

snoop vi (inf) to pry about in a sneaking way. * n an act of snooping; a person who pries into other people's business.—**snooper** n.

snooze vi (inf) to sleep lightly. * n (inf) a nap.

snore vi to breathe roughly and noisily while asleep.—also n.

snorkel n a breathing tube extending above the water, used in swimming just below the surface. * vi to swim using a snorkel.

snort vi to exhale noisily through the nostrils, esp as an expression of contempt or scorn. * vt to inhale (a drug) through the nose.

snout n the nose or muzzle of an animal.

snow n frozen water vapour in the form of white flakes; a snowfall; a mass of snow; (sl) cocaine or heroin. * vi to fall as snow.

snow apple n (Cdn) a white-fleshed eating apple first grown in Quebec.

snowball n snow pressed together in a ball for throwing; a drink made with advocaat and lemonade. * vi to throw snowballs; to increase rapidly in size.

snowbird n (Cdn) a small, mainly white bird of the finch or junco family, esp the snow bunting; a person from Canada or northern America who lives in a southern US state during the winter.

snowdrift n a bank of drifted snow.

snowfall n a fall of snow; the amount of snow that falls in a given time or area.

snowman n snow piled into the shape of a human figure.

snowplough, snowplow (US) n a vehicle designed for clearing away snow.

snow route n (Cdn) a major urban road that gets priority in the removal of snow.

snub[1] vt (pt **snubbed**) to insult by ignoring or making a cutting remark.—also n.

snub[2] adj short and turned up, as a nose.

snuff[1] n a powdered preparation of tobacco inhaled through the nostrils.

snuff[2] n the charred portion of a wick. * vt to extinguish (a candle flame).

snug adj (**snugger, snuggest**) cosy; warm; close-fitting.

snye n (Cdn) a side channel of a river, esp one that diverges from a river and then rejoins it.

so adv in this way; as shown; as stated; to such an extent; (inf) very much; therefore; more or less; also, likewise; then.

soak vt to submerge in a liquid; to take in, absorb; (sl) to extract large amounts of money from. * vi to become saturated; to penetrate. * n the act or process of soaking.

soap n a substance used with water to produce suds for washing; (inf) a soap opera. * vt to rub with soap.—**soapy** adj.

soar *vi* to rise high in the air; to glide along high in the air; to increase; to rise in status.

sob *vi* to weep with convulsive gasps. * *vt* to speak while sobbing.

sober *adj* not drunk; serious and thoughtful; realistic, rational; subdued in color. * *vt* to make or become sober (*often with* up *or* down).—soberly *adv.*

so-called *adj* commonly named or known as.

soccer *n* a football game played on a field by two teams of 11 players with a round inflated ball.

sociable *adj* friendly; companionable.—sociability *n.*—sociably *adv.*

social *adj* living or organized in a community, not solitary; relating to human beings living in society; of or intended for communal activities; sociable. * *n* an informal gathering of people, such as a party.—socially *adv.*

social insurance number *n* (*Cdn*) a nine-digit number issued by the federal government to individuals and used for identification purposes.

socialism *n* (a system based on) a political and economic theory advocating state ownership of the means of production and distribution.—socialist *n.*—socialistic *adj.*

social science *n* the study of human social organization and relationships using scientific methods.

social security *n* financial assistance for the unemployed, the disabled, etc to alleviate economic distress.

social work *n* any of various professional welfare services to aid the underprivileged in society.—social worker *n.*

society *n* the social relationships between human beings or animals organized collectively; the system of human institutional organization; a community with the same language and customs; an interest group or organization; the fashionable or privileged members of a community; companionship.

sociology *n* the study of the development and structure of society and social relationships.—sociologist *n.*—sociological *adj.*

sock[1] *n* a kind of short stocking covering the foot and lower leg.

sock[2] *vt* (*sl*) to punch hard.—*also n.*

socket *n* a hollow part into which something is inserted, such as an eye, a bone, a tooth, an electric plug, etc.

sod[1] *n* a lump of earth covered with grass; turf.

sod[2] *n* (*sl*) an obnoxious person; (*loosely*) a person, man.

soda *n* sodium bicarbonate; sodium carbonate; soda water.

soda water *n* a fizzy drink made by charging water with carbon dioxide under pressure.

sodden *adj* completely soaked through.

sodium *n* a metallic element.

sofa *n* an upholstered couch or settee with fixed back and arms.

soft *adj* malleable; easily cut, shaped, etc; not as hard as normal, desirable, etc; smooth to the touch; (*drinks*) nonalcoholic; mild, as a breeze; lenient; (*sl*) easy, comfortable; (*color, light*) not bright; (*sound*) gentle, low; (*drugs*) non-addictive.—softly *adv.*—softness *n.*

soften *vti* to make or become soft or softer.—softener *n.*

software *n* the programs used in computers.

soggy *adj* (soggier, soggiest) soaked with water; moist and heavy.

soil[1] *n* the ground or earth in which plants grow; territory.

soil[2] *vt* to make or become dirty or stained.

solar *adj* of or from the sun; powered by light or heat from the sun; reckoned by the sun.

sold *see* sell.

solder *n* a metal alloy used when melted to join or patch metal parts, etc.—*also vti.*

soldier *n* a person who serves in an army, esp a non-commissioned officer. * *vi* to serve as a soldier.—soldierly *adj.*

sole[1] *n* the underside of the foot or shoe. * *vt* to put a new sole on (a shoe).

sole[2] *n* (*pl* sole) a type of flatfish used as food.

sole[3] *adj* only, being the only one; exclusive.—solely *adv.*

solemn *adj* serious; formal; sacred; performed with religious ceremony.—solemnly *adv.*—solemness *n.*

solicitor *n* a lawyer.

solid *adj* firm; compact; not hollow; strongly constructed; having three dimensions; neither liquid nor gaseous; unanimous. * *n* a solid substance (not liquid or gas); a three dimensional figure.—solidly *adv.*—solidity *n.*

solidarity *n* unity of interest and action.

solidify *vti* to make or become solid, compact, hard, etc.

solitaire *n* a single gemstone, esp a diamond; a card game for one (—*also* patience).

solitary *adj* alone; only; single; living alone; lonely.

solitude *n* the state of being alone; lack of company.

solo *n* (*pl* solos) a musical composition for performance by one voice or instrument; a flight by a single person in an aircraft, esp a first flight. * *vi* to perform by oneself. * *adv* alone. * *adj* unaccompanied.—soloist *n.*

solstice *n* either of the two times in the year at which the sun is farthest from the equator (21 June and 21 December).

soluble *adj* capable of being dissolved (usu in water); capable of being solved or answered.—solubility *n.*

solution *n* the act or process of answering a problem; the answer found; the dispersion of one substance in another, usu a liquid, so as to form a homogeneous mixture.

solve *vt* to work out the answer to; to clear up, resolve.

solvent *adj* capable of dissolving a substance; able to pay all debts. * *n* a liquid that dissolves substances.—solvency *n.*

sombre, somber (*US*) *adj* dark, gloomy or dull;

dismal; sad.

some *adj* certain but not specified or known; of a certain unspecified quantity, degree, etc; a little; (*inf*) remarkable, striking, etc. * *pron* a certain unspecified quantity, number, etc.

somebody *n* an unspecified person; an important person.—*also pron.*

someday *adv* at some future day or time.

somehow *adv* in a way or by a method not known or stated.

someone *n* somebody.—*also pron.*

someplace *adv* somewhere.

somersault *n* a forward or backward roll head over heels along the ground or in mid-air.—*also vi.*

something *n, pron* a thing not definitely known, understood, etc; an important or notable thing. * *adv* to some degree. * *adj* having been formerly; being so occasionally or in only some respects.

sometime *adj* former. * *adv* at some unspecified future date.

sometimes *adv* at times, now and then.

somewhat *adv* to some extent, degree, etc; a little.

somewhere *adv* in, to or at some place not known or specified.

son *n* a male offspring or descendant.

song *n* a piece of music composed for the voice; the act or process of singing; the call of certain birds.

sonic *adj* of, producing, or involving sound waves.

son-in-law *n* a daughter's husband.

sonnet *n* a rhyming poem in a single stanza of fourteen lines.

sonny *n* a patronizing form of address to a boy.

soon *adv* in a short time; before long.

sooner or later *adv* at some future unspecified time, eventually.

soot *n* a black powder produced from flames.—**sooty** *adj.*

soothe *vt* to calm or comfort; to alleviate; to relieve (pain, etc).—**soothing** *adj.*

sophisticated *adj* refined; worldly-wise; intelligent; complex.—**sophistication** *n.*

soppy *adj* (**soppier, soppiest**) wet; (*inf*) sickly sentimental.—**soppily** *adv.*—**soppiness** *n.*

sorcerer *n* person who uses magic powers; a magician or wizard.—**sorceress** *nf.*

sordid *adj* filthy, squalid; vile; base; selfish.

sore *n* a painful or tender injury or wound; an ulcer or boil; grief; a cause of distress. * *adj* painful; tender; distressed.—**soreness** *n.*

sorely *adv* seriously, urgently.

sorrow *n* sadness; regret; an expression of grief. * *vi* to mourn, to grieve.—**sorrowful** *adj.*—**sorrowfully** *adv.*

sorry *adj* (**sorrier, sorriest**) feeling pity, sympathy, remorse or regret; pitiful; poor.

sort *n* a class, kind, or variety; quality or type. * *vt* to arrange according to kind; to classify.—**sorter** *n.*

SOS *n* an international signal code of distress;

an urgent call for help or rescue.

souffle *n* a baked dish made light and puffy by adding beaten egg whites before baking.

sought *see* **seek**.

soul *n* a person's spirit; the seat of the emotions, desires; essence; character; a human being.

soul-destroying *adj* extremely boring, depressing.

soulful *adj* expressing profound sentiment.—**soulfully** *adv.*

sound[1] *adj* healthy; free from injury or damage; substantial; stable; deep (as sleep) solid; thorough.—**soundly** *adv.*—**soundness** *n.*

sound[2] *n* a narrow channel of water connecting two seas or between a mainland and an island.

sound[3] *n* vibrations transmitted through the air and detected by the ear; the sensation of hearing; any audible noise; the impression given by something. * *vi* to make a sound; to give a summons by sound. * *vt* to cause to make a sound; to voice; to make a signal or order by sound.

sound[4] *vt* to measure the depth of; to seek to discover the views and intentions of.

sound barrier *n* the increase in air resistance experienced by objects travelling close to the speed of sound.

sounding[1] *n* measurement of the depth of water; a test, sampling, eg of public opinion.

sounding[2] *adj* resounding.

soundproof *adj* unable to be penetrated by sound. * *vt* to make soundproof by insulation, etc.

soundtrack *n* the sound accompanying a film; the area on cinema film that carries the sound recording.

soup *n* a liquid food made from boiling meat, fish, vegetables, etc, in water; (*inf*) a difficult or embarrassing situation.—**soupy** *adj.*

sour *adj* having a sharp, biting taste; spoiled by fermentation; cross; bad-tempered; distasteful or unpleasant; (*soil*) acid in reaction. * *vti* to make or become sour.—**sourly** *adv.*—**sourness** *n.*

source *n* a spring forming the head of a stream; an origin or cause; a person, book, etc, that provides information.

south *n* the direction to one's right when facing the the direction of the rising sun; the region, country, continent, etc, lying relatively in that direction. * *adj, adv* facing towards or situated in the south.

southeast *n* the point on a compass midway between south and east. * *adj, adv* at, towards, or from the southeast.—*also* **southeastern.**

southerly *adj* in, towards, or from the south. * *n* a wind from the south.

southern *adj* in, towards, or from the south; inhabiting or characteristic of the south.—**southernmost** *adj.*

southward *adj* towards the south.—**southwards** *adv.*

southwest *n* the point on a compass midway between south and west. * *adj, adv* at, towards, or from the southwest.—*also* **southwestern.**

souvenir *n* a keepsake, a memento.

sovereign *adj* supreme in authority or rank; (*country, state, etc*) independent. * *n* a supreme ruler; a monarch.—**sovereignty** *n.*

sovereignist, sovereigntist *n* (*Cdn*) a person who supports greater self-government for Quebec, esp its political independence. * of or pertaining to the movement for the political independence of Quebec.

sow[1] *n* an adult female pig. **sow**[2] *vt* (*pt* **sowed**, *pp* **sown** *or* **sowed**) to plant or scatter seed on or in the ground; to disseminate; to implant.—**sower** *n.*

soya bean, soybean (*US*) *n* a type of bean (orig from Asia) used as a source of food and oil.

spa *n* a mineral spring; a resort where there is a mineral spring.

space *n* the limitless three-dimensional expanse within which all objects exist; outer space; a specific area; an interval, empty area; room; an unoccupied area or seat. * *vt* to arrange at intervals.

spacecraft *n* a vehicle for travel in outer space.

spacious *adj* large in extent; roomy.—**spaciousness** *n.*

spade[1] *n* a tool with a broad blade and a handle used for digging.

spade[2] *n* a black symbol resembling a stylized spearhead marking one of the four suits of playing cards; a card of this suit.

span *n* a unit of length equal to a hand's breadth (about 9 inches/23 cm); the full extent between any two limits, such as the ends of a bridge or arch. * *vt* (*pt* **spanned**) to extend across.

spaniel *n* any of various breeds of dog with large drooping ears and a long silky coat.

Spanish *adj* of or pertaining to Spain. * *n* the language of Spain and Spanish Americans.

spank *vt* to slap with the flat of the hand, esp on the buttocks.—*also n.*

spanner *n* a tool with a hole or (often adjustable) jaws to grip and turn nuts or bolts, a wrench.

spare *vt* to refrain from harming or killing; to afford; to make (something) available (eg time). * *adj* kept as an extra, additional; scanty. * *n* a spare part; a spare tyre.—**sparely** *adv.*—**spareness** *n.*

sparing *adj* frugal, economical.—**sparingly** *adv.*

spark *n* a fiery or glowing particle thrown off by burning material or by friction; a flash of light from an electrical discharge; a trace. * *vt* to stir up; to activate. * *vi* to give off sparks.

sparrow *n* any of various small brownish songbirds related to the finch.

sparse *adj* spread out thinly; scanty.—**sparsely** *adv.*—**sparseness, sparsity** *n.*

Spartan *adj* of or relating to Sparta or its citizens; very austere. * *n* (*Cdn*) a crisp medium-sized red cooking or eating apple.

spasm *n* a sudden, involuntary muscular contraction; any sudden burst (of emotion or activity).

spasmodic *adj* intermittent; of or like a spasm.—**spasmodically** *adv.*

spastic *n* a person who suffers from cerebral palsy. * *adj* affected by muscle spasm.—**spasticity** *n.*

spat *see* **spit**[2].

spate *n* a large amount; a sudden outburst (as of words); a sudden flood.

spatter *vti* to scatter or spurt out in drops; to splash.—*also n.*

spatula *n* a tool with a broad, flexible blade for spreading or mixing foods, paints, etc.

spawn *n* a mass of eggs deposited by fish, frogs, or amphibians; offspring. * *vti* to lay eggs; to produce, esp in great quantity.

spay *vt* to render (a female animal) sterile by removing the ovaries.

speak *vi* (*pt* **spoke**, *pp* **spoken**) to utter words; to talk; to converse with; to deliver a speech; to be suggestive of something; to produce a characteristic sound.

speaker *n* a person who speaks, esp before an audience; the presiding official in a legislative assembly; a loudspeaker.

spear *n* a weapon with a long shaft and a sharp point; a blade or shoot (of grass, broccoli, etc). * *vt* to pierce with a spear.

spearing *n* an infraction in ice hockey for jabbing or poking an opponent with one's stick.

spec *vt* to write specifications for.

special *adj* distinguished; uncommon; designed for a particular purpose; peculiar to one person or thing.—**specially** *adv.*

specialist *n* a person who concentrates on a particular area of study or activity, esp in medicine.

speciality, specialty (*US*) *n* a special skill or interest; a special product.

specialize *vi* to concentrate on a particular area of study or activity. * *vt* to adapt to a particular use or purpose.—**specialization** *n.*

species *n* (*pl* **species**) a class of plants or animals with the same main characteristics, enabling interbreeding; a distinct kind or sort.

specific *adj* explicit; definite; of a particular kind. * *n* a characteristic quality or influence; a drug effective in treating a particular disease.—**specifically** *adv.*

specification *n* a requirement; (*pl*) detailed description of dimensions, materials, etc of something.

specify *vt* to state specifically; to set down as a condition.

specimen *n* (*plant, animal, etc*) an example of a particular species; a sample; (*inf*) a person.

speck *n* a small spot; a fleck.

speckle *n* a small mark of a different color. * *vt* to mark with speckles.

spectacle *n* an unusual or interesting scene; a large public show; an object of derision or ridicule; (*pl*) a pair of glasses.—**spectacled** *adj.*

spectacular *adj* impressive; astonishing.

spectator n an onlooker.

spectre, specter (US) n an apparition or ghost; a haunting mental image.

spectrum n (pl **spectra**) the range of color which is produced when a white light is passed through a prism; any similar distribution of wave frequencies; a broad range.

speculate vi to theorize, to conjecture; to make investments in the hope of making a profit.—**speculation** n.—**speculator** n.

speculative adj of or based on speculation; engaging in speculation in finance, etc.)—**speculatively** adv.

speech n the action or power of speaking; a public address or talk; language, dialect.

Speech from the Throne n (Cdn) a speech read on behalf of a government by a sovereign or the sovereign's representative that outlines proposed measures.—also **Throne Speech.**

speechless adj unable to speak; silent, as from shock; impossible to express in words.—**speechlessly** adv.

speed n quickness; rapidity or rate of motion; (photog) the sensitivity of film to light; (sl) an amphetamine drug. * vi (pt **sped**) to go quickly, to hurry; (pt **speeded**) to drive (a vehicle) at an illegally high speed.

speedometer n an instrument in a motor vehicle for measuring its speed.

speedway n the sport of racing light motorcycles around dirt or cinder tracks; a stadium for motorcycle racing; in US, a road reserved for fast traffic.

speedy adj (**speedier, speediest**) quick; prompt.—**speedily** adv.

spell¹ n a sequence of words used to perform magic; fascination.

spell² vb (pt **spelt** or **spelled**) vt to name or write down in correct order the letters to form a word; (letters) to form a word when placed in the correct order; to indicate. * vi to spell words.

spell³ n a usu indefinite period of time; a period of duty in a certain occupation or activity. * vt to relieve, stand in for.

spellbound adj entranced, enthralled.

spend vb (pt **spent**) vt to pay out (money); to concentrate (one's time or energy) on an activity; to pass, as time; to use up. * vi to pay out money.—**spender** n.

spendthrift n a person who spends money wastefully or extravagantly.

spent adj consumed, used up; physically drained, exhausted.

sperm n semen; the male reproductive cell.

spew vti to vomit; to flow or gush forth. * n something spewed.

sphere n a ball, globe or other perfectly round object; a field of activity or interest; a social class.—**spherical, spheric** adj.—**spherically** adv.

spice n an aromatic vegetable substance used for flavoring and seasoning food; these substances collectively; something that adds zest or interest. * vt to flavor with spice; to add zest to.

spicy adj (**spicier, spiciest**) flavored with spice; pungent; (inf) somewhat scandalous or indecent.—**spicily** adv.—**spiciness** n.

spider n a small wingless creature (arachnid) with eight legs, and abdominal spinnerets for spinning silk threads to make webs.

spike n long heavy nail; a sharp-pointed projection, as on a shoe to prevent slipping; an ear of corn, etc; a cluster of stalkless flowers arranged on a long stem. * vt to pierce with a spike.—**spiky** adj.

spill¹ vti (pt **spilt** or **spilled**) to cause, esp unintentionally, to flow out of a container; to shed (blood). * n something spilled.—**spillage** n.

spill² n a splinter or thin strip of wood or twisted paper for lighting a fire, etc.

spin vb (pr p **spinning**, pt **spun**) vt to rotate rapidly; to draw out and twist fibres into thread or yarn; (spiders, silkworm, etc) to make a web or cocoon; to draw out (a story) to a great length; (with **out**) to prolong, extend; to cause to last longer, eg money. * vi to seem to be spinning from dizziness; (wheels) to turn rapidly without imparting forward motion. * n a swift rotation; (inf) a brief, fast ride in a vehicle.

spinach n a plant with large, green edible leaves.

spinal adj of or relating to the spine or spinal cord.

spinal cord n the cord of nerves enclosed by the spinal column.

spindly adj (**spindlier, spindliest**) tall and slender; frail.

spine n a sharp, stiff projection, as a thorn of the cactus or quill of a porcupine; a spinal column; the backbone of a book.

spineless adj lacking a spine; weak-willed; irresolute.—**spinelessness** n.

spinning wheel n a small household machine with a wheel-driven spindle for spinning yarn from fibre.

spinster n an unmarried woman.

spiral adj winding round in a continuous curve up or down a centre or pole. * n a helix; a spiral line or shape; a continuous expansion or decrease, eg in inflation. * vi (pt **spiralled**) to move up or down in a spiral curve; to increase or decrease steadily.

spire n the tapering point of a steeple.

spirit n soul; a supernatural being, as a ghost, angel, etc; (pl) disposition; mood; vivacity, courage, etc; real meaning; essential quality; (usu pl) distilled alcoholic liquor. * vt to carry (away, off, etc) secretly and swiftly.

spirited adj full of life; animated.—**spiritedly** adv.

spirit level n a glass tube filled with liquid containing an air bubble and mounted in a frame, used for testing whether a surface is level.

spiritual adj of the soul; religious; sacred. * n an emotional religious song, originating among the Black slaves in the American South.—**spirituality** n.—**spiritually** adv.

spiritualism n the belief that the spirits of the dead can communicate with the living, as through mediums.—**spiritualist** n.

spirt see **spurt**.

spit[1] n a pointed iron rod on which meat is roasted; a long narrow strip of land projecting into the water. * vt (pr p **spitting**, pt **spitted**) to fix as on a spit, impale.

spit[2] vb (pr p **spitting**, pt **spat** or **spit**) vt to eject from the mouth; to utter with scorn. * vi to expel saliva from the mouth; (hot fat) to splutter; to rain lightly. * n saliva.

spite n ill will; malice. * vt to annoy spitefully, to vex.—**spiteful** adj.

spittle n saliva ejected form the mouth.

splake n a hybrid cross between a lake trout and a brook trout.

splash vt to spatter with liquid; to move with a splash; to display prominently. * n something splashed; a patch of color; a small amount, esp of a mixer added to an alcoholic drink.—**splashy** adj.

spleen n a large lymphatic organ in the upper left part of the abdomen which modifies the blood structure; spitefulness; ill humour.

splendid adj brilliant; magnificent; (inf) very good.—**splendidly** adv.

splendour, splendor (US) n brilliance; magnificence; grandeur.

splice vt to unite (two ends of a rope) by intertwining the strands; to connect (two pieces of timber) by overlapping.—also n.

splint n a rigid structure used to immobilize and support a fractured limb; a splinter of wood for lighting fires. * vt to put in splints.

splinter n a thin, sharp piece of wood, glass, or metal broken off. * vti to break off into splinters.—**splintery** adj.

split vti (pr p **splitting**, pt **split**) to break apart (usu into two pieces); to separate into factions; to divide into shares; to burst or tear. * n the act or process of splitting; a narrow gap made (as if) by splitting; a dessert consisting of sliced fruit, esp banana, with ice cream, nuts, etc; (often pl) the act of extending the legs in opposite directions and lowering the body to the floor. * adj divided; torn; fractured.

splutter vi to spit out food or drops of liquid noisily; to utter words confusedly and hurriedly.—also n.

spoil vb (pt **spoilt** or **spoiled**) vt to damage as to make useless, etc; to impair the enjoyment, etc, of; to overindulge (a child). * vi to become spoiled; to decay, etc, as food. * npl booty, valuables seized in war; the opportunities for financial gain from holding public office.

spoil-sport n (inf) a person who spoils the fun of others.

spoke[1], **spoken** see **speak**.

spoke[2] n any of the braces extending from the hub to the rim of a wheel.

spokesman n a person authorized to speak on behalf of others.—**spokeswomen** nf.

sponge n a plantlike marine animal with an internal skeleton of elastic interlacing horny fibres; a piece of natural or manmade sponge for washing or cleaning. * vt to wipe with a sponge. *vi (inf) to scrounge. —**sponginess** n.—**spongy** adj.

sponge cake n a sweet cake with a light porous texture.

sponsor n a person or organization that pays the expenses connected with an artistic production or sports event in return for advertising; in US, a business firm, etc that pays for a radio or TV programme advertising its product. * vt to act as sponsor for.—**sponsorship** n.

spontaneous adj arising naturally; unpremeditated.—**spontaneously** adv.—**spontaneity** n.

spook n (inf) a ghost; (inf) a spy. * vt to frighten.—**spooky** adj.

spool n a cylinder, bobbin, or reel, upon which thread, photographic film, etc, are wound. * vt to wind on a spool.

spoon n utensil with a shallow bowl and a handle, for eating, stirring, etc.—**spoonful** n.

sporadic adj occurring here and there; intermittent.—**sporadically** adv.

sport n an athletic game or pastime, often competitive and involving physical capability; good-humoured joking; (inf) a person regarded as fair and abiding by the rules. * vi to play, frolic. * vt (inf) to display, flaunt.

sporting adj interested in, concerned with, or suitable for sport; exhibiting sportsmanship; willing to take a risk.

sportsman n a person engaged in sport; a person who plays by the rules, is fair, is a good loser, etc.—**sportsmanlike**, **sportsmanly** adj.—**sportsmanship** n.

sporty adj (**sportier**, **sportiest**) (inf) fond of sport; flashy, ostentatious. —**sportily** adv.—**sportiness** n.

spot n a small area differing in color, etc, from the surrounding area; a stain, speck, etc; a taint on character or reputation; a small quantity or amount; a locality; (inf) a difficult or embarrassing situation; a place on an entertainment programme; a spotlight. * vt (pt **spotted**) to mark with spots; (inf) to identify or recognise; to glimpse.

spot check n a sudden random examination.

spotless adj immaculate.—**spotlessly** adv.

spotty adj (**spottier**, **spottiest**) marked with spots, esp on the skin; intermittent, uneven.—**spottiness** n.

spouse n (one's) husband or wife.

spout vti to eject in a strong jet or spurts; (inf) to drone on boringly. * n a projecting lip or tube for pouring out liquids.

sprain n a wrenching of a joint by sudden twisting or tearing of ligaments.—also vt.

sprang see **spring**.

sprawl vi to lie down with the limbs stretched out in an untidy manner; to spread out in a straggling way.—also n.

spray[1] n fine particles of a liquid; mist; an aerosol or atomizer. * vti to direct a spray (on); to apply as a spray.

spray[2] n a number of flowers on one branch; a

decorative flower arrangement; an ornament resembling this.

spread *vt* (*pt* **spread**) to extend; to unfold or open; to disseminate; to distribute; to apply a coating (eg butter). * *vi* to expand in all directions. * *n* an expanse; (*inf*) a feast; food which can be spread on bread; a bed cover.

spree *n* (*inf*) excessive indulgence, eg in spending money, alcohol consumption, etc.

sprig *n* a twig with leaves on it.

sprightly *adj* (**sprightlier, sprightliest**) full of life or energy.—**sprightliness** *n*.

spring *vb* (*pt* **sprang** *or* **sprung**, *pp* **sprung**) *vi* to move suddenly, as by elastic force; to arise suddenly; to originate. * *vt* to cause to spring up, to cause to operate suddenly. * *n* a leap; the season between winter and summer; a coiled piece of wire that springs back to its original shape when stretched; the source of a stream.—**springiness** *n*.—**springy** *adj*.

springboard *n* a flexible board used by divers and in gymnastics to provided added height or impetus.

spring break-up *n* (*Cdn*) the breakup of solid ice in a body of water in the spring.

spring-clean *vi* to clean (a house, etc) thoroughly.—*also n*.

sprinkle *vt* to scatter in droplets or particles (on something).—*also n*.

sprint *n* a short run or race at full speed. * *vi* to go at top speed.—**sprinter** *n*.

sprite *n* an elf or imp; a dainty person.

sprout *n* a new shoot on a plant; a small cabbage-like vegetable. * *vt* to put forth (shoots). * *vi* to begin to grow.

spruce[1] *adj* smart, neat, trim. * *vt* to smarten.

spruce[2] *n* an evergreen tree of the pine family with a conical head and soft light wood.

spruce grouse *n* a grouse of North American softwood forests.

sprung *see* **spring**.

spry *adj* (**spryer, spryest** *or* **sprier, spriest**) vigorous, agile.

spun *see* **spin**.

spur *n* a small metal wheel on a rider's heel, with sharp points for urging on the horse; encouragement, stimulus; a hard sharp projection. * *vt* (*pt* **spurred**) to urge on.

spurious *adj* not legitimate or genuine; false.—**spuriously** *adv*.—**spuriousness** *n*.

spurn *vt* to reject with disdain. * *n* disdainful rejection.

spurt *vi* to gush forth in a sudden stream or jet. * *n* a sudden stream or jet; a burst of activity.—*also* **spirt**.

spy *n* a secret agent employed to collect information on rivals. * *vi* to keep under secret surveillance, act as a spy (*usu with* **on**). * *vt* to catch sight of.

sq. *abbr* = square.

squabble *vi* to quarrel noisily. * *n* a noisy, petty quarrel.—*also n*.

squad *n* a small group of soldiers which form a working unit; a section of a police force;

(*sport*) a group of players from which a team is selected.

squadron *n* a unit of warships, cavalry, military aircraft, etc.

squalid *adj* filthy; neglected, sordid; degrading.—**squalidly** *adv*.—**squalor** *n*.

squander *vt* to spend extravagantly or wastefully.

square *n* a shape with four sides of equal length and four right angles; an open space in a town, surrounded by buildings; (*inf*) an old-fashioned person; an instrument for drawing right angles; the product of a number multiplied by itself. * *adj* square-shaped; (*financial account*) settled; fair, honest; equal in score; (*inf*) old-fashioned. * *vt* to make square; to multiply by itself. * *vi* to agree.—**squarely** *adv*.—**squareness** *n*.

square timber *n* (*Cdn*) (*hist*) logs cut into lengths with the round sides cut flat in order to be shipped more compactly.

squash[1] *vt* to squeeze, press, or crush; to suppress. * *vi* to squelch; to crowd. * *n* a crushed mass; a crowd of people pressed together; a fruit-flavored drink; a game played in a walled court with rackets and rubber ball.—**squashy** *adj*.

squash[2] *n* (*pl* **squashes, squash**) a marrow or gourd eaten as a vegetable.

squat *vi* (*pt* **squatted**) to crouch down upon the heels; to occupy land or property, without permission or title. * *adj* short and dumpy. * *n* the act of squatting; a house that is occupied by squatters.

squatter *n* a person who squats.

squawk *n* a loud, raucous call or cry, as of a bird; (*inf*) a loud protest.—*also vi*.

squeak *vi* to make a high-pitched cry. * *n* a squeaky noise.—**squeaker** *n*.—**squeaky** *adj*.

squeal *vi* to make a shrill and prolonged cry or sound; (*sl*) to be an informer; to protest.

squeamish *adj* easily nauseated; easily shocked or disgusted.—**squeamishly** *adv*.—**squeamishness** *n*.

squeeze *vt* to press firmly, compress; to grasp tightly; to hug; to force (through, into) by pressing; to extract liquid, juice, from by pressure; to obtain (money, etc) by force, to harass. * *n* squeezing or being squeezed; a hug; a small amount squeezed from something; a crowding together; financial pressure or hardship.

squelch *vi* to walk through soft, wet ground, making a sucking noise. * *vt* to crush or squash completely. * *n* a squelching sound.

squid *n* (*pl* **squid, squids**) an edible mollusc, related to the cuttlefish, with a long body and ten arms.

squid jigger *n* (*Cdn*) in Newfoundland, a weighted line with many hooks, used to catch squid for use as bait.—**squid jigging** *n*.

squint *vi* to half close or cross the eyes; to glance sideways. * *n* crossed eyes, as caused by a visual disorder; a glance sideways; (*inf*) a look. * *adj* squinting; (*inf*) crooked.

squire *n* a country gentleman, esp the leading landowner in a district.

squirm *vi* to writhe; to wriggle; to feel embarrassed or ashamed.

squirrel *n* a bushy tailed rodent with grey or reddish fur which lives in trees and feeds on nuts.

squirt *vt* to eject liquid in a jet. * *vi* to spurt. * *n* a jet of liquid; (*inf*) an insignificant person.

St *abbr* = Saint.

St. *abbr* = Street.

stab *vt* (*pt* **stabbed**) to injure with a knife or pointed weapon; to pain suddenly and sharply. * *vi* to thrust at (as if) with a pointed weapon. * *n* an act or instance of stabbing; a wound made by stabbing; a sudden sensation, as of emotion, pain, etc; (*inf*) an attempt.

stabilize *vti* to make or become stable or steady.

stable[1] *adj* steady or firm; firmly established; permanent; not decomposing readily.—**stability** *n*.

stable[2] *n* a building where horses or cattle are kept; a group of racehorses belonging to one owner; a group of people working for or trained by a specific establishment, as writers, performers, etc. * *vti* to put, keep, or live in a stable.

stack *n* a large neatly arranged pile (of hay, papers, records, etc); a chimney stack; (*inf*) a large amount of; a number of aircraft circling an airport waiting for permission to land. * *vt* to pile, arrange in a stack.

stadium *n* a sports ground surrounded by tiers of seats.

staff *n* (*pl* **staves**) a strong stick or pole; (*mus*) one of the five horizontal lines upon which music is written (—*also* **stave**); (*pl* **staffs**) a body of officers who help a commanding officer, or perform special duties; the workers employed in an establishment; the teachers or lecturers of an educational institution. * *vt* to provide with staff.

stag *n* a full-grown male deer. * *adj* (*party*) for men only.

stage *n* a degree or step in a process; a raised platform, esp for acting on; (*with* **the**) the theatre, the theatrical calling; any field of action or setting; a portion of a journey; a propulsion unit of a space rocket discarded when its fuel is spent. * *vt* to perform a play on the stage; to plan, organize (an event).

stage fright *n* nervousness at appearing before an audience.

stage manager *n* a person responsible for the stage arrangements prior to and during the performance of a play.

stagger *vi* to walk unsteadily, to totter. * *vt* to astound; to give a shock to; to arrange so as not to overlap; to alternate.

staggering *adj* astounding.—**staggeringly** *adv*.

stagnant *adj* (*water*) not flowing, standing still with a revolting smell; unchanging, dull.—**stagnancy** *n*.

stagnate *vi* to be, or become, stagnant.—**stagnation** *n*.

stagy, stagey *adj* (**stagier, stagiest**) theatrical, dramatic.

staid *adj* sober; sedate; old-fashioned.

stain *vt* to dye; to discolor with spots of something which cannot be removed. * *vi* to become stained; to produce stains. * *n* a discolored mark; a moral blemish; a dye or liquid for staining materials, eg wood.

stained glass *n* colored glass used in windows.

stainless *adj* free from stain; (materials) resistant to staining.

stair *n* a flight of stairs; a single step; (*pl*) a stairway.

staircase *n* a flight of stairs with banisters.

stairway *n* a staircase.

stake[1] *n* a sharpened metal or wooden post driven into the ground, as a marker or fence post; a post to which persons were tied for execution by burning; this form of execution. * *vt* to support with, tie or tether to a stake; to mark out (land) with stakes; (*with* **out**) to put under surveillance.

stake[2] *vt* to bet; (*inf*) to provide with money or resources. * *n* a bet; a financial interest; (*pl*) money risked on a race; (*pl*) the prize in a race

stalactite *n* an icicle-like calcium deposit hanging from the roof of a cave.

stalagmite *n* a cylindrical deposit projecting upwards from the floor of a cave, caused by the dripping of water and lime from the roof.

stale *adj* deteriorated from age; tainted; musty; stagnant; jaded.—**staleness** *n*.

stalemate *n* (*chess*) a situation in which a king can only be moved in and out of check, thus causing a draw; a deadlock.—*also vt*.

stalk[1] *n* the stem of a plant.

stalk[2] *vi* to stride in a stiff or angry way; to hunt (game, prey) stealthily.—**stalker** *n*.

stall[1] *n* a compartment for one animal in a stable; a table or stand for the display or sale of goods; a stalling of an engine; (*aircraft*) a loss of lift and downward plunge due to an excessive decrease in airspeed; (*pl*) the seats on the ground floor of a theatre. * *vti* (*car engine*) to stop or cause to stop suddenly, eg by misuse of the clutch; (*aircraft*) to lose or cause to lose lift because of an excessive reduction in airspeed.

stall[2] *vti* to play for time; to postpone or delay. * *n* (*inf*) any action used in stalling.

stalwart *adj* strong, sturdy; resolute; dependable. * *n* a loyal, hardworking supporter.

stamina *n* strength; staying power.

stammer *vti* to pause or falter in speaking; to stutter.—*also n*.—**stammerer** *n*.

stamp *vt* to put a mark on; to imprint with an official seal; to affix a postage stamp; (*with* **out**) to extinguish by stamping; to suppress, eradicate, by force. * *vi* to bring the foot down heavily (on). * *n* a postage stamp; the mark cancelling a postage stamp; a block for imprinting.

stampede *n* an impulsive rush of a panic-stricken herd; a rush of a crowd.—*also vti*.

stance *n* posture; the attitude taken in a given situation.

stand *vb* (*pt* **stood**) *vi* to be in an upright position; to be on, or rise to one's feet; to make resistance; to remain unchanged; to endure, tolerate; (*with* **by**) to look on without interfering; to be available for use if required; (*with* **down**) to withdraw, resign; to leave a witness box after testifying in court; (*soldier*) to go off duty; (*with* **off**) to remain at a distance; to reach a deadlock; (*with* **up**) to rise to one's feet. * *vt* to put upright; to endure, tolerate; (*with* **by**) to remain loyal to, to defend; (*with* **off**) to (cause to) keep at a distance; to lay off (employees) temporarily; (*with* **up**) to resist; to withstand criticism, close examination, etc; (*inf*) to fail to keep an appointment with. * *n* a strong opinion; a standing position; a standstill; a place for taxis awaiting hire; (*pl*) a structure for spectators; the place taken by a witness for testifying in court; a piece of furniture for hanging things from; a stall or booth for a small retail business.

standard *n* a flag, banner, or emblem; an upright pole, pillar; an authorized weight or measure; a criterion; an established or accepted level of achievement; (*pl*) moral principles. * *adj* serving as a standard; typical.—**standardize** *vt*.

stand-by *n* a person or thing held in readiness for use in an emergency, etc.—*also adj*.

stand-in *n* a substitute; a person who takes the place of an actor during the preparation of a scene or in stunts.—*also vi*.

standing *n* status or reputation; length of service, duration. * *adj* upright; permanent; (*jump*) performed from a stationary position.

standoffish *adj* aloof, reserved.

standpoint *n* a point of view, opinion.

standstill *n* a complete halt.

stand-up *adj* (*collar*) upright; (*fight*) furious; (*comedian*) telling jokes standing alone in front of an audience.

stank *see* **stink**.

staple¹ *n* a principal commodity of trade or industry of a region, etc; a main constituent. * *adj* chief.

staple² *n* a U-shaped thin piece of wire for fastening. * *vt* to fasten with a staple.

star *n* any one of the celestial bodies, esp those visible by night which appear as small points of light, including planets, comets, meteors, and less commonly the sun and moon; a figure with five points; an exceptionally successful or skilful person; a famous actor, actress, musician, dancer, etc. * *vti* (*pt* **starred**) to feature or be featured as a star.

starboard *n* the right side of a ship or aircraft when facing the bow.

starch *n* a white, tasteless, food substance found in potatoes, cereal, etc; a fabric stiffener based on this. * *vt* to stiffen with starch.—**starchy** *adj*.

stare *vi* to gaze fixedly, as in horror, astonishment,etc; to glare. * *n* a fixed gaze.

stark *adj* bare; plain; blunt; utter. * *adv* completely.—**starkly** *adv*.—**starkness** *n*.

start *vi* to commence, begin; to jump involuntarily, from fright. * *vt* to begin. * *n* a beginning; a slight involuntary body movement; a career opening.

starter *n* a person who starts something, esp an official who signals the beginning of a race; a competitor in a race; the first course of a meal; a small electric motor used to start an internal combustion engine.

startle *vti* to be, or cause to be, frightened or surprised.—**startling** *adj*.

starve *vi* to die or suffer from a lack of food. * *vt* deprive (a person) of food; to deprive (of) anything necessary.—**starvation** *n*.

state *n* condition; frame of mind; position in society; ceremonious style; (*with* *cap*) an area or community with its own government, or forming a federation under a sovereign government. * *adj* of the state or State; public; ceremonial. * *vt* to express in words; to specify, declare officially.

stately *adj* (**statelier**, **stateliest**) dignified; majestic.—**stateliness** *n*.

statement *n* a formal announcement; a declaration; a document showing one's bank balance.

statement of claim *n* (*Cdn*) a legal document that states what a plaintiff seeks to establish as the outcome of a civil suit.

statesman *n* a well-known and experienced politician.—**statesmanship** *n*.

static *adj* fixed; stationary; at rest. * *n* electrical interference causing noise on radio or TV.

station *n* a railway or bus terminal or stop; headquarters (of the emergency services); military headquarters; (*inf*) a TV channel; position in society, standing. * *vt* to assign to a post, place, office.

stationary *adj* not moving.

stationer *n* a dealer in stationery, office supplies, etc.

stationery *n* writing materials, esp paper and envelopes.

station wagon *n* an estate car.

statistic *n* a fact obtained from analysing information expressed in numbers.

statistics *n* (*used as sing*) the branch of mathematics dealing with the collection, analysis and presentation of numerical data.—**statistical** *adj*.—**statistician** *n*.

statue *n* a representation of a human or animal form that is carved or moulded.

stature *n* the standing height of a person; level of attainment.

status *n* (*pl* **statuses**) social or professional position or standing; prestige; condition or standing from the point of view of the law, position of affairs.

status Indian n (Cdn) a person who is officially registered as a member of a First Nations community.

status quo n the existing state of affairs.

statute n a law enacted by a legislature; a regulation.

statutory adj established, regulated, or required by statute.

staunch adj loyal; dependable.—**staunchly** adv.

stave n a piece of wood of a cask or barrel; (mus) a staff. * vt (pt **staved** or **stove**) (usu with **in**) to smash or dent inwards.

stay[1] n a rope supporting a mast

stay[2] vi to remain in a place; to wait; to reside temporarily. * vt to support; to endure; to stop, restrain. * n a suspension of legal proceedings; a short time spent as a visitor or guest.

STD abbr = sexually transmitted disease; subscriber trunk dialling.

steadfast adj firm, fixed; resolute.—**steadfastly** adv.

steady adj (**steadier, steadiest**) firm, stable; regular, constant; calm, unexcitable. * n (inf) a regular boyfriend or girlfriend. * vti to make or become steady.—**steadily** adv.—**steadiness** n.

steak n a slice of meat, esp beef or fish, for grilling or frying.

steal vt (pt **stole**, pp **stolen**) to take (from someone) dishonestly; to obtain secretly. * n (inf) an unbelievable bargain.

stealth n a manner of moving quietly and secretly.

stealthy adj (**stealthier, stealthiest**) acting or performed in a quiet, secret manner; unobtrusive, furtive.—**stealthily** adv.—**stealthiness** n.

steam n the hot mist or vapour created by boiling water. * vi to give off steam; to move by steam power; to cook with steam; (with **up**) (glasses, windows, etc) to become covered in condensation. * adj driven by steam.

steamie n (Cdn) in Quebec, a steamed hot dog.

steel n an alloy of iron and carbon; strength or courage. * adj of, or like, steel. * vt to cover with steel; to harden; to nerve (oneself).—**steely** adj.

steep[1] adj sloping sharply; (inf) excessive, exorbitant.—**steeply** adv.—**steepness** n.

steep[2] vti to soak or be soaked in a liquid; to saturate; to imbue.—also n.

steeple n a tower of a church, with or without a spire; the spire alone.

steeplechase n a horse race across country or on a course over jumps; a track race over hurdles and water jumps.—**steeplechaser** n.

steer[1] n a castrated male of the cattle family.

steer[2] vti to direct (a vehicle, ship, bicycle, etc) in the correct direction of travel.

Steller's jay n a blue jay with a dark crest found in central and western North America.

stem[1] n a plant stalk; the upright slender part of anything, such as a wineglass; the root of a word. * vi (pt **stemmed**) to originate (from).

stem[2] vt (pt **stemmed**) to stop, check (the flow or tide).

stench n a foul odour.

stencil n a pierced sheet of card or metal for reproducing letters by applying paint; a design so made. * vti (pt **stencilled**) to produce (letters, etc) or designs using a stencil.

step n one movement of the foot ahead in walking, running, or dancing; a pace; a grade or degree; a stage towards a goal; one tread of a stair, rung of a ladder. * vti (pt **stepped**) to take a step or a number of paces.

step- prefix related by remarriage of a spouse or parent.

stepladder n a short portable ladder with flat steps fixed within a frame.

stereo n (pl **stereos**) a hi-fi or record player with two loudspeakers; stereophonic sound. * adj stereophonic.

stereophonic adj (sound reproduction system) using two separate channels for recording and transmission to create a spatial effect.—**stereophonically** adv.—**stereophony** n.

stereotype n a fixed, general image of a person or thing shared by many people.—also vt.

sterile adj unable to produce offspring, fruit, seeds, or spores; fruitless; free from germs.

sterilize vt to render incapable of reproduction; to free from germs.—**sterilization** n.

sterling n the British system of money. * adj of excellent character.

stern[1] adj severe; austere, harsh.—**sternly** adv.—**sternness** n.

stern[2] n the rear part of a boat or ship

stethoscope n an instrument used to detect body sounds.—**stethoscopic** adj.

stew n a meal of cooked meat with vegetables. * vt to cook slowly.

steward n a manager (of property); a race organizer; a person who serves food on an aircraft or ship and looks after passengers.

stewardess n a woman steward on an aircraft or ship.

stick[1] vb (pt **stuck**) vt to pierce or stab; to attach with glue, adhesive tape, etc. * vi to cling to, to adhere; to stay close to; to be held up.

stick[2] n a broken off shoot or branch of a tree; a walking stick; a hockey stick; a rod.

sticker n an adhesive label or poster.

stickler n a person who is scrupulous or obstinate about something.

sticky adj (**stickier, stickiest**) covered with adhesive or something sweet; (weather) warm and humid; (inf) difficult.—**stickiness** n.

stiff adj not flexible or supple; rigid; firm; moving with difficulty; having aching joints and muscles; formal, unfriendly; (drink) potent; (breeze) strong; (penalty) severe. * n (sl) a corpse. * adv utterly.—**stiffly** adv.—**stiffness** n.

stiffen vti to make or become stiff.—**stiffener** n.

stifle vt to suffocate; to smother; to suppress, hold back.

stifling adj excessively hot and stuffy. —**stiflingly**

adv.

stigma n (pl **stigmas**) a social disgrace; the part of a flower that receives pollen; (pl **stigmata**) (*Christianity*) marks resembling the wounds of Christ thought to appear on the bodies of saintly people.

stile n a step, or set of steps, for climbing over a wall or fence.

still[1] adj motionless; calm; silent; (*drink*) not carbonated. * n a single photograph taken from a cinema film. *vti to make or become still. * adv continuously; nevertheless. — **stillness** n.

still[2] n an apparatus for distilling liquids, esp spirits.

stillborn adj born dead; (*idea, project, etc*) a failure from the start, abortive.

still life n (pl **still lifes**) a painting of inanimate objects, such as flowers, fruit, etc.

stilt n either of a pair of poles with footrests on which one can walk, as in a circus; a supporting column.

stilted adj (*speech, writing*) pompous, unnaturally formal; (*conversation*) forced, intermittent.

stimulate vt to excite, arouse.—**stimulation** n.

stimulus n (pl **stimuli**) something that acts as an incentive; an agent that arouses or provokes a response in a living organism.

sting n a sharp pointed organ of a bee, wasp, etc, or hair on a plant, used for injecting poison; a skin wound caused by injected poison from an insect or plant; (*sl*) a swindle. * vt to wound with a sting; to cause to suffer mentally; to goad, incite; (*sl*) to cheat by overcharging. * vi to feel a sharp pain.

stingy adj (**stingier, stingiest**) miserly, mean.—**stingily** adv.—**stinginess** n.

stink vi (pt **stank** or **stunk**) to give out an offensive smell; (*sl*) to possess something in an excessive amount; (*sl*) to be extremely bad in quality. * n a foul smell.

stipulate vt to specify as a condition of an agreement.—**stipulation** n.

stir[1] vb (pt **stirred**) vt to mix, as with a spoon; to rouse; to stimulate or excite. * vi to be disturbed; to move oneself; to be active. * n a stirring movement; tumult.

stir[2] n (*sl*) prison.

stirring adj rousing, exciting.

stirrup n a strap and flat-bottomed ring hanging from a saddle, for a rider's foot.

stitch n a single in-and-out movement of a threaded needle in sewing; a single loop of a yarn in knitting or crocheting; a sudden, sharp pain, esp in the side. * vti to sew.

stock n raw material; goods on hand; shares of corporate capital, or the certificates showing such ownership; lineage, family, race; a store; the cattle, horses, etc, kept on a farm; the broth obtained by boiling meat, bones, and vegetables as a foundation for soup, etc. * vt to supply; to keep in store. * adj standard; hackneyed.

stockade n a defensive enclosure or barrier of stakes fixed in the ground.

stockbroker n a person who deals in stocks.

stocking n a sock; a nylon covering for a woman's leg, supported by suspenders.

stock market, stock exchange n the market for dealing in stocks and shares.

stockpile n a reserve supply of essentials.—*also* vt.

stocky adj (**stockier, stockiest**) short and sturdy.—**stockily** adv.—**stockiness** n.

stodgy adj (**stodgier, stodgiest**) (*food*) thick, heavy and indigestible; uninteresting.

stoke vt to stir and feed (a fire) with fuel.

stole[1], **stolen** see **steal**.

stole[2] n a long scarf or piece of fur worn on the shoulders.

stolid adj impassive; unemotional.—**stolidity** n.—**stolidly** adv.

stomach n the organ where food is digested; the belly. * vt to put up with.

stone n a small lump of rock; a precious stone or gem; the hard seed of a fruit; (pl **stone**) a unit of weight (14 lb./6.35 kg). * vt to throw stones at; to remove stones from (fruit).

Stone sheep n a wild, thin-horned sheep of the mountainous parts othe Yukon and northern Brtish Columbia.

stony, stoney adj (**stonier, stoniest**) of, like, or full of stones; unfeeling, heartless.

stood see **stand**.

stool n a seat or a support for the back when sitting, with no back or arms; matter evacuated from the bowels.

stoop vti to bend the body forward and downward; to degrade oneself; to deign.—*also* n.

stop vb (pt **stopped**) vt to halt; to prevent; to intercept; to plug or block. * vi to cease; to come to an end; to stay. * n an act or instance of stopping; an impediment; (a knob controlling) a set of organ pipes; any of the standard settings of the aperture in a camera lens (—*also* **f-stop**); a regular stopping place for a bus or train; a punctuation mark, esp full stop.

stopover n a short break in a journey.

stoppage n stopping or being stopped; an obstruction; a deduction from pay; a concerted cessation of work by employees, as during a strike.

stopper n a cork or bung.

storage n storing or being stored; an area reserved for storing; (*comput*) the storing of data in a computer memory or on disk, tape, etc.

store n a large supply of goods for future use; a warehouse; a shop. * vt to set aside; to put in a warehouse, etc; (*comput*) to put (data) into a computer memory or onto a storage device.

storey, story (*US*) n a horizontal division of a building; a set of rooms occupying this space.

stork n a long-necked and long-legged wading bird.

storm n a heavy fall of rain, snow, etc with strong winds; a violent commotion; a furore; (mil) an attack on a fortified place.

* *vt* to rush, invade. * *vi* to be angry; to rain, snow hard.—**stormy** *adj*.

stormstayed *adj* (*Cdn*) stranded in a place because of severe weather conditions, esp a snowstorm.

story *n* a narrative of real or imaginary events; a plot of a literary work; an anecdote; an account; (*inf*) a lie; a news article.

stout *adj* strong; short and plump; sturdy. * *n* strong dark beer.—**stoutly** *adv*.—**stoutness** *n*.

stove[1] *n* a cooker; heating apparatus.

stove[2] *see* **stave.**

stow *vt* to store, pack, in an orderly way

stowaway *n* a person who hides on a ship, car, aircraft, etc to avoid paying the fare.

straddle *vt* to have one leg or support on either side of something.

strafe *vt* to machine-gun (troops, vehicles, etc) from the air.—*also n.*

straggle *vi* to stray; to wander.—**straggler** *n.*—**straggly** *adj*.

straight *adj* (*line*) continuing in one direction, not curved or bent; direct; honest; (*sl*) heterosexual; (*alcoholic drinks*) neat, not diluted. * *adv* directly; without delay. * *n* being straight; a straight line, form, or position; a straight part of a racetrack; (*poker*) a hand containing five cards in sequence.—**straightness** *n*.

straighten *vti* to make or become straight.

straightforward *adj* honest, open; simple; easy.—**straightforwardly** *adv*.—**straightforwardness** *n*.

strain[1] *vt* to tax; to stretch; to overexert; to stress; to injure (a muscle) by overstretching; (*food*) to drain or sieve. * *n* overexertion; tension; an injury from straining.

strain[2] *n* a plant or animal within a species having a common characteristic; a trait; a trace.

strained *adj* (*action, behaviour*) produced by excessive effort; (*mood, atmosphere*) tense, worried.

strainer *n* a sieve or colander used for straining liquids, pasta, tea, etc.

strait *n* a channel of sea linking two larger seas; (*usu pl*) difficulty, distress.

straitjacket, straightjacket *n* a coatlike device for restraining violent people; something that restricts or limits.—*also vt*.

strait-laced, straight-laced *adj* prim, morally strict.

strand[1] *vt* to run aground; to leave helpless, without transport or money.

strand[2] *n* a single piece of thread or wire twisted together to make a rope or cable; a tress of hair.—*also vt*.

strange *adj* peculiar; odd; unknown; unfamiliar.—**strangely** *adv*.—**strangeness** *n*.

stranger *n* a person who is unknown; a new arrival to a place, town, social gathering, etc; a person who is unfamiliar with or ignorant of something.

strangle *vt* to kill by compressing the windpipe, to choke; to stifle, suppress.—**strangler** *n*.

strap *n* a narrow strip of leather or cloth for carrying or holding (a bag, etc); a fastening, as on a shoe, wristwatch. * *vti* (*pt* **strapped**) to

fasten with a strap; to beat with a strap.

strapping *adj* tall, well-built.

strata *see* **stratum.**

strategic, strategical *adj* of, relating to, or important in strategy; (*weapons*) designed to strike at the enemy's homeland, not for use on the battlefield.—**strategically** *adv*.

strategy *n* the planning and conduct of war; a political, economic, or business policy.—**strategist** *n*.

stratum *n* (*pl* **strata, stratums**) a layer of sedimentary rock; a level (of society).

straw *n* the stalks of threshed grain; a tube for sucking up a drink.

strawberry *n* a soft red fruit used in desserts and jam.

stray *vi* to wander; to deviate; to digress. * *n* a domestic animal that has become lost. * *adj* random.

streak *n* a line or long mark of contrasting color; a flash of lightning; a characteristic, a trace. * *vti* to mark with or form streaks; to run naked in public as a prank.—**streaker** *n*.

streaky *adj* (**streakier, streakiest**) marked with streaks; (*bacon*) having alternate layers of fat and lean.

stream *n* a small river, brook, etc; a flow of liquid; anything flowing and continuous. * *vi* to flow, gush.

streamer *n* a banner; a long decorative ribbon.

streamline *vt* to shape (a car, boat, etc) in a way that lessens resistance through air or water; to make more efficient, to simplify.—**streamlined** *adj*.

street *n* a public road in a town or city lined with houses; such a road with its buildings and pavements; the people living,working, etc, along a given street.

streetcar *n* a tram.

street hockey *n* (*Cdn*) road hockey.

strength *n* the state or quality of being physically or mentally strong; power of exerting or withstanding pressure, stress, force; potency; effectiveness.

strengthen *vti* to make or become stronger.

strenuous *adj* vigorous; requiring exertion.—**strenuously** *adv*.—**strenuousness** *n*.

stress *n* pressure; mental or physical tension or strain; emphasis; (*physics*) a system of forces producing or sustaining strain. * *vt* to exert pressure on; to emphasize.

stretch *vt* to extend, to draw out. * *vi* to extend, spread; to extend (the limbs, body); to be capable of expanding, as in elastic material. * *n* the act of stretching or instance of being stretched; the capacity for being stretched; an expanse of time or space; (*sl*) a period of imprisonment.—**stretchy** *adj*.

stretcher *n* a portable frame for carrying the sick or injured.

strew *vt* (*pt* **strewed**, *pp* **strewn** *or* **strewed**) to scatter; to spread.

stricken *adj* suffering (from an illness); afflicted, as by something painful.

strict *adj* harsh, firm; enforcing rules rigorously; rigid.—**strictly** *adv*.—**strictness** *n*.

stride vi (pt **strode**, pp **stridden**) to walk with long steps. * vt to straddle.—also n.

strident adj loud and harsh.—**stridency** n.—**stridently** adv.

strife n a fight, quarrel; struggle.

strike vb (pt **struck**) vt to hit; to crash into; (mil) to attack; to ignite (a match) by friction; (disease, etc) to afflict suddenly; to come upon, esp unexpectedly; to delete; (clock) to indicate by sounding; to assume (eg an attitude); to occur to; (medal, coin) to produce by stamping; (flag, tent) to lower, take down; to come upon (oil, ore, etc) by drilling or excavation. * vi to cease work to enforce a demand (for higher wages or better working conditions). * n a stoppage of work; a military attack.

striker n a worker who is on strike; a mechanism that strikes, as in a clock; (soccer) a forward player whose primary role is to score goals.

striking adj impressive.—**strikingly** adv.

string n a thin length of cord or twine used for tying, fastening, etc; a stretched length of catgut, wire, or other material in a musical instrument; (pl) the stringed instruments in an orchestra; their players; a line or series of things. * vt (pt **strung**) to thread on a string.

stringent adj strict.—**stringently** adv.—**stringency** n.

strip vb (pt **stripped**) vt to peel off; to divest; to take away removable parts. * vi to undress. * n a long, narrow piece (of cloth, land, etc); an airstrip or runway.

stripe n a narrow band of a different color form the background; a chevron worn on a military uniform to indicate rank. * vt to mark with a stripe.—**striped** adj.—**stripy** adj.

stripper n a striptease artist; a device or solvent that removes paint.

striptease n an erotic show where a person removes their clothes slowly and seductively to music.

strive vi (pt **strove**, pp **striven**) to endeavour earnestly, labour hard, to struggle, contend.

strode see stride.

stroke[1] n a blow or hit; (med) a seizure; the sound of a clock; (sport) an act of hitting a ball; a manner of swimming; the sweep of an oar in rowing; a movement of a pen, pencil, or paintbrush.

stroke[2] vt to caress; to do so as a sign of affection.

stroll vi to walk leisurely, to saunter.—also n.

strong adj physically or mentally powerful; potent; intense; healthy; convincing; powerfully affecting the sense of smell or taste, pungent. * adv effectively, vigorously.—**strongly** adv.

stronghold n a fortress; a centre of strength or support.

strove see strive.

struck see strike.

structure n organization; construction; arrangement of parts in an organism, or of atoms in a molecule of a substance; system, framework; order. * vt to organize, to arrange; to build up.—**structural** adj.—**structurally** adv.

struggle vi to move strenuously so as to escape; to strive; to fight; to exert strength; to make one's way (along, through, up, etc) with difficulty. * n a violent effort; a fight.

strum vt (pt **strummed**) to play on (a guitar, etc), by moving the thumb across the strings.

strung see string.

strut[1] vi (pt **strutted**) to walk in a proud or pompous manner.

strut[2] n a brace or structural support. * vt to brace.

stub n a short piece left after the larger part has been removed or used; the counterfoil of a cheque, receipt, etc. * vt (pt **stubbed**) to knock (one's toe or foot) painfully; to extinguish (a cigarette).

stubble n the stubs or stumps left in the ground when a crop has been harvested; any short, bristly growth, as of beard.—**stubbly** adj.

stubborn adj obstinate; persevering; determined, inflexible.—**stubbornly** adv.—**stubbornness** n.

stuck see stick.

stuck-up adj (inf) conceited; proud; snobbish.

stud[1] n a male animal, esp a horse, kept for breeding; a collection of horses and mares for breeding; a farm or stable for stud animals.

stud[2] n a large-headed nail; an ornamental fastener. * vt (pt **studded**) to cover with studs.

student n a person who studies or investigates a particular subject; a person who is enrolled for study at a school, college, university, etc.

studied adj carefully planned.

studio n (pl **studios**) the workshop of an artist, photographer, etc; (pl) a building where motion pictures are made; a room where TV or radio programmes are recorded.

studious adj given to study; careful.

study vt to observe an investigate (eg phenomena) closely; to learn (eg a language); to scrutinize; to follow a course (at college, etc). * n the process of studying; a detailed investigation and analysis of a subject; the written report of a study of something; a room for studying.

stuff n material; matter; textile fabrics; cloth, esp when woollen; personal possessions generally. * vt to cram or fill.

stuffing n material used to stuff or fill anything; a seasoned mixture put inside poultry, meat, vegetables etc before cooking.

stuffy adj (**stuffier**, **stuffiest**) badly ventilated; lacking in fresh air; dull, uninspired.—**stuffiness** n.

stumble vi to trip up or lose balance when walking; to falter; (with across or on) to discover by chance. * n a trip; a blunder.

stump n the part of a tree remaining in the ground after the trunk has been felled; the part of a limb, tooth, that remains after the larger part is cut off or destroyed. * vt (inf) to confuse, baffle; to campaign for an election.

stun *vt* (*pt* **stunned**) to render unconscious due to a fall or blow; to surprise completely; to shock.

stung *see* **sting.**

stunk *see* **stink.**

stunning *adj* (*inf*) strikingly attractive.

stunt[1] *vt* to prevent the growth of, to dwarf.

stunt[2] *n* a daring or spectacular feat; a project designed to attract attention. * *vi* to carry out stunts.

stupefy *vt* to dull the senses of.—**stupefaction** *n.*

stupendous *adj* wonderful, astonishing.

stupid *adj* lacking in understanding or common sense; silly; foolish; stunned.—**stupidity** *n.*—**stupidly** *adv.*

stupor *n* extreme lethargy; mental dullness.

sturdy *adj* (**sturdier, sturdiest**) firm; strong, robust.—**sturdily** *adv.*—**sturdiness** *n.*

stutter *vi* to stammer.—*also n.*

sty[1], **stye** *n* (*pl* **sties, styes**) an inflamed swelling on the eyelid.

sty[2] *n* (*pl* **sties**) a pen for pigs; any filthy place.

style *n* the manner of writing, painting, composing music peculiar to an individual or group; fashion, elegance. * *vt* to design or shape (eg hair).

stylish *adj* having style; fashionable.—**stylishly** *adv.*—**stylishness** *n.*

stylize *vt* to give a conventional style to.—**stylization** *n.*

stylus *n* (*pl* **styli, styluses**) the device attached to the cartridge on the arm of a record-player that rests in the groove of a record and transmits the vibrations that are converted to sound.

suave *adj* charming, polite.—**suavely** *adv.*—**suaveness, suavity** *n.*

sub *n* (*inf*) a submarine; a substitute; a subscription; a subeditor.

sub- *prefix* under, below; subordinate, next in rank to.

subconscious *adj* happening without one's awareness. * *n* the part of the mind that is active without one's conscious awareness.—**subconsciously** *adv.*

subdue *vt* to dominate; to render submissive; to repress (eg a desire); to soften, tone down (eg color, etc).

subject *adj* under the power of; liable. * *n* a person under the power of another; a citizen; a topic; a theme; the scheme or idea of a work of art. * *vt* to bring under control; to make liable; to cause to undergo something.—**subjection** *n.*

subjective *adj* determined by one's own mind or consciousness; relating to reality as perceived and not independent of the mind; arising from one's own thoughts and emotions, personal.—**subjectively** *adv.*

subjunctive *adv* denoting that mood of a verb which expresses doubt, condition, wish, or hope. * *n* the subjunctive mood.

sublime *adj* noble; exalted.—**sublimely** *adv.*—**sublimity** *n.*

submarine *adj* underwater, esp under the sea.

* *n* a naval vessel capable of being propelled under water, esp for firing torpedoes or missiles.

submerge, submerse *vt* to plunge or sink under water; to cover, hide.—**submergence, submersion** *n.*

submission *n* an act of submitting; something submitted, as an idea or proposal; the state of being submissive, compliant; the act of referring something for another's consideration, criticism, etc.—**submissively** *adv.*—**submissiveness** *n.*

submit *vb* (*pt* **submitted**) *vt* to surrender (oneself) to another person or force; to refer to another for consideration or judgment; to offer as an opinion. * *vi* to yield, to surrender.

subordinate *adj* secondary; lower in order, rank. * *n* a subordinate person. * *vt* to put in a lower position or rank.—**subordination** *n.*

subscribe *vt* to pay to receive regular copies (of a magazine, etc); to donate money (to a charity, campaign); to support or agree with (an opinion, faith).—**subscriber** *n.*—**subscription** *n.*

subsequent *adj* occurring or following after.—**subsequently** *adv.*

subside *vi* to sink or fall to the bottom; to settle; to diminish; to abate.—**subsidence** *n.*

subsidiary *adj* secondary; supplementary; (*company*) owned or controlled by another.—*also n.*

subsidy *n* government financial aid to a private person or company to assist an enterprise.—**subsidize** *vt.*

subsistence *n* existence; livelihood.

substance *n* matter (such as powder, liquid); the essential nature or part; significance.

substantial *adj* of considerable value or size; important; strongly built.—**substantially** *adv.*

substantiate *vt* to prove, to verify.—**substantiation** *n.*

substitute *vt* to put or act in place of another person or thing (*with* **for**); to replace (by). * *n* a person or thing that serves in place of another.—*also adj.*—**substitution** *n.*

subtitle *n* an explanatory, usu secondary, title to a book; a printed translation superimposed on a foreign language film.—*also vt.*

subtle *adj* delicate; slight; not noticeable; difficult to define, put into words; ingenious.—**subtlety** *n.*—**subtly** *adv.*

subtract *vti* to take away or deduct, as one quantity from another.—**subtraction** *n.*

suburb *n* a residential district on the outskirts of a large town or city.—**suburban** *adj.*—**suburbia** *n.*

subversive *adj* liable to subvert established authority. * *n* a person who engages in subversive activities.

subway *n* a passage under a street; an underground metropolitan electric railway.

succeed *vt* to come after, to follow; to take the place of. * *vi* to accomplish what is attempted; to prosper.

success *n* the gaining of wealth, fame, etc; the favorable outcome (of anything attempted);

a successful person or action.

successful *adj* having success.—**successfully** *adv*.

succession *n* following in sequence; a number of persons or things following in order; the act or process of succeeding to a title, throne, etc; the line of descent to succeed to something.

successive *adj* following in sequence.—**successively** *adv*.

successor *n* a person who succeeds anothe.

succinct *adj* clear, concise.—**succinctly** *adv*.—**succinctness** *n*.

succulent *adj* juicy; moist and tasty; (*plant*) having fleshy tissue. * *n* a succulent plant (eg cactus).—**succulence** *n*.

succumb *vi* to yield to superior strength or overpowering desire; to die.

such *adj* of a specified kind (eg such people, such a film); so great. * *adv* so; very.

suck *vt* to draw (a liquid, air) into the mouth; to dissolve or roll about in the mouth (as a sweet); to draw in as if by sucking (*with* in, up etc).—*also n.*

sucker *n* (*sl*) a person who is easily taken in or deceived; a cup-shaped piece of rubber that adheres to surfaces.

suckle *vt* to feed at the breast or udder.

sucrose *n* sugar.

suction *n* the act or process of sucking; the exertion of a force to form a vacuum.

sudden *adj* happening quickly and unexpectedly, abrupt.—**suddenly** *adv*.—**suddenness** *n*.

sue *vt* (*pr p* suing, *pt* sued) to bring a legal action against.

suede *n* leather finished with a soft nap.

suet *n* white, solid fat in animal tissue, used in cooking.

suffer *vt* to undergo; to endure; to experience. * *vi* to feel pain or distress.—**sufferer** *n*.—**suffering** *n*.

sufferable *adj* endurable.

suffice *vi* to be sufficient, adequate (for some purpose).

sufficient *adj* enough; adequate—**sufficiency** *n*.—**sufficiently** *adv*.

suffix *n* (*pl* suffixes) a letter, syllable, or syllables added to the end of a word to modify its meaning or to form a new derivative.

suffocate *vti* to kill or be killed by depriving of oxygen, or by inhaling a poisonous gas; to feel hot and uncomfortable due to lack of air; to prevent from developing.—**suffocation** *n*.

sugar *n* a sweet white, crystalline substance obtained from sugarcane and sugar beet * *vi* to sweeten.

sugar maple *n* a North American maple from which sap is tapped to make maple syrup.

sugar shack *n* (*Cdn*) a building in which maple sap is boiled to make maple syrup.

sugary *adj* resembling or containing sugar; cloyingly sweet in manner, content, etc.—**sugariness** *n*.

suggest *vt* to put forward for consideration; to bring to one's mind; to evoke.—**suggestion** *n*.

suggestible *adj* easily influenced by others.—**suggestibility** *n*.

suggestive *adj* evocative; rather indecent, risqué.—**suggestively** *adv*.—**suggestiveness** *n*.

suicide *n* a person who kills himself intentionally; the act or instance of killing oneself intentionally; ruin of one's own interests.

suit *n* a set of matching garments, such as a jacket and trousers or skirt; one of the four sets of thirteen playing cards; a lawsuit. * *vt* to be appropriate; to be convenient or acceptable to.

suitable *adj* fitting; convenient (to, for).—**suitably** *adv*.—**suitability** *n*.

suitcase *n* a portable, oblong travelling case.

suite *n* a number of followers or attendants; a set, esp of rooms, furniture, pieces of music.

sulk *vi* to be sullen.

sulky *adj* (sulkier, sulkiest) bad-tempered, quiet and sullen, because of resentment.

sullen *adj* moody and silent; gloomy, dull.—**sullenly** *adv*.—**sullenness** *n*.

sulphur, sulfur (*US*) *n* a yellow nonmetallic element that is inflammable and has a strong odour.—**sulphuric** *adj*.

sulphuric acid *n* a powerfully corrosive acid.

sultana *n* a dried, white grape used in cooking; the wife or female relative of a sultan.

sultry *adj* (sultrier, sultriest) (*weather*) very hot, humid and close; (*person*) sensual; passionate.—**sultriness** *n*.

sum *n* the result of two or more things added together; the total, aggregate; a quantity of money; essence, gist. * *vt* (*pt* summed) to add (*usu with* up); to encapsulate; to summarize.

summarize *vt* to make or be a summary of.

summary *adj* concise; performed quickly, without formality. * *n* a brief account of the main points of something.—**summarily** *adv*.

summer *n* the warmest season of the year, between spring and autumn.—**summery** *adj*.

summit *n* the highest point, the peak; a meeting of world leaders.

summon *vt* to order to appear, esp in court; to convene; to gather (strength, enthusiasm, etc).

summons *n* a call to appear (in court). * *vt* to serve with a summons.

sump *n* a section of an engine for the oil to drain into.

sumptuous *adj* lavish; luxurious.—**sumptuously** *adv*.—**sumptuousness** *n*.

sun *n* the star around which the earth and other planets revolve which gives light and heat to the solar system; the sunshine. * *vt* (*pt* sunned) to expose oneself to the sun's rays.

sunbathe *vi* to lie in the rays of the sun or a sun lamp to get a suntan.—*also n.*

sunburn *n* inflammation of the skin from exposure to sunlight.—*also vti.*

Sunday *n* the day of the week after Saturday, regarded as a day of worship by Christians; a newspaper published on a Sunday.

sundial *n* a device that shows the time by casting a shadow on a graduated dial.

sundry *adj* miscellaneous, various. * *n* (*pl*) miscellaneous small things.

sunflower *n* a tall plant with large yellow flowers whose seeds yield oil.

sung *see* **sing**.

sunglasses *npl* tinted glasses to protect the eyes from sunlight.

sunk *see* **sink**.

sunny *adj* (**sunnier, sunniest**) (*weather*) bright with sunshine; (*person, mood*) cheerful.

sunrise *n* dawn.

sunset *n* dusk.

sunshine *n* the light and heat from the sun.

sunstroke *n* illness caused by exposure to the sun.

suntan *n* browning of the skin by the sun.

super *adj* (*inf*) fantastic, excellent; (*inf*) a superintendent, as in the police. * *n* a variety of high-octane petrol.

superannuation *n* regular contributions from employees' wages towards a pension scheme.

superb *adj* grand; excellent; of the highest quality.—**superbly** *adv*.

supercilious *adj* arrogant; haughty, disdainful.—**superciliously** *adv*.—**superciliousness** *n*.

superficial *adj* near the surface; slight, not profound; (*person*) shallow in nature.—**superficiality** *n*.—**superficially** *adv*.

superfluous *adj* exceeding what is required; unnecessary.—**superfluity** *n*.

superimpose *vt* to put or lay upon something else.

superintendent *n* a person who manages or supervises; a British police officer next above the rank of inspector.

superior *adj* higher in place, quality, rank, excellence; greater in number, power. * *n* a person of higher rank.—**superiority** *n*.

superlative *adj* of outstanding quality; (*gram*) denoting the extreme degree of comparison of adjectives and adverbs.—**superlatively** *adv*.

supermarket *n* a large self-service, shop selling food and household goods.

supernatural *adj* relating to things that cannot be explained by nature; involving ghosts, spirits, etc.—**supernaturally** *adv*.

superpower *n* a nation with great economic and military strength.

supersede *vt* to take the place of, replace.

supersonic *adj* faster than the speed of sound.—**supersonically** *adv*.

superstition *n* irrational belief based on ignorance or fear.—**superstitious** *adj*.

supervise *vti* to have charge of, direct, to superintend.—**supervision** *n*.—**supervisor** *n*.—**supervisory** *adj*.

supper *n* a meal taken in the evening, esp when dinner is eaten at midday; an evening social event; the food served at a supper; a light meal served late in the evening.

supple *adj* flexible, easily bent; lithe; (*mind*) adaptable.—**suppleness** *n*.

supplement *n* an addition or extra amount (usu of money); an additional section of a book,

periodical or newspaper. * *vt* to add to.—**supplemental** *adj*.

supply *vt* to provide, meet (a deficiency, a need); to fill (a vacant place). * *n* a stock; (*pl*) provisions.—**supplier** *n*.

support *vt* to hold up, bear; to tolerate, withstand; to assist; to advocate (a cause, policy); to provide for (financially). * *n* a means of support; maintenance.

supporter *n* a person who backs a political party, sports team, etc.

suppose *vt* to assume; to presume as true without definite knowledge; to think probable; to expect. * *vi* to conjecture.

supposed *adj* believed to be on available evidence.

supposedly *adv* allegedly.

supposition *n* an assumption, hypothesis.

suppress *vt* to crush, put an end to (eg a rebellion); to restrain (a person); to subdue.—**suppression** *n*.—**suppressor** *n*.

supreme *adj* of highest power; greatest; final; ultimate.—**supremacy** *n*.

surcharge *vt* to overcharge (a person); to charge an additional sum; to overload. * *n* an additional tax or charge; an additional or excessive load.

sure *adj* certain; without doubt; reliable, inevitable; secure; safe; dependable. * *adv* certainly.

surely *adv* certainly; securely; it is to be hoped or expected that.

surety *n* a person who undertakes responsibility for the fulfilment of another's debt; security given as a guarantee of payment of a debt.

surf *n* the waves of the sea breaking on the shore or a reef.

surface *n* the exterior face of an object; any of the faces of a solid; the uppermost level of sea or land; a flat area, such as the top of a table; superficial features. * *adj* superficial; external. * *vt* to cover with a surface, as in paving. * *vi* to rise to the surface of water.

surfboard *n* a long, narrow board used in the sport of surfing.

surfeit *n* an excessive amount.

surfing *n* the sport of riding in toward shore on the crest of a wave, esp on a surfboard.

surge *n* the rolling of the sea, as after a large wave; a sudden, strong increase, as of power.—*also vi*.

surgeon *n* a medical specialist who practices surgery.

surgery *n* the treatment of diseases or injuries by manual or instrumental operations; the consulting room of a doctor or dentist; the daily period when a doctor is available for consultation; the regular period when an MP, lawyer, etc is available for consultation.—**surgical** *adj*.—**surgically** *adv*.

surmise *n* guess, conjecture. * *vt* to infer the existence of from partial evidence.

surmount *vt* to overcome; to rise above.

surname *n* the family name. * *vt* to give a surname to.

surpass *vt* to outdo, to outshine; to excel; to exceed.

surplus *n* an amount in excess of what is required; an excess of revenues over expenditure in a financial year.

surprise *n* the act of catching unawares; an unexpected gift, event; astonishment. * *vt* to cause to feel astonished; to attack unexpectedly; to take unawares.—**surprising** *adj*.—**surprisingly** *adv*.

surreal *adj* bizarre.

surrender *vt* to relinquish or give up possession or power. * *vi* to give oneself up (to an enemy).—*also n*.

surreptitious *adj* done by stealth; clandestine, secret.—**surreptitiously** *adv*.

surround *vt* to encircle on all or nearly all sides; (*mil*) to encircle. * *n* a border around the edge of something.

surroundings *npl* the conditions, objects, etc around a person or thing; the environment.

surveillance *n* a secret watch kept over a person, esp a suspect.

survey *vt* to take a general view of; to appraise; to examine carefully; to measure and make a map of an area. * *n* a detailed study, as by gathering information and analysing it, a general view; the process of surveying an area or a house.

surveyor *n* a person who surveys land or buildings.

survival *n* surviving; a person or thing that survives; a relic.

survive *vt* to live after the death of another person; to continue, endure; to come through alive. * *vi* to remain alive (after experiencing a dangerous situation).—**survivor** *n*.

susceptible *adj* ready or liable to be affected by; impressionable.—**susceptibility** *n*.—**susceptibly** *adv*.

suspect *vt* to mistrust; to believe to be guilty; to think probable. * *n* a person under suspicion. * *adj* open to suspicion.

suspend *vt* to hang; to discontinue, or cease temporarily; to postpone; to debar temporarily from a privilege, etc.

suspender *n* a fastener for holding up stockings; (*pl*) braces.

suspense *n* mental anxiety or uncertainty; excitement.

suspension *n* suspending or being suspended; a temporary interruption or postponement; a temporary removal from office, privileges, etc; the system of springs, shock absorbers, etc that support a vehicle on its axles; (*chem*) a dispersion of fine particles in a liquid.

suspension bridge *n* a bridge carrying a roadway suspended by cables anchored to towers at either end.

suspicion *n* act of suspecting; a belief formed or held without sure proof; mistrust; a trace.—**suspicious** *adj*.—**suspiciously** *adv*.

sustain *vt* hold up, support; to maintain; to suffer (eg an injury); to nourish.

sustenance *n* nourishment.

swab *n* a wad of absorbent material, usu cotton, used to clean wounds, take specimens, etc; a mop.—*also vt*.

swagger *vi* to strut; to brag loudly. * *n* boastfulness; swinging gait.

swallow[1] *n* a small migratory bird with long wings and a forked tail.

swallow[2] *vt* to cause food and drink to move from the mouth to the stomach; to endure; to engulf; (*inf*) to accept gullibly; (*emotion, etc*) to repress.—*also n*.

swam *see* **swim**.

swamp *n* wet, spongy land; bog. * *vt* to overwhelm; to flood as with water.—**swampy** *adj*.

swan *n* a large, usu white, bird with a very long neck that lives on rivers and lakes. * *vi* (*pt* **swanned**) (*inf*) to wander aimlessly.

swap *vti* (*pt* **swapped**) (*inf*) to trade, barter. * *n* (*inf*) the act of exchanging one thing for another.—*also* **swop**.

swarm *n* a colony of migrating bees; a moving mass, crowd or throng. * *vi* to move in great numbers; to teem.

swarthy *adj* (**swarthier, swarthiest**) dark-complexioned.—**swarthiness** *n*.

swat *vt* (*pt* **swatted**) (*inf*) to hit with a sharp blow; to swipe.—*also n*.—**swatter** *n*.

sway *vi* to swing or move from one side to the other or to and fro; to lean to one side; to vacillate in judgment or opinion. * *n* influence; control.

swear *vi* (*pt* **swore**, *pp* **sworn**) to make a solemn affirmation, promise, etc, calling God as a witness; to give evidence on oath; to curse, blaspheme or use obscene language; to vow.

sweat *n* perspiration; (*inf*) hard work; (*inf*) a state of eagerness, anxiety.—*also vti*.—**sweaty** *adj*.

sweater *n* a knitted pullover.

sweat lodge *n* a structure used by North American Indians inside which water is poured on hot stones to induce sweating for religious or healing purposes.

Swede *n* a native of Sweden.

swede *n* a round root vegetable with yellow flesh.

swede saw *n* (*Cdn*) a hand saw with a bow-like tubular frame and many teeth.

Swedish *adj* pertaining to Sweden, its people or language. * *n* the language of Sweden.

sweep *vb* (*pt* **swept**) *vt* to clean with a broom; to remove (rubbish, dirt) with a brush. * *vi* to pass by swiftly. * *n* a movement, esp in an arc; a stroke; scope, range; a sweepstake.

sweeping *adj* wide-ranging; indiscriminate.—**sweepingly** *adv*.

sweet *adj* having a taste like sugar; pleasing to other senses; gentle; kind. * *n* a small piece of confectionery; a dessert.—**sweetly** *adv*.—**sweetness** *n*.

sweetbread *n* the pancreas or thymus of an animal used for food.

sweetcorn *n* maize, corn on the cob.

sweeten *vti* to make or become sweet or

sweeter; to mollify.

sweetheart *n* a lover.

swell *vi* (*pt* swelled, *pp* swollen *or* swelled) to increase in size or volume; to rise into waves; to bulge out. * *n* the movement of the sea; a bulge; a gradual increase in the loudness of a musical note; (*inf*) a socially prominent person. * *adj* excellent.

swelling *n* inflammation.

swelter *vi* to suffer from heat. * *n* humid, oppressive heat.

swept *see* **sweep**.

swerve *vi* to turn aside suddenly from a line or course; to veer.—*also n*.

swift *adj* moving with great speed; rapid. * *n* a swallow-like bird.—**swiftly** *adv*.—**swiftness** *n*.

swig *vt* (*pt* swigged) (*inf*) to take a long drink, esp from a bottle.—*also n*.

swill *vti* to drink greedily; to guzzle; to rinse with a large amount of water. * *n* liquid refuse fed to pigs.

swim *vi* (*pt* swam, *pp* swum) to move through water by using limbs or fins; to be dizzy; to be flooded with. * *n* the act of swimming.—**swimmer** *n*.

swimming costume, swimsuit *n* a one-piece garment for swinning in.

swindle *vti* to cheat (someone) of money or property.—*also n*.—**swindler** *n*.

swine *n* (*pl* swine) a pig; (*inf*) an contemptible person; (*inf*) an unpleasant thing.

swing *vb* (*pt* swung) *vi* to sway or move to and fro, as an object hanging in air; to pivot; to shift from one mood or opinion to another; (*music*) to have a lively rhythm; (*sl*) to be hanged. * *vt* to whirl; to play swing music; to influence; to achieve, bring about. * *n* a swinging, curving or rhythmic movement; a suspended seat for swinging in; a shift from one condition to another; a type of popular jazz played by a large band and characterized by a lively, steady rhythm.

swinging *adj* (*inf*) up-to-date; lively.

swing riding *n* (*Cdn*) a constituency in which more than one candidate in an election has a good chance of winning.

swipe *n* (*inf*) a hard, sweeping blow. * *vt* (*inf*) to hit with a swipe; (*sl*) to steal.

swirl *vti* to turn with a whirling motion.—*also n*.

swish *vi* to move with a soft, whistling, hissing sound. * *n* a swishing sound. * *adj* (*inf*) smart, fashionable.

Swiss *adj* of or belonging to Switzerland. * *n* (*pl* Swiss) a native of Switzerland.

switch *n* a control for turning on and off an electrical device; a sudden change; a swap. * *vt* to shift, change, swap; to turn on or off (as of an electrical device).

switchback *n* a zigzag road in a mountain region; a roller coaster.

switchboard *n* an installation in a building where telephone calls are connected.

swivel *n* a coupling that permits parts to rotate. * *vi* (*pt* swivelled) to turn (as if) on a pin or pivot.

swoon *vt* to faint.—*also n*.

swoop *vt* to carry off abruptly. * *vi* to make a sudden attack (*usu with* **down**) as a bird in hunting.—*also n*.

swop *see* **swap**.

sword *n* a weapon with a long blade and a handle a one end.

swordfish *n* a large marine fish with a sword-like upper jaw.

swore, sworn *see* **swear**.

swot *vi* (*pt* swotted) (*inf*) to study hard for an examination. * *n* (*inf*) a person who studies hard.

syllable *n* word or part of a word uttered by in a single sound; one or more letters written to represent a spoken syllable.

syllabus *n* (*pl* syllabuses) a summary or outline of a course of study or of examination requirements; the subjects studied for a particular course.

symbol *n* a representation; an object used to represent something abstract; an arbitrary or conventional sign standing for a quality, process, relation, etc as in music, chemistry, mathematics, etc.

symbolic, symbolical *adj* of, using, or constituting a symbol.—**symbolically** *adv*.

symbolism *n* the use of symbols; a system of symbolic representation.—**symbolist** *n*.

symbolize *vt* to be a symbol; to represent by a symbol.—**symbolization** *n*.

symmetrical, symmetric *adj* having symmetry.

symmetry *n* the corresponding arrangement of one part to another in size, shape and position; balance or harmony of form resulting from this.

sympathetic *adj* having sympathy; compassionate.—**sympathetically** *adv*.

sympathize *vi* feel sympathy for; to commiserate; to be in sympathy (with).

sympathy *n* agreement of ideas and opinions; compassion; (*pl*) support for an action or cause.

symphony *n* an orchestral composition in several movements; a large orchestra for playing symphonic works.—**symphonic** *adj*.—**symphonically** *adv*.

symposium *n* (*pl* symposiums, symposia) a conference at which several specialists deliver short addresses on a topic; an anthology of scholarly essays.

symptom *n* a bodily sensation experienced by a patient indicative of a particular disease; an indication.

synagogue *n* the building where Jews assemble for worship and religious study.

synchronize *vti* to occur at the same time and speed; (*watches*) to adjust to show the same time.—**synchronization** *n*.

syndicate *n* an association of individuals or corporations formed for a project requiring much capital; any group, as of criminals, organized for some undertaking; an organization selling articles or features to many newspapers, etc. * *vt* to manage as or form into a syndicate; to sell (an article, etc) through a syndicate. * *vi* to form a syndicate.—**syndication** *n*.

syndrome *n* a characteristic pattern of signs and symptoms of a disease.

synonym *n* a word that has the same, or similar, meaning as another or others in the same language.

synonymous *adj* having the same meaning; equivalent.

synopsis *n* (*pl* **synopses**) a summary or brief review of a subject.

syntax *n* (*gram*) the arrangement of words in the sentences and phrases of language; the rules governing this.—**syntactic** *adj*.—**syntactically** *adv*.

synthesis *n* (*pl* **syntheses**) the process of combining separate elements of thought into a whole; the production of a compound by a chemical reaction.

synthetic *adj* produced by chemical synthesis; artificial.—**synthetically** *adv*.

syphilis *n* a contagious, infectious venereal disease.—**syphilitic** *adj*.

syphon *see* **siphon**.

syringe *n* a hollow tube with plunger at one end and a sharp needle at the other by which liquids are injected or withdrawn, esp in medicine. * *vt* to inject or cleanse with a syringe.

syrup *n* a thick sweet substance made by boiling sugar with water; the concentrated juice of a fruit or plant.—**syrupy** *adj*.

system *n* a method of working or organizing by following a set of rules; routine; organization; structure; a political regime; an arrangement of parts fitting together.

systematic *adj* constituting or based on a system; according to a system.—**systematically** *adv*.

systems analysis *n* analysis of a particular task or operation to determine how computer hardware and software may best perform it.—**systems analyst** *n*.

T

T4 slip *n* (*Cdn*) an official statement of employment income and deductions for the year, used to calculate the amount of income taxes owed to the government.

tab *n* a small tag, label or flap; (*inf*) a bill, as for expenses. * *vt* to fix a tab on.

tabby *n* a domestic cat with a striped coat, esp a female.

table *n* a piece of furniture consisting of a slab or board on legs; the people seated round a table; supply of food; a list arranged for reference or comparison. * *vt* to submit, put forward; to postpone indefinitely. * *adj* of, on or at a table.

tablecloth *n* a cloth for covering a table.

table d'hôte *n* (*pl* **tables d'hôte**) a meal at a fixed price for a set number of courses.—*also*

adj.

tablespoon *n* a large serving spoon; a unit of measure in cooking.—**tablespoonful** *n*.

tablet *n* a pad of paper; a medicinal pill; a cake of solid substance, such as soap; a slab of stone.

table tennis *n* a game like tennis played on a table with small bats and balls.

taboo, tabu *n* a religious or social prohibition.—*also adj*.

tabulate *vt* to arrange (written material) in the form of a table.—**tabulation** *n*

tacit *adj* implied without being spoken; understood.—**tacitly** *adj*.

taciturn *adj* habitually silent and reserved.—**taciturnity** *n*.

tack¹ *n* a short, flat-headed nail; the course of a sailing ship; a course of action, approach; adhesiveness. * *vt* to fasten with tacks. * *vi* to change direction.

tack² *n* (*inf*) food.

tackle *n* a system of ropes and pulleys for lifting; equipment; rigging; (*sport*) an act of grabbing and stopping an opponent. * *vt* (*task, etc*) to attend to, undertake; (*a person*) to confront; (*sport*) to challenge with a tackle.

tacky *adj* (**tackier, tackiest**) (*paint, etc*) sticky.

tact *n* discretion in managing the feelings of others.—**tactful** *adj*.—**tactless** *adj*.

tactics *n sing* stratagem; ploy; the science or art of manoeuvring troops in the presence of the enemy.—**tactical** *adj*.—**tactician** *n*.

tadpole *n* the larva of a frog or toad, esp at the stage when the head and tail have developed.

tag¹ *n* a strip or label for identification. * *vt* to attach a tag; to mark with a tag. * *vi* (*with* **onto, after**) to trail along (behind).

tag² *n* a children's chasing game.

tail *n* the appendage of an animal growing from the rear; the rear part of anything; (*pl*) the side of a coin without a head on it; (*inf*) a person who keeps another under surveillance, esp a detective. * *vt* to follow closely, shadow.

tail coat *n* a man's black or grey coat cut horizontally just below the waist at the front with two long tails at the back.

tail-end *adj* tardy; being the last in line. * *n* the last.

tailor *n* a person who makes and repairs outer garments, esp. men's suits. * *vi* to work as a tailor. * *vt* to adapt to fit a particular requirement.

tailor-made *adj* specially designed for a particular purpose or person.

taint *vt* to contaminate; to infect. * *vi* to be corrupted or disgraced. * *n* a stain; corruption.

take *vb* (*pt* **took**, *pp* **taken**) *vt* to lay hold of; to grasp or seize; to gain, win; to choose, select; (*attitude, pose*) to adopt; to understand; to consume; to accept or agree to; to lead or carry with one; to use as a means of travel; (*math*) to subtract (from); to use; to steal; (*gram*) to be used with; to endure calmly. * *vi* (*plant, etc*) to start growing successfully; to become effective; to catch on; to have recourse to; to go to. * *n* (*film, TV*) the amount of film used without stopping the camera.

takeoff *n* the process of an aircraft becoming airborne.

takeover *n* the taking over of control, as in business.

taking *adj* attractive, charming; (*inf*) catching, contagious. * *n* the act of one that takes; (*pl*) earnings; profits.

talc *n* a type of smooth mineral used in ceramics and talcum powder; talcum powder.

talcum powder *n* perfumed powdered talc for the skin.

tale *n* a narrative or story; a fictitious account, a lie; idle or malicious gossip.

talent *n* any innate or special aptitude.—**talented** *adj*.

talk *vti* to speak; to converse; to discuss; to gossip; to divulge information. * *n* a discussion; a lecture; gossip; (*pl*) negotiations.

talkative *adj* given to talking a great deal.

tall *adj* above average in height; (*inf: story*) exaggerated.—**tallness** *n*.

tallboy *n* a high chest of drawers.

tally *n* reckoning, account; one score in a game. * *vi* to correspond; to keep score.

tambourine *n* a percussion hand instrument made of skin stretched over a circular frame with small jingling metal discs around the edge.

tame *adj* (*animal*) not wild, domesticated; compliant; dull, uninteresting. * *vt* (*animal*) to domesticate; to subdue; to soften.

tamper *vi* to meddle (with); to interfere (with).

tampon *n* a firm plug of cotton wool inserted in the vagina during menstruation.

tan *n* a yellowish-brown color; suntan. * *vti* (*pt* **tanned**) to acquire a suntan through sunbathing; (*skin, hide*) to convert into leather by processing.

tandem *n* a bicycle for two riders, one behind the other.

tang *n* sharp smell or a strong taste.—**tangy** *adj*.

tangent *n* a line that touches a curve or circle at one point, without crossing it. * *adj* touching at one point.

tangerine *n* a small, sweet orange with a loose skin; the color of this.—*also adj*.

tangible *adj* capable of being felt, seen or noticed; substantial; real.—**tangibility** *n*.

tangle *n* a mass of hair, string or wire knotted together confusedly; a complication. * *vi* to become tangled or complicated; (*with* **with**) to become involved in argument with.

tango *n* (*pl* **tangos**) a Latin American dance.—*also vi.*

tank *n* a large container for storing liquids or gases; an armoured combat vehicle, mounted with guns and having caterpillar tracks.

tankard *n* a tall, one-handled beer mug, often with a hinged lid.

tanker *n* a large ship or truck for transporting oil and other liquids.

tantalize *vt* to tease or torment by presenting something greatly desired, but keeping it inaccessible.

tantamount *adj* equivalent (to) in effect; as good as.

tantrum *n* a childish fit of bad temper.

tap[1] *n* a quick, light blow or touch; a piece of metal attached to the heel or toe of a shoe for reinforcement or to tap-dance. * *vti* (*pt* **tapped**) to strike lightly; to make a tapping sound.

tap[2] *n* a device controlling the flow of liquid through a pipe or from a container. * *vt* to pierce in order to draw fluid from; to connect a secret listening device to a telephone; (*inf*) to ask for money from; (*resources, etc*) to draw on.

tap-dance *vi* to perform a step dance in shoes with taps.—**tap-dancer** *n*.—**tap-dancing** *n*.

tape *n* a strong, narrow strip of cloth, paper, etc, used for tying, binding, etc; a tape measure; magnetic tape, as in a cassette or videotape. * *vt* to wrap with tape; to record on magnetic tape.

tape measure *n* a tape marked in inches or centimetres for measuring.

taper *n* a long thin candle. * *vti* to make or to become gradually narrower towards one end.—**tapering** *adj*.

tape recorder *n* a machine for recording and reproducing sounds or music on magnetic tape.—*also* **tape deck**.

tapestry *n* a heavy fabric woven with patterns or figures, used for wall hangings and furnishings.

tapioca *n* a starch extracted from the root of a tropical plant and used in puddings, etc.

tar *n* a thick, dark gluey substance obtained from wood, coal, peat, etc., used for surfacing roads. * *vt* to coat with tar.—**tarry** *adj*.

tarantula *n* a large, hairy spider with a poisonous bite.

tardy *adj* (**tardier, tardiest**) slow; later than expected.—**tardily** *adv.*—**tardiness** *n*.

target *n* a mark to aim at, esp in shooting; an objective or ambition.

tariff *n* a tax on imports; (*in a hotel*) a list of prices; the rate of charge for public services, such as gas or electricity.

Tarmac, Tarmacadam *n* (*trademark*) a material for surfacing roads made from crushed stones and tar; an airport runway. * *vti* (*pt* **tarmacked**) to lay down a tarmac surface.

tarnish *vi* (*metal*) to lose its lustre or discolor due to exposure to the air. * *vt* (*reputation*) to taint.—*also n.*

tarpaulin *n* canvas cloth coated with a waterproof substance.

tart[1] *adj* having a sour, sharp taste; (*speech*) sharp, severe.—**tartly** *adv.*—**tartness** *n*.

tart[2] *n* an open pastry case containing fruit, jam or custard; (*inf*) a prostitute.

tartan *n* a woollen cloth with a chequered pattern, having a distinctive design for each

Scottish clan.

tartar *n* a hard, yellow, crusty deposit that forms on the teeth; a salty deposit on the sides of wine casks.

tartar sauce *n* a mayonnaise sauce with herbs, etc, eaten esp with fish.

task *n* a specific amount of work to be done; a chore.

task force *n* a small unit with a specific mission, usu military.

tassel *n* an ornamental tuft of silken threads decorating soft furnishings, clothes, etc.—**tasselled** *adj*.

taste *vt* to perceive (a flavor) by taking into the mouth; to try by eating and drinking a little; to sample; to experience. * *vi* to try by the mouth; to have a specific flavor. * *n* the sense by which flavors are perceived; a small portion; the ability to recognize what is beautiful, attractive, etc; liking; a brief experience.

tasteful *adj* showing good taste.—**tastefully** *adv*.—**tastefulness** *n*.

tasteless *adj* without taste, bland; in bad taste.—**tastelessly** *adv*.

tasty *adj* (**tastier, tastiest**) savory; having a pleasant flavor.

tatter *n* a torn or ragged piece of cloth.—**tattered** *adj*.

tattoo[1] *n* (*pl* **tattoos**) a continuous beating of a drum; a military display of exercises and music.

tattoo[2] *vt* to make permanent patterns or pictures on the skin by pricking and marking with dyes. * *n* (*pl* **tattoos**) marks made on the skin in this way.

tatty *adj* (**tattier, tattiest**) shabby, ragged.

taught *see* **teach**.

taunt *vt* to provoke with mockery or contempt; to tease. * *n* an insult.

Taurus *n* the Bull, the second sign of the zodiac.

taut *adj* stretched tight; tense; stressed.

tavern *n* a pub, an inn.

tawdry *adj* (**tawdrier, tawdriest**) showy, cheap, and of poor quality.

tawny *adj* yellowish brown.

tax *n* a rate imposed by the government on property or persons to raise revenues; a strain. * *vt* to impose a tax (upon); to strain.

taxation *n* the act of levying taxes; the amount so raised.

taxi, taxicab *n* a car, usu fitted with a taximeter, that may be hired to transport passengers. * *vi* (*pr p* **taxiing**, *pt* **taxied**) (*aircraft*) to move along the runway before takeoff or after landing.

taxpayer *n* a person who or an organization that pays taxes.

TB *abbr* = tuberculosis.

tea *n* a shrub growing in China, India, Sri Lanka, etc; its dried, shredded leaves, which are infused in boiling water for a beverage; a light meal taken in mid-afternoon; a main meal taken in the early evening.

tea bag *n* a small porous bag containing tea leaves for infusing.

tea biscuit *n* (*Cdn*) a small baked cake leavened with baking powder or soda, often containing raisins or currants; (*Brit*) a semi-sweet, plain biscuit.

teach *vb* (*pt* **taught**) *vt* to impart knowledge to; to give lessons (to); to train; to help to learn. * *vi* to give instruction, esp as a profession.—**teachable** *adj*.

teacher *n* a person who instructs others, esp as an occupation.

teaching *n* the profession or practice of being a teacher; the act of giving instruction.

teacup *n* a small cup for drinking tea.

teak *n* a type of hard wood from an East Indian tree.

team *n* a group of people participating in a sport together; a group of people working together; two or more animals pulling a vehicle. * *vi* (*with* **up**) to join in cooperative activity.

teamwork *n* cooperation of individuals for the benefit of the team; the ability of a team to work together.

teapot *n* a vessel in which tea is made.

tear[1] *n* a drop of salty liquid appearing in the eyes when crying; anything tear-shaped.

tear[2] *vb* (*pt* **tore**, *pp* **torn**) *vt* to pull apart by force; to split. * *vi* to move with speed. * *n* a hole or split.

tearful *adj* weeping; sad.—**tearfully** *adv*.

tear gas *n* gas that irritates the eyes and nasal passages, used in riot control.

tease *vt* to separate the fibres of; to torment or irritate; to taunt playfully. * *n* a person who teases or torments; (*inf*) a flirt.—**teaser** *n*.

tea service, tea set *n* the set of cups and saucers, etc for serving tea.

teaspoon *n* a small spoon for use with tea or as a measure; the amount measured by this.—**teaspoonful** *n*.

teat *n* the nipple on a breast or udder; the mouthpiece of a baby's feeding bottle.

tea towel, tea cloth *n* a towel for drying dishes.

technical *adj* relating to, or specializing in practical, industrial, mechanical or applied sciences; (*expression, etc*) belonging to or peculiar to a particular field of activity.—**technically** *adv*.

technicality *n* a petty formality or technical point.

technician *n* a person skilled in the practice of any art, esp in practical work with scientific equipment.

technique *n* method of performing a particular task; knack.

technology *n* the application of mechanical and applied sciences to industrial use.—**technological** *adj*.—**technologist** *n*.

teddy bear *n* a stuffed toy bear.

tedious *adj* monotonous; boring.—**tedium** *n*.

tee *n* (*golf*) the place from where the first stroke is played at each hole; a small peg from which the ball is driven. * *vti* to position (the ball) on the tee.

teem[1] *vi* (*with* **with**) to be prolific or abundant in.

teem² *vi* to pour (with rain).

teenager *n* (*inf*) a person who is in his or her teens.

teens *npl* the years of one's life from thir*teen* to nine*teen*.—**teenage** *adj.*—**teenaged** *adj.*

tee-shirt *see* T-shirt.

teeter *vi* to move or stand unsteadily.

teeth *see* tooth.

teethe *vi* to cut one's first teeth.

teething *n* the condition in babies of the first growth of teeth.

teething troubles *npl* problems encountered in the early stages of a project, etc; pain caused by growing teeth.

teetotaller, teetotaler (*US*) *n* a person who abstains from alcoholic drinks.—**teetotal** *adj.*

telecommunication *n* communication of information over long distances by telephone and radio; (*pl*) the technology of telephone and radio communication.

telegram *n* a message sent by telegraph.

telegraph *n* a system for transmitting messages over long distances using electricity, wires and a code. * *vt* to transmit by telegraph.—**telegraphic** *adj.*—**telegraphy** *n.*

telepathy *n* the communication between people's minds of thoughts and feelings, without the need for speech or proximity.—**telepathic** *adj.*

telephone *n* an instrument for transmitting speech at a distance, esp by means of electricity. * *vt* (*someone*) to call by telephone.

telephonist *n* a person who operates a telephone switchboard.—*also* **telephone operator**.

telephoto lens *n* a camera lens that magnifies distant objects.

teleprinter *n* a telegraph apparatus with a keyboard that transmits and a printer that receives messages over a distance.

telescope *n* a tubular optical instrument for viewing objects at a distance.

televise *vt* (*a programme*) to transmit by television.

television *n* the transmission of visual images and accompanying sound through electrical and sound waves; a television receiving set; television broadcasting.

tell *vb* (*pt* **told**) *vt* to narrate; to disclose; to inform; to notify; to instruct; to distinguish. * *vi* to tell tales, to inform on; to produce a marked effect.

teller *n* a bank clerk; a person appointed to count votes in an election.

telling *adj* having great impact.

telltale *n* a person who tells tales about others. * *adj* revealing what is meant to be hidden.

telly *n* (*inf*) television.

temerity *n* rashness.

temp *n* (*inf*) a temporary employee.

temp. *abbr* = temperature.

temper *n* a frame of mind; a fit of anger. * *vt* to tone down, moderate; (*steel*) to heat and cool repeatedly to bring to the correct hardness.

temperament *n* one's disposition.

temperamental *adj* easily irritated; erratic.—

temperamentally *adv.*

temperance *n* moderation; abstinence from alcohol.

temperate *adj* mild or moderate in temperature; (*behaviour*) moderate, self-controlled.

temperature *n* degree of heat or cold; body heat above the normal.

tempest *n* a violent storm.

template *n* a pattern, gauge or mould used as a guide esp in cutting metal, stone or plastic.

temple¹ *n* a place of worship.

temple² *n* the region on either side of the head above the cheekbone.

tempo *n* (*pl* **tempos, tempi**) (*mus*) the speed at which music is meant to be played; rate of any activity.

temporal¹ *adj* relating to time; secular, civil.

temporal² *adj* of or relating to the temples of the head.

temporary *adj* lasting or used for a limited time only; not permanent.—**temporarily** *adv.*

tempt *vt* to entice to do wrong; to invite, attract, induce.—**tempter** *n.*—**temptress** *nf.*

temptation *n* the act of tempting or the state of being tempted; something or someone that tempts.

tempting *adj* attractive, inviting.

ten *adj, n* the cardinal number next above nine. * *n* the symbol for this (10, X, x).

tenacious *adj* grasping firmly; persistent; retentive; adhesive.

tenacity *n* the state or quality of being tenacious; doggedness, obstinacy; adhesiveness, stickiness.

tenancy *n* the temporary possession by a tenant of another's property; the period of this.

tenant *n* a person who pays rent to occupy a house or flat or for the use of land or buildings; an occupant.

tend¹ *vt* to take care of; to attend (to).

tend² *vi* to be inclined; to move in a specific direction.

tendency *n* an inclination or leaning.

tender¹ *n* a wagon attached to locomotives to carry fuel and water; a small ship that brings stores to a larger one.

tender² *vt* to present for acceptance; to offer as payment. * *vi* to make an offer. * *n* an offer to provide goods or services at a fixed price.

tender³ *adj* soft, delicate; fragile; painful, sore; sensitive; sympathetic.—**tenderly** *adv.*—**tenderness** *n.*

tenderize *vt* (*meat*) to make more tender, esp by pounding.

tendon *n* fibrous tissue attaching a muscle to a bone.

tenement *n* a building divided into flats, each occupied by a separate owner or tenant.

tenet *n* any belief or doctrine.

tennis *n* a game for two or four people, played by hitting a ball over a net with a racket.

tennis court *n* a court surfaced with clay, asphalt or grass on which tennis is played.

tenor *n* a general purpose or intent; the highest regular adult male voice, higher than a baritone and lower than an alto; a man who sings tenor.

tense[1] *n* (*gram*) the verb form that indicates the time of an action or the existence of a state.

tense[2] *adj* stretched, taut; apprehensive; nervous and highly strung. * *vti* to make or become tense.—**tensely** *adv.*—**tenseness** *n.*

tension *n* the act of stretching; the state of being stretched; (*between forces, etc*) opposition; stress; mental strain.

tent *n* a portable shelter of canvas, plastic or other waterproof fabric, which is erected on poles and fixed to the ground by ropes and pegs.

tentacle *n* a long, slender, flexible growth near the mouth of invertebrates, used for feeling, grasping or handling.

tentative *adj* provisional; not definite.—**tentatively** *adv.*—**tentativeness** *n.*

tenterhook *n* one of a series of hooks on which cloth is stretched to dry; (*pl: with* **on**) in a tense or anxious state.

tenth *adj* the last of ten; being one of ten equal parts. * *n* one of ten equal parts.

tent ring *n* (*Cdn*) a ring of stones used to hold down a tent or other temporary structure.

tenuous *adj* slight, flimsy, insubstantial.—**tenuousness** *n.*

tenure *n* the holding of property or a position; the period of time which a position lasts; a permanent job at a university.

tepid *adj* slightly warm, lukewarm.

term *n* a limit; any prescribed period of time; a division of an academic year; a word or expression, esp in a specialized field of knowledge; (*pl*) mutual relationship between people; (*pl*) conditions of a contract, etc. * *vt* to call, designate.

terminal *adj* being or situated at the end or extremity; (*disease*) fatal, incurable. * *n* a bus, coach or railway station at the end of the line; the point at which an electrical current enters or leaves a device; a device with a keyboard and monitor for inputting data into, or viewing it from, a computer.—**terminally** *adv.*

terminate *vti* to bring or come to an end.—**termination** *n.*

terminology *n* the terms used in any specialized subject.

terminus *n* (*pl* **termini, terminuses**) the final part; a limit; end of a transportation line.

termite *n* a wood-eating, white, ant-like insect.

terrace *n* a raised level area of earth, often part of a slope; an unroofed paved area between a house and a lawn; a row of houses; a patio or balcony; (*pl*) unroofed tiers in a football ground. * *vt* to make into a terrace.

terrain *n* the surface features of a tract of land; (*fig*) field of activity.

terrible *adj* causing great fear; dreadful; (*inf*) very unpleasant.

terribly *adv* frighteningly; (*inf*) very.

terrier *n* a type of small, active dog.

terrific *adj* of great size; (*inf*) excellent.

terrify *vt* to fill with terror, to frighten greatly.

territory *n* an area under the jurisdiction of a city or state; a wide tract of land; an area assigned to a sales person; an area of knowledge.

terror *n* great fear; an object or person inspiring fear or dread.

terrorism *n* the use of terror and violence to intimidate.— **terrorist** *n.*

terrorize *vt* to terrify; to control by terror.—**terrorization** *n.*

terse *adj* abrupt, to the point, concise.—**tersely** *adv.*

test *n* an examination; trial; a chemical reaction to test a substance or to test for an illness; a series of questions or exercises. * *vt* to examine critically.

testament *n* a will; proof; tribute; a covenant made by God with men; (*with cap*) one of the two main parts of the Bible.

test case *n* a legal action that establishes a precedent.

testicle *n* either of the two male reproductive glands that produce sperm.

testify *vti* to give evidence under oath; to serve as witness (to); (*with* **to**) to be evidence of.

testimonial *adj* relating to a testimony. * *n* a recommendation of one's character or abilities.

testimony *n* evidence; declaration of truth or fact.

testis *n* (*pl* **testes**) testicle.

test match *n* one of a series of international cricket or Rugby football matches.

test pilot *n* someone who flies new types of aircraft to test their performance and characteristics.

test tube *n* a cylinder of thin glass closed at one end, used in scientific experiments.

testy *adj* (**testier, testiest**) touchy, irritable.

tetanus *n* an intense and painful spasm of muscles, caused by the infection of a wound by bacteria; lockjaw.

tether *n* a rope or chain for tying an animal; the limit of one's endurance. * *vt* to fasten with a tether; to limit.

text *n* the main part of a printed work; the original or exact wording; a passage from the Bible forming the basis of a sermon; a subject or topic; a textbook.—**textual** *adj.*

textbook *n* a book used as a basis for instruction.

textile *n* a woven fabric or cloth. * *adj* relating to the making of fabrics.

texture *n* the characteristic appearance, arrangement or feel of a thing; the way in which threads in fabric are woven together.—**textural** *adj.*

than *conj* introducing the second element of a comparison.

thank *vt* to express gratitude to or appreciation for. * *npl* an expression of gratitude.—**thankful** *adj.*—**thankfully** *adv.*

thankless *adj* without thanks; unappreciated; fruitless, unrewarding.—**thanklessness** *n.*

Thanksgiving Day *n* a US legal holiday observed on the fourth Thursday of November.

that *demons adj, pron* (*pl* **those**) the (one) there

or then, esp the latter or more distant thing.
* *rel pron* who or which. * *conj* introducing
noun clause or adverbial clause of purpose
or consequence; because; in order that;
(*preceded by* **so, such**) as a result.

thatch *n* roofing straw. * *vt* to cover a roof with
thatch.

thaw *vi* to melt or grow liquid; to become
friendly. * *vt* to cause to melt. * *n* the melting of ice or snow by warm weather.

the *demons adj* denoting a particular person or
thing. * *adv* used before comparative adjectives or adverbs for emphasis.

theatre, theater (*US*) *n* a building where plays and
operas are performed; the theatrical world
as a whole; a setting for important events;
field of operations.

theatrical *adj* relating to the theatre; melodramatic, affected.—**theatrically** *adv.*

theft *n* act or crime of stealing.

their *poss adj* of or belonging to them; his, hers,
its.

theirs *poss pron* of or belonging to them; his,
hers, its.

them *pron* the objective case of **they**.

theme *n* the main subject of a discussion; an'
idea or motif in a work; a short essay;. a
leading melody.—**thematic** *adj.*

themselves *pron* the reflexive form of **they** or
them.

then *adv* at that time; afterwards; immediately;
next in time. * *conj* for that reason; in that
case.

theologian *n* a person who studies and interprets
religious texts, etc; a teacher of theology.

theology *n* the study of God and of religious doctrine and matters of divinity.

theorem *n* a proposition that can be proved from
accepted principles; law or principle.

theoretical *adj* of or based on theory, not practical application; hypothetical; conjectural.

theorize *vi* to form theories; to speculate.—**theo-
rist** *n.*

theory *n* an explanation or system of anything;
ideas and abstract principles of a science or
art; speculation; a hypothesis.

therapeutic *adj* relating to the treatment of disease; beneficial.

therapy *n* the treatment of physical or mental
illness.—**therapist** *n.*

there *adv* in, at or to, that place or point; in that
respect; in that matter.

thereabouts *adv* at or near that place or number.

thereafter *adv* after that; according to that.

therefore *adv* for that or this reason; consequently.

therein *adv* in that place or respect.

thereon *adv* on that or it; immediately following
that.

therm *n* a measurement of heat.

thermal *adj* generating heat; hot; warm; (*underwear*) of a knitted material with air spaces
for insulation. * *n* a rising current of warm
air.

thermometer *n* an instrument for measuring
temperature.

thermonuclear *adj* of or relating to nuclear fusion
or nuclear weapons that utilize fusion reactions.

Thermos *n* (*trademark*) a brand of vacuum flask.

thermostat *n* an automatic device for regulating
temperatures.

thesaurus *n* (*pl* **thesauri, thesauruses**) a reference
book of synonyms.

these *see* **this.**

thesis *n* (*pl* **theses**) a detailed essay written as
part of a university degree; a theory ex-
pressed as a statement for discussion.

they *pers pron, pl of* **he, she** *or* **it.**

thick *adj* dense; fat, broad; abundant, closely
set; in quick succession; crowded; (*inf*) stupid. * *adv* closely; frequently.

thicken *vti* to make or become thick.

thickset *adj* having a short, stocky body.

thick-skinned *adj* not sensitive.

thief *n* (*pl* **thieves**) a person who steals.

thigh *n* the thick part of the leg from the hip to
the knee.

thimble *n* a cap or cover worn to protect the finger when sewing.

thin *adj* (**thinner, thinnest**) narrow; slim; lean;
sparse, weak, watery; (*material*) fine; not
dense. * *vt* to make thin; to make less
crowded; to water down.—**thinly** *adv.*—**thin-
ness** *n.*

thing *n* an inanimate object; an event; an action;
(*pl*) possessions; (*inf*) an obsession.

think *vb* (*pt* **thought**) *vi* to exercise the mind in
order to make a decision; to revolve ideas
in the mind, to ponder; to remember; to
consider. * *vt* to judge, to believe or consider; (*with* **up**) to concoct, devise.—**thinker**
n.

third *adj* the last of three; being one of three
equal parts. * *n* one of three equal parts.

thirdly *adv* in the third place; as a third point.

third party *n* (*insurance*) involving a third person.

third rate *adj* inferior.

Third World *n* the underdeveloped countries of
the world (usu refers to Africa, Asia and
South America).

thirst *n* a craving for drink; a longing. * *vi* to
feel thirst; to have a longing.

thirsty *adj* (**thirstier, thirstiest**) having a desire to
drink; dry, arid; longing or craving for.—
thirstily *adv.*—**thirstiness** *n.*

thirteen *adj, n* three and ten.—**thirteenth** *adj, n.*

thirty *adj, n* three times ten.—**thirtieth** *adj, n.*

this *demons pron or adj* (*pl* **these**) denoting a
person or thing near, just mentioned, or
about to be mentioned.

thistle *n* a wild plant with prickly leaves and a
purple flower.

thong *n* a piece or strap of leather to lash things
together; the lash of a whip.

thorn *n* a shrub or small tree having thorns, esp
hawthorn; a sharp point or prickle on the
stem of a plant or the branch of a tree.

thorny *adj* (**thornier, thorniest**) prickly; (*problem*)
knotty.

thorough *adj* complete, very detailed and painstaking, exhaustive.—**thoroughness** n.

thoroughbred adj bred from pure stock. * n a pedigree animal, esp a horse.

thoroughfare n a way through; a street; right of passing through.

thoroughly adv completely, fully; entirely, absolutely.

those adj, pron, pl of that.

though conj yet, even if. * adv however; nevertheless.

thought pt, pp of think. * n the act of thinking; reasoning; serious consideration; an idea; opinions collectively; design, intention.

thoughtful adj pensive; considerate.

thoughtless adj without thought; inconsiderate.

thousand adj ten times one hundred; (pl) denoting any large but unspecified number. * n the number 1000.—**thousandth** adj, n.

thrash vt to beat soundly; to defeat; (with out) to discuss thoroughly, until agreement is reached. * vi to thresh grain; to writhe.

thread n a fine strand or filament; a long thin piece of cotton, silk or nylon for sewing; the spiral part of a screw; (of reasoning) a line. * vt to pass a thread through the eye of a needle; to make one's way (through).

threadbare adj worn, shabby.

threat n a declaration of an intention to inflict harm or punishment upon another.

threaten vti to utter threats to; to be a threat.

three adj, n the cardinal number next above two. * n the symbol (3, III, iii) expressing this.

three-dimensional adj having three dimensions.

thresh vti to beat out (grain) from (husks).

threshold n the sill at the door of a building; doorway, entrance; the starting point, beginning.

threw see throw.

thrift n careful management of money.—**thrifty** adj.

thrill vti to tingle with pleasure or excitement. * n a sensation of pleasure and excitement; a trembling or quiver.

thriller n a novel, film or play depicting an exciting story of mystery and suspense.

thrive vi (pt thrived or throve, pp thrived or thriven) to prosper, to be successful; to grow vigorously.—**thriving** adj.

throat n the front part of the neck; the passage from back of the mouth to the top part of the tubes into the lungs and stomach; an entrance.

throb vi (pt throbbed) to beat or pulsate rhythmically, with more than usual force; to vibrate.—also n.

throes npl violent pangs or pain.

thrombosis n (pl thromboses) the forming of a blood clot in the heart or in a blood vessel.

throne n a chair of state occupied by a monarch; sovereign power. * vt to place on a throne.

Throne Speech n (Cdn) Speech from the Throne.

throttle n a valve controlling the flow of fuel or steam to an engine. * vt to choke or strangle.

through prep from one side or end to the other; into and then out of; covering all parts; from beginning to end of; by means of; in consequence of; up to and including. * adv from one end or side to the other; completely. * adj going without interruption; unobstructed.

throughout prep in every part of; from beginning to end. * adv everywhere; at every moment.

throw vb (pt threw, pp thrown) vt to hurl, to fling; to cast off; (party) to hold; (inf) to confuse or disconcert. * vi to cast or hurl through the air (with the arm and wrist); to cast dice. * n the act of throwing; the distance to which anything can be thrown; a cast of dice.

throwaway adj disposable.

throw-in n (soccer) a throw from touch to resume play.

thrush¹ n a bird with a brown back and spotted breast.

thrush² n a fungal disease occurring in the mouths of babies or in women's vaginas.

thrust vti (pt thrust) to push with force; to stab, pierce; to force into a situation. * n a forceful push or stab; pressure; the driving force of a propeller; forward movement; the point or basic meaning.

thud n a dull, heavy sound, caused by a blow or a heavy object falling. * vi (pt thudded) to make such a sound.

thug n a violent and rough person, esp a criminal.

thumb n the first, short, thick finger of the human hand. * vt (book) to turn (the pages) idly.

thumb index n a series of semicircular notches cut in the edge of a book for easier reference to particular parts.

thumbtack n a drawing pin.

thump n a heavy blow; a thud. * vt to strike with something heavy. * vi to throb or beat violently.

thunder n the deep rumbling or loud cracking sound after a flash of lightning; any similar sound. * vi to sound as thunder. * vt (words) to utter loudly.

thunderclap n a loud bang of thunder.

thunderous adj very loud; producing thunder.

thunderstorm n a storm with thunder and lightning.

thundery adj indicating thunder.

Thursday n the fifth day of the week.

thus adv in this or that way; to this degree or extent; so; therefore.

thwart vt to prevent, to frustrate.

thyme n a herb with small leaves used for flavoring savory food.

thyroid n the gland in the neck affecting growth and metabolism.

tiara n a semicircular crown decorated with jewels.

tic n any involuntary, regularly repeated, spasmodic contraction of a muscle.

tick¹ n a small bloodsucking insect that lives on people and animals.

tick² *vi* to make a regular series of short sounds; to beat, as a clock; (*inf*) to work, function. * *n* the sound of a clock; a moment.

tick³ *n* (*inf*) account, credit.

tick⁴ *vt* (*often with* off) to check off, as items in a list. * *n* a check mark (v) to check off items on a list or to indicate correctness.

ticket *n* a printed card, etc, giving right of travel or entry; a label on merchandise giving size, price, etc.

tickle *vt* to touch lightly to provoke pleasure or laughter; to please or delight.

ticklish, tickly *adj* sensitive to being tickled; easily offended; difficult or delicate.

tidal *adj* relating to, or having, tides.

tiddlywinks *npl* a game whose object is to flick small plastic discs into a container by snapping them with a larger disc.

tide *n* the regular rise and fall of the seas, oceans, etc usu twice a day; a current of water; a tendency; a flood. * *vt* (*with* over) to help along temporarily.

tidy *adj* (tidier, tidiest) neat; orderly. * *vt* to make neat; to put things in order.—**tidily** *adv.*—**tidiness** *n.*

tie *vb* (*pr p* tying, *pt* tied) *vt* to bind; to fasten with a string or thread; to make a bow or knot in; to restrict. * *vi* to score the same number of points (as an opponent). * *n* a knot, bow, etc; a bond; a long narrow piece of cloth worn with a shirt; an equality in score.

tier *n* a row or rank in a series when several rows are placed one above another.

tiff *n* a petty quarrel or disagreement.

tiger *n* a large, fierce carnivorous animal of the cat family, having orange and black stripes.—**tigress** *nf.*

tight *adj* taut; fitting closely; not leaky; constricted; miserly; difficult; providing little space or time for variance; (*contest*) close; (*inf*) drunk.

tighten *vti* to make or grow tight or tighter

tightrope *n* a taut rope on which acrobats walk.

tights *npl* a one-piece garment covering the legs and lower body.

tile *n* a thin slab of baked clay used for covering roofs, floors, etc. * *vt* to cover with tiles.

till¹ *n* a drawer inside a cash register for keeping money.

till² *prep* until. * *conj* until.

till³ *vt* (*land*) to cultivate for raising crops, as by ploughing.

tiller *n* the handle or lever for turning a rudder in order to steer a boat.

tilt *vi* to slope, incline, slant. * *vt* to raise one end of. * *n* a slope or angle.

timber *n* wood when used as construction material; a beam; trees collectively. * *vt* to provide with timber or beams.

time *n* the past, present and future; a particular moment; hour of the day; an opportunity; the right moment; duration; occasion; musical beat. * *vt* to regulate as to time; to measure or record the duration of.

time bomb *n* a bomb designed to explode at a predetermined time; something with a potentially delayed reaction.

timekeeper *n* a person or instrument that records or keeps time; an employee who records the hours worked by others.—**timekeeping** *n.*

time lag *n* the interval between two connected events.

timeless *adj* eternal; ageless.

timely *adj* at the right time, opportune.—**timeliness** *n.*

timer *n* a device for measuring, recording or controlling time; a device for controlling lights, heating, etc by setting an electrical clock to regulate their operations.

timetable *n* a list of times of arrivals and departures or trains, aeroplanes, etc; a schedule showing a planned order or sequence.

time zone *n* a geographical region throughout which the same standard time is used.

timing *n* the control and expression of speech or actions to create the best effect, esp in the theatre, etc.

timpani *npl* a set of kettledrums.

tin *n* a malleable metallic element; a container of tin, a can. * *adj* made of tin or tin plate. * *vt* (*pt* tinned)to put food into a tin.

tinfoil *n* baking foil for wrapping food; silver paper.

tinge *vt* to tint or color. * *n* a slight tint, color or flavor.

tingle *vi* to feel a prickling, itching or stinging sensation.—*also n.*

tinker *n* (*formerly*) a travelling mender of pots and pans. * *vi* to fiddle with; to attempt to repair.

tinkle *vi* to make a sound like a small bell ringing; to clink, to jingle; to clink repeatedly. * *n* a tinkling sound; (*inf*) a telephone call.

tin plate *n* thin sheets of iron or steel plated with tin.

tinsel *n* a shiny Christmas decoration made of long pieces of thread wound round with thin strips of metal or plastic foil; something showy but of low value.

tint *n* a shade of any color, esp a pale one; a tinge; a hair dye. * *vt* to color or tinge.

tiny *adj* (tinier, tiniest) very small.

tip¹ *n* the pointed end of anything; the end, as of a billiard cue, etc. * *vt* (*pt* tipped) to put a tip on.

tip² *vti* (*pt* tipped) to tilt or cause to tilt; to overturn; to empty (out, into, etc); to give a gratuity to, as a waiter, etc; (*rubbish*) to dump; to give a helpful hint or inside information to. * *n* a light tap; a gratuity; a rubbish dump; an inside piece of information; a helpful hint.

tip-off *n* a warning based on inside information.

tipple *vi* to drink alcohol regularly in small quantities. * *n* an alcoholic drink.

tipsy *adj* (tipsier, tipsiest) slightly drunk.

tiptoe *vi* (*pt* tiptoed) to walk very quietly or carefully.

tire *vt* to exhaust the strength of, to weary. * *vi* to become weary; to lose patience; to become bored.

tired *adj* weary, sleepy; hackneyed, conventional, flat; (*with* of) exasperated by, bored with.

tiresome *adj* tedious.

tissue *n* thin, absorbent paper used as a disposable handkerchief, etc; a very finely woven fabric; a mass of organic cells of a similar structure and function.

tit¹ *n* a songbird such as a blue tit or great tit.

tit² *n* (*vulg*) a woman's breast.

titanic *adj* monumental; huge.

titbit *n* a tasty morsel of food; a choice item of information.

titillate *vt* to tickle; to arouse or excite pleasurably.

title *n* the name of a book, play, piece of music, work of art, etc; the heading of a section of a book; a name denoting nobility or rank or office held, or attached to a personal name; (*law*) that which gives a legal right (to possession).

title deed *n* a deed or document proving a title or right to possession.

title role *n* the character in a play, film, etc after whom it is named.

titter *vi* to giggle, snigger. * *n* a suppressed laugh.

tittle-tattle *n* idle chat, empty gossip.

to *prep* in the direction of; towards; as far as; expressing the purpose of an action; indicating the infinitive; introducing the indirect object; in comparison with. * *adv* towards.

T.O. *abbr* (*inf*) = Toronto.

toad *n* an amphibious reptile, like a frog, but having a drier skin and spending less time in water.

toadstool *n* a mushroom, esp a poisonous or inedible one.

toady *n* a person who flatters insincerely. * *vi* (*with* to) to act in a servile manner.

toast *vt* to brown over a fire or under a grill; to warm; to drink to the health of. * *n* toasted bread; the sentiment or person to which one drinks.

toaster *n* a person who toasts; a thing that toasts, esp an electrical appliance.

toastmaster *n* the proposer of toasts at public dinners.—**toastmistress** *nf*.

tobacco *n* a plant whose dried leaves are used for smoking, chewing or snuff.

tobacconist *n* a person or shop that sells cigarettes, etc.

toboggan *n* a sledge, sled.

today *n* this day; the present age. * *adv* on this day; nowadays.

toddler *n* a young child.

toddy *n* a drink of whisky, sugar, and hot water.

toe *n* one of the five digits on the foot; the part of the shoe or sock that covers the toes.

toenail *n* the thin, hard, covering on the end of the toes.

toe rubbers *npl* (*Cdn*) low rubber overshoes that extend from the heel of a man's shoe under the sole and over the tip of the toe.

toffee, toffy *n* a sweet of brittle but tender texture made by boiling sugar and butter together.

toga *n* a piece of cloth draped around the body, as worn by citizens in ancient Rome.

together *adv* in one place or group; in cooperation with; in unison; jointly.

toil *vi* to work strenuously; to move with great effort. * *n* hard work.

toilet *n* a lavatory; the room containing a lavatory; the act of washing and dressing oneself.

toilet paper, toilet tissue *n* an absorbent paper for cleansing after urination, etc.

toilet roll *n* a cardboard cylinder around which toilet paper is wound.

toiletry *n* a lotion, perfume, etc used in washing and dressing oneself.

toilet water *n* a diluted perfume.

token *n* a symbol, sign; an indication; a metal disc for a slot machine; a souvenir; a gift voucher. * *adj* nominal; symbolic.

told *see* tell.

tolerable *adj* bearable; fairly good.—**tolerably** *adv*.

tolerance *n* open-mindedness; forbearance; (*med*) ability to resist the action of a drug, etc; ability of a substance to endure heat, stress, etc without damage.

tolerant *adj* able to put up with the beliefs, actions, etc of others; broad-minded; showing tolerance to a drug, etc; capable of enduring stress, etc.

tolerate *vt* to endure, put up with, suffer.

toll¹ *n* money levied for passing over a bridge or road; the number of people killed in an accident or disaster.

toll² *vt* (*bell*) to ring slowly and repeatedly, as a funeral bell. * *vi* to sound, as a bell. * *n* the sound of a bell when tolling.

tomato *n* (*pl* tomatoes) a plant with red pulpy fruit used as a vegetable.

tomb *n* a vault in the earth for the burial of the dead.

tomboy *n* a girl who likes rough outdoor activities.

tombstone *n* a memorial stone over a grave.

tomcat *n* a male cat.

tomorrow *n* the day after today; the future.—*also adv*.

ton *n* a unit of weight equivalent to 2,000 pounds in US or 2,240 pounds in UK; (*inf*) 100 mph; (*inf*: *pl*) a great quantity.

tone *n* the quality of a sound; pitch or inflection of the voice; color, shade; body condition. * *vt* to give tone to. * *vi* to harmonize (with).

tongs *npl* an instrument consisting of two arms that are hinged, used for grasping and lifting.

tongue *n* the soft, moveable organ in the mouth, used in tasting, swallowing, and speech; the ability to speak; a language; (*shoe*) a piece of leather under the laces; a jet of flame; the tongue of an animal served as food; the catch of a buckle.

tongue-tied *adj* speechless.

tongue-twister n a sequence of words that it is difficult to pronounce quickly and clearly.

tonic n a medicine that improves physical well-being; something that imparts vigour; a fizzy mineral water with a bitter taste. * adj relating to tones or sounds.

tonight n this night; the night or evening of the present day.—also adv.

tonnage n a merchant ship's capacity measured in tons; the weight of its cargo; the amount of shipping of a country or port; merchant ships collectively; a duty levied on ships based on tonnage or capacity.

tonne n metric ton, 1,000 kg.

tonsil n one of the two oval organs of soft tissue situated one on each side of the throat.

tonsillitis n inflammation of the tonsils.

too adv in addition; also; likewise; extremely; very.

took see **take**.

tool n an implement that is used by hand; a means for achieving any purpose.

toonie n (Cdn) (inf) the Canadian two-dollar coin.

toot vi to hoot a car horn, whistle, etc in short blasts. * n a hoot.—also vt.

tooth n (pl **teeth**) one of the white, bone-like structures arranged in rows in the mouth, used in biting and chewing; the palate; a tooth-like projection on a comb, saw, or wheel.

toothache n a pain in a tooth.

toothbrush n a small brush for cleaning teeth.

toothpaste n a paste for cleaning teeth, used with a toothbrush.

toothpick n a sliver of wood or plastic for removing food particles from between the teeth.

top[1] n the highest, or uppermost, part or surface of anything; the highest in rank; the crown of the head; the lid. * adj highest; greatest. * vt to cover on the top; to remove the top of or from; to rise above; to surpass.

top[2] n a child's toy, which is spun on its pointed base.

top hat n a man's tall, silk hat.

top-heavy adj having an upper part too heavy for the lower, causing instability.

topic n a subject for discussion; the theme of a speech or writing.

topical adj of current interest.

topless adj lacking a top; (garment) revealing the breasts; wearing such a garment.

topmost adj nearest the top, highest.

topple vi to fall over. * vt to cause to overbalance and fall; (government) to overthrow.

topsy-turvy adj, adv turned upside down; in confusion.

toque n a small brimless hat for women; (Cdn) a close-fitting, stretchable knitted hat.

torch n a portable light powered by batteries; a device for giving off a hot flame.

torment n torture, anguish; a source of pain. * vt to afflict with extreme pain, physical or mental.—**tormentor, tormenter** n.

torn see **tear**[2].

tornado n (pl **tornadoes**) a violently whirling column of air seen as a funnel-shaped cloud that usu destroys everything in its narrow path.

torpedo n (pl **torpedoes**) a self-propelled submarine offensive weapon, carrying an explosive charge. * vt to attack, hit, or destroy with torpedo(es).

torpor n a state of lethargy.

torque n (physics) a force that causes rotation around a central point, such as an axle.

torrent n a rushing stream; a flood of words.—**torrential** adj.

torso n (pl **torsos**) the trunk of the human body.

tortoise n a slow-moving reptile with a dome-shaped shell into which it can withdraw.

tortoiseshell n a brown and yellow color.

tortuous adj full of twists, involved.—**tortuously** adv.

torture n subjection to severe physical or mental pain to extort a confession, or as a punishment. —also vt. —**torturer** n.

Tory n a member or supporter of the Progressive Conservative Party of Canada; a member of the Conservative Party in UK politics.—also adj.

toss vt to throw up; to pitch; to fling; (head) to throw back. * vi to be tossed about; to move restlessly.—also n.

toss-up n the throwing of a coin to decide a question.

tot[1] n anything little, esp a child; a small measure of spirits.

tot[2] vt (pt **totted**) (with **up**) to add up or total.

total adj whole, complete; absolute. * n the whole sum; the entire amount. * vt (pt **totalled**) to add up.—**totally** adv.

totalitarian adj relating to a system of government in which one political group maintains complete control, esp under a dictator. —**totalitarianism** n.

totter vi to walk unsteadily; to shake or sway as if about to fall.—**tottery** adj.

touch vt to come in contact with, esp with the hand or fingers; to reach; to affect with emotion; to tinge or tint; to border on; (sl) to ask for money (from). * vi to be in contact; to be adjacent; to allude to. * n the act of touching; the sense by which something is perceived through contact; a trace; understanding; a special quality or skill.

touch-and-go adj precarious, risky.

touchdown n the moment when an aircraft or spaceship lands; (Rugby football, American football) a placing of the ball on the ground to score.

touched adj emotionally affected; mentally disturbed.

touching adj affecting, moving.

touchline n (football, etc) the side boundary of a pitch.

touchy adj (**touchier, touchiest**) irritable; very risky.

tough adj strong; durable; hardy; rough and violent; difficult; (inf) unlucky.—**toughen** vti.—**toughness** n.

toupee *n* a wig or section of hair to cover a bald spot, esp worn by men.

tour *n* a turn, period, etc as of military duty; a long trip, as for sightseeing. * *vti* to go on a tour (through).

tourism *n* travelling for pleasure; the business of catering for people who do this; the encouragement of touring.

tourist *n* one who makes a tour, a sightseer, travelling for pleasure.—*also adj.*

tournament *n* a sporting event involving a number of competitors and a series of games.

tourtière *n* (*Cdn*) a French-Canadian pie of ground pork and spices.

tousle *vt* to make untidy, ruffle, make tangled (esp hair).

tout *vti* (*inf*) to praise highly; (*inf*) to sell betting tips on (race horses); (*inf*) to solicit business in a brazen way. * *n* (*inf*) a person who does so.

tow *vt* to pull or drag with a rope. * *n* the act of towing; a towrope.

towards, toward (*US*) *prep* in the direction of; concerning; just before; as a contribution to.

towel *n* an absorbent cloth for drying the skin after it is washed, and for other purposes.

towelling, toweling (*US*) *n* cloth for towels; a rubbing with a towel.

tower *n* a tall, narrow building, standing alone or forming part of another; a fortress. * *vi* (*with* **over**) to rise above; to loom.

tower block *n* a skyscraper.

town *n* a densely populated urban centre, smaller than a city and larger than a village; the people of a town.

townhall *n* a large building housing the offices of the town council, often with a hall for public meetings.

towpath *n* the footpath beside a river or canal.

towrope, towline *n* a strong rope or cable for towing a wheeled vehicle, ship, etc.

toxic *adj* poisonous; harmful; deadly.

toy *n* an object for children to play with; a replica; a miniature. * *vi* to trifle; to flirt.

trace *n* a mark etc left by a person, animal or thing; a barely perceptible footprint; a small quantity. * *vt* to follow by tracks; to discover the whereabouts of; (*map, etc*) to copy by following the lines on transparent paper.

track *vt* to follow the tracks of; (*satellite, etc*) to follow by radar and record position. * *n* a mark left; a footprint; parallel steel rails on which trains run; a course for running or racing; sports performed on a track, as running, hurdling; the band on which the wheels of a tractor or tank run; one piece of music on a record; a soundtrack.

tracksuit *n* a loose suit worn by athletes to keep warm.

tract[1] *n* an expanse of land or water; a part of a bodily system or organ.

tract[2] *n* a treatise.

tractor *n* a motor vehicle for pulling heavy loads and for working ploughs.

trade *n* buying and selling (of commodities); commerce; occupation; customers; business. * *vi* to buy and sell; to exchange.—**trader** *n*.

trade-in *n* a used item given in part payment when buying a replacement.

trademark *n* a name used on a product by a manufacturer to distinguish it from its competitors, esp when legally protected.—*also vt.*

tradesman *n* (*pl* **tradesmen**) a shopkeeper; a skilled worker.

trade(s) union *n* an organized association of employees of any trade or industry for the protection of their income and working conditions.

tradition *n* the handing down from generation to generation of opinions and practices; the belief or practice thus passed on; custom.—**traditional** *adj.*—**traditionally** *adv.*

traffic *n* trade; the movement or number of vehicles, pedestrians, etc, along a street, etc. * *vi* (*pt* **trafficked**) to do business (esp. in illegal drugs).

traffic circle *n* a roundabout.

traffic light *n* one of a set of colored lights used to control traffic at street crossings, etc.

traffic warden *n* a person who is authorized to control traffic and to report parking violations, etc.

tragedy *n* a play or drama that is serious and sad, and the climax a catastrophe; an accident or situation involving death or suffering.—**tragic** *adj.*—**tragically** *adv.*

trail *vt* to drag along the ground; to have in its wake; to follow behind. * *vi* to hang or drag loosely behind; (*plant*) to climb; (*with* **off** *or* **away**) to grow weaker or dimmer. * *n* a path or track; the scent of an animal; something left in the wake.

trailer *n* a wagon, van, etc designed to be towed by a motor vehicle; a caravan; an advertisement for a film or television programme.

train *vt* to teach, to guide; to tame for use, as animals; to prepare for racing, etc; (*gun, etc*) to aim. * *vi* to do exercise or preparation. * *n* a series of railway carriages pulled by a locomotive; a sequence; the back part of a dress that trails along the floor; a retinue.

trained *adj* skilled.

trainee *n* a person who is being trained.

trainer *n* a coach or instructor in sports; a person who prepares horses for racing.

training *n* practical instruction; a course of physical exercises.

trait *n* a characteristic feature.

traitor *n* a person who commits treason or betrays his country, friends, etc.—**traitorous** *adj.*

tram *n* an electrically powered vehicle for public transport that travels along rails set into the ground.

tramlines *npl* rails for trams; the sidelines on a tennis court.

tramp *vti* to walk heavily; to tread or trample; to wander about as a tramp. * *n* a vagrant.

trample *vti* to tread under foot.

trampoline *n* a sheet of strong canvas stretched tightly on a frame, used in acrobatic tumbling.

trance *n* a state of unconsciousness, induced by hypnosis, in which some of the powers of the waking body, such as response to commands, may be retained.

tranquil *adj* quiet, calm, peaceful.—**tranquillity, tranquility** *n.*

tranquillizer *n* a drug that calms.

transact *vt* (*business*) to conduct or carry out.

transaction *n* the act of transacting; something transacted, esp a business deal; (*pl*) a record of the proceedings of a society.

transatlantic *adj* crossing the Atlantic Ocean; across, beyond the Atlantic.

trans-Canada *adj* (*Cdn*) across, including, or involving all of Canada.

transcend *vt* to rise above or beyond; to surpass.—**transcendent** *adj.*

transcript *n* a written or printed copy made by transcribing; an official copy of proceedings, etc.

transcription *n* the act of transcribing; something transcribed, esp a piece of music; a transcript; a recording made for broadcasting.

transept *n* one of the two wings of a church, at right angles to the nave.

transfer *vb* (*pt* **transferred**) *vt* to carry, convey, from one place to another; (*law*) to make over (property) to another; (*money*) to move from the control of one institution to another. * *vi* to change to another bus, etc. * *n* the act of transferring; the state of being transferred; someone or something that is transferred; a design that can be moved from one surface to another.—**transferable** *adj.*

transform *vti* to change the shape, appearance, or condition of; to convert.—**transformation** *n.*

transformer *n* a device for changing alternating current with an increase or decrease of voltage.

transfusion *n* the injection of blood into the veins of a sick or injured person.—**transfuse** *vt.*

transient *adj* temporary; of short duration, momentary.—**transience** *n.*

transistor *n* a device for amplifying sound, as in a radio or television; a small portable radio.

transit *n* a passing over or through; the carrying of people or goods.

transition *n* passage from one place or state to another; change.—**transitional** *adj.*

transitive *adj* (*gram*) denoting a verb that requires a direct object; of or relating to transition.

transitory *adj* lasting only a short time.

translate *vti* to express in another language; to explain, interpret.—**translator** *n.*

translation *n* the act of translating; something translated into another language or state; an interpretation.

transmission *n* the act of transmitting; something transmitted; a system using gears, etc, to transfer power from an engine to a moving part, esp wheels of a car; a radio or television broadcast.

transmit *vt* (*pt* **transmitted**) to send from one place or person to another; to communicate; to convey; (*radio or TV signals*) to send out.

transmitter *n* an apparatus for broadcasting television or radio programmes.

transparency *n* the state of being transparent; (*photog*) a slide.

transparent *adj* that may be easily seen through; clear, easily understood.

transplant *vt* (*plant*) to remove and plant in another place; (*med*) to remove an organ from one person and transfer it to another.—*also n.*

transport *vt* to convey from one place to another; to delight. * *n* the system of transporting goods or passengers; the carrying of troops and their equipment by sea or land; a vehicle for this purpose.—**transportable** *adj.*—**transportation** *n.*

transvestite *n* a person who gains sexual pleasure from wearing the clothes of the opposite sex.—**transvestism** *n.*

trap *n* a mechanical device or pit for snaring animals; an ambush; a trick to catch someone out; a two-wheeled horsedrawn carriage. * *vt* (*pt* **trapped**) to catch in a trap; to trick.

trapdoor *n* a hinged or sliding door in a roof, ceiling or floor.

trapeze *n* a gymnastic apparatus consisting of a horizontal bar suspended by two parallel ropes.

trapper *n* a person who traps animals, esp for their skins.

trappings *npl* trimmings; additions; ornaments.

trash *n* nonsense; refuse; rubbish.

trash can *n* a dustbin.

trauma *n* an emotional shock that may cause long-term psychological damage; an upsetting experience.—**traumatic** *adj.*

travel *vb* (*pt* **travelled**) *vi* to journey or move from one place to another. * *vt* to journey across, through. * *n* journey.

traveller, traveler (*US*) *n* a person who travels; a salesman who travels for a company.

traveller's cheque *n* a draft purchased from a bank, etc signed at the time of purchase and signed again at the time of cashing.

travesty *n* a misrepresentation; a poor imitation; a parody.

trawler *n* a boat used for trawling.

tray *n* a flat board, or sheet of metal or plastic, surrounded by a rim, used for carrying food or drink.

treacherous *adj* untrustworthy, disloyal; unstable, dangerous.

treachery *n* disloyalty, betrayal of trust.

treacle *n* a thick sticky substance obtained during the refining of sugar.—**treacly** *adj.*

tread *vti* (*pt* **trod**, *pp* **trodden**) to step or walk on, along, in, over or across; to crush or squash (with the feet); to trample (on). * *n* a step, way of walking; the part of a shoe, wheel, or tyre that touches the ground.

treason *n* the crime of betraying one's government or attempting to overthrow it; treachery.—**treasonable** *adj*.

treasure *n* wealth and riches hoarded up; a person or thing much valued. * *vt* to hoard up; to prize greatly.

treasurer *n* a person appointed to take charge of the finances of a society, government or city.

treasury *n* a place where valuable objects are deposited; the funds or revenues of a government.

Treasury Board *n* (*Cdn*) a government department responsible for reviewing planned expenditures.

treat *vt* to deal with or regard; to subject to the action of a chemical; to apply medical treatment to; to pay for another person's entertainment; to deal with in speech or writing. * *n* an entertainment paid for by another person; a pleasure seldom indulged; a unusual cause of enjoyment.

treatise *n* a formal essay in which a subject is treated systematically.

treatment *n* the application of drugs, etc, to a patient; the manner of dealing with a person or thing, esp in a novel or painting; behaviour towards someone.

treaty *n* a formal agreement between states.

treble *adj* triple, threefold; (*mus*) denoting the treble. * *n* the highest range of musical notes in singing. * *vti* to make or become three times as much.

tree *n* a tall, woody, perennial plant having a single trunk, branches and leaves.

trek *vi* (*pt* **trekked**) to travel slowly or laboriously; (*inf*) to go on foot (to). * *n* a long and difficult journey; a migration.

trellis *n* a structure of lattice work, for supporting climbing plants, etc.—**trelliswork** *n*.

tremble *vi* to shake, shiver from cold or fear; to quiver.—*also n*.

tremendous *adj* awe-inspiring; very large or great; (*inf*) wonderful; marvellous.

tremor *n* a vibration; an involuntary shaking.

trench *n* a long narrow channel in the earth, used for drainage; such an excavation made for military purposes.

trend *n* tendency; a current style or fashion.

trendy *adj* (**trendier**, **trendiest**) (*inf*) fashionable. * *n* (*inf*) a person who tries to be fashionable.—**trendily** *adv*.—**trendiness** *n*.

trepidation *n* a state of fear or anxiety.

trespass *vi* to intrude upon another person's property without their permission; to encroach upon, or infringe, another's rights. * *n* act of trespassing.—**trespasser** *n*.

trestle *n* a wooden framework for supporting a table top.

triactor *n* (*Cdn*) a bet on the first three finishers in a horse race, specifying the order of their finish.

trial *n* a test or experiment; judicial examination; an attempt; a preliminary race, game in a competition; suffering; hardship; a person causing annoyance.

triangle *n* (*math*) a plane figure with three angles and three sides; a percussion instrument consisting of a triangular metal bar beaten with a metal stick.—**triangular** *adj*.

tribe *n* a group of people of the same race, sharing the same customs, religion, language or land.—**tribal** *adj*.—**tribesman** *n*.

tribulation *n* distress, difficulty, hardship.

tribunal *n* a court of justice; a committee that investigates and decides on a particular problem.

tribune[1] *n* in ancient Rome, a magistrate appointed to protect the rights of common people; a champion of the people.

tribune[2] *n* a raised platform or dais from which speeches are delivered.

tributary *n* a stream or river flowing into a larger one.

tribute *n* a speech, gift or action to show one's respect or thanks to someone; a payment made at certain intervals by one nation to another in return for peace.

trick *n* fraud; deception; a mischievous plan or joke; a magical illusion; a clever feat; skill, knack; the playing cards won in a round. * *adj* using fraud or clever contrivance to deceive. * *vt* to deceive, cheat.—**trickster** *n*.

trickery *n* the practice or an act of using underhand methods to achieve an aim; deception.

trickle *vti* to flow or cause to flow in drops or in a small stream.—*also n*.

tricky *adj* (**trickier**, **trickiest**) complicated, difficult to handle; risky; cunning, deceitful.—**trickily** *adv*.—**trickiness** *n*.

tricycle *n* a three-wheeled pedal cycle, esp for children.

trifle *vi* to treat lightly; to dally. * *n* anything of little value; a dessert of whipped cream, custard, sponge cake, sherry, etc.

trifling *adj* insignificant.

trigger *n* a catch that when pulled activates the firing mechanism of a gun. * *vt* (*with* **off**) to initiate; to set (off).

trigonometry *n* the branch of mathematics concerned with calculating the angles of triangles or the lengths of their sides.

trim *adj* (**trimmer**, **trimmest**) in good condition; tidy, neat; slim. * *vt* (*pt* **trimmed**) to neaten; to cut or prune; to decorate; (*aircraft*) to balance the cargo weight in. * *n* a decorative edging; a haircut that tidies.

trimming *n* decorative part of clothing; (*pl*) accompaniments.

trinity *n* a group of three; (*with cap*) in Christianity, the union of Father, Son and Holy Spirit in one God.

trinket *n* a small or worthless ornament.

trio *n* (*pl* **trios**) a set of three; (*mus*) a group of three singers or instrumentalists.

trip *vb* (*pt* **tripped**) *vi* to move or tread lightly; to stumble and fall; to make a blunder. * *vt* (*a* *person: often with* **up**) to cause to stumble; to activate a trip. * *n* a stumble; a journey, tour, or voyage; a slip; a mistake; a light step; a mechanical switch; (*sl*) a hallucinatory experience under the influence of a drug.

tripe *n* the stomach lining of an ox, prepared for cooking; (*inf*) rubbish, nonsense.

triple *adj* threefold; three times as many. * *vti* to treble.

triplet *n* one of three children born at one birth.

triplicate *adj* threefold.

tripod *n* a three-legged stand, as for supporting a camera.

trite *adj* dull; hackneyed.

triumph *n* a victory; success; a great achievement. * *vi* to win a victory or success; to rejoice over a victory.—**triumphal** *adj*.

triumphant *adj* feeling or showing triumph; celebratory; victorious.—**triumphantly** *adv*.

trivia *npl* unimportant details.

trivial *adj* unimportant; commonplace.

trod, trodden *see* **tread**.

trolley *n* (*pl* **trolleys**) a table on wheels for carrying or serving food; a cart for transporting luggage or shopping in a supermarket; a device that transmits electric current from an overhead wire.

trolleybus, trolley car *n* an electric bus powered from an overhead wire by means of a trolley.

trombone *n* a brass musical wind instrument whose length is varied with a U-shaped sliding section.

troop *n* a crowd of people; a group of soldiers within a cavalry regiment; (*pl*) armed forces; soldiers. * *vi* to go in a crowd.

trooper *n* a cavalryman; in US, a mounted policeman or a state policeman.

trophy *n* a cup or shield won as a prize in a competition or contest; a memento , as taken in battle or hunting.

tropic *n* one of the two parallel lines of latitude north and south of the equator; (*pl*) the regions lying between these lines.

tropical *adj* relating to the tropics; (*weather*) hot and humid.

trot *vi* (*pt* **trotted**) (*horse*) to go, lifting the feet higher than in walking and moving at a faster rate. * *n* the gait of a horse; a brisk pace.

trouble *vti* to cause trouble to; to worry; to pain; to upset; to cause inconvenience; to take pains (to). * *n* an anxiety; a medical condition causing pain; a problem; unrest or disturbance.—**troublesome** *adj*.

troubleshooter *n* a person whose work is to locate and eliminate a source of trouble or conflict.—**troubleshooting** *n*.

trough *n* a long, narrow container for water or animal feed; a channel in the ground; an elongated area of low barometric pressure.

trounce *vt* to defeat completely.

troupe *n* a travelling company, esp of actors, dancers or acrobats.—**trouper** *n*.

trousers *npl* an item of clothing covering the body from waist to ankle, with two tubes of material for the legs; pants.

trousseau *n* (*pl* **trousseaux**) the clothes and linen a bride collects for her marriage.

trout *n* (*pl* **trout**) a game fish of the salmon family living in fresh water.

trowel *n* a hand tool for gardening; a flat-bladed tool for spreading cement, etc.

truant *n* a pupil who is absent from school without permission. * *vi* to play truant.—*also* *adj*.—**truancy** *n*.

truce *n* an agreement between two armies or states to suspend hostilities.

truck *n* a heavy motor vehicle for transporting goods; a lorry; a vehicle open at the back for moving goods or animals. * *vt* (*goods*) to convey by truck. * *vi* to drive a truck.

trudge *vti* to travel on foot, heavily or wearily. * *n* a tiring walk.

true *adj* (**truer, truest**) conforming with fact; correct, accurate; genuine; loyal; perfectly in tune. * *adv* truthfully; rightly.

truffle *n* a round, edible underground fungus; a sweet made with chocolate, butter and sugar.

truly *adv* completely; genuinely; to a great degree.

trump *n* (*cards*) the suit that is chosen to have the highest value in one game. * *vt* to play a trump card on.

trumpet *n* a brass wind instrument consisting of a long tube with a flared end and three buttons. * *vti* to proclaim loudly.—**trumpeter** *n*.

truncate *vt* to cut the top end off; to shorten.—**truncation** *n*.

truncheon *n* a short, thick club carried by a policeman.

trundle *vt* (*an object*) to push or pull on wheels. * *vi* to move along slowly.

trunk *n* the main stem of a tree; the torso; the main body of anything; the long nose of an elephant; a strong box or chest for clothes, etc, esp on a journey; the boot of a car.

trunks *npl* a man's short, light pants for swimming.

truss *n* a supporting framework for a roof or bridge; a hernia brace. * *vt* to bind (up).

trust *n* firm belief in the truth of anything, faith in a person; confidence in; custody; a financial arrangement of investing money for another person; a business syndicate. * *adj* held in trust. * *vti* to have confidence in; to believe.—**trustful** *adj*.

trustee *n* a person who has legal control of money or property that they are keeping or investing for another.—**trusteeship** *n*.

trustworthy *adj* reliable, dependable.

trusty *adj* (**trustier, trustiest**) trustworthy, faithful. * *n* a prisoner granted special privileges as a trustworthy person.—**trustily** *adv*.—**trustiness** *n*.

truth *n* that which is true, factual or genuine; agreement with reality.

truthful *adj* telling the truth; accurate, realistic; honest, frank.—**truthfulness** *n*.

try *vt* to test the result or effect by experiment;

to determine judicially; to put strain on. * *vi* to attempt; to make an effort. * *n* an attempt, an effort; (*Rugby football*) a score made with a touchdown.

trying *adj* exasperating.

tsar *n* the title of the former ruler of Russia.—*also* **czar**.

TSE *abbr* = Toronto Stock Exchange.

T-shirt *n* an informal knitted cotton sweater.—*also* **tee-shirt**.

T-square *n* a T-shaped instrument for drawing and determining right angles.

tub *n* a circular container, esp for holding water.

tuba *n* a large brass instrument of bass pitch.

tubby *adj* (**tubbier, tubbiest**) plump.

tube *n* a long, thin, hollow pipe; a soft metal or plastic cylinder in which thick liquids or pastes are stored; (*inf*) in UK, the underground railway system.—**tubular** *adj*.

tuberculosis *n* an infectious disease of the lungs.—**tubercular** *adj*.

tubing *n* tubes collectively; a length of tube; the material from which tubes are made; a circular fabric.

TUC *abbr* = Trades Union Congress.

tuck *vt* to draw or gather together in a fold; (*with* **up**) to wrap snugly. * *vi* (*inf*) (*with* **into**) to eat greedily. * *n* a fold in a garment.

Tuesday *n* the third day of the week.

tuft *n* a bunch of grass, hair or feathers held together at the base; a clump.

tug *vti* (*pt* **tugged**) to pull with effort or to drag along. * *n* a strong pull; a tugboat.

tugboat *n* a small powerful boat for towing ships.

tug of war *n* a contest in which two teams tug on opposite ends of a rope to pull the opposing team over a central line; a struggle for supremacy between two opponents.

tuition *n* teaching, instruction.

tulip *n* a highly-colored cup-shaped flower grown from bulbs.

tullibee *n* (*Cdn*) a North American whitefish.

tumble *vi* to fall over; to roll or to twist the body, as an acrobat. * *vt* to push or cause to fall. * *n* a fall; a somersault.

tumble-drier, tumble dryer *n* a machine for drying clothes with warm air.

tumbler *n* a large drinking glass without a handle or stem; an acrobat.

tummy *n* (*inf*) stomach.

tumour, tumor (*US*) *n* an abnormal growth of tissue in any part of the body.

tumult *n* a commotion; an uproar.

tumultuous *adj* disorderly; rowdy, noisy; restless.—**tumultuously** *adv*.—**tumultuousness** *n*.

tuna *n* (*pl* **tuna, tunas**) a large ocean fish of the mackerel group.

tune *n* a melody; correct musical pitch; harmony. * *vt* (*musical instrument*) to adjust the notes of; (*radio, TV etc*) to adjust the resonant frequency, etc, to a particular value.—**tuneful** *adj*.—**tunefully** *adv*.

tungsten *n* a hard malleable greyish white metallic element used in lamps, etc, and in alloys with steel.

tunic *n* a hip or knee-length loose, usu belted blouse-like garment; a close-fitting jacket worn by soldiers and policemen.

tunnel *n* an underground passage, esp one for cars or trains. * *vb* (*pt* **tunnelled**) *vt* to make a way through. * *vi* to make a tunnel.

tunny *n* (*pl* **tunnies, tunny**) tuna.

turban *n* a headdress consisting of cloth wound in folds around the head worn by men; a woman's hat of this shape.

turbine *n* a machine in which power is produced when the forced passage of steam, water, etc causes the blades to rotate.

turbot *n* a large, flat, round edible fish.

turbulent *adj* disturbed, in violent commotion.

tureen *n* a large dish for serving soup, etc.

turf *n* (*pl* **turf, turves**) the surface layer of grass and its roots; (*with* **the**) horse racing; a racetrack. * *vt* to cover with turf.

turgid *adj* swollen; pompous, bombastic.—**turgidity** *n*.—**turgidness** *n*.

turkey *n* (*pl* **turkeys, turkey**) a large bird farmed for its meat.

Turkish bath *n* a bath with steam rooms, showers, massage, etc.

turmoil *n* agitation; disturbance, confusion.

turn *vi* to revolve; to go in the opposite direction; to depend on; to appeal (to) for help; to direct (thought or attention) away from; to change in character; to be shaped on the lathe. * *vt* to change the position or direction of by revolving; to reverse; to transform; (*age, etc*) to have just passed; to change or convert; to invert. * *n* a rotation; new direction or tendency; a place in sequence; a turning point, crisis; performer's act; an act of kindness or malice; a bend.

turning point *n* the point at which a significant change occurs.

turnip *n* a plant with a large white or yellow root, cultivated as a vegetable.

turnout *n* a gathering of people.

turnover *n* the volume of business transacted in a given period; a fruit or meat pasty; the rate of replacement of workers.

turnpike *n* a toll road, esp one that is an expressway.

turnstile *n* a mechanical gate across a footpath or entrance, which admits only one person at a time.

turntable *n* a circular, horizontal revolving platform, as in a record player.

turn-up *n* the cuff of a trouser; (*inf*) a surprise.

turpentine *n* an oily resin secreted by coniferous trees, used as a solvent and thinner for paints.—*also* **turps**.

turquoise *n* an opaque greenish-blue mineral, valued as a gem; the color of turquoise.—*also adj*.

turret *n* a small tower on a building rising above it; a dome or revolving structure for guns, as on a warship, tank or aeroplane.—**turreted** *adj*.

turtle *n* any of an order of land, freshwater or marine reptiles having a soft body encased in a hard shell.

turtleneck *n* a high close-fitting neckline on a sweater.

tusk *n* a long, projecting tooth on either side of the mouth, as of the elephant.—**tusked** *adj*.

tussle *n* a scuffle.

tutor *n* a private teacher who instructs pupils individually; a member of staff responsible for the supervision and teaching of students in a university. * *vt* to instruct; to act as a tutor.

tutorial *n* a period of tuition by a tutor to an individual or a small group. * *adj* of or pertaining to a tutor.

tuxedo *n* a man's semi-formal suit with a tailless jacket; a dinner jacket.

TV *abbr* = television.

twang *n* a sharp, vibrant sound, as of a taut string when plucked; a nasal tone of voice. * *vt* to make a twanging sound.

tweed *n* a twilled woollen fabric used in making clothes.

tweezers *n sing* small pincers.

twelfth *adj* the last of twelve; being one of twelve equal parts.

twelve *adj* the cardinal number next after eleven. * *n* the symbol for this (12, XII, xii).

twenty *adj*, *n* two times ten. * *n* the symbol for this (20, XX, xx). —**twentieth** *adj*.

twice *adv* two times; two times as much; doubly.

twig[1] *n* a small branch or shoot of a tree.—**twiggy** *adj*.

twig[2] *vti* (*pt* **twigged**) (*inf*) to grasp the meaning of.

twilight *n* the dim light just after sunset and before sunrise; the final stages of something.

twill *n* a cloth woven in such a way as to produce diagonal lines across it.—**twilled** *adj*.

twin *n* either of two persons or animals born at the same birth; one thing resembling another. * *adj* double; very like another; consisting of two parts nearly alike. * *vt* (*pt* **twinned**) to pair together.

twine *n* a string of twisted fibres or hemp. * *vti* to twist together; to wind around.

twinge *n* a sudden, stabbing pain; an emotional pang.

twinkle *vi* to sparkle; to flicker.

twirl *vt* to whirl; to rotate; to wind or twist. * *vi* to turn around rapidly.

twist *vt* to unite by winding together; to coil; to confuse or distort (the meaning of); to bend. * *vi* to revolve; to write. * *n* the act or result of twisting; a twist of thread; a curve or bend; an unexpected event; a wrench.

twitch *vt* to pull with a sudden jerk. * *vi* to be suddenly jerked. * *n* a sudden muscular spasm.

two *adj*, *n* the cardinal number next above one. * *n* the symbol for this (2, II, ii).

two-faced *adj* deceitful, hypocritical.

two-four *n* (*Cdn*) (*inf*) a case of twenty-four bottles of beer.

two-piece *n* a garment consisting of two separate matching bits.—*also adj*.

two solitudes *npl* (*Cdn*) the French- and English-speaking peoples of Canada, considered as being independent and isolated from each other.

twosome *n* a group of two; a game for two people.

tycoon *n* a powerful industrialist, etc.

type *n* a kind, class or group; sort; model; a block of metal for printing letters; style of print. * *vt* to write by means of a typewriter; to classify.

typecast *vt* (*pt* **typecast**) (*actor*) to cast in the same role repeatedly because of physical appearance, etc.

typescript *n* a typed copy of a book, document, etc.

typewriter *n* a keyboard machine for printing characters.

typhoid *n* an acute infectious disease acquired from contaminated food or water.

typhoon *n* a violent tropical cyclone originating in the western Pacific.

typhus *n* a highly contagious acute disease spread by body lice and characterized by fever, a rash and headache.—**typhous** *adj*.

typical *adj* representative of a particular type; characteristic.—**typically** *adv*.

typify *vt* to characterize.

typist *n* a person who uses a typewriter, esp as a job.

tyranny *n* the government or authority of a tyrant; harshness; oppression.

tyrant *n* a person who uses his or her power arbitrarily and oppressively.—**tyrannical** *adj*.

tyre, tire (*US*) *n* a protective, usu rubber, covering around the rim of a wheel.

ubiquitous *adj* existing, or seeming to exist everywhere at once.—**ubiquity** *n*.

udder *n* a milk-secreting organ containing two or more teats, as in cows.

UEL *abbr* (*Cdn*) = United Empire Loyalist.

UFO *abbr* = unidentified flying object.

ugly *adj* (**uglier, ugliest**) unsightly; unattractive; repulsive; ill tempered.—**ugliness** *n*.

UHF *abbr* = ultrahigh frequency.

UI *abbr* (*Cdn*) = Unemployment Insurance.

UK *abbr* = United Kingdom.

ulcer *n* an open sore on the surface of the skin or a mucous membrane.—**ulcerous** *adj*

ulterior *adj* (*motives*) hidden, not evident; subsequent.

ultimate *adj* last; final; most significant; essential. * *n* the most significant thing.—**ultimately** *adv*.

ultimatum *n* (*pl* **ultimatums**) the final proposal, condition or terms in negotiations.

ultraviolet *adj* of light waves shorter than the wavelengths of visible light and longer than

X-rays.

ulu *n* a traditional large knife used by the Inuit.

umbilical cord *n* the vascular tube connecting a foetus with the placenta through which oxygen and nutrients are passed.

umbrage *n* resentment; offence.

umbrella *n* a cloth-covered collapsible frame carried in the hand for protection from rain or sun; a general protection.

umiak *n* a large, open, flat-bottomed boat used by the Inuit.

umpire *n* an official who enforces the rules in sport; an arbiter.—*also vti.*

umpteen *adj* (*inf*) an undetermined large number.—**umpteenth** *adj.*

UN *abbr* = United Nations.

un- *prefix* not; opposite of; contrary to; reversal of an action or state.

unable *adj* not able; lacking the strength, skill, power or opportunity (to do something).

unanimous *adj* showing complete agreement.—**unanimity** *n.*—**unanimously** *adv.*

unassuming *adj* unpretentious; modest.

unattached *adj* unmarried, not engaged to be married; not belonging to a particular group, organization, etc.

unattended *adj* not supervised; not accompanied.

unauthorized *adj* not endorsed by authority.

unavoidable *adj* bound to happen, inevitable; necessary, compulsory.—**unavoidably** *adv.*

unaware *adj* not conscious or aware (of); ignorant (of).

unawares *adv* by surprise; unexpectedly, without warning.

unbalanced *adj* mentally unstable; having bias or over-representing a particular view, group, interest, etc; (*bookkeeping*) not having equal debit and credit totals.

unbeliever *n* a person who does not believe, esp in a religion.

unbending *adj* severe, stern; inflexible, unchanging; rigid in behaviour or attitude.

unbridled *adj* unrestrained; (*horse*) having no bridle.

unburden *vt* to reveal or confess one's troubles, secrets, etc to another in order to relieve the mind; to take off a burden.

uncalled-for *adj* unnecessary, unwanted, unwarranted.

uncanny *adj* (**uncannier, uncanniest**) odd; unexpected; suggestive of supernatural powers; unearthly.

uncertain *adj* not knowing accurately, doubtful; (*with* **of**) not confident or sure; not fixed, variable, changeable.—**uncertainty** *n.*

uncle *n* the brother of one's father or mother; the husband of one's aunt.

uncommon *adj* rare, unusual; extraordinary.

uncompromising *adj* not prepared to compromise; inflexible, obstinate.

unconditional *adj* without restrictions or conditions, absolute.

unconscious *adj* not aware (of); lacking normal perception by the senses, insensible; unintentional. * *n* the deepest level of mind containing feelings and emotions of which one is unaware and unable to control.—**unconsciously** *adv.*

uncouth *adj* lacking in manners; rough; rude.—**uncouthness** *n.*

unctuous *adj* oily; smarmy,; too suave; insincerely charming.—**unctuously** *adv.*—**unctuousness** *n.*

undaunted *adj* fearless; not discouraged.—**undauntedly** *adv.*

undecided *adj* doubtful, hesitant; (*solution, etc*) not determined.—**undecidedly** *adv.*

under *prep* lower than; beneath the surface of; below; covered by; subject to; less than, falling short of. * *adv* beneath, below, lower down. * *adj* lower in position, degree or rank; subordinate.

under- *prefix* beneath, below.

undercarriage *n* the landing gear of an aeroplane; a car's supporting framework.

underclothes *npl* underwear.—*also* **underclothing**.

undercoat *n* a coat of paint, etc, applied as a base below another; a growth of hair or fur under another; a coat worn under an overcoat.

undercover *adj* done or operating secretly.

undercurrent *n* a hidden current under water; an emotion, opinion, etc, not apparent.

undercut *vt* (*pt* **undercut**) to charge less than a competitor; to undermine.

underdog *n* the loser in an encounter, contest, etc; a person in an inferior position.

underdone *adj* not sufficiently or completely cooked.

underestimate *vti* to set too low an estimate on or for. * *n* too low an estimate.

underexpose *vt* (*photog*) to fail to expose (film) to light sufficiently long to produce a good image.—**underexposed** *adj.*—**underexposure** *n.*

underfoot *adv* underneath the foot or feet; on the ground.

undergo *vt* (*pt* **underwent**, *pp* **undergone**) to experience, suffer, endure.

undergraduate *n* a student at a college or university studying for a first degree.

underground *adj* situated under the surface of the ground; secret; of noncommercial newspapers, movies, etc that are unconventional, radical, etc. * *n* a secret group working for the overthrow of the government or the expulsion of occupying forces; an underground railway system; a subway.

undergrowth *n* shrubs, plants, etc growing beneath trees.

underhand *adv* (*sport*) with an underarm motion; underhandedly.

underhanded *adj* sly, secret, deceptive.—**underhandedly** *adv.*

underlie *vt* (*pr p* **underlying**, *pt* **underlay**, *pp* **underlain**) to be situated under; to form the basis of.

underline *vt* to put a line underneath; to emphasize.

underling *n* a person of inferior rank or status to someone else; a subordinate.

undermine *vt* to wear away, or weaken; to injure or weaken, esp by subtle or insidious means.

underneath adv under. * adj lower. * n the underside.—also prep.

underpants npl pants worn as an undergarment by men and boys.

underpass n a section of road running beneath another road, a railway, etc.

underprivileged adj lacking the basic rights of other members of society; poor.

underrate vt to undervalue, to underestimate.

underside n the lower surface.

underskirt n a woman's undergarment worn beneath the skirt, a petticoat.

understand vb (pt **understood**) vt to comprehend; to realize; to believe; to assume; to know thoroughly (eg a language); to accept; to be sympathetic with. * vi to comprehend; to believe.—**understandable** adj.

understanding n comprehension; compassion, sympathy; personal opinion, viewpoint; mutual agreement. * adj sympathetic.

understate vt to state something in restrained terms; to represent as less than is the case.—**understatement** n.

understudy vti to learn a role or part so as to be able to replace (the actor playing it); to act as an understudy (to).—also n

undertake vt (pt **undertook**, pp **undertaken**) to attempt to; to agree to; to commit oneself to; to promise; to guarantee.

undertaker n a funeral director.

undertaking n enterprise; task; promise; obligation.

underwater adj being, carried on under the surface of the water, esp the sea; submerged; below the water line of a vessel.—also adv.

underwear n garments worn underneath one's outer clothes, next to the skin.

underworld n criminals as an organized group; (myth) Hades.

undesirable adj not desirable; not pleasant; objectionable.—**undesirability** n.—**undesirably** adv.

undies npl (inf) women's underwear.

undo vt (pt **undid**, pp **undone**) to untie or unwrap; to reverse (what has been done); to bring ruin on.

undoubted adj without doubt; definite, certain.—**undoubtedly** adv.

undress vt to remove the clothes from. * vi to take off one's clothes.

undue adj improper; excessive.

unduly adv too; excessively; improperly.

unearth vt to dig up from the earth; to discover; to reveal.

unearthly adj mysterious; eerie; supernatural; absurd, unreasonable.

uneasy adj uncomfortable; restless; anxious; disquieting.—**uneasily** adv.—**uneasiness** n.

uneconomic adj wasteful; unprofitable.

unemployed adj not having a job, out of work.—**unemployment** n.

unerring adj sure, unfailing.

uneven adj not level or smooth; variable; not divisible by two without leaving a remainder.—**unevenness** n.

unexpected adj not looked for, unforeseen.—**unexpectedly** adv.

unfailing adj not failing or giving up; persistent; constant, dependable.—**unfailingly** adv.

unfair adj unjust; unequal; against the rules.—**unfairly** adv.—**unfairness** n.

unfaithful adj disloyal; not abiding by a promise; adulterous.—**unfaithfully** adv.—**unfaithfulness** n.

unfasten vt to open or become opened; to undo or become undone; to loose.

unfeeling adj callous, hardhearted.—**unfeelingly** adv.

unfinished adj not finished, incomplete; in the making; crude, sketchy.

unfit adj unsuitable; in bad physical condition.

unflappable adj (inf) calm, not easily agitated.

unfold vti to open or spread out; to become revealed; to develop.

unforeseen adj unsuspected.

unfortunate adj unlucky; disastrous; regrettable. * n an unlucky person.

unfortunately adv regrettably, unluckily, unhappily.

unfounded adj groundless; baseless.

ungainly adj (**ungainlier, ungainliest**) awkward; clumsy.—**ungainliness** n.

ungodly adj (**ungodlier, ungodliest**) not religious; sinful; wicked; (inf) outrageous.

unguarded adj without protection, vulnerable; open to attack; careless; candid, frank.—**unguardedly** adv.

unguent n a lubricant or ointment.

unhappy adj (**unhappier, unhappiest**) not happy or fortunate; sad; wretched; not suitable.—**unhappily** adv.—**unhappiness** n.

unhealthy adj (**unhealthier, unhealthiest**) not healthy or fit, sick; encouraging or resulting from poor health; harmful, degrading; dangerous.—**unhealthily** adv.—**unhealthiness** n.

unicorn n an imaginary creature with a body like a horse and a single horn on the forehead.

uniform adj unchanging in form; consistent; identical. * n the distinctive clothes worn by members of the same organization, such as soldiers, schoolchildren.—**uniformly** adv.

uniformity n the state of being consistent or the same; dullness, monotony.

unify vt to make into one; to unite.—**unification** n.

unilateral adj involving one only of several parties; not reciprocal.—**unilateralism** n.—**unilaterally** adv.

uninhibited adj not repressed or restrained; relaxed, spontaneous.—**uninhibitedly** adv.

union n the act of uniting; a combination of several things; a confederation of individuals or groups; marriage; a trades union.

unique adj without equal; the only one of its kind.—**uniquely** adv.

unison n accordance of sound, concord, harmony; **in unison** simultaneously; in agreement; in harmony.

unit n the smallest whole number, one; a single or whole entity; (measurement) a standard amount; an establishment or group of people who carry out a specific function; a piece of furniture fitting together with other pieces.—**unitary** *adj*.

unite *vti* to join into one, to combine; to be unified in purpose.

United Nations *n sing or pl* an international organization of nations for world peace and security formed in 1945.

United States *n* a federation of states, esp the United States of America.

unit trust *n* a company that manages a range of investments on behalf of members of the public whose interests are looked after by an independent trust.

unity *n* oneness; harmony; concord.

universal *adj* widespread; general; relating to all the world or the universe; relating to or applicable to all mankind.—**universally** *adv*.—**universality** *n*.

universe *n* all existing things; (*astron*) the totality of space, stars, planets and other forms of matter and energy; the world.

university *n* an institution of higher education which confers bachelors' and higher degrees; the campus or staff of a university.

unkempt *adj* uncombed; slovenly, dishevelled

unkind *adj* lacking in kindness or sympathy; harsh; cruel.—**unkindly** *adv*.—**unkindness** *n*.

unknown *adj* not known; not famous; not understood; with an unknown value. * *n* an unknown person or thing.

unleash *vt* to release from a leash; to free from restraint.

unless *conj* if not; except that.

unlikely *adj* improbable; unpromising.

unlimited *adj* without limits; boundless; not restricted.—**unlimitedly** *adv*.

unload *vti* to remove a load, discharge freight from a truck, ship, etc; to relieve of or express troubles, etc; to dispose of, dump; to empty, esp a gun.

unlock *vt* (*door, lock, etc*) to unfasten; to let loose; to reveal; to release.

unlucky *adj* (**unluckier, unluckiest**) not lucky, not fortunate; likely to bring misfortune; regrettable.—**unluckily** *adv*.

unmask *vti* to remove the mask from; to expose, show up.

unmitigated *adj* unqualified, absolute.

unnatural *adj* abnormal; contrary to nature; artificial; affected; strange; wicked.—**unnaturally** *adv*.

unpack *vti* (*suitcase, etc*) to remove the contents of; (*container, etc*) to take things out of; to unload.

unpleasant *adj* not pleasing or agreeable; nasty; objectionable.—**unpleasantly** *adv*.—**unpleasantness** *n*.

unpopular *adj* disliked; lacking general approval.—**unpopularity** *n*.

unprecedented *adj* having no precedent; unparalleled.

unpretentious *adj* modest, not boasting.

unqualified *adj* lacking recognized qualifications; not equal to; not restricted, complete.

unravel *vt* (*pt* **unravelled**) to disentangle; to solve.

unreasonable *adj* contrary to reason; lacking

reason; immoderate; excessive.—**unreasonably** *adv*.

unrelenting *adj* relentless; continuous.—**unrelentingly** *adv*.

unremitting *adj* incessant.

unrest *n* uneasiness; anxiety; angry discontent verging on revolt.

unroll *vti* to open out or down from a roll; to unfold; to straighten out; to reveal or become revealed.

unruly *adj* (**unrulier, unruliest**) hard to control, restrain, or keep in order; disobedient.

unsavory *adj* distasteful; disagreeable; offensive.

unscathed *adj* unharmed.

unscrew *vti* to remove a screw from; (*lid, etc*) to loosen by turning.

unscrupulous *adj* without principles.

unseemly *adj* unbecoming; inappropriate.

unsettled *adj* changeable; lacking stability; unpredictable; not concluded.

unsightly *adj* unattractive; ugly.

unskilled *adj* without special skill or training.

unspeakable *adj* bad beyond words, indescribable.

unsteady *adj* (**unsteadier, unsteadiest**) shaky, reeling; facillating.—**unsteadily** *adv*.

unthinkable *adj* inconceivable; out of the question; improbable.—**unthinkably** *adv*.

untidy *adj* (**untidier, untidiest**) not neat, disordered. * *vt* to make untidy.—**untidily** *adv*.

untie *vt* to undo a knot in, unfasten.

until *prep* up to the time of; before. * *conj* up to the time when or that; to the point, degree, etc that; before.

untimely *adj* premature; inopportune.

untold *adj* not told; too great to be counted; immeasurable.

untoward *adj* unseemly; unfavorable; adverse.

unusual *adj* uncommon; rare.

unveil *vt* to reveal; to disclose.

unwell *adj* ill, not well; (*inf*) suffering from a hangover.

unwieldy *adj* not easily moved or handled, as because of large size; awkward.—**unwieldily** *adv*.—**unwieldiness** *n*.

unwilling *adj* not willing, reluctant; said or done with reluctance.—**unwillingly** *adv*.—**unwillingness** *n*.

unwind *vt* to untangle; to undo. * *vi* to relax.

unwitting *adj* not knowing; unintentional.—**unwittingly** *adv*.

unworldly *adj* spiritual, not concerned with the material world.

unwritten *adj* not written or printed; traditional; oral.

up *adv* to, towards, in or on a higher place; to a later period; so as to be even with in time, degree, etc. * *prep* from a lower to a higher point on or along. * *adj* moving or directed upward; at an end; (*inf*) well-informed. * *vt* (*pt* **upped**) to raise; to increase; to take up. * *n* ascent; high point.

upalong *adv* (*Cdn*) in Newfoundland, to or on a distant location, esp to or on the mainland of Canada. * *n* such a location.

up-and-coming adj promising for the future; likely to succeed.

upbringing n the process of educating and nurturing (a child).

update vt to bring up to date.

upgrade vt to improve, raise to a higher grade.

upheaval n radical or violent change.

uphill adj ascending, rising; difficult, arduous. * adv up a slope or hill; against difficulties.

uphold vt (pt upheld) to support, sustain; to defend.

upholstery n materials used to make a soft covering esp for a seat.

upkeep n maintenance; the cost of it.

upon prep on, on top of.

upper adj farther up; higher in position, rank, status. * n the part of a boot or shoe above the sole; (sl) a drug used as a stimulant.—also **upmost**.

upper case n capital letters.—**upper-case** adj.

upper class n people occupying the highest social rank.—also adj.

upright adj vertical, in an erect position; righteous, honest, just. * n a vertical post or support. * adv vertically.

uprising n a revolt; a rebellion.

uproar n a noisy disturbance; a commotion; an outcry.

uproot vt to tear out by the roots; to remove from established surroundings.

upset[1] vt (pr p upsetting, pt upset) to overturn; to spill; to disturb; to put out of order; to distress; to overthrow; to make physically sick.

upset[2] n an unexpected defeat; distress or its cause. * adj distressed; confused; defeated.

upshot n the conclusion; the result.

upside down adj inverted; the wrong way up; (inf) topsy turvy.

upstairs adv up the stairs; to an upper level or storey. * n an upper floor.

upstart n a person who has suddenly risen to a position of wealth and power; an arrogant person.

up-to-date adj modern; fashionable.

upturn n an upward trend; an (economic) improvement. * vt to turn upside down.

upward, upwards adj from a lower to a higher place.—also adv.

uranium n a metallic element used as a source of nuclear energy.

urban adj of or relating to a city.—**urbanization** n.

urbane adj sophisticated; refined.—**urbanity** n.

urchin n a raggedly dressed mischievous child; a sea urchin.

urge vt to drive forward; to press, plead with. * n an impulse, yearning.

urgency n the quality or condition of being urgent; compelling need; importance.

urgent adj impelling; persistent; calling for immediate attention.—**urgently** adv.

urinate vi to pass urine.

urn n a vase or large vessel; a receptacle for preserving the ashes of the dead; a large metal container for boiling water for tea or coffee.

US abbr = United States.

us pron the objective case of **we**.

USA abbr = United States of America.

usage n customary use; practice, custom; use of language.

use[1] vt to put to some purpose; to utilize; to exploit (a person); to partake of (drink, drugs, tobacco, etc).

use[2] n act of using or putting to a purpose; usage; usefulness; need (for); advantage; practice, custom.—**usable, useable** adj.

used adj not new; second-hand.

useful adj able to be used to good effect; (inf) capable, commendable.—**usefully** adv.

useless adj of no use.—**uselessly** adv.—**uselessness** n.

usher n one who shows people to their seats in a theatre, church, etc; a doorkeeper in a law court. * vt to escort to seats, etc.

USSR abbr = (formerly) Union of Soviet Socialist Republics.

usual adj customary; ordinary; normal.—**usually** adv.

usurer n a person who lends money at an excessively high rate of interest.

usurp vt to seize or appropriate unlawfully.—**usurper** n.

utensil n an implement or container, esp one for use in the kitchen.

uterus n (pl uteri) the womb.—**uterine** adj.

utilitarian adj designed to be of practical use.

utility n usefulness; a public service, such as telephone, electricity, etc; a company providing such a service.

utilize vt to make practical use of.—**utilization** n.

utmost adj of the greatest degree or amount; furthest. * n the most possible.

utter[1] adj absolute; complete.

utter[2] vt to say; to speak.—**utterance** n.

V

V abbr = volt(s).

v abbr = velocity; versus against; vide see; verb.

vacancy n emptiness; an unoccupied job or position.

vacant adj empty; unoccupied; (expression) blank.—**vacantly** adv.

vacate vt to leave empty; to give up possession of.

vacation n a holiday; a period of the year when universities, colleges and law courts are closed. * vi to go on holiday.—**vacationer** n.

vacation pay n (Cdn) the wages to which an employee is legally entitled to receive as a paid vacation, or a sum of money equivalent to it.

vaccinate vt to inoculate with vaccine as a protection against a disease.—**vaccination** n.

vaccine n a preparation used for inoculation to give immunity from certain diseases.

vacuum *n* (*pl* **vacuums**) a region devoid of all matter; a region in which gas is present at low pressure; a vacuum cleaner. * *vt* to clean with a vacuum cleaner.

vacuum cleaner *n* an electrical appliance for removing dust from carpets, etc, by suction.

vacuum flask *n* a container for keeping liquids hot or cold.

vagina *n* in female mammals and humans, the canal connecting the uterus and the external sex organs.—**vaginal** *adj*.

vagrant *n* a person who has no settled home, a tramp.—**vagrancy**.

vague *adj* unclear; indistinct, imprecise; (*person*) absent-minded.—**vaguely** *adv*.—**vagueness** *n*.

vain *adj* conceited; excessively concerned with one's appearance; senseless; worthless.—**vainly** *adv*.

valentine *n* a lover or sweetheart chosen on St Valentine's Day, 14th February; a card or gift sent on that day.

valiant *adj* courageous; brave.—**valiantly** *adv*.

valid *adj* based on facts; (*objection, etc*) sound; legally acceptable; binding.—**validity** *n*.—**validly** *adv*.

valley *n* (*pl* **valleys**) low land between hills or mountains.

valuable *adj* having considerable importance or monetary worth. * *n* a personal possession of value, esp jewellery; (*pl*) valuable possessions.

valuation *n* the act of valuing; an estimated price or worth; an estimation.—**valuator** *n*.

value *n* worth, merit, importance; market value; purchasing power; relative worth; (*pl*) moral principles. * *vt* to estimate the worth of; to regard highly; to prize.—**valued** *adj*.—**valuer** *n*.

value added tax *n* a tax levied on the difference between the production cost of an item and its selling price.

valve *n* a device for controlling the flow of a gas or liquid through a pipe; (*anat*) a tube allowing blood to flow in one direction only.

van *n* a covered motor vehicle for transporting goods, etc.

Vancouverite *n* a person who lives in or is from Vancouver, British Columbia.

vandal *n* a person who wilfully damages property.—**vandalism** *n*.—**vandalize** *vt*.

vanguard *n* the front part of an army; the leading position of any movement.

vanilla *n* extract from the orchid pod used as a flavoring.

vanish *vi* to disappear; to fade away.

vanity *n* conceit; worthlessness; something worthless.

vanity case, vanity box *n* a small case used for carrying cosmetics, etc.

vantage *n* a favorable position; a position allowing a clear view or understanding.

vapour, vapor (*US*) *n* the gaseous state of a substance normally liquid or solid; particles of water or smoke in the air.

variable *adj* liable to change; not constant. * *n*

(*math*) a quantity that varies.—**variability** *n*.

variance *n* discrepancy.

variant *n* a different form.—*also adj*.

variation *n* diversity; deviation; modification.

varicose *adj* (*veins*) abnormally swollen and dilated.

variety *n* diversity; an assortment.

variety show *n* an entertainment made up of various acts, such as songs, comedy turns, etc.

various *adj* varied, different; several.—**variously** *adv*.

varnish *n* a sticky liquid which dries and forms a hard, glossy coating. * *vt* to coat with varnish.

vary *vti* to change, to diversify, modify; to become altered.

vase *n* a vessel for displaying flowers.

vast *adj* immense.—**vastly** *adv*.—*n* **vastness**.

VAT *abbr* = value added tax.

vat *n* a large barrel or tank.

Vatican *n* the residence of the pope in Rome; papal authority.

vault[1] *n* an arched ceiling or roof; a burial chamber; a strongroom for valuables; a cellar.—**vaulted** *adj*.

vault[2] *vti* to leap or jump over an obstacle.—*also n*.

VD *abbr* = venereal disease.

veal *n* the edible flesh of a calf.

veer *vi* (*wind*) to change direction; to swing around; to change from one mood or opinion to another.

vegetable *n* a herbaceous plant grown for food; (*inf*) a person who has suffered brain damage.—*also adj*.

vegetarian *n* a person who consumes a diet that excludes meat and fish. —*also adj*.—**vegetarianism** *n*.

vegetate *vi* to grow like a plant; to sprout; to lead a mentally inactive, aimless life.

vegetation *n* vegetable growth; plants in general.

vehement *adj* passionate; forceful; furious.—**vehemence** *n*.

vehicle *n* a conveyance, such as a car, bus or truck, for carrying people or goods; a medium.—**vehicular** *adj*.

veil *n* a thin fabric worn over the head or face of a woman; a nun's headdress; anything that conceals. * *vt* to put on a veil; to cover; to conceal.

vein *n* one of the vessels that convey the blood back to the heart; a seam of mineral within a rock; a branching rib in a leaf; a streak of different color; a style or mood. * *vt* to streak.

velocity *n* speed.

velvet *n* a fabric made from silk, rayon, etc with a soft, thick pile; anything like velvet in texture.

vending machine *n* a coin-operated machine which dispenses goods.

vendor, vender *n* a person selling something.

veneer *n* an overlay of fine wood or plastic; a superficial appearance. * *vt* to cover with veneer.

venerable *adj* worthy of reverence or respect.

venereal *adj* (*disease*) resulting from sexual intercourse.

Venetian blind *n* a window blind formed of long thin horizontal slips of wood that can be pivoted.

vengeance *n* the act of taking revenge; retribution.—**vengeful** *adj*.

venison *n* the edible flesh of the deer.

venom *n* poison; spite, malice.—**venomous** *adj*.

vent *n* a small opening or slit; an outlet or flue for the escape of fumes. * *vt* to release; (*temper*) to give expression to.

ventilate *vt* to supply with fresh air; to express, to discuss.

ventilation *n* the act of ventilating; the state of being ventilated; free discussion. .

ventilator *n* an appliance for ventilating a room, etc.

ventriloquism *n* the act or art of speaking so that the sounds appear to come from a source other than the actual speaker.

venture *n* a dangerous expedition; a risky undertaking. * *vti* to risk; to dare.—**venturesome** *adj*.

venue *n* the place of an action or event.

veranda, verandah *n* a roofed porch, supported by light pillars.

verb *n* (*gram*) the part of speech that expresses an action, a process, state or condition or mode of being.

verbal *adj* spoken; literal; pertaining to or characteristic of a verb.—**verbally** *adv*.

verbiage *n* use of too many words.

verbose *adj* wordy.

verdict *n* the decision of a jury at the end of a trial; decision, judgment.

verge *n* the brink; the extreme edge or margin; a grass border beside a road. * *vi* to border (on).

verger *n* a church official.

verify *vt* to confirm the truth of; to substantiate.—**verifiable** *adj*.—**verification** *n*.

vermin *n* (*used as pl*) pests, such as insects and rodents; persons dangerous to society.—**verminous** *adj*.

vermouth *n* a white wine flavored with herbs, used in cocktails and as an aperitif.

vernacular *n* the commonly spoken language or dialect of a country or region. * *adj* native.

versatile *adj* changeable, adaptable; able to move or turn freely.—**versatility** *n*.

verse *n* a line of poetry; a stanza of a poem; a short section of a chapter in the Bible.

versed *adj* skilled or learned in a subject.

version *n* a translation from one language into another; a particular account or description.

versus *prep* against; in contrast to.

vertebra *n* (*pl* **vertebrae, vertebras**) one of the interconnecting bones of the spinal column.

vertebrate *n* an animal with a backbone.

vertical *adj* perpendicular to the horizon; upright. * *n* a vertical line or plane.

vertigo *n* a sensation of dizziness and sickness caused by a disorder of the sense of balance.—**vertiginous** *adj*.

verve *n* enthusiasm; liveliness; energy.

very *adj* complete; absolute; same. * *adv* extremely; truly; really.

vespers *npl* (*used as sing*) an Anglican service held daily in the evening.

vessel *n* a container; a ship or boat; a tube in the body along which fluids pass.

vest *n* a sleeveless undergarment; a waistcoat. * *vt* to place or settle (power, authority, etc.); to confer.

vested interest *n* a strong reason for acting in a certain way, usu for personal gain.

vestibule *n* an entrance hall or lobby.

vestige *n* a hint; a trace.

vestry *n* a room in a church where vestments, etc, are kept and parochial meetings held; a meeting for parish business.

vet *n* a veterinary surgeon. * *vt* (*pt* **vetted**) to examine, check for errors, etc.

veteran *adj* old, experienced; having served in the armed forces. * *n* a person who has served in the armed forces; a person who has given long service in a particular activity.

veterinary surgeon *n* a person trained in treating sick or injured animals.—*also* **veterinarian**.

veto *n* (*pl* **vetoes**) the right of a person or group to prohibit an action or legislation; a prohibition. * *vt* to refuse to agree to; to prohibit.

vex *vt* to annoy; to puzzle, confuse.—**vexation** *n*.

VHF *abbr* = very high frequency.

via *prep* by way of.

viable *adj* capable of growing or developing; workable; practicable.—**viability** *n*.

viaduct *n* a road or railway carried by a bridge with arches over a valley, river, etc.

vibrate *vti* to shake; to move quickly backwards and forwards; to quiver; to oscillate.—**vibration** *n*.—**vibratory** *adj*.

vicar *n* a parish priest; a clergyman in charge of a chapel.

vice[1] *n* an evil action or habit.

vice[2], **vise** (*US*) *n* a clamping device with jaws, used for holding objects firmly.

vice- *prefix* who acts in place of, or as a deputy to, another.

vice versa *adv* conversely; the other way round.

vicinity *n* a nearby area; proximity.

vicious *adj* cruel; violent; malicious; ferocious.—**viciously** *adv*.

vicissitudes *npl* ups and downs; successive changes of fortune.

victim *n* a person who has been killed or injured by an action beyond his or her control; a dupe.

victimize *vt* to make a victim.—**victimization** *n*.

victor *n* a winner; a conqueror.

Victoria Day *n* (*Cdn*) a public holiday celebrated on the Monday on or preceding May 25.

Victorian *adj* of or living in the reign of Queen Victoria; old-fashioned, prudish.

victorious *adj* having won in battle or contest; emblematic of victory; triumphant.—**victoriously** *adv*.

victory *n* triumph in battle; success; achievement.

video *n* (*pl* **videos**) the transmission or recording of television programmes or films, using a television set and a video recorder and tape. * *vt* to record on video tape.

video recorder *n* the machine that plays or records on video tape.

video tape *n* a magnetic tape on which images and sounds can be recorded for reproduction on television.—**video-tape** *vt*.

vie *vi* (*pr p* **vying**, *pt* **vied**) to contend or strive for superiority.

view *n* sight; range of vision; inspection, examination; intention; scene; opinion. * *vt* to see; to consider; to examine intellectually.

viewer *n* a person who views, esp television; an optical device used in viewing.

viewfinder *n* a device in a camera showing the view to be photographed.

viewpoint *n* opinion; a place from which something can be viewed, esp a scenic panorama.

vigil *n* keeping watch at night.

vigilance *n* watchfulness; alertness.—**vigilant** *adj*.

vigour, vigor (*US*) *n* physical or mental strength; vitality.—**vigorous** *adj*.—**vigorously** *adv*.

vile *adj* wicked; evil; offensive; very bad.

villa *n* a large country or suburban house.

village *n* a collection of houses smaller than a town.

villager *n* an inhabitant of a village.

villain *n* a scoundrel; the main evil character in a play, film or novel.—**villainous** *adj*.

vindicate *vt* to justify; to absolve from blame.—**vindication** *n*.—**vindicator** *n*.

vindictive *adj* vengeful; spiteful.—**vindictiveness** *n*.

vine *n* any climbing plant, or its stem; a grapevine.

vinegar *n* a sour-tasting liquid containing acetic acid, used as a condiment and preservative.

vineyard *n* a plantation of grapevines.

vintage *n* the grape harvest of one season; wine, esp of good quality made in a particular year; wine of a particular region; the product of a particular period. * *adj* (*cars*) classic; (*wine*) of a specified year and of good quality; (*play*) characteristic of the best.

vinyl *n* a strong plastic used in floor coverings, furniture, records, etc.

viola *n* a stringed instrument of the violin family, and tuned a fifth below it.

violate *vt* to break or infringe (an agreement); to rape; to disturb (one's privacy).

violence *n* physical force intended to cause injury or destruction; natural force; passion, intensity.

violent *adj* urged or driven by force; vehement; impetuous; forcible; furious; severe.—**violently** *adv*.

violet *n* a small plant with bluish-purple flowers; a bluish-purple color.

violin *n* a four-stringed musical instrument, played with a bow.

violinist *n* a person who plays the violin.

VIP *abbr* = Very Important Person.

viper *n* a common European venomous snake.

virgin *n* a person (esp a woman) who has never had sexual intercourse. * *adj* chaste; pure; untouched.—**virginal** *adj*.

virginity *n* the state of being a virgin; the state of being chaste, untouched, etc.

Virgo *n* the Virgin, the 6th sign of the zodiac.

virile *adj* manly; sexually potent.—**virility** *n*.

virtual *adj* in effect or essence, though not in fact or strict definition.—**virtually** *adv*.

virtue *n* moral excellence; any admirable quality; chastity; merit.

virtuoso *n* (*pl* **virtuosi, virtuosos**) a person highly skilled in an activity, esp in playing a musical instrument.—*also adj*.—**virtuosity** *n*.

virtuous *adj* righteous; upright; pure.—**virtuously** *adv*.

virus *n* (*pl* **viruses**) a very simple microorganism capable of replicating within living cells, producing disease; the disease caused by a virus; a harmful influence.

visa *n* an endorsement on a passport allowing the bearer to travel in the country of the government issuing it.

vis-à-vis *prep* opposite to; in face of. * *adv* facing.

viscount *n* in UK, a title of nobility next below an earl.—**viscountess** *nf*.

visibility *n* clearness of seeing or being seen.

visible *adj* that may be seen; evident.

vision *n* the power of seeing, sight; a supernatural appearance; foresight; imagination.

visionary *adj* imaginative; having foresight; existing in imagination only, not real. * *n* an imaginative person.

visit *vt* to go to see; to pay a call upon a person or place; to punish or reward with. * *vi* to see or meet someone regularly. * *n* act of going to see.

visiting card *n* a small card with the name left when paying visits.

visitor *n* a person who visits; a caller.

visor *n* a movable part of a helmet protecting the face; the peak of a cap.

vista *n* a view, as from a high place; a mental picture.

visual *adj* relating to vision or sight; visible.

visual aid *n* a film, slide or overhead projector, etc used to aid teaching.

visualize *vt* to form a mental picture of.—**visualization** *n*.

vital *adj* necessary to life; essential; lively.—**vitally** *adv*.

vitality *n* vigour; spirits; animation.

vitamin *n* organic substance, occurring naturally in foods, which is essential for good health.

vivacious *adj* lively; animated; spirited.—**vivacity** *n*.

vivid *adj* brightly colored; graphic; lively; intense.—**vividly** *adv*.

vivisection *n* the practice of performing surgical operations on living animals for scientific research.

vocabulary *n* an alphabetical list of words with their meanings; the words of a language; an individual's use of particular words.

vocal *adj* relating to the voice; outspoken, noisy; (*phonetics*) having a vowel function.—**vocally** *adv*.

vocalist *n* a singer.

vocation *n* calling to a particular career or occupation.— **vocational** *adj*.

vociferous *adj* clamorous, noisy.—**vociferously** *adv*.

vodka *n* a spirit distilled from rye.

vogue *n* the fashion at a specified time; popularity.

voice *n* sound from the mouth; sound produced by speaking or singing; expressed opinion; the relation between a verb and its subject. * *vt* to express; to speak.

void *adj* unoccupied, empty; not legally binding. * *n* an empty space; a vacuum. * *vt* to empty; to make invalid.

volatile *adj* evaporating very quickly.

volcano *n* (*pl* **volcanoes, volcanos**) a hill or mountain formed by ejection of lava, ashes, etc through an opening in the earth's crust.— **volcanic** *adj*.

volition *n* the exercise of the will; choice.

volley *n* (*pl* **volleys**) the multiple discharge of many missiles or small arms; a barrage; (*tennis, volleyball*) the return of the ball before it reaches the ground. * *vt* to return (a ball) before it hits the ground.

volleyball *n* a team game played by hitting a large inflated ball over a net with the hands; the ball used.

volt *n* the unit of measure of the force of an electrical current.

voltage *n* electrical force measured in volts.

volume *n* the amount of space occupied by an object; quantity; amount; intensity of sound; a book; one book of a series.

voluntary *adj* acting by choice; willing; brought about by free will; without remuneration.— **voluntarily** *adv*.

volunteer *n* a person who carries out work voluntarily; a person who freely undertakes military service.—*also vti*.

voluptuous *adj* excessively fond of pleasure; having an attractive figure.

vomit *vi* (*pt* **vomited**) to eject the contents of the stomach through the mouth, to spew. * *n* matter ejected from the stomach when vomiting.

vote *n* an indication of a choice or opinion as to a matter on which one has a right to be consulted; a ballot; decision by a majority; the right to vote; franchise. * *vi* to cast one's vote. * *vt* to elect.—**voter** *n*.

vouch *vt* to provide evidence or proof of. * *vi* to give assurance; to guarantee.

voucher *n* a written record of a transaction; a receipt; a token that can be exchanged for something else.

vow *n* a solemn or binding promise. * *vt* to promise; to resolve.

vowel *n* an open speech sound produced by continuous passage of the breath; a letter representing such a sound, as *a, e, i, o, u*.

voyage *n* a long journey, esp by ship or spacecraft. * *vi* to journey.—**voyager** *n*.

voyageur *n* (*Cdn*) (*hist*) a French-speaking paddler of a canoe employed to transport goods to and from trading posts in the interior of the country.

vulgar *adj* common; coarse; offensive; vernacular.—**vulgarly** *adv*.

vulnerable *adj* capable of being wounded physically or mentally; open to persuasion; easily influenced.—**vulnerability** *n*.

vulture *n* a large bird of prey having no feathers on the neck or head.

W

wad *n* a small, soft mass, as of cotton or paper; a bundle of paper money.

wade *vti* to walk through water; to pass (through) with difficulty.

wader *n* a bird that wades, eg the heron.

waferboard *n* (*Cdn*) a rigid sheet or panel composed of wood chips.

waffle[1] *n* a thick, crisp pancake baked in a waffle iron.

waffle[2] *vi* (*inf*) to speak or write at length without saying anything substantial.

waft *vt* to drift or float through the air. * *n* a breath, scent or sound carried through the air.

wag[1] *vti* (*pt* **wagged**) to move rapidly from side to side or up and down (as of a finger, tail).— *also n*.

wag[2] *n* a joker, a wit.

wage *vt* to carry on, esp war. * *n* (*often pl*) payment for work or services.

wager *n* a bet. * *vti* to bet.

waggle *vti* to wag.—*also n*.

wagon, waggon *n* a four-wheeled vehicle pulled by a horse or tractor, for carrying heavy goods.

wail *vi* to make a long, loud cry of sorrow or grief; to howl, to moan.—*also n*.

waist *n* the narrowest part of the human trunk, between the ribs and the hips; the narrow part of anything that is wider at the ends; the part of a garment covering the waist.

waistcoat *n* a waist-length, sleeveless garment worn immediately under a suit jacket; a vest.

waistline *n* the narrowest part of the waist; its measurement; the seam that joins the bodice and skirt of a dress, etc; the level of this.

wait *vti* to stay, or to be, in expectation or readiness; to defer or to be postponed; to remain; (*with* **at** *or* **on**) to serve food at a meal. * *n* act or period of waiting.

waiter *n* a man or woman who serves at table, as in a restaurant.—**waitress** *nf*.

waiting list *n* a list of people applying for or waiting to obtain something.

waiting room *n* a room for people to wait in at a station, hospital, etc.

waive *vt* to refrain from enforcing; to relinquish voluntarily.

wake[1] *vb* (*pt* **woke** *or* **waked,** *pp* **woken** *or* **waked**) *vi* to emerge from sleep; to become awake. * *vt* to rouse from sleep. * *n* a watch or vigil beside a corpse, on the eve of the burial.—**wakeful** *adj.*—**waken** *vti.*

wake[2] *n* the waves or foamy water left in the track of a ship; a trail.

walk *vi* to travel on foot with alternate steps. * *vt* to pass through or over; (*a dog*) to exercise; to escort on foot. * *n* the act of walking; distance walked over; gait; a ramble or stroll; a profession.—**walker** *n.*

walkie-talkie *n* a portable two-way radio transmitter and receiver.

walking stick *n* a stick used in walking, a cane.

walkover *n* an unopposed or easy victory; a horse race with only one starter.

wall *n* a vertical structure of brick, stone, etc for enclosing, dividing or protecting. * *vt* to enclose with a wall; to close up with a wall.

wallet *n* a flat pocketbook for paper money, cards etc.

walleye *n* a large North American freshwater fish with prominent eyes.

wallflower *n* a fragrant plant with red or yellow flowers; a person who does not dance for lack of a partner.

wallop *vt* (*pt* **walloped**) (*inf*) to beat or defeat soundly; (*inf*) to strike hard. * *n* (*inf*) a hard blow.

wallow *vi* (*animal*) to roll about in mud; to indulge oneself in emotion.—*also n.*

wallpaper *n* decorated paper for covering the walls of a room.

walnut *n* a tree producing an edible nut with a round shell and wrinkled seed; its nut; its wood used for furniture.

walrus *n* (*pl* **walruses, walrus**) a large, thick-skinned aquatic animal, related to the seals, having long canine teeth and coarse whiskers.

waltz *n* a piece of music with three beats to the bar; a whirling or slowly circling dance. * *vti* to dance a waltz; to lead (someone) in waltz time.

wan *adj* (**wanner, wannest**) pale and sickly; feeble or weak.—**wanly** *adv.*—**wanness** *n.*

wand *n* a magician's rod.

wander *vi* to ramble with no definite destination; to go astray; to lose concentration.—*also n.*

wane *vi* to decrease, esp of the moon; to decline. * *n* decrease, decline.

want *n* lack; poverty. * *vt* to need; to require; to lack; to wish (for).

wanted *adj* sought after.

wanting *adj* lacking.

wanton *adj* malicious; wilful; sexually provocative.

war *n* military conflict between nations or parties; a conflict; a contest. * *vi* (*pt* **warred**) to make war.

ward *n* a section of a hospital; an electoral district; a division of a prison; a child placed under the supervision of a court.—**wardship** *n.*

warden *n* an official; a person in charge of a building or home; a prison governor;

warder *n* a prison officer.

wardrobe *n* a cupboard for clothes; one's clothes.

ware *n* (*pl*) merchandise, goods for sale; pottery.

warehouse *n* a building for storing goods.

warfare *n* armed hostilities; conflict.

warhead *n* the section of a missile containing the explosive.

warlike *adj* hostile.

warm *adj* moderately hot; friendly, kind; (*colors*) rich; enthusiastic. * *vt* to make warm. * *vi* to become enthusiastic (about). —**warmly** *adv.*—**warmth** *n.*

warm-hearted *adj* kind, sympathetic; affectionate.

warn *vt* to notify of danger; to caution or advise (against).—**warning** *n.*

warp *vti* to twist out of shape; to distort; to corrupt. * *n* the threads arranged lengthwise on a loom across which other threads are passed.

warrant *vt* to guarantee; to justify. * *n* a document giving authorization; a writ for arrest.

warranty *n* a pledge to replace something if it is not as represented, a guarantee.

warrior *n* a soldier, fighter.

warship *n* a ship equipped for war.

wart *n* a small, hard projection on the skin.— **warty** *adj.*

wartime *adj, n* (of) a period or time of war.

wary *adj* (**warier, wariest**) watchful; cautious.— **warily** *adv.*—**wariness** *n.*

was *see* **be.**

wash *vti* to cleanse with water and soap; to flow against or over; to sweep along by the action of water; to separate gold, etc, from earth by washing; to cover with a thin coat of metal or paint. * *n* a washing; the break of waves on the shore; the waves left behind by a boat; a liquid used for washing.

washbasin, washbowl *n* a basin or bowl, esp a bathroom fixture, for use in washing one's hands, etc.—*also* **wash-hand basin.**

washed-out *adj* faded; limp; exhausted.

washer *n* a flat ring of metal, rubber, etc, to give tightness to joints; a washing machine.

washing *n* the act of cleansing with water; a number of items washed together.

washing machine *n* a device for washing clothes.

washroom *n* cloakroom, lavatory.

wasp *n* a winged insect with a black and yellow striped body, which can sting.

wastage *n* anything lost by use or natural decay; wasteful or avoidable loss of something valuable.

waste *adj* useless; left over; uncultivated or uninhabited. * *vt* to ravage; to squander; to use foolishly; to fail to use. * *vi* to lose strength, etc as by disease. * n uncultivated or uninhabited land; discarded material, garbage, excrement.—**wasteful** adj.—**wastefully** adv.—**wastefulness** n.

watch n surveillance; close observation; vigil; guard; a small timepiece worn on the wrist, etc; (naut) a period of duty. * vi to look with attention; to wait for; to keep vigil. * vt to keep one's eyes fixed on; to guard; to tend; to observe closely; (chance, etc) to wait for.—**watcher** n.—**watchful** adj.—**watchfully** adv.—**watchfulness** n.

watchdog n a dog that guards property; a person or group that monitors safety, standards, etc.

watchmaker n a person who makes and repairs watches.

water n the substance H2O, a clear, thin liquid, lacking taste or smell, and essential for life; any body of it, as the ocean, a lake, river, etc; bodily secretions such as tears, urine. * vt to moisten with water; to irrigate; to dilute with water. * vi (eyes) to smart; to salivate; to take in water.

water bomber n (Cdn) an aircraft used to drop water on a forest fire.

water-closet n a lavatory.

watercolor n a water-soluble paint; a picture painted with watercolors.

watercress n a plant growing in ponds and streams, used in a salad.

waterfall n a fall of water over a precipice or down a hill.

watering can n a container with a spout for watering plants.

water line n a line up to which a ship's hull is submerged.

waterlogged adj soaked or saturated with water.

water main n a main pipe or conduit for carrying water.

watermark n a line marking the height to which water has risen; a mark impressed on paper which can only be seen when held up to the light.

watermelon n a large fruit with a hard green rind and edible red watery flesh.

waterproof adj impervious to water; watertight.—also vt.

watershed n a turning point.

water-skiing n the sport of planing on water by being towed by a motorboat—**water-skier** n.

watertight adj not allowing water to pass through; foolproof.

waterworks n (as sing) an establishment that supplies water to a district; (pl: inf) the urinary system; (inf) tears.

watt n a unit of electrical power.

wave n an undulation travelling on the surface of water; the form in which light and sound are thought to travel; an increase or upsurge (eg of crime); a hair curl; a movement of the hand in greeting or farewell. * vti to move freely backward and forward; to flutter; to undulate; to move the hand to and fro in greeting, farewell, etc.—**wavy** adj.

wavelength n the distance between the crests of

successive waves of light or sound; radio frequency.

waver vi to hesitate; to falter.—**waverer** n.

wax[1] n beeswax; an oily substance used to make candles, polish, etc. * vt to rub, polish, cover or treat with wax.

wax[2] vi to increase in strength, size, etc.

waxwork n a figure or model formed of wax; (pl) an exhibition of such figures.

way n path, route; road; distance; room to advance; direction; state; means; possibility; manner of living; (pl) habits.

waylay vt (pt **waylaid**) to lie in wait for; to accost.

wayward adj wilful, stubborn; unpredictable.—**waywardness** n.

WC abbr = water-closet.

WCB abbr (Cdn) = Workers' Compensation Board.

we pron pl of I; I and others.

weak adj lacking power or strength; feeble; ineffectual.—**weakness** n.

weaken vti to make or grow weaker.

weakling n a person who lacks strength of character.

wealth n a large amount of possessions or money; affluence; an abundance (of).—**wealthy** adj.

wean vt (baby, animal) to replace the mother's milk with other nourishment; to dissuade (from indulging a habit).

weapon n any instrument used in fighting.

wear vb (pt **wore**, pp **worn**) vt to have on the body as clothing; (hair, etc) to arrange in a particular way; to display; to rub away; to impair by use; to exhaust, tire. * vi to be impaired by use or time; to be spent tediously. * n deterioration from frequent use; articles worn.—**wearer** n.

weary adj (**wearier**, **weariest**) tired; bored. * vti to make or become tired.—**weariness** n.—**wearisome** adj.

weasel n a small carnivorous animal with a long slender body and reddish fur.

weather n atmospheric conditions, such as temperature, rainfall, cloudiness, etc. * vt to expose to the action of the weather; to survive. * vi to withstand the weather.

weathercock n a weather vane in the form of a cock to show the wind direction.

weave vb (pt **wove**, pp **woven**) vt to interlace threads in a loom to form fabric; to construct. * vi to make a way through (eg a crowd), to zigzag.—**weaver** n.

web n a woven fabric; the network of fine threads spun by a spider; the membrane joining the digits of birds and animals.

webbed adj (ducks, etc) having the digits connected by a fold of skin.

wed vti (pt **wedded** or **wed**) to marry; to join closely.

wedding n marriage; the ceremony of marriage.

wedge n a v-shaped block of wood or metal for splitting or fastening; a wedge-shaped object. * vti to split or secure with a wedge; to thrust (in) tightly; to become fixed tightly.

wedlock n marriage.

Wednesday n fourth day of the week, between Tuesday and Thursday.

wee adj small, tiny.

weed n any undesired plant, esp one that crowds out desired plants; (sl) marijuana. * vt to remove weeds or anything troublesome.

weedkiller n a chemical or hormonal substance used to kill weeds.

week n the period of seven consecutive days, esp from Sunday to Sunday.

weekday n a day of the week other than Saturday or Sunday.

weekend n the period from Friday night to Sunday night—also adv.

weekly adj happening once a week or every week.

weep vti (pt **wept**) to shed tears, to cry; (wound) to ooze.—**weepy** adj.

weigh vt to measure the weight of; to consider carefully. * vi to have weight; to be burdensome.

weight n the amount which anything weighs; influence; any unit of heaviness. * vt to attach a weight to.

weightlessness n the state of having no or little reaction to gravity, esp in space travel.

weightlifting n the sport of lifting weights of a specific amount in a particular way.—**weightlifter** n.

weighty adj (**weightier, weightiest**) heavy; serious.—**weightily** adv.

weir n a low dam across a river which controls the flow of water.

weird adj unearthly, mysterious; eerie; bizarre.—**weirdly** adv.

welcome adj gladly received; pleasing. * n reception of a person or thing. * vt to greet kindly.

welch see **welsh**.

weld vt to unite, as metal by heating until fused or soft enough to hammer together; to join closely. * n a welded joint.

welfare n wellbeing; health; assistance or financial aid granted to the poor, the unemployed, etc.

well[1] n a spring; a hole bored in the ground to provide a source of water, oil, gas, etc; the open space in the middle of a staircase. * vi to pour forth.

well[2] adj (**better, best**) agreeable; comfortable; in good health. * adv in a proper, satisfactory, or excellent manner; thoroughly; prosperously; with good reason; to a considerable degree; fully. * interj an expression of surprise, etc.

well-heeled adj (inf) wealthy.

wellies npl (sl) wellingtons.

wellington (boot) n a rubber, waterproof boot.

well-off adj in comfortable circumstances; prosperous.

well-to-do adj prosperous.

Welsh adj relating to the people of Wales or their language.—also n.

welsh vti to avoid paying a gambling debt; to run off without paying.—also **welch.**—**welsher, welcher** n.

went see **go**.

wept see **weep**.

were see **be**.

we're = we are.

weren't = were not.

west n the direction of the sun at sunset; one of the four points of the compass; the region in the west of any country; (with cap) Europe and the Western Hemisphere. * adj situated in, or toward the west. * adv in or to the west.

westerly adj towards the west; blowing from the west. * n a wind blowing from the west.—also adv.

western adj of or in the west. * n a film, novel, etc about the usu pre-20th century American West.

Western Canadian n a person who lives in or is from Manitoba, or one of the provinces west of it. * adj of or pertaining to such a person.

westward adj towards the west.—also adv.

wet adj (**wetter, wettest**) covered or saturated with water or other liquid; rainy; misty; not yet dry. * n water or other liquid; rain or rainy weather. * vti (pt **wet** or **wetted**) to soak; to moisten.—**wetness** n.

wet suit n a close-fitting suit worn by divers, etc, to retain body heat.

whack vti (inf) to strike sharply, esp making a sound. * n (inf) a sharp blow.

whale n a very large sea mammal that breathes through a blowhole, and resembles a fish in shape. * vi to hunt whales.

wharf n (pl **wharfs, wharves**) a platform for loading and unloading ships in harbour.

what adj of what sort, how much, how great. * relative pron that which; as much or many as. * interj used as an expression of surprise or astonishment.

whatever pron anything that; no matter what.

whatsoever adj whatever.

wheat n a cereal grain usu ground into flour for bread.

wheat pool n (Cdn) a farmer's cooperative in western Canada for the sale of wheat and other cereal crops.

wheel n a solid disc or circular rim turning on an axle; a steering wheel; (pl) the moving forces. * vt to transport on wheels. * vi to turn round or on an axis; to move in a circular direction, as a bird.

wheelbarrow n a cart with one wheel in front and two handles and legs at the rear.

wheelchair n a chair with large wheels for invalids.

wheeze vi to breathe with a rasping sound; to breathe with difficulty.—also n.

when adv at what or which time * conj at the time at which; although; relative pron at which.

where adv at which or what place; to which place; from what source; relative pron in or to which.

whereabouts *adv* near or at what place; about where. * *n* approximate location.

whereas *conj* since; on the contrary.

wherever *adv* at or to whatever place.

whet *vt* (*pt* **whetted**) to sharpen by rubbing, to stimulate.

whether *conj* introducing an alternative possibility or condition.

which *adj* what one (of). * *pron* which person or thing; that. * *relative pron* person or thing referred to.

whichever *pron* whatever one that; whether one or the other; no matter which.—*also adj.*

whiff *n* a sudden puff of air, smoke or odour.

while *n* a period of time. * *conj* during the time that; whereas; although. * *vt* to pass (the time) pleasantly.

whim *n* a fancy; an irrational thought.

whimper *vi* to make a low, unhappy cry.—*also n.*

whimsical *adj* unusual, odd, fantastic.—**whimsicality** *n.*

whine *vi* (*dog*) to make a long, high-pitched cry; (*person*) to complain childishly. * *n* a plaintive cry.

whip *n* a piece of leather attached to a handle used for punishing people or driving on animals; an officer in parliament who maintains party discipline. * *vb* (*pt* **whipped**) *vt* to move, pull, throw, etc suddenly; to strike, as with a lash; (*eggs, etc*) to beat into a froth. * *vi* to move rapidly.

whip-round *n* (*inf*) an appeal among friends for contributions.

whir, whirr *n* a humming or buzzing sound. * *vti* to revolve with a buzzing noise.

whirl *n* a swift turning; confusion, commotion; (*inf*) an attempt or try. * *vti* to turn around rapidly; to spin.

whirlpool *n* a circular current or vortex of water.

whirlwind *n* a whirling column of air; rapid activity.

whisk *vt* to make a quick sweeping movement; (*eggs, cream*) to beat, whip. * *vi* to move nimbly and efficiently. * *n* a kitchen utensil for whisking; (*inf*) a small amount.

whisker *n* any of the sensory bristles on the face of a cat, etc; (*pl*) the hair growing on a man's face, esp the cheeks.—**whiskered** *adj.*

whiskey *n* whisky distilled in the US or Ireland.

whisky *n* a spirit distilled from barley or rye.

whisper *vti* to speak softly; to spread a rumour. * *n* a hushed tone; a hint, trace.

whist *n* a card game for four players in two sides, each side attempting to win the greater number of the 13 tricks.

whistle *vti* to make a shrill sound by forcing the breath through the lips; to make a similar sound with a whistle; (*wind*) to move with a shrill sound. * *n* a whistling sound; a musical instrument; a metal tube that is blown to make a shrill warning sound.

white *adj* of the color of snow; pure; bright; (*skin*) light-colored. * *n* the color white; the white part of an egg or the eye.—**whiten** *vti.*

white-collar *adj* of office and professional workers.

whitefish (*pl* same or **whitefishes**) *n* a freshwater fish of the trout family in northern North America.

whitewash *n* a mixture of lime and water, used for whitening walls; concealment of the truth.—*also vt.*

Whitsun *n* the seventh Sunday after Easter; the following week.—*also* **Whit Sunday, Whitsuntide.**

whittle *vt* to pare or cut thin shavings from (wood) with a knife; (*with away or down*) to reduce.

whiz, whizz *vi* (*pt* **whizzed**) to make a humming sound. * *n* (*pl* **whizzes**) a humming sound; (*inf*) an expert.

WHO *abbr* = World Health Organization.

who *pron* what or which person; that.

whodunit, whodunnit *n* (*inf*) a detective novel, play, etc.

whoever *pron* anyone who; whatever person.

whole *adj* not broken, intact; containing the total amount, number, etc.; complete. * *n* the entire amount; a thing complete in itself.

wholehearted *adj* sincere, single-minded, enthusiastic.—**wholeheartedly** *adv.*

whole note *n* a semibreve.

wholesale *n* selling of goods, usu at lower prices and in quantity, to a retailer.

wholesome *adj* healthy; mentally beneficial.—**wholesomeness** *n.*

whom *pron* objective case of **who.**

whoop *n* a loud cry of excitement.

whooping cough *n* an infectious disease, esp of children, causing coughing spasms.

whore *n* a prostitute.

whose *pron* the possessive case of **who** or **which.**

why *adv* for what cause or reason? * *interj* exclamation of surprise. * *n* (*pl* **whys**) a cause.

wick *n* a cord, as in a candle or lamp, that supplies fuel to the flame.

wicked *adj* evil, immoral, sinful.—**wickedly** *adv.*—**wickedness** *n.*

wicker *n* a long, thin, flexible twig; such twigs woven together, as in making baskets.—**wickerwork** *n.*

wicket *n* a small door or gate; (*croquet*) any of the small wire arches through which the balls must be hit; (*cricket*) the stumps at which the bowler aims the ball; the area between the bowler and the batsman; a batsman's innings.

wide *adj* broad; extensive; of a definite distance from side to side; (*with of*) far from the aim; open fully. * *n* (*cricket*) a ball bowled beyond the reach of the batsman.—**widely** *adv.*

wide-angle *adj* (*photog*) with an angle of view of 60 degrees or more.

wide-awake *adj* fully awake; ready, alert.

widen *vti* to make or grow wide or wider.

widespread *adj* widely extended; general.

widow *n* a woman whose husband has died. * *vt* to cause to become a widow.—**widowhood** *n.*

widower *n* a man whose wife has died.

width *n* breadth.

wield *vt* (*a weapon, etc*) to brandish; to exercise

power.

wife *n* (*pl* **wives**) a married woman.

wig *n* an artificial covering of real or synthetic hair for the head.

wiggle *vti* to move from side to side with jerky movements.

wild *adj* in its natural state; not tamed or cultivated; uncivilized; lacking control; disorderly; furious. —**wildly** *adv.* —**wildness** *n.*

wilderness *n* an uncultivated and desolate place.

wild-goose chase *n* a futile pursuit of something.

wildlife *n* animals in the wild.

wilful, willful (*US*) *adj* stubborn; done intentionally.—**wilfully** *adv.* —**wilfulness** *n.*

will[1] *n* power of choosing or determining; desire; determination; desire; attitude, disposition; a legal document directing the disposal of one's property after death. * *vt* to bequeath; to command.

will[2] *aux vb* used in constructions with 2nd and 3rd persons; used to show futurity, determination, obligation.

willow *n* a tree or shrub with slender, flexible branches; the wood of the willow.

willpower *n* the ability to control one's emotions and actions.

wilt *vi* to become limp, as from heat; (*plant*) to droop; to become weak or faint.

wily *adj* (**wilier, wiliest**) crafty; sly.—**wiliness** *n.*

win *vti* (*pr p* **winning**, *pt* **won**) to gain with effort; to succeed in a contest; to gain eg by luck; to achieve influence over. * *n* a success.—**winner** *n.*

wince *vi* to shrink back; to flinch (as in pain).—*also n.*

winch *n* a hoisting machine. * *vt* to hoist or lower with a winch.

wind[1] *n* a current of air; breath; scent of game; (*inf*) flatulence; tendency; (*mus*) wind instrument(s). * *vt* (*pt* **winded**) to cause to be short of breath; to perceive by scent.

wind[2] *vb* (*pt* **wound**) *vt* to turn by cranking; to tighten the spring of a clock; to coil around something else; to encircle or cover, as with a bandage. * *vi* to turn, to twist, to meander.

windbreak *n* a shelter that breaks the force of the wind, as a line trees.

windfall *n* fruit blown off a tree; any unexpected gain, esp financial.

winding *adj* meandering.

wind instrument *n* a musical instrument played by blowing into it or by passing a current of air through it.

windmill *n* a machine operated by the force of the wind turning a set of sails.

window *n* a framework containing glass in the opening in a wall of a building, or in a vehicle, etc, for air and light.

window box *n* a narrow box on a windowsill for growing flowers, etc.

windowsill *n* a sill beneath a window.

windpipe *n* the air passage from the mouth to the lungs.

windrow *n* a row of leaves or pile of soil heaped up by or as if by the wind; (*Cdn*) a ridge of snow or gravel heaped up at the side of a road by a snow plough or grader.

windscreen, windshield *n* a protective shield of glass in the front of a vehicle.

windscreen wiper, windshield wiper *n* a metal blade with a rubber edge that removes rain, etc, from a windscreen.

windy *adj* (**windier, windiest**) exposed to the winds; stormy; verbose.

wine *n* fermented grape juice used as an alcoholic beverage; the fermented juice of other fruits or plants.

wineglass *n* a glass, usu with a stem, for drinking wine.

wing *n* the forelimb of a bird, bat or insect, by which it flies; the main lateral surface of an aeroplane; a projecting part of a building; the side of a stage; a section of a political party. * *vti* to make one's way swiftly; to wound without killing.

wink *vi* to quickly open and close one's eye; to give a hint by winking. * *n* the act of winking; an instant.

winning *n* a victory; (*pl*) money won in gambling. * *adj* charming.

Winnipeg goldeye *n* goldeye.

winter *n* the coldest season of the year: in the northern hemisphere from November or December to January or February. * *vi* to spend the winter.

winter road *n* (*Cdn*) a road made of compacted snow or ice over a frozen lake or land impassable in warmer weather.

wintry, wintery *adj* (**wintrier, wintriest**) typical of winter, cold, stormy, snowy; unfriendly, frigid.

wipe *vt* to rub a surface with a cloth in order to clean or dry it; (*with* **out**) to remove; to erase; to kill off; to destroy. * *n* a wiping.

wire *n* a flexible thread of metal; a length of this; (*US horse racing*) the finish line of a race; a telegram. * *adj* formed of wire. * *vt* to fasten, furnish, connect, etc with wire; in US, to send a telegram.

wireless *n* (*formerly*) a radio.

wiry *adj* (**wirier, wiriest**) lean, supple and sinewy.—**wiriness** *n.*

wisdom *n* the ability to use knowledge; sound judgment.

wisdom tooth *n* one of four teeth set at the end of each side of the upper and lower jaw in humans and grown last.

wise *adj* having knowledge or common sense; learned; prudent.— **wisely** *adv.*

wish *vti* to long for; to express a desire. * *n* desire; thing desired.

wishful *adj* having a wish; hopeful.

wisp *n* a thin strand; a small bunch, as of hay; anything slender.—**wispy** *adj.*

wistful *adj* pensive; sad; yearning.—**wistfully** *adv.*—**wistfulness** *n.*

wit *n* (*speech, writing*) the facility of combining ideas with humorous effect; a person with this ability; (*pl*) ability to think quickly.

witch *n* a woman who practises magic and is considered to have dealings with the devil.

witchcraft *n* the practice of magic.

with *prep* denoting nearness or agreement; in the company of; in the same direction as; among; by means of; possessing.

withdraw *vb* (*pt* **withdrew**, *pp* **withdrawn**) *vt* to draw back or away; to remove; to retract. * *vi* to retire; to retreat.—**withdrawal** *n*.

wither *vi* to fade or become limp or dry, as of a plant. * *vt* to cause to dry up or fade.

withhold *vt* (*pt* **withheld**) to hold back; to deduct; to restrain; to refuse to grant.

within *prep* inside; not exceeding; not beyond.

without *prep* outside or out of, beyond; not having, lacking. * *adv* outside.

withstand *vt* (*pt* **withstood**) to oppose or resist, esp successfully; to endure.

witness *n* a person who gives evidence or attests a signing; testimony (of a fact). * *vt* to have first hand knowledge of; to see; to be the scene of; to serve as evidence of; to attest a signing. * *vi* to testify.

witness box, witness stand *n* an enclosure for witnesses in a court of law.

witticism *n* a witty remark.

witty *adj* (**wittier, wittiest**) full of wit.—**wittily** *adv*.—**wittiness** *n*.

wives *see* **wife**.

wizard *n* a magician; a man who practises witchcraft or magic; an expert.—**wizardry** *n*.

wk *abbr* = week.

wobble *vi* to sway unsteadily from side to side; to waver, to hesitate.—**wobbly** *adj*.

woe *n* grief, misery; (*pl*) misfortune.—**woeful** *adj*.—**woefully** *adv*.

wok *n* a large, metal, hemispherical pan used for Chinese-style cooking.

woke, woken *see* **wake**[1].

wolf *n* (*pl* **wolves**) a wild animal of the dog family that hunts in packs; a flirtatious man.

woman *n* (*pl* **women**) an adult human female; the female sex.

womanly *adj* having the qualities of a woman.

womb *n* the female organ in which offspring are developed until birth, the uterus; any womb-like cavity; a place where something is produced.

women *see* **woman**.

won *see* **win**.

wonder *n* a feeling of surprise or astonishment; something that excites such a feeling; a prodigy. * *vi* to feel wonder; to be curious; to speculate; to marvel.

wonderful *adj* marvellous.—**wonderfully** *adv*.

won't = will not.

woo *vt* to seek to attract with a view to marriage; to court; to solicit eagerly.—**wooer** *n*.

wood *n* the hard fibrous substance under the bark of trees; trees cut or sawn, timber; a thick growth of trees.

wooded *adj* covered with trees.

woodlot *n* an area of treed land, esp on a far, from which firewood can be cut.

woodpecker *n* a bird that pecks holes in trees to extract insects.

woodwind *n* section of an orchestra in which wind instruments, originally made of wood, are played.

woodwork *n* carpentry.

woodworm *n* an insect larva that bores into wood; the damage in furniture so caused.

wool *n* the fleece of sheep and other animals; thread or yarn spun from the coats of sheep; cloth made from this yarn.

woollen, woolen (*US*) *adj* made of wool.

woolly *adj* (**woollier, woolliest**) of, like or covered with wool; indistinct, blurred; muddled. * *n* (*inf*) a woollen garment.—**woolliness** *n*.

word *n* a single unit of language in speech or writing; talk, discussion; a message; a promise; a command; information; a password; (*pl*) lyrics; (*pl*) a quarrel. * *vt* to put into words, to phrase; to flatter.

wording *n* the way in which words are used, esp in written form; a choice of words.

wordy *adj* (**wordier, wordiest**) verbose.

wore *see* **wear**.

work *n* employment, occupation; a task; the product of work; manner of working; place of work; a literary composition; (*pl*) a factory, plant. * *vi* to be employed, to have a job; to operate (a machine, etc); to produce effects. * *vt* to effect, to achieve.—**workable** *adj*.—**worker** *n*.

working *adj* spent in or used for work; functioning. * *n* operation; mode of operation; (*pl*) the manner of functioning or operating; (*pl*) the parts of a mine that are worked.

working class *n* people who work for wages, esp manual workers.

workmanship *n* technical skill; the way a thing is made, style.

work-out *n* a session of strenuous physical exercises.

workshop *n* a room or building where work is done; a seminar for specified intensive study, work, etc.

world *n* the planet earth and its inhabitants; mankind; the universe; a sphere of existence; the public.

worldly *adj* (**worldlier, worldliest**) earthly, rather than spiritual; material; experienced.

worldwide *adj* universal.

worm *n* an earthworm; an insect larva; the thread of a screw. * *vt* to work (oneself into a position) slowly or secretly; to extract information by slow and persistent means.

worn *see* **wear**.

worn-out *adj* (*machine, etc*) past its useful life; (*person*) depressed, tired.

worry *vb* to bother, pester, harass. * *vi* to be uneasy or anxious; to fret. * *n* a cause or feeling of anxiety.—**worrier** *n*.

worse *adj* (used as compar of **bad** and **ill**) less favorable; not so well as before. * *adv* with great severity.—**worsen** *vti*.

worship *n* religious adoration; a religious ritual, eg prayers; devotion. * *vb* (*pt* **worshipped**) *vt* to adore or idolize. * *vi* to participate in a religious service.—**worshipper** *n*.

worst *adj* (used as superl of **bad** or **ill**; see also

worse) bad or ill in the highest degree; of the lowest quality. * *adv* to the worst degree. * *n* the least good part.

worsted *n* twisted thread or yarn made from long, combed wool.

worth *n* value; price; excellence; importance. * *adj* equal in value to; meriting.

worthless *adj* valueless; useless; of bad character.—**worthlessness** *n*.

worthwhile *adj* important or rewarding enough to justify effort.

worthy *adj* (**worthier, worthiest**) virtuous; deserving. * *n* a worthy person, a local celebrity.—**worthily** *adv*.

would *see* will².

would-be *adj* aspiring or professing to be.

wound¹ *n* any cut, bruise, hurt, or injury caused to the skin; hurt feelings. * *vt* to injure.

wound² *see* wind².

wove, woven *see* weave.

Wpg. *abbr* = Winnipeg.

wrangle *vi* to argue; to dispute noisily. * *n* a noisy argument.

wrap *vt* (*pt* **wrapped**) to fold (paper) around (a present, purchase etc); to wind (around); to enfold. * *n* a shawl.

wrapper *n* one who or that which wraps; a book jacket; a light dressing gown.

wrath *n* intense anger; rage.—**wrathful** *adj*.

wreak *vt* inflict or exact (eg vengeance, havoc).

wreath *n* (*pl* **wreaths**) a twisted ring of leaves, flowers, etc; something like this in shape.

wreck *n* accidental destruction of a ship; a badly damaged ship; a run-down person or thing. * *vt* to destroy; to ruin.

wreckage *n* the process of wrecking; remnants from a wreck.

wren *n* small brownish songbird, with a short erect tail.

wrench *vt* to give something a violent pull or twist; to injure with a twist, to sprain; to distort. * *n* a forceful twist; a sprain; a spanner; emotional upset caused by parting.

wrestle *vti* to fight by holding and trying to throw one's opponent down; to struggle.—**wrestler** *n*.

wretch *n* a miserable or despised person.

wretched *adj* very miserable; in poor circumstances; despicable.—**wretchedly** *adv*.—**wretchedness** *n*.

wriggle *vi* to move with a twisting motion; to squirm, to writhe; to use evasive tricks.—*also n*.—**wriggler** *n*.

wring *vt* (*pt* **wrung**) to twist; to compress by twisting to squeeze water from; to pain; to obtain forcibly.

wrinkle *n* a small crease or fold on a surface. * *vti* to make or become wrinkled.

wrist *n* the joint connecting the hand with the forearm.

writ *n* (*law*) a written court order.

write *vb* (*pr p* **writing**, *pt* **wrote**, *pp* **written**) *vt* to form letters on paper with a pen or pencil; to express in writing; to compose (music, literary work, etc); to communicate by let-

ter; (*with* **off**) to cancel a bad debt as a loss; (*inf*) to damage (a vehicle) beyond repair. * *vi* to be a writer.

write-off *n* a debt cancelled as a loss; (*inf*) a badly damaged car.

writer *n* an author; a scribe or clerk.

writhe *vi* to twist the body violently, as in pain; to squirm (under, at).

writing *n* the act of forming letters on paper, etc; a written document; authorship; (*pl*) literary works.

writing paper *n* paper treated to accept ink and used esp for letters.

written *see* write.

wrong *adj* not right, incorrect; mistaken, misinformed; immoral. * *n* harm; injury done to another. * *adv* incorrectly. * *vt* to do wrong to.—**wrongly** *adv*.

wrongful *adj* unwarranted, unjust.—**wrongfully** *adv*.

wrote *see* write.

wrought *adj* formed; made; (*metals*) shaped by hammering, etc.

wrung *see* wring.

wry *adj* (**wryer, wryest** *or* **wrier, wriest**) twisted, contorted; ironic.—**wryly** *adv*.—**wryness** *n*.

wt *abbr* = weight.

XYZ

Xmas *abbr* = Christmas.

X-ray, x-ray *n* radiation of very short wavelengths, capable of penetrating solid bodies, and printing on a photographic plate a shadow picture of objects not permeable by light rays. * *vt* to photograph by x-rays.

xylophone *n* a percussion instrument consisting of a series of wooden bars which are struck with small hammers.

yacht *n* a sailing or mechanically driven vessel, used for pleasure cruises or racing. * *vi* to race or cruise in a yacht.—**yachting** *n*.—**yachtsman** *n*.—**yachtswoman** *nf*.

Yank, Yankee *n* (*inf*) a citizen of the US, an American.

yank *vti* to pull suddenly, to jerk.—*also n*.

yap *vi* (*pt* **yapped**) to yelp, bark; (*sl*) to talk constantly, esp in a noisy or irritating manner.

yard¹ *n* a unit of measure of 3 feet and equivalent to 0.9144 metres.

yard² *n* an enclosed concrete area, esp near a building; an enclosure for a commercial activity (eg a shipyard); a garden.

yardstick *n* a standard used in judging.

yarn *n* fibres of wool, cotton etc spun into strands for weaving, knitting, etc; (*inf*) a tale or story. * *vi* to tell a yarn; to talk at length.

yawn *vi* to open the jaws involuntarily and inhale, as from drowsiness; to gape.—*also n*.

yawning *adj* gaping; wide-open; drowsy.—**yawningly** *adv*.

yd., yds *abbr* = yard(s).

year *n* a period of twelve months, or 365 or 366 days, beginning with 1 January and ending with 31 December.

yearly *adj* occurring every year; lasting a year. * *adv* once a year; from year to year.

yearn *vi* to feel desire (for); to long for.—**yearning** *n*.

yeast *n* a fungus that causes alcoholic fermentation, used in brewing and baking.

yell *vti* to shout loudly; to scream. * *n* a loud shout.

yellow *adj* of the color of lemons, egg yolk, etc; having a yellowish skin; (*inf*) cowardly. * *n* the color yellow. * *i* to become or turn yellow.

Yellow Transparent *n* (*Cdn*) an early yellow-skinned cooking and eating apple.

yelp *vti* to utter a sharp, shrill cry or bark.—*also n*.

yen[1] *n* (*pl* **yen**) the monetary unit of Japan.

yen[2] *n* (*inf*) a yearning, an ambition.

yes *adv* a word of affirmation or consent.

yesterday *n* the day before today; the recent past. * *adv* on the day before today; recently.

yet *adv* still; so far; even. * *conj* nevertheless; however; still.

yew *n* an evergreen tree or shrub with thin, sharp leaves and red berries.

Yiddish *n* a mixed German and Hebrew dialect spoken by Jews.

yield *vt* to resign; to give forth, to produce, as a crop, result, profit, etc. * *vi* to submit; to give way to physical force, to surrender. * *n* the amount yielded; the profit or return on a financial investment.

yodel *vti* (*pt* **yodelled**) to sing, alternating from the ordinary voice to falsetto.

yoga *n* a system of exercises for attaining bodily and mental control and well-being.

yoghurt, yogurt *n* a semi-liquid food made from milk curdled by bacteria.

yoke *n* a bond or tie; slavery; the wooden frame joining oxen to make them pull together; part of a garment that is fitted below the neck. * *vt* to put a yoke on; to join together.

yolk *n* the yellow part of an egg.

yonder *adv* over there.

you *pron* (*gram*) 2nd person singular or plural; the person or persons spoken to.

you'd = you would; you had.

you'll = you will; you shall.

young *adj* in the early period of life; in the first part of growth; new; inexperienced. * *n* young people; offspring.

youngster *n* a young person; a youth.

your *poss adj* of or belonging to or done by you.

you're = you are.

yours *poss pron* of or belonging to you.

yourself *pron* (*pl* **yourselves**) the emphatic and reflexive form of **you**.

youth *n* the period between childhood and adulthood; young people collectively; the early stages of something; a young man or boy.—**youthful** *adj*.—**youthfully** *adv*.

youth hostel *n* a supervised lodging for usu young travellers.

you've = you have.

YST *abbr* = Yukon Standard Time.

YT *abbr* = Yukon Territories; Yukon Time.

Yukon Gold *n* (*Cdn*) a smooth-skinned, yellow-fleshed, early-maturing variety of potato.

Yukoner *n* (*Cdn*) a person who lives in or is from Yukon.

zany *adj* (**zanier, zaniest**) comical; eccentric.—**zaniness** *n*.

zeal *n* fervent devotion; fanaticism.

zealous *adj* full of zeal; ardent.—**zealously** *adv*.

zebra *n* (*pl* **zebras, zebra**) a black and white striped wild animal related to the horse.

zebra crossing *n* a street crossing for pedestrians marked by black and white strips on the road.

zed *n* the letter z.

zero *n* (*pl* **zeros**) the symbol 0; nothing; the lowest point; freezing point, 0 degrees Celsius.

zest *n* the outer part of the skin of an orange or lemon used to give flavor; enthusiasm; excitement.—**zestful** *adj*.

zigzag *n* a series of short, sharp angles in alternate directions. * *adj* having sharp turns. * *vti* (*pt* **zigzagged**) to move or form in a zigzag.

zinc *n* a bluish-white metallic element used in alloys and batteries.

zip *n* a slide fastener on clothing, bags, etc with interlocking teeth. * *vt* (*pt* **zipped**) to fasten with a zip.

zipper *n* a zip.

zither *n* a stringed instrument played by plucking.

zodiac *n* an imaginary belt in the heavens, along which the sun, moon, and planets appear to move, divided into twelve equal areas; a diagram representing this.

zombie *n* a person who is lifeless and apathetic; an automaton.

zone *n* a region, area; a subdivision; any area with a specified use or restriction.—**zonal** *adj*.

zoo *n* (*pl* **zoos**) a place where wild animals are kept for public show.

zoology *n* the study of animals with regard to their classification, structure and habits.—**zoological** *adj*.—**zoologist** *n*.

zoom *vi* to go quickly, to speed; to climb upwards sharply in an aeroplane; to rise rapidly; (*photog*) to focus in on, using a zoom lens.

zoom lens *n* (*photog*) a camera lens that makes distant objects appear closer without moving the camera.